financial accounting theory

fifth edition

William R. Scott

UNIVERSITY OF WATERLOO

QUEEN'S UNIVERSITY

PEARSON

Prentice
Hall

Toronto

Library and Archives Canada Cataloguing in Publication

Scott, William R. (William Robert), 1931–

Financial accounting theory / William R. Scott. — 5th ed.

Includes bibliographical references and index.
ISBN 978-0-13-207286-1

1. Accounting—Textbooks.   I. Title.
HF5635.S36 2009   657'.044   C2008-900661-5

ISBN-13: 978-0-13-207286-1
ISBN-10: 0-13-207286-6

Vice President, Editorial Director: Gary Bennett
Executive Editor: Samantha Scully
Executive Marketing Manager: Cas Shields
Developmental Editors: Megan Dunkley and Rema Celio
Production Editor: Imee Salumbides
Copy Editor: Melissa Hajek
Proofreader: Laurel Sparrow
Production Coordinator: Deborah Starks
Compositor: Hermia Chung
Permissions Researcher: Amanda McCormick
Art Director: Julia Hall
Cover Designer: Miguel Acevedo
Cover Image: Masterfile, Andrew Olney

7   12 11 10

Printed and bound in the United States of America.

To Mary Ann, Julie, Martha, Kathy, Paul, and Cary

Contents

Preface

This book began as a series of lesson notes for a financial accounting theory course of the Certified General Accountants' Association of Canada (CGA). The lesson notes grew out of a conviction that we have learned a great deal about the role of financial accounting and reporting in our society from securities markets and information economics–based research conducted over many years, and that financial accounting theory comes into its own when we formally recognize the information asymmetries that pervade business relationships.

The challenge was to organize this large body of research into a unifying framework and to explain it in such a manner that professionally oriented students would both understand and accept it as relevant to the financial accounting environment and ultimately to their own professional careers.

This book seems to have achieved its goals. In addition to being part of the CGA program of professional studies for a number of years, it has been extensively used in financial accounting theory courses at the University of Waterloo, Queen's University, and numerous other universities, both at the senior undergraduate and professional Master's levels. I am encouraged by the fact that, by and large, students comprehend the material and, indeed, are likely to object if the instructor follows it too closely in class. This frees up class time to expand coverage of areas of interest to individual instructors and/or to motivate particular topics by means of articles from the financial press and professional and academic literature.

Despite its theoretical orientation, the book does not ignore the institutional structure of financial accounting and standard setting. It features considerable coverage of financial accounting standards. Many important standards, such as reserve recognition accounting, management discussion and analysis, employee stock options, post-employment benefits, financial instruments, ceiling tests, hedge accounting, and comprehensive income are described and critically evaluated. The structure of standard-setting bodies is also described, and the role of structure in helping to engineer the consent necessary for a successful standard is evaluated. While the text discussion concentrates on relating standards to the theoretical framework of the book, the coverage provides students with the occasion to learn the contents of the standards themselves.

I have also used this material in Ph.D. seminars. Here, I concentrate on the research articles that underlie the text discussion. Nevertheless, the students appreciate the framework of the book as a way of putting specific research papers into perspective. Indeed, the book proceeds in large part by selecting important research papers for description and commentary, and provides extensive references to other research papers underlying the text discussion. Assignment of the research papers themselves could be especially useful for instructors who wish to dig into methodological issues that, with some exceptions, are downplayed in the book itself.

A major change in this fifth edition is to orient the coverage of accounting standards to those of the International Accounting Standards Board (IASB), in place of Canadian standards in the *CICA Handbook*. This is because of the planned adoption in 2011 of IASB standards for public companies by the Canadian Accounting Standards Board. This change does not affect the approach and structure of the book. While there are numerous differences in detail, international and Canadian accounting standards are already similar at a conceptual level, and are continuing to move closer together. Consequently, prior to 2011, Canadian readers can accept IASB standards as roughly equivalent to those in Canada. Of course, this change to IASB standards should appeal to the numerous users of this book in other countries that have adopted IASB standards.

As in previous editions, coverage of major U.S. accounting standards is included, particularly where these differ from, or are in advance of, international and Canadian standards. Other changes include expanded coverage of financial reporting issues arising from global integration of capital markets, and improvements to the discussion and presentation of agency theory.

I have updated references and discussion of recent research articles, revised the exposition as a result of comments received and experience in teaching from earlier editions, and added new problem material. I have also expanded the number of optional sections for those who do not wish to delve too deeply into certain topics.

This edition now accepts that securities markets are not fully efficient, although it continues to argue that markets are close enough to full efficiency that the efficient market model provides useful guidance to theory and practice. In part, this continuing acceptance of the efficient market model reflects my perception from the academic literature that the efficiency model is recovering somewhat from the onslaught of behavioural finance. More fundamentally, however, research suggests that departures from full efficiency can be just as well explained by rational investor behaviour as by non-rational behavioural characteristics. Consequently, this edition retains its acceptance of the rational Bayesian decision theory model of the average investor.

SUPPLEMENTS

Instructor's Resource CD-ROM (ISBN 978-0-13-604110-8)

This resource CD includes the following instructor supplements:

- **Instructor's Manual** The Instructor's Manual includes suggested solutions to all the end-of-chapter Questions and Problems. It also offers learning objectives for each chapter and suggests teaching approaches that could be used. In addition, it comments on other issues for consideration, suggests supplementary references, and contains some additional problem material.

- **PowerPoint® Lecture Slides** PowerPoint presentations offer a comprehensive selection of slides covering theories and examples presented in the text. They are designed to organize the delivery of content to students and stimulate classroom discussion.

Acknowledgments

I have received a lot of assistance in writing this book. First, I thank CGA Canada for their encouragement and support over the past years. Much of the material in the questions and problems has been reprinted or adapted from the *Accounting Theory I* course and examinations of the Certified General Accountants' Association of Canada. These are acknowledged where used.

I acknowledge the financial assistance of the Ontario Chartered Accountants' Chair in Accounting at the University of Waterloo, which enabled teaching relief and other support in the preparation of the original manuscript. Financial support of the School of Business of Queen's University is also gratefully acknowledged.

I extend my thanks and appreciation to the following instructors who provided formal reviews for this fifth edition:

- Granville Ansong (Saint Mary's University)
- Sati P. Bandyopadhyay (University of Waterloo)
- Paul Berry (Mount Allison University)
- Kate Bewley (York University)
- Carla Carnaghan (University of Lethbridge)
- James C. Gaa (University of Alberta)
- Maureen P. Gowing (University of Windsor)
- Irene M. Gordon (Simon Fraser University)
- Mary Oxner (St. Francis Xavier University)

I also thank numerous colleagues and students for advice and feedback. These include Sati Bandyopadhyay, Phelim Boyle, Dennis Chung, Len Eckel, Haim Falk, Steve Fortin, Irene Gordon, Jennifer Kao, David Manry, Patricia O'Brien, Bill Richardson, Gordon Richardson, Dean Smith, Dan Thornton, and Mike Welker. Special thanks to Alex Milburn for invaluable assistance in understanding IASB standards, and to Dick VanOfferen for helpful comments and support on all editions of this work.

I thank the large number of researchers whose work underlies this book. As previously mentioned, numerous research papers are described and referenced. However, there are many other worthy papers that I have not referenced. This implies no disrespect or lack of appreciation for the contributions of these authors to financial accounting theory. Rather, it has been simply impossible to include them all, both for reasons of space and the boundaries of my own knowledge.

I am grateful to Carolyn Holden for skilful, timely, and cheerful typing of the original manuscript in the face of numerous revisions, and to Jill Nucci for research assistance.

At Pearson Education Canada I would like to thank Samantha Scully, Gary Bennett, Cas Shields, Megan Dunkley, Imee Salumbides, Melissa Hajek, Laurel Sparrow, Leanne Rancourt, Deborah Starks, Hermia Chung, and Miguel Acevedo.

Finally, I thank my wife and family who, in many ways, have been involved in the learning process leading to this book.

William Scott

Chapter 1
Introduction

Figure 1.1 Organization of the Book

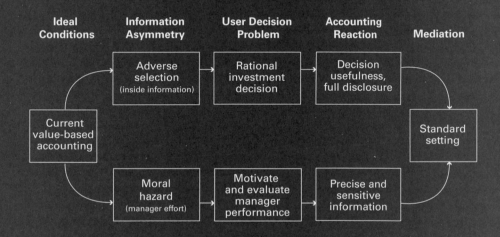

1.1 THE OBJECTIVE OF THIS BOOK

This book is about accounting, not how to account. It argues that accounting students, having been exposed to the methodology and practice of accounting, need to critically examine the broader implications of financial accounting for the fair and efficient working of our economy. Our objective is to give the reader an understanding of the current financial accounting and reporting environment, taking into account the diverse interests of both external users and management.

1.2 SOME HISTORICAL PERSPECTIVE

Accounting has a long history. The first complete description of the double entry bookkeeping system appeared in 1494, authored by Luca Paciolo, an Italian monk/mathematician.[1] Paciolo did not invent this system—it had developed over a long period of time. Segments that developed first included, for example, the collection of an account receivable. "Both sides" of such a transaction were easy to see, since cash and accounts receivable have a physical and/or legal existence, and the amount of the increase in cash was equal to the decrease in accounts receivable. The recording of other types of transactions, such as the sale of goods or the incurring of expenses, however, took longer to develop. In the case of a sale, it was obvious that cash or accounts receivable increased, and that goods on hand decreased. But, what about the difference between the selling price and the cost of the goods sold? There is no physical or legal representation of the profit on the sale. For the double entry system to handle transactions such as this, it was necessary to create *abstract* concepts of income and capital. By Paciolo's time, these concepts had developed, and a complete double entry system, quite similar to the one in use today, was in place. The abstract nature of this system, including the properties of capital as the accumulation of income and income as the rate of change of capital,[2] attracted the attention of mathematicians of the time. The "method of Venice," as Paciolo's system was called, was frequently included in mathematics texts in subsequent years.

Following 1494, the double entry system spread throughout Europe, and Paciolo's work was translated into English in 1543. It was in England that another sequence of important accounting developments took place.

By the early eighteenth century, the concept of a joint stock company had developed in England to include permanent existence, limited liability of shareholders, and transferability of shares. Transferability of shares led in turn to the development of a stock market where shares could be bought and sold. Obviously, investors needed financial information about the firms whose shares they were trading. Thus began a long transition for financial accounting, from a system to enable a merchant to control his/her own operations to a system to inform investors who were not involved in the day-to-day operations of the firm. It was in the joint interests of the firm and investors that financial information provided by the firm was trustworthy, thereby laying the groundwork for the development of an auditing profession and government regulation. In this regard, the 1844 Companies Act was notable. It was in this act that the concept of providing an audited balance sheet to shareholders first appeared in the law, although this requirement was dropped in subsequent years[3] and not reinstated until the early 1900s. During the interval, voluntary provision of information was common, but its effectiveness was hampered by a lack of accounting principles. This was demonstrated, for example, in the controversy of whether amortization of capital assets had to be deducted in determining income available for dividends (the courts ruled it did not).

In the twentieth century, major developments in financial accounting shifted to the United States, which was growing rapidly in economic power. The introduction of a corporate income tax in the United States in 1909 provided a major impetus to income measurement, and, as noted by Hatfield (1927, p. 140), was influential in persuading business managers to accept amortization as a deduction from income.

Nevertheless, accounting in the United States continued to be relatively unregulated, with financial reporting and auditing largely voluntary. However, the stock market crash of 1929 and resulting Great Depression led to major changes. The most noteworthy was the creation of the Securities and Exchange Commission (SEC) by the Securities Act of 1934, with a focus on protecting investors by means of a disclosure-based structure. The Act regulates dealing in the securities of firms that meet certain size tests and whose securities are traded in more than one state. As part of its mandate, the SEC has the responsibility to ensure that investors are supplied with adequate information.

Merino and Neimark (1982) (MN) examined the conditions leading up to the creation of the SEC. In the process, they reported on some of the securities market practices of the 1920s and prior. Apparently, voluntary disclosure was widespread, as also noted by Benston (1973). However, MN claim that such disclosure was motivated by big business's desire to avoid disclosure regulations that would reduce their monopoly power.

Disclosure regulations would reduce monopoly power by better enabling potential entrants to identify high-profit industries. Presumably, if voluntary disclosure was adequate, the government would not feel that regulated disclosure was necessary. Thus, informing investors was not the main motivation of disclosure. Instead, investors were "protected" by a "two-tiered" market structure whereby prices were set by knowledgeable insiders, subject to a self-imposed "moral regulation" to control misleading reporting. Unfortunately, moral regulation was not always effective, and MN refer to numerous instances of manipulative financial reporting and other abuses, which were widely believed to be major contributing factors to the 1929 crash.

The 1934 securities legislation can then be regarded as a movement away from an avoidance-of-regulation rationale for disclosure towards the supplying of better-quality information to investors as a way to control manipulative financial practices.[4]

One of the practices of the 1920s that received criticism was the frequent appraisal of capital assets, the values of which came crashing down in 1929. A major lesson learned by accountants as a result of the Great Depression was that values were fleeting. The outcome was a strengthening of the historical cost basis of accounting. This basis received its highest expression in the famous Paton and Littleton monograph, *An Introduction to Corporate Accounting Standards*, of 1940. This document elegantly and persuasively set forth the case for historical cost accounting, based on the concept of the firm as a going concern. This concept justifies important attributes of historical cost accounting such as waiting to recognize revenue until objective evidence of realization is available, the matching against realized revenues of the allocated costs of earning those revenues, and the deferral of unrealized gains and losses on the balance sheet until the time came to match them with revenues. As a result, the income statement reliably shows the current "installment" of the firm's earning power. The income statement replaced the balance sheet as the primary focus of financial reporting.

It is sometimes claimed that the Paton and Littleton monograph was too persuasive, in that it shut out exploration of alternative bases of accounting. However, alternative valuation bases have become more common over the years, to the point where we now have a **mixed measurement system**. Historical cost is still the primary basis of accounting for important asset and liability classes, such as capital assets, inventories, and long-term debt. However, if assets are impaired, they are frequently written down to a lower value. Ceiling tests for capital assets and the lower-of-cost-or-market rule for inventories are examples. Under International Accounting Standards Board standards, capital assets can sometimes be written up over cost if their value has increased. Generally speaking, standard setters have moved steadily towards current cost alternatives to historical cost accounting over the past number of years.

There are two main current cost alternatives to historical cost for assets and liabilities. One is **value-in-use**, such as discounted present value of future cash flows. The other is **fair value**, also called **exit value** or **opportunity cost**, the amount that would be received or paid should the firm dispose of the asset or liability. These valuation bases will be discussed in Chapter 7. When distinguishing between them is not necessary, we shall refer to valuations that depart from historical cost as **current values**.

While the lesson favouring historical cost learned by accountants from the Great Depression may be in the process of being forgotten, another lesson remains. This is how to survive in a disclosure-regulated environment. In the United States, for example, the SEC has the power to establish the accounting standards and procedures used by firms under its jurisdiction. If the SEC chose to use this power, the prestige and influence of the accounting profession would be greatly eroded, possibly to the point where financial reporting becomes a process of "manual thumbing" with little basis for professional judgement and little influence on the setting of accounting standards. However, the SEC chose to delegate most standard setting to the profession.[5] To retain this delegated authority, however, the accounting profession had to retain the SEC's confidence that it was doing a satisfactory job of creating and maintaining a financial reporting environment that protects and informs investors and encourages the proper working of capital markets. Thus began the search for basic accounting concepts, those underlying truths on which the practice of accounting is, or should be, based. This was seen as a way to improve practice by reducing inconsistencies in choice of accounting policies across firms and enabling the accounting for new reporting challenges[6] to be deduced from basic principles rather than developing in an ad hoc and inconsistent way.

Accountants have laboured long and hard to find these basic concepts, but with relatively little success.[7] Indeed, they have never fully agreed on a definition of what accounting concepts are, let alone a list of them.

As a result, accounting theory and research up to the late 1960s consisted largely of a priori reasoning as to which accounting concepts and practices were "best." For example, should the effects of changing prices and inflation on financial statements be taken into account, and, if so, how? This debate can be traced back at least as far as the 1920s. Some accountants argued that the current values of specific assets and liabilities held by the firm should be recognized, with the resulting unrealized holding gains and losses included in net income. Other accountants argued that inflation-induced changes in the purchasing power of money should be recognized. During a period of inflation, the firm suffers a purchasing power loss on monetary assets such as cash and accounts receivable, since the amounts of goods and services that can be obtained when they are collected and spent is less than the amounts that could have been obtained when they were created. Conversely, the firm enjoys a purchasing power gain on monetary liabilities such as accounts payable and long-term debt. Separate reporting of these gains and losses would better reflect real firm performance, it was argued. Still other accountants argued that the effects of *both* specific and inflation-induced changes in prices should be taken into account. Others, however, often including firm management, resisted these suggestions. One argument, based in part on experience from the Great Depression, was that measurement of inflation was problematic, and current values were very volatile, so that taking them into account would not necessarily improve the measurement of the firm's (and the manager's) performance.

Nevertheless, standard setters in numerous countries did require some disclosures of the effects of changing prices. In Canada, for example, Section 4510 of the *CICA Handbook*, issued in 1982, required disclosure in the notes to the financial statements of the current values of inventories and capital assets, and of purchasing power gains and losses resulting from inflation. Section 4510 was subsequently withdrawn. However, this withdrawal was due more to the decline in inflation in the years following introduction of the section than to the debate having been settled.

The basic problem with debates such as how to account for changing prices was that there was little theoretical basis for choosing among the various alternatives, particularly since, as mentioned, accountants were unable to agree on a set of basic accounting concepts.

During this period, however, major developments were taking place in other disciplines. In particular, a theory of rational decision-making under uncertainty developed as a branch of statistics. This theory prescribes how individuals may revise their beliefs upon receipt of new information. The theory of efficient securities markets developed in economics and finance, with major implications for the role of information in capital markets. Another development was the Possibility Theorem of Arrow (1963), which demonstrated that, in general, it is not possible to combine differing preferences of individual members of society into a social preference ordering that satisfies reasonable conditions. This implies that there is no such thing as perfect or true accounting concepts, since, for example, investors will prefer different accounting concepts than managers. Arrow's theorem demonstrates that no set of concepts will be fully satisfactory to both parties. Instead, concepts must be hammered out strategically through negotiation and compromise to the point where both parties are willing to accept them even though they are not perfectly satisfactory to either side. The difficulties that accountants have had in agreeing on basic concepts are thus not surprising. Without a set of basic concepts, accounting standards, which are derived from the concepts, are subject to the same challenges.

These theories, which began to show up in accounting theory in the latter half of the 1960s, generated the concept of decision useful (in place of true) financial statement information. This view of the role of financial reporting first appeared in the American Accounting Association (AAA)[8] monograph, *A Statement of Basic Accounting Theory*, in 1966. Current statements of basic accounting concepts, most notably the Conceptual

Frameworks of the Financial Accounting Standards Board (FASB), International Accounting Standards Board (IASB), and the Canadian Accounting Standards Board (AcSB) are based on decision usefulness.

Equally important was the development of the economics of imperfect information, a branch of economics that formally recognizes that some individuals have an information advantage over others. This led to the development of the theory of agency, which has greatly increased our understanding of the legitimate interests of business management in financial reporting and standard setting.

These theories suggest that the answer to which way to account, if any, for changing prices outlined above will be found in the extent to which they lead to good investment decisions. Furthermore, any resolution will have to take the concerns of management into account.

In Canada, the development of financial accounting and reporting has proceeded differently, although the end result is basically similar to that of the United States. Financial reporting requirements in Canada were laid down in federal and provincial corporations acts, along the lines of the English corporations acts referred to earlier. The ultimate power to regulate financial reporting rests with the legislatures concerned. However, in 1946, the Committee on Accounting and Auditing Research, now the Accounting Standards Board, of the Canadian Institute of Chartered Accountants (CICA) began to issue bulletins on financial accounting issues. These were intended to guide Canadian accountants as to best practices, and did not have force of law. In 1968, these were formalized into the *CICA Handbook*. At first, adherence to these provisions was voluntary, but, given their prestigious source, they were difficult to ignore. Over time, the *Handbook* gained recognition as the authoritative statement of Generally Accepted Accounting Principles (GAAP) in Canada. Ultimately, provincial securities commissions and the corporations acts formally recognized this authority. For example, in 1975, for federally regulated companies, the Canada Business Corporations Act required adherence to the *CICA Handbook* to satisfy reporting requirements under the act. The end result, then, is similar to that in the United States in that the body with ultimate authority to set accounting standards has delegated this function to a private professional body.

More recently, several notable events have had a major impact on financial accounting and reporting. These followed from the stock market boom in the late 1990s and its collapse in the early 2000s. During the collapse, share prices of many firms, especially those in the "high-tech" industry, fell precipitously. For example, while the share price of General Electric Corp., a large U.S. conglomerate firm, fell from a high of about $55 U.S. in August 2000 to a low of about $21 in October 2002, that of telecommunications firm Nortel Networks fell from a high of about $82 U.S. to a low of 44 cents over the same period.

A contributing factor to the market collapse was the revelation of numerous financial reporting irregularities. Frequently, these involved revenue recognition, which has long been a problem in accounting theory and practice. Palmose and Scholz (2004), in a study of 492 U.S. corporations that reported restatements of prior years' incomes during

1995–1999, report that revenue restatements were the single most common type of restatement in their sample. In part, this problem is due to the vagueness and generality of revenue recognition criteria under GAAP. For example, revenue can be recognized when the significant risks and rewards of ownership have been transferred to the buyer and collection is reasonably assured.

During the boom of the late 1990s and early 2000s, many firms, especially newly established ones with little or no history of profits, attempted to impress investors and enhance their stock prices by reporting a rapidly growing stream of revenue. Subsequently, when the boom collapsed, much recognized revenue proved to be premature and had to be reversed.

Numerous other, even more serious, failures of financial reporting also came to light. Two of these are particularly notable. Enron Corp. was a large U.S. corporation with initial interests in natural gas distribution. Following substantial deregulation of the natural gas market in the United States during the 1980s, Enron successfully expanded its operations to become an intermediary between natural gas producers and users, thereby enabling them to manage their exposures to fluctuating natural gas prices. For example, it offered long-term fixed-price contracts to public utilities and natural gas producers. Subsequently, Enron extended this business model to a variety of other trading activities, including steel, natural gas, electricity, and weather futures. Its stock market performance was dramatic, rising to a high of about $90 U.S. per share in late 2000. To finance this rapid expansion, and support its share price, Enron needed both large amounts of capital and steadily increasing earnings. Meeting these needs was complicated by the fact that its forays into new markets were not always profitable, creating a temptation to disguise losses.[9]

In the face of these challenges, Enron resorted to devious tactics. One tactic was to create various special purpose entities (SPEs). These were limited partnerships formed for specific purposes, and effectively controlled by senior Enron officers. These SPEs were financed largely by Enron's contributions of its own common stock, in return for notes receivable from the SPE. The SPE could then borrow money using the Enron stock as security, and use the borrowed cash to repay its note payable to Enron. In this manner, much of Enron's debt did not appear on its balance sheet—it appeared on the books of the SPEs instead.

In addition, Enron received fees for management and other services supplied to its SPEs, and also investment income. This investment income is particularly worthy of note. By applying current value accounting to its holdings of Enron stock, the SPE included increases in the value of this stock in its income. As an owner of the SPE, Enron included its share of the SPE's income in its own earnings. In effect, Enron was able to include increases in the value of its own stock in its reported earnings! Reuters (2006), reporting on a 5 1/2 year jail sentence of Enron's chief accounting officer for his part in the Enron fraud, notes that $85 million of Enron's 2000 reported operating earnings came from this source.

Of course, if the SPEs had been consolidated with Enron's financial statements, as they should have been, the effects of these tactics would disappear. The SPE debt would

In July 2002, Qwest Communications International Inc., a large provider of Internet-based communications services, announced that it was under investigation by the SEC. Its share price immediately fell by 32%. In February 2003, the SEC announced fraud charges against several senior Qwest executives, alleging that they had inflated revenues during 2000 and 2001 in order to meet revenue and earnings projections.

One tactic used was to separate long-term sales of equipment and services into two components. Full revenue was immediately recognized on the equipment component despite the obligation to honour the service component over an extended period. A related tactic was to price services at cost, putting all profit into the equipment component, which was immediately recognized as revenue despite a continuing obligation to protect the customer from risk of obsolescence on the equipment "sold." Yet another tactic was to recognize revenue from the sale of fibre-optic cable despite an ability of the purchaser to exchange the cable at a later date. In retrospect, Qwest's revenue recognition practices were premature, to say the least.

In June 2004, the SEC announced settlements with some of the officers charged. One officer, for example, repaid $200,000 of "ill-gotten gains," plus a penalty of $150,000, and agreed to "cease and desist" from any future violations.

then have shown on Enron's consolidated balance sheet, fees billed would have been offset against the corresponding expense recorded by the SPE, and Enron's investment in its SPEs would have been deducted from its shareholders' equity.

However, the SPEs were not consolidated, seemingly with the agreement of Enron's auditor. But, in late 2001, Enron announced that it would now consolidate, apparently in response to an inquiry from the SEC. This resulted in an increase in its reported debt of some $628 million, a decrease in its shareholders' equity of $1.1 billion, and large reductions in previously reported earnings. Investors quickly lost all confidence in the company. Its share price fell to almost zero and it filed for bankruptcy protection in December 2001.

A second major abuse was relatively less complex. WorldCom Inc. was a large U.S. telecommunications carrier. During the years 1999 to 2002, the company overstated its earnings by about $11 billion. Almost $4 billion of this amount arose from capitalization of network maintenance and other costs that should have been charged to expense as incurred—a tactic that overstated both reported earnings and operating cash flow. Another $3.3 billion of overstatement arose from reductions in the allowance for doubtful accounts. Again, when these abuses came to light, investor confidence collapsed and WorldCom applied for bankruptcy protection in 2002.

These, and numerous other, reporting abuses took place regardless of the fact that the financial statements of the companies involved were audited and certified as in accordance with GAAP. As a result, public confidence in financial reporting and the working of capital markets was severely shaken.

One result of this collapse of confidence was increased regulation. The most notable example is the Sarbanes-Oxley Act, passed by the U.S. Congress in 2002. This wide-ranging act is designed to restore public confidence by reducing the likelihood of accounting horror stories such as those just described. The act does this by improving corporate governance and tightening the audit function. One of its major provisions is to create the Public Company Accounting Oversight Board. This agency has the power to set auditing standards and to inspect and discipline auditors of public companies. The act also restricts several of the non-audit services offered by auditing firms to their clients, such as information systems and valuation services. Furthermore, the auditor now reports to the audit committee of the client's board of directors, rather than to management. The audit committee must be composed of directors independent of the company.

Other provisions of Sarbanes-Oxley include a requirement that firms' financial reports shall include "all material correcting adjustments," and disclose all material off-balance-sheet loans and other relations with "unconsolidated entities." Furthermore, the Chief Executive Officer and Chief Financial Officer must certify that the financial statements present fairly the company's results of operations and financial position. Section 404 of the act required these two officers and an independent auditor to certify the proper operation of the company's internal controls over financial reporting, although these requirements were relaxed somewhat in 2007.

The standard-setting bodies themselves moved to restore public confidence. One move was to tighten the rules surrounding SPEs so that it is more difficult to avoid their consolidation with the financial statements of the parent entity. In Canada, the Accounting Standards Board (AcSB) has implemented two new accounting standards that, presumably, are intended to further reduce the likelihood of Enron- and WorldCom-style reporting failures. Section 1100 of the *CICA Handbook*, adopted in 2003, clarifies the meaning of Canadian GAAP and removes the ability of a firm to depart from GAAP. Prior to Section 1100, firms had some room to adopt accounting policies that departed from GAAP by claiming that use of GAAP would result in misleading financial statements. Section 1400 of the *Handbook*, adopted at the same time, requires that financial statements present fairly the firm's financial position and results of operations, and asserts that fair presentation includes the provision of sufficient information about significant transactions that their effects on the financial statements can be understood. These requirements of Section 1400 are similar to some of the requirements of the Sarbanes-Oxley Act outlined above.

Earlier in this section, we noted that one of the effects of the stock market crash of 1929 was a strengthening of the historical cost basis of accounting. This raises the question of whether the 2001 stock market crash and revelation of accounting abuses will result in a similar movement back to a more conservative basis of accounting in the 2000s. Basu (1997) defines conservatism as the requiring of a higher standard of verification to record gains than to record losses, resulting in persistent understatement of assets, earnings, and shareholders' equity relative to their actual values. Thus, unrealized losses from declines in value are recognized when they take place, but gains from increases in value are not recognized until they are realized. For example, as mentioned earlier, inventories and capital assets are generally valued on the basis of historical cost unless a decline in value below cost has occurred, in which case a lower-of-cost-or-market rule or ceiling test is applied.

Indeed, there is evidence of increasing conservatism in recent years. For example, standard setters extended ceiling tests to include purchased goodwill in 2001. Also, it seems that managers are becoming more conservative in applying accounting standards. Thus, Lobo and Zhou (2006) document a decrease in aggressive accounting practices subsequent to the passage of the Sarbanes-Oxley Act, and Graham, Harvey, and Rajgopal (2005) report survey evidence that managers are now more likely to manage earnings using real variables (e.g., cutting R&D) than risk the legal and reputation consequences of aggressive accounting policies.

As a result of developments such as these, some accountants are giving greater attention to the usefulness of conservatism. Time will tell whether an increased understanding of its role will moderate standard setters' movements towards a current value approach to financial reporting.

These various developments set the stage for the current financial accounting and reporting environment that is the subject of this book.

1.3 A NOTE ON ETHICAL BEHAVIOUR

The collapse of Enron and WorldCom, and subsequent collapse of public confidence in financial reporting, raise questions about how to restore this confidence. One response is increased regulation, as in the Sarbanes-Oxley Act described above. However, **ethical behaviour** by accountants and auditors is also required, since numerous accountants designed, were involved in, or at least knew about the reporting irregularities. Also, the financial statements of the firms involved were certified by their auditors as being in accordance with GAAP.

By ethical behaviour, we mean that accountants and auditors should "do the right thing." In our context, this means that accountants must behave with integrity and independence in putting the public interest ahead of the employer's and client's interests should these conflict.

It is important to realize that there is a social dimension to integrity and independence. That is, a society depends on shared beliefs and common values. This notion goes back to Thomas Hobbes, a seventeenth-century philosopher, in his book *The Leviathan*. Hobbes argued that if people acted solely as selfish individuals, society would collapse to the point where force, or the threat of force, would prevail—there would be no cooperative behaviour. He also argued that rules, regulations, and the courts were not enough to restore cooperative behaviour, since no set of rules could possibly anticipate all human interaction. What is needed, in addition, is that people must recognize that it is in their joint interests to cooperate.

Clearly, the force of Hobbes' arguments can be seen in the Enron and WorldCom disasters. We have a set of rules governing financial reporting (e.g., GAAP). However, GAAP was not followed and/or was bent so as to conform to its letter but not its intent.

Cooperative behaviour broke down because certain individuals behaved in a manner that broke the rules—they did not behave with integrity and independence. This was good for them, at least in the short run, but bad for society. Hobbes' theory predicts that increased regulation will not suffice to prevent a repetition of these reporting disasters. What is also needed is ethical behaviour.

Note, however, that there is a time dimension to ethical behaviour. An accountant can act in his/her own self-interest and still behave ethically. This is accomplished by taking a longer-run view of the consequences of one's actions. For example, suppose that an accountant is instructed to understate a firm's environmental liabilities. In the short run, doing so will benefit the accountant through job retention, promotion, and higher compensation. In the longer run, though, future generations will suffer through increased pollution, shareholders will suffer from reduced share price when the extent of environmental liability becomes known, and investors as a whole will suffer when reduced public confidence in financial reporting lowers the prices of all shares. The accountant will suffer through dismissal, professional discipline or expulsion, and reduced compensation due to reduced stature of all accountants. By taking account of these longer-run costs, the accountant is motivated to behave ethically. In effect, in the longer run, self-interested behaviour and ethical behaviour merge.[10]

In this book, we will often cast our discussion in terms of full disclosure, usefulness of financial statements, cooperative behaviour, and reputation, all of which benefit society. However, in acting so as to meet these desirable characteristics of financial reporting, the accountant is, in effect, acting ethically.

1.4 THE COMPLEXITY OF INFORMATION IN FINANCIAL ACCOUNTING AND REPORTING

The environment of accounting is both very complex and very challenging. It is complex because the product of accounting is **information**—a powerful and important commodity. The main reason for this complexity is the absence of perfect or true accounting concepts and standards, as discussed in Section 1.2. As a result, individuals will not be unanimous in their reaction to even the same information. For example, a sophisticated investor may prefer the valuation of certain firm assets and liabilities at value-in-use on grounds that this will help to predict future firm performance Other investors may prefer fair value accounting on grounds that this better reports on manager stewardship (to be discussed in Chapter 7). Others may be less positive towards any form of current value accounting, perhaps because they feel that current value information is unreliable, or simply because they are used to historical cost information. Furthermore, managers, who will have to report the current values, might react quite negatively. Management typically objects to inclusion of unrealized gains and losses resulting from changes in asset and liability values in net income, arguing that these items introduce excessive volatility into earnings, do not reflect their performance, and should not be included when evaluating the results of their efforts. These arguments may be somewhat self-serving, since part of management's job is to anticipate changes in values and take steps to protect the firm from adverse effects of these changes. For example, management may hedge against increases in prices of raw materials and changes in interest rates. Nevertheless, management's objections remain. As a result, accountants quickly get caught up in whether reported net income should fulfill a primary role of reporting useful information to investors or reporting on management's stewardship of the firm's resources.

Another reason for the complexity of information is that it does more than affect individual decisions. In affecting decisions it also affects the working of markets, such as securities markets and managerial labour markets. It is important to the efficiency and fairness of the economy itself that these markets work well.

The challenge for financial accountants, then, is to survive and prosper in a complex environment characterized by conflicting preferences of different groups with an interest in financial reporting. This book argues that the prospects for survival and prosperity will be enhanced if accountants have a critical awareness of the impact of financial reporting on investors, managers, and the economy. The alternative to awareness is simply to accept the reporting environment as given. However, this is a very short-term strategy, since environments are constantly changing and evolving.

1.5 THE ROLE OF ACCOUNTING RESEARCH

A book about accounting theory must inevitably draw on accounting research, much of which is contained in academic journals. There are two complementary ways that we can view the role of research. The first is to consider its effects on accounting practice. For example, a decision usefulness approach underlies Section 1000 of the CICA *Handbook*, and the Conceptual Framework of the FASB in the United States. The essence of this approach is that investors should be supplied with information to help them make good investment decisions. One has only to compare the current annual report of a public company with those issued in the 1960s and prior to see the tremendous increase in disclosure over the 40 years or so since decision usefulness formally became an important concept in accounting theory.

Yet, this increase in disclosure did not "just happen." It, as outlined in Section 1.2, is based on fundamental research into the theory of investor decision-making and the theory of capital markets, which have guided the accountant in what information is useful. Furthermore, the theory has been subjected to extensive empirical testing, which has established that, on average, investors use financial accounting information much as the theory predicts.

Independently of whether it affects current practice, however, there is a second important view of the role of research. This is to improve our *understanding* of the accounting environment, which we argued above should not be taken for granted. For example, fundamental research into models of conflict resolution, in particular agency theory models, has improved our understanding of managers' interests in financial reporting, of the role of executive compensation plans in motivating and controlling management's operation of the firm, and of the ways in which such plans use accounting information. This in turn leads to an improved understanding of managers' interests in accounting policy choice and why they may want to bias or otherwise manipulate reported net income, or, at least, to have some ability to manage the "bottom line." Research such as this enables us to better understand corporate governance issues such as the boundaries of management's legitimate role in financial reporting. It also helps us understand why the accountant is frequently caught between the interests of investors and managers. In this book, we use both of the above views. Our approach to research is twofold. In some cases, we choose important research papers, describe them intuitively, and explain how they fit into our overall framework of financial accounting theory and practice. In other cases, we simply refer to research papers on which our discussion is based. The interested reader can pursue the discussion in greater depth if desired.

1.6 THE IMPORTANCE OF INFORMATION ASYMMETRY

This book is based on information economics. This is a unifying theme that formally recognizes that some parties to business transactions may have an information advantage over others. When this happens, the economy is said to be characterized by **information asymmetry**. We shall consider two major types of information asymmetry.

The first is **adverse selection**. For our purposes, adverse selection occurs because some persons, such as firm managers and other insiders, will know more about the current condition and future prospects of the firm than outside investors. There are various ways that managers and other insiders can exploit their information advantage at the expense of outsiders. For example, managers may behave opportunistically by biasing or otherwise managing the information released to investors, perhaps to increase the value of stock options they hold. They may delay or selectively release information early to selected investors or analysts, enabling insiders, including themselves, to benefit at the expense of ordinary investors. Such tactics are *adverse* (hence the term) to the interests of ordinary investors, since it reduces their ability to make good investment decisions. Then, investors' concerns about the possibility of biased information release and favouritism will make them wary of buying firms' securities, with the result that capital markets will not function as well as they should. We can then think of financial accounting and reporting as a mechanism to control adverse selection by timely and credible conversion of inside information into outside information.

> *Adverse selection* is a type of information asymmetry whereby one or more parties to a business transaction, or potential transaction, have an information advantage over other parties.

The second type of information asymmetry is **moral hazard**. Moral hazard exists in many situations. A medical doctor may give a patient a cursory examination. A trustee for a bond issue may shirk his/her duties, to the disadvantage of the bondholders. In our context, moral hazard occurs because of the separation of ownership and control that characterizes most large business entities. It is effectively impossible for shareholders and creditors to observe directly the extent and quality of top manager effort on their behalf. Then, the manager may be tempted to shirk on effort, blaming any deterioration of firm performance on factors beyond his or her control, or biasing reported earnings to cover up. Obviously, if this happens, there are serious implications both for investors and for the efficient working of the economy. We can then view accounting net income as a measure of managerial performance. This helps to control moral hazard in two complementary ways. First, net income can serve as an input into executive compensation contracts to motivate manager performance. Second, net income can inform the managerial labour market, so that a manager who shirks will suffer a decline in income, reputation, and market value in the longer run.

> **Moral hazard** is a type of information asymmetry whereby one or more parties to a business transaction, or potential transaction, can observe their actions in fulfillment of the transaction but other parties cannot.

1.7 THE FUNDAMENTAL PROBLEM OF FINANCIAL ACCOUNTING THEORY

Given the absence of perfect or true accounting concepts, it turns out that the most useful measure of net income to inform investors, that is, to control adverse selection, need not be the same as the best measure to motivate manager performance, that is, to control moral hazard. This was recognized by Gjesdal (1981). Investors' interests are best served by information that enables better investment decisions and better-operating capital markets. Providing it is reasonably reliable, current value accounting fulfills this role, since it provides up-to-date information about assets and liabilities, hence of future firm performance, and reduces the ability of insiders to take advantage of changes in asset and liability values.

Managers' legitimate interests are best served by information that is highly informative about their performance in running the firm, since this enables efficient compensation contracts and better working of managerial labour markets. This is the **stewardship** role of financial reporting, one of the oldest concepts in accounting. While fair value accounting can improve reporting on stewardship, it can also interfere. Current values are very volatile in their impact on reported earnings and, unless market values are readily available, may be more subject to bias and manipulation by the manager than historical cost-based information. Both of these effects reduce the informativeness of earnings about manager stewardship. Thus, from a managerial perspective, a less volatile and more conservative income measure, such as one based on historical cost, or at least a measure that excludes certain unrealized gains and losses, may better fulfill a role of motivating and evaluating managers.

Given that there is only one bottom line, the fundamental problem of financial accounting theory is how to design and implement concepts and standards that best trade off the investor-informing and manager performance–evaluating roles for accounting information.

Some policies require tradeoffs between these roles, as in current value versus historical cost accounting just described. Other policies, such as expanded disclosure, may facilitate both roles. In this regard, it is interesting to note that the IASB and FASB, in a joint financial statement presentation project, may dichotomize the income statement into separate components for operating, financing, investing, and tax activities, as well as an "other comprehensive income" section, which includes unrealized gains and losses on items such as financial instruments. The extent to which such proposals, if adopted, will solve the fundamental problem remains to be seen. For now, it is largely correct to say that there is only one bottom line.[11]

1.8 REGULATION AS A REACTION TO THE FUNDAMENTAL PROBLEM

There are two basic reactions to the fundamental problem. One is, in effect, to ask, "What problem?" That is, why not keep regulation to the minimum needed to provide a stable environment for trade, resolution of disputes, and punishment for wrongdoing? Then, let market forces determine how much and what kinds of information firms should produce? We can think of investors and other financial statement users as demanders of information and of managers as suppliers. Just as in markets for apples and automobiles, the forces of demand and supply can determine the quantity produced.

This view argues, in effect, that market forces can sufficiently control the adverse selection and moral hazard problems so that investors are protected, and managerial labour markets and securities markets will work reasonably well. Indeed, as we shall see, there is a surprising number of ways for managers to credibly supply information. Furthermore, investors as a group are surprisingly sophisticated in ferreting out the implications of information for future firm performance. Consequently, according to this view, unregulated market prices reasonably reflect firm and manager value.

The second reaction is to turn to **regulation** to protect investors, on the grounds that information is such a complex and important commodity that market forces alone fail to adequately control the problems of moral hazard and adverse selection. This leads directly to the role of standard setting, which is viewed in this book as a form of regulation that lays down generally accepted accounting concepts and standards.

Of course, consistent with the theorem of Arrow (Section 1.2) and the arguments of Hobbes (Section 1.3), we cannot expect regulation to completely protect investors. Consequently, the rigorous determination of the right amount of regulation is an extremely complex issue of social choice. At the present time we simply do not know which of the above two reactions to the fundamental problem is on the right track. Certainly, we witness lots of regulation in accounting, and there appears to be no slowing down in the rate at which new standards are coming on line. Consequently, it may seem that society has resolved the question of extent of regulation for us.

Yet, we live in a time of deregulation. Past years have witnessed substantial deregulation of major industries such as transportation, telecommunications, financial services, and electric power generation, where deregulation was once thought unthinkable. The reason it is important to ask whether similar deregulation should take place in the information "industry" is that regulation has a cost—a fact often ignored by standard setters. Again, the answer to the question of whether the benefits of regulation outweigh the costs is not known. However, we shall pursue this issue later in the book.

1.9 THE ORGANIZATION OF THIS BOOK

Figure 1.1 summarizes how this book operationalizes the framework for the study of financial accounting theory outlined above. There are four main components of the figure, and we will outline each in turn.

1.9.1 Ideal Conditions

Before considering the problems introduced into accounting by information asymmetry, it is worthwhile to consider what accounting would be like under ideal conditions. This is depicted by the leftmost box of Figure 1.1. By ideal conditions we mean an economy where firms' future cash flows and their probabilities are known. Also, the economy has perfect and complete markets or, equivalently, a lack of information asymmetry and other barriers to fair and efficient working of markets. Such conditions are also called "first best." Then, asset and liability valuation is on the basis of expected present values of future cash flows (i.e., value-in-use). Arbitrage ensures that present values and market values are equal. Investors and managers would have no scope for disagreement over the role of financial reporting and no incentives to call for regulation. Under such conditions, there would be no fundamental problem of financial accounting theory.

Unfortunately, or perhaps fortunately, ideal conditions do not prevail in practice. Nevertheless, they provide a useful benchmark against which more realistic "second best" accounting conditions can be compared. For example, we will see that there are numerous instances of the actual use of current value-based accounting techniques in financial reporting. Reserve recognition accounting for oil and gas companies is an example. Furthermore, the use of such techniques is increasing, as in standards requiring fair value accounting for financial instruments. A study of accounting under ideal conditions is useful not only because practice is moving to increased use of current values, but more importantly, it helps us to see what the real problems and challenges of current value accounting are when the ideal conditions that it requires do not hold.

1.9.2 Adverse Selection

The top three boxes of Figure 1.1 represent the second component of the framework. This introduces the adverse selection problem. As discussed in Section 1.6, this is the problem of communication from the firm to outside investors. Here, the accounting role is to provide a "level playing field" through full disclosure of useful and cost-effective information to investors and other financial statement users.

To understand how financial accounting can help to control the adverse selection problem, it is desirable to have an appreciation of how investors make decisions. This is because knowledge of investor decision processes is essential if the accountant is to know what information they need. The study of investment decision-making is a large topic, since investors undoubtedly make decisions in a variety of ways, ranging from intuition to "hot tips" to random occurrences such as a sudden need for cash to sophisticated computer-based models.

The approach we will take in this book is to assume that most investors are **rational**, that is, they make decisions so as to maximize their expected utility, or satisfaction, from wealth. This theory of rational investment decision has been widely studied. In making the rationality assumption we do not imply that all investors make decisions this way. Indeed, there is increasing recognition that many investors do not behave rationally in the sense of maximizing their expected utility of wealth. We do claim, however, that the theory captures the average behaviour of those investors who want to make informed investment decisions, and this claim is backed up by substantial empirical evidence.

The reporting of information that is useful to rational investors is called the **decision usefulness** approach. As suggested in Section 1.2, this approach underlies the pronouncements of major standard-setting bodies, such as the Conceptual Framework of the FASB.

There are two versions of decision usefulness. One is called the **information approach**. This perspective takes the view that the form of disclosure does not matter—it can be in notes, or in supplementary disclosures such as reserve recognition accounting and management discussion and analysis, in addition to the financial statements proper.[12] Rational investors are regarded as sufficiently sophisticated on average that they can digest the implications of public information from any source.

Recent years, however, have seen a considerable increase in the use of current values, including for leases, pensions, other postretirement benefits, and financial instruments. This version is called the **measurement approach** to decision usefulness. Under this perspective, accountants expand their approach to decision usefulness by taking more responsibility for incorporating measurements of current asset and liability values into the financial statements proper. Whether this means that accountants have forgotten the lessons of the 1920s and 1930s, or whether improvements in measurement tools, such as statistical analysis of large databases and the use of mathematical models to estimate fair values, and new regulations such as Sarbanes-Oxley, will help to avoid the reporting abuses discussed in Section 1.2, is difficult to say. Only time will tell if these developments will slow down or reverse the measurement approach.

1.9.3 Moral Hazard

The bottom three boxes of Figure 1.1 represent the third component of the book. Here, the information asymmetry problem is moral hazard, arising from the unobservability of the manager's effort in running the firm. That is, the manager's decision problem is to decide on how much effort to devote to running the firm on behalf of the shareholders. Since effort is unobservable, the manager may be tempted to shirk on effort. However, since net income reflects manager performance, it operates as an indirect measure of the manager's effort decision. Consequently, the user decision problem is how to design financial reporting to motivate and evaluate manager performance. To be informative about performance, net income should be a precise and sensitive measure of this performance.

1.9.4 Standard Setting

We can now see the source of the fundamental problem of financial accounting theory more clearly. Current values of assets and liabilities are of greater interest to investors than their historical costs, since current values provide the best available indication of future firm performance and investment returns. However, as mentioned, managers may feel that unrealized gains and losses from adjusting the carrying values of assets and liabilities to current value do not reflect *their own* performance. Accounting standard setters quickly get caught up in mediation between the conflicting preferences of investors and managers. This is depicted by the rightmost box in Figure 1.1.

1.9.5 The Process of Standard Setting

We have pointed out that, in practice, the setting of accounting concepts and standards requires negotiation and compromise. Also, their application must be enforced. We now give a brief description of the structure of accounting standard-setting bodies, to show how these requirements are operationalized.

The International Accounting Standards Board (IASB) The IASB was established in 2001, assuming standard-setting responsibility from a predecessor body, the International Accounting Standards Committee. This earlier body was created in 1973 by agreement between accountancy bodies in Australia, Canada, France, Germany, Japan, Mexico, the Netherlands, the United Kingdom and Ireland, and the United States.

The basic objective of the IASB is to develop a single set of high quality, understandable, and enforceable global accounting standards, now called International Financial Reporting Standards (IFRS).[13] These standards are developed by a board of 14 individuals, most of whom are full-time. They must possess technical skills and suitable international business and market experience.

A majority of nine of 14 votes is required to pass new standards, a requirement called **super-majority voting**. Super-majority voting decreases the possibility of approval of a standard that is only marginally acceptable to the Board, and also tends to produce a process of negotiation and compromise in the creation of a new standard. Dissenting members will be in a stronger position than they would be if only a simple majority was required and thus would be less likely to feel that their views and concerns had been ignored.

In designing standards, the IASB follows **due process**. This includes broad consultation with interested parties before admitting a topic to the Board's agenda, and the issuing of exposure drafts of new standards, possibly preceded by a discussion paper, to enable interested parties, including management, to react and comment. Public hearings may also take place. Comments are analyzed and a revised standard is prepared. A statement of basis for conclusions is issued to explain the standard. Representation of diverse constituencies on the Board and super-majority voting also contribute to due process. Note that the following of due process is consistent with a need for compromise and negotiation in setting accounting standards.

Many countries, including Canada from 2011, have adopted IASB standards, as has the European Union. Some countries, such as China, have adopted most of them. Other countries, notably the United States and Canada prior to 2011, prefer to use their own accounting standards, with the ultimate goal of integrating with IASB standards.

The Financial Accounting Standards Board (FASB) The FASB was established in 1973 to assume from earlier bodies the role of standard setting in the United States. Its purpose is to establish and improve standards of financial accounting and reporting for the guidance and education of the public. To accomplish this, its mission includes developing accounting concepts, improving the usefulness of financial reporting, keeping standards current to reflect changes in the business and economic environment, addressing financial reporting deficiencies, improving the understanding of the nature and purpose of information contained in financial reports, and promoting international convergence of accounting standards.

The FASB consists of five full-time board members, appointed for a maximum of two, five-year terms. They must have knowledge and experience in investing, accounting, finance, business, education and research, and concern for the investor and the public interest. Unlike the IASB, simple-majority voting is required, with three of the five members in favour required to pass a new standard.

The FASB, like the IASB, is independent of other business and professional organizations. For example, the FASB is distinct from the American Institute of Certified Public Accountants (AICPA), the major American professional accounting body. While the AICPA is one of the sponsoring bodies and endorses FASB standards, many other bodies are also involved in sponsoring the FASB.

In 2002, the FASB established a **User Advisory Council**. This is a group of over 40 investment professionals to assist the FASB in raising awareness of how investors, analysts, and rating agencies use financial information and how to better design accounting standards to meet their needs.

In setting and updating accounting and reporting concepts and standards, the FASB, like the IASB, places heavy emphasis on due process. Procedures for initiating and adopting new standards are broadly similar to those of the IASB outlined above.

The Canadian Accounting Standards Board (AcSB) The AcSB is the Canadian accounting standard-setting body. It is authorized by the Board of Governors of the Canadian Institute of Chartered Accountants to publish reports "on its own responsibility." Presumably, this is to give it a measure of independence from the CICA itself and reduce the possibility of interference in its deliberations. This organizational structure differs from that of the IASB and FASB, which, as mentioned, are independent of related professional organizations.

The AcSB consists of a maximum of nine members, chosen to represent diverse constituencies. Unlike the IASB and FASB, most members serve on a voluntary basis. That is, with the exception of the Chairperson, these are not full-time, salaried positions. The AcSB's accounting standards are contained in the *CICA Handbook*. The origins and authority of the *Handbook* were outlined in Section 1.2. To pass a new standard, a super-majority of two-thirds of Board members voting in favour is required.

With its adoption of IASB accounting standards from 2011, the activities of the AcSB will change somewhat. The Board will give increased attention to special problems of financial reporting for non-public enterprises (who do not necessarily report under GAAP) and to not-for-profit enterprises. Also, of course, the Board will continue to take part in the setting of international standards through IASB representation and contributions to the development of concepts and new IFRSs.

Securities Commissions If standard-setting bodies are to achieve their objectives, financial statements must adhere to GAAP. Adherence to GAAP is accomplished in a variety of ways. Ethical behaviour by managers and accountants is obviously desirable. Also, as we shall see, securities markets and managerial labour markets are important contributors to responsible reporting. When these motivations fail, enforcement takes over. Discipline committees of professional accounting bodies play an important enforcement role, as does the prospect of legal liability for reporting failures.

From our perspective, securities commissions are one of the most important enforcers of accounting standards. Notable among these is the SEC in the United States. Its creation, and its delegation of standard setting to the FASB, were outlined in Section 1.2. However, the SEC also fulfills an important enforcement role by investigating firms and managers for failures to adhere to GAAP and prosecuting and penalizing them if appropriate. The SEC's reach extends to many Canadian and other foreign firms whose shares are traded in the United States. We shall see several examples of the SEC's enforcement activities in this book.

The SEC also issues accounting standards, mainly for disclosures outside of the financial statements. These include reserve recognition accounting for oil and gas firms, management discussion and analysis, and disclosures of management compensation, all of which will be discussed in later chapters.

In Canada, securities regulation is a provincial jurisdiction. Consequently, Canada does not at present have a national securities regulator. However, the provincial and territorial securities regulators have created the Canadian Securities Administrators (CSA), a forum to coordinate and harmonize Canadian capital markets regulation. Its mission includes the protection of investors, securing the proper working of capital markets, and reducing risk. Of the provincial securities commissions, the most important is the Ontario Securities Commission (OSC). Later chapters contain several references to OSC regulations.

The International Organization of Securities Commissions (IOSCO) represents the world's securities regulators, including Canadian regulators and the SEC. It recommends to its members that they use IASB standards, although individual member countries may require reconciliation of IASB standards with their own GAAP. For example, foreign firms that wish to trade their securities in the United States must meet SEC requirements. These include filing financial statements with the SEC either in accordance with IASB GAAP or with U.S. GAAP.[14]

Unlike domestic securities commissions, IOSCO does not have the authority to enforce IASB standards. Enforcement is up to the authorities in the respective jurisdictions that adopt these standards. Consequently, analysis of financial statements from foreign jurisdictions should include careful awareness of local customs and business practices and the legal and other institutional characteristics of those jurisdictions. Research shows that even in the presence of the same set of accounting standards (i.e., IASB standards), the quality of financial reporting varies across countries. Some of this research is discussed in Chapter 13.

1.10 RELEVANCE OF FINANCIAL ACCOUNTING THEORY TO ACCOUNTING PRACTICE

The framework just described provides a way of organizing our study of financial accounting theory. However, this book also recognizes an obligation to convince you that the theory is relevant to accounting practice. This is accomplished in two main ways. First, the various theories and research underlying financial accounting are described and explained in plain language, and their relevance is demonstrated by means of numerous references to accounting practice. For example, Chapter 3 describes how investors may make rational investment decisions, and then goes on to demonstrate that this decision theory underlies the Conceptual Framework of the FASB. Also, the book contains numerous instances where accounting standards are described and critically evaluated. In addition to enabling you to learn some of the contents of these standards, you can better understand and apply them when you have a grounding in the underlying reasoning on which they are based. The second approach to demonstrating relevance is through assignment problems. A concerted attempt has been made to select relevant problem material to illustrate and motivate the concepts.

Recent years have been challenging, even exciting, times for financial accounting theory. We have learned a tremendous amount about the important role of financial accounting in our economy from the information economics research outlined above. If this book enables you to better understand and appreciate this role, it will have attained its objective.

Notes

1. For some information about Paciolo, a translation of his bookkeeping treatise, and a copy of an Italian version, see *Paciolo on Accounting*, by R. Gene Brown and Kenneth S. Johnston (1963).

2. Readers with a mathematical background will recognize these relationships as related to the fundamental theorem of calculus.

3. The dropping of these requirements did not mean that firms should not supply information to shareholders, but that the amount and nature of information supplied was a matter between the firm and its shareholders. In effect, it was felt that market forces, rather than legal requirement, were sufficient to motivate information production.

4. Actually, MN pose a much deeper question. Widespread share ownership had long been seen as a way of reconciling increasingly large and powerful corporations with the popular belief in individualism, property rights, and democracy, whereby the "little guy" could take part in the corporate governance process. With the 1929 crash and subsequent revelation of manipulative abuses, a new approach was required that would both restore public confidence in securities markets and be acceptable to powerful corporate interest groups. MN suggest that the creation of the SEC was an embodiment of such a new approach.

5. This is not to say that the SEC stands aloof from accounting standards. If it perceives that standards as set by the profession are straying too far from what it wants, the SEC can bring considerable pressure to bear short of taking over the process. In this regard, see Note 6. However, the SEC reaffirmed its delegation of standard setting to the FASB in 2003.

6. The controversy over the investment tax credit in the United States provides an excellent example. The 1962 Revenue Act provided firms with a credit against taxes payable of 7% of current investment in capital assets. The controversy was whether to account for the credit as a reduction in current income tax expense or to bring all or part of it into income over the life of the capital assets to which the credit applied. The Accounting Principles Board (the predecessor body to the FASB) issued APB2, requiring the latter alternative. The SEC, however, objected and issued its own standard, allowing greater flexibility in accounting for the credit. The Accounting Principles Board backed down and issued APB4 in 1964 allowing either alternative. The basic problem, as seen by the standard setters, was the lack of a set of basic accounting concepts from which the correct accounting for the credit could be deduced.

7. For a detailed description of the search for basic accounting concepts in the United States from the inception of the SEC to the 1990s, see Storey and Storey (1998).

8. The American Accounting Association is an association of academic accountants. It does not have standard-setting authority like the FASB. Nevertheless, professional accountants later picked up on the decision usefulness concept. See *Study Group on the Objectives of Financial Statements* (1973), also called the Trueblood Committee report.

9. For further discussion of Enron's business model, see Healy and Palepu (2003).

10. This argument derives from the **folk theorem** of game theory. In its simplest form, this theorem states that for a non-cooperative game that is repeated indefinitely, without discounting of future payoffs, a cooperative solution can be attained if the players adopt a rational strategy. In our context, the rational strategy is for the accountant to forgo a short-term gain resulting, say, from bending or violating GAAP to please the client. The accountant will forgo the short-term gain if the strategy of the other players (investors, standard setters, lawmakers, courts) is to sufficiently punish the accountant for deviating from the cooperative strategy. That is, in the longer run, the accountant's payoffs are higher if he/she acts cooperatively.

    The folk theorem originated in the 1960s. It is so named because it is not known who established it first. Subsequently, game theorists have strengthened the theorem, for example by deriving conditions under which the theorem can be extended to finite periods, and with some discounting.

See Friedman (1996), pp.103-104. See also Robert Aumann's 2005 Nobel Prize Lecture: (**http://nobelprize.org/nobel_prizes/economics/laureates/2005/aumann-lecture.html**).

It should be noted, however, that while the folk theorem can produce ethical behaviour, the two mindsets are different. Ethical behaviour is driven by a desire to do the right thing. Folk theorem is driven by a rational calculation by the players that if they deviate from the cooperative solution they will be sufficiently punished.

11. We say "largely" since current IASB and FASB standards already include other comprehensive income, which is reported after net income. However, unlike for net income, there is little evidence that other comprehensive income is decision useful. Thus, net income is the main "bottom line." Other comprehensive income is discussed in Chapter 13.

12. Strictly speaking, the term "financial statements" includes the notes to the statements. When we refer to disclosure within the financial statements themselves, we will use the term "financial statements proper." Thus, if a firm values an asset at current value in its accounts and reports the resulting number on the balance sheet, it reports current value in the financial statements proper. If it discloses current value only in a note, this would be reported in the financial statements but not in the financial statements proper.

13. IFRS were called International Accounting Standards (IAS) prior to the issuance of IFRS 1, effective in 2004. We will use both names, as appropriate, in subsequent discussions.

14. In Canada, IASB-based financial statements of foreign firms are accepted without the need to reconcile to Canadian GAAP, under National Instrument 52-107 of the CSA. For Canadian firms with shares traded in the United States, the Multi-jurisdictional Disclosure System allows them to file SEC reports using the documents they file in Canada, and vice versa. Canadian firms taking advantage of the Multi-jurisdictional Disclosure System must meet the requirements of the Sarbanes-Oxley Act, however.

Chapter 2
Accounting Under Ideal Conditions

Figure 2.1 Organization of Chapter 2

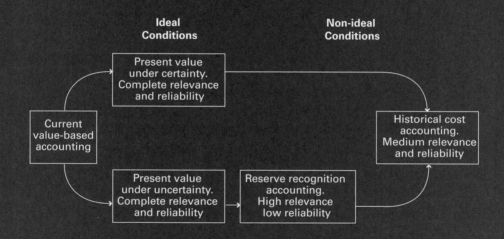

2.1 OVERVIEW

We will begin our study of financial accounting theory by considering the present value model. This model provides the utmost in **relevant information** to financial statement users. In this context we define relevant information as information about the firm's future economic prospects, that is, its dividends, cash flows, and profitability.

Our concern is with the conditions under which relevant financial statements will also be reliable, where **reliable information** faithfully represents without bias what it is intended to represent. We will also explore the conditions under which market values of assets and liabilities can serve as indirect measures of present value. This will be the case under ideal conditions (to be defined later). If conditions are not ideal (which is usually the case), fundamental problems are created for asset valuation and income measurement.

Figure 2.1 outlines the organization of this chapter.

2.2 THE PRESENT VALUE MODEL UNDER CERTAINTY

The present value model is widely used in economics and finance and has had considerable impact on accounting over the years. We first consider a simple version of the model under conditions of certainty. By "certainty" we mean that the future cash flows of the firm and the interest rate in the economy are publicly known with certainty. We denote these as **ideal conditions**.

Example 2.1
Illustration of the Present Value Model Under Certainty

Consider P.V. Ltd., a one-asset firm with no liabilities. Assume that the asset will generate end-of-year cash flows of $150 each year for two years and then will have zero value. Assume also that the risk-free interest rate in the economy is 10%. Then, at time 0 (the beginning of the first year of the asset's life), the present value of the firm's future cash flows, denoted by PA_0, is:

$$PA_0 = \frac{150}{1.10} + \frac{150}{1.10^2} = 136.36 + 123.97 = \$260.33$$

We can then prepare a present value opening balance sheet as follows:

P.V. Ltd.
Balance Sheet
As at Time 0

Capital asset, at present value $260.33	Shareholders' equity $260.33

The firm's income statement for year 1 is:

P.V. Ltd.
Income Statement
For Year 1

Accretion of discount	$26.03

Since future net revenues are capitalized into asset value, net income is simply interest on opening asset value, just as income from a savings account is interest on the opening account balance.[1] Thus, net income for the year is equal to $PA_0 \times 10\% = \$260.33 \times 10\% = \$26.03$. This amount is called **accretion of discount**. It is opening present value multiplied by the interest rate. The term arises because the stream of cash receipts is one year closer at the end of the year than it was at the beginning.[2]

At the end of year 1, the present value of the remaining cash flows from the firm's asset is:

$$PA_1 = \frac{150}{1.10} = \$136.36$$

Then, the end-of-year-1 balance sheet is:

P.V. Ltd.			
Balance Sheet			
As at End of Year 1			
Financial Asset		**Shareholders' Equity**	
Cash	$150.00	Opening value	$260.33
		Net income	26.03
Capital Asset, at present value	136.36		
	$286.36		$286.36

This assumes that the firm pays no dividend. A dividend can be easily incorporated by reducing cash and shareholders' equity by the amount of the dividend.

Note the following points about Example 2.1:

1. The net book value of the capital asset at any year-end is equal to its present value, or value-in-use (see the discussion of value-in-use in Section 1.2), where value-in-use is here determined as the present value of the future cash flows from that asset, discounted at 10%.

2. The $26.03 accretion of discount is also referred to as *ex ante* or **expected net income** since, at time 0, the firm expects to earn $26.03. Of course, since all conditions are known with certainty, the expected net income will equal the *ex post* or **realized net income**.

3. **Relevant** financial statement information gives information to investors about the firm's future economic prospects. The information in Example 2.1 is entirely relevant. To see this, note first that, fundamentally, economic prospects are defined by the firm's stream of future dividends—it is dividends that provide a payoff to investors, the present value of which serves to establish firm value.

   Then, it might seem that the firm's dividend policy will affect its value, since the timing of dividends will affect their present value. However, under ideal conditions, this is not the case, due to **dividend irrelevancy**.

   To see why dividend policy does not matter under ideal conditions, note that as long as investors can invest any dividends they receive at the *same rate* of return as the firm earns on cash flows *not* paid in dividends, the present value of an investor's overall interest in the firm is independent of the timing of dividends. This holds in our example since there is only one interest rate in the economy. In effect, the firm's cash flows establish the size of the "pot" that is ultimately available to investors and it does not matter if this pot is distributed sooner or later. If it is distributed during the current year, investors can earn 10% on the distributions. If it is distributed in a subsequent year, the firm earns 10% on amounts not distributed, but this accrues to investors through an increase in the value of their investment. The present value to the investor is the same either way.

Under dividend irrelevancy, cash flows are just as relevant as dividends, because cash flows establish the firm's dividend-paying ability. As a result, the financial statements under Example 2.1 are entirely relevant.

4. As an accountant, you might be wondering why the firm's net income seems to play no role in firm valuation. This is quite true—it doesn't, under ideal conditions of certainty. The reason is that future cash flows are known and hence can be discounted to provide balance sheet valuations. Net income is then perfectly predictable, being simply accretion of discount as pointed out above. In effect, under ideal conditions, the balance sheet contains all the relevant information and the income statement contains none.[3] Even though net income is "true and correct," it conveys no information because investors can always figure it out by multiplying the opening balance sheet value by the interest rate. To put this another way, there is no information in the current net income that helps investors predict future economic prospects of the firm. These are already known to investors, and capitalized into asset valuation, by assumption. This is an important point and we shall return to it later. For now, suffice it to say that when ideal conditions do not hold, the income statement assumes a much more significant role.

5. **Reliable** financial statement information faithfully represents without bias what it is intended to represent. Reliability has several dimensions. The first is **representational faithfulness**, that is, a correspondence between the accounting valuation or description of an item and the real item the information represents. For example, the balance sheet valuation of capital assets and resulting amortization would not be representationally faithful if operating expenses are capitalized, as in the case of WorldCom described in Section 1.2. Nor would the valuation of long-term debt be representationally faithful if some debt is off-balance-sheet, as in the case of Enron. Errors in estimation also violate representational faithfulness. Freedom from **bias** is another reliability dimension. For example, an accounting valuation will be biased if management has manipulated its valuation for its own purposes. **Verifiability** is a third dimension. Different accountants and auditors should be able to come up with the same value if information is verifiable.

The information in Example 2.1 is entirely reliable, since we have assumed that future cash flows and the interest rate are known with certainty. Then, balance sheet valuations faithfully represent the real underlying assets and liabilities of the firm. Any attempt by management to bias valuations would be immediately detected.

Asset and liability values are determined by straightforward calculation, hence verifiable.

6. Under the ideal conditions of future cash flows known with certainty and the economy's risk-free interest rate given, the present value of an asset or liability will equal its market value. To see this, consider the following argument: Given an interest rate of 10%, no one would be willing to pay more than $260.33 for P.V.'s asset at time 0— if they did, they would be earning less than 10%. Also, the owners of the asset would not sell it for less than $260.33—if offered less than $260.33, they would be better off to retain it and earn 10%. If they needed the money they could borrow at 10% against the asset as security. Thus, the only possible equilibrium market price is $260.33. This argument is a simple example of the principle of **arbitrage**. If market prices for identical goods and services are such that it is possible to make a profit by simply buying in one market and selling in another, these are called arbitrage profits. However, it seems reasonable to expect that, if future cash flows and the risk-free rate are publicly known, the scramble of self-interested individuals to make these quick profits would eliminate any price discrepancies.[4] In terms of the different ways to measure current value outlined in Section 1.2, value-in-use and fair value (i.e., market, or exit, value) are equal under ideal conditions.

7. As P.V. Ltd. owns only one asset and has no liabilities, the firm's market value would also be $260.33 at time 0, being the sum of the financial assets[5] and the present value of future cash receipts from the capital asset. Thus, the total market value of P.V.'s shares outstanding would be $260.33. In more general terms, if a firm has more than one asset, the market value of the firm would be the sum of the value of its financial assets plus the present value of the joint future receipts from its capital assets, including intangibles, less the present value of any liabilities. At points in time after time 0, the firm's market value continues to equal the sum of its financial assets plus capital assets, net of liabilities. Note, however, that dividend policy affects the amount of financial assets. To the extent that the firm does not pay out all of its profits in dividends, it will earn a return on reinvested assets. Question 2, at the end of this chapter, illustrates this point. See also the discussion of dividend irrelevancy above.

2.2.1 Summary

The purpose of Example 2.1 is to demonstrate that under the ideal conditions of future cash flows known with certainty and a fixed risk-free interest rate in the economy, it is possible to prepare relevant financial statements that are also reliable. The process of arbitrage ensures that the market value of an asset equals the present value of its future cash flows. The market value of the firm is then the value of its net financial assets plus the value of its capital assets (less any liabilities).

Since all future cash flows are capitalized into the present value of assets, revenue is, in effect, recognized upon asset acquisition. Net income for the period is simply interest on opening present value. However, even though net income can be perfectly calculated, it has no information content, because investors can easily calculate it for themselves. All of the "action" is on the balance sheet, which shows the value of the firm. Because of dividend irrelevancy, all of these conclusions are independent of the firm's dividend policy.

2.3 THE PRESENT VALUE MODEL UNDER UNCERTAINTY

It is instructive to extend the present value model to the presence of uncertainty. With one major exception, most of the concepts carry over from Example 2.1. Again, we will proceed by means of an example.

Example 2.2
Illustration of the Present Value Model Under Uncertainty

Let us continue Example 2.1 taking into account that the economy can be in a "bad" state or a "good" state during each year. If it is in the bad state, cash flows will be $100 for the year. If it is in the good state, however, cash flows will be $200 for the year. Assume that during each year the bad state and the good state each occur with probability 0.5. Our assumption that state probabilities are the same each year implies that the state realizations are independent. That is, the state realization in year 1 does not affect the probabilities[6] of state realization in year 2.

Uncertain future events such as the state of the economy are called **states of nature**, or **states** for short. Thus the states in this example are, for each year:

State 1: Economy is bad.
State 2: Economy is good.

Note that no one can control which of the states is realized—this is why they are called states of *nature*. Other examples of states that affect cash flows are weather, government policies, strikes by suppliers, equipment breakdowns, etc. In any realistic situation there will be a large number of possible states. However, our two-state example is sufficient to convey the idea—states of nature are a conceptual device to model those uncertain, uncontrollable future events whose realizations affect the cash flows of the firm.

While at time 0 no one knows which state will occur, we assume that the set of possible states is publicly known and complete. That is, every possible future event that can affect cash flows is known to everyone. Thus, while no one knows for sure which state will occur, it is known that whatever state does happen must be an element of the set. Furthermore, we assume that the state realization is publicly observable—everyone will know which state actually happens. Finally, we assume that the state probabilities are **objective** and publicly known. By objective we mean that if we imagine a long-run sequence of repetitions of our two-period economy, the bad state will occur with relative frequency 0.5 (or whatever other state probability we were to assume). Think by analogy with rolling a pair of fair dice. We know that the probability of a seven, say, is 1/6, and that if we were to roll the dice a large number of times a seven will appear with relative frequency 1/6. Thus, 1/6 is an objective probability of rolling seven, just as 0.5 is an objective probability that the economy is in a good state this period. Note that an implication of objective probabilities here is that any particular outcome tells us nothing about what the state probabilities are—these are already known by assumption. Thus, the probability of a seven on the next roll of the dice remains at 1/6, just as the probability of the good state remains at 0.5 regardless of the state realization this period.

These assumptions extend the concept of ideal conditions, also called "first-best" conditions, to take uncertainty into account. To summarize,[7]

> **Ideal conditions** under uncertainty are characterized by: (1) a given, fixed interest rate at which the firm's future cash flows are discounted, (2) a complete and publicly known set of states of nature, (3) state probabilities objective and publicly known, and (4) state realization publicly observable.

Another way to think about ideal conditions here is that they are similar to conditions of certainty except that future cash flows are known *conditionally* on the states of nature. That is, *if* state 1 happens, *then* cash flows will be $100, etc. We will assume that P.V. Ltd.'s future cash flows are discounted at 10%.

Given these ideal conditions, we can now calculate the **expected present value** of P.V.'s future cash flows at time 0:

$$PA_0 = 0.5 \left(\frac{\$100}{1.10} + \frac{\$200}{1.10} \right) + 0.5 \left(\frac{\$100}{1.10^2} + \frac{\$200}{1.10^2} \right)$$
$$= (0.5 \times \$272.73) + (0.5 \times \$247.93)$$
$$= \$136.36 + \$123.97$$
$$= \$260.33$$

We can then prepare P.V.'s opening balance sheet as follows:

P.V. Ltd. Balance Sheet As at Time 0			
Capital asset, at expected present value	$260.33	Shareholders' equity	$260.33

It is worthwhile to ask whether the time 0 market value of the asset, and hence of the firm, would be $260.33, as per the balance sheet. It is tempting to answer yes, since this is the firm's expected value given dividend irrelevance. But uncertainty introduces an additional consideration not present in the certainty model of Section 2.2. This is that investors may be averse to risk. While the *expected* value of the firm is $260.33 at time 0, it is shown below that the expected value of the firm at the *end* of year 1 will be $236.36 or $336.36 depending on whether the bad state or the good state happens in that year.

Ask yourself whether you would be indifferent between having $260.33 in your pocket or a 50/50 gamble of $236.36 or $336.36. The present value of the 50/50 gamble is:

$$PA_0 = 0.5 \times \frac{\$236.36}{1.10} + 0.5 \times \frac{\$336.36}{1.10}$$
$$= (0.5 \times \$214.87) + (0.5 \times \$305.78)$$
$$= \$107.44 + \$152.89$$
$$= \$260.33$$

the same as the sure thing. But, most people would prefer the sure thing, because it is less risky. Then, the market value of the firm will be less than $260.33, since to the extent that investors are collectively risk-averse they will value the risky firm at less than its present value.

In this chapter, we will ignore this complication by assuming that investors are risk-neutral. That is, they are indifferent between the sure thing and the 50/50 gamble above. Then, the firm's market value will be $260.33 at time 0. This assumption of risk-neutral investors will be relaxed later, since accountants have a role to play in informing investors about the firm's riskiness as well as its expected value. The concept of a risk-averse investor is introduced in Section 3.4 and the impact of risk on firm valuation is shown in Section 4.5. For now, suffice it to say that the expected value of future cash flows or, more generally, future firm performance, is relevant for investors irrespective of their attitudes to risk.

Given risk-neutral valuation, the arbitrage principle will ensure that the market value of the firm's asset, and of the firm itself, is $260.33. The arbitrage principle would still hold if investors were averse to risk but the market value would be driven to an amount less than $260.33.

To return to the example, accretion of discount is now based on *expected* net income for year 1, calculated as 0.10 × $260.33 = $26.03.

The major difference between the uncertainty and certainty cases is that *expected net income and realized net income need not be the same under uncertainty*. To analyze this further, assume that the year 1 state realization is a bad economy. Thus *realized* cash flows in year 1 are $100, whereas *expected* cash flows were 0.5 × 100 + 0.5 × 200 = $150. Realized net income is then the sum of expected net income plus the difference between expected and actual cash flows, as per the following income statement:

P.V. Ltd. Income Statement (bad economy) For Year 1		
Accretion of discount (0.10 × $260.33)		$26.03
Less: Abnormal earnings, as a result of bad-state realization:		
Expected cash flows (0.5 × $100 + 0.5 × $200)	$150	
Actual cash flows	100	50.00
Net loss		$23.97

The negative $50 of unexpected cash flows results in a $50 "shock" to earnings for the year. The negative $50 earnings shock is called **abnormal earnings**, or, equivalently, **unexpected earnings**, since it reduces expected earnings of $26.03 to a loss of $23.97. Under uncertainty, net income consists of *expected* net income plus or minus abnormal earnings for the year.[8]

Now, at the end of year 1 the expected present value of the remaining cash flows from the asset is:

$$PA_1 = 0.5\left(\frac{\$100}{1.10} + \frac{\$200}{1.10}\right) = \$136.36$$

The year-end balance sheet is:

<table>
<tr><td colspan="4" align="center">**P.V. Ltd.**
Balance Sheet
(bad economy)
As at End of Year 1</td></tr>
<tr><td>**Financial Asset**</td><td></td><td>**Shareholders' Equity**</td><td></td></tr>
<tr><td>Cash</td><td>$100.00</td><td>Opening value</td><td>$260.33</td></tr>
<tr><td>**Capital Asset**</td><td></td><td>Net loss</td><td>23.97</td></tr>
<tr><td>End of year value</td><td>136.36</td><td></td><td></td></tr>
<tr><td></td><td>$236.36</td><td></td><td>$236.36</td></tr>
</table>

Again, arbitrage ensures that the market value of the asset is $136.36 and of the firm is $236.36 at time 1. We continue the assumption that the firm pays no dividend. Ideal conditions ensure that it makes no difference whether the firm pays a dividend or not, as in the certainty case. In other words, dividend irrelevancy continues to hold. Question 4 pursues this point.

It should be noted that in our example abnormal earnings do not **persist**. That is, their effect dissipates completely in the year in which they occur. In general, this need not be the case. For example, if the bad-state realization was due to, say, a tax increase that affected economic activity, the abnormal effect on earnings may persist for several periods. We ignore this possibility here to keep the example simple. However, we will return to the concept of persistence in Chapters 5 and 6.

Now, let's consider the accounting if the state realization is a good economy. The year 1 income statement is:

```
                         P.V. Ltd.
                      Income Statement
                      (good economy)
                        For Year 1

Accretion of discount                                      $26.03

Add: Abnormal earnings, as a result of good-state
        realization ($200 – $150)                           50.00

Net income                                                 $76.03
```

The abnormal earnings of $50 is the difference between actual and expected cash flows for year 1, and these abnormal earnings increase expected earnings up to a profit of $76.03.

At the end of year 1, the present value of the remaining cash flows is still $136.36. The year-end balance sheet is:

```
                              P.V. Ltd.
                            Balance Sheet
                            (good economy)
                          As at End of Year 1

Financial Asset                       Shareholders' Equity

Cash                    $200.00       Opening value           $260.33

Capital Asset                         Net income                76.03

End of year value        136.36

                        $336.36                               $336.36
```

Again, arbitrage ensures that the firm's market value at time 1 will be $336.36, given risk-neutral investors.

Note the following points about Example 2.2:

1. It continues to be the case that financial statement information is both completely relevant and completely reliable. Relevance holds because balance sheet values are based on expected future cash flows, and dividend irrelevancy holds. Reliability holds because ideal conditions ensure that present value calculations are verifiable and incapable of management bias. Thus the resulting values faithfully represent the firm's assets and liabilities.

   Note that financial statement reliability and **volatility** are different concepts. For reasons just given, present value calculations are reliable under ideal conditions. However, net income and balance sheet values are volatile since end-of-period present values depend on which state is realized. This volatility is demonstrated by abnormal earnings in our example, where net income varied from –$23.97 to +$76.03 under bad and good economy realizations respectively, leading to ending firm value of $236.36 or $336.36. Thus, the investor bears risk even when the financial statements are completely reliable.[9]

2. Like the certainty case, there are still two ways of calculating balance sheet current values: we can calculate expected present values directly or we can use market values. Under ideal conditions, arbitrage forces the two ways to yield identical results. Thus, as in Example 2.1, value-in-use and fair value are equal.

3. Despite the fact that expected and realized net income need not be equal, the income statement still has no information content when abnormal earnings do not persist. Investors have sufficient information to calculate for themselves what realized net income will be, once they know the current year's state realization. This calculation is programmable and no accounting policy decisions are needed. We can now say that net income is predictable *conditional on* the state of nature.

4. At the risk of getting ahead of ourselves, let us see how the income statement *can* be informative. For this, we need only relax the assumption that state probabilities are objective. This puts us into the realm of **subjective probabilities**, which are formally introduced in Chapter 3. Then, investors no longer have "ready-made" state probabilities available to them for purposes of calculating expected future firm performance. Rather, they must assess these probabilities themselves, using whatever information is available. There is no longer any guarantee that in a long-run sequence of repetitions of the two-period economy, the bad and good states will occur with the same relative frequencies as the probabilities assigned by the investor. The reason, of course, is that individuals are limited in their knowledge and forecasting ability. Note that if state probabilities are subjective, so are the resulting expected values. That is, the value of the firm is also subjective.

Subjective probabilities are a more reasonable assumption than objective probabilities, because the future performance of a business entity is much more complex and difficult to predict than a simple roll of fair dice. Since investors know that their predictions are subject to error, they will be alert for information sources that enable them to revise their probability assessments. The income statement is one such source. When state probabilities are subjective, the income statement can provide information about what these probabilities are. For example, observing a net income of $76.03 this year in Example 2.2 may cause you to increase your probability of the good state in future years. This would improve your ability to predict firm cash flows and profitability.

If this argument is unclear to you, return to the analogy of rolling dice, but now assume that you do not know whether the dice are fair. What is your probability of rolling a seven? Obviously, this probability is no longer objective, and you must assess it on the basis of whatever information and prior experience you have. However, rolling the dice (analogous to observing the income statement) provides information, and after a few rolls you should have a better idea whether their true state is fair or not fair. For example, if you rolled five times and a seven came up each time, you would probably want to increase from 1/6 your subjective probability of rolling a seven. Just as improved knowledge of the true state of the dice will help you to predict future rolls, improved knowledge of the true state of the firm will help you to predict future firm performance and investment returns. In Chapter 3 we will show how investors can use financial statement information to revise their subjective probabilities of future firm performance.

2.3.1 Summary

The purpose of Example 2.2 is to extend the present value model to formally incorporate uncertainty, using the concepts of states of nature and objective probabilities. The definition of ideal conditions must be extended to include a complete and publicly known set of states of nature, with future cash flows known *conditionally* on state realization. Also, ideal conditions now specify objective state probabilities and that the state realization be publicly observable. The logic of the present value model under certainty then carries over, except that market values are based on *expected* cash flows, assuming investors are risk-neutral.

The major difference between the certainty and uncertainty cases is that *expected* and *realized* net income need no longer be the same under uncertainty, and the difference is called abnormal earnings. Nevertheless, financial statements based on expected present values continue to be both relevant and reliable. They are relevant because they are based on expected future cash flows. They are reliable because financial statement values faithfully represent these expected future cash flows and, as in the certainty case, management bias is not possible. All of these conclusions are independent of the firm's dividend policy, since dividend irrelevancy continues to hold.

2.4 RESERVE RECOGNITION ACCOUNTING (RRA)
2.4.1 An Example of RRA

By now, you probably want to point out that the real world is *not* characterized by ideal conditions. This is quite true. Nevertheless, accounting practice is moving strongly towards increased use of current values for major classes of assets and liabilities. For example, defined post-employment benefits to retirees, such as pensions, healthcare, and disability, are accounted for on the basis of expected future benefit payments under current accounting standards. Also, current standards require that derivative financial instruments be measured at fair value. These and other examples of a measurement approach are reviewed in Chapter 7.

However, the present value model encounters serious reliability problems when we try to apply it without ideal conditions. To illustrate these problems, we now consider reserve recognition accounting for oil and gas companies.

In 1982, the FASB issued Statement of Financial Accounting Standards No. 69 (SFAS 69), which requires supplemental disclosure of certain information about the operations of publicly traded oil and gas companies. An interesting aspect of SFAS 69 is that disclosure of the estimated present value of future receipts from a company's proved oil and gas reserves is required. The estimate is known as the "standardized measure." The intent, presumably, is to provide investors with more relevant information about future cash flows than that contained in the conventional, historical cost-based financial statements. Oil and gas companies, it can be argued, particularly need to give this type of supplementary disclosure because the historical cost of oil and gas properties may bear little relationship to their value.

In Canada, National Instrument (NI) 51-101 of the CSA requires similar, but considerably expanded, present value disclosures. However, firms can apply for exemption from this standard to instead report under SFAS 69. Since most large Canadian oil and gas firms have received exemption, we shall consider SFAS 69 here. For an illustration of reporting under NI 51-101, see problem 24.

It can hardly be said that oil and gas companies operate under conditions of certainty. Consequently, we shall consider SFAS 69 in relation to our present value model under uncertainty, which was illustrated in Example 2.2. Present value accounting applied to oil and gas reserves is known as **reserve recognition accounting (RRA)**.

Consider first Table 2.1, adapted from the 2006 annual report of Suncor Energy Inc., a Canadian corporation with shares traded on the Toronto and New York stock exchanges. Note that the undiscounted future net cash flows are shown, and also the present value of these cash flows, discounted at 10%. When estimating future cash flows, SFAS 69 requires that the present value calculations use year-end oil and gas prices (as opposed to prices expected to be in effect when the reserves are lifted and sold). No information is given about the riskiness of the estimates. That is, no states of nature and probabilities are given, only the end results of the expectation calculation.

Table 2.1 Suncor Energy, Inc. Present Value of Estimated Future Cash Flows (millions of dollars)

December 31	2006	2005	2004
Future cash inflows	$32,882	$16,444	$3,355
Future production costs	(12,264)	(10,181)	(640)
Future development costs	(5,648)	(1,705)	(64)
Other related future costs	(612)	(464)	(367)
Future income tax expenses	(4,221)	(1,216)	(460)
Subtotal	10,137	2,878	1,824
Discount at 10%	(6,768)	(1,214)	(750)
Standardized measure	$ 3,369	$ 1,664	$1,074

Source: Reprinted by permission of Suncor Energy Inc.

This disclosure seems to conform fairly well to our theoretical Example 2.2. The $3,369 is the amount that would appear on Suncor's December 31, 2006, present value-based balance sheet for the asset "proved oil and gas reserves" if one was prepared. It corresponds to the $136.36 valuation of the capital asset at time 1 in Example 2.2. It should be noted, however, that the 10% discount rate used by Suncor is not the single known rate in the economy. Rather, this rate is mandated by SFAS 69, presumably for comparability across firms. Also, as mentioned, the figures apply only to proved reserves and not all of Suncor's assets.

Table 2.2 gives changes in the standardized measure.

Table 2.2 Suncor Energy, Inc. Changes in the Standardized Measure of Discounted Future Net Cash Flows (millions of dollars)

	2006	2005	2004
Balance, beginning of year	$1,664	$1,074	$1,851
Sales and transfers..., net of production costs	(559)	(456)	(359)
Net changes in prices and production costs	1,907	737	(1,786)
Changes in estimated future development costs	(1,141)	(573)	14
Extensions, discoveries and improved recovery, less related costs	59	162	131
Development costs incurred during the period	772	557	524
Revisions to previous quantity estimates	1,051	440	(47)
Purchase of reserves in place	–	–	32
Sale of reserves in place	(2)	(4)	–
Accretion of discount	231	125	245
Net changes in income taxes	(714)	(470)	426
Other related cost changes	101	72	43
Balance, end of year	$3,369	$1,664	$1,074

Source: Reprinted by permission of Suncor Energy Inc.

To understand this statement, we prepare in Table 2.3 an income statement in the same format as the income statement for P.V. Ltd. in Example 2.2.

Check each of the numbers in Table 2.3 from the original Suncor statement in Tables 2.1 and 2.2.[10]

The changes in estimates of $1,204 in Table 2.3 should be considered carefully. Note, in particular, that there are a number of changes, including revisions of quantities, prices, and costs as well as related income taxes. Note also that the amounts are quite material, netting out to over 72% of the opening standardized measure amount, and dwarfing expected net income of $231. The number and magnitude of these changes are the main differences between our Example 2.2, which assumed ideal conditions, and the "real world" environment in which Suncor operates.[11] We shall return to this point shortly.

Table 2.3 Suncor Energy, Inc. Income Statement for 2006 From Proved Oil and Gas Reserves (millions of dollars)

Expected net income—accretion of discount		$ 231
Abnormal Earnings:		
Net present value of additional reserves added during year (59 − 2)		57
Unexpected items—changes in estimates		
Net changes in prices and production costs	1,907	
Revisions to previous quantity estimates	1,051	
Changes in estimated future development costs	(1,141)	
Net changes in income taxes	(714)	
Other related cost changes	101	1,204
Net income from proved oil and gas reserves		$1,492

Source: Reprinted by permission of Suncor Energy Inc.

Note that the accretion of discount is not 10% of beginning-of-year present value, as it was in Example 2.2. Suncor does not disclose how this amount is calculated. Presumably, its failure to agree with its theoretical counterpart derives from the impact of the various changes to estimates during the year.

2.4.2 Summary

The procedures used by Suncor to account for the results of its oil and gas operations under RRA seem to conform to the theoretical present value model under uncertainty, except that it is necessary to make material changes to previous estimates.

2.4.3 Critique of RRA

This necessity to make changes in estimates seems to be the Achilles heel of RRA. Oil company managers, in particular, tend to regard RRA with reservation and suspicion. As an example, the following statement appears in Suncor's 2006 RRA disclosure:

> In computing the standardized measure . . . , assumptions other than those mandated by Statement 69 could produce substantially different results. We caution against viewing this information as a forecast of future economic conditions or revenues, and do not consider it to represent the fair market value of our Firebag in-situ and Natural Gas properties.

One might ask why Suncor reports under SFAS 69 instead of CSA NI 51-101, since SFAS 69 is a U.S. accounting standard. However, since its shares are traded on an American stock exchange, Suncor must meet U.S. reporting requirements. Also, it may want to report information with which U.S. investors are familiar. Since the RRA information has been prepared, it can also be reported to Canadian shareholders at little additional cost.

Table 2.4 Suncor Energy, Inc. Results of Operations for Oil and Gas Production for the Year Ended December 31, 2006 (millions of dollars)

December 31	2006	2005	2004
Total revenues	$903	$722	$533
Production and other expenses	(414)	(306)	(233)
Depletion, depreciation and amortization	(215)	(145)	(130)
Income taxes	(38)	(98)	(48)
Results of operations	$236	$173	$122

Source: Reprinted by permission of Suncor Energy Inc.

While it is clear that management is cautious about RRA, this does not necessarily mean that it does not provide useful information to investors. Certainly, RRA is more relevant than historical cost information, so it has the potential to be useful. To see the potential for relevance, compare the present value-based 2006 net income from Table 2.3 with Suncor's historical cost-based earnings from oil and gas[12] summarized in Table 2.4.

Comparison of net income under the two bases is complicated by the fact that the present value calculations relate only to proved reserves. However, let us take the $236 results of operations for 2006 in Table 2.4 as the historical cost analogue of the $1,492 present value-based income in Table 2.3. This seems reasonable since, if oil and gas has been sold, the reserves it came from are obviously proved.

We see that the present value-based earnings are *much* higher than their historical cost-based counterpart. What accounts for the difference? The difference can be explained by different bases of asset valuation. Under RRA, oil and gas assets are valued at expected present value, which is generally higher than historical cost. Thus, shareholders' equity is also higher under RRA, implying that earnings are higher.

We can also account for the difference in terms of revenue recognition. Under RRA, changes in the value of proved reserves are included in income as they occur, as witnessed by the various estimate changes included in RRA net income in Table 2.3. We see there that increases in prices and reserve quantities are major earnings components. Under historical cost accounting, as you know, these increases in the value of the proved reserves would not show up in the income statement until the proved reserves were produced and sold. In effect, the present value-based income statement recognizes the increase sooner. Thus, present value information has the potential for usefulness because of this greater relevance.

Note that asset valuation and revenue recognition are two sides of the same coin. We can discuss the timing of revenue recognition (the credit side of the coin), as in the previous paragraph. Or, we can discuss whether reserves should be valued at present value, as in RRA, or whether they should be valued at cost, as in historical cost accounting (the debit side of the coin). The same tradeoff between relevance and reliability applies. Recognizing unrealized increases in asset value and, equivalently, recognizing revenue sooner increases relevance, since the investor receives an earlier reading on future cash flows. However, early recognition decreases reliability. Representational faithfulness is reduced due to the large number and amounts of changes to estimates under RRA. Verifiability is questionable since different individuals may come up with different values due, for example, to different estimates of proved reserves or different timing assumptions for lifting and selling the oil and gas. As evidenced by the quotation at the beginning of this section, Suncor's management agrees with these concerns. The need for estimates also creates opportunity for manager bias (see Theory in Practice 2.1 on p. 41).

This same equivalence between asset valuation and revenue recognition appears in Examples 2.1 and 2.2. There, we concentrated on the valuation of assets at present value. Alternatively, we could have emphasized that under ideal conditions revenue is recognized when capital assets are acquired, since future cash flows (i.e., revenues) are inputs into the present value calculations.

Regardless of whether investors focus on revenue recognition or asset valuation, we should observe some reaction in the price of Suncor's shares to the release of RRA information if RRA is in fact useful. Empirical evidence on the usefulness of RRA is reviewed in Chapter 5. For now, suffice it to say that evidence of usefulness is mixed, at best.

Given questions about empirical evidence of usefulness, questions about reliability, and management's concerns, what is the basic problem of RRA? The main point to realize is that Suncor does not operate under the ideal conditions of Examples 2.1 and 2.2. Consider the difficulties that Suncor's accountants face in applying ideal conditions. First, interest rates in the economy are not fixed, although SFAS 69 deals with this by requiring a fixed, given rate of 10% for the discounting. Second, the set of states of nature affecting the amounts, prices, and timing of future production is much larger than the simple two-state set in Example 2.2, due to the complex environment in which oil and gas companies operate. SFAS 69 reduces some of this complexity by requiring that reserves be valued using year-end prices. However, reserve quantity states, and the timing of their extraction, are still needed. Third, it is unlikely that the state realization would be publicly observable. Events like equipment breakdowns, production problems, and minor oil spills would most likely be inside information of the firm. Under ideal conditions, there is no inside information.

A fourth problem is more fundamental. Objective state probabilities are not available. Consequently, subjective state probabilities need to be assessed by Suncor's engineers and accountants, with the result that the standardized measure is itself a subjective estimate. In effect, it is difficult to apply present value accounting when the ideal conditions it requires do not hold.

Because of these difficulties in applying ideal conditions, the reliability of RRA information is severely compromised. This shows up in the number and materiality of quantity and price revisions to estimates, as shown in Table 2.2. It is not that estimates of expected future cash flows cannot be made. After all, RRA is on line. Rather, lacking objective probabilities, these estimates become subject to revisions that threaten reliability to the point where the benefit of increased relevance is compromised. The important point is

The subjectivity of reserve quantity estimates is illustrated by the case of Royal Dutch/Shell. Long a respected company, Shell's reputation suffered a severe blow when, in January 2004, it reduced its "proved" reserves by 20%, reclassifying them as "probable." This was followed by several smaller reductions. Apparently, the company had been overstating its proved reserves as far back as 1997 to disguise falling behind its competitors in replacing its reserves. Such overstatements were enabled by relatively vague SEC rules (which Shell purported to follow) that require "reasonable certainty" of recovery under existing economic and operating conditions to classify reserves as proved. Also, the reserve quantities were unaudited.

This scandal, which resulted in the dismissals of Shell's chairman and head of exploration and development, and a preliminary fine by the SEC of $150 million U.S., led to a major drop in Shell's share price as investors revised downwards their probabilities of Shell's future performance. The relevance of Shell's reserve information was overwhelmed by low reliability introduced by manager bias.

In April 2007, Shell agreed to pay $352.6 million U.S. to non-U.S. investors in settlement of their claims for damages. It also offered $80 million to U.S. investors, bringing its total fines and damage payments to almost $700 million.

that, without ideal conditions, complete relevance and reliability are no longer jointly attainable. One must be traded off against the other.

2.4.4 Summary

RRA represents a valiant attempt to convey relevant information to investors. On the surface, the present value information conforms quite closely to the theoretical present value model under uncertainty. If one digs deeper, however, serious problems of estimation are revealed. This is because oil and gas companies do not operate under the ideal conditions assumed by the theoretical model. As a result, reserve information loses reliability, as evidenced by the need for substantial annual revisions and possible bias, as it gains relevance. It seems necessary to trade off these two desirable information qualities.

2.5 HISTORICAL COST ACCOUNTING REVISITED

2.5.1 Comparison of Different Measurement Bases

To this point, we have mainly considered ideal conditions, which lead to a present value (i.e., value-in-use) version of current value accounting. But, as we outlined in Section 1.2, present-day accounting practice can be described as a mixed measurement model. While, over the past number of years, standard setters have introduced numerous current value-based standards, extension of current value accounting will run into increasing volatility and reliability issues, as our discussion of RRA in Section 2.4 demonstrates.

Consequently, it is likely that historical cost-based accounting for major classes of assets and liabilities, including inventories, capital assets, and long-term debt, will continue for some time. In this section, we consider some of the characteristics of historical cost accounting in relation to current value. We also consider historical cost in relation to cash basis accounting. Since cash flows are a fundamental determinant of firm value, why not prepare financial statements on a cash basis?

Relevance Versus Reliability Relevance and reliability are important characteristics of accounting information. As we concluded in the previous section, it is necessary to trade them off. However, different measurement bases imply different tradeoffs. Historical cost accounting is relatively reliable since the cost of an asset or liability to a firm is usually a verifiable number that is less subject to errors of estimation and bias than are present value calculations. However, historical costs may be low in relevance. While cost may equal current value at date of acquisition, this equality will soon be lost as current values change over time. Consequently, the relevance of current value accounting generally exceeds that of historical cost. But, the need for estimates when conditions are not ideal opens current value accounting up to problems of reliability.

With respect to cash flow accounting, relevance is low since cash flows are usually received after the economic event that generates them. However, since cash is relatively easy to measure, reliability is high. Note, however, that reliability is not complete, as illustrated in the case of WorldCom (Section 1.2), where both operating cash flow and net income were overstated.

Revenue Recognition As discussed in Section 1.2, the timing of revenue recognition is controversial. We can also characterize accounting measurement bases in terms of revenue recognition. Recall that for each basis of asset and liability measurement there is an associated basis of revenue recognition. In Section 2.4.3, we demonstrated this for RRA. Valuing proved reserves at current value (i.e., the standardized measure) implies revenue recognition as reserves are proved. More generally, current valuation of assets and liabilities implies revenue recognition as changes in current value occur. Under historical cost, valuation of inventories at cost and accounts receivable at selling price implies revenue recognition as inventory is sold. Under cash flow accounting, revenue is recognized as cash is collected, implying that accounts receivable are valued at the cost of goods sold. Thus, current value accounting implies early revenue recognition. Cash flow accounting implies late recognition. Historical cost accounting is in between.

Recognition Lag This same ordering of measurement bases appears in the concept of **recognition lag**, which is the extent to which the timing of revenue recognition lags behind changes in real economic value. Current value accounting has little recognition lag, since changes in economic value are recognized as they occur. Historical cost accounting has greater recognition lag. As just pointed out, revenue is not recognized until increases in inventory value are validated, usually through realization as sales. Thus revenue recognition lags the economic value of inventory. Operating cash flows have even greater recognition lag, since the accountant waits until cash is received or paid.

Matching of Costs and Revenues Finally, we consider the matching of costs and revenues. As pointed out in Section 1.2, matching is primarily associated with historical cost accounting, since net income under historical cost accounting is a result of matching realized revenues with the costs of earning those revenues. There is little matching under current value accounting, since net income is essentially an explanation of how current values of assets and liabilities have changed during the period. Matching is not required for this since value changes in assets and liabilities are driven by market forces and the firm's response to these forces. Little matching is required under cash flow accounting either, since cash flow is simply the difference between cash in and cash out.

Characterizations of measurement bases in terms of relevance and reliability, revenue recognition, recognition lag, and matching are basically similar, and we shall use them interchangeably in this book. Thus, to say that historical cost accounting is low in relevance but reasonably reliable is to also say that the accountant waits until objective evidence is available before recognizing revenue, that historical cost lags in recognizing changes in asset and liability values, and that historical cost is a process of matching.

2.5.2 Accruals

The question then is, which measurement basis provides the most useful information about the firm's *future* economic prospects (the primary interest of investors)? Accountants have debated this question for many years, and we return to it often in later chapters. For now, suffice it to say that arguments can be made in favour of historical cost. One argument is its reliability relative to current value when conditions are not ideal. Another is its relevance relative to cash flows—by matching costs and revenues, historical cost accounting "smooths out" current period operating cash flows into a measure of the longer-run or persistent earning power that is implied by those cash flows. For example, if a firm pays for inventory and sells it in December, but collects the cash in January, operating cash flow does not match December costs and revenues. By recording an account receivable, historical cost accounting puts costs and revenues into the same period, enabling a smoother, more relevant measure of persistent earning power than cash flow accounting. Persistent earning power provides the basis for an assessment of future economic prospects. This is why the income statement is the primary focus of financial reporting under historical cost accounting.[13]

However, to match costs and revenues, the accountant has to calculate **accruals** (accounts receivable are an accrual, for example). At this point, historical cost accounting faces a major challenge. There is usually no unique way to match costs with revenues. This complicates the ability of historical cost-based earnings to reveal persistent earning power. With respect to accounts receivable, this complication shows up in the necessity to estimate an allowance for doubtful accounts. To illustrate further, we consider two additional examples.

Amortization of Capital Assets A major problem with matching is the amortization of capital assets. The matching principle deems it necessary to deduct amortization of capital assets (an accrual) from revenue for the period to arrive at net income. Yet, it does not state how much amortization should be accrued except for a vague indication that it should be systematic and rational. For example, under IAS 16, amortization should be charged systematically over the asset's useful life and reflect the pattern of benefit consumption.

As a result of this vagueness, the door is opened to a variety of amortization methods, such as straight-line, declining-balance, and so on. This complicates the comparison of profitability across firms, because we must ascertain the amortization methods firms are using before making comparisons. It also means that firm managers have some room to bias their reported profitability through choice of amortization method or through changes to the method used. Verifiability is also reduced, since different accountants may have different opinions as to the appropriate policy to reflect benefit consumption.

Note that if capital assets were valued at current value, we would need only *one* amortization method—the change in the current value of the assets during the period.

Full-Cost Versus Successful-Efforts in Oil and Gas Accounting

Under historical cost accounting, we need to know the cost of assets, so that they can be amortized (matched) against revenues over their useful lives. We suggested earlier in this section that the cost of assets is usually reliably determinable. However, in some cases, even the cost of assets is not clear. Oil and gas accounting provides an interesting and important example.

There are two basic methods of determining the cost of oil and gas reserves. The **full-cost method** capitalizes all costs of discovering reserves (subject to certain exceptions), including the costs of unsuccessful drilling. The argument is that the cost of successful wells includes the costs of dry holes drilled in the search for the successful ones. The **successful-efforts method** capitalizes only the costs of successful wells and expenses dry holes, the rationale being that it is difficult to regard a dry hole in the ground as an asset.

Clearly, these two approaches can produce materially different recorded costs for oil and gas reserves of actively exploring companies, with the result that amortization accruals can also be materially different. In turn, this complicates the comparison of the reported net incomes of oil and gas firms, because different firms may use different methods for determining the cost of their reserves. For our purposes, however, simply note that the historical cost basis of accounting cannot settle the question of which method is preferable. The historical cost basis requires only that a cost of oil and gas reserves be established. It does not require a particular method for establishing what the cost should be. In fact, both methods are currently allowed in Canada and the United States. Under IASB standards, IFRS 6 allows successful efforts and full cost subject to a ceiling test. The extent to which full-cost accounting will remain following Canada's adoption of IFRS standards is unclear at the present time since this depends on the outcome of an IASB research project on extractive industries.

The use of RRA in the firm's accounts would eliminate the full-cost versus successful-efforts controversy. RRA values proved oil and gas reserves at their present values. It is *not* a cost-based approach, so the question of how to determine cost does not arise.

On the basis of the above examples, we conclude that while historical cost accounting may be more reliable than current value-based methods, and more relevant than cash accounting, it is by no means completely relevant and reliable. To increase the usefulness of historical cost accounting in the face of this difficulty, accountants have adopted a strategy of **full disclosure**. For example, disclosure of accounting policies used enables investors to at least be aware of the particular policies the firm has chosen out of the multiplicity of policies that are available for most assets and liabilities. Also, **supplementary information** is given to help investors project current performance into the future. The RRA disclosure discussed in Section 2.4 is an example of such supplementary information.

2.5.3 Summary

The continued use of historical cost accounting in financial reporting can be thought of as a consequence of the impossibility of preparing reliable financial statements on a current value basis, and the low relevance of cash flow accounting. The use of historical cost accounting represents an intermediate tradeoff between measurement characteristics, such as relevance and reliability. Complete relevance is not attained, since historical cost-based asset values need bear little resemblance to current values. However, complete reliability is not attained either, since the possibility of imprecision and bias remains. The measurement of net income becomes a process of matching, rather than a simple calculation of accretion of discount, and the matching process usually allows different ways of accounting for the same item.

Given the continuing use of historical cost-based accounting in practice, accountants have tried to make the historical cost framework more useful. One way of increasing usefulness is to retain the historical cost framework but expand disclosure in the annual report, so as to help investors to make their own estimates of future economic prospects.

2.6 THE NON-EXISTENCE OF TRUE NET INCOME

To prepare a complete set of financial statements on a current value basis, it is necessary to value *all* of the firm's assets and liabilities this way, with net income being the change in the firm's current value during the period (adjusted for capital transactions such as dividends). Yet, we saw with RRA that severe problems arise when we try to apply a present value approach to even a single type of asset. These problems would be compounded if the approach was incorporated into the financial statements proper and extended to all other assets and liabilities.

This leads to an important and interesting conclusion, namely that under the real-world conditions in which accounting operates, *net income does not exist as a well-defined economic construct*. As evidence, simply consider Suncor's RRA net income of $1,492 in Table 2.3. How can we take this as well-defined, or "true," income when we know that next year there will be another flock of unanticipated changes to the estimates that underlie the 2006 income calculation?

A fundamental problem is the lack of objective state probabilities. With objective probabilities, present values of assets and liabilities correctly reflect the uncertainty facing the firm, since present values then take into account all possible future events and their probabilities. In this case, accounting information is completely relevant as well as completely reliable and true economic income exists.

The equality of present values and market values under ideal conditions suggests an indirect approach to true economic income—base the income calculation on changes in market values rather than present values. However, this approach runs into the problem that market values need not exist for all firm assets and liabilities, a condition known as **incomplete markets**. For example, while there may be a market price for a barrel of crude oil, what is the market value of Suncor's reserves? In the face of uncertainties over quantities, prices, and lifting costs, an attempt to establish their market value runs into the same estimation problems as RRA. As a result, a ready market value is not available. If market values are not available for all firm assets and liabilities, an income measure based on changes in market values is not possible. Beaver and Demski (1979) give formal arguments to show that income is not well defined when markets are incomplete.[14] Lacking objective probabilities, the door is opened for subjective estimates of future firm performance. These estimates can suffer from lack of precision and possible bias. As a result, accounting estimates based on present value lose reliability as they strive to maintain relevance.

Thus, a second conclusion is that accountants feel that historical cost-based accounting for major classes of operating assets and liabilities represents a more useful way to account, since we observe historical cost accounting for these classes strongly rooted in practice. Some relevance is lost, but hopefully this is more than made up for by increased reliability.

You may be bothered by the claim that true net income does not exist. Should we devote our careers to measuring something that doesn't exist? However, we should be glad of the impossibility of ideal conditions. If they existed, no one would need accountants! As discussed in Examples 2.1 and 2.2, net income has no information content when conditions are ideal. The present value calculations and related income measurement could then be programmed in advance. All that is needed is the set of states, their probabilities, and knowledge of which state is realized, and accountants would not be needed for this. Thus, we can say of income measurement, "If we can solve it, we don't need it."

This lack of a theoretically correct concept of income is what makes accounting both frustrating and fascinating at the same time. It is frustrating because of the difficulty of agreeing on accounting policies. Different users will typically want different tradeoffs between relevance and reliability. As a result, there are often several ways of accounting for the same thing. It is fascinating because the lack of a well-defined concept of net income means that a great deal of *judgement* must go into the process of asset valuation and income measurement. It is judgement that makes accounting valuable and, indeed, provides the very basis of a profession.

2.7 CONCLUSION TO ACCOUNTING UNDER IDEAL CONDITIONS

Instead of dwelling on questions of existence of net income, accountants turned their efforts to making financial statements useful. We will now proceed to study decision usefulness.

Questions and Problems

1. Prepare the income statement for year 2 and the balance sheet at the end of year 2 for P.V. Ltd. in Example 2.1 under the assumption that P.V. Ltd. pays no dividends.

2. Show that an owner of P.V. Ltd. in Example 2.1 would not care whether P.V. Ltd. paid any dividend at the end of year 1. State precisely why this is the case.

3. Verify the expected net income for P.V. Ltd. for year 1 in Example 2.2 by calculating the expected value of *ex post* net income. How much is expected net income for year 2? Show calculations. Explain why expected net income is also called "accretion of discount."

4. Show that an owner of P.V. Ltd. in Example 2.2 would not care whether P.V. Ltd. paid any dividend at the end of year 1. Assume that the good-economy state was realized in year 1.

5. In Example 2.2, assume that P.V. Ltd. pays no dividends over its life, until a liquidating dividend is paid at the end of year 2 consisting of its cash on hand at that time.

   Required
   Verify that the market value of P.V. Ltd. at time 0 based on the present value of dividends equals $260.33, equal to P.V.'s market value based on expected future cash flows.

6. A simple example of the difference between ideal and non-ideal conditions is the rolling of a die.

   Required
   a. Calculate the expected value of a single roll of a fair die.

   b. Now suppose that you are unsure whether the die is fair. How would you then calculate the expected value of a single roll?

   c. Continuing part **b**, now roll the die four times. You obtain 6, 4, 1, 3. Does this information affect your belief that the die is fair? Explain.

7. Explain why, under ideal conditions, there is no need to make estimates when calculating expected present value.

8. Explain why estimates are required to calculate expected present value when conditions are *not* ideal. (CGA-Canada)

9. Do you think that the market value of an oil and gas firm will be affected when RRA information is presented in addition to historical cost-based earnings from oil and gas producing activities? Explain why or why not.

10. Explain why, under non-ideal conditions, it is necessary to trade off relevance and reliability. Define these two terms as part of your answer.

11. Why do you think Suncor's management expresses severe reservations about RRA?

12. The text discussion of RRA is primarily in terms of the relevance and reliability of the asset valuation of oil and gas reserves. RRA can also be evaluated in terms of the criteria for revenue recognition. IAS 18 states that revenue involving the sale of goods should be measured at the fair value of the consideration received or to be received. Revenue should be recognized when significant risks and rewards of ownership are transferred to the buyer, the seller has lost effective control, and the consideration that will be received can be reliably measured.

    Required

    a. At what point in their operating cycle do most industrial and retail firms regard revenue as having been earned (i.e., realized)? Use the three revenue recognition criteria above to explain why.

    b. Suppose that X Ltd. is an oil and gas producer. X Ltd. uses RRA on its books and prepares its financial statements on this basis. When (i.e., at what point in the operating cycle) is revenue recognized under RRA? Does this point meet the criteria for revenue recognition under GAAP as given in IAS 18? Explain why or why not.

13. Inventory is another asset for which there is a variety of ways to account under historical cost accounting, including first-in, first-out; last-in, first-out; average cost; etc.

    a. How would inventory be accounted for under ideal conditions? In your answer, consider both balance sheet and revenue recognition approaches.

    b. Give reasons why inventory is usually accounted for on a historical cost basis. Is accounting on this basis completely reliable? Why?

14. Sure Corp. operates under ideal conditions of certainty. It acquired its sole asset on January 1, 2008. The asset will yield $500 cash at the end of each year from 2008 to 2010, inclusive, after which it will have no market value and no disposal costs. The interest rate in the economy is 6%. Purchase of the asset was financed by the issuance of common shares. Sure Corp. will pay a dividend of $50 at the end of 2008 and 2009.

    Required

    a. Prepare a balance sheet for Sure Corp. as at the end of 2008 and an income statement for the year ended December 31, 2008.

    b. Prepare a balance sheet for Sure Corp. as at the end of 2009 and an income statement for the year ended December 31, 2009.

    c. Under ideal conditions, what is the relationship between present value (i.e., value-in-use) and market value (i.e., fair value)? Why? Under the real conditions in which accountants operate, to what extent do market values provide a way to implement fair value accounting? Explain.

    d. Under real conditions, present value calculations tend to be of low reliability. Why? Does this mean that present value-based accounting for assets and liabilities is not decision useful? Explain.

Note: In the following problem, the capital asset is financed in part by means of interest-bearing bonds.

15. P Ltd. operates under ideal conditions. It has just bought a capital asset for $3,100, which will generate $1,210 cash flow at the end of one year and $2,000 at the end of the second year. At that time, the asset will be useless in operations and P Ltd. plans to go out of business. The asset will have a known salvage value of $420 at the end of the second year. The interest rate in the economy is constant at 10% per annum.

    P Ltd. finances the asset by issuing $605 par value of 12% coupon bonds to yield 10%. Interest is payable at the end of the first and second years, at which time the bonds mature. The balance of the cost of the asset is financed by the issuance of common shares.

    Required

    a. Prepare the present value-based balance sheet as at the end of the first year and an income statement for the year. P Ltd. plans to pay no dividends in this year.

    b. Give two reasons why ideal conditions are unlikely to hold.

    c. If ideal conditions do not hold, but present value-based financial statements are prepared anyway, is net income likely to be the same as you calculated in part **a**? Explain why or why not.

16. Rainy Ltd. operates under ideal conditions of uncertainty. Its cash flows depend crucially on the weather. On January 1, 2008, Rainy acquired equipment to be used in its operations. The equipment will last two years, at which time its salvage value will be zero. Rainy financed the equipment purchase by issuing common shares.

    In 2008, net cash flows will be $700 if the weather is rainy and $200 if it is dry. In 2009, cash flows will be $900 if the weather is rainy and $300 if it is dry. Cash flows are received at year-end. In each year, the probability that the weather is rainy is 0.3 and 0.7 that it is dry. The interest rate in the economy is 6% in both years.

    Rainy pays a dividend of $50 at the end of 2008.

    Required

    a. In 2008, the weather is rainy. Prepare a balance sheet as at the end of 2008 and an income statement for 2008.

    b. If we attempt to apply the present value model under uncertainty to the more realistic conditions under which accountants operate, the expected present value calculations become unreliable. Explain why.

    c. Explain why well-defined (i.e., "true") net income does not exist under the realistic conditions under which accountants operate. In place of true net income, what criterion have accountants adopted to guide their financial accounting and reporting decisions?

17. QC Ltd. operates under ideal conditions of uncertainty. On January 1, 2008, it purchased a capital asset that will last for two full years and then will be retired with zero salvage. The purchase price was financed with an issue of common stock. QC Ltd. plans to pay no dividends until after the end of 2009. The interest rate in the economy is 6%.

    QC Ltd. identifies two states of nature: Net cash flows from the asset will be $100 in 2008 and $200 in 2009 (the high state) or $100 in 2008, and $50 in 2009 (the low state). The objective probability of the high state is 0.60. All cash flows are received at their respective year-ends. At the end of year 2 it becomes known that the high state is realized.

Required

a. How much did QC Ltd. pay for its capital asset? Show calculations.

b. Prepare, in good form, an income statement for QC Ltd. for the *second year* of operations, that is, 2009.

c. Prepare, in good form, a balance sheet for QC Ltd. as at the end of 2009 operations (before any dividend payments).

Note: In the following problem, state probabilities are not independent over time. Part **b** requires calculations not illustrated in the text.

18. Conditional Ltd. operates under ideal conditions of uncertainty. It has just purchased a new machine, at a cost of $3,575.10, paid for entirely from the proceeds of a stock issue. The interest rate in the economy is 8%. The machine is expected to last for two years, after which time it will have zero salvage value.

    The new machine is an experimental model, and its suitability for use in Conditional's operations is not completely known. Conditional assesses a 0.75 probability that there will be a major machine failure during the first year of operation, and a 0.25 probability that the machine will operate as planned. If there is a major failure, cash flow for the year will be $1,000. If the machine operates as planned, cash flow will be $3,000 for the year. If there is no major failure in the first year, the probability of a major failure in the second year, and resulting cash flows of $1,000, falls to 0.60. If there is no major failure in the second year, cash flows for that year will again be $3,000. However, if there is a major failure in the first year, the lessons learned from correcting it will result in only a 0.10 probability of failure in the second year.

    It turns out that there is no major failure in the first year.

Required

a. Verify that the cost of $3,575.10 for the machine is correct.

b. Prepare an income statement for year 1.

c. Prepare a balance sheet as at the end of the first year.

19. On January 1, 2008, ABC Ltd. started its business by purchasing a productive oil well. The proved oil reserves from the well are expected to generate $7,000 cash flow at the end of 2008, $6,000 at the end of 2009, and $5,000 at the end of 2010. Net sales is gross revenues less production costs. Net sales equals cash flows. On January 1, 2011, the oil well is expected to be dry, with no environmental liabilities. The management of ABC Ltd. wishes to prepare financial statements based on RRA in accordance with SFAS 69. The following information is known about the well at the end of 2008:

    ■ Actual cash flows in 2008 amounted to $6,500, that is, $500 less than expected.
    ■ Changes in estimates: Due to improved recovery (of oil from the well), cash flows in 2009 and 2010 are estimated to be $6,500 and $6,000 respectively.

Required

a. Prepare the income statement of ABC Ltd. for 2008 from its proved oil reserves.

b. Managements of some firms have expressed serious concerns about the reliability of the RRA information. Outline two of these concerns.

20. The following RRA information is taken from the December 31, 2008, annual report of FX Energy, Inc.

FX Energy, Inc.
Changes in the Standardized Measure of Discounted Future Cash Flows
For the year ended December 31, 2008
($ thousands)

Present value at January 1, 2008	$5,460
Sales of oil produced, net of production costs	(1,172)
Net changes in prices and production costs	(159)
Extensions and discoveries, net of future costs	2,511
Changes in estimated future development costs	(53)
Previously estimated development costs incurred during the year	202
Revisions in previous quantity estimates	(31)
Accretion of discount	546
Changes in rates of production and other	116
Present value at December 31, 2008	$7,420

Required

a. Prepare an income statement for FX Energy for 2008.

b. FX Energy reports elsewhere in its annual report an (historical cost-based) operating loss from exploration and production for 2008 of $7,245. While all of this amount may not derive from proved reserves, take this operating loss as a reasonable historical cost-based analogue of the RRA income you calculated in part **a**. Also explain why RRA income for 2008 is different from the $7,245 loss under historical cost.

c. The standardized measure is applied only to proved reserves under SFAS 69, using year-end oil and gas prices. Explain why.

d. SFAS 69 mandates a discount rate of 10% for the RRA present value calculations, rather than allowing each firm to choose its own rate. Why? Can you see any disadvantages to mandating a common discount rate?

Note: The item "extensions and discoveries, net of future costs" represents additional reserves proved during the year. Treat it as a separate abnormal earnings item in the 2008 income statement. The item "changes in rates of production and other" represents changes in timing of extraction from the timing that was expected at the beginning of 2008.

21. The following RRA information is taken from the 2008 annual report of Moonglo Energy Inc.

Balance of proved reserves: beginning of year	$1,070
Sales, net of production costs	(456)
Sales of reserves in place	(4)
Accretion of discount	125
Extensions and discoveries, net of related costs	162
Development costs incurred in year	629
Changes in estimates	134
Balance of proved reserves: end of year	$1,660

Required

a. Prepare 2008 income statements for Moonglo on an RRA basis.

b. Moonglo reports a profit on its 2008 oil and gas operations, on a historical cost basis, of $173. Explain (in words only) why this profit differs from the RRA income you calculated in part **a**.

c. Which income number (RRA or historical cost basis) is more relevant? Which is more reliable? Explain why.

22. The text states that matching of costs and revenues is a major challenge of historical cost accounting. A related challenge is revenue recognition, that is, when to recognize revenue as realized, or earned. Most firms recognize revenue as earned at the point of sale. More generally, according to IAS 18, revenue from sale of goods should be recognized when the significant risks and rewards of ownership are transferred to the buyer, the seller loses effective control of the goods, and the amount of consideration to be received can be reliably measured. For services and long-term contracts, revenue should be recognized on a percentage of completion basis.

    It is often not clear just when these general criteria are met. For example, revenue recognition at point of sale may be a reasonable tradeoff between relevance and reliability in most cases. However, relevance is increased (and reliability decreased) if revenue is recognized earlier than point of sale.

    Furthermore, revenue recognition policy may be used by firms to impress investors. For example, firms with no earnings history (e.g., startup firms) and firms that are incurring significant losses or declines in earnings have an incentive to record revenue as early as possible, so as to improve the appearance of their financial statements.

    Consider the case of Lucent Technologies Inc. In December 2000, Lucent restated its revenue for its fiscal year ended September 30, 2000, reducing the amounts originally reported as follows:

Vendor financing	$199 (million)
Partial shipments	28
Distribution partners	452
Total	$679

The vendor financing component of the restatement represents previously unrecorded credits granted by Lucent to customers, to help them finance purchases of Lucent products. That is, the customer sales were originally recorded gross, rather than net, of the credits. The distribution partners' component represents product shipped to firms with which Lucent did not deal at arm's length, but which was not resold by these firms at year-end. These firms included certain distributors in which Lucent had an ownership interest. The practice of overshipping to distributors is called "stuffing the channels."

In its 2000 annual report, Lucent reported net income of $1,219 million, compared to $4,789 million for 1999 and $1,065 million for 1998.

On May 17, 2004, the SEC announced charges against Lucent and several of its officers for overstating revenues by $1,148 million in 2000 in order to meet sales targets. The company's share price fell by 5.5% on that day. Tactics used, the SEC claimed, included the granting of improper credits to customers to encourage them to buy company products, and invoicing sales to customers that were subject to renegotiation in subsequent periods.

Subsequently, Lucent paid a fine of $25 million for "lack of cooperation." In addition, the company, and some of the executives charged, settled the allegations by paying penalties, without admitting or denying guilt.

Required

a. What is the most relevant point of revenue recognition? The most reliable? Explain. In your answer, consider manufacturing firms, oil and gas exploration firms, retail firms, and firms with long-term contracts.

b. Do you feel that Lucent's original recognition of the above components as revenue was consistent with the general revenue recognition criteria given above? Explain why or why not. In your answer, consider the tradeoff between relevance and reliability.

c. What additional revenue recognition questions arise when the vendor has an ownership interest in the customer?

23. Refer to the revenue recognition practices of Qwest Communications outlined in Theory in Practice 1.1.

Required

a. Use the concept of relevance to argue that firms should record revenue as earned as early as possible in their operating cycles. Was Qwest's revenue recognition policy relevant? Explain.

b. Use the concept of reliability to argue that firms should wait until the significant risks and rewards of ownership are transferred to the buyer, and there is reasonable assurance of collection, before recording revenue. Was Qwest's revenue recognition policy reliable? Explain.

c. When is revenue recognized under ideal conditions? Why?

24. National Instrument 51-101 of the Canadian Securities Administrators, effective September 30, 2003, lays down disclosure requirements for Canadian oil and gas firms. These requirements include:

- Proved reserve quantities, defined as reserves that can be estimated with a high degree of certainty (operationalized as at least 90% probability) to be recoverable.

- Probable reserve quantities, defined as additional reserves such that there is at least a 50% probability that the amounts actually recovered will exceed the sum of estimated proved and probable reserves.

- Future net revenues from proved reserves and changes therein, discounted at 10% and undiscounted, using
  i) year-end prices and costs
  ii) forecasted prices and costs

- Future net revenues from probable reserves, discounted at 5%, 10%, 15%, and 20%, and undiscounted, using forecasted prices and costs.

In addition, reserves data must be verified by an independent qualified reserves evaluator or auditor and reviewed by the board of directors.

Reproduced below in Table 2.5 are portions of the NI 51-101 disclosure of Western Oil Sands Inc., from its 2006 *Annual Information Form* (AIF).

Table 2.5 Net Present Values of Future Net Revenue Based on Forecast Prices and Costs

	Before Deducting Income Taxes Discounted At					After Deducting Income Taxes Discounted At				
	0% (MMS)	5% (MMS)	10% (MMS)	15% (MMS)	20% (MMS)	0% (MMS)	5% (MMS)	10% (MMS)	15% (MMS)	20% (MMS)
Proved Developed Producing	7,684	4,561	3,049	2,239	1,762	5,819	3,569	2,470	1,873	1,515
Proved Developed Non-producing	281	196	127	80	49	192	131	81	47	25
Proved Undeveloped	4,699	1,059	(220)	(706)	(898)	3,292	617	(343)	(718)	(871)
Total Proved	12,663	5,816	2,957	1,613	913	9,303	4,317	2,208	1,201	668
Total Probable	3,554	1,616	912	607	451	2,510	1,158	669	459	352
Total Proved Plus Probable	16,217	7,432	3,868	2,220	1,365	11,813	5,475	2,877	1,660	1,020

Reconciliation of Changes in Net Present Values of Future Net Revenue Discounted at 10% Based on Constant Prices and Costs

The following table sets forth changes between future net revenue estimates attributable to net proved reserves as at December 31, 2006, against such reserves as at December 31, 2005:

	(MMS)
Estimated Future Net Revenue at December 31, 2005	2,575
Sales and Transfers of Oil and Gas Produced. Net of Production Costs and Royalties	(339)
Net Change in Prices. Production Costs and Royalties Related to Future Production	(232)
Changes in Previously Estimated Development Costs Incurred During the Period	66
Changes in Estimated Future Development Costs	(256)
Extensions and Improved Recovery	507
Discoveries	—
Acquisitions of Reserves	41
Dispositions of Reserves	—
Net Change Resulting from Revisions in Quantity Estimates	—
Accretion of Discount Pre Tax	334
Net Change in Income Taxes	30
Changes Resulting from Technical Revisions	—
Estimated Future Net Revenue at December 31, 2006	2,726

Notes:
(1) Reserve definitions consistent with National Instrument 51–101—Standards of Disclosure for Oil and Gas Activities ("N1 51–101") have been used in the GI.J Reserves Report where
"Proved" reserves are those reserves that can be estimated with a high degree of certainty to be recoverable. The targeted level of certainty under a specific set of economic conditions is at least a 90 percent probability that the quantities actually recovered will equal or exceed the estimated proved reserves
"Proved Undeveloped" reserves are those reserves expected to be recovered from known accumulations where a significant expenditure is required to render them capable of production
"Probable" reserves are those reserves that are less certain to be recovered than proved reserves
"Proved Plus Probable" reserves include those additional reserves that are less certain to be recovered than proved reserves. The targeted level of certainty under a specific set of economic conditions is at least a 50 percent probability that the quantities actually recovered will equal or exceed the sum of the estimated proved plus probable reserves

Source: Western Oil Sands Inc. 2006 *Annual Information Form*. Reprinted by permission.

Required

a. Evaluate the relevance of National Instrument 51-101 disclosures in comparison to those of SFAS 69. In your answer, include consideration of whether or not discounting expected future receipts at various rates (rather than at 10% as per SFAS 69) adds to relevance.

b. Evaluate the reliability of National Instrument 51-101 disclosures in comparison to those of SFAS 69.

c. In its AIF, Western Oil Sands states "The estimated future net revenues contained in the following tables do not necessarily represent the fair market value of the Corporation's reserves. There is no assurance that the forecast price and cost assumptions contained in the . . . reserves report will be attained and variances could be material." Give reasons why the company gives this disclaimer.

25. "A theoretically correct measure of income does not exist in the real world in which accountants must operate."

Required

a. What is meant by the phrase "a theoretically correct measure of income"?

b. Why does a theoretically correct measure of income not exist in the real world? Discuss.

c. Discuss how the historical cost basis of accounting trades off relevance against reliability.

d. Give two examples of problems or weaknesses associated with historical cost accounting. (CGA-Canada)

Notes

1. Net income for year 1 can also be calculated in a more familiar format as:

Cash flow (i.e., sales)	$150.00
Amortization expense	123.97
Net income	$ 26.03

Amortization expense is calculated as $260.33 - $136.36 = $123.97—that is, the decline in the present value of the future receipts from the asset over the year. This way of calculating amortization differs from the way that accountants usually calculate it. Nevertheless, it is the appropriate approach under the ideal conditions of this example, namely, future cash flows known with certainty and a fixed risk-free interest rate.

We view this approach to measuring income under ideal conditions as inferior to the accretion of discount approach illustrated in the example. It creates the impression that revenue is recognized as sales are made, whereas, as explained in the example, revenue is recognized when assets are acquired. The reason why the same net income number results is that the difference between sales-based and asset acquisition–based revenue is captured in amortization expense.

2. Yet another way to calculate income, familiar from introductory accounting, is to calculate the change in balance sheet net assets for the year, adjusted for capital transactions. In this example, we have:

$$\text{Net income} = \$286.37 - \$260.33 - \$0 = \$26.03$$

where capital transactions are zero. Thus, knowing the present values of all assets and liabilities enables one to calculate present value–based net income.

3. This argument can be turned around. We could argue that if the firm's future income statements were known with certainty, in conjunction with the interest rate, then they would contain all relevant information and the balance sheet could be easily deduced. In effect, each statement contains all the information needed for the other. We view the balance sheet as more fundamental under ideal conditions of certainty, however.

4. To illustrate arbitrage, assume a share of ABC Ltd. is selling in Toronto for $10, and the same share is selling in New York for $10.50 (in Canadian dollars). Ignoring commissions, ABC shares could be purchased on the Toronto market for $10 and sold in New York for $10.50, for a profit of $0.50 per share. However, share price will quickly rise in Toronto because of greater demand, and will just as quickly fall in New York because of greater supply. This change in the supply/demand relationship will bring the market prices into equality in the two markets.

5. Here, the only financial item is cash. Generally, financial assets are assets whose values are fixed in terms of money, such as accounts receivable and investments with a fixed face value, such as bonds. Certain other assets, such as investments in shares, are also regarded as financial assets if a ready market value is available. Financial liabilities, such as accounts payable, bank loans, and bonds issued, are defined similarly.

6. The independence assumption is not crucial to the example. With slight added complexity we could allow for conditional probabilities, where the probability of state realization in year 2 depends on the state realization in year 1. For example, if the good state happened in year 1, this might increase the probability that the good state would also happen in year 2. See problem 18. The important point for ideal conditions to hold, however, is that if probabilities will change over time, the pattern of changes is publicly known.

7. Somewhat weaker conditions than these would be sufficient to give a first-best economy. Our purpose here, however, is only to give a set of conditions sufficient to ensure that net income is well defined and without information content.

8. We can also calculate net income as

Cash flow (sales)	$100.00
Amortization expense ($260.33 − $136.36)	123.97
Net loss	$ 23.97

See Note 1 for reasons why we prefer the net income format used in the example.

9. Of course, if investors are risk-neutral, this risk will not matter to them. However, under more realistic conditions, which we will introduce later, risk does matter. Note that the firm can use hedging to reduce this volatility.

10. As is the case in Examples 2.1 and 2.2, we can also prepare an income statement in a more conventional format:

Cash flow from operations (sales in year)	$ 559
Development costs incurred in year	(772)
Amortization "expense" (increase in present value of proved reserves during the year) ($3,369 − $1,664)	1,705
Net income from proved oil and gas reserves	$1,492

Note also that amortization expense is negative for the year. This can happen under present value accounting, and simply means that present value increased over the year. The $772 of development costs incurred during the year is not a change in estimates. It represents the expenditure of some of the development costs allowed for in the beginning-of-year present value.

See also Notes 1 and 8.

11. Note that these changes in estimates contain two components. One component derives from state realization. As illustrated in Example 2.2, state realization introduces volatility into earnings. The second component derives from errors in estimation of cash flow amounts that result from particular state realizations. Under ideal conditions, there are no such errors of estimation. Since Suncor does not disclose the states of nature it has taken into account when preparing its future cash flow estimates and which states actually happened, we cannot separate changes in estimates into these two components. The significance of such a separation is that while state realization generates volatility, it does not reduce reliability. Consequently, attributing all changes in estimates to errors, as we do in our discussion, tends to understate RRA reliability.

12. SFAS 69 also requires the reporting of historical cost-based results of operations for oil and gas producing activities.

13. For an extensive discussion of the balance sheet versus income statement approaches, and the inability of the income statement approach to resolve the question of how to match costs and revenues, see Storey and Storey (1998).

14. For a counterargument, see Ohlson (1987).

Chapter 3
The Decision Usefulness Approach to Financial Reporting

Figure 3.1 Organization of Chapter 3

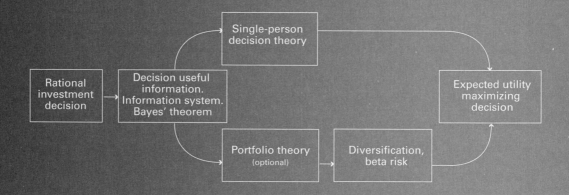

3.1 OVERVIEW

In Chapter 2 we concluded that the present value model faces some severe problems in practice. It is doubtful that a complete set of financial statements on this basis is feasible. This inability to value the whole firm on a present value or market value basis means that a theoretically well-defined concept of net income does not exist in the complex real world in which accountants operate.

In this chapter we will begin our study of how to tackle this problem. In Chapter 2 we suggested that historical cost accounting produces relatively reliable information, even though historical cost is not as relevant as present value or market-based approaches to current value.

Given that the mixed measurement model retains historical cost accounting for major classes of assets and liabilities, the next question is: How can financial statements be made more *useful*? This leads to an important concept in accounting—the concept of **decision usefulness**. To properly understand this concept, we need to consider other theories (that is, other than the present value model) from economics and finance. We, as accountants, cannot proceed to make financial statements more useful until we know just what usefulness means. We also need a precise definition of information. Decision theories and capital market theories assist in conceptualizing the meaning of useful financial statement information.

The main purpose of this chapter is to introduce you to some of these theories and to discuss their relevance to accounting. As we shall see, major accounting standard-setting bodies have picked up on these theories, to such an extent that they underlie many of the accounting standards and pronouncements issued by these bodies.

Figure 3.1 outlines the organization of this chapter.

3.2 The Decision Usefulness Approach

As we can infer from Section 2.5, the decision usefulness approach to accounting theory takes the view that "if we can't prepare theoretically correct financial statements, at least we can try to make financial statements more useful." First enunciated in 1966,[1] and reinforced by the influential 1973 report of the Trueblood Commission,[2] this simple observation has had major implications for accounting theory and practice. In particular, we must now pay much closer attention than we did in Chapter 2 to financial statement users and their decision needs, since under non-ideal conditions it is not possible to read the value of the firm directly from the financial statements.

Decision usefulness is contrasted with another view of the role of financial reporting, namely stewardship, whereby the role is to report on management's success, or lack thereof, in managing the firm's resources. As stated in Chapter 1, we regard each role as equally important. In this chapter, we begin our discussion of decision usefulness. Discussion of the second role begins in Chapter 8.

In adopting the decision usefulness approach, two major questions must be addressed. First, who are the users of financial statements? Clearly, there are many users. It is helpful to categorize them into broad groups, such as investors, lenders, managers, unions, standard setters, and governments. These groups are called **constituencies** of accounting.

Second, what are the decision problems of financial statement users? By understanding these decision problems, accountants will be better prepared to meet the information needs of the various constituencies. Financial statements can then be prepared with these information needs in mind. In other words, tailoring financial statement information to the specific needs of the users of those statements will lead to improved decision-making. In this way, the financial statements are made more *useful*.

Of course, determining the specific decision needs of users is by no means an obvious process. For example, what information does a holder of the firm's long-term debt need to make a rational decision about whether to sell certain holdings? Would this decision be helped or hindered by valuing long-term debt at fair value?

In the face of difficult questions like these, accountants have turned to various theories in economics and finance for assistance. In this chapter we consider the single-person **theory of decision**. This theory is a good place to begin to understand how individuals may make rational decisions under uncertainty.

The theory enables us to appreciate the concept of information, which enables decision-makers to update their subjective beliefs about future payoffs from their decisions.

We also consider the **theory of investment**, a specialization of decision theory to model the decision processes of a rational investor. In particular, the theory of investment helps us to understand the nature of *risk* in a portfolio investment context.

These theories are important to accountants because they have been adopted by major professional accounting standard-setting bodies. An examination of some of the pronouncements of the Conceptual Framework project of the FASB (Section 3.8) shows that the above theories lurk just under the surface. Consequently, an understanding of the theories enables a deeper understanding of the pronouncements themselves.

3.2.1 Summary

Accountants have adopted a decision usefulness approach to financial reporting as a reaction to the impossibility of preparing theoretically correct financial statements. However, the decision usefulness approach leads to the problem of identifying the users of financial statements and the information they need to make good decisions. Accountants have decided that investors are a major constituency of users and have turned to various theories in economics and finance—in particular, to theories of decision and investment— to understand the type of financial statement information investors need.

3.3 SINGLE-PERSON DECISION THEORY

Single-person decision theory takes the viewpoint of an individual who must make a decision under conditions of uncertainty.[3] It recognizes that state probabilities are no longer objective, as they are under ideal conditions, and sets out a formal procedure whereby the individual can make the best decision by selecting from a set of alternatives. This procedure allows additional information to be obtained to revise the decision-maker's subjective assessment of the probabilities of what might happen after the decision is made (i.e., the probabilities of states of nature). Decision theory is relevant to accounting because financial statements provide additional information that is useful for many decisions, as illustrated in Example 3.1.

3.3.1 Decision Theory Applied

Example 3.1
A Typical Investment Decision

Bill Cautious has $10,000 to invest for one period. He has narrowed down his choice to two investments: shares of X Ltd. or government bonds yielding 2 1/4%. We will denote the act of buying the shares by a_1, and the bonds by a_2.

If he buys the shares, Bill faces risk. That is, the future performance of X Ltd. is not known when Bill makes his decision. Consequently, he defines two states of nature:

State 1: X Ltd. future performance high

State 2: X Ltd. future performance low

We can think of X Ltd.'s future performance in terms of its future dividends, cash flows, or earnings, all of which affect the end-of-period market value of its shares. Assume that if X Ltd. is in state 1, Bill's net return on the X shares will be $1,600, where net return is calculated as:

Net return = End-of-period market value + Dividends in period − Original investment

If X Ltd. is in state 2, assume that Bill's net return will be zero.

If Bill buys the bonds, he receives interest of $225 next period, regardless of the state of nature. That is, the bond investment is treated as riskless.

The amounts to be received from a decision are called **payoffs**, which we can summarize by a **payoff table**, as shown in Table 3.1.

Table 3.1 Payoff Table for Decision Theory Example 3.1

Act	State	
	High	**Low**
a_1 (buy shares)	$1,600	$0
a_2 (buy bonds)	$225	$225

Now consider the state probabilities. Bill subjectively assesses the probability of state 1 (the high-performance state) as $P(H) = 0.30$. The probability of state 2 is then $P(L) = 0.70$. These subjective probabilities incorporate all that Bill knows about X Ltd. to this point in time. They are called **prior probabilities**. He could base these probabilities on an analysis of X Ltd.'s past financial statements, plus other news to date about the company. Instead, or in addition, he could study the current market price of X Ltd. shares. If share price is low, it could indicate an unfavourable market evaluation of X's future prospects, and Bill might also take this into account when assessing his state probabilities.

Bill is risk-averse. Let us assume that the amount of utility, or satisfaction, he derives from a payoff is equal to the square root of the amount of the payoff.[4] Thus, if he receives a payoff of $1,600, his utility is 40. This assumption of risk aversion is not necessary to our example. We could just as easily assume Bill was risk-neutral and evaluate the expected *dollar* amounts of the various payoffs. However, investors are generally risk-averse, so we will work in utilities rather than dollars. Section 3.4 considers risk aversion in greater detail.

In view of our discussion of ethical issues in Section 1.3, a complete evaluation of the utility of an act requires Bill to evaluate any effects of his decision on others. Here, however, Bill's decision is relatively self-contained. That is, whether he buys the shares or the bonds will have little or no effect on anyone else. Consequently, we evaluate his utility in terms of its effect on his own wealth. In other decision problems, for example whether to buy the shares of a firm that is a heavy polluter, Bill may reduce the utility of his payoffs to recognize the adverse social effects of a decision to buy.

Figure 3.2 gives a decision tree diagram for this decision problem. The numbers in parentheses in the middle column of the figure are the probabilities of the states, the second column from the right shows the dollar amounts of the payoffs, and the right-most column gives Bill's utility for each amount.

The decision theory tells us that, if he must decide now, Bill should choose the act with the highest **expected utility**. We will denote the expected utility of act a_1 by $EU(a_1)$, and so on.

$$EU(a_1) = (0.30 \times 40) + (0.70 \times 0) = 12$$
$$EU(a_2) = 1.00 \times 15 = 15$$

Therefore, it appears that Bill should choose a_2 and buy the bonds.[5]

However, Bill has another alternative: to obtain *more information* before deciding. Accordingly, let's assume that he decides to become more informed. The annual report of X Ltd. is to be released within the next few days and Bill decides to wait for it, since it provides readily available and cost-effective evidence about the state of the firm. When the annual report comes, Bill notes that net income is quite high and the firm's net current assets and debt-to-equity ratio are improved from last year. In effect, the current financial statements show "good news" (GN).[6]

Figure 3.2 Decision Tree for Bill's Choice

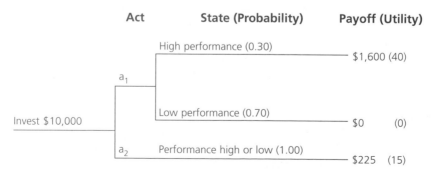

On the basis of extensive experience in financial statement preparation and analysis, Bill knows that if X Ltd. really is a high-state firm, there is an 80% probability that the current year's financial statements will show GN and 20% probability that they will show bad news (BN). Denote these conditional probabilities by P(GN/H) = 0.80 and P(BN/H) = 0.20, respectively. Note that even if the firm is in the high state, there is still a 20% probability that the financial statements show BN. This is because accounting standards do not generate complete relevance and reliability. For example, the 20% value of P(BN/H) may be due to accounting standards designed to prevent premature revenue recognition. Then, expected profit from a major new contract may not be included in current earnings even though it is relevant information about future payoffs. Alternatively, or in addition, BN may be reported by a high-state firm to disguise high profits. Such firms may wish to smooth earnings to a sustainable level, or reduce the likelihood of attracting competitors.

Bill also knows that if X Ltd. is a low-state firm, it is still possible that the financial statements show GN, Again, this is because accounting standards are not completely relevant and reliable. Assume that if X Ltd. really is in a low state, the probability that the current year's financial statements will show GN is 10%, giving a 90% probability that they will show BN. Denote these conditional probabilities by P(GN/L) = 0.10 and P(BN/L) = 0.90, respectively.

Now, armed with the GN evidence from the current financial statements and the above conditional probabilities, Bill can use Bayes' theorem to calculate his **posterior state probabilities** (that is, posterior to the financial statement evidence). The posterior probability of the high-performance state is:

$$P(H/GN) = \frac{P(H)\ P(GN/H)}{P(H)\ P(GN/H) + P(L)\ P(GN/L)}$$

$$= \frac{0.30 \times 0.80}{(0.30 \times 0.80) + (0.70 \times 0.10)}$$

$$= 0.77$$

where:

P(H/GN) is the (posterior) probability of the high state given the good-news financial statement

P(H) is the prior probability of the high state

P(GN/H) is the probability that the financial statements show good news given that the firm is in the high state

P(L) is the prior probability of the low state

P(GN/L) is the probability that the financial statements show good news given that the firm is in the low state

Then, Bill's posterior probability P(L/GN) of X Ltd. being in the low-performance state is 1.00 − 0.77 = 0.23. Recall that if the state is high, the payoff from Bill's share investment will be high ($1,600), and if it is low, the payoff will be low ($0).

Bill can now calculate the expected utility of each act on the basis of his posterior probabilities:

$$EU(a_1/GN) = (0.77 \times 40) + (0.23 \times 0) = 30.8$$
$$EU(a_2/GN) = 1.00 \times 15 = 15$$

Thus, the GN current financial statement information has caused Bill's optimal decision to change to a_1—he should buy the shares of X Ltd.

3.3.2 The Information System

It is important to understand why financial statement information is useful here. To be useful, it must help predict future investment returns. Under non-ideal conditions, the financial statements do not show expected future firm performance directly. Nevertheless, financial statements will still be useful to investors to the extent that the good or bad news they contain will persist into the future. Think of a progression, from current good or bad news in the financial statements to future expected firm performance to future expected investment returns.

To return to our example, the good news was that current earnings and liquidity were high. This information enabled Bill to predict high future X Ltd. performance with probability 0.77, and this is also the probability of the high payoff on his investment. Of course, such information is a double-edged sword. Had the financial statements contained bad news, Bill's probability of high payoff would have been lowered just as surely as it was raised by good news.

We may conclude that financial statements can still be useful to investors even though they do not report directly on future cash flows by means of present value-based calculations. Here, it is the lack of ideal conditions that gives the financial statements their information content—recall that there was really no information in net income in Examples 2.1 and 2.2. While Examples 2.2 and 3.1 both allow for uncertainty, the fundamental difference between them is that state probabilities were objective in Example 2.2, but subjective in Example 3.1. This opens a role for information to help the decision-maker update subjective state probabilities and predict investment returns.

The heart of the linkage between current financial statement information and future firm performance is the conditional probabilities $P(GN/H)$ and $P(BN/L)$. These probabilities are called an **information system**, which can be summarized by a table such as Table 3.2. Recall that, in our example, the probability that the current financial statements of X Ltd. show good news, conditional on the firm being in the high performance state, is 0.80. The probability they show bad news conditional on the low performance state is 0.90. The 0.80 and 0.90 probabilities are called **main diagonal probabilities**; the others are called **off-main diagonal probabilities**.

> An **information system** is a table giving, conditional on each state of nature, the objective[7] probability of each possible financial statement evidence item.

Table 3.2 Information System for Decision Theory Example 3.1

		Current Financial Statement Evidence	
		GN	BN
	High	0.80	0.20
State			
	Low	0.10	0.90

Note that financial statements are not perfect, or "true"—this would be the case only under ideal conditions. As mentioned above, there is a 20% probability that even if the firm is in the high state the financial statements would show BN, and a 10% probability that if it is in the low state the financial statements would show GN. This weakening of the relationship between current financial statement information and future firm performance is sometimes described as **noise** or as low **earnings quality** in the financial statements. Nevertheless, the information system is **informative**, since it enables Bill to update his prior probabilities to reflect what he now knows, thereby affecting his decision. For cases of fully informative and non-informative information systems, see question 1 at the end of this chapter.

It should be noted that the information system concept is decision-specific. The system in Table 3.2 is geared to a decision whether or not to buy a firm's shares. Other decisions would involve a different table. For example, a decision whether or not to buy or sell a firm's bonds could define states of nature as "principal and interest repaid" and "principal and interest not repaid." The GN or BN in the financial statements would thus be more oriented to measures of liquidity and dividends and less to net income than described in Example 3.1, with different conditional probabilities.

Financial statements that are highly informative, and the information system that underlies them, are often called **transparent**, **precise**, or **high quality**, since they convey lots of information to investors. In this book, we shall often use the term "informative" to refer to financial statement quality since it is a more primitive concept. However, we shall also use the other terms, particularly in relation to earnings, since various measures of earnings informativeness are used to evaluate the usefulness of reported net income.

Note also that the extent of informativeness depends on the relevance and reliability of the financial statements. For example, suppose a new accounting standard required X Ltd. to switch to fair value from historical cost[8] for its capital assets. The resulting increase in relevance would tend to increase the main diagonal probabilities of the information system and lower the off-main diagonal ones. This is because fair values, for example, current market values, of assets are better predictors of their future values (and hence of future firm performance) than are historical costs of capital assets. However, the use of fair values would also decrease reliability since, due to market incompleteness, current market values need not be available. Then, less reliable estimates of fair value must be made, and these are subject to errors and possible managerial bias. This would have the opposite effect on the main diagonal probabilities. Thus, it is difficult to say whether such an accounting policy change would increase or decrease the informativeness of the information system.

However, if it were possible to increase relevance without sacrificing reliability or vice versa, the result would be to increase financial statement usefulness. One way to accomplish this would be to present **supplementary current value information**, as in RRA. This increases relevance for those who want to use supplemental information. However, the financial statements proper are still available for those who want the somewhat greater reliability of historical cost accounting for oil and gas operations.

The concept of informativeness of an information system is useful in understanding the role of information in decision-making. The higher the main diagonal probabilities relative to the off-main diagonal ones, the more informative the system. Consequently, the more informative an information system, the more decision useful it is. It enables better predictions of relevant states of nature and resulting payoffs. In an investment context, these payoffs are returns on investments.

While thinking of financial statements as a table of conditional probabilities may take some getting used to, the concept of an information system is one of the most powerful and useful concepts in financial accounting theory. This is because it captures the information content of financial statements, thereby determining their usefulness for investor decision-making. Furthermore, many practical accounting problems can be framed in terms of their impact on the information system. For example, we pointed out above that if a move to fair value accounting for capital assets is to be decision useful, the increase in relevance (which increases the main diagonal probabilities) must outweigh any decrease in reliability (which decreases them). Similar reasoning can be applied to other new or proposed accounting standards. Standards requiring fair value accounting for financial instruments, for example, will be decision useful only if the increased relevance of reporting is not outweighed by decreased reliability. Since most financial reporting debates can be cast in terms of relevance versus reliability, the information system provides a useful framework for evaluation.

As mentioned (see Note 7) the information system probabilities are objective. This raises the question, how does Bill know what these probabilities are? One response is simply to *assume* they are known. We made this assumption in Example 3.1 and Table 3.2. This is an example of **rational expectations**—investors are assumed to quickly form accurate estimates of unknown, underlying firm parameters, in this case the information system probabilities. This assumption is common in much theoretical economics and accounting research.

One approach to forming accurate estimates is by sampling. Bill can take a sample of several years of past X Ltd. financial statements (possibly including other firms similar to X Ltd.) and record the number of times GN is followed by high performance, and similarly for BN. If the information system probabilities are stationary, these frequencies will equal the probabilities in Table 3.2, for a large enough sample. Completely accurate estimates are unlikely, however, since new accounting standards will change information system probabilities over time. Thus, a sampling approach is subject to errors of estimation.

A different approach to evaluating information system informativeness was taken by Easton and Zmijewski (1989) (EZ). They examined Value Line analysts' revisions of future quarterly earnings forecasts following the GN or BN in firms' current quarterly earnings.

That is, analysts are viewed as rational investors who use financial statement earnings information to revise their beliefs about future firm performance, similar to Bill Cautious in Example 3.1. Future quarterly earnings are analogous to the states of nature in Table 3.2 (Value Line predicts future firm performance in terms of earnings), and the GN or BN in current quarterly earnings constitutes the financial statement evidence in that table. Value Line provides forecasts for a large number of firms, and these forecasts are revised quarterly.

For a sample of 150 large U.S. corporations followed by Value Line over the period 1975–1980, EZ found that for every $1 of GN or BN in reported earnings, the Value Line analysts increased or decreased next quarter's earnings forecast by about 34 cents on average. This implies that the information systems underlying the sample firms' financial statements are informative, that is, analysts use current financial statement information to revise their beliefs about future firm performance. EZ called the effect of current financial statement information on analysts' next quarter earnings forecast a "revision coefficient." This coefficient is a proxy for earnings quality, that is, it reflects the magnitude of the information system probabilities.

EZ also found that the higher a firm's revision coefficient is (recall that the 34 cents above is an average), the stronger was the effect of the GN or BN in current earnings on the market price of the firm's shares. This is consistent with investors accepting the analysts' evaluation of the information system, bidding share price up or down more strongly the higher the quality of the system.

EZ's results suggest that quarterly earnings are decision useful, consistent with the decision theory model of Example 3.1. Empirical studies of the response of share price to financial statement information are considered in greater detail in Chapter 5.

Theory in Practice 3.1

Decision theory methods are finding applications in several areas other than accounting. Consider, for example, the evaluation of new medical discoveries. Suppose that a drug company has developed a new, expensive, test for a deadly disease. It has administered the test to a sample of persons and has compiled the test's success rates (correct identification of persons who do and do not have the disease) and failure rates (incorrect identification). The success rates correspond to the main diagonal probabilities of the information system in Table 3.2, and the failure rates correspond to the off-main diagonal probabilities. The higher the main diagonal probabilities relative to off-main diagonal, the better the test discriminates (i.e., predicts future performance) between persons who do and do not have the disease.

The company is now trying to decide whether to proceed with marketing the test. Commercial success will be assured if the test is demanded by a large number of people. That is, the test will be popular if persons with low prior probability of having the disease (i.e., most persons) will want to take it. The drug company uses Bayes' theorem to calculate the posterior probability of having the disease for a person with an assumed low prior probability. If it finds the posterior probability to be high (indicating that the test discriminates very well), such persons will be likely to want to take the expensive test. Consequently, the drug company may decide to proceed.

3.3.3 Information Defined

Decision theory and the concept of informativeness give us a precise way to define information:

> *Information* is evidence that has the potential to affect an individual's decision.

Notice that this is an *ex ante* definition. We would hardly expect an individual to gather evidence if he or she didn't expect to learn enough so as to possibly affect a decision. Bayes' theorem is simply a device to process what has been learned. The crucial requirement for evidence to constitute information is that for at least some evidence that might be received, beliefs will be sufficiently affected that the optimal decision will change.

Also, the definition is individual-specific. As pointed out in Chapter 1, individuals may differ in their reaction to the same information, even for similar decisions. For example, their prior probabilities may differ, so that posterior probabilities, and hence their investment decisions, may differ even when confronted with the same evidence.

The definition should really be interpreted net of cost. An information source may have the potential to affect an individual's decision but, if it is too costly, it is not information since it will not be used. It can be argued, however, that financial statements are a cost-effective information source because of the large number of potential users.

Finally, it should be emphasized that an individual's receipt of information and subsequent belief revision is really a continuous process. We can think of the individual as using Bayes' theorem every time a new information item comes along. Example 3.1 concentrated on belief revision following receipt of the annual report, but obviously there are many other information sources, such as media, websites, speeches and announcements, statistical reports, etc. that can also affect decisions. Hopefully, by supplying relevant and reliable information, financial statements will continue their role as an important source of information.

3.3.4 Summary

Decision theory is important because it helps us to understand why information is such a powerful commodity—it can affect the actions taken by investors. Accountants, who prepare much of the information required by investors, need to understand this powerful role.

3.4 THE RATIONAL, RISK-AVERSE INVESTOR

In decision theory, the concept of a rational individual simply means that in making decisions, the chosen act is the one that yields the highest expected utility.[9] This implies that the individual may search for additional information relating to the decision, using it to revise state probabilities by means of Bayes' theorem.

We emphasize that the decision theory described above is a *model* of rational decision-making. Whether individuals actually make decisions this way is difficult to say. Nevertheless, in thinking about questions of decision usefulness, it is helpful to assume that they do. As we will discuss in Section 6.2, we do not mean to imply that all individuals make decisions as the theory suggests, but only that the theory captures the average behaviour of investors who want to make good investment decisions. Alternatively, we can argue that if investors want to make good decisions this is how they *should* proceed. If individuals do not make decisions in some rational, predictable manner it is difficult for accountants, or anyone else, to know what information they find useful. At any rate, implications of the theory have been subjected to much empirical testing, as we shall see in Chapter 5. To the extent that predictions of the theory are confirmed empirically, our confidence that the decision theory model is a reasonable one is strengthened.

It is also usually assumed that rational investors are **risk-averse**.[10] To see the intuition underlying this concept, think of yourself as an investor who is asked to flip a fair coin with your university or college instructor—suppose the coin is a penny. You would probably be willing to flip for pennies, if for no other reason than to humour the instructor. If the ante were raised, you would probably be willing to flip for dimes, quarters, even dollars. However, there would come a point where you would refuse—say, flipping for $100,000 (if you didn't refuse, the instructor would).

Remind yourself that the expected payoff of flipping a fair coin is zero, regardless of the amount at stake, since you have a 50% chance of winning and a 50% chance of losing in all cases. Thus, your increasing nervousness as the stakes are raised means that another effect, beyond the expected value of the gamble, is operating. This is risk aversion.

Note also that risk-averse individuals trade off expected return and risk. For example, if the coin was biased in your favour—say you have a 75% chance of winning—you would probably be willing to flip for higher stakes than if the coin was fair. In effect, you are now willing to bear more risk in exchange for a higher expected value—the expected payoff of your gamble is now $0.50 per dollar rather than 0.

To model risk aversion, decision theorists use the device of a **utility function**, which relates payoff amounts to the decision-maker's utility for those amounts.

To portray a utility function, consider Figure 3.3. The solid line shows the utility function of Bill Cautious in Example 3.1. Bill's utility function is:

$$U(x) = \sqrt{x}, x \geq 0$$

where x is the amount of the payoff. Note that the utility function of a risk-averse individual is concave.

Based on his prior probabilities, Bill's expected payoff for act a_1 is $(0.3 \times \$1,600) + (0.7 \times 0) = \$480$. The expected *utility* of the payoff is at point C on the dotted line joining A and B. This expected utility of $(0.3 \times 40) + (0.7 \times 0) = 12$ is less than the utility of 15 for the risk-free investment at point D on Figure 3.3. Consequently, Bill's rational decision is to choose the risk-free investment, if he were to act on the basis of his prior probabilities. This is the case even though the expected payoff of the risky investment ($480) is greater than the risk-free payoff ($225). This demonstrates that Bill is averse to risk.

Figure 3.3 Risk-Averse Utility Function

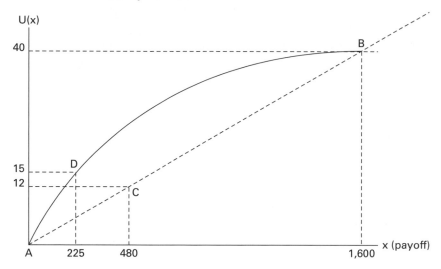

To see how Bill's decision may change if the risky investment were less risky, assume that the possible payoffs are now $200 (with probability 0.7) and $1,133.33 (with probability 0.3) instead of the earlier $0 and $1,600. You should verify that the expected payoff is still $480 but the expected utility rises to 20.[11] Then, Bill's rational decision is to buy the risky investment. The reduction in risk raises expected utility, even though the expected payoff has not changed.

Despite the intuitive appeal of risk aversion, it is sometimes assumed that decision-makers are **risk-neutral**. This means that they evaluate risky investments strictly in terms of expected payoff—risk itself does not matter per se. We made this assumption in Example 2.2. Figure 3.4 shows the utility function of a risk-neutral decision-maker. A

Figure 3.4 Risk-Neutral Utility Function

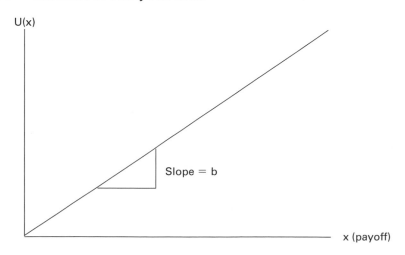

typical risk-neutral utility function is $U(x) = bx$, where b is the slope of the line. Here, utility is simply a linear function of the payoff.

Risk neutrality may be a reasonable assumption when the payoffs are small. However, risk aversion is the more realistic assumption in most cases. The concept of risk aversion is important to accountants, because it means that investors need information concerning the risk, as well as the expected value, of future returns.

*3.5 THE PRINCIPLE OF PORTFOLIO DIVERSIFICATION

In Section 3.4, we stated that individual investors were typically assumed to be risk-averse. Consequently, for a given expected payoff from investments the rational investor wants the lowest possible risk or, equivalently, for a given risk, will want the highest possible expected payoff. In effect, the investor adopts a tradeoff between risk and return; greater risk will be borne only if expected return is higher and vice versa.

One way investors can lower risk for a given expected return is to adopt a strategy of diversification, that is, to invest in a portfolio of securities. The principle of portfolio diversification shows us that some, but not all, risk can be eliminated by appropriate investment strategy. This principle has important implications for the nature of the risk information that investors need. The risk reported on by many common accounting-based risk measures, such as debt to equity, times interest earned (ratio of net income before interest and taxes to interest expense), or the current ratio, can be reduced or eliminated a priori by appropriate diversification.

Before illustrating the diversification principle, we return briefly to our risk-averse investor. Note that before we can calculate an individual's expected utility for different investment acts, we need to know what that individual's utility function looks like. For example, Bill Cautious' utility function in Example 3.1 was $U(x) = \sqrt{x}$, $x \geq 0$. With this utility function and payoff probabilities, Bill's expected utilities for different acts were calculated and compared.

One might reasonably ask, "How do we know what an individual's utility function is?" To avoid this question, we shall now assume **mean-variance utility**:

$$U_i(a) = f_i(\bar{x}_a, \sigma_a^2)$$

where symbol a represents an investment act. For example, investment act a could be an investment in a riskless government bond, or in a firm's shares, as in Example 3.1. Alternatively, it could be an investment in a portfolio of securities.

The equation states that the utility of an investment act a to investor i is a function f_i of the expected rate of return from that act $\bar{x}_a$ and the risk as measured by its variance

---

*Sections 3.5, 3.6, and 3.7 can be ignored with little loss of continuity. However, diversification and beta are referred to frequently in subsequent chapters. Readers with no previous exposure to these concepts should read at least Sections 3.5 and 3.7.1.

$\sigma_a{}^2$. We assume that f_i is increasing in $\bar{x}_a$ and decreasing in $\sigma_a{}^2$. A specific example of a mean variance utility function is:

$$U_i(a) = 2\bar{x}_a - \sigma_a{}^2$$

which can be seen to increase in $\bar{x}_a$ and decrease in $\sigma_a{}^2$. Individuals will have different tradeoffs between expected rate of return and risk—for example, a more risk-averse investor might have $-2\sigma_a{}^2$ rather than $-\sigma_a{}^2$ as shown above. It is not true in general that the utility of an act depends only on its mean and variance. However, investigation of this is beyond our scope.

The significance of a mean-variance utility assumption to accountants is that it makes investors' decision needs more explicit—all investors need information about the expected values and riskiness of returns from investments, regardless of the specific forms of their utility functions. Without such an assumption, specific knowledge of investors' utility functions would be needed to fully deduce their information requirements.

With this background in mind, we now illustrate the principle of portfolio diversification by means of two examples.

Suppose that a risk-averse investor (Toni Difelice) has $200 to invest and is considering investing all of it in the shares of firm A, currently trading for $20. Assume that Toni assesses a 0.74 probability[12] that the shares will increase in market value to $22 over the coming period and a 0.26 probability that they will decrease to $17. Assume also that A will pay a dividend of $1 per share at the end of the period (we could also make the dividend uncertain, but this would just add complexity without affecting the point to be made).

Example 3.2
The Principle of Portfolio Diversification (Part 1)

As in our decision theory Example 3.1, Toni's subjective probabilities could be posterior to her analysis of firm A's financial statements and the resulting application of Bayes' theorem. Alternatively, they could be her prior probabilities based on whatever other information is at her disposal. For present purposes, the extent to which Toni may have become informed does not matter. The important point is that she has assessed probabilities.

The payoffs from Toni's proposed investment are as follows:

If shares increase: $22 × 10 shares + $10 dividend = $230

If shares decrease: $17 × 10 shares + $10 dividend = $180

Table 3.3 shows the calculation of the expected rate of return and variance of this investment. Henceforth, we will work with the *rate* of return. As can be seen from Table 3.3, this just involves dividing net returns by the amount of original investment ($200). The division by original investment is a standardization device—rates of return can be directly compared across securities while amounts of returns cannot. Also, rate of

Table 3.3 Calculating Expected Rate of Return and Variance

Payoff	Rate of Return	Probability	Expected Rate of Return	Variance
$230	$\dfrac{230 - 200}{200} = 0.15$	0.74	0.1110	$(0.15 - 0.0850)^2 \times 0.74 = 0.0031$
$180	$\dfrac{180 - 200}{200} = -0.10$	0.26	$\underline{-0.0260}$	$(-0.10 - 0.0850)^2 \times 0.26 = \underline{0.0089}$
			$\overline{X}_a = \underline{0.0850}$	$\sigma_a^2 = \underline{0.0120}$

return fits in nicely with the assumption of mean-variance utility, which is in terms of the expected value and variance of rate of return.

The variance of return is 0.0120. The variance of an investment return serves as a measure of its riskiness. Since Toni is risk-averse, increasing riskiness will lower her utility, other things equal.

Assume that Toni's utility function is:

$$U_i(a) = 2\overline{X}_a - \sigma_a^2$$

as given above. Then, her utility for this investment is:

$$(2 \times 0.0850) - 0.0120 = 0.1580$$

Toni now has to decide whether to take this investment act. If she feels that this utility is not sufficiently high, further research would be necessary to find a more attractive investment, or some other use for the $200 of capital.

Example 3.3
The Principle of Portfolio Diversification (Part 2)

It turns out that Toni would not be rational to accept the above investment—a more attractive investment can be found. It is possible to find another investment decision that has the same expected return but lower risk. This is because of the **principle of portfolio diversification**.

To illustrate, assume that shares of firm B are also traded on the market, with a current market value of $10. These shares also pay a dividend of $1. Assume there is a 0.6750 probability that firm B's shares will increase in market value to $10.50 at the end of the period, and a 0.3250 probability that they will decrease to $8.50.

Now suppose that Toni decides to invest $200 in six shares of firm A at $20 and eight shares of firm B at $10. We must calculate Toni's expected utility for the portfolio consisting of six shares of firm A and eight shares of firm B. Notice that the same amount ($200) is invested, but that it is now spread over two different securities.

Four possible payoffs now exist from the portfolio: both shares increase in market value, one share increases and the other decreases, or both shares decrease. The amounts of the payoffs and their assumed probabilities are as follows in Table 3.4:

Table 3.4 Payoffs and Their Probabilities

A		B		Dividends		Total Payoff	Probability
132	+	84	+	14	=	$230	0.5742
132	+	68	+	14	=	$214	0.1658
102	+	84	+	14	=	$200	0.1008
102	+	68	+	14	=	$184	0.1592
							1.0000

Recall that six shares of firm A and eight shares of firm B are held, and that the high payoff is $22 per share for firm A and $10.50 for firm B, plus a $1 dividend from each share. This gives the $230 payoff on the first line of the table. The other payoffs are similarly calculated.

Now let us consider more closely the probabilities we have assumed for the four possible payoffs. The returns from shares of firm A and firm B are correlated in our example. To see this, consider the first row in Table 3.4 with a total payoff of $230. This payoff will be realized if both shares A and B realize their high-payoff values. On the basis of our assumption about the probabilities of the individual payoffs of shares A and B, the probabilities of these two payoffs, when each share is considered separately, are 0.74 for A and 0.6750 for B. If the payoffs of shares A and B were independent, the probability of both shares realizing their high payoffs would be $0.74 \times 0.6750 = 0.4995$.

However, in any economy, there are states of nature, also called factors, which affect the returns of *all* shares, such as levels of interest rates, foreign exchange rates, the level of economic activity, and so on. These are called **market-wide** or **economy-wide factors**. Their presence means that if the return on one share is high, it is more likely that the returns on most other shares in the economy will also be high—more likely, that is, than would be the case if the returns on shares were independent. Thus, we have assumed that the probability that both shares A and B realize their high payoffs is 0.5742, greater than the 0.4995 that we would obtain under independence, to reflect these underlying common factors.

Similar reasoning applies to the last row of Table 3.4 with a payoff of $184. Here we have assumed that the joint probability of both firm A and firm B realizing their low payoffs is 0.1592, greater than the ($0.26 \times 0.3250 = 0.0845$) probability under independence. If market-wide state realizations are such that they work against high returns (i.e., if the economy is performing poorly), then the probability that both shares realize low payoffs is greater than what would be expected under independence.

Of course, while share returns may be correlated due to common factors, they will not be perfectly correlated. It is still possible that one firm realizes a high return and another a low return—witness the two middle rows of Table 3.4. This is because, in addition to economy-wide factors, there are also **firm-specific factors** that affect the return of one firm only. Examples include the quality of a firm's management, new patents, strikes, machine breakdowns, and so on. Thus, the second row of the table represents a situation where firm A realizes a high return (say, because of a new invention it has just patented) and firm B realizes a low return (say, because of a critical machine failure in its assembly line). However, due to the presence of economy-wide factors, the probabilities for these high/low payoff realizations will also be different than under independence. This is true of Example 3.3.

It should be pointed out that the preceding argument assumes that the *only* source of correlation between returns on firms' shares is market-wide factors. In effect, we have partitioned states of nature that can affect share returns into two components—economy-wide and firm-specific. This is a simplification, since, for example, industry-wide factors could introduce additional returns correlation. However, the simplification is a widely used one and is sufficient for our purposes. It leads to an important measure of share riskiness (beta), which we will discuss shortly. For now, you should realize that the assumption implies that if *all* factors were economy-wide, returns on firms' shares would be perfectly correlated. If *all* factors were firm-specific, returns would be independent. As is usually the case, the truth lies somewhere in between. Consequently, the probabilities given in Table 3.4 assume that both types of factors are present.

The expected rate of return and variance of Toni's portfolio of A and B shares are calculated in Table 3.5 using the correlated probabilities. Thus, the expected rate of return of the portfolio is 0.0850, as before (we have forced this result by appropriate choice of the probabilities, to facilitate comparison), but the variance has decreased to 0.0074, from 0.0120. Since Toni is risk-averse, she would be better off buying the portfolio of A and B shares rather than just A, because the expected return is the same, but the risk is lower.

Table 3.5 Calculating Expected Rate of Return and Variance

Payoff	Rate of Return		Probability	Expected Rate of Return	Variance	
$230	$\dfrac{230-200}{200} =$	0.15	0.5742	0.0861	$(0.15-0.0850)^2 \times 0.5742$	$= 0.0024$
$214	$\dfrac{214-200}{200} =$	0.07	0.1658	0.0116	$(0.07-0.0850)^2 \times 0.1658$	$= 0.0000$
$200	$\dfrac{200-200}{200} =$	0.00	0.1008	0.0000	$(0.00-0.0850)^2 \times 0.1008$	$= 0.0007$
$184	$\dfrac{184-200}{200} =$	-0.08	0.1592	$-\underline{0.0127}$	$(-0.08-0.0850)^2 \times 0.1592$	$= \underline{0.0043}$
				$\bar{x}_a = \underline{0.0850}$		$\sigma_a^2 = \underline{0.0074}$

In fact, her utility now is:

$$U_i(a) = (2 \times 0.0850) - 0.0074$$
$$= 0.1626$$

up from 0.1580 for the single-share investment.

3.5.1 Summary

Risk-averse investors can take advantage of the principle of portfolio diversification to reduce their risk, by investing in a portfolio of securities. This is because realizations of firm-specific states of nature tend to cancel out across securities, leaving economy-wide factors as the main contributors to portfolio risk.

While individual attitudes to risk may differ, we can see investors' decision needs with particular clarity if we assume mean-variance utility. Then, regardless of the degree of risk aversion, we know that utility increases in expected rate of return and decreases in variance of the portfolio.

*3.6 THE OPTIMAL INVESTMENT DECISION

If a portfolio of two shares is better than one, then a three-share portfolio should be better than two, and so on. Indeed, this is the case and, assuming there are no transaction costs such as brokerage fees, Toni should continue buying until the portfolio includes some of every security traded on the market. This is called "holding the market portfolio." Note again that the total amount invested remains at $200, but is spread over a greater number of securities.

Be sure you understand *why* the same amount invested in a portfolio can yield lower risk than if it were invested in a single firm for the same expected rate of return. To repeat, when more than one risky investment is held, *the firm-specific risks tend to cancel out*. If one share realizes a low return, there is always the chance that another share will realize a high return.[13] The larger the number of different firms' shares in the portfolio, the more this effect can operate. As a result, the riskiness of returns is reduced, which we have illustrated above by means of our variance calculations. Of course, in the presence of economy-wide risk, there is not a complete cancelling out. At a minimum, that is, when the market portfolio is held, the economy-wide factors will remain to contribute to portfolio risk, and this risk cannot be diversified away. Such non-diversifiable risk is called **systematic risk**.

Conceptually, the market portfolio includes all assets available for investment in the economy. As a practical matter, the market portfolio is usually taken as all the securities traded on a major stock exchange. The return on the market portfolio can then be proxied by the return on a market index for that exchange, such as the Dow Jones Industrial Average index of the New York Stock Exchange, the S&P/TSX Composite Index, etc.

---

*This section can be omitted without loss of continuity.

Now return to our investor, Toni Difelice. Toni decides to buy the market portfolio after hearing about the benefits of diversification. Her first task is to assess the expected return and variance of the market portfolio. She subjectively assesses a 0.8 probability that the S&P/TSX Composite Index will increase by 10% for the coming period and a 0.2 probability that it will increase by $2\,^{1}/_{2}\%$. Then, denoting the expected return and variance of the market portfolio by $\bar{x}_M$ and σ_M^2 respectively:

$$\bar{x}_M = (0.10 \times 0.8) + (0.0250 \times 0.2) = 0.0850$$
$$\sigma_M^2 = [(0.10 - 0.0850)^2 \times 0.8] + [(0.0250 - 0.0850)^2 \times 0.2]$$
$$= 0.0002 + 0.0007$$
$$= 0.0009$$

This gives Toni a utility of:

$$2\bar{x}_M - \sigma_M^2 = 0.1700 - 0.0009$$
$$= 0.1691$$

which is greater than the 0.1626 utility of the two-share portfolio in Example 3.3.

The question now is: Is this Toni's optimal investment decision? The answer is probably not. If Toni were quite risk-averse, she might prefer a portfolio with lower risk than 0.0009, and would be willing to have a lower expected return as a result.

One strategy she might follow would be to sell some of the high-risk stocks in her portfolio. But, if she does this, she is no longer holding the market portfolio, so some of the benefits of diversification are lost. How can Toni adjust portfolio risk to her desired level without losing the benefits of diversification?

The answer lies in the **risk-free asset**. If a risk-free asset, such as treasury bills yielding, say, 4%, is available, an investor could sell some of the market portfolio (that is, sell some of each security, so that the market portfolio is still held but total investment in it is lower) and use the proceeds to buy the risk-free asset. This strategy is depicted in Figure 3.5 as a move

Figure 3.5 The Optimal Portfolio Investment Decision

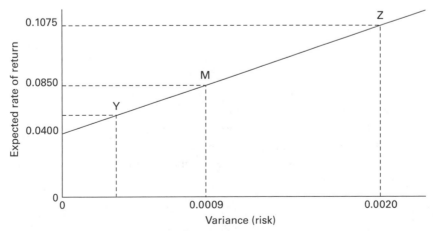

from M, where only the market portfolio is held, to Y. Risk is lower at Y, but so is expected return, compared to M. However, if the investor is quite risk-averse this could raise utility.

Conversely, if Toni were less risk-averse, she may prefer to borrow at the risk-free rate and buy more of the market portfolio, thereby moving to Z, with higher expected return and risk.

In this way, each investor can secure a desired risk–return tradeoff while continuing to enjoy the maximum risk-reduction effects of diversification.

To illustrate, suppose that Toni borrows $100 at a rate of 0.04 and buys an additional $100 of the market portfolio. Toni now has $300 of market portfolio, on which she expects to earn 0.0850, and owes $100 at 4% interest. But her own investment is still $200. Consequently, her expected return is now:

$$\bar{x}_a = \left(\frac{300}{200} \times 0.0850\right) - \left(\frac{100}{200} \times 0.0400\right)$$
$$= (0.1275 - 0.0200)$$
$$= 0.1075$$

The variance of her return also increases, since she now has $300 at risk on an investment of $200. There is no variance attached to the $100 borrowed, of course, since interest and principal payments are fixed. The variance of her return is now:

$$\sigma_a^2 = (300/200)^2 \times 0.0009$$
$$= 0.0020$$

yielding utility of $(2 \times 0.1075) - 0.0020 = 0.2130$. This yields Toni a higher utility than simply holding the market portfolio (0.1691). Toni will continue to borrow until the amount borrowed and reinvested yields an $\bar{x}_a$ and σ_a^2 that maximizes her utility. In fact, if she can borrow all she wants at 4%, she would borrow $9,800, which would yield her utility of 2.33.

3.6.1 Summary

When transaction costs are ignored, a risk-averse investor's optimal investment decision is to buy that combination of market portfolio and risk-free asset that yields the best tradeoff between expected return and risk. This tradeoff is individual-specific—it depends on the investor's utility function. Some investors may wish to reduce their investment in the market portfolio and buy the risk-free asset with the proceeds. Others may wish to borrow at the risk-free rate and increase their investment. Either way, all investors can enjoy the full benefits of diversification while at the same time attaining their optimal risk–return tradeoff.

*3.7 PORTFOLIO RISK

3.7.1 Calculating and Interpreting Beta

The principle of diversification leads to an important risk measure of a security in the theory of investment. This is **beta**, which measures the co-movement between changes in the price of a security and changes in the market value of the market portfolio. To illustrate, we will calculate the betas of shares of firms A and B in Example 3.3, in relation to the market portfolio M given in Section 3.6.

Beta is an important and useful concept in financial accounting. As we shall see in Chapter 5, a stock's beta is a crucial component of empirical studies of the usefulness to investors of financial accounting information. Also, it is a "launching pad" for reporting on firm risk. Reporting on risk is discussed in Section 7.5. Consequently, an understanding of what a stock's beta is and what it tells us about firm risk is an important part of an accountant's knowledge base.

Example 3.4
Calculating Beta

The beta of A shares, denoted by β_A, is given by:

$$\beta_A = \frac{Cov(A,M)}{Var(M)}$$

where $Cov(A,M)$ is the covariance of the returns on A with the returns on the market portfolio M. In effect, β_A measures how strongly the return on A varies as the market varies. For example, a high-beta security would undergo wide swings in rate of return as market conditions change. Shares of airlines and aircraft manufacturers are examples, since these industries are sensitive to economic conditions. Shares of electric utilities and fast food firms would be low-beta, since the returns of such firms are less subject to the state of the economy.

Division by $Var(M)$ is simply a standardization device, to express $Cov(A,M)$ in units of market variance. For example, if the returns on the Toronto and New York Stock Exchanges have different variances, standardization by the variance of returns on the respective exchanges makes betas of Canadian and U.S. firms more comparable.

To calculate the beta of security A, assume that the conditional payoff probabilities of A are as follows:

■ When return on M is high:
Probability that return on A is high = 0.90
Probability that return on A is low = 0.10

---

*This section can be omitted without loss of continuity.

- When return on M is low:

    Probability that return on A is high = 0.10
    Probability that return on A is low = 0.90

These probabilities could be estimated by examining past data on the returns on A shares in relation to the returns on M. Cov(A,M) is calculated in Table 3.6.

Table 3.6 Calculation of Covariance

Returns		Joint
A	**M**	**Probabilities**
High	High	$(0.15 - 0.0850)(0.10 - 0.0850) \times 0.72 = \quad 0.0007$
High	Low	$(0.15 - 0.0850)(0.0250 - 0.0850) \times 0.02 = \quad -0.0001$
Low	High	$(-0.10 - 0.0850)(0.10 - 0.0850) \times 0.08 = \quad -0.0002$
Low	Low	$(-0.10 - 0.0850)(0.0250 - 0.0850) \times 0.18 = \quad \underline{0.0020}$
		Cov(A,M) = $\quad \underline{0.0024}$

In the first row of the table, the values 0.15 and 0.0850 are the high return and the expected return respectively of A (see Table 3.3). Similarly 0.10 and 0.0850 are the high return and the expected return of M (see Section 3.6). The joint probability that both A and M pay off high is:

$$\text{Prob(A high and M high)} = \text{Prob(M high) Prob(A high/M high)}$$
$$= 0.8 \times 0.9$$
$$= 0.72$$

You should verify the remaining rows in the table.
Then, recalling from Section 3.6 that $\sigma_M^2 = \text{Var(M)} = 0.0009$, we obtain:

$$\beta_A = \frac{0.0024}{0.0009} = 2.6667$$

For security B in Example 3.3, assume that the conditional payoff probabilities are:

- When return on M is high:

    Probability that return on B is high = 0.7917
    Probability that return on B is low = 0.2083

- When return on M is low:

    Probability that return on B is high = 0.2083
    Probability that return on B is low = 0.7917

Then, similar calculations give:

$$\beta_B = \frac{0.0014}{0.0009} = 1.5556$$

You should verify this calculation.[14]

Since β_B is lower than β_A, an investor who buys only B shares is more insulated from the ups and downs of the stock market than if he/she buys only A shares. This is the sense in which a low-beta security has low risk.[15]

3.7.2 Portfolio Expected Value and Variance

Since risk-averse investors with mean-variance utility functions need to know the expected value and variance of their investment portfolios, we give here formulae for their calculation. In the process, we shall see that beta measures the amount of systematic risk contributed by a security to a portfolio.

The expected value of return on a portfolio P is calculated as a weighted average of the expected returns on the securities in the portfolio:

$$\bar{x}_p = k_1\bar{x}_1 + k_2\bar{x}_2 + ... + k_n\bar{x}_n$$

where $\bar{x}_p$ is the expected return on P, $\bar{x}_1$ is the expected return on security 1, etc., k_1 is the proportion of total portfolio investment in security 1, etc., and there are n securities in the portfolio.

In Example 3.3, $n = 2$, $k_1 = \$120/\$200 = 0.6$, $k_2 = (1 - k_1) = 0.4$, and the expected returns on the two securities A and B in Toni's portfolio were both 0.0850. Then, the formula gives:

$$\bar{x}_{A + B} = (0.6 \times 0.0850) + (0.4 \times 0.0850) = 0.0850$$

which, of course, agrees with the direct calculation in Table 3.5.

For the variance of portfolio return, we have the following standard formula for the variance of a sum of random variables:

$$Var(P) = \sigma_p^2 = k_1^2\sigma_1^2 + k_2^2\sigma_2^2 + ... + k_n^2\sigma_n^2 + 2k_1k_2\,Cov(x_1,x_2) + 2k_1k_3\,Cov(x_1,x_3)$$
$$+ ... + 2k_{n-1}k_n\,Cov(x_{n-1},x_n)$$

That is, the variance of P is the weighted sum of the variances of the individual securities in P plus the weighted sum of covariances of all the pairs of securities in P.

In Example 3.3, the formula reduces to:

$$Var(A + B) = k_1^2\,Var(A) + (1 - k_1)^2\,Var(B) + 2k_1(1 - k_1)\,Cov(A,B)$$

The main point here is that portfolio variance depends not only on the variances of the component securities, but also, if the security returns are correlated, on the covariance between them (if the returns on A and B are uncorrelated, $Cov(A,B) = 0$).

In an investment context, the returns on A and B are most definitely correlated because of economy-wide factors. In fact, we have assumed that economy-wide factors are the *only* source of correlation between security returns. Then, we can write the covariance between A and B in terms of their covariances with the market portfolio M:

$$\text{Cov(A,B)} = \frac{\text{Cov(A,M) Cov(B,M)}}{\text{Var(M)}}$$

$$= \text{Var(M)}\beta_A\beta_B$$

The portfolio variance becomes:[16]

$$
\begin{aligned}
\text{Var(A + B)} &= 0.6^2\,\text{Var(A)} + 0.4^2\,\text{Var(B)} + 2 \times 0.6 \times 0.4\,\text{Var(M)}\beta_A\beta_B \\
&= (0.36 \times 0.0120) + (0.16 \times 0.0088) + (0.48 \times 0.0009 \times 2.6667 \times 1.5556) \\
&= 0.0043 + 0.0014 + 0.0017 \\
&= 0.0074
\end{aligned}
$$

which agrees with the direct calculation in Table 3.5. Thus, we see that securities A and B contribute systematic risk of 0.0017 to the portfolio variance of 0.0074, or about 23%.

3.7.3 Portfolio Risk as the Number of Securities Increases

A contribution of 23% may not seem like much, but this results from the presence of only two securities in the portfolio. Consider what happens as the number of securities in the portfolio increases. Let there now be n securities in portfolio P. To simplify a bit, we will assume that an equal amount is invested in each security, so that the proportion of each security in P is $1/n$ of the total amount invested. Then:

$$\text{Var(P)} = \frac{1}{n^2}\sigma_1^2 + \frac{1}{n^2}\sigma_2^2 + ... + \frac{1}{n^2}\sigma_n^2 + \frac{2}{n^2}\,\text{Cov}(x_1,x_2) + \frac{2}{n^2}\,\text{Cov}(x_1,x_3) + ... + \frac{2}{n^2}\,\text{Cov}(x_{n-1},x_n)$$

$$= \frac{1}{n^2}\left[\sigma_1^2 + \sigma_2^2 + ... + \sigma_n^2\right] + \frac{2}{n^2}\,\text{Var(M)}\left[\beta_1\beta_2 + \beta_1\beta_3 + ... + \beta_{n-1}\beta_n\right]$$

There are n variance terms in the formula. However, the number of covariance terms goes up quite quickly relative to n. In fact, there are $n(n-1) \div 2$ covariance terms. For example, if n = 10, there are 10 variance terms but 45 covariance terms.

This means that, even for portfolios that contain a modest number of securities, *most of the risk is systematic risk*, from the covariance terms. For example, for n = 10, the coefficient of the variance terms is only 1/100, so that the variances of the 10 securities contribute only 10% of their average variance to the portfolio variance. However, while the coefficient of the systematic risk terms is only 2/100, there are 45 terms, so the covariances contribute fully 90% of their average covariance to the portfolio variance. In other words, *most of the benefits of diversification can be attained with only a few securities in the portfolio*. This is fortunate, since brokerage and other transactions costs would prevent most investors from buying the market portfolio.[17]

Note that we have made a rational expectations assumption that the investor knows the expected returns and risk of the securities being considered for the portfolio, analogous to our assumption in Section 3.3.2 that the information system probabilities were known. As a practical matter, these items are not known with complete accuracy. This creates a more specialized role for financial reporting relative to its rather abstract role in Example 3.1 of supplying GN or BN. That is, useful information is information that helps investors assess securities' expected returns and betas.

3.7.4 Summary

When transactions costs are not ignored, a risk-averse investor's optimal investment decision is to buy relatively few securities, rather than the market portfolio. In this way, most of the benefits of diversification can be attained, at reasonable cost.

Information about securities' expected returns and betas is useful to such investors. This enables them to assess the expected return and riskiness of various portfolios that they may be considering. They can then choose the portfolio that gives them their most preferred risk–return tradeoff, subject to the level of transactions costs that they are willing to bear.

3.8 THE REACTION OF PROFESSIONAL ACCOUNTING BODIES TO THE DECISION USEFULNESS APPROACH

It is interesting to note that major professional accounting bodies have adopted the decision usefulness approach. For example, according to the *IASB Framework* (2001), the goal of financial statements is to provide information about the financial position, performance, and changes in financial position of the firm that is useful to a wide range of users in making economic decisions.

Section 1000 of the *CICA Handbook* states, in part:

The objective of financial statements is to communicate information that is useful to investors, members, contributors, creditors and other users . . . in making their resource allocation decisions and/or assessing management stewardship.

However, the earliest and most complete statement of this adoption comes from the FASB in its Conceptual Framework project.[18]

According to *Statement of Financial Accounting Concepts* (1978) (SFAC 1), the purpose of the concepts project is to set forth fundamentals on which financial accounting and reporting standards will be based. SFAC 1 gives a series of objectives of financial reporting. Its first objective of financial reporting (p. 5) is to:

provide information that is useful to present and potential investors and creditors and other users in making rational investment, credit, and similar decisions.

Note particularly the use of the word "rational" in this objective. This is the tie-in to the economic decision theory. As pointed out in Section 3.4, decision-makers who proceed in accordance with the theory, that is, those who make decisions so as to maximize their expected utility, are referred to as rational.

Note also that, like the IASB framework, a variety of constituencies is included in this most general objective (present and potential investors and creditors and other users) and also that a wide variety of decisions are contemplated (investment, credit, and similar decisions). This immediately raises the question of what particular decision-makers and decisions are involved. Thus, SFAC 1 states that the second objective of financial reporting (p. 17, para. 37) is to:

> *provide information to help present and potential investors and creditors and other users in assessing the amounts, timing, and uncertainty of prospective cash receipts from dividends or interest and the proceeds from the sale, redemption, or maturity of securities or loans.*

Thus, we can see that the primary decision addressed in SFAC 1 is the investment decision in firms' shares or debt. Specifically, cash receipts from dividends or interest are *payoffs*, similar to those in the payoff table (Table 3.1) of Example 3.1. Note that these investment decisions apply to potential investors as well as present ones. This means that financial statements must communicate useful information to the market, not just to existing investors in the firm.

Note also that the second objective is future-oriented—it calls for information about "prospective" cash receipts from dividends or interest. There is a clear recognition that investors need information to help them estimate *future* payoffs from their investments. In particular, the second objective states that investors need to assess "the amounts, timing, and uncertainty" of prospective returns. While the terms used are somewhat different, these will be recognized as relating to the expected value and risk of future returns. Thus, the second objective also contains a clear recognition that investors will want information about risk of returns as well as their expected amounts. That is, use of the term "uncertainty" indicates an implicit assumption that investors are risk-averse since, as we pointed out in Section 3.4, if they were risk-neutral they would not care about uncertainty.

The question now arises: How can historical cost-based financial statements be useful in predicting future returns? This is probably the major difficulty that the FASB's Conceptual Framework has faced. Given that historical cost accounting remains an important component of the mixed measurement model, it is necessary to establish some linkage between past firm performance and future prospects. Without such linkage, the decision-oriented objectives of SFAC 1 would not be attainable.

We can see the linkage clearly, however, by drawing on the decision theory model. In particular, refer to the information system (Table 3.2) for Example 3.1. The table provides a probabilistic relationship between current financial statement information (GN or BN) and the future-oriented states of nature (high or low performance), that will determine future investment payoffs. In effect, current financial statement information and future returns are linked via the conditional probabilities of the information system.

Consistent with the information system linkage, SFAC 1 states (p. 19, para. 42):

Although investment and credit decisions reflect investors' and creditors' expectations about future enterprise performance, those expectations are commonly based at least partly on evaluations of past enterprise performance.

This is the crucial argument that enables the Conceptual Framework to maintain that even though the financial statements report on past and current performance and financial position, this information can be useful to forward-looking investors. It is consistent with the decision usefulness approach, which purports that information is useful if it helps investors make their own estimates of future returns.

SFAC 1 also relates to the concept of accruals introduced in Section 2.5.2. SFAC 1 states (p. 5):

Information about enterprise earnings based on accrual accounting generally provides a better indicator of an enterprise's present and continuing ability to generate favourable cash flows than information limited to the financial effects of cash receipts and payments.

Here, the FASB envisages future firm performance (states of nature) in terms of future cash flows, consistent with its second objective stated above. The FASB is arguing that net income is a better predictor of future cash flows than current cash flows themselves. This may seem surprising. Nevertheless, several researchers, for example, Kim and Kross (2006), have documented this statement empirically. For a large sample of U.S. firms over 1974–2000, they report that the ability of current earnings to predict next period's operating cash flows exceeds that of current operating cash flows.

In Section 2.5.2, we described accruals as a device to match costs and revenues. The FASB statement highlights a more fundamental accruals role, namely to anticipate future cash flows and thus future firm performance. For example, an account receivable (an accrual) anticipates the sales proceeds to be received next period, and current net income includes this amount. Current cash flows (zero, for this particular sale) would not predict next period's cash receipts from this sale very well.

Kim and Kross also find that the ability of earnings to predict next period's operating cash flows increased over 1974–2000. Furthermore, Ball and Shivakumar (2006), in a study over 1987–2003, find that the ability of earnings to predict future cash flows increases substantially for years in which the firm is performing poorly, compared to years of good performance. This suggests that practice has moved towards increasing use of accruals to anticipate unrealized losses while avoiding anticipation of unrealized gains. Since accruals to anticipate unrealized losses predict future cash flow reductions, the combination of these two findings provides empirical evidence of increasing conservatism. This may seem strange, in view of standard setters' movements towards current value accounting. However, conservatism can be regarded as a "one-sided" version of current value. In Section 6.7 we will argue that conservatism can increase financial statement usefulness for investors.

In SFAC 2, the FASB goes on to consider the characteristics that are necessary if financial statement information is to be useful for investor decision-making. This is another crucial and delicate aspect of the whole conceptual framework—how can financial statement information be presented so as to be of maximum use to investors in predicting future returns? Once again, the answer lies in the concepts of **relevance** and **reliability**.

In Chapter 2, we defined relevant financial statements as those that give information to investors about the firm's future economic prospects. The SFAC 2 definition (p. 5) is somewhat broader:

> *Relevant accounting information is capable of making a difference in a decision by helping users to form predictions about the outcomes of past, present, and future events or to confirm or correct prior expectations. Information can make a difference to decisions by improving decision makers' capacities to predict or by providing feedback on earlier expectations. Usually, information does both at once, because knowledge about the outcomes of actions already taken will generally improve decision makers' abilities to predict the results of similar future actions. Without a knowledge of the past, the basis for a prediction will usually be lacking. Without an interest in the future, knowledge of the past is sterile.*

The essence of the SFAC 2 definition is that information is relevant if it helps financial statement users to form their own predictions of events (such as future performance and resulting payoffs). Again, this is consistent with the decision usefulness approach. Thus, we can say that under the ideal conditions of Chapter 2, relevant financial statement information consists of (the discounted present values of) future payoffs, or expected future payoffs. Under less-than-ideal conditions, relevant financial statement information consists of information that helps investors form *their own* expectations of future payoffs. By extending the definition of relevance to include information that can help investors form their own payoff estimates, the scope for information to be relevant is greatly enlarged.

It is also worth noting that the FASB notion of relevance is consistent with the definition of information in decision theory. Recall that information is that which has the potential to change individual decisions, that is, it can "make a difference." In effect, evidence is not really information unless it is capable of affecting user decisions. This role of information comes across with particular clarity in Bayes' theorem. Recall that Bayes' theorem provides a vehicle for investors to update their prior beliefs about relevant states of nature on the basis of new information, as illustrated in Example 3.1.

Another desirable information characteristic in SFAC 2 is reliability. In Section 2.2, we defined reliable information as information that is representationally faithful, free from bias, and verifiable. According to SFAC 2 (p. 5):

> *To be reliable, information must have representational faithfulness and it must be verifiable and neutral.*

Neutrality means the absence of intention to influence action or to attain a predetermined result. The SFAC reliability definition is consistent with ours, since if information is neutral, it is unbiased, and vice versa. SFAC 2 (para. 90) also recognizes that relevance and reliability have to be traded off, consistent with our conclusion from RRA (Section 2.4.4).

SFAC 2 continues on to explore other desirable characteristics of useful financial statement information. One of these is **timeliness**, which is best thought of as a constraint on relevance. That is, if a manager delays the release of information, it loses any relevance it may have had if it had been released promptly.

As previously mentioned, the main point to realize is that, to be useful for investment decision purposes, financial statement information need not necessarily involve a direct prediction of future firm payoffs. Rather, if the information has certain desirable characteristics, such as relevance, reliability, and timeliness, it can be an informative input to help investors form their own predictions of these payoffs.

3.8.1 Summary

The FASB's SFAC 1 represents an important adaptation of decision theory to financial accounting and reporting. Furthermore, this theory is oriented in SFAC 1 to the theory of decision-making for investors, which has been much studied in economics and finance.

SFAC 2 operationalizes the decision usefulness approach by developing the characteristics that accounting information should have in order to be useful. In essence, accounting information should provide an informative information system that links current financial statements with future state realizations and payoffs. Two major informative characteristics are *relevance* and *reliability*. Relevant information is information that has the capacity to affect investors' beliefs about future returns, and it should be released in a timely manner. Reliable information faithfully represents what it purports to measure. It should be precise and free from bias. SFAC 2 recognizes the tradeoff between relevance and reliability.

3.9 CONCLUSIONS ON DECISION USEFULNESS

Following from the pioneering *ASOBAT* and Trueblood Committee reports, the decision usefulness approach to financial reporting implies that accountants need to understand the decision problems of financial statement users. Single-person decision theory and its specialization to the portfolio investment decision provide an understanding of the needs of rational, risk-averse investors. This theory tells us that such investors need information to help them assess securities' expected returns and the riskiness of these returns. In the theory of investment, beta is an important risk measure, being the standardized covariance of a security's return with the return on the market portfolio. This covariance risk is the main component of the riskiness of a diversified portfolio, even if the portfolio contains only relatively few securities.

Financial statements are an important and cost-effective source of information for investors, even though they do not report directly on future investment payoffs. They provide an information system that can help investors to predict future firm perform-ance, which, in turn, predicts future investment returns. This predictive role is enhanced to the extent that financial statements provide a useful tradeoff between relevance and reliability.

Major accounting standard-setting bodies such as the IASB and FASB have adopted the decision usefulness approach. This is evidenced by their conceptual frameworks, which show a clear recognition of the role of financial reporting in providing relevant and reliable information for investors.

Questions and Problems

1. Refer to Table 3.2, the information system table for Example 3.1. Prepare a similar table for a **perfect**, or **fully informative**, information system, that is, an information system that perfectly reveals the true state of nature. Do the same for a **non-informative** infor-mation system, that is, one that reveals nothing about the true state.

    Use the probabilities from the two tables you have prepared to revise state probabilities by means of Bayes' theorem, using the prior probabilities and GN message given in Example 3.1. Comment on the results. (CGA-Canada)

2. What would the utility function of a **risk-taking** investor look like? What sort of portfolio would such an individual be likely to invest in? What information would the investor need? (CGA-Canada)

3. An investor's utility function is:

$$U_i(a) = 3\bar{x} - \frac{1}{2}\,\sigma_x^2$$

    Act a_1 has $\bar{x} = 0.88$, $\sigma_x^2 = 0.512$, yielding $U_i(a_1) = 2.384$. Act a_2 has $\bar{x} = 0.80$.

    What σ_x^2 would this act require to yield the same utility as a_1? Comment on the result with regard to risk and expected return. (CGA-Canada)

4. Refer to Figure 3.5. Suppose Toni's utility function is:

$$U_i(a) = \frac{1}{2}\bar{x} - 16\sigma_x^2$$

    Calculate Toni's utility at point Z on Figure 3.5 and compare it with her utility at point M. Which act does Toni prefer? Explain. (CGA-Canada)

5. What is the beta of:
    a. The market portfolio
    b. The risk-free asset
    c. Portfolio A + B in Example 3.3 and Section 3.7? (CGA-Canada)

6. Explain why most of the benefits of diversification can be attained with only a relatively few securities in the portfolio. Assume that an equal amount is invested in each security. Does the riskiness of the return on a diversified portfolio approach zero as the number of securities in the portfolio gets larger? Explain. (CGA-Canada)

7. As noted in Section 3.8, the FASB states in SFAC 1:

> *Information about enterprise earnings based on accrual accounting generally provides a better indicator of an enterprise's present and continuing ability to generate favourable cash flows than information limited to the financial effects of cash receipts and payments.*

In other words, the FASB is arguing that net income is a better predictor of future cash flows than current cash flows themselves. This may seem surprising.

Why do you think the FASB makes this argument? (CGA-Canada)

8. Verify the statement made at the end of Section 3.6 that if Toni Difelice can borrow all she wants at 4% she would borrow $9,800, yielding utility of 2.33.

9. Give some reasons why the off-main diagonal probabilities of an information system such as that depicted in Table 3.2 are non-zero. Use the concepts of relevance and reliability in your answer. Explain why an information system is more useful the lower the off-main diagonal probabilities are.

10. a. State the decision usefulness approach to accounting theory.

   b. What two questions arise once the decision usefulness approach is adopted?

   c. What primary constituency of financial statement users has been adopted by a major accounting standard setting body as a guide to the reporting of decision-useful financial information?

   d. According to the FASB Conceptual Framework's second objective of financial reporting, what information is needed by the constituency of users that you have identified in part **c**?

   e. Explain why information about the riskiness of securities is useful to investors.

11. Mr. Smart is an investor with $15,000 to invest. He has narrowed his choice down to two possible investments:

■ Mutual fund

■ Common shares in Buyme Corporation

A decision tree for Mr. Smart's situation can be found in Figure 3.6 on p. 90. Mr. Smart is risk-averse. The amount of utility he derives from a payoff is:

$$\text{Utility} = 2\ln(\text{payoff})$$

Because of a planned major purchase, Mr. Smart intends to sell his investment one year later. The payoffs represent the proceeds from the sale of the investment and receipt of any dividends, net of initial investment. The probabilities represent Mr. Smart's prior probabilities about the state of the economy (good or bad) over the coming year.

Required

a. Calculate Mr. Smart's expected utility for each action and indicate which action he would choose if he acted on the basis of his prior information.

b. Now, suppose Mr. Smart decides that he would like to obtain more information about the state of the economy rather than simply accepting that it is just as likely to be good as bad. He decides to take a sample of current annual reports of major corporations.

Figure 3.6 Decision Tree for Mr. Smart's Problem

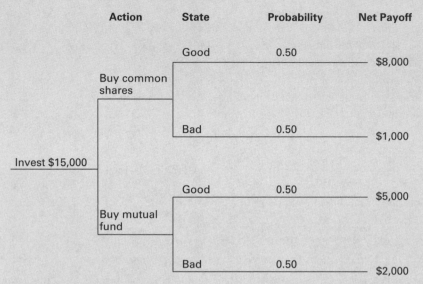

Every annual report shows that its firm is doing well, with increased profits over the previous year. The probability that there would be such healthy profits if the state of the economy actually was good is 0.75. The probability of such healthy profits is only 0.10 if the state of the economy actually was bad.

Use Bayes' theorem to calculate Mr. Smart's posterior probabilities of the high and low states of the economy. Will he change his decision?

Note: Round your calculations to two decimal places.

12. John Save plans to invest $5,000 in one of the following instruments:

■ Bonds of J Ltd., yielding 12%

■ Canada Savings Bonds, yielding 8%

On the basis of his knowledge of current economic conditions and the outlook for the industry of J Ltd., John assesses the prior probability that J Ltd. will go bankrupt as 0.05. If this happens, John will lose both principal and interest and receive no money at the end of the year. If J Ltd. does not go bankrupt, John plans to sell the bonds, plus interest, at the end of one year.

Of course, the probability that the Canada Savings Bonds will fail to pay off is zero. John also plans to sell these, plus interest, one year later.

John is risk-averse, and decides to choose the investment that yields the highest expected utility. Assume that John's utility for an amount of $x is given by $\sqrt{x}$, where x is the gross payoff.

Required

a. On the basis of his prior probabilities, which investment should John choose?

b. Rather than choosing on the basis of his prior probabilities, assume that John decides to analyze the current financial statements of J Ltd. These financial statements can look "good" (G) or "bad" (B). After his analysis, John realizes that the statements look good. On the basis of his extensive understanding of financial statement analysis, he knows that the probability that the financial statements would look good given that the firm was actually heading for bankruptcy is 0.10, that is:

$$P(G/S_1) = 0.10$$

where S_1 denotes the state of heading for bankruptcy.

Similarly, John knows that:

$$P(G/S_2) = 0.80$$

where S_2 denotes the state of not heading for bankruptcy.

Which investment should John now take? Explain why. Use Bayes' theorem.

13. Consider the common stock of A Ltd. and the common stock of B Ltd. These two common stocks have the same expected return and the same variance of return.

You are a risk-averse investor and have a fixed sum of money to invest. You are considering the following two choices:

a. Investing the entire sum of money in common stock of A Ltd.

b. Investing in a portfolio with the investment equally distributed between common stock of A Ltd. and common stock of B Ltd.

Required

Discuss whether you would choose alternative **a** or **b** or whether you are indifferent between them. Explain your choice. (CGA-Canada)

14. "It is possible to reduce risk in a portfolio by diversification."

Required

a. Do you agree with this statement? If so, why? Explain.

b. Can the risk of a portfolio be reduced to zero by diversification? Explain.

c. Why is beta the most relevant measure of risk in a diversified portfolio?

15. Marie has $1,000 that she wishes to invest for one year. She has narrowed her choices down to one of the following two actions:

a_1: Buy bonds of Risky Mining Ltd. These pay 14.4% interest, unless Risky goes bankrupt, in which case Marie will lose her principal and interest.

a_2: Buy Canada Savings Bonds, paying 6.4% interest.

Marie assesses her prior probability of Risky Mining Ltd. going bankrupt as 0.40. Marie's utility for money is given by the square root of the amount of her gross payoff. That is, if she buys the Canada Savings Bonds her gross payoff is $1,064, etc. Marie is a rational decision-maker.

Required

a. Based on her prior probabilities, which action should Marie take? Show your calculations.

b. Before making a final decision, Marie decides she needs more information. She obtains Risky Mining's current financial statements and examines its debt-to-equity ratio. This ratio can be either "HI" or "LO." Upon calculating the ratio, Marie observes that it is

LO. On the basis of her prior experience in bond investments, Marie knows the following conditional probabilities:

Future State	Debt-to-Equity Ratio	
	LO	HI
NB (Not Bankrupt)	0.50	0.50
B (Bankrupt)	0.05	0.95

Which action should Marie now take? Show your calculations, taken to two decimal places.

c. The Accounting Standards Board adopts a major new standard affecting Risky Mining Ltd.'s financial statements. Pension liabilities and other post-employment benefits must now be measured in the financial statements at their expected discounted present values, instead of the previous pay-as-you-go accounting.

Evaluate the likely impact of the new standard on the main diagonal probabilities of the information system in part **b**.

16. A rational investor has $1,000 to invest. She is contemplating investing the full amount in shares of Company A (a_1) or investing it in a risk-free government bond (a_2).

The investor identifies two states of nature:

State H: Company A has high future performance.

State L: Company A has low future performance.

On the basis of her prior information about Company A, the investor assesses the following subjective prior probabilities:

State H: 0.2

State L: 0.8

The following is the payoff table for these two investments. Payoffs are net of (i.e., they exclude) the original investment.

		State	
		H	L
Act	a_1	$324	$0
	a_2	$36	$36

The investor is risk-averse, with utility equal to the square root of the net dollar payoff.

Required

a. On the basis of her prior probabilities, which act should the investor take? Show calculations.

b. Instead of acting now, the investor decides to obtain more information about Company A by careful reading of its annual report. The investor, who is an expert in financial accounting and reporting standards, knows that they are based primarily on historical cost accounting and the lower-of-cost-or-market rule. The quality of financial statements prepared according to these standards is expressed in the following information system:

		Current Annual Report Evidence	
		GOOD	BAD
State	H	0.6	0.4
	L	0.1	0.9

Good evidence means that a company reports increased profits and adequate working capital. Bad evidence means that the company's profits are down and working capital is low.

Upon reading the current annual report, the investor finds it is Good.

Which act should the investor take now? Show calculations.

c. Assume that the accounting standards are revised to require fair value accounting for major asset classes. Evaluate, in words, the impact of this revision on the quality of the information system.

17. Ajay is a rational, risk-averse investor with $5,000 to invest for one year. He has decided to invest this amount in a high-technology firm and has narrowed his choice down to either AB Ltd. or XY Ltd. AB is a highly speculative firm with good prospects but no established products. XY is a well-established firm with stable performance. The payoffs (net of amount invested) for each firm depend on its next year's performance, as follows:

		Return	
		AB Ltd.	XY Ltd.
Next Year's Performance	High	$1,089	$324
	Low	$0	$196

For each firm, Ajay assesses prior probabilities of 0.5 for the high- and low-performance states. His utility for his investment return is equal to the square root of the amount of net payoff received.

Required

a. On the basis of his prior probabilities, should Ajay invest in AB Ltd. (a_1) or XY Ltd. (a_2)? Show calculations.

b. XY Ltd. has just released its annual report. Ajay decides to analyze it before investing. His analysis shows "good news" (GN). He consults Al, an expert in financial reporting standards, who is quite critical of the quality of current GAAP. Al advises that, based on current GAAP, the information system for firms' annual reports is as follows:

		Financial Statement Information	
		GN	BN
Next Year's Performance	High	0.6	0.4
	Low	0.5	0.5

The annual report of AB Ltd. is not due for some time, and nothing else has happened to cause Ajay to change his prior probabilities of AB's next year performance. Which investment should Ajay make now? Show calculations.

c. Concerned by several recent financial reporting failures, the regulatory authorities decide to act. They quickly introduce several new accounting standards, including tighter controls over revenue recognition and greater conservatism in asset valuation. New corporate governance regulations and restrictions on the ability of auditors to engage in non-audit services for their clients are also implemented. Al advises Ajay that the information system for annual reports following these new standards and regulations is as follows:

		Financial Statement Information	
		GN	BN
Next Year's Performance	High	0.8	0.2
	Low	0.2	0.8

Al advises Ajay to ignore the information system in part **b** and instead use this one to revise his prior probabilities of XY Ltd.'s next year's performance based on the GN in its annual report. AB Ltd. still has not reported and Ajay's prior probabilities of its performance are unchanged. Which act should Ajay now take? Show calculations.

18. You are an expert on financial statement analysis and the quality of financial reporting, with extensive experience in rational investing. You determine that the current quality of financial reporting is summarized in the following information system:

		Financial Statement Information	
		GN	BN
State of Nature	High	0.8	0.2
	Low	0.1	0.9

The states of nature refer to future firm performance. GN (good news) and BN (bad news) summarize the information content of current financial statements.

You are a shareholder of CG Ltd., which has just released its quarterly financial report. You analyze this report, and decide that it shows GN. Your decision problem is to sell your shares now (a_1) or hold them for another quarter (a_2).

Your prior probability of the high state is 0.7. The current market value of your CG Ltd. shares is $81. If CG is in the high state, your payoff will be $100 if you sell at the end of the next quarter. If CG is in the low state, your payoff will be $36. You are risk-averse, with utility equal to the square root of your payoff.

Required

a. What information is included in your prior probabilities? Are they subjective or objective? Why?

b. Are the information system probabilities subjective or objective? What determines these probabilities?

c. Should you sell or hold your CG shares? Show calculations.

19. The following problem is designed to encourage your consideration of Bayes' theorem. It shows how unaided judgement about probabilities can often be far off the mark. The problem is adapted from one appearing in an article in *The Economist*, "Getting the goat," February 20, 1999, p. 72. This article discusses how people who guess at probabilities can frequently be wrong:

A disease is present in the population at the rate of one person per thousand. A test for the disease becomes available. The drug company that is marketing the test randomly selects you to take the test. You agree, and the test results are positive. If the disease is present, the test always shows a positive result. However, the test has a 5% probability of showing a positive result when in fact the disease is not present. What is the probability that you have the disease?

Notes

1. As mentioned in Section 1.2, decision usefulness was the focus of the 1966 AAA monograph, *A Statement of Basic Accounting Theory* (*ASOBAT*).

2. The Trueblood Commission was a study group of the American Institute of Certified Public Accountants, which, in its 1973 report, *Objectives of Financial Statements*, accepted the decision usefulness approach of *ASOBAT*. The significance of this acceptance is that the AICPA is a professional accounting body, whereas the AAA is an association of academics.

3. For a formal development of the concepts of decision theory, including utility theory, the information system, and the value of information, see Laffont (1989), especially Chapters 1, 2, and 4. See also Demski (1972), especially Chapters 1 to 3. For an excellent intuitive development of the theory, see Raiffa (1968).

4. We define utility here in terms of the net payoff. Conceptually, utility should be defined in terms of the investor's total wealth. However, we opt for the simplest presentation in this example. Note also that the payoff for square root utility must be positive. If a negative (net) payoff is possible, we could work with gross payoffs or assume some other measure of utility, such as the log of the payoff.

5. A possible alternative would be to diversify, that is, buy some of each type of security. We will rule this out for now by assuming that the brokerage fees for buying small amounts are prohibitive.

6. Evaluation of the information in financial statements requires complete and careful analysis. For example, suppose earnings are up this year but sales are down. On closer inspection, the reason for higher earnings may be due to some non-recurring item, such as a gain on sale of land, or to cost-cutting because of declining market share. Alternatively, earnings may be up due to some fortunate but temporary realization of states of nature, such as a strike at a competitor's factory. In both cases, Bill may interpret higher earnings as bad news. Note that full disclosure is necessary here.

7. While the decision-maker's prior and posterior probabilities are subjective, the information system probabilities are objective. As explained below, these objective probabilities are determined by the quality of the financial statements. For the distinction between objective and subjective probabilities, see the discussion in Example 2.2.

8. The main diagonal probabilities of the information system in Table 3.2 are chosen to be consistent with the concept of conservatism. Recall from our discussion in Section 1.2 that conservatism is defined as the requiring of a higher standard of verification to record gains than to record losses. That

is, the firm waits to record gains until there is objective evidence of their realization, but records unrealized losses by writing assets down (or liabilities up) when a loss in value occurs. In Section 1.2, we used ceiling tests and the lower-of-cost-or-market rule for inventories as examples. Recognition of unrealized losses raises the information system probability of BN/low state, assuming reasonable reliability. This *ex post* type of conservatism is called **conditional conservatism** by Beaver and Ryan (2005), since writedowns are conditional on a loss in value actually taking place.

Historical cost accounting also introduces conservatism into the information system. For example, profitable capital investments are recorded at historical cost rather than current value, and inventories are carried at cost until objective evidence of realization is achieved. This recognition lag for good news in the financial statements lowers the probability of GN/high state. Beaver and Ryan call this *ex ante* type of conservatism **unconditional conservatism**, since assets are valued at less than their current value even though a loss in value has not taken place. Both types of conservatism are captured in Table 3.2 by the BN/low state probability (0.90) being higher than the GN/high state probability (0.80).

9. Strictly speaking, choosing the act that maximizes expected utility is a *consequence* of rationality, not rationality itself. Savage (1954) defines a set of axioms of rational behaviour under uncertainty with subjective probabilities. If an individual behaves according to these axioms, it can be shown that that individual will prefer one act to another if and only if its expected utility is higher than the other, where the expectation is with respect to the individual's subjective state probabilities. See, for example, Laffont (1989, pp. 14–17) for a demonstration.

10. For a formal development and analysis of risk aversion, see Pratt (1964), or Laffont (1989), Chapter 2.

11. The expected payoff is:

$$(0.7 \times \$200) + (0.3 \times \$1{,}133.33) = \$480$$

Expected utility is:

$$(0.7 \times \sqrt{200}) + (0.3 \times \sqrt{1{,}133.33}) = (0.7 \times 14.14) + (0.3 \times 33.66)$$
$$= 9.90 + 10.10$$
$$= 20$$

12. Note that we have suppressed the set of states of nature in this example. That is, Toni assesses payoff probabilities directly, rather than routing them through states. Thus, instead of saying "The probability that firm A is in high-performance state is 0.74 and if A really is in this state the payoff will be \$230," we simply say "The probability of the \$230 payoff is 0.74." This simplification has certain analytical advantages and is frequently used.

13. The risk we are referring to here is *ex ante* risk. That is, the investor is in the process of an investment decision and is looking ahead. This is not to say that if a firm in the portfolio realizes, say, a low return because some unfortunate firm-specific risk factor has happened, the investor will not be angry at that firm *ex post*.

14. The expected return of B is:

$$\left(0.6750 \times \frac{92 - 80}{80}\right) + \left(0.3250 \times \frac{76 - 80}{80}\right)$$
$$= (0.6750 \times 0.15) + (0.3250 \times -0.05) = 0.0850$$

(See Example 3.3.)

Cov(B,M) is calculated as:

Returns		Joint Probabilities				
B	**M**					
High	High	$(0.15 - 0.085)(0.10 - 0.085)$	$\times$	0.6333	$=$	0.0006
High	Low	$(0.15 - 0.085)(0.025 - 0.085)$	$\times$	0.0417	$=$	-0.0002
Low	High	$(-0.05 - 0.085)(0.10 - 0.085)$	$\times$	0.1667	$=$	-0.0003
Low	Low	$(-0.05 - 0.085)(0.025 - 0.085)$	$\times$	0.1583	$=$	0.0013
				Cov(B,M)	$=$	0.0014

The joint probability of B high and M high is given by $0.8 \times 0.7917 = 0.6333$. You should now verify the remaining lines.

15. Note that A shares have the same expected return as B shares (0.085), but higher risk since $\beta_A = 2.6667$ while $\beta_B = 1.5556$. Then, it might seem that Toni should buy only B shares. However, this is not the case—Toni will still want to hold both A and B shares in her portfolio. If she invests all of her $200 in B, her expected return is 0.085 and variance of return is 0.0088 (see Note 16), giving expected utility of 0.1612, which is less than expected utility of 0.1626 from holding both A and B. In this case, the benefits of diversification outweigh the fact that B shares by themselves have lower risk.

16. $\text{Var(B)} = \sigma_B^2 = [0.6750 \times (0.15 - 0.0850)^2] + [0.3250 \times (-0.05 - 0.0850)^2]$

$\quad = 0.0029 + 0.0059$

$\quad = 0.0088$

17. An alternative to buying the market portfolio is to invest in an index fund. This is a fund that tracks the rate of return on a stock market index. This attains the benefits of full diversification, but with lower transactions costs. However, unless he/she buys every stock in the index, the manager of such a fund would be crucially interested in stocks' expected returns and betas.

18. The IASB framework is currently under revision as part of a project to bring the FASB and IASB versions into conformity.

Chapter 4
Efficient Securities Markets

Figure 4.1 Organization of Chapter 4

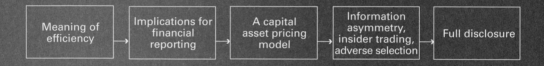

4.1 OVERVIEW

In this chapter, we consider the interaction of rational investors in a securities market. The theory of efficient securities markets predicts that the security prices that result from this interaction have some appealing properties. In essence, these prices "fully reflect" the collective knowledge and information-processing expertise of investors. The process by which prices do this is quite complex and not fully understood. Nevertheless, the general outlines of the process are easy to see, and we shall concentrate on these.

Securities market efficiency has important implications for financial accounting. One implication is that it leads directly to the concept of *full disclosure*. Efficiency implies that it is the information content of disclosure, not the form of disclosure itself, that is valued by the market. If so, information can be released as easily in notes and supplementary disclosures as in the financial statements proper. The theory also affects how the accountant should think about reporting on firm risk.

In efficient markets theory, accounting is viewed as being in competition with other information sources such as news media, financial analysts, and even market price itself. As a vehicle for informing investors, accounting will survive only if it is relevant, reliable, timely, and cost effective, relative to other sources.

Efficient securities market theory also alerts us to what is the primary reason for the existence of accounting, namely information asymmetry. When some market participants know more than others, pressure arises to find mechanisms whereby the better informed, who wish to do so, can credibly communicate their information to others, and whereby those with information disadvantage can protect themselves from possible exploitation by the better informed. Insider trading is an example of such exploitation.

We can then think of accounting as a mechanism to enable communication of useful information from inside the firm to outside. In addition to enabling better investor decisions, this has social benefits through improving the working of securities markets.

As mentioned in Section 1.2, accounting theorists began to realize the importance of securities market efficiency in the late 1960s. Since that time, the theory has guided much accounting research and has had major implications for accounting practice. By and large, financial accounting standard-setting bodies and regulators have accepted the full disclosure and decision usefulness implications of securities market efficiency. To illustrate this, we will examine management discussion and analysis (MD&A), an important disclosure standard, from an informational perspective.

While, in this chapter, we outline the properties of a fully efficient securities market and their implications for accountants, it should be emphasized that efficiency is a *model* of how a securities market operates. Like any model, it does not capture the full complexity of such a market. Indeed, recent years have seen an increasing number of questions about whether investors are as rational as the model assumes, and increasing evidence questioning market efficiency.

These questions are examined in Chapter 6, where we conclude that while actual securities markets are not fully efficient, they are close enough that accountants can be guided by efficiency implications and the rational decision theory underlying them. We also conclude that to the extent securities markets are not fully efficient, this further increases the importance of financial reporting.

Figure 4.1 outlines the organization of this chapter.

4.2 EFFICIENT SECURITIES MARKETS

4.2.1 The Meaning of Efficiency

In Chapter 3 we studied the optimal investment decisions of rational investors. Now consider what happens when a large number of rational individuals interact in a securities market. Our interest is in the characteristics of the market prices of securities traded in the market, and how these prices are affected by new information.

If information was free, it is apparent that investors would want to take advantage of it. For instance, under the ideal conditions of Example 2.2, investors would want to know which state of nature was realized, since this affects the future share price and dividends of the firm. By assumption, information is free under ideal conditions since state realization is publicly observable. Thus, all investors would use this information, and the process of arbitrage ensures that the market value of the firm then adjusts to reflect the revised cash flow expectations that result, as illustrated in Example 2.2.

Unfortunately, information is not free under non-ideal conditions. Investors have to decide how much accounting expertise and information to acquire, and then to form their own subjective estimates of firms' future performance. Furthermore, these estimates will need revision as new information comes along. Each investor then faces a cost–benefit tradeoff with respect to how much information to gather. There is a variety of relevant information sources—the financial press, tips from friends and associates, changes in economic conditions, advice from analysts and brokers, etc. We can think of rational investors as continuously revising their subjective state probabilities as such information is received. From our standpoint, of course, a major source of cost-effective information is firms' quarterly and annual reports. Probability revision arising from financial statement information was illustrated in Example 3.1.

At least some investors spend considerable time and money to use these information sources to guide their investment decisions. Such expert investors are called **informed**. Bill Cautious, in Example 3.1, is an example of such an investor.

It should be apparent that informed investors will want to move *quickly* upon receipt of new information. If they do not, other investors will get there first and the market value of the security in question will adjust so as to reduce or eliminate the benefit of the new information.

When a sufficient number of investors behave this way, the market becomes **efficient**. There are several definitions of an efficient securities market. The definition that we shall use here is the **semi-strong form**.

*An **efficient securities market** is one where the prices of securities traded on that market at all times fully reflect all information that is publicly known about those securities.*

Three points are particularly noteworthy. First, market prices are efficient with respect to *publicly known* information. Thus, the definition does not rule out the possibility of inside information. Persons who possess inside information, in effect, know more than the market. If they wish to take advantage of their inside information, insiders may be able to earn excess profits on their investments at the expense of outsiders. This is because the market prices of these investments, reflecting only outside or publicly available information, do not incorporate the knowledge that insiders possess. Not every insider is "bad," of course. Some managers may seek ways to credibly communicate their inside information to the market, perhaps to bolster their firms' share price and their reputations. Nevertheless, investors will still be worried about the *possibility* of insider trading.

A second, related point is that market efficiency is a *relative* concept. The market is efficient relative to a stock of publicly available information. There is nothing in the definition to suggest that the market is omniscient and that market prices always reflect real underlying firm value. Market prices can certainly be wrong in the presence of inside information, for example.

The definition of efficiency does imply, however, that once new or corrected information becomes publicly available, the market price will quickly adjust to it. This adjustment occurs because rational investors will scramble to revise their beliefs about future performance as soon as new information, from whatever source, becomes known. As a result, the expected returns and risk of their existing portfolios will change and they will enter the market to restore their optimal risk–return tradeoffs. The resulting buy-and-sell decisions will quickly change security prices to fully reflect the new information.

A third implication is that investing is **fair game** if the market is efficient. This means that investors cannot expect to earn excess returns on a security, or portfolio of securities, over and above the normal expected return on that security or portfolio, where the normal expected return allows for risk. One way to establish a normal return benchmark is by means of a capital asset pricing model, as will be illustrated in Section 4.5.

Finally, given market efficiency, a security's market price should fluctuate randomly over time. That is, there should be no serial correlation of share returns. Thus, if a firm reports GN today, its share price should rise to reflect this news the same day. If, in the absence of any further news, its price continues to rise during succeeding days, this is evidence of inefficiency. The reason why price fluctuations are random is that anything about a firm that can be *expected*, such as the seasonal nature of its business, the retirement of its chief executive, or the expected profit on a major new contract, will be fully reflected in its security price by the efficient market as soon as the expectation is formed. That is, the market's expectation of the effect of such events on the value of the firm is on average *unbiased*. The only reason that prices will change is if some relevant but *unexpected* information comes along. By definition, unexpected events occur randomly. For example, an accident may change the expected profit on a contract, and share price will quickly respond to reflect this random event. Thus, if we examine the time series formed by the sequence of price changes for a particular security, this series should fluctuate randomly over time according to market efficiency theory. A time series that exhibits such serially uncorrelated behaviour is sometimes called a **random walk**.[1]

4.2.2 How Do Market Prices Fully Reflect All Available Information?

We now consider *how* market prices fully reflect all available information. This process is by no means obvious. As described previously, rational, informed investors will demand information about securities. However, there is no guarantee that all individuals will react identically to the same information. For example, they may have different prior beliefs. Some may have superior expertise to analyze financial statement information. In a sense, the decision theory model is like an automobile. It provides a vehicle to process information, but nothing guarantees that everyone's driving habits are identical or that they all take the same route to a destination.

As a result, it is quite likely that different investors will react to the same information differently, even though they all proceed rationally. Yet, investors interact in a market, each making buy/sell decisions about various securities. Since the market price of a security is the result of the demand for and supply of the security by investors, how can the market price fully reflect all available information when the individuals making the demand and supply decisions are different?

An interesting insight into this question can be gained from an example in Beaver (1981, p. 162, Table 6-1). The example relates to forecasting the results of football games. The *Chicago Daily News*, during 1966–1968, printed weekly the predictions of each of its sports staff as to who would win that weekend's college football games. Table 4.1, taken from Beaver, summarizes the outcomes of these predictions.

Note the following points from Table 4.1. First, there were a number of different forecasters (15–16) and a large number of forecasts were made (619 over the three years). Second, no one individual forecaster dominated in terms of forecasting ability. The best forecasters in 1966 were well down the list in subsequent years, and vice versa. Third, note the consistent performance of the consensus forecast. The consensus forecast was also published weekly by the *Chicago Daily News* and, for each game, consisted of the team favoured to win by the majority of those forecasting. It is clear that the consensus forecast has a quality that transcends the forecasting ability of the individual forecasters from which the consensus is derived.

To translate the example into a securities market context, we can think of the forecasters as investors in a security and the forecasts as their various buy/sell decisions. The

Table 4.1 Forecasting Outcomes of Football Games

	1966	1967	1968
Total forecasters (including consensus)	15	15	16
Total forecasts made per forecaster	180	220	219
Rank of consensus*	1 (tie)	2	2
Median rank of forecasters	8	8	8.5
Rank of best forecasters:			
J. Carmichael (1966)	1 (tie)	8	16
D. Nightingale (1966)	1 (tie)	11	5
A. Biondo (1967)	7	1	6
H. Duck (1968)	8	10	1

*When all three years are combined, the consensus outperforms every one of the forecasters (that is, ranks first).

Source: William H. Beaver, *Financial Reporting: An Accounting Revolution*® 1981, p. 162, Table 6-1. Reprinted by permission of Prentice-Hall Inc., Upper Saddle River, New Jersey. Data are from "Here's How Our Staff Picks 'Em," as published in the *Chicago Sun-Times*. Copyright 1966, 1967, 1968 by Chicago Sun-Times Inc. Reprinted with permission.

consensus forecast is analogous to the market price, since it is a type of average of the various individual forecasting decisions.

The rationale behind the example is not hard to see. It appears that the differences in forecasting ability of individual forecasters tend to cancel out when the consensus is formed, leaving a "market price" that outperforms the ability of any of the market participants.

Of course, just because a consensus forecast outperforms individual forecasters of football games does not by itself mean that the same phenomenon carries over to security prices. Essentially, what is required is that investors' estimates of security values must on average be unbiased. That is, the market does not systematically misinterpret the valuation implications of a stock of information, but rather puts a valuation on securities that is *on average* correct or unbiased. As mentioned, this does not mean that any individual investor will necessarily be correct, but it does mean that *on average* the market uses all available information. This is the meaning of the term "fully reflects" in the definition of securities market efficiency given earlier.

It should be emphasized that this argument assumes that individual decisions are independent, so that individual differences cancel out in their effect on price. If this is not the case, efficiency arguments break down.[2] Thus, if our football forecasters got together to work out and agree on a consensus forecast, their forecasts would not be independent if they reflected the views of, say, a dominant and persuasive member of the group. Similarly, if a sufficient number of investors display a collective bias in their reaction to new information about a firm, the resulting share price will be biased. For example, a firm may have reported a pattern of increasing earnings. If investors expect future earnings growth to continue simply because of growth in the past, share price momentum may develop. Then, share prices may be "too high," driven by past price increases rather than by rational evaluation of information by independent investors. We will return to this point in Chapter 6, where we discuss whether securities markets are fully efficient.

Theory in Practice 4.1

Prof. Burton Malkiel, in his 1973 book *A Random Walk Down Wall Street,* argued that randomly throwing darts at a list of shares traded on the New York Stock Exchange would earn just as high a return as the returns earned by professional money managers. His argument drew on efficient markets theory, which predicts that, since share price always fully reflects all publicly available information, there are no "bargain" stocks. Then, professional money managers cannot do better than a strategy of random stock choice.

During the 1990s, *The Wall Street Journal* tested this argument. It sponsored a monthly series of contests, whereby four investment analysts each picked a favoured stock. The return on each stock over the next six months was tallied and compared with the return on a randomly chosen stock for the same period. For the first 100 contests, the pros earned an average six-months return of 10.9% while the darts earned a 4.5% return. The average six-months return of the Dow Jones index was 6.8%.

(continued)

When asked to explain these results, Prof. Malkiel defended the efficiency theory, arguing that the results could be explained by risk differences. He also pointed out that stock market performance during the 1990s was driven by very large firms. But, since there are many more relatively small firms on the market than large firms, the probability that a randomly thrown dart would pick a small firm was quite high. Also, as investors learned of the stocks picked by the pros they would revise upwards their opinions of these stocks. The resulting increase in demand would raise their prices and returns relative to the randomly chosen stocks.

4.2.3 Summary

In an efficient securities market, prices fully reflect all available information, and the price changes on such a market will behave randomly over time. Efficiency is defined relative to a stock of information. If this stock of information is incomplete, say due to inside information, or wrong, security prices will be wrong. Thus, market efficiency does not guarantee that security prices fully reflect real firm value. It does suggest, however, that prices are unbiased relative to publicly available information and will react quickly to new or revised information.

The quantity and quality of publicly available information will be enhanced by prompt and full reporting. However, individual investors may have different prior beliefs and/or may interpret the same information differently. Nevertheless, roughly speaking, we can think of these differences as averaging out, so that the market price has superior quality to the quality of the information processing of the individuals trading on the market. This argument assumes, however, that investors evaluate new information independently.

4.3 IMPLICATIONS OF EFFICIENT SECURITIES MARKETS FOR FINANCIAL REPORTING

4.3.1 Implications

An early examination of the reporting implications of efficient securities markets appeared in an article by W. H. Beaver, "What Should Be the FASB's Objectives?" (1973). Here, we will outline Beaver's arguments.

According to Beaver, the first major implication is that accounting policies adopted by firms do not affect their security prices, as long as these policies have no differential cash flow effects, the particular policies used are disclosed, and sufficient information is given so that the reader can convert across different policies. Thus, Beaver would regard accounting disputes such as a firm's choice of amortization method or the full-cost versus successful-efforts approach for oil and gas firms as, essentially, "tempests in a teapot." Notice that a firm's choice between different accounting policies in each of these disputes involves only "paper" effects. The policy chosen will affect reported net income, but will not directly affect future cash flows and dividends. For example, an oil and gas firm's proceeds from sale of crude and refined products will not depend directly on whether it uses full-cost or successful-efforts accounting. In particular, the amount of income tax the firm must pay will not be affected by its accounting policy choice in either of these areas since the tax department has its own way of calculating expenses and income in each area, independent of how the firm accounts for them on its books. If investors are interested in future cash flows and dividends and their impact on security returns, and if choosing between accounting policies does not directly influence these variables, the firm's choice between accounting policies should not matter.

Thus, the efficient market argument is that as long as firms disclose their selected policy and any additional information needed to convert from one method to another, investors are able to make the necessary calculations to see through to the resulting differences in reported net income. The market can see through to the ultimate cash flow and dividend implications regardless of which accounting policy is actually used for reporting. Thus, the efficient market is not "fooled" by differing accounting policies when comparing different firms' securities. This suggests that management should not care about which particular accounting policies they use as long as those policies have no direct cash flow effects.

We thus see that full disclosure extends to disclosure of the firm's accounting policies. This is recognized by standard setters. For example, IAS 1 states that a complete set of financial statements includes disclosure of accounting policies. Also, the CICA *Handbook*, paragraph 1505.04, currently states:

> *A clear and concise description of the significant accounting policies of an enterprise should be included as an integral part of the financial statements.*

A second implication follows—namely, efficient securities markets go hand in hand with full disclosure. If a firm's management possesses relevant information about the firm and if this can be disclosed at little or no cost, management should then disclose this information on a timely basis unless it is certain that the information is already known to investors from other sources. More generally, management should develop and report information about the firm as long as the benefits to investors exceed the costs. The reasons are twofold. First, market efficiency implies that investors will use all available information about the firm as they strive to improve their predictions of future returns, so that additional information will not be wasted. Second, the more information a firm discloses about itself, the greater is investors' confidence in the working of the securities market, since there is less inside information to worry about.

Third, market efficiency implies that firms should not be overly concerned about the naïve investor—that is, financial statement information need not be presented in a manner so simple that everyone can understand it. The reasoning, from Fama (1970), is that if *enough* investors understand the disclosed information, the market price of a firm's shares is the same as it would be if all investors understood it. This is because informed investors will engage in buy/sell decisions on the basis of the disclosed information, moving the market price towards its efficient level. Also, naïve investors can hire their own experts, such as financial analysts or investment fund managers, to interpret the information for them, or can mimic the buy/sell decisions of informed investors. As a result, any information advantage that informed investors have is quickly dissipated. In other words, naïve investors can *trust* the efficient market to price securities so that they always reflect all that is publicly known about the firms that have issued them, even though these investors may not have complete knowledge and understanding themselves. This is referred to as investors being **price-protected** by the efficient market.

Since Beaver's paper, accountants have recognized that there is a variety of reasons for trading securities. For example, some investors may make a rational decision to rely on market price as a good indicator of future payoffs, rather than incur the costs of becoming informed. Others may trade for a variety of non-portfolio reasons—perhaps an unexpected need for cash has arisen. Consequently, "naïve" may not be the best word to describe uninformed investors. This is considered further in Section 4.4.

A final implication is that accountants are in competition with other providers of information, such as websites and other media, disclosures by management, and various financial institutions. That is, belief revision is a continuous process, as pointed out in Section 3.3.3. Thus, if accountants do not provide useful, cost-effective information, the role of the accounting function will decline over time as other information sources take over—accountants have no *inherent* right to survive in the competitive marketplace for information. However, survival will be more likely if accountants recognize that the ultimate responsibility of their profession is to society. This longer-run point of view is encouraged by standards that promote useful information, by penalties for individuals who abuse public trust for short-term gain, and by encouragement of ethical behaviour.

Beaver's paper was published in 1973. Consequently, it predates SFAC 1 (issued in 1978) and SFAC 2 (1980) by several years. However, it provides a good example of the early enthusiasm of accounting theorists for efficient securities markets. It also highlights the type of disclosure-oriented thinking that led to the formal statement of the usefulness criterion by the FASB in SFAC 1.

4.3.2 Summary

Beaver argues that securities market efficiency has several implications for financial reporting. First, managers and accountants should not be concerned about which accounting policies firms use unless different accounting policies have direct cash flow effects. Many accounting policy alternatives, about which accountants have argued long and hard, do not have such cash flow effects. Second, firms should disclose as much information about themselves as is cost-effective—the fact of disclosure and not the form it takes is what is important. The efficient market will prefer the least costly form of disclosure, other things equal. One can argue, however, that financial statements are a cost-effective disclosure medium. Third, firms need not be concerned about the naïve investor when choosing disclosure policies and formats. Such persons are price-protected, because efficient security prices fully reflect all that is publicly known about those securities. Furthermore, there is a variety of media, including websites, management disclosures, and financial institutions, whereby investors can take advantage of sophisticated information without needing to fully understand it themselves. Finally, the efficient market is interested in useful information from any source, not just accounting reports.

4.4 THE INFORMATIVENESS OF PRICE

4.4.1 A Logical Inconsistency

The careful reader may have noticed an inconsistency in our discussion of efficient securities markets to this point. Recall that efficiency implies that the market price of a security at all times fully reflects all that is publicly known about that security. What is it that drives market price to have this "fully reflects" characteristic? It is the actions of informed investors who are always striving to obtain and process information so as to make good buy/sell decisions.

However, by the definition of market efficiency, all available information is already reflected in market price. That is, the price is **fully informative**.[3] Since information acquisition is costly, and investors could not expect to beat the market when the market price already reflects all publicly known information, investors would simply stop gathering information and rely on market price as the best indicator of future security returns. For example, a simple decision rule would be to buy and hold a diversified investment portfolio, changing its composition only if the risk–return tradeoff of the portfolio gets out of line.

The logical inconsistency, then, is that if prices fully reflect available information, there is no motivation for investors to acquire information; hence, prices will not fully reflect available information. In terms of football forecasting, the forecasters would stop putting effort into their forecasts because they can't beat the consensus forecast, but then the consensus forecast would lose its superior forecasting ability. Technically speaking, the problem here is that stable equilibrium prices do not exist, as shown by Grossman (1976).

This has potentially serious implications for accounting theory, since a lack of equilibrium makes it problematic whether financial statement information is useful to investors. Also, it is contrary to what we observe. SFAC 1 (Section 3.8) certainly implies that investors find financial reporting useful, for example.

However, there is a way out of the inconsistency. This is to recognize that there are other sources of demand and supply for securities than the buy/sell decisions of rational, informed investors. For example, people may buy or sell securities for a variety of unpredictable reasons—they may decide to retire early, they may need money to pay gambling debts, they may have received a "hot tip," etc. Such persons are called **liquidity traders** or **noise traders**. Their buy/sell decisions will affect a security's market price, but the decisions come at random—they are not based on a rational evaluation of information.

To illustrate how market price is affected by the presence of noise trading, suppose that a rational investor observes a security's price to be higher than he/she had expected based on all the information currently possessed by that investor. Now, our investor knows that other rational investors also have their own information about the security and that this information may well be more favourable. These other investors may be buying and driving up the security's price. As a result, our investor is inclined to raise his/her expectation of the security's value. While the investor does not know what information other investors have, it is rational to believe that the information is favourable and this may be what is driving up the security's price.

However, our investor also knows that the higher-than-expected security price may simply be due to noise trading. Perhaps someone has temporarily invested a large cash windfall in a randomly chosen portfolio of securities, including the security in question. If so, our investor would *not* want to increase his/her expectation of the security's value. Since each scenario is possible, the investor will increase his/her expectation of the security's value, but to an amount *less than* the security's current market price. That is, the rational investor responds by putting some weight on each possibility. In effect, the current share price conveys *some* information about share value but not *all* information as in the fully informative case.

For our purposes, an important point to note is that investors now have an incentive to update their beliefs by gathering more information. If they can find out which explanation is the correct one, this can quickly be turned into a profitable investment opportunity. For example, if further investigation reveals that the firm is undervalued, the investor will buy. If, instead, investigation reveals that the share price is temporarily high due to noise trading, the investor will sell short. The efforts of investors to do this will then drive share price towards its efficient value. Presumably, at least some of this additional information will come from analysis of financial statements.

Investor behaviour such as this is another example of rational expectations—the investor quickly figures out how much weight to put on the possibility that share price reflects noise trading and how much on the possibility that other investors have better information. Security prices are said to be **partially informative** in the presence of noise trading and rational expectations. Note that market prices are still efficient in the presence of noise trading, but in an *expected value* sense, since noise has expectation zero. That is, the investor expects *a priori* that a security's market price fully reflects all publicly available information, but, *ex post*, further investigation may reveal that this is not the case.

The extent to which investors gather additional information depends on a number of factors, such as how informative price is, the quality of financial statement information, and the costs of analysis and interpretation. These factors lead to empirical predictions about how security market prices respond to financial statement information. For example, we might expect that price will be more informative for large firms, since they are more "in the news" than small firms, hence their market price will incorporate considerable information. This reduces the ability of financial statements to add to what is already known about such firms. Thus, we would predict that security prices respond less to financial statement information for large firms than for small firms.

Furthermore, note that firm management has an incentive to cater to the desire of investors to ferret out information. For example, management may have inside information that leads it to believe the firm is undervalued. To correct this, management may engage in **voluntary disclosure**, that is, disclosure of information beyond the minimum requirement of GAAP and other reporting standards. Such disclosure can have credibility, even if unaudited, since legal liability and reputation damage impose discipline on managers' reporting decisions. Unfortunately, there are limitations on voluntary disclosure, not only because the legal system and reputation concerns may be unable to completely enforce credibility but because management will not want to reveal information that would give away competitive advantage.

However, voluntary disclosure is much more complex and subtle than simply disclosing information. Management can signal inside information by its choice of accounting policies and, indeed, by the nature and extent of voluntary disclosure itself. The rational investor will thus look carefully at what the manager *does* in terms of accounting policy choice and disclosure. For example, instead of directly revealing good news about a secret research program, a firm that feels it is undervalued could choose very conservative accounting policies. This reveals inside information about the firm's future performance since management would not likely adopt conservative policies unless it felt that future cash flows and earnings would be high enough to absorb the resulting conservative "hit." Even though they may not know what the specific inside information is, rational investors would respond to these conservative policies by bidding up the firm's share price. This means that there are potential rewards to investors, and analysts, for careful and complete analyses of firms' annual reports. Such analyses may identify mispricing and can quickly be turned into profitable investment decisions.

Also, an increase in the quality of financial statement disclosure, other things equal, should lead investors to increase their utilization of financial statement information relative to price. For example, the requirement by securities commissions that firms include **management discussion and analysis (MD&A)** in their annual reports may increase market price reactions to annual reports. Annual reports should have higher information content with MD&A than without it. MD&A is discussed in Section 4.8.

We conclude that the term "fully reflects" in the efficient securities market definition has to be interpreted with care. It does not mean that security prices are fully informative with respect to available information at all points in time. Indeed, if it did, this would have adverse implications for the usefulness of financial statements. Rather, the term should be interpreted as reflecting a tension between the level of informativeness allowed by noise and liquidity traders, and the ability of investors and analysts to identify mispriced securities through analysis of the financial statements proper, supplementary disclosures, accounting policy choice, the nature and extent of voluntary disclosure, and, indeed, of all other available information. With this interpretation in mind, it is important to point out that the implications of security market efficiency as outlined by Beaver in Section 4.3 continue to apply. In particular, the importance of full disclosure remains.

4.4.2 Summary

While the ability of a market price to *average out* individual differences in information processing, as we saw in the football forecasting example, is on the right track, the process of price formation in securities markets is much more complex than this. Through consideration of ways that rational investors can become more informed by careful analysis of managers' disclosure decisions, and by allowing for other sources of demand and supply for securities than from rational, informed investors, accountants are beginning to understand the role of information in price. The presence of non-rational traders does not necessarily mean that the efficient securities market concept that share prices "fully reflect" information is invalid, but rather that this concept must be interpreted with care.

Improved understanding of the process of price formation leads to empirical predictions of how security prices respond to accounting information and, ultimately, enables accountants to prepare more useful financial statements.

4.5 A CAPITAL ASSET PRICING MODEL

We are now in a position to formalize the relationship between the efficient market price of a security, its risk, and the expected rate of return on a security. We shall do so by means of the well-known Sharpe-Lintner capital asset pricing model (CAPM) (Sharpe, 1964; Lintner, 1965).

First, we need some preliminaries. Define R_{jt}, the net rate of return on the shares of firm j for time period t, as:

$$R_{jt} = \frac{P_{jt} + D_{jt} + P_{j, t-1}}{P_{j, t-1}} = \frac{P_{jt} + D_{jt}}{P_{j, t-1}} - 1 \qquad (4.1)$$

where:

P_{jt} is the market price of firm j's shares at the end of period t
D_{jt} is dividends paid by firm j during period t
$P_{j, t-1}$ is the market price of firm j's shares at the beginning of period t

This is the return concept used in Examples 3.1, 3.2, and 3.3. It is a *net* rate of return given that the opening market price is subtracted in the numerator. We can also define a *gross rate of return* as $1 + R_{jt}$, where:

$$1 + R_{jt} = \frac{P_{jt} + D_{jt}}{P_{j, t-1}}$$

Since the only difference between the two rates of return concepts is the 1, we can use them interchangeably. In fact, to conform to common practice, we will usually refer to both net and gross rates of return as simply **returns**.

We can think of returns as either *ex post* or *ex ante*. *Ex post*, we are at the end of period t and looking back to calculate the return actually realized during the period, as in Equation 4.1. Alternatively, we can stand at the beginning of period t (i.e., at time $t-1$) and think of an *ex ante* or expected return as:

$$E(R_{jt}) = \frac{E(P_{jt} + D_{jt})}{P_{j,\,t-1}} - 1 \qquad (4.2)$$

That is, expected return for period t is based on the expected price at the end of the period plus any dividends expected during the period, divided by the current price.

Now, consider an economy with a large number of rational, risk-averse investors. Assume that there is a risk-free asset in the economy, with return R_f. Assume also that security markets are efficient and transaction costs are zero. Then, the Sharpe-Lintner CAPM shows that:

$$E(R_{jt}) = R_f(1 - \beta_j) + \beta_j E(R_{Mt}) \qquad (4.3)$$

where β_j is the beta of share j and R_{Mt} is the return on the market portfolio for period t.

Note that the model is in terms of the market's *expected* returns. Equation 4.3 states that at the beginning of period t, firm j's expected return for the period equals a constant $R_f(1 - \beta_j)$ plus another constant β_j times the expected return on the market portfolio. $E(R_{jt})$ can also be interpreted as the firm's cost of equity capital, since it represents the expected return demanded by the market on that firm's shares.

Strictly speaking, markets do not have expectations—individuals do. One way to think of the market's expectations is that the price of a share behaves *as if* the market holds a certain expectation about its future performance. More fundamentally, the market price of a share includes a sort of average of the expectations of all informed investors, much like the consensus forecast in the Beaver football example (Section 4.2.2) includes an average expectation of the forecasters.

It is not difficult to see the intuition of the model. Since rational investors will fully diversify when transactions costs are zero, the only risk measure in the formula is β_j. Firm-specific risk does not affect share price because it disappears in fully diversified portfolios. Also, note that the higher is β_j the higher is expected return, other things equal. This is consistent with risk aversion, since risk-averse investors will require a higher expected return to compensate for higher risk.

Note also the role of the current market price $P_{j,t-1}$ in the model. The return demanded by the market on share j for period t, that is, $E(R_{jt})$ in Equation 4.3, is a function only of R_f, R_{Mt}, and β_j. The current market price does not appear. However, in Equation 4.2, given expected end-of-period price P_{jt} and dividends D_{jt}, we see that $P_{j,t-1}$ in the denominator will adjust so that the right-hand side of Equation 4.2 equals $E(R_{jt})$. That is, a share's current price will adjust so that its expected return equals the return demanded by the market for that share as given by Equation 4.3.

We can now see how new information affects firm j's share price. Suppose that at time t − 1 (now) some new firm-specific information comes along that raises investors' expectations of P_{jt} (and possibly also of D_{jt}), without affecting R_f, β_j, or $E(R_{Mt})$. This will throw Equation 4.2 out of balance, since $E(R_{jt})$ from Equation 4.3 does not change. Thus, $P_{j,t-1}$, the current price, must rise to restore equality. This, of course, is consistent with market efficiency, which states that the market price of a security will react immediately to new information.

To pursue further the effect of information on share price in the CAPM, suppose that in addition to any effect on P_{jt}, the new information is more informative, in the sense of higher main diagonal probabilities of the firm's information system (Section 3.3.2). Then, greater financial reporting informativeness can reduce β_j, thereby reducing cost of capital. This was shown by Lambert, Leuz, and Verrecchia (2007). They point out that information about one firm often affects the market's expectations about other firms. For example, suppose firm j is General Electric Co. (GE). If GE adopts a more informative financial reporting system for its quarterly earnings, the market, and thus GE's share price, is better able to predict GE's future performance. However, due to GE's size and diversity, its performance provides the market with information about the future performance of other firms, so that the market is also better able to predict the future performance and share price of these firms. That is, with more informative reporting, *each* firm's share price better reflects that firm's *firm-specific* performance, so that the co-movement between them (i.e., the covariance between GE's share price and share prices of other firms) falls. Since a stock's beta is essentially the covariance between its return and the return of other firms in the market (Section 3.7.1), GE's beta will fall, reducing its cost of capital. Lambert, Leuz, and Verrecchia point out that lack of informativeness in financial reporting cannot be diversified away when reporting precision affects the covariance terms, since these terms increase in number as the number of firms in the portfolio increases. Consequently, the possibility of reducing investor risk by more informative reporting is of interest to accountants.

For our purposes, there are three main uses for the CAPM formula. First, it brings out clearly how share prices depend on investors' expectations of future share price and dividends. If these expectations change (the numerator of Equation 4.2), current price $P_{j,t-1}$ (the denominator) will immediately change to reflect these new expectations. For a given change in expectations, and given R_f and $E(R_{Mt})$, the amount of the change in current price depends only on the share's beta. To put this another way, the larger the change in expectations, the larger the change in price, other things equal.

Second, by reverting to an *ex post* view of returns, the CAPM provides us with a way of separating the realized return on a share into expected and unexpected components. To see this, consider the following version of the model, where we are now at the end of period t and looking back:

$$R_{jt} = \alpha_j + \beta_j R_{Mt} + \epsilon_{jt} \tag{4.4}$$

This version of CAPM is called the **market model**. It states that the realized return R_{jt} for the period is the sum of the beginning-of-period *expected* return ($\alpha_j + \beta_j R_{Mt}$) and the *unexpected* or **abnormal**[4] return ϵ_{jt}. The expected return comes from the CAPM, with $\alpha_j = R_f(1 - \beta_j)$. The ϵ_{jt} captures the impact on R_{jt} of all those events during period t that were not expected at the beginning of the period. By definition in an efficient market, $E(\epsilon_{jt}) = 0$, since new information comes along randomly. But, in any period t the *realized* value of ϵ_{jt} need not be zero. Its realized value will depend on just what information did come along. Thus, the market model enables an *ex post* separation of the realized return R_{jt} into expected $(\alpha_j + \beta_j R_{Mt})$ and unexpected or abnormal (ϵ_{jt}) components.

Third, the market model provides a convenient way for researchers and analysts to estimate a stock's beta. Notice that the market model is presented in the form of a regression equation. By obtaining past data on R_{jt} and R_{Mt}, the coefficients of the regression model can be estimated by least-squares regression. If we assume that the market is able to form unbiased expectations of R_{Mt} (so that R_{Mt} is a good proxy for $E(R_{Mt})$, which is unobservable), and if we assume that β_j is stationary over time, then the coefficient of R_{Mt} from least-squares regression is a good estimate[5] of β_j. Furthermore, the reasonableness of the estimation can be checked by comparing the estimated coefficient α_j with $R_f(1 - \beta_j)$—the two should be the same.

As we will see in Chapter 5, much empirical research in accounting has required an accurate estimate of beta, and we will return to its estimation in Section 7.5.1. For now, it is important to realize that the CAPM provides an important and useful way to model the market's expectation of a share's returns and a firm's cost of capital, and that the model depends crucially on securities market efficiency. Also, it shows clearly how new information affects current share price.

For later reference, two points about the CAPM should be noted. First, it assumes rational expectations. That is, investors are assumed to know stock's betas and the expected return on the market. As a practical matter, these may not be accurately known. Then, an additional source of risk arises, called **estimation risk**. For example, as described above, the market model can be used to estimate beta. However, this estimate is unlikely to be completely accurate, especially if only a few periods of data are available for the estimation, or if beta changes. Then, the actual risk borne by the investor will differ from desired risk, distorting his/her risk–return tradeoff. To some extent, this estimation risk may be diversified away (overestimates of beta for some shares may be offset by underestimates for others). However, if different investors have different beta estimates, this will affect their investment decisions, thereby introducing additional volatility into share returns over and above that recognized by the CAPM. To compensate for this added risk, investors will demand an extra return.

Second, the CAPM considers information asymmetry only to a limited extent. With information asymmetry, outside investors face the risk that insiders may profit at their expense. We will regard this as another component of estimation risk, since investors' estimates of underlying firm parameters, such as the ability and integrity of management, may be incorrect if management exploits inside information. If we regard the exploiting of inside information as contributing to low informativeness of financial reporting, the

CAPM model of Lambert, Leuz, and Verrecchia (2007), discussed earlier, suggests that more informative reporting will reduce estimation risk.

However, since inside information, and the possibility that insiders will exploit it, are omnipresent, estimation risk may loom sufficiently large in investors' minds that, in addition to any effect on beta, it becomes an additional risk factor *to* beta. If so, investors will demand higher expected return than given by the CAPM.

Thus, while it is a good place to start, the CAPM may understate cost of capital for many firms. As we point out in the next section, estimation risk is important for accountants, since it may be reduced by full and timely disclosure.

4.6 INFORMATION ASYMMETRY

4.6.1 A Closer Look at Information Asymmetry

In this section, we take a closer look at the notion of "publicly available" information in the efficient securities market definition. This leads directly to what is undoubtedly the most important concept of financial accounting theory—*information asymmetry*. Frequently, one type of participant in the market (sellers, for example) will know something about the asset being traded that another type of participant (buyers) does not know. When this situation exists, the market is said to be characterized by information asymmetry. As mentioned in Section 1.6, there are two major types of information asymmetry—adverse selection and moral hazard. We now consider these in greater detail.

First, note that information asymmetry is an important reason for market incompleteness (Section 2.6). That is, in extreme cases, a market may collapse, or fail to develop in the first place, as a result of information asymmetry. To illustrate, consider the market for insurance policies. Assuming you are risk-averse, you may wish to buy insurance against the possibility of failing to attain your university or college degree or professional accounting designation. You would be better off with such a policy, at least if the cost was fair. Serious illness or accident may prevent your completion of the course of studies, and you could eliminate this risk if you had a policy that reimbursed you for your loss of the present value of the increased future income that would follow the attainment of your degree or designation. However, offering such a policy would create severe difficulties for the insurance company. One difficulty is that people who were sick would flock to enroll in educational programs (called an adverse selection problem because people whose health is adverse to the insurance company's best interests self-select themselves to buy insurance). Then, when their illness led to their failure, they could collect on their policies and still enjoy the monetary fruits of a degree.

Another problem is that if you owned such a policy, you would probably shirk your studies, even if you were perfectly healthy. Why put in all the time and effort to complete your course of studies when, by merely failing, you could receive equivalent compensation from your insurance policy? This is a moral hazard problem, for you are tempted to cheat the company by shirking your studies. Note that requiring a medical certificate would not be of much use here, because of the difficulty in establishing that it was the illness that led to the failure.

As a result, no insurance company would sell you a policy that would reimburse you for your full income loss if you failed to attain your degree. The problem is information asymmetry. You have a major information advantage over the company, because the company can only observe whether you fail, not whether your illness, accident, or shirking caused you to fail.

Faced with information disadvantages of this magnitude, the company responds by not writing insurance policies of the type described, contributing to the market incompleteness noted in Section 2.6.

In other cases, information asymmetry is not so severe as to prevent the market from developing. Nevertheless, the market does not work as well as it might. This situation was studied by Akerlof (1970). An example of a market characterized by information asymmetry is the used car market. The owner of a car will know more about its true condition, and hence its future stream of benefits, than would a potential buyer. This creates an adverse selection problem, since the owner may try to take advantage of this inside information by bringing a "lemon" to market, hoping to get more than it is worth from an unsuspecting buyer. However, buyers will be aware of this temptation and, since they don't have the information to distinguish between lemons and good cars, will lower the price they are willing to pay for any used car, a process called **pooling**. As a result, many cars—the good ones—will have a market value that is less than the real value of their future stream of benefits. The arbitrage effect, whereby cars of similar service potential must sell for similar prices, operates less effectively when it is difficult to know exactly what the service potential of a used car is. Thus, owners of good cars are less likely to bring them to market. In other words, the market for used cars does not work as well as it might. This is another source of market incompleteness—a market can exist but be incomplete in the sense that purchasers cannot always buy a car of the exact type and condition they want.

It is interesting to note the variety of devices that markets use to reduce the effects of information asymmetry. Thus, used car markets are characterized by guarantees, safety certificates, test drives, dealers who attempt to establish a good reputation, and so on. Insurance markets are characterized by medical examinations for life and health insurance, co-insurance and deductible clauses for fire insurance, premium reductions for good driving records, and so on. However, because they are costly, these disclosure devices do not completely eliminate the problem. Nevertheless, they may be sufficiently effective to at least allow the market to operate, albeit not as well as it would in the absence of information asymmetry.

One of the reasons why information asymmetry is of such importance to accounting theory is that *securities markets* are subject to information asymmetry problems, such as insider information and insider trading. Even if security market prices fully reflect all publicly available information, it is still likely that insiders know more than outsiders about the true state of the firm. If so, they may take advantage of their information to earn excess profits by biasing, delaying, or withholding its public release while they buy or sell shares on the basis of this information. This is another example of the adverse selection problem, since insiders will be attracted by these opportunities, which are *adverse* to the interests of investors. Of course, investors will be aware of this estimation risk and will lower the amounts that they would otherwise be willing to pay for all shares to reflect their expected losses at the hands of insiders. Just like the used car market, the efficient securities market is subject to incompleteness. It does not work as well as it might since investors cannot be sure of buying a security with the exact expected return and risk that they want.

The collapse of Enron and WorldCom outlined in Section 1.2 is an example of the adverse effects of information asymmetry on securities markets. Following these and other financial reporting failures, investors realized that the shares of many firms were lemons. As a result, their confidence in the informativeness of financial statements of all firms collapsed as they realized they were facing much higher estimation risk than they had thought. A major fall in share prices took place as investors reduced the amounts they were willing to pay or, in extreme cases, withdrew from the market completely.

It may seem strange that markets can be efficient but yet investor confidence can collapse. However, we can reconcile these seemingly conflicting notions by introducing the concept of the **fundamental value** of a share:

> The **fundamental value** of a share is the value it would have in an efficient market if there is no inside information. That is, all information about the share is publicly available.

Obviously, prior to their collapse, the market prices of Enron and WorldCom shares did not reflect fundamental value, even though the market may have been efficient relative to the information about these firms that *was* publicly available. As a result of these and other such episodes, investors realized that many other firms' shares may have the same problem, leading to a general loss of confidence.

Of course, fundamental value is a theoretical ideal. We would not expect that inside information can be completely eliminated. It may not be cost effective for a firm to directly reveal strategic information about research in process or plans for a takeover bid, for example.

The steps taken by governments and accounting bodies to restore public confidence following the Enron and WorldCom collapses, outlined in Section 1.2, can be regarded as attempts to reduce adverse selection and estimation risk by improving financial reporting informativeness. Many of these steps involve policies of full disclosure, to expand the set of information that is publicly available and reduce biases resulting from incorrect or misleading information in the public domain. Also, timeliness of reporting will reduce the ability of insiders to profit from their information advantage. Thus, we can think of financial reporting as a device to control the adverse selection problem and estimation risk, thereby improving the working of securities markets and reducing incompleteness. Figure 4.2 illustrates this role.

The outer circle of the figure depicts the firm's fundamental value. The inner circle depicts the information underlying the efficient market price of the share, being all

Figure 4.2 Role of Financial Reporting in an Efficient Market

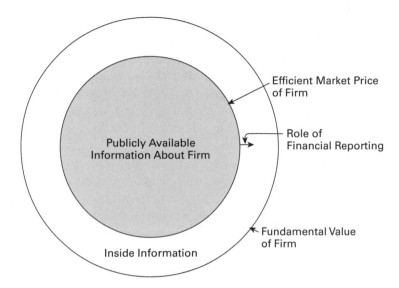

publicly available information. The difference between the inner and outer circle depicts inside information. Inside information is subject to adverse selection, creating estimation risk. The role of financial reporting is to convert inside information into outside information, thereby enlarging the inner circle. Obviously, the inner circle cannot fully reach the outside, since the cost of eliminating all inside information would be astronomic. Nevertheless, we frequently refer to markets where the inner circle is "large" relative to the outside circle as markets that **work well**.[6]

Market collapse, as in the case of Enron and WorldCom, will take place if investors realize that much of the information in the inner circle is not useful, that is, not informative of the true state of the firm. In effect, the inner circle collapses, taking fundamental value and share price with it.

4.6.2 Summary

Under ideal conditions, the firm's market value fully reflects *all* information. That is, price equals fundamental value. When conditions are not ideal, market value fully reflects all *publicly available* information, if security markets are efficient.

The difference between these two information sets includes **inside information**. The ability of insiders to profit from their information advantage is an example of the adverse selection problem. The possibility of adverse selection creates estimation risk for investors, which can increase firms' costs of capital above their CAPM values. Full and timely disclosure will reduce this problem, thereby improving the working of securities markets. Since reporting of all inside information is too costly, however, the adverse selection problem will still be present.

4.7 THE SOCIAL SIGNIFICANCE OF SECURITIES MARKETS THAT WORK WELL

In a capitalist economy, securities markets are the primary vehicle whereby capital is raised and allocated to competing investment needs. Consequently, it is socially desirable that these markets work well in the sense that security prices provide correct values to guide the flow of investment funds. For example, a firm that has high-expected-value capital projects will be encouraged to invest in them if it receives a high price for its securities, and investment should be discouraged in firms that do not have high-expected-value capital projects. This will happen to the extent that security prices are close to fundamental value. Of course, this is what society wants, since investment capital is in scarce supply. Social welfare will be enhanced if scarce capital goes to the most productive alternatives.

However, as mentioned, security prices do not fully reflect fundamental value in the presence of inside information. Investors will be aware of the estimation risk resulting from adverse selection and insider trading. Then, a "lemons" phenomenon comes into play. Investors recognize that the market is not a "level playing field" and either withdraw from the market or lower the amount they are willing to pay for *any* security. As a result, firms with high-quality investment projects will not receive a high price for their securities, and the market is not working as well as it should. A related problem is that if too many investors withdraw, the market becomes **thin** or, equivalently, it loses **depth**, where depth is the number of shares that investors can buy or sell without affecting the market price. When depth is low, potential investors may not be able to buy or sell all they want of a security at the market price, which further hampers investment.

Empirical evidence on the importance of markets that work well for efficient capital allocation is provided by Wurgler (2000). He estimates the efficiency of capital allocation for 65 countries over the years 1963–1995 and finds that countries with more firm-specific information incorporated into share prices (relative to industry- and economy-wide information, which affects all share prices) enjoy greater capital allocation efficiency.[7] Note that more firm-specific information incorporated into share prices is just another way of saying that the market is working better, or, equivalently, that there is less inside information.

Of course, developed capitalist economies have a variety of mechanisms for promoting the operation of securities markets. One such approach is regulation. Thus, we witness government securities commissions, as outlined in Section 1.9.5. These agencies create and enforce regulations to, for example, control insider trading and promote prompt disclosure of significant events, with penalties for violation. If such regulation is effective, estimation risk resulting from inside information is reduced. Investors will then remove firms from the lemons category and, as a result, will be willing to pay higher prices for securities than they otherwise would.

However, the efficient market can provide **incentives** for the release of inside information over and above that required by regulation. Just as a used car dealer who develops a reputation for honesty and fair dealing will enjoy higher sales prices, a firm with a credible policy of full disclosure beyond the regulatory minimum will enjoy higher share prices and lower cost of capital. This is because full disclosure reduces investors' concerns about inside information.

Obviously, regulations and market incentives are not mutually exclusive—we witness both in our economy. Regulation is like a "stick" and requires penalties to enforce it. The need for regulation will be reduced, however, to the extent that "carrots," such as improved reputation and higher share price, operate to motivate full disclosure. In both cases, the economy benefits since security prices are closer to fundamental firm value.

We may conclude that the social benefits of securities markets that work reasonably well will be attained if the following two conditions are met:

- All useful information is publicly available, at least up to the ability of penalties and incentives to cost-effectively motivate full disclosure.
- Securities market prices are efficient relative to publicly available information.

4.8 AN EXAMPLE OF FULL DISCLOSURE

4.8.1 Introduction

In this section, we consider an important full-disclosure accounting standard. Specifically, we outline and illustrate **management discussion and analysis (MD&A)**. This is a standard that requires firms to provide a narrative explanation of company performance, financial condition, and future prospects. The intent is to assist investors to interpret the firm's financial statements.

While of interest in its own right, this standard also provides an important illustration of how the amount of useful information in the public domain can be increased. The MD&A standard lies between the carrot-and-stick approaches to information release. While all public companies have to provide MD&A, there is some latitude in the extent to which they meet the letter of its disclosure requirements. For example, while some firms may provide what is mainly a rehash of information already available from the financial statements, others may go beyond the minimum requirements by releasing inside information about, for example, future business strategies, plans, and prospects.

4.8.2 Management Discussion and Analysis

Objectives of MD&A Our coverage of MD&A is based on the requirements of National Instrument 51-102 of the OSC, effective in 2004. Through the Canadian Securities Administrators, harmonized MD&A regulations now apply across Canada. Similar requirements are laid down in other jurisdictions, such as that of the SEC in the United States.

MD&A is a narrative explanation, through the eyes of management, of company performance, financial condition, and future prospects. It is to be written in language that investors are able to understand. Its objectives include:

■ To help current and prospective investors understand the financial statements.

■ To discuss information not fully reflected in the financial statements.

■ To discuss important trends and risks.

■ To provide information about the quality, and potential variability, of earnings and cash flow, to help investors determine if past performance is indicative of future performance.

To implement these objectives, specific disclosure requirements include:

■ Discuss overall firm performance, and revenue, asset, and liability items. Explain factors that have caused period-to-period variations, such as acquisitions and dispositions. Indicate with which set of accounting principles the financial statements are consistent.

■ Discuss the firm's ability to meet short- and long-term liquidity needs.

■ Discuss important commitments and off-balance-sheet arrangements.

■ Discuss changes in accounting policies.

■ Explain and discuss trends, risks, and uncertainties that are expected to affect future performance. Describe how financial instruments are used to manage risks. Explain needed changes to forward-looking information previously provided that is now known to be in error because of subsequent developments.

Several aspects of these requirements should be noted:

■ The MD&A standard has a clear forward-looking orientation. For example, known trends affecting future performance should be discussed. This orientation is consistent with the conceptual frameworks, outlined in Section 3.8, which assert investors' interests in assessing prospective cash receipts from their investments.

■ The concept of an information system is implicit in the MD&A standard. As discussed in Section 3.3.2, the information system specifies the relationship between current financial statement evidence and future firm performance. This is recognized in the standard's objective of helping investors to determine if past firm performance is indicative of future performance.

■ Also consistent with its future orientation, the standard tilts towards relevance in the relevance/reliability tradeoff. That is, there is less need to wait until objective evidence is available than in the financial statements. However, MD&A does not completely ignore reliability considerations. For example, NI 51-102 requires that the firm's MD&A be approved by its board of directors. Presumably, this is to reduce the likelihood of manager manipulation and bias. Also, reminiscent of the adjustments of previous estimates in RRA, the firm is required to discuss any needed changes to forward-looking information provided in previous MD&A that is now known to be in error as a result of further developments. This requirement helps with reliability since the manager knows that errors or biases in estimates will have to be explained later.

- The MD&A standard seems reasonably consistent with the theories of rational investor decision-making and market efficiency. For example, it emphasizes full disclosure and recognizes that investors need forward-looking information and information about risk. Indeed, the standard can be regarded as an attempt to make securities markets work better by providing a vehicle for management to disclose inside information. This consistency with theory is not complete, however. For example, the emphasis is on firm-specific risk disclosure. Yet, the theory of investment suggests that much of this risk can be diversified away. Nevertheless, the disclosures should help to reduce investors' estimation risk.

MD&A is to be written in plain language. While this is difficult to disagree with, it is not consistent with the argument of Beaver (Section 4.3) that firms need not be too concerned about the naïve investor, due to the price protection characteristic of efficient market prices.

With this background in mind, we now illustrate some of these considerations by means of the MD&A of a large Canadian corporation.

An Example of MD&A Disclosure Exhibit 4.1 reproduces portions of the MD&A and related disclosures in the 2006 *Annual Report* of Canadian Tire Corporation, Limited, including all of its risk management discussion. Canadian Tire won the Award of Excellence in Annual Reporting of the 2006 CICA Corporate Reporting Awards for the best overall annual report for its industry category.

Canadian Tire's MD&A begins with an overview of the business, then describes its strategic plan, including the performance indicators (financial aspirations) it uses to monitor its financial goals. Recent performance relative to these goals is also disclosed. The firm also provides extensive discussion of current operations and financial conditions, but this is not reproduced here.

Canadian Tire discusses the performance and prospects of its major divisions, including its retail division reproduced in the exhibit. The discussion covers market trends, how Canadian Tire positions itself in its markets, and new initiatives. Note, in particular, its focus on the scope for growth.

With respect to its discussion of risk management, note the variety of risks Canadian Tire faces. These range from information management risk to the risk to its profitability resulting from the actions of competitors, to the seasonal nature of its business, to credit risks arising from failure of contracting parties to fulfil their obligations, to price risks, to disclosure and insider trading risk. The steps that Canadian Tire takes to control these risks, such as its hedging policies, and credit granting and collection policies, are outlined.

Discussion MD&A represents a major step taken by securities commissions to set standards that go beyond the requirements of GAAP. The reason why securities commissions become involved in MD&A disclosure regulation, presumably, is that the accounting recommendations of the *CICA Handbook* relate to the financial statements, whereas the concern of the OSC and other securities regulators is with the disclosures by management contained elsewhere in the annual report, to which the *CICA Handbook* does not apply.

Exhibit 4.1
MD&A Extracts, from 2006 Annual Report,
Canadian Tire Corporation, Limited

1.0 OUR COMPANY
1.1 Overview of the Business

Canadian Tire has been in business for 85 years, offering everyday products and services to Canadians throughout its growing network of interrelated businesses. Canadian Tire, our Associate Dealers, franchises and Petroleum agents operate more than 1,100 general merchandise and apparel retail stores, gas stations and car washes. The Company also provides a variety of financial services to Canadians, primarily its proprietary Options MasterCard™ and Canadian Tire-branded credit cards, personal loans, insurance and warranty products. In October 2006, Financial Services began offering high interest savings accounts, guaranteed investment certificates and residential mortgages in two pilot markets.

Canadian Tire's model of interrelated businesses provides market differentiation and competitive advantage. Canadian Tire's businesses benefit from the Company's key capabilities in merchandising, marketing and advertising, supply chain and real estate, which enable us to achieve a greater level of efficiency. Canadian Tire's primary loyalty program, Canadian Tire 'Money'—shared by CTR, Financial Services and Petroleum—is an example of how interrelationships between the businesses create a strong competitive advantage for the Company.

The success of the loyalty program has proven—through high customer acceptance and redemption—to be a key element of Canadian Tire's total customer value proposition and is designed to drive higher total sales across CTR, Financial Services and Petroleum. For example, a customer who fills up with gas at Petroleum's gas stations and uses Canadian Tire credit cards spends considerably more at Canadian Tire stores, on average, than a customer who only shops at Canadian Tire stores.

Mark's has already derived meaningful cost and operating synergies from Canadian Tire's strengths in real estate and supply chain since its acquisition by the Company in 2002. Canadian Tire co-locates Mark's and Canadian Tire stores in certain locations and, increasingly, is extending its national marketing and advertising channels to boost customer traffic and loyalty to Mark's and increase its brand penetration.

Canadian Tire's four main businesses are described below:

CTR is Canada's most shopped general merchandise retailer with a network of 468 Canadian Tire stores that are operated by Associate Dealers, who are independent business owners. Associate Dealers buy merchandise from the Company and sell it to consumers in Canadian Tire stores. CTR also includes our online shopping channel and PartSource.

Management's Discussion and Analysis

PartSource is a chain of 63 specialty automotive hard parts stores that cater to serious "do-it-yourselfers" and professional installers of automotive parts. The PartSource network consists of 46 franchise stores and 17 corporate stores.

Mark's is one of Canada's leading clothing and footwear retailers, operating 339 stores nationwide, including 287 corporate and 52 franchise stores that offer men's wear, women's wear and industrial apparel. Mark's operates under the banner "Mark's", and in Quebec, "L'Équipeur". Mark's also conducts a business-to-business operation under the "Imagewear by Mark's Work Wearhouse" brand.

Petroleum is Canada's largest independent retailer of gasoline with a network of 260 gas stations, 251 convenience stores and kiosks, 74 car washes, 13 Pit Stops and 92 propane stations. The majority of Petroleum's sites are co-located with Canadian Tire stores as a deliberate strategy to attract customers to Canadian Tire stores. Substantially all of Petroleum's sites are operated by agents.

Financial Services markets a range of Canadian Tire-branded credit cards, including the Canadian Tire Options MasterCard, Commercial Link MasterCard and Gas Advantage MasterCard. Financial Services also offers personal loans, insurance and warranty products and an emergency roadside assistance service called "Canadian Tire Roadside Assistance". Canadian Tire Bank, a wholly-owned subsidiary of Financial Services, is a federally regulated bank that manages and finances Canadian Tire's MasterCard and retail credit card portfolios, as well as the personal loan portfolio. In October 2006, Canadian Tire Bank began offering high interest savings accounts, guaranteed investment certificates and residential mortgages in two pilot markets.

3.0 OUR STRATEGY

3.1 Five-year Strategic Plan

Canadian Tire has a five-year Strategic Plan to guide the Company's growth from 2005 to 2009. The Plan has five strategic imperatives outlined below. Each of these imperatives is supported by specific initiatives, outlined in section 4.2, on business segment performance.

1 — grow sales and revenues

2 — improve our earnings performance

3 — embed a *Customer for Life* culture across our entire organization

4 — extend growth and performance beyond 2009

5 — enhance value creation through financial flexibility and maximization of the value of real estate assets

3.2 Financial Aspirations

As part of our initial strategic planning process, we developed five financial aspirations that we believe are important and logical metrics for both the Company and its shareholders to track progress against the Plan. These metrics are not to be construed as guidance or forecasts for any individual year within the Plan, but rather as long-term targets that

Management's Discussion and Analysis

we aspire to achieve over the life of the Plan, based on the successful execution of our various initiatives.

Financial aspirations	2005–2009 Strategic Plan	2005–2006 performance	2006 performance	2006 adjusted[1]
Same store sales (see note below) (simple average of annual percentage growth, CTR stores only)	3% to 4%	3.4%	3.4%	3.4%
Gross operating revenue[2] (compound annual growth rate)	7% to 9%	8.1%	7.1%	7.1%
EBITDA[3] and minority interest (compound annual growth rate)	10% to 15%	7.8%	3.6%	6.3%
Basic earnings per share (compound annual growth rate)	12% to 15%	9.9%	7.7%	11.0%
After-tax return on invested capital (annual simple average)	10%	9.6%	9.6%	9.4%

[1]Excludes non-operating items.
[2]Gross operating revenue for 2005 has been restated for the impact of EIC–156 as required by CICA.
[3]Earnings before interest, income taxes, depreciation and amortization. See section 12.0 on non-GAAP measures.

Same store sales Previously, we reported on CTR's comparable store sales growth as part of our overall financial aspirations. We will now report solely on CTR's same store sales growth and accordingly, we have changed our financial aspirations to reflect our new practice. There are three key reasons for the change in reporting: same store sales growth is the metric used by management and most commonly used in the retail industry; and, the same store sales calculation will include the large number of store expansions included in the Concept 20/20 store rollout.

3.3 2007 Strategic Plan Outlook

Canadian Tire will continue to invest in existing growth initiatives with a renewed focus on enhancing productivity. Our growth initiatives for 2007 include:

> continued rollout of approximately 70 CTR Concept 20/20 projects, including the addition of nine stores in new markets. Total retail square feet will increase approximately 10 percent by the end of the year

> addition of eight new PartSource stores and continued acquisitions of regional competitors

> continued expansion of Mark's retail space through approximately 55 projects, including adding 29 new stores to the network, increasing retail square footage by 14 percent

> developing and testing at least one new store format integrating the complete Mark's concept with a larger Canadian Tire store

> addition of nine new Petroleum sites and additional re-branded sites, in line with the interrelated marketing objective to enhance traffic and customer loyalty to CTR and Financial Services credit cards

Management's Discussion and Analysis

> further regional expansion of the Gas Advantage MasterCard business and the testing of at least one additional new card product

> continued testing of the new high interest savings accounts, guaranteed investment certificates and residential mortgages in the two pilot regions

In addition, a number of new initiatives will be launched within CTR to enhance the long-term competitiveness and productivity of its operations, including:

> the upgrade and simplification of information technology (IT) infrastructure and applications to reduce IT operating costs and enhance the productivity of Canadian Tire's workforce

> improvements to Associate Dealer ordering and shipping processes to better align the flow of product to CTR stores with customer purchasing patterns, thereby reducing corporate and store inventory levels and operational complexity

> enhancements to automotive parts supply chain capabilities to support the expansion of PartSource and continued growth and efficiencies at CTR

Consolidated quarterly results

($ in millions except per share amounts)	Q4 2006	Q3 2006	Q2 2006	Q1 2006	Q4 2005	Q3 2005	Q2 2005	Q1 2005
Gross operating revenue[1]	$2,426.1	$2,023.3	$2,247.6	$1,572.1	$2,304.3	$1,888.6	$2,020.6	$1,508.1
Net earnings	108.3	95.4	103.3	47.6	118.2	84.4	92.2	35.3
Basic earnings per share	1.33	1.17	1.27	0.58	1.44	1.03	1.13	0.43
Fully diluted earnings per share	1.32	1.16	1.25	0.58	1.43	1.02	1.11	0.43

[1]Quarterly gross operating revenue for 2005 has been restated for the impact of EIC–156 as required by CICA. See section 11.3 for additional information.

CTR sales in the fourth quarter were adversely affected by unseasonably warm weather in December in Ontario and Quebec. See section 4.2.1.2 for more information on the factors that affected CTR's retail sales performance.

4.2 BUSINESS SEGMENT PERFORMANCE

4.2.1 Canadian Tire Retail

4.2.1.1 Strategic Plan update and outlook

The following outlines CTR's performance in 2006 in the context of the 2005–2009 Strategic Plan, and provides an outlook for 2007 and for the full Plan period.

Strategic Plan update and outlook

Concept 20/20 store program

Concept 20/20 is the cornerstone of Canadian Tire Retail's current growth agenda. Concept 20/20 stores are experiencing strong first-, second- and third-year sales, caused by increases in customer traffic and average transaction value, thereby providing the potential for a more attractive return on investment than previous store formats.

Management's Discussion and Analysis

Concept 20/20 same store sales were very strong in 2006, up 8.0 percent year-over-year. On average, customers spend 40 percent more time in Concept 20/20 stores than in other store formats, demonstrating that the attractive Concept 20/20 store design, product displays and open-plan layout encourage customers to browse the stores, increasing the likelihood of incremental purchases. The strong sales performance of Concept 20/20 led to the decision to accelerate the store rollout in 2006 and 2007.

2006 Performance

Fourth quarter

CTR opened 15 new stores in the quarter, 11 of which are replacement stores and four of which are new to the network. Eleven of the 15 stores opened in the quarter are Concept 20/20–Mark's Work Wearhouse combination stores.

CTR also expanded and retrofitted 18 new-format stores to the Concept 20/20 format.

Full year 2006

CTR completed a total of 73 Concept 20/20 projects in 2006, opening 19 new stores and expanding and retrofitting 54 existing stores to the Concept 20/20 format. Seven of the new Concept 20/20 stores are additions to the network.

At the end of 2006, CTR had 468 stores, including 126 Concept 20/20 stores (20 Concept 20/20 Canadian Tire–Mark's Work Wearhouse combination stores). CTR added approximately 1.3 million retail square feet to the network for a total of 16.2 million retail square feet at the end of the year.

2005–2009 Plan

CTR plans to open approximately 270 Concept 20/20 stores between 2005 and 2009.

2007 Outlook

CTR plans to open approximately 70 new Concept 20/20 stores, adding 1.6 million retail square feet as follows:

> 19 new Concept 20/20 stores, including 10 replacement stores

> 51 expansions and retrofits

9.0 ENTERPRISE RISK MANAGEMENT

To preserve and enhance shareholder value, the Company approaches the management of risk strategically through its Enterprise Risk Management (ERM) framework. Introduced in 2003, the ERM framework sets out principles and tools for identifying, evaluating, prioritizing and managing risk effectively and consistently across the Company.

The intent of introducing our ERM framework was to establish an integrated approach to managing risks to assist in achieving our strategic objectives. Our ERM framework is:

> designed to provide an understanding of risks across the Company, and the potential impacts of risks on every part of the organization;

> cross-functional in its perspective to provide a consistent discipline for managing risk;

> designed to allow for improved capital allocation decisions to optimize risk and reward; and

> designed to incorporate a number of tools for managing risk, including avoidance, mitigation, insurance and acceptance.

Management's Discussion and Analysis

Our first steps were to develop a process for identifying our Principal Risks and to carry out an initial risk assessment, which we completed in 2004. We define a Principal Risk (Principal Risks) as one that can have a significant adverse impact on Canadian Tire's performance, reputation and ability to service its customers and has, in the absence of controls, a reasonable possibility of occurring.

Based on our experience since 2004, we are now enhancing the processes and procedures that support the ERM framework, including performance metrics and Board reporting. We are also reviewing and enhancing policies relating to the management of our Principal Risks.

The officer in charge of each business and support unit is accountable for ensuring that risks are managed effectively within his or her business area.

A management Enterprise Risk Committee was formed in 2006 to enhance the sustainability of the ERM framework. The Enterprise Risk Committee was created to oversee the management of Principal Risks and other enterprise-wide risks under the leadership of the Chief Executive Officer (CEO) and has the responsibility for reviewing and approving the recommendation to the Board of Directors, the ERM policy and framework.

The Company's Internal Audit Services (IAS) division also supports the Company's overall risk management program. The primary role of IAS is to assist the Audit Committee and the Social Responsibility and Risk Governance Committee (SRRG) in the discharge of their responsibilities relating to risk and uncertainty, financial controls and control deviations, compliance with laws and regulations and compliance with the Company's Code of Business Conduct for Employees and Directors. To this end, IAS is responsible for conducting independent assessments of the effectiveness of risk management and control processes across the Company.

9.1 Board Accountability

The mandate of the Board of Directors includes overseeing the development of an ERM process, for which the Board has delegated initial responsibility to the SRRG. The SRRG, and in certain instances the Audit Committee, is responsible for gaining and maintaining reasonable assurance that management:

> appropriately identifies and manages risks;

> develops a policy that accurately sets out our risk philosophy, risk tolerance and the expectations and accountabilities for identifying, assessing, monitoring and managing risk (the ERM Policy);

> fully implements and sustains the ERM process in compliance with the ERM Policy and that the ERM Policy continues to accurately state our risk philosophy and risk tolerance, as well as our expectations and accountabilities for managing risks;

> identifies Principal Risks in a timely manner, including those risks relating to or arising from any weaknesses or threats to our business and our assumptions underlying our Strategic Plan; and

> effectively assesses, monitors and manages Principal Risks in compliance with ERM Policy.

9.2 Principal Risks

Canadian Tire has policies and practices mandated by the Board of Directors to manage the Company's Principal Risks. The following commentary provides a high level perspective on the nature of each identified Principal Risk and describes the main practices that we have in place to mitigate the potential impacts of Principal Risks on our business activities.

9.2.1 Information Management

The integrity, reliability and security of information in all its forms are critical to the Company's daily and strategic operations. Inaccurate, incomplete and unavailable information and/or inappropriate access to information could lead to incorrect financial and/or operational reporting, poor decisions, privacy breaches and/or inappropriate disclosure or leaks of sensitive information.

Information management risk was recently identified as a Principal Risk in its own right, separate from the technology risk described below. Canadian Tire recognizes that information is a critical enterprise asset. Currently, the information management risk is being managed at the individual business unit level through the development of policies and procedures pertaining to security access, system development, change management and problem and incident management. With a view to enhancing and standardizing the controls to manage the information management risk, the Company is developing corporate operating policies which establish minimum standards for the usage, security and appropriate destruction of information. Furthermore, enterprise metrics are being identified to assist in monitoring significant information management risks.

9.2.2 Technology

Technology is critical to Canadian Tire's operations and is a key enabler of the Strategic Plan. Any system inefficiency or failure could negatively affect our performance, reputation and/or our ability to service customers. Monitoring the availability of Canadian Tire's information technology and assessing the efficiency, stability and scalability of our systems is key to managing this risk. Canadian Tire's technology must also be sufficiently current to ensure that we are able to service our customers and that our business units remain competitive in the marketplace.

Numerous controls are in place to manage the technology risk, including system and disaster recovery procedures and monitoring of system availability, capacity and inappropriate external access attempts. Since the beginning of 2003, our Information Technology group has been planning and implementing a simpler technical environment with the appropriate standardized processes to minimize the risks associated with operating on a number of differing technology platforms.

9.2.3 Product Safety

The Company's brand equity and reputation are integrally linked to the safety of its products and services. Unsafe products and services or products that do not meet regulatory requirements could pose a risk to the health and safety of customers, employees, and other members

Management's Discussion and Analysis

of the public or to the environment. This risk, should it materialize, could negatively impact the Company's relationship with its customers, or the Canadian Tire, Mark's Work Wearhouse, and PartSource brands, and result in lost sales due to product re-work and recalls.

We are committed to mitigating the risks associated with our products and services. To this end, we employ quality assurance processes that test products for durability, safety and functionality. These processes are periodically reviewed and enhanced. We also analyze product returns, review consumer reports and use the resulting information to include quality provisions in supplier contract negotiations. Further, all of our vendors are required to carry insurance to cover product liability and indemnify us.

9.2.4 Consumer Credit

With a growing portfolio of consumer lending products, our Financial Services business assumes certain risks that include our failure or inability to accurately predict the creditworthiness of our customers. Financial Services manages credit risks to maintain and improve the quality and profitability of its consumer lending portfolio by:

> employing sophisticated credit-scoring models to constantly monitor the creditworthiness of customers;

> using the latest technology to make informed credit decisions for each customer account to limit credit risk exposure;

> adopting technology to improve the effectiveness of the loan collection process; and

> monitoring the macro-economic environment, especially with respect to interest rates, employment levels and income levels.

9.2.5 Competitive

We compete for customers, employees, products and services against international, national and regional retailers (department stores, mass merchandisers, home-improvement stores and warehouses, petroleum retailers and specialty marketers), banks and other financial services institutions which currently operate in one or more of our business segments. Material changes in the strategic direction and positioning or other practices of those competitors could create material competitive risk to the Company.

We actively monitor and analyze competitive activity as part of our strategic planning process, collecting competitive information, identifying material changes in the competitive environment, identifying material competitive risks and developing strategies to mitigate these risks. Each of our businesses has core strengths and initiatives that provide differentiation in the marketplace and enhance our competitive position, reducing our overall competitive risk. The unique strengths and strategies of our businesses are described in more detail in sections 2.0 and 4.2 of this MD&A.

9.2.6 Economic

Shifts in the fundamentals of the economic environment in which we operate—such as economic growth, inflation, exchange rates, levels of taxation and interest rates—could affect consumer confidence and spending and impact our ability to source products at a competitive cost. We constantly monitor economic developments in the markets where we operate and where we source our products. We use this information in our continuous strategic and operational reviews to adjust our initiatives as economic conditions dictate and to facilitate ongoing innovation in stores, merchandising concepts and products and Financial Services.

9.2.7 Hazards, Disasters and Business Interruptions

Natural disasters, war, or random occurrences or acts could result in a material change to economic and market performance, consumer behaviour and business conditions or operations. We have established emergency response protocols and business continuity plans that are currently being reviewed and enhanced. Our emergency response teams have been trained to respond to situations as they arise. Our business continuity management team monitors business continuity plans to ensure that they are adequately prepared and tested, particularly with respect to our critical processes and systems. We also maintain insurance coverage to offset physical loss and loss of profits to mitigate the financial impact of an unusual event. The recovery under any insurance claim is subject to limitations set by the insurer.

9.2.8 Geopolitical

Changes in the domestic and international political environment could impact the Company's strategic and operational capabilities. The Company's ability to source products and services could be compromised. These risks can arise from domestic and foreign trade agreements, policies, laws and regulations and other political events and could result in significant material losses or damage to our reputation.

The Company mitigates this risk by monitoring the geopolitical environment of the countries in which we do business. When we contemplate a new vendor relationship, we undertake a risk assessment to evaluate the vendor's fit as well as the vendor country's political environment. We monitor for political changes that could impact our ability to remain competitive.

9.2.9 Legislative Compliance

In operating our business, we must comply with a variety of laws and regulations to meet our corporate and social responsibilities and to avoid the risk of financial penalties and/or criminal and civil liability to our officers and directors. Areas of principal risk are environment, health and safety, competition law, privacy, disclosure, insider trading and laws and regulations which govern financial institutions. Failure to comply with applicable regulations could result in sanctions and financial penalties by regulatory bodies that could impact our earnings and reputation. At the corporate level, we have established a Risk Management and Compliance Services Department to provide, among other things, a framework for compliance oversight with laws and regulations applicable to our businesses.

Environment, Health and Safety We are required to comply with various environmental, health and safety (EHS) laws and regulations which govern how the Company must manage and monitor its EHS activities. Effective and safe management of the EHS aspects of the business mitigates the risk of financial penalties and criminal or civil liability for officers and directors, and at the same time allows the Company to achieve its committed objective of protecting the environment and the healthy and safety of employees, customers, and the communities in which we do business. In order to ensure that we meet our obligations and mitigate EHS risks, we have in place an EHS policy and management system to guide compliance across the enterprise.

We also recognize that a healthy and safe workplace minimizes injuries and other risks employees face in carrying out their duties. A healthy, safe workplace also improves productivity and avoids penalties or other liabilities for our officers and directors. To this end, we have a number of practices in place to ensure a quality workplace, including guidelines for physical and ergonomic workspaces and shared facilities. Our EHS policies and management systems are designed to ensure that appropriate procedures are followed to minimize workplace injuries. We also offer programs which are designed to promote healthy lifestyles. The incidence of workplace injuries is monitored and reports are reviewed by the SRRG on a quarterly basis.

Competition Law The retail operations of CTR, PartSource, Mark's and Petroleum and certain aspects of Financial Services' businesses are required to comply with the federal *Competition Act* which regulates: (a) certain advertising activities such as ordinary price claims and claims concerning the attributes and performance of our products and services, and (b) other practices related to the lessening of competition in the marketplace. Failure to comply with the requirements of the *Competition Act* could lead to substantial civil and criminal liabilities, administrative penalties and damage to the Company's reputation.

The primary manner in which the Company mitigates the risks associated with failure to comply with the *Competition Act* is to provide ongoing, periodic training to personnel involved in marketing and advertising our products and services. The Company also employs legal personnel with expertise in competition law who regularly review the format and content of our various advertising vehicles and provide ongoing advice to our marketing and advertising staff in respect to other competition law matters.

Privacy In accordance with the *Personal Information Protection and Electronic Documents Act* (PIPEDA) and similar provincial legislation, we introduced a set of privacy policies in 2003. These policies address the privacy issues surrounding the collection, use, disclosure and retention of personal information used in our workplace and identify guiding principles for ensuring that our practices protect the privacy and security of all personal information. In order to reinforce the understanding of these policies and promote compliance, a privacy training lesson was developed in 2006 which will be completed by employees in 2007.

Disclosure We are required to comply with securities reporting legislation and accounting standards that are intended to ensure the full, accurate and timely communication of financial and other material information to the public. To ensure that we meet our obligations and mitigate risks associated with either the disclosure of inaccurate or incomplete information or

Management's Discussion and Analysis

a failure to disclose required information, we have in place a Disclosure Policy and a management Disclosure Committee to guide compliance:

> The Disclosure Policy sets out our accountabilities, authorized spokespersons and our approach to the identification and dissemination of material information. The policy also defines restrictions on insider trading and the handling of confidential information.

> The Disclosure Committee reviews all financial information prepared for communication to the public to ensure that it meets regulatory requirements. The Committee is also responsible for raising all potentially material issues to the Audit Committee prior to making any disclosure recommendations.

> The CEO, Chief Financial Officer (CFO), Senior Vice-President, Secretary and General Counsel, Chairman of the Board and Chairman of the Audit Committee review all financial disclosures prior to submission to the Audit Committee for the Audit Committee's review and recommendation to the Board.

The Disclosure Policy was reviewed and amended in 2006 in order to reflect recent changes to the Ontario *Securities Act*.

Insider Trading As a publicly traded issuer, Canadian Tire is subject to the insider trading provisions of the securities legislation in each province and territory of Canada. These laws prohibit directors and officers and significant shareholders from trading in the Company's securities when in possession of undisclosed material information about the Company. The legislation also prohibits the Company and its insiders from "tipping" undisclosed material information to third parties except in the necessary course of business. Insiders are required to publicly report any trades in the Company's securities in accordance with the insider trading laws. Failure to abide by the insider trading laws could undermine public confidence in the integrity of the Company's management and its systems of compliance which could, in turn, damage the Company's reputation. Any such failure could also result in fines and imprisonment to the offending individuals.

The Company mitigates the risks of illegal insider trading by adopting a policy on insider trading which requires insiders to comply with the laws applicable thereto. In addition, the policy requires each member of the Board of Directors, senior management and certain other designated employees to pre-clear any trades with the General Counsel of the Company in order to ensure that no trades are made while such individuals possess undisclosed material information during predetermined quarterly blackout periods established pursuant to the policy. The Company also has a robust Disclosure Policy and associated procedures in order to ensure that material information about the Company is properly disclosed to the public in a timely manner.

Financial Services Our Financial Services division relies on its Compliance Department to assist Canadian Tire Bank in meeting all applicable financial services legislative and regulatory requirements.

9.2.10 Accounting, Valuation and Reporting

In any organization, there is a risk of incorrect application of the rules or standards governing accounting. We employ numerous professionally accredited accountants throughout our finance group, and all of our divisional financial officers have a dotted line reporting relationship to our CFO. Senior finance representatives are assigned to all significant projects. Policies are in place to ensure the completeness and accuracy of reported transactions. Key transaction controls are in place, there is a segregation of duties between transaction initiation, processing and cash disbursement, and there is restricted physical access to the Treasury and cash settlements area. Accounting, measurement, valuation and reporting of accounts which involve estimates and/or valuations are reviewed quarterly by the CFO, the external auditor and the Audit Committee. Significant accounting and financial topics and issues are presented to and discussed with the Audit Committee, and a presentation of quarterly scorecards on operational results is made to the Audit Committee and Board of Directors.

9.2.11 Capital

We must maintain sufficient capital to operate our business and absorb the potential impact of unexpected losses. We maintain adequate access to debt markets to meet our funding requirements. Our Treasurer is responsible for the effective management of capital within the target limits approved by the Board. To monitor our adherence to established policies, a Financial Risk Management Report—which sets out targets and performance on debt to capital ratios, liquidity ratios and foreign exchange management—is provided to the Audit Committee on a quarterly basis. Our Financial Risk Management group approves financial risk management policies for recommendation to the Audit Committee and monitors compliance with those policies. The Funding Plan for the Company is prepared by the Treasury department and approved by the Board.

9.2.12 Financial Instruments

The use of derivative products to manage currency, interest rates and equity exposures and the use of other complex financial instruments pose certain risks. To reduce our risk, our Treasury department does not operate as a profit centre. Controls are in place to detect and prevent speculative activity.

It is our policy to identify and manage currency and interest-rate risk proactively and conservatively. To attempt to ensure that any counterparty to our financial transactions has the ability to meet its financial commitments, we deal only with highly rated financial institutions. We also ensure that there is no undue concentration with any single counterparty. Our Treasury department also monitors activity against policy limits and reports to the Financial Risk Management group and Audit Committee.

9.2.13 Effective Management

Lack of effective recruitment programs, succession planning and compensation structures, as well as performance management and development would present risks to our ability to

Management's Discussion and Analysis

implement our strategic initiatives and to attract, motivate and retain talented people. We have well-established recruitment and performance practices that are facilitated and monitored by our Human Resources group.

Our compensation structure emphasizes employee share ownership and profit sharing, and is reviewed regularly to ensure it is competitive with the marketplace. Twice annually, the executive team undertakes a Leadership Review Process to identify high-potential individuals for development and to identify viable successors for all key management positions.

9.2.14 Ethical Business Practices

Any violation of law, breach of corporate policy or unethical behaviour poses significant risk to our reputation, our brand name and our ability to operate. Commitment to ethical business practices is core to our values and is reflected in a number of policies and practices which are reviewed and strengthened on an ongoing basis to ensure that our employees and directors uphold the highest standard of ethical behaviour.

In order to oversee implementation and compliance with the Code of Business Conduct for Employees and Directors (the Code), the Business Conduct Compliance Office (BCCO) was established and became fully operational in 2005. The BCCO is structured so as to provide multiple channels through which individuals can report (confidentially and anonymously) breaches of the Code for investigation and follow-up. The office also provides assistance and support to employees and directors with respect to interpreting the application of the Code. In late 2006, a review of the Code was commenced in order to ensure that we continue to strengthen our commitment to ethical business practices and remain current with recent developments in the field of ethical business management.

In order to ensure that our suppliers and vendors also abide by the same high standards of ethical business conduct, the Supplier Code of Conduct was introduced in 2005.

Source: Reprinted by permission of Canadian Tire Corporation, Limited.

Canadian Tire's MD&A seems to fully meet the objectives and requirements of the standard given earlier. Indeed, its disclosures exceed a minimal rehashing of financial statement information and vague gestures to future prospects. The information provided goes well beyond what can be learned from the financial statements themselves. In particular, the discussion is from management's perspective, and contains considerable forward-looking information to assist investors to assess the probabilities of future firm performance.

It is interesting to speculate why some firms go beyond minimal reporting requirements, particularly due to the potential for lawsuits if the forward-looking disclosures are not met. One possibility is that the Canadian reporting environment may be less litigious than others, such as the United States. Another is that by building investor confidence through reducing estimation risk, the firm's cost of capital will be reduced. This is discussed in Chapter 12. Yet another possibility is that a full-disclosure reputation may also affect customer, as well as investor, confidence.

The potentially serious consequences of violating MD&A requirements are illustrated by the case of Kmart Corp., a giant Michigan-based retail chain.

In August 2005, the SEC announced civil charges against the former CEO and CFO of Kmart, including a ban on their serving as officers or directors of public corporations. These charges arose from the summer of 2001, when Kmart acquired excess inventory of approximately $850 million U.S. This created a serious liquidity problem, as Kmart did not have enough cash and bank credit to pay for the overbuy.

To alleviate this liquidity crunch, Kmart decided to delay payments to its suppliers, creating serious concerns in the vendor community. Several major suppliers withheld further shipments. Kmart declared bankruptcy in January 2002, resulting in a $4.5 billion loss to shareholders, a loss of many jobs, and losses of retirement savings.

The SEC charges arose out of claimed fraudulent misstatements in Kmart's 2001 MD&A. For example, there was no disclosure of why approximately $570 million of accounts payable were past due, despite MD&A requirements to discuss short- and long-term liquidity needs, to discuss asset and liability items, and to explain factors that have caused period-to-period variations, as well as discussing important trends and risks that are expected to affect future performance.

Instead, the company blamed the accounts payable increase on glitches in a system update. It also reported, vaguely, that the $440 million increase in inventory (about a 6% increase) was due to "seasonal inventory fluctuations and actions taken to improve overall in-stock position."

4.9 CONCLUSIONS ON EFFICIENT SECURITIES MARKETS

Efficient securities market theory has major implications for financial accounting. One of these is that supplementary information in financial statement notes or elsewhere is just as useful as information in the financial statements proper. Another is that efficiency is defined relative to a stock of publicly known information. Informative financial reporting has a role to play in improving the amount, timing, and accuracy of this stock, thereby enabling capital markets to work better and improve the operation of the economy.

MD&A is an important example of a full disclosure standard. This standard has the potential to convey information beyond that contained in the conventional historical cost-based financial statements. This potential is not only in the information contained in the disclosure per se. The extent to which the firm goes beyond minimal MD&A requirements tells the market something more. Superior disclosure signals a confident, well-planned management approach (otherwise, why release the information?), suggesting that good performance in the face of changing opportunities, risks, and uncertainties will continue.

Full disclosure has two main benefits, which can be attained simultaneously. One is to enable investors to make better decisions. The other is to improve the ability of securities markets to direct investment to its most productive uses. The reason why these benefits are attained simultaneously, of course, is that better information enables more-informed buy/sell decisions, helping share price to better reflect fundamental firm value. Share price, in turn, affects the firm's investment decisions.

Another implication of efficient securities market theory appears in Beaver's 1973 analysis. This is that the specific accounting policies adopted by firms do not matter as long as they have no differential cash flow effects across those policies, full disclosure is made of the particular policies used, and investors have sufficient information to convert from one policy to another. The reason, according to efficient markets theory, is that investors as a whole will *look through* reported net income to its underlying implications for future cash flows. In so doing, they will take into account the specific accounting policies used in calculating net income. Thus, firms' choices of amortization policy, of successful-efforts or full-cost accounting for oil and gas exploration, and so on, will not affect the efficient market prices of their securities, providing the specific accounting policies they are using are fully disclosed. Thus, we see that the full-disclosure principle extends to disclosure of accounting policies.

Accountants are improving their understanding of the role of information in determining price. In essence, market price aggregates the collective information processing and decision-making expertise of investors. Thus, market price itself has considerable information content, which individuals may use as input into their decisions. A "buy and hold" investment strategy is an example of a decision that relies on the information content of market price.

This aggregation of information into market price contains a logical contradiction, however. If price is fully informative, no one would bother to collect additional, costly, information. In effect, market price contains within it the seeds of its own destruction. However, we can identify two factors to prevent this from happening:

- Noise and liquidity traders introduce a random component to market price, which prevents market price from being fully informative about future value.

- Information asymmetry, in particular the presence of inside information, means that not all relevant information is in the public domain. Then, investors have the potential to earn extra profits if they can ferret out some of this inside information. Improved disclosure, as in MD&A, provides investors with some help in this regard.

As Beaver (1973) put it, accountants are in competition with other information sources. We now know that market price is one of these other sources. Think of market price as aggregating all relevant "other" information up to the time of release of the financial statements. The question then is: Is it cost effective for rational investors to inform themselves by utilizing the financial statements?

Again, the accountants' answer is the concept of full disclosure. By increasing the information content of financial reporting, including supplementary information in notes and MD&A, not only do accountants help preserve their competitive advantage, they also improve social welfare by reducing the adverse impacts of inside information.

If investors do in fact find accounting information useful, this should show up as a response of security prices to this information. In the next chapter, we will examine empirical evidence in this regard.

Questions and Problems

1. Two firms, of the same size and risk, release their annual reports on the same day. It turns out that they each report the same amount of net income. Following the release, the share price of one firm rose strongly while the other rose hardly at all.

   Explain how it is possible for the market to react positively to one firm's annual report and hardly at all to the other when the firms are similar in size, risk, and reported profitability.

2. Shares of firm A and firm B are traded on an efficient market. The two firms are of the same size and risk. They both report the same net income. However, you see in the financial statement notes that firm A uses the LIFO inventory method and declining-balance amortization for capital assets, while firm B uses the FIFO inventory method and straight-line amortization.

   Which firm's shares should sell at the higher price-to-earnings ratio, all other things being equal? Explain. Assume a period of rising prices. (CGA-Canada)

3. Using the concept of information asymmetry, answer the following questions:

   a. You observe that used cars sold by new car dealers sell for a higher price, for models of same make, year, and condition, than used cars sold by used car dealers. Why?

   b. Why would a fire insurance policy contain a $150 deductible provision?

   c. Why would a life insurance company require a medical examination before approving applications for new policies?

   d. A firm plans to raise additional capital by means of a new issue of common shares. Before doing so, it hires a well-known investment house to help design and market the issue, and also switches auditors from a small, local firm to a "Big Four" firm. Why? (CGA-Canada)

4. To what extent might the financial press provide a relevant source of information for investors? Would this information source conflict with or complement financial statement information? Explain.

5. On January 21, 1993, *The Wall Street Journal* reported that General Electric Co.'s fourth-quarter 1992 earnings rose 6.2% to $1.34 billion or $1.57 a share, setting a new record and bringing the earnings for 1992 to $4.73 billion or $5.51 a share. After adjusting for extraordinary items, 1992 earnings from continuing operations were up about 10% from the previous year.

   The *Journal* also reported that forecasts made by analysts averaged $1.61 per share for the fourth quarter of 1992, and from $5.50 to $5.60 per share for the whole year. One analyst was quoted as saying that 1992 "wasn't a bad year for GE" despite the downturn in the stock market on the day of the earnings announcement.

   Yet, on the same day the fourth-quarter earnings were announced, General Electric Co.'s stock price fell $1.50 to $82.625 on the New York Stock Exchange.

Required

a. Give three reasons to explain why this could happen.

b. Use the Sharpe-Lintner CAPM (Equations 4.2 and 4.3) to explain how the new information caused the current price slip. Calculations are not required.

6. On February 27, 2007, Laurentian Bank of Canada released results for its first quarter, ending on January 31, 2007. It reported profit of 74 cents per share (70 cents per share before a non-recurring gain). Analysts' estimates of profit for the quarter were 65 cents per share. For the same quarter of the previous year, profit was 59 cents per share. Total revenue increased 6%. The bank announced a quarterly dividend of 29 cents per share, unchanged from the two previous quarters. The CFO of Laurentian stated that its loan exposure to struggling forestry and manufacturing firms was better, although there was still room for improvement.

Laurentian's shares are traded on the S&P TSX exchange. The TSX index rose 5 points on February 27, closing at 13,040.11. Laurentian's share price fell 34 cents for the day, to $30.71.

Required

Why did Laurentian's share price fall? Assume efficient securities markets, and consider both economy-wide and firm-specific factors in your answer.

7. Atlas Ltd. is a listed public company. It is in a volatile industry. The market price of its shares is highly sensitive to its earnings. The company's annual meeting is to be held soon, and the president is concerned, expecting to be attacked strongly by a dissident group of shareholders.

One issue the dissidents are expected to focus on is the company's amortization policy. They will claim that the annual declining-balance amortization charges are excessive—that the company's conservative amortization policy seriously understates annual earnings per share, causing the shares' market price to be artificially low. Threats have even been made of suing management and the board of directors to "recover the resulting loss in market value, relative to shareholders in companies with less conservative amortization policies, suffered by Atlas shareholders."

The president has asked you to help prepare a defence against the expected attack on the company's amortization policy.

Required

Write a memo summarizing how you would recommend the president respond to this attack. (CGA-Canada)

8. The article "GM to Take Charge of $20.8-Billion" here reproduced from *The Globe and Mail* (February 2, 1993) describes the potential impact of SFAS 106, "Accounting for Postretirement Benefits Other Than Pensions," on General Motors and Ford. For example, it appears that General Motors will be required to record a liability of $20.8 billion, reducing its shareholders' equity from $27.8 billion to $7 billion, about a 75% reduction.

GM to Take Charge of $20.8-Billion

Atlanta—General Motors Corp. will take a $20.8-billion (U.S.) charge against 1992 earnings to account for a new way of estimating retiree health care costs, the auto maker's directors decided yesterday.

The charge, which will not affect the struggling auto maker's cash flow, will leave GM with the largest annual loss of any U.S. corporation, eclipsing the company's 1991 loss of $4.45-billion, which was a record at that time.

Including accounting changes, other charges and losses on its North American operations, GM's 1992 loss could approach $23-billion.

The $20.8-billion is a non-cash charge. It reduces GM's net worth to about $7-billion, still sufficient to pay stock dividends under the laws of Delaware, where GM is incorporated.

Separately, GM said it would take a $744-million fourth-quarter restructuring charge for its National Car Rental Systems business. In a recent U.S. Securities and Exchange Commission filing, GM estimated that charge at about $300-million.

The accounting change, required by the Financial Accounting Standards Board of all publicly traded U.S. companies, has had a major effect on each of the Big Three U.S. auto makers.

Ford Motor Co. said it would take a $7.5-billion charge against 1992 earnings to account for the change. Chrysler Corp. said it has not decided whether to take its $4.7-billion charge as a lump sum in the first quarter or spread it over 20 years, as the standard allows.

GM had estimated its charge for adopting the new accounting standard at $16-billion to $24-billion. The $20.8-billion actual charge includes its workers, GM Hughes Electronics Corp. and its financial subsidiary, General Motors Acceptance Corp.

The company's EDS Corp. subsidiary does not pay health benefits, so it was exempt.

Source: *The Globe and Mail*, February 2, 1993. Reprinted by permission of The Associated Press.

Required

Describe and explain how you would expect the efficient securities market to react to this information.

9. You have just obtained inside information about a firm that employs you and in which you own shares. The information is that the current quarter's earnings will be substantially below forecast. Should you sell your shares before the bad news becomes publicly known? Outline arguments for and against this temptation.

10. A major reason for the rarity of formal financial forecasts in annual reports is the possibility of lawsuits if the forecast is not met, particularly in the United States. On November 17, 1995, *The Wall Street Journal* reported that the SEC was supporting a bill before the U.S. Senate to provide protection from legal liability resulting from forecasts, providing that "meaningful cautionary statements" accompanied the forecast.

Required

a. To the extent that firms are discouraged from providing financial forecasts by the prospect of litigation, how could this lead to a negative impact on the working of securities markets? Can you give an argument that a litigious environment might actually improve the working of securities markets?

b. Explain how the passage of a bill such as that mentioned above might benefit investors.

c. Explain how passage might benefit firms.

11. Refer to Theory in Practice 4.1 in Section 4.2.2.

Required

a. Use efficient securities market theory to explain how "dart-throwing" may be a desirable investment strategy.

b. Explain Prof. Malkiel's argument that risk differences may be driving the superior average returns earned by the pros and the Dow Jones index. How would you determine whether risk differences were affecting the results?

c. Explain another possible reason, not mentioned by Prof. Malkiel, for the superior returns earned by the pros.

12. For companies with no history of positive earnings, such as startup companies, growth of revenues provides an alternative performance measure and indicator of possible future earning power. This is particularly the case if the new company incurs high R&D costs, advertising, and other startup expenditures that delay the advent of reported earnings. Without reported earnings, such companies may inflate reported revenues to impress investors. In an article in *The Globe and Mail*, December 30, 2000, Janet McFarland discusses some of these practices. They include:

■ Recognizing full revenue even though products or systems can be returned, or when there are future obligations such as servicing the products and systems sold.

■ Recording revenue on long-term contracts in advance of billings to the customer (billings may be delayed as a form of vendor financing to the customer, a practice frequently used to attract business from cash-short firms).

■ Recording revenue from gross sales when the company is an agent rather than a principal.

Examples of such practices include Imax Corp., which reported the (discounted) full amounts of minimum royalties due under 10-year or more leases of its theatre systems (in accordance with GAAP for long-term leases), leaving itself open to the possibility that customers may default on payments due in future. JetForm Corp. recognized revenue from consulting contracts on the percentage-of-completion method, although amounts billed to customers were less. Bid.Com, a firm that conducted on-line auctions as agent for the seller, included the purchase price, rather than its commission on the purchase, as revenue.

One of the problems surrounding reporting of revenue is that while a firm's revenue recognition policy must be disclosed, the disclosure standards are vague. Thus companies typically state that revenue is recognized as goods are shipped or services rendered, or that revenues on long-term contracts are recognized on a percentage-of-completion basis. These statements are sufficiently general that practices such as the above may be unknown to the market.

Required

a. To what extent can revenue growth substitute for net income as a predictor of future earning power? Explain. Use efficient securities market concepts in your answer, and consider the requirement under GAAP for immediate writeoff of research and startup costs.

b. Use the concept of relevance to defend the revenue recognition policies outlined above.

c. Use the concept of reliability to criticize the revenue recognition policies outlined above.

d. To the extent that investors are aware of the possible use of revenue recognition policies that overstate revenues (even though, for a specific firm, they may not know the extent to which that firm is using such policies), what is the effect on the operation of the capital market? Explain.

13. Zhang (2005) examined revenue recognition practices in the software industry. Software firms derive revenue from software licensing and post-contract customer support. In both cases, the point in time when significant risks and rewards of ownership are transferred to the buyer and amounts to be received can be reliably measured are unclear. Consequently, there is scope for alternative revenue recognition practices in the industry.

With respect to licensing, one alternative is to recognize revenue when the licensing contract is signed (early recognition). Another is to wait until the software is delivered to the customer, consistent with the usual sale basis of revenue recognition (late recognition). With respect to post-contract customer support, alternatives are to recognize revenue when contracts are signed (early recognition) or recognize revenue ratably over the term of the contract (late recognition).

Zhang examined a sample of 122 firms over 1987–1997, of which 22 firms were early recognizers and 93 late. He measured the relevance of a firm's quarterly revenue by its association with its share returns for the quarter. Given securities market efficiency, revenues of early recognizers should be more highly associated with their share returns than revenues of late recognizers. Zhang reported significant statistical evidence consistent with this expectation.

Zhang measured the reliability of revenue information by examining the cash flows from quarter-end accounts receivable collected over the following two quarters. Recall that in Section 3.8 we pointed out the role of accruals in anticipating future cash flows. Thus, the closer are the amounts of cash collections over these following two quarters to opening net accounts receivable, the more reliable the revenue information. Zhang found that the reliability of revenue information measured this way was significantly less for early recognizers than for late recognizers.

Combination of these two findings suggests that relevance and reliability must be traded off, since the greater relevance of early revenue recognition is accompanied by reduced reliability.

Required

a. Explain why securities market efficiency implies that revenues of early recognizers should be more highly associated with their share returns than revenues of late recognizers. In your answer, assume that information about licensing contracts becomes public information when the contract is signed.

b. Explain why the closer are cash collections for the following two quarters to opening accounts receivable, the more reliable is revenue information.

c. Do Zhang's findings imply that early revenue recognition for licensing contracts has the potential to be decision useful for investors? Use the concept of an information system (in particular, the effects of relevance and reliability on the main diagonal probabilities) in your answer.

14. What implications does estimation risk have for the working of securities markets, and for social welfare, in a capitalist economy? Explain how estimation risk can be reduced in our economy. Can estimation risk be eliminated?

Notes

1. More generally, the random fluctuation could be about a trend line. For example, the price of a security may have an upward trend over time.

2. This phenomenon, that the collective judgements of a large group can be surprisingly accurate, has been documented in numerous contexts. Surowiecki (2004) gives four conditions needed for the effect to operate: diversity of information, independence, decentralization, and aggregation.

3. In Section 3.3.2, we applied the term "informative" to the information system. An informative information system leads the decision-maker to revise his/her prior probabilities. In that context, a *fully* informative information system perfectly reveals the state of nature (see question 1 of Chapter 3). In the context of this chapter, "fully informative" applies to share price rather than to an information system, but the reasoning is similar—current share price fully reflects or, equivalently, perfectly reveals all publicly available information. Note that if share price is fully informative, the information system formed by financial statements is non-informative—it reveals nothing new about the firm since share price already reveals all. Hence the logical inconsistency—if share prices are fully informative, no one would use financial statements. But, if no one used financial statements, share prices would no longer be fully informative.

4. This abnormal return should not be confused with abnormal earnings like those of P.V. Ltd. in Example 2.2. While the idea of differing from expectations is the same, abnormal security return here refers to a *market* return, whereas abnormal earnings refer to *accounting* net income.

5. Estimating beta by least-squares regression is not inconsistent with the calculation of beta described in Section 3.7.1. The regression approach merely provides a convenient framework to carry out the estimation. To see this, note the definition of the coefficient of an independent variable in a regression model—it is the amount of change in the dependent variable (R_{jt}) for a unit change in the independent variable (R_{Mt}). This is exactly the definition of beta. As explained in Section 3.7.1, beta measures the strength of the variation in a security's return as the market return varies.

6. This view of market efficiency differs from many economic analyses, where the outside circle, which we call fundamental value, is regarded as the efficient market price, and the inside circle represents a less-than-efficient market price. In such analyses, the role of financial reporting is to improve market efficiency. We use a "two-stage" view of market efficiency because it is consistent with the definition of semi-strong efficiency given in Section 4.2.1, where efficiency is *relative to* a stock of information. This enables us to emphasize the role of financial reporting in improving the stock of information, thereby reducing adverse selection and estimation risk and improving social welfare.

7. Wurgler estimates a country's efficiency of capital allocation by the relationship between its growth in investment and its growth in output—more output from a unit of growth in investment implies higher capital allocation efficiency. He estimates the amount of firm-specific information in a country's share prices by their **synchronicity** (the extent to which share prices move together)—less synchronicity or, equivalently, less co-movement between share prices, implies more firm-specific information relative to industry- and economy-wide information. In obtaining his result, Wurgler controls for shareholder minority rights and extent of state ownership in the economy, which also affect capital allocation efficiency.

Chapter 5

The Information Approach to Decision Usefulness

Figure 5.1 Organization of Chapter 5

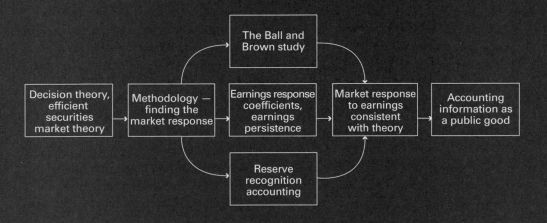

5.1 OVERVIEW

There is a saying that "the proof of the pudding is in the eating." If the efficient markets theory and the decision theories underlying it are reasonable descriptions of reality on average, we should observe the market values of securities responding in predictable ways to new information.

This leads to an examination of empirical research in accounting. Despite the difficulties of designing experiments to test the implications of decision usefulness, accounting research has established that security market prices do respond to accounting information. The first solid evidence of this security market reaction to earnings announcements was provided by Ball and Brown in 1968. Since then, a large number of empirical studies have documented additional aspects of securities market response.

On the basis of these studies, it does seem that accounting information is useful to investors in helping them estimate the expected values and risks of security returns. One has only to contemplate the use of Bayes' theorem in Example 3.1 to see that if accounting information did not have information content there would be no revision of beliefs upon receipt, hence no triggering of buy/sell decisions. Without buy/sell decisions, there would be no trading volume or price changes. In essence, information is useful if it leads investors to change their beliefs and actions. Furthermore, the degree of usefulness for investors can be measured by the extent of volume or price change following release of the information.

This equating of usefulness to information content is called the **information approach** to decision usefulness of financial reporting, an approach that has dominated financial accounting theory and research since 1968, and has only within the last few years yielded to a measurement approach, to be discussed in Chapters 6 and 7. As we have seen in Sections 3.8 and 4.8, the information approach has been adopted by major accounting standard-setting bodies. This approach takes the view that investors want to make *their* own predictions of future security returns (instead of having accountants do it for them, as under ideal conditions) and will "gobble up" all useful information in this regard. As mentioned, empirical research has shown that at least some accounting information is perceived as useful. Furthermore, the information approach implies that empirical research can help accountants to further increase usefulness by letting market response guide them as to what information is and is not valued by investors.

> The **information approach** to decision usefulness is an approach to financial reporting that recognizes individual responsibility for predicting future firm performance and that concentrates on providing useful information for this purpose. The approach assumes securities market efficiency, recognizing that the market will react to useful information from any source, including financial statements.

One must be careful, however, when equating usefulness with the extent of security price change. While investors, and accountants, may benefit from useful information, it does *not* follow that *society* will necessarily be better off. Information is a very complex commodity and its private and social values are not the same. One reason is *cost*. Financial statement users do not generally pay directly for this information. As a result, they may find information useful even though it costs society more (e.g., in the form of higher product prices to help firms pay for generating and reporting the information) than the increased usefulness is worth. Furthermore, information affects people differently, requiring complex cost–benefit tradeoffs to balance the competing interests of different constituencies.

These social considerations do not invalidate the information approach. Accountants can still strive to improve their competitive position in the information marketplace by providing useful information. And, it is still true that securities markets will work better to allocate scarce capital if security prices provide good indicators of investment opportunities. However, what accountants cannot do is claim that the best accounting policy is the one that produces the greatest market response.

Figure 5.1 outlines the organization of this chapter.

5.2 OUTLINE OF THE RESEARCH PROBLEM

5.2.1 Reasons for Market Response

We begin by reviewing the reasons why we would predict that the market price of a firm's shares will respond to its financial statement information. For most of this chapter we will confine financial statement information to reported net income. The information content of net income is a topic that has received extensive empirical investigation. Information content of other financial statement components will be discussed in Section 5.7 and in Chapter 7.

Consider the following predictions about investor behaviour, in response to financial statement information:

1. Investors have prior beliefs about a firm's future performance, that is, its dividends, cash flows, and/or earnings, which affect the expected returns and risk of the firm's shares. These prior beliefs will be based on all available information, including market price, up to just prior to the release of the firm's current net income. Even if they are based on publicly available information, these prior beliefs need not all be the same, because investors will differ in the amount of information they have obtained and in their abilities to interpret it.

2. Upon release of current year's net income, certain investors will decide to become more informed by analyzing the income number. For example, if net income is high, or higher than expected, this may be good news. If so, investors, by means of Bayes' theorem, would revise upward their beliefs about future firm performance. Other investors, who perhaps had overly high expectations for what current net income should be, might interpret the same net income number as bad news.

3. Investors who have revised their beliefs about future firm performance upward will be inclined to buy the firm's shares at their current market price, and vice versa for those who have revised their beliefs downward. Investors' evaluations of the riskiness of these shares may also be revised.

4. We would expect to observe the volume of shares traded to increase when the firm reports its net income. Furthermore, this volume should be greater the greater are the differences in investors' prior beliefs and in their interpretations of the current financial information. If the investors who interpret reported net income as good news (and hence have increased their expectations of future performance) outweigh those who interpret it as bad news, we would expect to observe an increase in the market price of the firm's shares, and vice versa.

Beaver (1968), in a classic study, examined trading volume reaction. He found a dramatic increase in volume during the week of release of earnings announcements. Further details of Beaver's findings are included in question 9 of this chapter. In the balance of this chapter we will concentrate on market price reaction. Market price reaction may provide a stronger test of decision usefulness than volume reaction. For example, the model of Kim and Verrecchia (1997) suggests that volume is noisier than price change as a measure of decision usefulness of financial statement information.

You will recognize that the preceding predictions follow the decision theory and efficient markets theory of Chapters 3 and 4 quite closely. If these theories are to have relevance to accountants, their predictions should be borne out empirically. An empirical researcher could test these predictions by obtaining a sample of firms that issue annual reports and investigating whether the volume and price reactions to good or bad news in earnings occur as the theories lead us to believe. This is not as easy as it might seem, however, for a number of reasons, as we will discuss next.

5.2.2 Finding the Market Response

1. Efficient markets theory implies that the market will react quickly to new information. As a result, it is important to know *when* current year's reported net income first became publicly known. If the researcher looked for volume and price effects even a few days too late, no effects may be observed even though they had existed.

    Researchers have solved this problem by using the date the firm's net income was reported in the financial media such as *The Wall Street Journal*. If the efficient market is going to react, it should do so in a **narrow window** of a few days surrounding this date.

2. The good or bad news in reported net income is usually evaluated relative to what investors *expected*. If a firm reported net income of, say, $2 million, and this was what investors had expected (from quarterly reports, speeches by company officials, analysts' predictions, forward-looking information in MD&A and, indeed, in share price itself), there would hardly be much information content in reported net income. Investors would have already revised their beliefs on the basis of the earlier information. Things would be different, however, if investors had expected $2 million and reported net income was $3 million. This good news would trigger rapid belief revision about the future performance of the firm. This means that researchers must obtain a proxy for what investors expected net income to be.

3. There are always many events taking place that affect a firm's share volume and price. This means that a market response to reported net income can be hard to find. For example, suppose a firm released its current year's net income, containing good news, on the same day the federal government first announced a substantial decrease in the surplus. Such a public announcement would probably affect prices of all or most securities on the market, which in turn might swamp the price impact of the firm's earnings release. Thus, it is desirable to separate the impacts of market-wide and firm-specific factors on share returns.

5.2.3 Separating Market-Wide and Firm-Specific Factors

As described in Section 4.5, the market model is widely used to *ex post* separate market-wide and firm-specific factors that affect security returns. Figure 5.2 gives a graphical illus-

Figure 5.2 Separating Market-Wide and Firm-Specific Security Returns Using the Market Model

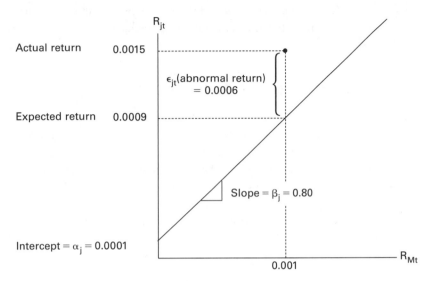

R_{Mt} = Return on market portfolio for period t
R_{jt} = Return on firm j's shares for period t

tration of the market model for firm j for period t, where we take the length of the period as one day. Longer time periods, such as a week, month, or year, and even shorter periods, are also used by researchers.

The figure shows the relationship between the return on firm j's shares and the return on the market portfolio (proxied, for example, by the Dow Jones Industrial Average index or the S&P/TSX Composite index).

Consider the equation of the market model, repeated here from Section 4.5 (Equation 4.4):

$$R_{jt} = \alpha_j + \beta_j R_{Mt} + \epsilon_{jt}$$

As described in Section 4.5, the researcher will obtain past data on R_{jt} and R_{Mt} and use regression analysis to estimate the coefficients of the model. Suppose that this yields $\alpha_j = 0.0001$ and $\beta_j = 0.80$, as shown in the figure.[1]

Now, armed with this estimate of the market model for firm j, the researcher can consult *The Wall Street Journal* to find the day of the firm's current earnings announcement. Call this day "day 0." Suppose that for day 0 the return on the Dow Jones Industrial index was 0.001.[2] Then, the estimated market model for firm j is used to predict the return on firm j's shares for this day. As shown in Figure 5.2, this expected return[3] is 0.0009. Now assume that the *actual* return on firm j's shares for day 0 is 0.0015. Then, the difference between actual and expected returns is 0.0006 (that is, $\epsilon_{jt} = 0.0006$ for this day). This 0.0006 is an estimate of the abnormal, or firm-specific, return on firm j's shares for that day.[4] This abnormal return is also interpreted as the rate of return on firm j's shares for day 0 *after removing* the influence of market-wide factors. Note that this interpretation is consistent with Example 3.3, where we separated the factors that affect share returns into market-wide and firm-specific categories. The present procedure provides an operational way to make this separation.

5.2.4 Comparing Returns and Income

The empirical researcher can now compare the abnormal share return on day 0 as calculated above with the unexpected component of the firm's current reported net income. If this unexpected net income is good news (that is, a positive unexpected net income) then, given securities market efficiency, a positive abnormal share return constitutes evidence that investors on average are reacting favourably to the unexpected good news in earnings. A similar line of reasoning applies if the current earnings announcement is bad news.

To increase the power of the investigation, the researcher may wish to also examine a few days on either side of day 0. It is possible, for example, that the efficient market might learn of the good or bad earnings news a day or two early. Conversely, positive or negative abnormal returns may continue for a day or two after day 0 while the market digests the information, although market efficiency implies that any excess returns should die out quickly. Consequently, the summing of abnormal returns for a three-to-five-day narrow window around day 0 seems more reasonable than examining day 0 only. It also helps protect against the possibility that the date of publication of current earnings in the financial media may not be a completely accurate estimate of the date of their public availability.

If positive and negative abnormal returns surrounding good or bad earnings news are found to hold across a sample of firms, the researcher may conclude that predictions based on the decision theory and efficient securities market theory are supported. This would in turn support the decision usefulness approach to financial accounting and reporting, because, if investors did not find the reported net income information useful, a market response would hardly be observed.

Of course, this methodology is not foolproof—a number of assumptions and estimations have to be made along the way. One complication is that other firm-specific information frequently comes along around the time of a firm's earnings announcement. For example, if firm j announced a stock split or a change in its dividend on the same day that it released its current earnings, it would be hard to know if a market response was due to one or the other. However, researchers can cope with this by simply removing such firms from the sample.

Another complication is the estimation of a firm's beta, needed to separate market-wide and firm-specific returns as in Figure 5.2. As mentioned, this estimation is usually based on a regression analysis of past data using the market model. Then, the estimated beta is the slope of the regression line. However, as we will discuss in Section 6.2.3, a firm's beta may change over time, for example as the firm changes its operations and/or its capital structure. If the estimated beta is different from the true beta, this affects the calculation of abnormal return, possibly biasing the results of the investigation.

There is a variety of ways to cope with this complication. For example, it may be possible to get a "second opinion" on beta by estimating it from financial statement information rather than from market data. (This is considered in Section 7.5.1.) Alternatively, beta may be estimated from a period after the earnings announcement and compared with the estimate from a period before the announcement.

Also, there are ways to separate market-wide and firm-specific returns that ignore beta. For example, we can estimate firm-specific returns by the difference between firm j's stock return during period 0 and the average return on its shares over some prior period. Or, we can take the difference between firm j's return during period 0 and the return on the market portfolio for the same period. Alternatively, as in Easton and Harris (1991), we can simply work with total share returns and not factor out market-wide returns at all.

The rationale for these simpler procedures is that there is no guarantee that the market model adequately captures the real process generating share returns—the impact of estimation risk on the CAPM was discussed in Chapter 4. To the extent that the market model does not fully capture reality, its use may introduce more error in estimating beta and abnormal returns than it reduces by removing market-wide returns and controlling for risk. A further complication is that there is a variety of market portfolio return indices available, of which the Dow Jones Industrial Average is only one. Which one should be used?

These issues were examined by Brown and Warner (1980) in a simulation study. Despite modelling and measurement problems such as those just mentioned, Brown and Warner concluded that, for monthly return windows, the market model–based procedure outlined in Section 5.2.3 performed reasonably well relative to the above alternatives. Consequently, this is the procedure we will concentrate on.

Using this procedure, it does appear that the market reacts to earnings information much as the theories predict. We will now review the first solid evidence of this reaction, the famous 1968 Ball and Brown study.

5.3 THE BALL AND BROWN STUDY

5.3.1 Methodology and Findings

In 1968, Ball and Brown (BB) began a tradition of empirical capital markets research in accounting that continues to this day. They were the first to provide convincing scientific evidence that firms' share returns respond to the information content of financial statements. This type of research is called an **event study**, since it studies the securities market reaction to a specific event, in this case a firm's release of its current net income. A review of the BB paper is worthwhile because its basic methodology, and adaptations and extensions of it, are still used. Their paper continues to provide guidance, as well as encouragement, to those who wish to better understand the decision usefulness of financial reporting.

BB examined a sample of 261 New York Stock Exchange (NYSE) firms over nine years from 1957 to 1965. They concentrated on the information content of earnings, to the exclusion of other potentially informative financial statement components such as liquidity and capital structure. One reason for this, as mentioned earlier, was that earnings for NYSE firms were typically announced in the media prior to actual release of the annual report so that it was relatively easy to determine when the information first became publicly available.

BB's first task was to measure the information content of earnings, that is, whether reported earnings were greater than what the market had expected (GN), or less than expected (BN). Of course, this requires a proxy for the market's expectation. One proxy they used was last year's actual earnings, from which it follows that unexpected earnings is simply the change in earnings.[5] Thus, firms with earnings higher than last year's were classified as GN, and firms with earnings lower than last year's were classified as BN.

The next task was to evaluate the market return on the shares of the sample firms near the time of each earnings announcement. This was done according to the abnormal returns procedure illustrated in Figure 5.2. The only difference was that BB used monthly returns (daily returns were not available on databases in 1968).

Analogously to Figure 5.2, suppose that firm j reported its 1957 earnings in February 1958, and that these earnings were GN. Suppose also that the return on the NYSE market portfolio in February 1958 was 0.001, yielding an expected firm j return of 0.0009. BB would then calculate the actual return on firm j shares for February 1958. Suppose this was 0.0015, yielding an abnormal return for February of 0.0006. Since firm j's 1957 earnings were reported in February 1958 and since its shares earned 0.0006 over and above the market in this month, one might suspect that the reason for the positive abnormal return was that investors were reacting favourably to the GN information in earnings.

The question then was: Was this pattern repeated across the sample? The answer was yes. If we take all the GN earnings announcements in the sample (there were 1,231), the *average* abnormal security market return in the month of earnings release was strongly positive. Conversely, the average abnormal return for the 1,109 bad news earnings announcements in the sample was strongly negative. This provides substantial evidence that the market did respond to the good or bad news in earnings during a narrow window consisting of the month of earnings announcement release.

An interesting and important aspect of the BB study was that they repeated their abnormal security market returns calculation for a **wide window** consisting of each of the 11 months prior to and the six months following the month of earnings release (month 0). BB calculated average abnormal returns for each month of this 18-month window. The results are shown in Figure 5.3, taken from BB.

The upper part of Figure 5.3 shows cumulative average abnormal returns for the GN earnings announcement firms in the sample; the bottom part shows the same for the BN announcement firms. As can be seen, the GN firms strongly outperformed the total sample (which approximates the market-wide return), and the BN firms strongly underperformed, over the 11-month period leading up to the month of earnings release.

5.3.2 Causation Versus Association

Note that the returns are *cumulative* in the diagram. While there was a substantial increase (for GN) and decrease (for BN) in average abnormal returns in the narrow window consisting of month 0, as described above, Figure 5.3 suggests that the market began to *anticipate* the GN or BN as much as a year early, with the result that returns accumulated steadily over the period. As can be seen, if an investor could have bought the shares of all GN firms one year before the good news was released and held them until the end of the month of release, there would have been an extra return of about 6% over and above the

Figure 5.3 Abnormal Returns for GN and BN Firms

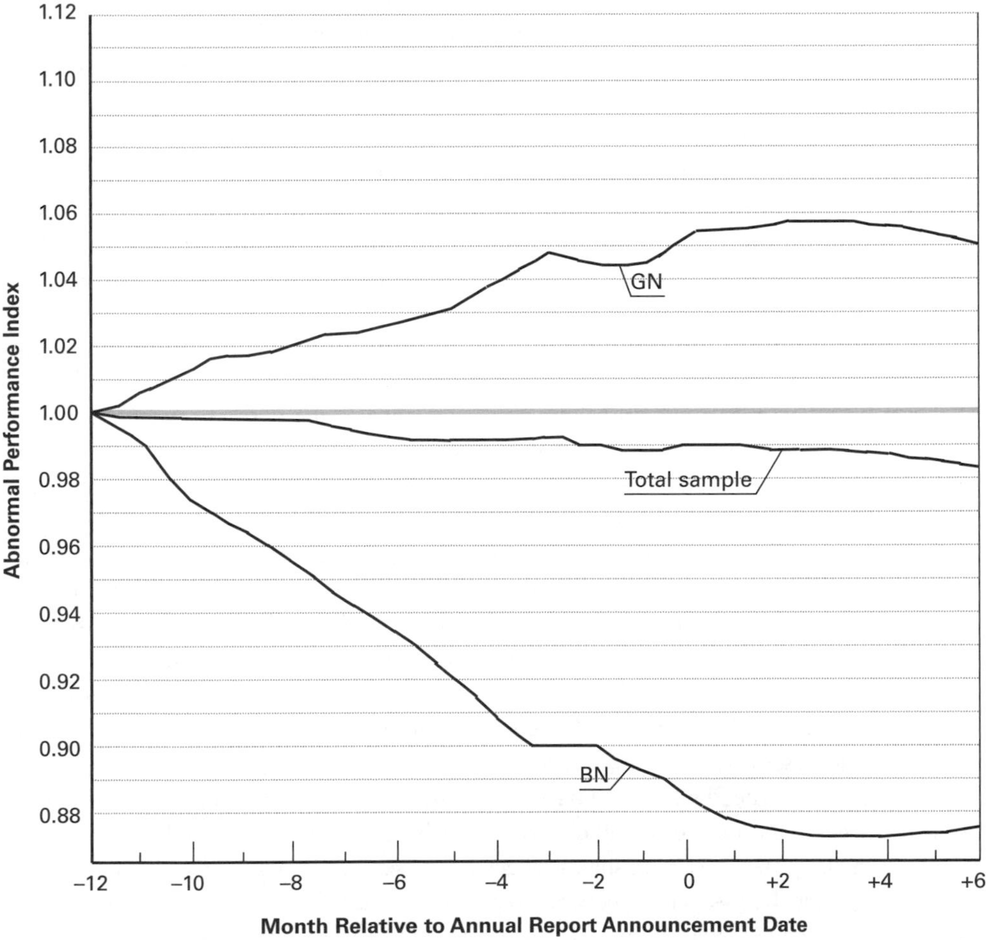

Source: Ray Ball and P. Brown, "An Empirical Evaluation of Accounting Income Numbers," *Journal of Accounting Research* (Autumn 1968), p. 169. Reprinted by permission.

market-wide return. Similarly, an abnormal loss of over 9% would have been incurred on a portfolio of BN firms bought one year before the bad news was released.[6]

This leads to an important distinction between narrow and wide window studies. If a security market reaction to accounting information is observed during a narrow window of a few days (or, in the case of BB, a month) surrounding an earnings announcement, it can be argued that the accounting information is the *cause* of the market reaction. The reason is that during a narrow window there are relatively few firm-specific events other than net income to affect share returns. Also, if other events do occur, such as stock splits or dividend announcements, the affected firms can be removed from the sample, as mentioned. Thus, a narrow-window association between security returns and accounting information suggests that accounting disclosures are the *source* of new information to investors.

Evaluation of security returns over a wide window, however, opens them up to a host of other value-relevant events. For example, a firm may have discovered new oil and gas reserves, be engaged in promising R&D projects, or have rising sales and market share. As the market learns this information from more timely sources, such as media articles, firm announcements, conditions in the economy and industry, quarterly reports, etc., share price would begin to rise. This reflects the partly informative nature of security prices since, in an efficient market, security prices reflect all available information, not just accounting information. Thus, firms that in a real sense are doing well would have much of the effect on their share prices anticipated by the efficient market before the GN appears in the financial statements. That is, because of recognition lag, *prices lead earnings* over a wide window.

Clearly, this effect was taking place in the BB study. As a result, it cannot be claimed that reported net income *causes* the abnormal returns during the 11 months leading up to month 0. The most that can be argued is that net income and returns are *associated*. That is, for wide windows, it is the real, underlying, economic performance of the firm that generates the association, since both share price and (with a lag) net income reflect real performance.

To pursue this "prices lead earnings" effect, suppose that we continue to widen the window, perhaps up to several years. We will find that the association between share returns and earnings increases as the window widens. While historical cost-based net income tends to lag behind the market in reflecting value-relevant events, as the window is widened the relative effect of the lag decreases. Over a long period of time the sum of net incomes reported over that period captures more of the effects of economic factors such as those described above, even though there may be a lag in their initial recognition. This effect was studied by Easton, Harris, and Ohlson (1992), who found that the association between security returns and historical cost-based earnings improved as the window was widened, up to 10 years. A similar effect was observed by Warfield and Wild (1992), who found that the association between security returns and earnings for annual reporting periods averaged over 10 times the association for quarterly periods.

In the long run, the total income earned by the firm, regardless of the basis of accounting, will approach total income under ideal conditions (on this point, see question 16).

But a narrow window association, as BB found for month 0, provides stronger support for decision usefulness, since it suggests that it is the accounting information that actually causes investor belief revision and hence security returns.

5.3.3 Outcomes of the BB Study

One of the most important outcomes of BB was that it opened up a large number of additional usefulness issues. A logical next step is to ask whether the *magnitude* of unexpected earnings is related to the *magnitude* of the security market response—recall that BB's analysis was based only on the *sign* of unexpected earnings. That is, the information content of earnings in BB's study was classified only into GN or BN, a fairly coarse measure.

The question of magnitude of response was investigated, for example, by Beaver, Clarke, and Wright (BCW) in 1979. They examined a sample of 276 NYSE firms with December 31 year-ends, over the 10-year period from 1965 to 1974. For each sample firm, for each year of the sample period, they estimated the unexpected earnings changes. They then used the market model procedure described in Sections 4.5 and 5.2.3 to estimate the abnormal security returns associated with these unexpected earnings changes.

Upon comparison of unexpected earnings changes with abnormal security returns, BCW found that the greater the change in unexpected earnings, the greater the security market response. This result is consistent with the CAPM (Section 4.5) and with the decision usefulness approach, since the larger are unexpected earnings changes the more investors on average will revise their estimates of future firm performance and resulting returns from their investments, other things equal.[7]

Also, since 1968, accounting researchers have studied securities market response to net income on other stock exchanges, in other countries, and for quarterly earnings reports, with similar results. The approach has been applied to study market response to the information contained in new accounting standards, auditor changes, etc. Here, however, we will concentrate on what is probably the most important extension of BB, earnings response coefficients. This line of research asks a different question than BCW, namely, for a *given* amount of unexpected earnings, is the security market response greater for some firms than for others?

5.4 EARNINGS RESPONSE COEFFICIENTS

Recall that the abnormal securities market returns identified by BB were *averages*, that is, they showed that on average their GN firms enjoyed positive abnormal returns, and negative for their BN firms. Of course, an average can conceal wide variation about the average. Thus, it is likely that some firms' abnormal returns were well above average and others' were well below.

This raises the question of *why* the market might respond more strongly to the good or bad news in earnings for some firms than for others. If answers to this question can be found, accountants can improve their understanding of how accounting information is useful to investors. This, in turn, could lead to the preparation of more useful financial statements.

Consequently, one of the most important directions that empirical financial accounting research took following the BB study was the identification and explanation of differential market response to earnings information. This is called **earnings response coefficient (ERC)** research.[8]

> An *earnings response coefficient* measures the extent of a security's abnormal market return in response to the unexpected component of reported earnings of the firm issuing that security.

5.4.1 Reasons for Differential Market Response

A number of reasons can be suggested for differential market response to reported earnings. We will review these in turn.

Beta The riskier is the sequence of a firm's future expected returns, the lower will be its value to a risk-averse investor, other things equal. For a diversified investor, the relevant risk measure of a security is its beta, explained in Section 3.7. Since investors look to current earnings as an indicator of future firm performance and share returns, the riskier these future returns are the lower investors' reactions to a given amount of unexpected earnings will be.

To illustrate, think of a typical risk-averse, rational investor whose utility increases in the expected value and decreases in the risk of the return on his or her portfolio. Suppose that the investor, upon becoming aware that a portfolio security has just released GN earnings information, revises upwards the expected rate of return on this security, and decides to buy more of it. However, if this security has high beta, this will increase portfolio risk.[9] Consequently, the investor would not buy as much more as if the security was low beta. In effect, the high beta acts as a brake on the investor's demand for the GN security. Since all risk-averse, rational, informed investors will think this way, the demand for the GN firm's shares will be lower the higher is its beta, other things equal. Of course, lower demand implies a lower increase in market price and share return in response to the GN, hence, a lower ERC.

Empirical evidence of a lower ERC for higher-beta securities was found by Collins and Kothari (1989) and by Easton and Zmijewski (1989).

Capital Structure For highly levered firms, an increase, say, in earnings (before interest) adds strength and safety to bonds and other outstanding debt, so that much of the good news in earnings goes to the debtholders rather than the shareholders. Thus, the ERC for a highly levered firm should be lower than that of a firm with little or no debt, other things equal.

Empirical evidence of a lower ERC for more highly levered firms was reported by Dhaliwal, Lee, and Fargher (1991).

Earnings Quality Recall from Section 3.3.2 that we define the quality (i.e., the informativeness) of earnings by the magnitude of the main diagonal probabilities of the associated information system. The higher these probabilities, the higher we would expect the ERC to be, since investors are better able to infer future firm performance from current performance.

As a practical matter, measurement of earnings quality is less clear, since information system probabilities are not directly observable and a sampling approach runs into problems of estimation risk due to sampling error. An indirect approach, discussed in Section 3.3.2, is to infer earnings quality by the magnitude of analysts' earnings forecast revisions following earnings announcements. However, this just raises the question of *why* analysts revise their forecasts more for some firms than others.

Fortunately, other dimensions of earnings quality are available, including the important concept of **earnings persistence**. We would expect that the ERC will be higher the more the good or bad news in current earnings is expected to persist into the future, since current earnings then provide a better indication of future firm performance. Thus, if current GN is due to the successful introduction of a new product or cost-cutting by management, the ERC should be higher than if the GN was due to, say, an unanticipated gain on disposal of plant and equipment. In the latter case, the firm's market value increases dollar-for-dollar with the amount of the gain, since there is little reason to expect the unusual gain to recur. In the new product and cost-cutting cases, the revenue increases or cost savings will persist to benefit future income statements as well, so the ERC should be higher.

Evidence that ERCs are higher the higher the persistence of unexpected current earnings changes was presented by Kormendi and Lipe (1987), whose measure of persistence was the extent to which earnings changes of the last two years continued into the current year—the greater the influence of the last two years' earnings changes on the current year's earnings change, the greater the persistence of these previous earnings.

Persistence is a challenging and useful concept. One reason, advanced by Ramakrishnan and Thomas (1991) (RT), is that different components of net income may have different persistence. For example, suppose that in the same year a firm successfully introduces a new product it also reports a gain on disposal of plant and equipment. Then, the persistence of earnings is an average of the differing persistence of the components of earnings. RT distinguish three types of earnings events:

- Permanent, expected to persist indefinitely
- Transitory, affecting earnings in the current year but not future years
- Price-irrelevant, persistence of zero

The ERCs per dollar of unexpected earnings for these are $(1 + R_f)/R_f$ (where R_f is the risk-free rate of interest under ideal conditions), 1, and 0 respectively.[10]

In effect, there are three ERCs, all of which may be present in the same income statement. RT suggest that instead of trying to estimate an average ERC, investors should attempt to identify the three types separately and assign different ERCs to each. In so doing, they can identify the firm's permanent, or persistent, earning power. This implies that accountants should provide lots of classification and detail on the income statement.

To understand the ERC for permanent earnings, note that it can be written as $1 + 1/R_f$. Thus, under ideal conditions, the market response to $1 of permanent earnings consists of the current year's installment of $1 plus the present value of the perpetuity of future installments of $1/R_f$. (This ignores riskiness of the future installments, which is appropriate if investors are risk-neutral or the permanent earnings are firm-specific.) Writing the ERC this way also shows that when earnings persist beyond the current year, the magnitude of the ERC varies inversely with the interest rate.

Another aspect of ERCs is that their persistence can depend on the firm's accounting policies. For example, suppose that a firm uses current value accounting, say for a capital asset, and that the fair value of the asset increases by $100. Assume that the increase results from an increase in the price of the product produced by the asset. Then, assuming that changes in current value are included in income, net income for the period will include[11] GN of $100. Since unexpected changes in value occur randomly, by definition, the market will not expect the $100 to persist. Thus, the ERC is 1.

Suppose instead that the firm uses historical cost accounting for the asset and that the annual increase in contribution margin is $9.09. Then there will be only $9.09 of GN in earnings this year. The reason, of course, is that under historical cost accounting the $100 increase in current value is brought into income only as it is realized. The efficient market will recognize that the current $9.09 GN is only the "first installment."[12] If it regards the value increase as permanent and $R_f = 10\%$, the ERC will be 11 (1.10/0.10).

Zero-persistence income statement components can result from choice of accounting policy. Suppose, for example, that a firm capitalizes a large amount of organization costs. This could result in GN on the current income statement, which is freed of the costs because of their capitalization. However, assuming the organization costs have no salvage value, the market would not react to the "GN," that is, its persistence is zero. As another example, suppose that a firm writes off research costs currently in accordance with GAAP. This could produce BN in current earnings. However, to the extent the market perceives the research costs as having future value, it would react positively to this BN so that persistence is negative. The possibility of zero or negative persistence suggests once more the need for detailed income statement disclosure, including a statement of accounting policies.

A second dimension of earnings quality is **accruals quality**. This approach was proposed by DeChow and Dichev (2002). They pointed out that net income is composed of:

$$\text{Net income} = \text{cash flow from operations} \pm \text{net accruals}$$

where net accruals, which can be positive or negative, include changes in non-cash working capital accounts such as receivables, allowance for doubtful accounts, inventories, accounts payable, etc., as well as amortization expense. They then argued that earnings quality depends primarily on the quality of working capital accruals, since cash flow from operations is relatively less subject to errors and manager bias, and therefore of reasonably high quality to start with.

To measure accrual quality, DeChow and Dichev suggested that to the extent current period working capital accruals show up as cash flows next period, those accruals are of high quality. This is consistent with SFAC 1, discussed in Section 3.8, where the role of accruals is envisaged as one of anticipating future cash flows. Thus, if accounts receivable at the end of the current period are $1,000, less an allowance for doubtful accounts of $100, and if $900 is collected next period, then the accounts receivable and doubtful accounts accruals are of high quality since they match perfectly with the cash subsequently collected. However, if only $800 is subsequently collected, the accruals are of lower quality since there has been an error in their estimation or, perhaps, deliberate net overstatement by management so as to increase current reported net income.

A similar argument applies to last period's accruals. Suppose, for example, that accounts receivable last period were $700, less an allowance for doubtful accounts of $60, and that they realized $600 in the current period. This lowers the quality of current accruals and earnings since current bad debts expense includes the $40 underprovision, which really belongs to last period.

To test this concept of accrual quality, DeChow and Dichev suggested estimating the following regression equation:

$$\Delta WC_t = b_0 + b_1 CFO_{t-1} + b_2 CFO_t + b_3 CFO_{t+1} + \varepsilon_t$$

where ΔWC_t is the change in net non-cash working capital for the firm in question for period t, that is, working capital accruals. For example, in our illustration above, if accounts receivable and allowance for doubtful accounts are the only non-cash working capital items, working capital has increased by $\Delta WC_t = \$260$ (i.e., $900 - $640) in period t. This is an accrual because net income includes this amount (assuming the firm recognizes income at point of sale) but it has not yet been received in cash.

CFO_{t-1} is cash flow from operations in period $t - 1$, etc., b_0, b_1, and b_2 are constants to be estimated, and ε_t is the residual error term, that is, the portion of total accruals not explained by cash from operations.

Accrual quality, hence earnings quality, is measured by the magnitude of ε_t, that is, high ε_t indicates a poor match between current accruals ΔWC_t and actual operating cash flow realizations.

Evidence that firms' ERCs and share prices respond positively to accrual quality as measured by this procedure is reported by Francis, LaFond, Olsson, and Schipper (2004 and 2005) and Ecker, Francis, Kim, Olsson, and Schipper (2006).[13]

Growth Opportunities The GN or BN in current earnings may suggest future growth prospects for the firm, and hence a higher ERC. One might think that since financial statements contain a considerable historical cost component, net income really cannot say much about the future growth of the firm. However, this is not necessarily the case. Suppose that current net income reveals unexpectedly high profitability for some of the firm's recent investment projects. This may indicate to the market that the firm will enjoy strong growth in the future. One reason, of course, is that to the extent the high profitability persists, the future profits will increase the firm's assets. In addition, success with current projects may suggest to the market that this firm is also capable of identifying and implementing additional successful projects in future, so that it becomes labelled as a growth firm. Such firms can easily attract capital and this is an additional source of growth. Thus, to the extent that current good news in earnings suggests growth opportunities, the ERC will be high.

To illustrate, extend the persistence example above by assuming that the $9.09 of current permanent earnings increase is expected to grow by 5% per year. The present value at 10% of a perpetuity that increases by 5% per year is $1/(0.10 - 0.05) = 20$, greater than $1/0.10 = 10$ under no-growth. Thus, the ERC is 21 rather than 11 as before.

Evidence that the ERC is higher for firms that the market regards as possessing growth opportunities was shown by Collins and Kothari (1989). They used the ratio of market value of equity to book value of equity as a measure of growth opportunities, the rationale being that the efficient market will be aware of the growth opportunities before they are recognized in net income and will bid up share price accordingly. Collins and Kothari find a positive relationship between this measure and the ERCs of their sample firms.

The Similarity of Investor Expectations Different investors will have different expectations of a firm's next-period earnings, depending on their prior information and the extent of their abilities to evaluate financial statement information. However, these differences will be reduced to the extent that they draw on a common information source, such as analysts' consensus forecasts, when forming their expectations. Consider a firm's announcement of its current earnings. Depending on their expectations, some investors will regard this information as GN, others as BN, hence some will be inclined to buy and some to sell. However, to the extent that investors' earnings expectations were "close together," they will put the same interpretation on the news. For example, if most investors base their earnings expectation on the analysts' consensus forecast, and current earnings are less than forecast, they will all regard this as BN and will be inclined to sell rather than buy. Thus, the more similar the earnings expectations the greater the effect of a dollar of abnormal earnings on share price. In effect, the more precise are analysts' forecasts the more similar are investors' earnings expectations and the greater the ERC, other things equal. For an analysis of conditions under which the ERC is increasing in the precision of analysts' earnings forecasts and how this precision is affected by factors such as the number of analysts forecasting the firm, see Abarbanell, Lanen, and Verrecchia (1995).

The Informativeness of Price We have suggested on several previous occasions that market price itself is partially informative about the future value of the firm. In particular, price is informative about (i.e., leads) earnings. Recall that the reason is that market price aggregates all publicly known information about the firm, much of which the accounting system recognizes with a lag. Consequently, the more informative is price, the less will be the information content of current accounting earnings, other things equal, hence the lower the ERC.

A proxy for the informativeness of price is *firm size*, since larger firms are more in the news. However, Easton and Zmijewski (1989) found that firm size was not a significant explanatory variable for the ERC. The reason is probably that firm size proxies for other firm characteristics, such as risk and growth, as much as it proxies for the informativeness of share price. Once these factors are controlled for, any significant effect of size on the ERC seems to go away. Collins and Kothari (1989) dealt with size by moving the wide window over which security returns were measured earlier in time for large firms, on the grounds that share price is more informative for such firms. They found that this substantially improved the relationship between changes in earnings and security returns, since a more informative share price implies that the market anticipates changes in earning power sooner. Once this time shifting was done, size appeared to have no explanatory power for the ERC.

5.4.2 Implications of ERC Research

Be sure that you see the reason *why* accountants should be interested in the market's response to financial accounting information. Essentially, the reason is that improved understanding of market response suggests ways that they can further improve the decision usefulness of financial statements. For example, lower informativeness of price for smaller firms implies that expanded disclosure for these firms would be useful for investors, contrary to a common argument that larger firms should have greater reporting responsibilities.

Also, the finding that ERCs are lower for highly levered firms supports arguments to expand disclosure of the nature and magnitude of financial instruments, including those that are off-balance-sheet. If the relative size of a firm's liabilities affects the market's response to net income, then it is desirable that all liabilities be disclosed.

The importance of growth opportunities to investors suggests, for example, the desirability of disclosure of segment information, since profitability information by segments would better enable investors to isolate the profitable, and unprofitable, operations of the firm. Also, MD&A enables the firm to communicate its growth prospects, as illustrated in Section 4.8.2.

Finally, the importance of earnings persistence to the ERC means that disclosure of the *components* of net income is useful for investors. In sum, lots of detail in the income statement, the balance sheet, and in supplemental information helps investors interpret the current earnings number.

5.4.3 Measuring Investors' Earnings Expectations

As mentioned previously, researchers must obtain a proxy for expected earnings, since the efficient market will only react to that portion of an earnings announcement that it did not expect. If a reasonable proxy is not obtained, the researcher may fail to identify a market reaction when one exists, or may incorrectly conclude that a market reaction exists when it does not. Thus, obtaining a reasonable estimate of earnings expectations is a crucial component of information approach research.

Under the ideal conditions of Example 2.2, expected earnings is simply accretion of discount on opening firm value. When conditions are not ideal, however, earnings expectations are more complex. One approach is to project the time series formed by the firm's past reported net incomes, that is, to base future expectations on past performance. A reasonable projection, however, depends on earnings persistence. To see this, consider the extremes of 100% persistent earnings and zero persistent earnings. If earnings are completely persistent, expected earnings for the current year are just last year's actual earnings. Then, unexpected earnings are estimated as the *change* from last year. This approach was used by Ball and Brown, as described in Section 5.3. If earnings are of zero persistence, then there is no information in last year's earnings about future earnings, and all of current earnings are unexpected. That is, unexpected earnings are equal to the *level* of current year's earnings. This approach was used by Bill Cautious in Example 3.1.

Which extreme is closer to the truth? This can be evaluated by the degree of correlation between security returns and the estimate of unexpected earnings, a question examined by Easton and Harris (1991). Using regression analysis of a large sample of U.S. firms over the period 1969–1986, they documented a correlation between one-year security returns and the change in net income, consistent with the approach of Ball and Brown. However, there was an even stronger correlation between returns and the level of net income. Furthermore, when both earnings changes and levels were used, the two variables combined did a significantly better job of predicting returns than either variable separately. These results suggest that the truth is somewhere in the middle, that is, both changes in and levels of net income are components of the market's earnings expectations, where the relative weights on the two components depend on earnings persistence.

The foregoing discussion is based solely on a time series approach, however. Another source of earnings expectations is analysts' forecasts. These are now widely available for most large firms. If analysts' forecasts are more accurate than time series forecasts, they provide a better estimate of earnings expectations, since rational investors will presumably use the most accurate forecasts. Evidence by Brown, Hagerman, Griffin, and Zmijewski (1987), who studied the quarterly forecasting performance of one forecasting organization (Value Line), suggests that analysts outperform time series models in terms of accuracy. O'Brien (1988) also found that analysts' quarterly earnings forecasts were more accurate than time series forecasts. These results are what we would expect, since analysts can bring to bear information beyond that contained in past earnings when making their earnings projections.

When more than one analyst follows the same firm, it seems reasonable to take the consensus, or average, forecast as the proxy for the market's earnings expectation, following the reasoning underlying the football forecasting example of Section 4.2.2. O'Brien pointed out, however, that the age of a forecast has an important effect on its accuracy. She found that the single most recent earnings forecast provided a more accurate earnings prediction in her sample than the average forecast of all analysts following the firm, where the average ignored how old the individual forecasts were. This suggests that the timeliness of a forecast dominates the cancelling-out-of-errors effect of the average forecast.

Despite evidence that analysts' forecasts tend to be more accurate than forecasts based on time series, other evidence, discussed by Kothari (2001), suggests that analysts' forecasts are optimistically biased, although the bias may have decreased in recent years. Nevertheless, recent studies of the information content of earnings tend to base earnings expectations on analysts' forecasts.

Theory in Practice 5.1

Cisco Systems Inc. is a large provider of networking equipment, based in San Jose, California. In August 2004, it released financial results for the quarter ended July 30, 2004. Its revenues increased by 26% over the same quarter of 2003. Its net income for the quarter was $1.4 billion or 21 cents per share, a 41% increase over the same quarter of 2003, and 5% in excess of the average analysts' forecast of 20 cents.

Yet, Cisco's share price fell almost 18% to $18.29 following the announcement. This fall in price seems contrary to the results of Ball and Brown and subsequent researchers, who have documented a positive market response to good earnings news. However, certain balance sheet and supplemental information was not so favourable. For example, inventory turnover declined to 6.4 from 6.8 in 2003, gross margin declined slightly, order backlog was down and, while revenue was growing, its rate of growth appeared to be declining. Also, several analysts commented on an increase in inventories, suggesting lower earnings persistence and accrual quality to the extent these inventories would be slow in selling. Furthermore, Cisco's CEO, commenting on the quarter's results, mentioned that the firm's customers were becoming more cautious about spending.

These negative signals implied low quality and negative persistence for the good earnings news, probably compounded by very similar investor expectations. The result was a negative ERC.

5.4.4 Summary

The information content of reported net income can be measured by the extent of security price change or, more specifically, by the size of the security's abnormal market return, around the time the market learns the current net income. This is because rational, informed investors will revise their expectations about future firm performance and share returns on the basis of current earnings information. Revised beliefs trigger buy/sell decisions, as investors move to restore the risk–return tradeoffs in their portfolios to desired levels. If there was no information content in net income there would be no belief revision, no resulting buy/sell decisions, and hence no associated price changes.

For a given amount of unexpected net income, the extent of security price change or abnormal returns depends on factors such as firm size, capital structure, risk, growth prospects, persistence, the similarity of investor expectations, and earnings quality.

Following the pioneering study of Ball and Brown, empirical research has demonstrated a differential market response depending on most of these factors. These empirical results are really quite remarkable. First, they have overcome substantial statistical and experimental design problems. Second, they show that the market is, on average, very sophisticated in its ability to evaluate accounting information. This supports the theory of securities market efficiency and the decision theories that underlie it. Finally, they support the decision usefulness approach to financial reporting.

Indeed, the extent to which historical cost-based net income can provide "clues" about future firm performance may seem surprising. The key, of course, is the information system probabilities, as shown in Table 3.2. In effect, the higher the main diagonal probabilities, the greater we would expect the ERC to be. This supports the FASB's contention in its Conceptual Framework that investors' expectations are based "at least partly on evaluations of past enterprise performance" (Section 3.8). As accountants gain a better understanding of investor response to financial statement information, their ability to provide useful information to investors will further increase.

5.5 UNUSUAL, NON-RECURRING, AND EXTRAORDINARY ITEMS

In Section 5.4.1, we mentioned Ramakrishnan and Thomas' (1991) suggestion that investors separately estimate permanent, transitory, and price-irrelevant components of earnings. An interesting example of the importance of earnings persistence can be found in the reporting of events that are unusual and/or infrequent. Since these items may not recur regularly, their persistence will be transitory or price-irrelevant. This means that they must be fully disclosed; otherwise, the market may get an exaggerated impression of earnings persistence.

For accounting standards on the reporting of **extraordinary items**, we consider Section 3480 of the *CICA Handbook*. In 1989, Section 3480 was revised to introduce greater consistency in the reporting of extraordinary items on the income statement. According to paragraph 3480.02:

> *Extraordinary items* are items that result from transactions or events that have all of the following characteristics:
> (a) they are not expected to occur frequently over several years;
> (b) they do not typify the normal business activities of the entity; and
> (c) they do not depend primarily on decisions or determinations by management or owners.

The last characteristic in the definition was added in the 1989 revision. Prior to that time, only the first two characteristics applied. The result was to eliminate a large number of former extraordinary items such as, for example, gains or losses on disposals of capital assets. After 1989 such unusual and non-recurring gains or losses would be included *before* income from continuing operations, since management controls the timing of such transactions.

This revision was designed to resolve the issue of **classificatory smoothing**, whereby management could smooth (or otherwise manage) earnings from continuing operations by choosing to classify unusual items above or below the operating earnings line. Evidence that managers in the United States, prior to 1989, behaved as if they smoothed earnings from continuing operations by means of classificatory smoothing was reported by Barnea, Ronen, and Sadan (1976). By requiring those unusual items whose amounts and/or timing could be controlled by management to be consistently reported as part of operating income, the 1989 revision effectively eliminated the ability to engage in classificatory smoothing. It therefore appeared that the new Section 3480 represented an improvement in financial reporting.

However, the nature of the improvement can be questioned, based on the ERC research outlined in Section 5.4. Specifically, unusual items have low persistence. For example, a gain on sale of capital assets would have persistence of 1 or less. Other unusual items could have persistence as low as zero, to the extent that they are not value-relevant at all.

The impact of the 1989 revisions to Section 3480 caused a number of low-persistence, unusual, and non-recurring items to move from extraordinary items up to the operating section of the income statement. The income statement format following from Section 3480 is summarized as follows (we ignore income taxes for simplicity):

Net income before unusual and non-recurring items, also called core earnings	x x
Unusual and non-recurring items	<u>x x</u>
Income from continuing operations, also called operating income	x x
Extraordinary items	<u>x x</u>
Net income	<u>x x</u>

Core earnings represents the persistent component of income, and is the basis of investors' estimates of future earning power. Unusual and non-recurring items are items that do not qualify as extraordinary items under Section 3480. As mentioned, they are of low persistence, by definition.

We can now see two related problems arising from the 1989 revisions to Section 3480. First, if unusual and non-recurring items are not fully disclosed, investors may overestimate the persistence of operating income, although Section 1520 and, more recently, Section 1400 of the *Handbook* do require disclosure of these items. Second, and of greater concern, the amounts and timing of the recording of unusual and non-recurring items are subject to strategic manipulation by management. For example, if management chooses to recognize an unusual loss currently, income from continuing operations is reduced. Furthermore, if the loss had been building up for some time, earnings of previous periods are, in retrospect, overstated. More serious, management may overstate the amount of the loss—the amounts of many losses, such as a writedown of the value of property, plant, and equipment, are highly subjective and difficult for investors to verify. Then, by excessively relieving *future* periods of charges for amortization, core earnings in future years are over-stated. There is no requirement under current GAAP to separate out the effects of prior writedowns from core earnings.[14] Thus, the accounting for unusual and non-recurring items has the potential to confuse the evaluation of earnings persistence.

These issues were investigated by Elliott and Hanna (1996), who found a significant decline in the core earnings ERC in quarters following the reporting of a large unusual item (usually, these were losses rather than gains). Furthermore, the ERC declined further if the firm reported numerous large special items over time. This latter evidence is consistent with the market interpreting the frequency of recording of unusual and non-recurring items as a proxy for their potential misuse. We will return to the impact of extraordinary, unusual, and non-recurring items on core earnings in our discussion of earnings management in Chapter 11.

Thus, the question appears to be open whether Section 3480 actually succeeded in improving financial reporting. From our standpoint, however, Section 3480 represents an interesting example of how theory can be brought to bear to reexamine an issue that was thought resolved.

Theory in Practice 5.2

As a result of the September 11 terrorist attacks in the United States, numerous companies incurred substantial expenses and revenue losses. For example, airlines were unable to fly for two days.

In the United States, accounting standards for extraordinary items are similar to those given above for Canada. In a 2001 news release, the FASB decided against allowing costs resulting from the attacks to be treated as extraordinary items. The FASB had originally considered allowing at least some costs as extraordinary, but came to the conclusion that it would be impossible to reliably separate direct costs (e.g., airlines' losses of revenue during the two-day shutdown) from indirect costs (e.g., continuing loss of customers from public concerns about safety, and general loss of business and consumer confidence). Also, some of these costs would be recovered through insurance and government assistance. Consequently, the FASB concluded that all costs resulting from September 11 be classified as part of income from continuing operations, with any government assistance also reported in continuing operations, as a separate line item.

In this regard, *The Globe and Mail*, in an October 29, 2001, article, quoted Patricia O'Malley, a prominent Canadian accountant and member of the International Accounting Standards Board, as saying, "Given the world we live in, it would be hard to call them extraordinary."

5.6 A CAVEAT ABOUT THE "BEST" ACCOUNTING POLICY

To this point, we have argued that accountants can be guided by securities market reaction in determining usefulness of financial accounting information. From this, it is tempting to conclude that the best accounting policy is the one that produces the greatest market price response. For example, if net income reported by oil and gas firms under successful-efforts accounting produces a greater market reaction than net income reported under full-cost accounting, successful-efforts should be used, because investors find it more useful.

However, we must be extremely careful about this conclusion. Accountants may be better off to the extent that they provide useful information to investors, but it does not follow that *society* will necessarily be better off.

The reason is that information has characteristics of a **public good**. A public good is a good such that consumption by one person does not destroy it for use by another. Consumption of a **private good**—such as an apple—eliminates its usefulness for other consumers. However, an investor can use the information in an annual report without eliminating its usefulness to other investors. Consequently, suppliers of public goods may have trouble charging for these products, so that we often witness them being supplied by governmental or quasi-governmental agencies—roads and national defence, for example. If a firm tried to charge investors for its annual report, it would probably not attract many customers, because a single annual report, once produced, could be downloaded to many users. Instead, we observe governments through securities legislation and corporations acts, *requiring* firms to issue annual reports.

Of course, firms' annual reports are not "free." Production of annual reports is costly. Other, more significant, costs include the disclosure of valuable information to competitors and the likelihood that manager operating decisions will be affected by the amount of information about those decisions that has to be released. For example, managers may curtail plans for expansion if too much information about them has to be disclosed. Investors will eventually pay for these costs through higher product prices. Nevertheless, investors perceive annual reports as free, since the extent to which they use them will not affect the product prices they pay. Also, investors may incur costs to inform themselves, either directly, or indirectly by paying for analyst or other information services. Nevertheless, the basic "raw material" is perceived as free and investors will do what any other rational consumer will do when prices are low—consume more of it. As a result, *investors may perceive accounting information as useful even though from society's standpoint the costs of this information outweigh the benefits to investors.*

Also, as mentioned in Chapter 1, information affects different people differently. Thus, information may be useful to potential investors and competitors but current shareholders may be harmed by supplying it. As a result, the social value of such information depends on both the benefits to potential investors and competitors, and the costs to shareholders. Such cost–benefit tradeoffs are extremely difficult to make.

Think of information as a commodity, demanded by investors and supplied by firms through accountants. Because of the public-good aspect of information, we cannot rely on the forces of demand and supply to produce the socially "right" or first-best amount of production, as we can for private goods produced under competition. The essential reason is that the price system does not, and probably cannot, operate to charge investors the full costs of the information they use. Consequently, from a social perspective we cannot rely on the extent of security market response to tell us which accounting policies should be used (or, equivalently, "how much" information to produce). Formal arguments to support this conclusion were given by Gonedes and Dopuch (1974).

We will return to the question of regulation of information production in Chapters 12 and 13. For now, the point to realize is that it is still true that accountants can be guided by market response to maintain and improve their competitive position as suppliers to the marketplace for information. It is also true that securities markets will work better to the extent security prices provide good indications of underlying real investment opportunities. However, these social considerations do suggest that, as a general rule, accounting standard-setting bodies should be wary of using securities market response to guide their decisions.

Interestingly, an exception to this rule seems to have occurred with respect to standard setters' decisions to eliminate current cost accounting for capital assets. SFAS 33, which required U.S. firms to report supplemental current cost information for certain assets, was discontinued in 1986. Discontinuance was based in part on the influential study by Beaver and Landsman (1983), who failed to find any incremental securities market reaction to current cost information over and above the information content of historical cost-based net income.[15] In Canada, Hanna, Kennedy, and Richardson (1990) recommended the discontinuance of Section 4510 of the *CICA Handbook*, which laid down procedures for supplemental current cost disclosures for capital assets. They were unable to find evidence of usefulness of this information and the section was withdrawn in 1992. It is difficult to disagree with decisions to cease production of information that no one finds useful. Nevertheless, from a social perspective, no one knows whether this decision was correct, due to the difficulties of measuring social costs and benefits.

5.7 THE INFORMATION CONTENT OF OTHER FINANCIAL STATEMENT INFORMATION

In this section we depart from our concentration on the information content of net income in order to consider the informativeness of other financial statement components, such as the balance sheet and supplementary information.

Overall, it has been difficult to find direct evidence of usefulness of other financial statement information, unlike the impressive evidence of market reaction to earnings described earlier. Despite the relevance of RRA information (Section 2.4), studies by Magliolo (1986) and Doran, Collins, and Dhaliwal (1988) were unable to find more than a weak market reaction to RRA. Boone (2002) reported a stronger market reaction to RRA information than to historical cost-based information, and argued that the relatively weak reaction reported by earlier researchers is due to statistical problems in their methodology. However, it seems that the question of whether or not RRA provides useful information is open.

Low reliability is one possible explanation for these mixed results, of course. Another possibility is that RRA is pre-empted by more timely sources of reserves information, such as announcements of discoveries, and analyst forecasts. Also, the point in time that the market first becomes aware of the RRA information is often unclear. For net income, media publication of the earnings announcement provides a reasonable event date. However, given the inside nature of oil and gas reserves information and its importance to firm value, analysts and others may work particularly hard to ferret it out in advance of the annual report. If a reasonable event date for the release of other financial statement information cannot be found, return studies must use wide windows, which are open to a large number of influences on price in addition to accounting information.

However, there is an indirect approach to finding evidence of usefulness that links other information to the quality of earnings. To illustrate, suppose that an oil company reports high earnings this year, but supplemental oil and gas information shows that its reserves have declined substantially over the year. An interpretation of this information is that the firm has used up its reserves to increase sales in the short run. If so, the quality of current earnings is reduced, since they contain a non-persistent component that will dissipate if new reserves are not found. Then, the market's reaction to the bad news in the supplemental reserve information may be more easily found in a low ERC than in a direct reaction to the reserve information itself. Conversely, a higher ERC would be expected if reserves had increased.

This approach was generalized by Lev and Thiagarajan (1993) (LT). They identified 12 "fundamentals" used by financial analysts in evaluating earnings quality. For example, one fundamental was the change in inventories, relative to sales. If inventories increase, this may suggest a decline in earnings quality—the firm may be entering a period of low sales, or simply be managing its inventories less effectively. Other fundamentals include change in capital expenditures, order backlog, and, in the case of an oil and gas company, the change in its reserves.

For each firm in their sample, LT calculated a measure of earnings quality by assigning a score of 1 or 0 to each of that firm's 12 fundamentals, then adding the scores. For example, for inventories, a 1 is assigned if that firm's inventories, relative to sales, are down for the year, suggesting higher earnings quality, and a 0 score is assigned if inventories are up.

When LT added these fundamental scores as an additional explanatory variable in an ERC regression analysis, there was a substantial increase in ability to explain abnormal security returns beyond the explanatory power of unexpected earnings alone. This suggests that the market, aided perhaps by analysts, is quite sophisticated in its use of balance sheet and supplementary information. Instead of a direct reaction to this information, it seems to use it to augment the information content of earnings.

5.8 CONCLUSIONS ON THE INFORMATION APPROACH

The empirical literature in financial accounting is vast, and we have looked only at certain parts of it. Nevertheless, we have seen that, for the most part, the securities market response to reported net income is impressive in terms of its sophistication. Results of empirical research in this area support the efficient markets theory and underlying decision theories.

The market does not seem to respond to other financial statement information as strongly as it does to earnings information. The extent to which the lack of strong market response to this other information is due to methodological difficulties, to low reliability, to availability of alternative information sources, or to failure of efficient markets theory itself is not fully understood, although it may be that investors anticipate balance sheet and supplementary information to fine-tune the ERC, rather than using such information directly.

As stated earlier, the approach to financial accounting theory that equates the extent of security price change with information content and hence with decision usefulness is known as the information approach. The essence of this approach is that investors are viewed as attempting to predict future returns from their investments. They seek all relevant information in this regard, not just accounting information. To maximize their competitive position as suppliers of information, accountants may then seek to use the extent of security market response to various types of accounting information as a guide to its usefulness to investors. This motivates their interest in empirical research on decision usefulness. Furthermore, the more information accountants can move from inside to outside the firm, the better can capital markets guide the flow of scarce investment funds.

Despite these considerations, accountants must be careful of concluding that the accounting policies and disclosures that produce the greatest market response are the best for society. This is not necessarily true, due to the public-good nature of accounting information. Investors will not necessarily demand the "right" amount of information, since they do not bear its full costs. These concerns limit the ability of decision usefulness research to guide accounting standard setters.

Nevertheless, until relatively recently, the information approach has dominated financial accounting theory and research, beginning with the Ball and Brown paper of 1968. It has led to a tremendous amount of empirical investigation that has enriched our understanding of the decision usefulness of accounting information for investors.

Questions and Problems

1. Explain the information approach to financial reporting. Does it rely on the historical cost basis of accounting?

2. Refer to the separation of market-wide and firm-specific security returns as shown in Figure 5.2. What factors could reduce the accuracy of the estimate of abnormal returns? (CGA-Canada)

3. Explain why the market might begin to anticipate the GN or BN in earnings as much as a year in advance, as Ball and Brown found in Figure 5.3. (CGA-Canada)

4. Give examples of components of net income with:

   a. High persistence

   b. Persistence of 1

   c. Persistence of 0 (CGA-Canada)

5. Explain why it is desirable to find the exact time that the market first became aware of an item of accounting information if any security price reaction to this information is to be detected. Can such a time always be found? Explain why or why not. What can researchers do when the exact time cannot be isolated? (CGA-Canada)

6. Is a negative ERC possible? Explain why or why not.

7. A researcher finds evidence of a security price reaction to an item of accounting information during a narrow window of three days surrounding the date of release of this information and claims that it was the accounting information that caused the security price reaction. Another researcher finds evidence of security price reaction to a different item of accounting information during a wide window beginning 12 months prior to the release of the financial statements containing that item. This researcher does not claim that the accounting information caused the security price reaction but only that the information and the market price reaction were associated.

   Explain why one can claim causation for a narrow window but not for a wide window. Which price reaction constitutes the stronger evidence for usefulness of accounting information? Explain.

8. XYZ Ltd. is a large retail company listed on a major stock exchange, and its reported net income for the year ended December 31, 2009, is $5 million. The earnings were announced to the public on December 31, 2009.

   Financial analysts had predicted the company's net income for 2009 to be $7 million. The financial analysts' prediction of $7 million net income was in effect up until the release of the 2009 earnings on December 31, 2009.

   Assumptions

   ■ No other news about XYZ Ltd. was released to the public on December 31, 2009.

   ■ No significant economy-wide events affecting share prices occurred on December 31, 2009.

   ■ Financial analysts' forecasts about XYZ Ltd.'s net income represented the market's expectations about XYZ Ltd.'s income.

   Required

   a. Would you expect a change in price of XYZ Ltd.'s common stock on December 31, 2009? If so, why? Explain.

   b. Consider the two situations below:

      i. The deviation of forecasted earnings from actual earnings of $2 million (i.e., $7 million − $5 million) is completely accounted for by the closing down of a number of its retail outlets.

      ii. The deviation of the forecasted earnings from actual earnings of $2 million is completely accounted for by a fire in XYZ Ltd.'s largest retail outlet, which had caused the outlet to be closed temporarily for six months.

In which of these two scenarios would you expect the price change of XYZ Ltd.'s common stock to be greater? Explain.

9. In a classic study, Beaver (1968) examined the trading volume of firms' securities around the time of their earnings announcements. Specifically, he examined 506 annual earnings announcements of 143 NYSE firms over the years 1961–1965 inclusive (261 weeks).

   For each earnings announcement, Beaver calculated the average daily trading volume (of the shares of the firm making that announcement) for each week of a 17-week window surrounding week 0 (the week in which the earnings announcement was made). For each firm in the sample, he also calculated the average daily trading volume outside its 17-week window. This was taken as the normal trading volume for that firm's shares.

   For each week in the 17-week window, Beaver averaged the trading volumes over the 506 earnings announcements in the sample. The results are shown in Figure 5.4 below. The dotted line in the figure shows the average normal trading volume outside the 17-week window.

   As can be seen from the figure, there was a dramatic increase in trading volume, relative to normal, in week 0. Also, volume is below normal during most of the weeks leading up to week 0.

Figure 5.4 Volume Analysis

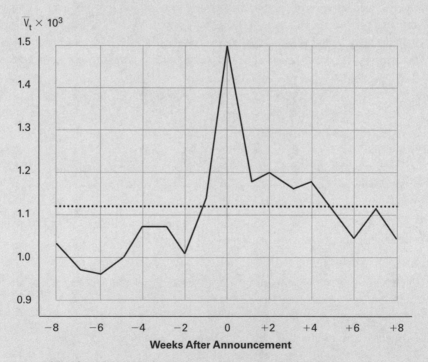

Source: W. Beaver, "The Information Content of Annual Earnings Announcements," *Journal of Accounting Research*, Supplement, 1968: 67–92. Reprinted by permission.

Required

a. Why do you think trading volume increased in week 0?

b. Why do you think trading volume was below normal in the weeks leading up to week 0?

c. Do Beaver's volume results support the decision usefulness of earnings information? Explain.

d. Which is the better indicator of decision usefulness, the abnormal return measure (Figure 5.2) or the volume measure? Explain. (CGA-Canada)

10. Discuss the impact of firm size on the ERC.

11. X Ltd. is a growth firm that uses very conservative accounting policies. Y Ltd. is growing more slowly and uses current value accounting for its capital assets and related amortization.
    Otherwise, X Ltd. and Y Ltd. are quite similar. They are the same size and have similar capital structures and similar betas.

Required

a. Both X Ltd. and Y Ltd. report the same GN in earnings this year. Which firm would you expect to have the greater security market response (ERC) to this good earnings news? Explain.

b. Suppose that X Ltd. had a much higher debt-to-equity ratio and beta than Y Ltd. Would your answer to part **a** change? Explain.

12. On the basis of the empirical evidence presented in this chapter, do you feel the FASB is correct in its claim in SFAC 1 (see Section 3.8) that investors' expectations about future enterprise performance "are commonly based at least partly on evaluations of past enterprise performance?" Explain.

13. By defining extraordinary items to be infrequent, not typical of normal business activities, and not depending on management decision, Section 3480 of the *CICA Handbook* greatly increases the need for adequate disclosure of the components of reported net income. Explain why.

14. Explain why financial statement information has characteristics of a public good. Include a definition of a public good in your answer. What does this imply about using the *extent* of security market reaction to accounting information to guide accountants? Standard setters?

15. You estimate empirically the ERC of firm J as 0.38. Firm K is identical to firm J in terms of size, earning power, persistence of earnings, and risk. Unlike firm J, however, firm K includes a high-quality financial forecast in its MD&A. You estimate firm K's ERC as 0.57. Which firm's net income report appears to be more useful to investors? Explain. Does this mean that all firms should be required to prepare high-quality financial forecasts? Explain.

16. It is important to realize that different bases of accounting, such as current value accounting and historical cost-based accounting, do not affect total earnings over the life of the firm, but only the *timing* of the recognition of those earnings. In effect, over the life of the firm, the firm "earns what it earns," and different bases of accounting will all produce earnings that add up to this total.

If this is so, then we would expect that the greater the number of time periods over which we aggregate a firm's historical cost earnings, the closer the resulting total will be to economic earnings, that is, the earnings total that would be produced over the same periods under ideal conditions.

This was studied by Easton, Harris, and Ohlson (1992) (EHO) and by Warfield and Wild (1992) (WW). EHO proxied economic income by the return on the firm's shares on the securities market. When this return was aggregated over varying periods of time (up to 10 years) and compared with aggregate historical cost-based earnings returns for similar periods, the comparison improved as the time period lengthened. WW studied a similar phenomenon for shorter periods. They found, for example, that the association between economic and accounting income for quarterly time periods was on average about 1/10 of their association for an annual period, consistent with mixed measurement model-based net income lagging behind economic income in its recognition of relevant economic events.

Required

a. In Example 2.1, calculate net income for years 1 and 2 assuming that P.V. Ltd. uses historical cost accounting with straight-line amortization for its capital asset, while retaining all other assumptions. Verify that total net income over the two-year life of P.V. Ltd. equals the total economic net income that P.V. Ltd. would report using present value amortization.

b. Do the same in Example 2.2, assuming that the state realization is bad and good in years 1 and 2 respectively.

c. Use the fact that accruals reverse to explain why total net income over the two years in parts **a** and **b** above are the same under economic and straight-line amortization. Are these results consistent with the empirical results of EHO and WW outlined above?

17. On May 8, 2001, the *Financial Post* reported "The Street Turns Against Canadian Tire." Canadian Tire Corporation, Ltd.'s share price had risen by $0.75 to $24.90 on May 2, 2001, following a news release in which Wayne Sales, president and CEO at the time, said "We are pleased with our ability to deliver double digit growth...." Canadian Tire's reported earnings of $0.37 per share exceeded analysts' expectations.

The market soon learned, however, that reported earnings included an $8 million one-time gain on sale of certain Canadian Tire assets. Without this gain, earnings were $0.29 per share, 6% below earnings for the same quarter of 2000. Canadian Tire's share price quickly fell back to $22.95.

The *Post* reported that "passing off" a one-time gain as part of operating earnings "didn't fool or impress analysts" and is something they "hoped not to see again."

Required

a. Use efficient securities market theory to explain the rise in Canadian Tire's share price on May 2, 2001, and the rapid subsequent fall in share price.

b. Was Canadian Tire correct in including the $8 million one-time gain in operating income? Explain.

c. Evaluate the persistence of Canadian Tire's reported net income of $0.37 per share (no calculations required). Does the fact of Mr. Sales' ignoring of this item in his press release affect your evaluation? Explain why or why not.

18. On October 19, 2000, *The Globe and Mail* reported on Imperial Oil Ltd.'s earnings for the third quarter ended on September 30, 2000, released on October 18. Net income was a record $374 million, up from $191 million for the same quarter of the previous year. Return on equity was 25.7%, up from 10.1% a year earlier. Earnings for the quarter included a $60 million gain on Imperial's sale of its Cynthia pipeline and other assets. Cash flow for the quarter was $433 million, up from $270 million in the previous year's third quarter. The reported profit of $374 million was in line with analysts' expectations.

On October 18, the TSE oil and gas index rose by 0.6%, as the market anticipated higher prices for oil and gas. Yet, Imperial's share price fell on the day by $1.25, to close at $37.35. *The Globe and Mail* also reported analysts' comments about a widening discount for heavy crude oil, relative to light crude. Imperial is Canada's biggest producer of heavy crude. Also, Imperial's production from its oil sands projects declined in the quarter, due to maintenance and temporary production problems.

Required

a. Use the market model to calculate the abnormal return, relative to the TSE oil and gas index, on Imperial Oil's shares for October 18, 2000. Imperial Oil's beta is approximately 0.65. The risk-free interest rate at this time was approximately 0.0002 per day. Note the theoretical relationship $\alpha_j = R_f (1 - \beta_j)$.

b. Is the abnormal decline in Imperial's share price on October 18 consistent with efficient securities market theory? Explain why or why not. Consider earnings persistence in your answer.

c. In what section of the income statement should the $60 million gain on the sale of the Cynthia pipeline be reported? Explain.

19. Refer to Theory in Practice 5.2 in Section 5.5 concerning the September 11 terrorist attacks in the United States.

Required

a. Do you agree that the costs resulting from September 11 are not extraordinary items? Explain why or why not.

b. Evaluate the persistence (in words—no calculations required) of these costs.

c. From the standpoint of efficient markets theory, how should these costs be disclosed? Does it matter whether or not they are classified as extraordinary?

20. On October 21, 2004, Abitibi-Consolidated Inc., a large Canadian-based newsprint and groundwood producer, reported income from continuing operations for its third quarter, 2004, of $182 million, or $0.41 per share. This compares with a net loss from continuing operations for the same quarter of 2003 of $70 million, or $0.16 per share. Sales for the quarter were $1,528 million, and core earnings (i.e., excluding unusual and non-recurring items) were $82 million. The analyst forecast for the third quarter, 2004, was a loss of $0.06 per share.

Income from continuing operations included unusual and non-recurring items of $239 million, being a gain of $239 million from foreign exchange conversion. Much of the company's long-term debt is denominated in U.S. dollars. The foreign exchange gain arose because of the rising value of the Canadian dollar, relative to the U.S. dollar, during the quarter.

Comparable figures for the third quarter of 2003 were: sales of $1,340 million, a core loss of $32 million, and foreign exchange conversion gain of $13 million.

There is no mention of R&D costs in the company's third quarter report. Its 2003 annual report mentions R&D only in passing, with reference to forest conservation. Presumably, R&D expenditures are relatively low.

Abitibi-Consolidated's share price rose $0.59 to $7.29 on the Toronto Stock Exchange on October 21, 2004. The S&P/TSX index gained 59 points to close at 8,847 on the same day. According to media reports, the increases were driven by a "red-hot" materials and energy sector (including Abitibi-Consolidated). In a conference call accompanying its third quarter report, Abitibi-Consolidated's CEO complained that investors were too pessimistic about the company. The company's beta, according to Yahoo! Finance, is 0.779. The risk-free interest rate at this time was approximately 0.00020 per day. Note the theoretical relationship $\alpha_j = R_f (1 - \beta_j)$.

Required

a. Evaluate (in words only) the persistence of Abitibi-Consolidated's operating income for the third quarter of 2004.

b. The company reported no extraordinary items in its third quarter report. Do you feel that the foreign exchange gain of $239 million should have been reported as extraordinary, rather than included in income from continuing operations? Explain why or why not.

c. Do you feel that the increase in Abitibi-Consolidated's share price on October 21 was consistent with efficient securities market theory or do you agree with the CEO? Explain, and show any calculations.

21. On September 13, 2005, the shares of Best Buy Co. fell $5.14 to $45.22 on the New York Stock Exchange, a decline of 10.2%. The decline followed the release of its second quarter 2005 financial results. Best Buy is a large North American retailer of consumer electronics and appliances, with over 700 stores in the United States and Canada, including the Future Shop chain. Best Buy reported earnings of 37 cents per share, compared with 30 cents for the same quarter of 2004. However, its 2005 earnings included an expense for stock-based compensation. If the second quarter 2004 had included this expense, earnings for that 2004 quarter would have been 26 cents per share. Sales revenue rose 10% for the quarter, including a 3.5% increase in same-store sales (same-store sales, which exclude the effects of new store openings, are a closely watched indicator of retail company performance). Its gross profit rose to 25.5% of sales from 24.2% a year earlier. In its news release accompanying the financial results, management predicted earnings of 28 to 32 cents per share for its third 2005 quarter. This prediction included the effects of Hurricane Katrina which, in late August 2005, caused widespread devastation in parts of the southern United States and led to a brief closing of 15 company stores. Management also announced plans to open 86 new stores in the United States and Canada during the fiscal year ending February 25, 2006. While management expressed concerns about the effects of high gasoline prices on consumer spending, it reiterated its guidance that future annual growth in earnings from continuing operations would be about 26%.

Analysts had estimated second quarter 2005 earnings of 38 cents per share, and third quarter earnings of 34 cents.

The New York Stock Exchange Composite Index closed at 7,578.25 on September 13, 2005, and at 7,762.60 on September 12, 2005. Best Buy's stock beta, as per its website, is 1.84. The risk-free interest rate at this time was approximately 0.0001 per day.

Required

a. What percentage return on Best Buy's stock price would you expect on September 13, 2005, strictly as a result of market-wide (i.e., systematic) factors? Use the market model and show your calculations. Note the theoretical relationship $\alpha_j = R_f (1 - \beta_j)$.

b. What was the abnormal return on Best Buy's stock on September 13, 2005? Is this return consistent with securities market efficiency? Explain why or why not.

c. Evaluate (in words only—no calculations required) the persistence of the news (i.e., the increase from 26 cents per share to 37 cents per share) in Best Buy's second quarter 2005 earnings.

22. An article in *The Globe and Mail*, February 16, 2002, reported that IBM used the $300 million proceeds of a sale of one of its business units to reduce operating expenses in its fourth quarter 2001 income statement. This added about 8 cents per share to its fourth quarter earnings. As a result, IBM beat analysts' forecasts by 1 cent per share.

IBM defended its treatment by claiming that buying and selling businesses is a normal business practice, and that most of the sale proceeds related to intellectual property that it had developed. The article quotes a Merrill Lynch analyst as saying, "Our only concern is that the company could have done more to call out the magnitude of the transaction." According to the article, IBM's share price fell by 4% as a result of this news.

While not mentioned in this article, the SEC opened a preliminary inquiry into IBM's accounting practice, expressing concerns that IBM had let it be known that the reason for its higher operating earnings was tight cost controls, rather than the sale proceeds. This inquiry was subsequently dropped, but the SEC issued a bulletin reminding firms to report gains or losses on asset sales separately from operating costs.

Required

a. Suppose that IBM was subject to the provisions of Section 3480 of the *CICA Handbook* (actually, a similar standard exists in the United States). Was its treatment of the sale of its business unit consistent with the definition of an extraordinary item under Section 3480? Explain why or why not.

b. Explain why IBM's share price dropped following the Merrill Lynch analyst's comment and the news of the SEC's preliminary inquiry.

Notes

1. As mentioned in Section 4.5, this estimate of α_j should equal $(1 - \beta_j)R_f$, where R_f is the risk-free rate of interest. Here, $\alpha_j = 0.0001$ implies $R_f = 0.0005$ per day for $\beta_j = 0.80$.

2. The market return for day 0 is calculated as follows:

$$R_{MO} = \frac{\text{Level of D / J index, end day 0} + \text{Dividends D / J index, day 0}}{\text{Level of D / J index, beginning day 0}} - 1$$

Sometimes, because of data problems, the dividends are omitted.

3. Calculated as:

$$E(R_{jt}) = \alpha_j + \beta_j R_{M0}$$
$$= 0.0001 + (0.80 \times 0.001)$$
$$= 0.0009$$

4. Again, this abnormal return should not be confused with abnormal earnings like those of P.V. Ltd. in Example 2.2. While the idea is the same, abnormal return here refers to a *market* return, whereas abnormal earnings refer to *accounting* net income.

5. Other ways to estimate investor expectations are discussed in Section 5.4.3.

6. Note that the loss on bad news firms can be converted into a gain by selling short the shares of the bad news firms.

7. The information system described in Section 3.3.2 contained only two columns—GN and BN. To model the market response to the *magnitude* of GN or BN, we would add additional columns—VGN (very GN), MGN (moderate GN), VBN, etc. The information system concept can be extended to any number of information refinements. Our two-column example is only for simplicity.

8. For reasons explained in Section 5.3.2, the interpretation of a narrow-window ERC is different from a wide-window ERC. Here we will refer, somewhat loosely, to both types as simply ERCs.

9. Recall from Section 3.7 that in reasonably diversified portfolios, most of the portfolio risk stems from the betas of the securities in the portfolio. Thus, if the investor were to buy more shares of a security whose beta is greater than the average beta of the securities currently in the portfolio, this will raise the average, hence increasing portfolio risk.

10. These are "market value" ERCs, where the market's response to GN or BN is expressed in terms of the abnormal change in market value, rather than the abnormal return as in our ERC definition. To convert a market value ERC to a rate of return ERC, divide it by opening firm value.

11. This is analogous to the inclusion of unexpected oil and gas price changes in income under RRA. See Table 2.3.

12. This assumes that the market knows that the increase in market value is $100. Possibly, this would be known from sources other than the financial statements. If not, considerable onus is put on the firm for full disclosure. Perhaps MD&A provides a vehicle for management to reveal this information.

13. However, accrual "quality" is perhaps not the best term for the ε_t residuals. As DeChow and Dichev point out, they contain a mixture of discretionary and non-discretionary items. For example, firms that have high volatility in their operating and policy environments will experience larger and more frequent inventory writedowns, greater swings in bad debts and, generally, more accruals with greater estimation errors. Consequently, a careful scrutiny by the investor of firm characteristics and manager strategies and incentives is needed to fully understand whether accrual quality is good or bad.

14. Note that under RRA, adjustments to prior period estimates are reported separately. Perhaps this approach could be adopted for the effects of current write-offs on future core earnings. If so, this would constitute a major extension of full disclosure. We will return to this possibility in Section 11.6.3.

15. A number of reasons other than lack of usefulness can be suggested for these results. First, the market may value the information but is able to estimate it from other sources. Second, the information may be relevant but unreliable, since a large number of assumptions and estimates go into its preparation. Third, the market may have reacted to the information but the research methodology was not sufficiently powerful to find it. For example, the Beaver and Landsman (1983) study was criticized by Bernard (1987) on methodological grounds. Indeed, some evidence of securities market reaction has been found in studies subsequent to Beaver and Landsman. Thus, Bernard and Ruland (1987) found some information content for current cost information, at least in certain industries.

hapter 6

The Measurement Approach to
Decision Usefulness

Figure 6.1 Organization of Chapter 6

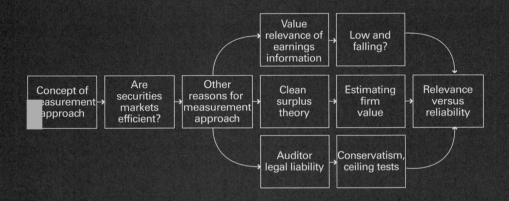

6.1 OVERVIEW

The **measurement approach** to decision usefulness implies greater usage of current values in the financial statements proper. We define the measurement approach as follows:

> The **measurement approach** to decision usefulness is an approach to financial reporting under which accountants undertake a responsibility to incorporate current values into the financial statements proper, providing that this can be done with reasonable reliability, thereby recognizing an increased obligation to assist investors to predict firm performance and value.

The measurement approach does not invalidate our argument in Section 3.1 that it is the investor's responsibility to make his/her own predictions of future firm performance. Rather, the intent is to enable better predictions of this performance by means of a more informative information system. Of course, if a measurement approach is to be useful, it must not be at the cost of a substantial reduction in reliability. While it is unlikely that current values will completely replace historical cost in the mixed measurement model, it is the case that the relative balance of cost-based versus current value-based information in the financial statements is moving in the measurement direction. This may seem strange, given the problems that techniques such as RRA accounting have experienced. However, a number of reasons can be suggested for the change in emphasis.

One such reason involves investor rationality and securities market efficiency. Despite the impressive results outlined in Chapter 5 in favour of the decision usefulness of reported net income, recent years have seen increasing theory and evidence suggesting that securities markets may not be as efficient as originally believed—recall our statement in Section 4.1 that we view efficiency as a matter of degree, rather than efficient/not efficient.

Our interest in the extent of efficiency arises because lack of efficiency has major implications for accounting, the most basic being whether or not the theory of rational decision-making outlined in Chapter 3 underlies investor behaviour. To the extent that markets are not efficient and investors are not rational, reliance on these theories to justify historical cost-based financial statements enhanced by much supplementary disclosure, which underlies the information approach to decision usefulness, is threatened. If investors collectively are not as adept at processing information as rational decision theory assumes, perhaps usefulness would be enhanced by greater use of current values in the financial statements proper. Furthermore, while beta is the only relevant risk measure according to the CAPM, there is evidence that other variables, such as firm size and book-to-market ratio, do a better job than beta of predicting share return. If so, perhaps accountants should take more responsibility for reporting on firm risk.

We shall conclude that while securities markets are not fully efficient, they are sufficiently so that accountants can be guided by efficient markets theory. We shall also conclude that lack of full efficiency can be explained equally well by rational decision theory as by non-rational investor behaviour. Furthermore, to bring our discussion back to financial reporting, we shall argue that the extent of inefficiency and non-rational investor behaviour can be reduced by a measurement approach.

Other reasons for moving towards a measurement approach derive from a low proportion of share price variability explained by historical cost-based net income, from the Ohlson clean surplus theory that provides support for increased measurement, and from the legal liability to which accountants are exposed when firms become financially distressed. In this chapter we will outline and discuss these various reasons.

Figure 6.1 outlines the organization of this chapter.

6.2 ARE SECURITIES MARKETS FULLY EFFICIENT?

6.2.1 Introduction

In recent years, increasing questions have been raised about investor rationality and securities market efficiency. That is, there is evidence that shares are mispriced relative to their efficient market values. Questions of investor rationality and market efficiency are of considerable importance to accountants since, if these questions are valid, the practice of relying on supplementary information in notes and elsewhere to augment historical cost-based financial statements proper may not be completely effective in conveying useful information to investors. Furthermore, if shares are mispriced, improved financial reporting may be helpful in reducing inefficiencies, thereby improving the working of securities markets. In the next few sub-sections we will outline and discuss the major questions that have been raised about market efficiency.

The basic premise of these questions is that average investor behaviour may not correspond with the rational decision theory and investment models outlined in Chapter 3. For example, individuals may have **limited attention**. That is, they may not have time and ability to process all available information. Then, they will concentrate on information that is readily available, such as the "bottom line," and ignore information in notes and elsewhere in the annual report. Furthermore, investors may be biased in their reaction to information, relative to how they should react according to Bayes' theorem. For example, there is evidence that individuals are **conservative** (not to be confused with conservatism in accounting as in lower-of-cost-or-market and ceiling tests) in their reaction to new evidence. Conservative individuals revise their beliefs by *less than* Bayes' theorem implies.

Psychological theory and evidence also suggests that individuals are often **overconfident**—they overestimate the precision of information they collect themselves. For example, an investor that privately researches a firm may overreact to the evidence he or she obtains. If we equate the individual's self-collected information with prior probabilities in Bayes' theorem, this implies that the overconfident individual will *underreact* to new information that is not self-collected relative to information that is. This underreaction seems to be particularly apparent if the new information, such as an earnings report, is perceived as statistical and abstract.

Another individual characteristic from psychology is **representativeness**. Here, the individual assigns too much weight to evidence that is consistent with the individual's impressions of the population from which the evidence is drawn. For example, suppose that a firm's profits have grown strongly for several years. The investor subject to representativeness will assign this firm to the growth firm category, ignoring the fact that true growth firms are a rare event in the economy—the individual assigns too much weight to the recent evidence of earnings growth and not enough to the prior information that the base rate of growth firms in the population is low. This behaviour seems particularly likely if the evidence is salient, anecdotal, or extreme—for example, a firm's earnings growth may be the subject of sensational media articles. Thus, the investor overreacts to the evidence, revising his/her beliefs that the firm in question is a growth firm by *more than* prescribed by Bayes' theorem. In effect, the individual takes the evidence of a few years of growth in earnings as *representative* of a growth firm, ignoring the fact that it is quite likely that earnings will revert to normal in the future. If enough investors behave this way, share price will *overreact* to the reported growth in earnings.

Yet another attribute of many individuals is **self-attribution bias**, whereby individuals feel that good decision outcomes are due to their abilities, whereas bad outcomes are due to unfortunate realizations of states of nature, hence not their fault. Suppose that following an overconfident investor's decision to purchase a firm's shares, its share price rises (for whatever reason). Then, the investor's faith in his or her investment ability rises. If share price falls, faith in ability does not fall. If enough investors behave this way, share price **momentum** can develop. That is, reinforced confidence following a rise in share price leads to the purchase of more shares, and share price rises further. Confidence is again reinforced, and the process feeds upon itself, that is, it gains momentum. Daniel, Hirshleifer, and Subrahmanyam (1998) present a model whereby momentum develops when investors are overconfident and self-attribution biased. Daniel and Titman (1999), in an empirical study, report that over the period 1968–1997 a strategy of buying portfolios of high-momentum shares and short-selling low-momentum ones earned high and persistent abnormal returns (i.e., higher than the return from holding the market portfolio), consistent with the overconfidence and momentum arguments.[1]

These various behavioural characteristics are, of course, inconsistent with securities market efficiency and underlying rational decision theory. According to the CAPM, higher returns can only be earned if higher beta risk is borne. Yet Daniel and Titman report that the average beta risk of their momentum portfolios was less than that of the market portfolio.

As is apparent from the foregoing, behavioural characteristics can produce a wide variety of share price behaviours over time. For example, overconfidence leading to share price momentum implies positive serial correlation of returns while the momentum continues (and negative longer-term correlation as the overconfidence is eventually revealed), whereas representativeness implies negative serial correlation (i.e., share price overreacts to evidence, leading to subsequent price correction as overvaluation is revealed). All of these patterns are contrary to the random walk behaviour of returns under market efficiency.

The study of behavioural-based securities market inefficiencies is called **behavioural finance**, which began with the seminal paper of De Bondt and Thaler (1985). For a comprehensive review of the theory and evidence of behavioural finance, see Hirshleifer (2001). We now review several other questions about efficiency that have been raised in this theory.

6.2.2 Prospect Theory

The **prospect theory** of Kahneman and Tversky (1979) provides a behavioural-based alternative to the rational decision theory described in Section 3.3. According to prospect theory, an investor considering a risky investment (a "prospect") will separately evaluate prospective gains and losses. This separate evaluation contrasts with decision theory where investors evaluate decisions in terms of their effects on their total wealth (see Chapter 3, Note 4). Separate evaluation of gains and losses about a reference point is an implication of the psychological concept of **narrow framing**, whereby individuals analyze problems in too isolated a manner, as a way of economizing on the mental effort of decision-making. This economizing on mental effort may derive from limited attention, as mentioned above. As a result, an individual's utility in prospect theory is defined over deviations from zero for the prospect in question, rather than over total wealth.

Figure 6.2 shows a typical investor utility function under prospect theory.

The investor's utility for gains is assumed to exhibit the familiar risk-averse, concave shape as illustrated in Figure 3.3. However, prospect theory assumes **loss aversion**, a behavioural concept whereby individuals dislike even very small losses. Thus, beginning at the point where the investment starts to lose in value, the investor's rate of utility loss is greater than the rate of utility increase for a gain in value.[2] Indeed, the utility for losses is assumed to be convex rather than concave, so that the investor exhibits risk-taking behaviour with respect to losses. This leads to a **disposition effect**, whereby the investor holds on to losers and sells winners, and, indeed, may even buy more of a loser security. The disposition effect was studied by Shefrin and Statman (1985). They identified a sample of investors whose rational decision was to sell loser securities before the end of the taxation year. They found, however, that the investors tended to avoid selling, consistent with the disposition effect.

Prospect theory also assumes that when calculating the expected value of a prospect, individuals under- or overweight their probabilities (i.e., posterior probabilities are less than or greater than those resulting from application of Bayes' theorem). Underweighting

Figure 6.2 Prospect Theory Utility Function

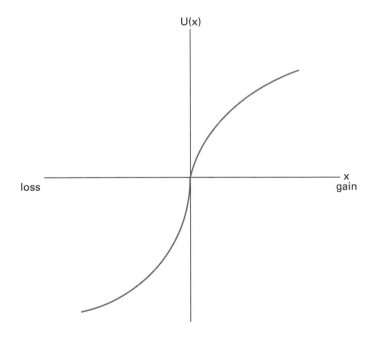

of probabilities is a ramification of overconfidence. Thus, information not generated by the investor him/herself, such as GN in reported earnings, will be underweighted relative to other evidence. As a result, the individual's posterior probability of the high future performance state may be too low. BN will be underweighted for similar reasons, in which case the posterior probability of low future performance may also be underweighted.

Overweighting of probabilities is a ramification of representativeness, whereby individuals tend to overweight current evidence that, for example, a stock's value is about to take off, even though realization of the state "taking off" is a rare event.

These tendencies can lead to "too low" posterior probabilities on states that are likely to happen, and "too high" on states that are unlikely to happen. The posterior probabilities need not sum to one.

The combination of separate evaluation of gains and losses and the weighting of probabilities can lead to a wide variety of "irrational" behaviours. For example, fear of losses may cause investors to stay out of the market even if prospects have positive expected value according to a decision theory calculation. Also, they may underreact to bad news by holding on to "losers" so as to avoid realizing a loss and, as mentioned above, may even buy more of a loser stock, thereby taking on added risk. Thus, under prospect theory, investor behaviour depends in a complex way on payoff probabilities that may differ from those obtained from Bayes' theorem, risk aversion with respect to gains, and risk taking with respect to losses.

Theory in Practice 6.1

A number of experiments have tested the predictions of prospect theory. In one experiment (Knetsch 1989), a group of student subjects was each given a chocolate bar and another group each given a mug. The two items (i.e., prospects) were of roughly equal monetary value. The subjects were then allowed the option of trading with other subjects. For example, a student who had received a chocolate bar but who preferred a mug could exchange with someone who wanted a chocolate bar. While the longevity of the two items did differ, they were of equal monetary value, and were assigned randomly to the subjects. Then, rationality predicts that about half of them would trade. However, only about 10% traded.

These results are consistent with prospect theory. This can be seen from Figure 6.2. Since the rate at which investor utility decreases for small losses is greater than the rate at which it increases

for small gains, disposing of ("losing") an item already owned creates a larger utility loss than the utility gained by acquiring another item of equal value. As a result, the subjects tended to hold on to the item they had been given.

Subsequent experiments by List (2003) cast these results in a different light, however. List conducted experiments in real markets, rather than in simulated markets with student subjects as above. A distinguishing feature of real markets is that they contain traders with varying degrees of experience. List found that as their experience increased, the behaviour of market participants converged towards that predicted by rational decision theory. He also showed how more experienced traders could buy and sell from less sophisticated ones so as to drive market prices towards their efficient levels.[3] Consequently, List's results tend to support the rational decision theory over prospect theory.

There are few empirical accounting tests of prospect theory. However, one such test was conducted by Burgstahler and Dichev (1997) (BD). In a large sample of U.S. firms from 1974–1976, these researchers documented that relatively few firms in their sample reported small losses. A relatively large number of firms reported small positive earnings. That is, there is a "gap" just below zero in the distribution of firms' reported earnings. Burgstahler and Dichev interpreted this result as evidence that firms that would otherwise report a small loss manipulate cash flows and accruals to manage their reported earnings upwards, so as to instead show small positive earnings (techniques of earnings management are discussed in Chapter 11).

As Burgstahler and Dichev point out, this result is consistent with prospect theory. To see why, note again from Figure 6.2 that the rate at which investor utility decreases for small losses is greater than the rate at which it increases for small gains. This implies a relatively strong negative investor reaction to a small reported loss. Managers of firms that would otherwise report a small loss thus have an incentive to avoid this negative investor reaction, and enjoy a positive reaction, by managing reported earnings upwards. (Of course, managers of firms with *large* losses have similar incentives, but as the loss increases it becomes more difficult to manage earnings sufficiently to avoid the loss. Also, the incentive to manage earnings upwards declines for larger losses since the rate of negative investor reaction is not as great.)

However, Burgstahler and Dichev suggest that their evidence is also consistent with managers behaving rationally. Lenders will demand better terms from firms that report losses, for example. Also, suppliers may cut the firm off, or demand immediate payment for goods shipped. To avoid these consequences, managers have an incentive to avoid reporting losses if possible. Also, firms in a loss position may be eligible for income tax refunds, which could put them into a small profit position even without deliberate earnings management.

BD's interpretation that a gap in reported earnings just below zero indicates earnings management has generated considerable subsequent research. For example, Durtschi and Easton (2005) conclude that the apparent gap may result instead from the statistical methods used by the authors. Subsequently, however, evidence consistent with BD is reported by Jacob and Jorgenson (2007). Indeed, these authors find that earnings management extends to well above and below the small gains and losses documented by BD. To the extent that prospect theory predicts earnings management only in small intervals around zero, this finding suggests other motivations (to be discussed in Chapter 11) also operate. The extent to which the BD results support prospect theory is thus unclear.

6.2.3 Is Beta Dead?

As mentioned in Section 4.5, an implication of the CAPM is that a stock's beta is the sole firm-specific determinant of the expected return on that stock. If the CAPM reasonably captures rational investor behaviour, share returns should be increasing in β_j and should be unaffected by other measures of firm-specific risk, which are diversified away. However, in a large sample of firms traded on major U.S. stock exchanges over the period 1963–1990, Fama and French (1992) found that beta, and thus the CAPM, had little ability to explain stock returns. Instead, they found significant explanatory power for the book-to-market ratio (B/M) (ratio of book value of common equity to market value). They also found explanatory power for firm size. Their results suggest that rather than looking to beta as a risk measure, the market acts as if firm risk increases with book-to-market and decreases with firm size.

Fama and French's findings are not necessarily inconsistent with rational investor behaviour and efficient securities markets. For example, investors may purchase shares of low B/M firms to protect themselves against undiversifiable risk of, say, a downturn in the economy that would lead many firms into financial distress. Purchasing shares of low B/M firms provides such protection since one reason that the market assigns high market value, relative to book value, to a firm is that the firm is unlikely to become financially distressed. The $E(R_{Mt})$ term of the market model (see Section 4.5) may not fully capture the risk of financial distress since it is an average across all firms in the market. As a result, rational investors will look to other risk measures, such as book-to-market, when making their portfolio decisions.[4]

The Fama and French results do threaten the CAPM, however, since they imply that beta is not an important risk measure. The low explanatory power for beta documented by Fama and French has led some to suggest that beta is "dead."

Somewhat different results are reported by Kothari, Shanken, and Sloan (1995), however. They found that over a longer period of time (1941–1990) beta *was* a significant predictor of return. Book-to-market also predicted return, but its effect was relatively weak. They attributed the difference between their results and those of Fama and French to differences in methodology and time period studied.

Behavioural finance, however, provides a different perspective on the validity of the CAPM and beta. That is, share return behaviour inconsistent with the CAPM is viewed as evidence of market inefficiency. In this regard, Daniel, Hirshleifer, and Subrahmanyam (2001) present a model that assumes two types of investors—rational and overconfident. Because of rational investors, a stock's beta is positively related to its returns, as in the CAPM. However, overconfident investors overreact as they self-collect information. This drives share price too high or low, driving the firm's book-to-market ratio too low or high. Over time, share price reverts towards its efficient level as the overconfidence is revealed. As a result, both beta and book-to-market ratio are positively related to future share returns. Thus, in the Daniel, Hirshleifer, and Subrahmanyam model, the positive book-to-market relation to future share returns found by Fama and French is not driven by rational investors protecting themselves against financial distress. Rather, it is driven by overconfidence, a behavioural effect inconsistent with rationality and efficiency.

The status of the CAPM and its implications for beta thus seem unclear. A possible way to rescue beta is to recognize that it may change over time. Our discussion in Section 4.5 assumed that beta was **stationary**. However, changes in interest rates and firms' capital structures, improvements in firms' abilities to manage risk, and development of global markets may affect the relationship between the return on individual firms' shares and the market-wide return, thereby affecting the value of firms' betas. If so, evidence of share return behaviour that appears to conflict with the CAPM could perhaps be explained by shifts in beta.

If betas are non-stationary, rational investors will want to figure out when and by how much firms' betas change. This is a difficult question to answer in a timely manner, and different investors will have different opinions. Different estimates of beta introduce differences in investment decisions, even though all investors have access to the same information and proceed rationally with respect to their estimate of what beta is. In effect, another source of estimation risk is introduced into the market. As a result, additional volatility is introduced into share price behaviour, but beta remains as a variable that explains this behaviour. According to this argument, the CAPM implication that beta is an important risk variable is reinstated, with the proviso that beta is non-stationary. Models that assume rational investor behaviour in the face of non-stationarity[5] are presented by Kurz (1997). Evidence that non-stationarity of beta explains much of the apparent anomalous behaviour of share prices is provided by Ball and Kothari (1989).[6]

From an accounting standpoint, to the extent that beta is not the only relevant firm-specific risk measure, this can only increase the role of financial statements in reporting useful risk information (the book-to-market ratio is an accounting-based variable, for example). Nevertheless, in the face of the mixed evidence reported above, we conclude that beta is not dead. However, it may change over time and may have to "move over" to share its status as a risk measure with accounting-based variables.

6.2.4 Excess Stock Market Volatility

Further questions about securities market efficiency derive from evidence of excess stock price volatility at the market level. Recall from the CAPM that, holding beta and the risk-free interest rate constant, a change in the expected return on the market portfolio, $E(R_{Mt})$, is the only reason for a change in the expected return of firm j's shares. Now the fundamental determinant of $E(R_{Mt})$ is the aggregate expected dividends across all firms in the market—the higher are aggregate expected dividends the more investors will invest in the market, increasing demand for shares and driving the stock market index up (and vice versa). Consequently, if the market is efficient, changes in $E(R_{Mt})$ should not exceed changes in aggregate expected dividends.

This reasoning was investigated by Shiller (1981), who found that the variability of the stock market index was several times greater than the variability of aggregate dividends. Shiller interpreted this result as evidence of market inefficiency.

Subsequently, Ackert and Smith (1993) argued that while expected future dividends are the fundamental determinant of firm value, they should be defined broadly to include all cash distributions to shareholders, such as share repurchases and distributions following takeovers, as well as ordinary dividends. In a study covering the years 1950–1991,

Ackert and Smith showed that when these additional items were included, excess volatility disappeared.

However, despite Ackert and Smith's results, there are reasons why excess volatility at the market level may exist. One reason, consistent with efficiency, derives from non-stationarity, as outlined in the previous section. Other reasons derive from behavioural factors. The momentum model of Daniel, Hirshleifer, and Subrahmanyam (2001) implies excess market volatility as share prices overshoot and then fall back. A different argument is made by DeLong, Shleifer, Summers, and Waldmann (1990). They assume a capital market with both rational and positive feedback investors. Positive feedback investors are those who buy in when share price begins to rise, and vice versa. One might expect that rational investors would then sell short, anticipating the share price decline that will follow the price run-up caused by positive feedback buying. However, the authors argue that rational investors will instead "jump on the bandwagon," to take advantage of the price run-up while it lasts. As a result, there is excess volatility in the market.

In sum, it seems that the question of excess market volatility raised by Shiller is unresolved. The results of Ackert and Smith suggest it does not exist if dividends are defined broadly. Even if excess market volatility does exist, it can possibly be explained by rational models based on non-stationarity. Alternatively, volatility may be driven by behavioural factors that cause share prices to overreact then fall back as the overreaction is revealed, inconsistent with full market efficiency.

6.2.5 Stock Market Bubbles

Stock market bubbles, wherein share prices rise far above rational values, represent an extreme case of market volatility. Shiller (2000) investigated bubble behaviour with specific reference to the surge in share prices of technology companies in the United States in the years leading up to 2000. Bubbles, according to Shiller, derive from a combination of biased self-attribution and momentum, positive feedback trading, and "herd" behaviour reinforced by optimistic media predictions of market "experts." These reasons underlie then Federal Reserve Board Chairman Greenspan's famous "irrational exuberance" comment on the stock market in a 1996 speech.

Shiller argues that bubble behaviour can continue for some time, and that it is difficult to predict when it will end. Eventually, however, it will burst because of growing beliefs of, say, impending recession or increasing inflation.

6.2.6 Efficient Securities Market Anomalies

We now consider evidence of market inefficiency that specifically involves financial accounting information. Recall that the evidence described in Chapter 5 generally supports efficiency and the rational investor behaviour underlying it. There is, however, other evidence suggesting that the market may not respond to information exactly as the efficiency theory predicts. For example, share prices may not fully react to financial statement information right away, so that abnormal security returns persist for some time following the release of the information. Also, it appears that the market may not always extract all the information content from financial statements. In statistical terms, share returns are serially correlated. Cases such as these that appear inconsistent with securities market efficiency are called **efficient securities market anomalies**. We now consider two such anomalies.

Post-Announcement Drift Once a firm's current earnings become known, the information content should be quickly digested by investors and incorporated into the efficient market price. However, it has long been known that this is not exactly what happens. For firms that report good news (GN) in quarterly earnings, their abnormal security returns tend to drift upwards for some time following their earnings announcement. Similarly, firms that report bad news (BN) in earnings tend to have their abnormal security returns drift downwards for a similar period. This phenomenon is called **post-announcement drift** (PAD). Traces of this behaviour can be seen in the Ball and Brown study reviewed in Section 5.3—see Figure 5.3 and notice that abnormal share returns drift upwards and downwards for some time following the month of release of GN and BN, respectively.

Bernard and Thomas (1989) (BT) further examined this issue. In a large sample of firms over the period 1974–1986, they documented the presence of PAD in quarterly earnings. Indeed, an investor following a strategy of buying the shares of GN firms and selling short BN on the day of earnings announcement, and holding for 60 days, would have earned an average return of 18% per annum over and above the market-wide return, before transactions costs, in their sample. By GN or BN here, BT mean the difference between current quarterly reported earnings and those of the same quarter last year. These differences are called **quarterly seasonal earnings changes**. The assumption is that investors' expectations of current quarterly earnings are based on those of the same quarter of the previous year.[7]

It seems that *investors underestimate the implications of current earnings for future earnings*. As BT point out, it is a known fact that quarterly seasonal earnings changes are positively correlated for up to three subsequent quarters. Thus, if a firm reports, say, GN this quarter, in the sense that this quarter's earnings are greater than the same quarter last year, there is a greater than 50% chance that its future-quarter earnings will also be GN. Rational investors should anticipate this and, as they bid up the price of the firm's shares in response to the *current* GN, they should bid them up some more due to the increased probability of GN in *future* quarters. However, BT's evidence suggests that this does not happen. The implication is that PAD results from investors taking considerable time to figure this out, or at least that they underestimate the magnitude of the correlation (Ball and Bartov, 1996). In terms of the information system given in Table 3.2, BT's results suggest that Bill Cautious evaluates the main diagonal probabilities as less than they really are.[8]

Be sure you see the significance of PAD. If it exists, sophisticated investors could earn arbitrage profits, at least before transactions costs, by modifying the diversified investment strategy described in Section 3.7. For example, an investor could buy GN shares on the day the GN was announced. If he or she could then sell short other companies' shares whose returns were perfectly correlated with the efficient market price changes of the GN shares, the combined portfolio would be riskless—all price changes other than those arising from PAD would cancel out since gains and losses on the GN shares are offset by losses and gains on the short sales shares. Then, the investor will earn a riskless profit as the value of the GN shares drifts upwards over future quarters. Furthermore, proceeds from the short sales can be used to buy the GN shares, so little if any capital is required.

The existence of such a "money machine" seems hard to imagine. One would expect that the scramble of investors to exploit a riskless profit opportunity would immediately bid up the prices of GN shares, thereby restoring them to their efficient market value. Yet, the results of BT suggest this does not happen.

Indeed, PAD continues to exist. In a more recent study involving a large sample of firms over 1980–2004, Narayanamoorthy (2006) documented the continued existence of PAD. He showed that a strategy of investing only in GN firms earned an abnormal return even greater than BT's 18%.[9]

Researchers continue to try to understand the PAD puzzle. Chordia and Shivakumar (2005) suggest that investors do not fully incorporate the effects of inflation on firms' future profits into their decisions, and present evidence that this is at least partly responsible for PAD.[10]

Bartov, Radhakrishnan, and Krinsky (2000) find that PAD is less if a greater proportion of a firm's shares is held by institutions, such as banks, investment houses, and insurance companies. Institutions may possess greater expertise and economies of scale than behaviourally biased or unsophisticated investors. This finding implies that institutional investors earn arbitrage profits, thereby eliminating at least some PAD. Ke and Ramalingegowada (2005), who studied a large sample of quarterly earnings announcements over 1986–1999, also report that some institutions earn arbitrage profits by trading to take advantage of PAD. The proportion of their profits from PAD is quite small, however, being dominated by other strategies such as buy and hold or momentum trading.

Market Response to Accruals Sloan (1996), for a large sample of 40,769 annual earnings announcements over the years 1962–1991, separated reported net income into operating cash flow and accrual components. This can be done by drawing again on the formula:

$$\text{Net income} = \text{cash flow from operations} \pm \text{net accruals}$$

As pointed out in Section 5.4, net accruals, which can be positive (i.e., income-increasing) or negative, include changes in non-cash working capital accounts such as receivables, allowance for doubtful accounts, inventories, accounts payable, and amortization expense.

Sloan pointed out that accruals are more subject to errors of estimation and possible manager bias than cash flows, and argued that this lower reliability should reduce the association between current accruals and next period's net income. Operating cash flows, however, result from continuing operations. They are less likely to reverse and are less subject to error and bias. Recall from Section 5.4 that persistence is the extent to which the good or bad news in current earnings is expected to continue into the future. Since accruals are less reliable than cash flows, the good or bad news they contain in the current period is less likely to continue into the next period than good or bad news in cash flows. In effect, Sloan argued, the cash flow component of earnings is more persistent than the accrual component.

Sloan examined separately the persistence of the operating cash flows and accruals components of net income for the firms in his sample, and found that next year's reported net income was more highly associated with the operating cash flow component of the current year's income than with the accrual component, supporting his argument of greater cash flow persistence.

If this is the case, we would expect the efficient market to respond more strongly to the GN or BN in earnings the greater is the cash flow component relative to the accrual component in that GN or BN, and vice versa.

Sloan found that this did not happen. While the market did respond to the GN or BN in earnings, it did not seem to "fine-tune" its response to take into account the cash flow and accruals composition of those earnings. Instead, share returns of high positive accrual firms tended to drift downwards over time rather than falling right away, and vice versa. Sloan designed a simulated investment strategy to exploit the apparent market mispricing. By buying shares of low-accrual firms and selling short shares of high-accrual firms, and holding for one year, he demonstrated a return of 10.4% per annum over and above the market return, before transactions costs.

Sloan's results raise questions about securities market efficiency similar to PAD. It seems that a money machine is available for accruals as well.

As with PAD, researchers continue to try to understand the accruals anomaly. For example, Lev and Nissim (2006) studied a large sample of firms over 1965–2002. They found that the accruals anomaly continues, even subsequent to publication of Sloan's results (1996). They did find that institutional investors trade on the anomaly, indicating that they are aware of it. But, similar to the PAD findings of Ke and Ramalingegowada referenced above, the amount of their trading is quite low, well short of what would be needed to arbitrage the accruals anomaly away. Lev and Nissim point out that the firms in their sample tend to be small, young, with relatively low share prices, low dividend yield, and low book-to-market ratios, and argue that these are not investment characteristics favoured by financial institutions.

6.2.7 Implications of Securities Market Inefficiency for Financial Reporting

To the extent that securities markets are not fully efficient, this can only increase the importance of financial reporting. To see why, let us expand the concept of noise traders introduced in Section 4.4.1, as suggested by Lee (2001). Specifically, now define noise traders to also include investors subject to the behavioural biases outlined earlier. An immediate consequence is that noise no longer has expectation zero. That is, even in terms of expectation, share prices may be mispriced relative to the prices they would have if markets were fully efficient. Over time, however, rational investors, including analysts, will discover such mispricing and take advantage of it, driving prices towards fundamental values. This is what we observed in the anomalies studies. In both cases, share price did not fully respond right away. Instead, share returns drifted up or down following the reporting of accounting information as its full information content became apparent over time.

Improved financial reporting, by giving investors more help in predicting efficient firm value, will speed up share price response to the full information content of financial statements. Examples of improved reporting include full disclosure of low persistence components of earnings, high quality MD&A and, as we suggest in this chapter, moving current value information into the financial statements proper. Indeed, by reducing the costs of rational analysis, better reporting may reduce the extent of investors' behavioural biases. In effect, securities market inefficiency supports a measurement approach.

This argument is shown in Figure 6.3, which is an extension of Figure 4.2.

Figure 6.3 adds an inner circle to Figure 4.2, representing the information included in actual share price when markets are not fully efficient. Then, share price does not incorporate all publicly available information. This adds a second role for financial reporting: to reduce inefficiencies by making the mispricing area between the two inner circles as small as possible.

Figure 6.3 Roles of Financial Reporting When Securities Market Is Not Fully Efficient

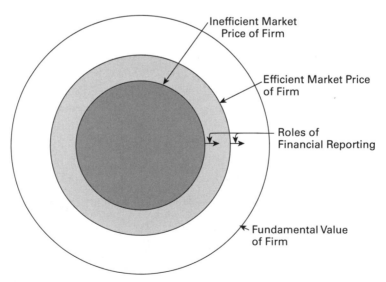

6.2.8 Discussion of Market Efficiency Versus Behavioural Finance

Collectively, the behavioural finance theory and evidence discussed in the previous sections raise serious questions about the extent of securities market efficiency and rational investor behaviour. Fama (1998), however, evaluated much of this evidence and concluded that it did not explain the "big picture." That is, while there is evidence of market behaviour inconsistent with efficiency, there is not a unified alternative theory that predicts and integrates the anomalous evidence. For example, Fama pointed out that apparent overreaction of share prices to information is about as common as underreaction. What is needed to meet Fama's concern is a theory that predicts when the market will overreact and when it will underreact.

This lack of a unified theory may be changing. For example, Barberis, Shleifer, and Vishny (1998) draw on the behavioural concept of conservatism to explain underreaction. That is, conservative investors underweight new evidence relative to their prior information. As a result, share price underreacts, relative to an efficient market reaction, and drifts upwards or downwards over time as the under/overvaluation becomes apparent from future earnings reports or other sources.

With respect to overreaction, Barberis, Shleifer, and Vishny draw on representativeness. Suppose that an investor subject to this characteristic observes a firm's earnings increasing steadily over time. This investor will regard (i.e., represent) this firm as a growth firm, despite the fact that real growth firms are rare. That is, the investor downgrades the prior information of a low population base rate for growth firms. Then, relative to an efficient market, share price overreacts to reported earnings, and continues to increase until, as is likely to happen, an earnings reversal eventually takes place.

As another example, Hirshleifer and Teoh (2003) present a model in which some investors are fully rational but others have limited attention, which affects their ability to process publicly available information. Limited attention implies that the *form* of presentation, as opposed simply to its information content, affects investors' interpretations of the information. Then, the market may underreact to supplemental information. For example, consider the difficulty researchers have had in documenting a securities market response to RRA, discussed in Section 5.7. We suggested there that low reliability and availability of alternate reserves information were responsible. Another explanation derives from limited attention. Suppose that the present value of proved reserves has decreased sharply this year. The Hirshleifer and Teoh model predicts that the market will underreact to this information, since investors with limited ability to process information concentrate on reported net income, ignoring the RRA information included in MD&A or the notes. Thus, instead of fully reacting right away, the firm's share price will drift downwards as the bad news about reserves becomes apparent over time. Bringing current value accounting for proved reserves into the financial statements proper would make it easier for these investors to realize the implications for future firm performance, speeding up the market reaction.

Empirical support for this argument is provided by Ahmed, Kilic, and Lobo (2006), who studied a sample of U.S. banks that disclosed values of their derivatives as supplemental information prior to SFAS 133, and valued them at fair value in their financial statements proper subsequent to SFAS 133 (SFAS 133, which requires all derivatives to be valued on the balance sheet at fair value, is discussed in Section 7.3.4). They found no significant share price reaction to the value of derivatives disclosed as supplemental information but a significantly positive reaction when disclosed on the balance sheet. This finding contrasts with efficient securities market theory, which predicts that as long as the derivative values are disclosed, and assuming equal reliability, the location of disclosure does not matter.

Thus, by setting out how different behavioural characteristics lead to overreaction and underreaction, behavioural researchers are responding to Fama's concern.

If share mispricing results from behavioural factors, why do sophisticated investors not step in to earn arbitrage profits, thereby eliminating the mispricing? An answer is that there are **limits to arbitrage**, which constrain the market's ability to eliminate share mispricing. One such limit is transactions costs. The investment strategies required to earn arbitrage profits may be quite costly. Costs include more than brokerage commissions. They also include costs of short selling, which can be high. Time and effort are also required, including continuous monitoring of earnings announcements, annual reports, market prices, overcoming any behavioural biases, and development of the required expertise.[11] In this regard, Mashruwala, Rajgopal, and Shevlin (2006) (MRS), in a study of the accruals anomaly, use share price and trading volume as proxies for transactions costs. Trading volume is a proxy because low trading volume suggests that transactions costs are high. Share price is a proxy because buying and selling commissions are relatively higher for low-priced shares. MRS studied a large sample of firms over 1975–2000. They found that firms with very high (income-increasing) and very low (income-decreasing) accruals exhibited lower and greater, respectively, average share returns for the year following their earnings announcements than firms with intermediate accruals levels, and that these extreme-accruals firms had on average low share prices and trading volume. That is, the accruals anomaly was greater for these firms. This suggests that transactions costs at least partially constrain sophisticated investors' abilities to exploit the accruals anomaly—the highest amounts of money left "on the table" are for firms where the money machine is most costly to access.

In their study of PAD, Ke and Ramalingegowada (2005) estimated the transactions costs for the institutions in their sample, and found that PAD arbitrage profits earned are confined largely to institutions with low costs, suggesting again that high costs do indeed limit arbitrage. The results of Bartov et. al, and Lev and Nissim referenced earlier also support a transactions cost argument.

A second reason why arbitrage does not eliminate mispricing is risk. As mentioned earlier, a portfolio containing shares for which mispricing exists, such as that produced by the PAD and accruals anomalies, represents a departure from a fully diversified investment strategy. Instead, the investor tries to earn a return greater than that of the market portfolio by investing in shares that he or she perceives as mispriced. As a result of less diversification, firm-specific variance of returns assumes a greater role. This firm-specific risk of an arbitrage investment strategy is called **idiosyncratic risk**.

In our money-machine investment strategy described above, idiosyncratic risk was eliminated, since the investor sold short shares with efficient market price changes perfectly correlated with those of the mispriced shares in his/her portfolio. MRS argue, however, that as a practical matter it is difficult, if not impossible, to find such shares. Consequently, idiosyncratic risk remains to limit the arbitrage of rational, risk-averse investors. MRS report that the highest levels of return to a strategy of investing in extreme-accrual firms in their sample are concentrated in shares of high idiosyncratic risk, consistent with their argument. Mendenhall (2004) reports similar results for the PAD anomaly.

It thus seems that transactions costs and idiosyncratic risk are major barriers to arbitraging away share mispricing. As a result, anomalies such as PAD and accruals persist.

A more fundamental question, however, is why the anomalies appear in the first place. Do they necessarily result from behavioural characteristics, or can rational investor behaviour produce similar observations? If the latter, the theory of rational investor behaviour can be salvaged, even though markets may not be fully efficient.

Indeed, share price behaviour similar to that predicted by behavioural finance can be generated by rational investors, if we relax the assumption that parameters underlying firm performance are stationary and known by the decision-maker. This was shown by Brav and Heaton (2002). To see their argument, suppose that a firm has just reported a substantial increase in earnings. The question then is, has the firm's expected earning power increased, or is this simply a one-time blip produced by some low-persistence earnings item or short-run favourable state realization? While careful analysis of the financial statements may help, the rational investor is unlikely to know the answer with complete accuracy, due, for example, to inside information, possibly compounded by poor disclosure. That is, the investor faces estimation risk with respect to the underlying non-stationary firm parameter of expected earning power.

In the face of this estimation risk, the rational investor will place some probability on each possibility. His/her estimate of expected future earnings will increase, but by less than the increase in current earnings. Other rational investors will do the same. The additional demand will trigger an immediate share price increase. This increase will be less than it would be if investors were certain of the increase in expected earning power, but more than if they knew there was no expected earning power increase.

To reduce their estimation risk, investors will watch for additional information. If expected earning power has in fact increased, new information that is on balance favourable will be observed over time. For each information item, investors will revise their expected earning power estimate and will buy additional shares. The firm's share price will drift upwards.

Notice that this upward drift produces a time pattern of share returns similar to the behavioural concept of conservatism. It is also similar to the upward drift for GN firms' share prices documented in the PAD studies, and for the upward drift of share prices of low-accrual firms.

Conversely, if expected earning power has not increased, unfavourable information will be observed over time. Then, we would expect the share overvaluation to reverse as the overvaluation is revealed. This overreaction to net income produces a time pattern of share returns similar to the behavioural concept of representativeness, and is consistent with PAD for BN firms, and with high-accrual firms.

The point is that if we relax the assumption of stationarity of underlying financial reporting parameters, rational investor behaviour can produce similar patterns of under-reaction and overreaction to accounting information as behavioural finance.

This argument can possibly explain the findings of Doyle, Lundholm, and Soliman (2006) (DLS). These authors examined a large sample of quarterly earnings announcements over 1988–2000. They found that the share returns of those firms reporting large positive earnings surprises (actual reported earnings less analysts' consensus forecasts) on average drifted upwards for three years following the earnings announcement. Similarly, share returns of firms with large negative earnings surprises drifted downwards over the same period. DLS reported an average three-year return of 24% to a strategy of buying shares of sample firms in the top 10% of earnings surprises and selling short shares of firms in the lowest 10% category. Furthermore, these returns continued to hold after allowing for the effects on returns of risk (e.g., beta) and other anomalies (e.g., accruals anomaly).[12]

The three-year upward drift reported by DLS suggests that their firms reporting extreme earnings surprises have in fact experienced an upward or downward shift in expected earning power on average, but that it takes investors up to three years to find enough confirming evidence to fully accept the shift. This result is consistent with the Brav and Heaton argument. Of course, this result is also consistent with behaviourally biased investors. However, DLS report that their extreme sample firms are relatively small, with relatively little analyst following and relatively few institutional shareholders, leading to high transactions costs. Furthermore, it is likely that investors trying to earn the 24% excess return reported by DLS would bear idiosyncratic risk. As discussed earlier, all of these considerations lead to high limits to arbitrage. Nevertheless, as Brav and Heaton point out, it is difficult to distinguish convincingly which theory is operative, since both theories predict the same share price behaviour over time.

This last observation leads to an interesting possibility, namely that behavioural theories of investment and the theory of rational investment that underlies market efficiency may be moving together. Is there a great difference in claiming, on the one hand, that failure of share prices to fully reflect accounting information is due to behavioural characteristics such as conservatism and representativeness, and claiming, on the other hand, that such failures are driven by investor uncertainty about underlying firm parameters? Perhaps it is not cost effective for rational investors to fully remove this uncertainty, so that they behave as predicted by behavioural finance. In both cases, the market is not fully efficient. However, the inefficiency can be attributed just as well to rational investor behaviour, to behavioural biases, or to both.

6.2.9 Conclusions About Securities Market Efficiency

With respect to securities market efficiency, efficient or not efficient is the wrong question. Instead, the question is one of the *extent* of efficiency. We conclude that securities markets are not fully efficient, based largely on the continued existence of anomalies such as those described above. However, we also conclude that securities markets are sufficiently close to full efficiency that accountants can be guided by its implications, as outlined in Chapter 4. Our conclusion is based in part on the evidence described in Chapter 5, which suggests considerable efficiency. It is also based on increasing evidence that limits to arbitrage, such as cost and risk, make it difficult, if not impossible, for investors to actually earn riskless profits by taking advantage of anomalies. We can hardly expect the market to be efficient with respect to more information than it is cost effective to exploit.

With respect to whether investor rationality or behavioural theories best underlie securities market behaviour, the question seems to be open. Undoubtedly, investors exhibit each type of behaviour. However, a strong argument can be made that the rational decision theory model is still the most useful model for accountants to understand investor needs. This argument is based on theoretical arguments that non-stationarity of underlying earnings quality parameters provides a rational explanation for what is often interpreted as evidence of inefficiency, and on the fact that bounds on investor behaviour imposed by the costs and risks of earning arbitrage profits are consistent with rationality.

However, in the final analysis, it may not matter to accountants whether the rational model or behavioural models are most descriptive of investors, since the action implications are similar. One can argue that reducing the costs and risks of rational investing, by bringing current values into the financial statements proper, will increase decision usefulness and market efficiency. Alternatively, one can argue that helping investors overcome behavioural biases by bringing current values into the financial statements proper will increase decision usefulness and market efficiency. In either case, a measurement approach should help attain these desirable goals.

6.3 OTHER REASONS SUPPORTING A MEASUREMENT APPROACH

A number of considerations come together to suggest that the decision usefulness of financial reporting may be enhanced by increased attention to measurement. As just discussed, securities markets may not be as efficient as previously believed. Thus, investors may need more help in assessing probabilities of future firm performance than they obtain from historical cost statements. Also, we shall see that reported net income explains only a small part of the variation of security prices around the date of earnings announcements, and the portion explained may be decreasing. This raises questions about the relevance of historical cost-based reporting in the mixed measurement model.

From a theoretical direction, the clean surplus theory of Ohlson shows that the market value of the firm can be expressed in terms of income statement and balance sheet variables. While the clean surplus theory applies to any basis of accounting, its demonstration that firm value depends on fundamental accounting variables is consistent with a measurement approach.

Finally, increased attention to measurement is supported by more practical considerations. In recent years, auditors have been subjected to major lawsuits. In retrospect, it appears that net asset values of failed firms were seriously overstated. Conservative accounting standards that require current value-based techniques, such as ceiling tests, may help to reduce auditor liability in this regard.

We now review these other considerations in more detail.

6.4 THE VALUE RELEVANCE OF FINANCIAL STATEMENT INFORMATION

In Chapter 5 we saw that empirical accounting research has established that security prices do respond to the information content of net income. The ERC research, in particular, suggests that the market is quite sophisticated in its ability to extract value implications from financial statements.

However, Lev (1989) pointed out that the market's response to the good or bad news in earnings is really quite small, even *after* the impact of economy-wide events has been allowed for as explained in Figure 5.2. In fact, only 2 to 5% of the abnormal variability of narrow-window security returns around the date of release of earnings information can be attributed to earnings itself.[13] The proportion of variability explained goes up somewhat for wider windows—see our discussion in Section 5.3.2. Nevertheless, most of the variability of security returns seems due to factors other than the change of earnings. This finding has led to studies of the **value relevance** of financial statement information. Value relevance is closely related to the concept of earnings quality, since it uses securities market reaction to measure the extent to which financial statement information assists investors to predict future firm performance.

An understanding of Lev's point requires an appreciation of the difference between **statistical significance** and **practical significance**. Statistics that measure value relevance such as R^2 (see Note 13) and the ERC can be significantly different from zero in a statistical sense, but yet can be quite small. Thus, we can be quite sure that there *is* a security market response to earnings (as opposed to *no* response), but at the same time we can be disappointed that the response is not larger than it is. To put it another way, suppose that, on average, security prices change by $1 during a narrow window of three or four days around the date of earnings announcements. Then, Lev's point is that only about two to five cents of this change is due to the earnings announcement itself, even after allowing for market-wide price changes during this period.

Indeed, value relevance may be deteriorating. Brown, Lo, and Lys (1999), for a large sample of U.S. stocks, examined the wide-window relationship between share price and annual earnings, concluding that R^2 has decreased over the period 1958–1996. Similar results are reported by Kim and Kross (2005). Lev and Zarowin (1999), in a study covering 1978–1996, found similar results of declining R^2. They also reported a falling ERC. A falling ERC is more ominous than a falling R^2, since a falling R^2 is perhaps due to an increased impact over time of other information sources on share price, rather than a decline in the value relevance of accounting information. The ERC, however, is a direct measure of accounting value relevance, regardless of the magnitude of other information sources.[14]

Contrasting evidence, however, is provided by Landsman and Maydew (2002) for a sample of quarterly earnings announcements over 1972–1988. Instead of R^2 and ERC, they measured the information content of quarterly earnings by the abnormal security return (i.e., by the residual of the market model [Section 4.5]) over a three-day window surrounding the earnings release date. Recall from Section 5.2.3 that the residual term of the market model measures the firm-specific information content of an earnings announcement. By this measure, Landsman and Maydew found that the information content of earnings had *increased* over the period they studied.

This raises the question, how can the R^2 and ERC fall but abnormal return increase? A reconciliation is suggested by Francis, Schipper, and Vincent (2002). They point out an increasing tendency for large firms to report other information, such as sales, unusual and non-recurring items, and forward-looking information, at the same time as they make their earnings announcements. Thus, while the share price response to net income as such (measured by R^2 and ERC) may be falling, the response to the earnings announcement taken as a whole (measured by abnormal return) is increasing. Francis, Schipper, and Vincent examined the three-day abnormal returns to a sample of quarterly earnings announcements containing other information, during 1980–1999, and report results consistent with this argument.

Of course, we would never expect net income to explain *all* of a security's abnormal return, except under ideal conditions. Historical cost accounting and conservatism mean that net income lags in recognizing much economically significant information, such as increased value of intangibles. Recognition lag lowers R^2 by waiting longer than the market before recognizing value-relevant events.

Even if accountants were the *only* source of information to the market, our discussion of the informativeness of price in Section 4.4, and the resulting need to recognize the presence of noise and liquidity traders, tells us that accounting information cannot explain all of abnormal return variability. Also, non-stationarity of parameters such as beta (Section 6.2.3) and excess volatility introduced by non-rational investors (Section 6.2.4) further increase the amount of share price volatility to be explained.

Nevertheless, a "market share" for net income of only 2 to 5% and falling seems low, even after the above counterarguments are taken into account. Lev attributed this low share to poor earnings quality. This suggests that earnings quality could be improved by introducing a measurement approach into the financial statements. At the very least, evidence of low value relevance of earnings suggests that there is still plenty of room for accountants to improve the usefulness of financial statement information.

6.5 OHLSON'S CLEAN SURPLUS THEORY

6.5.1 Three Formulae for Firm Value

The Ohlson **clean surplus theory** provides a framework consistent with the measurement approach, by showing how the market value of the firm can be expressed in terms of fundamental balance sheet and income statement components. The theory assumes ideal conditions in capital markets, including dividend irrelevancy.[15] Nevertheless, it has had some success in explaining and predicting actual firm value. Our outline of the theory is based on a simplified version of Feltham and Ohlson (1995) (FO). The clean surplus theory model is also called the **residual income** model.

Much of the theory has already been included in earlier discussions, particularly Example 2.2 of P.V. Ltd. operating under ideal conditions of uncertainty. You may wish to review Example 2.2 at this time. In this section we will pull together these earlier discussions and extend the P.V. Ltd. example to allow for earnings persistence. The FO model can be applied to value the firm at any point in time for which financial statements are available. For purposes of illustration, we will apply it at time 1 in Example 2.2, that is, at the end of the first year of operation.

FO point out that the fundamental determinant of a firm's value is its dividend stream. Assume, for P.V. Ltd. in Example 2.2, that the bad-economy state was realized in year 1 and recall that P.V. pays no dividends, until a liquidating dividend at time 2. Then, the expected present value of dividends at time 1 is just the expected present value of the firm's cash on hand at time 2:

$$PA_1 = \frac{0.5}{1.10} (\$110 + \$100) + \frac{0.5}{1.10} (\$110 + \$200)$$

$$= \$95.45 + \$140.91$$

$$= \$236.36$$

Recall that cash flows per period are $100 if the bad state happens and $200 for the good state. The $110 term inside the brackets represents the $100 cash on hand at time 1 invested at a return of $R_f = 0.10$ in period 2.

Given dividend irrelevancy, P.V.'s market value can also be expressed in terms of its future cash flows. Continuing our assumption that the bad state happened in period 1:

$$PA_1 = \$100 + \left(0.5 \times \frac{\$100}{1.10}\right) + \left(0.5 \times \frac{\$200}{1.10}\right)$$

$$= \$100 + \$136.36$$

$$= \$236.36$$

where the first term is cash on hand at time 1, that is, the present value of $100 cash is just $100.

The market value of the firm can also be expressed in terms of financial statement variables. FO show that:

$$PA_t = bv_t + g_t \qquad (6.1)$$

at any time t, where bv_t is the net book value of the firm's assets per the balance sheet and g_t is the expected present value of future abnormal earnings, also called **goodwill**. For this relationship to hold it is necessary that all items of gain or loss go through the income statement, which is the source of the term "clean surplus" in the theory.

To evaluate goodwill for P.V. Ltd. as at time t = 1, look ahead over the remainder of the firm's life (one year in our example).[16] Recall that **abnormal earnings** are the difference between actual and expected earnings. Using FO's notation, define ox_2 as earnings for year 2 and $ox_2{}^a$ as abnormal earnings for that year.[17] From Example 2.2, we have:

If the bad state happens for year 2, net income for year 2 is

$$(100 \times 0.10) + 100 - 136.36 = -\$26.36$$

where the bracketed expression includes interest earned on opening cash.

If the good state happens, net income is

$$10 + 200 - 136.36 = \$73.64$$

Since each state is equally likely, expected net income for year 2 is

$$E\{ox_2\} = (0.5 \times -26.36) + (0.5 \times 73.64) = \$23.64$$

Expected abnormal earnings for year 2, the difference between expected earnings as just calculated and accretion of discount on opening book value, is thus

$$E\{ox_2{}^a\} = 23.64 - (0.10 \times 236.36) = \$0$$

Goodwill, the expected present value of future abnormal earnings, is then

$$g_1 = 0/1.10 = 0$$

Thus, for P.V. Ltd. in Example 2.2 with no persistence of abnormal earnings, goodwill is zero. This is because, under ideal conditions, arbitrage ensures that the firm expects to earn only the given interest rate on the opening value of its net assets. As a result, we can read firm value directly from the balance sheet:

$$PA_1 = \$236.36 + \$0$$
$$= \$236.36$$

Zero goodwill represents a special case of the FO model called **unbiased accounting**, that is, all assets and liabilities are valued at current value. When accounting is unbiased, and abnormal earnings do not persist, all of firm value appears on the balance sheet. In effect, the income statement has no information content, as we noted in Example 2.2.

Unbiased accounting represents the extreme of the measurement approach. Of course, as a practical matter, firms do not account for all assets and liabilities this way. For example, if P.V. Ltd. uses historical cost accounting or, more generally, conservative accounting for its capital asset, bv_1 may be biased downwards relative to current value. FO call this **biased accounting**. When accounting is biased, the firm has *unrecorded* goodwill g_t. However, the clean surplus formula (Equation 6.1) for PA_t holds for any basis of accounting, not just unbiased accounting under ideal conditions. To illustrate, suppose that P.V. Ltd. uses straight-line amortization for its capital asset, writing off $130.17 in year 1 and $130.16 in year 2. Note that year 1 present value–based amortization in Example 2.2 is $123.97. Thus, with straight-line amortization, earnings for year 1 and capital assets as at the end of year 1 are biased downwards relative to their ideal conditions counterparts. We now repeat the calculation of goodwill and firm value as at the end of year 1, continuing the assumption of bad state realization for year 1.

With straight-line amortization, expected net income for year 2 is:

$$E\{ox_2\} = (100 \times 0.10) + 0.5\,(100 - 130.16) + 0.5\,(200 - 130.16) = \$29.84$$

Expected abnormal earnings for year 2 is:

$$E\{ox_2{}^a\} = 29.84 - (0.10 \times 230.16) = \$6.82$$

where $230.16 is the firm's book value at time 1, being $100 cash plus the capital asset book value on a straight-line basis of $130.16.

Goodwill is then

$$g_1 = 6.82/1.10 = \$6.20$$

giving firm market value of

$$PA_1 = 230.16 + 6.20$$
$$= \$236.36$$

the same as the unbiased accounting case.

While firm value is the same, the goodwill of $6.20 is unrecorded on the firm's books. This again illustrates the point made in Section 2.5.1 that under historical cost accounting net income lags real economic performance. Here, historical cost-based net income for year 1 is $100 − $130.17 = –$30.17, less than net income of –$23.97 in Example 2.2. Nevertheless, if unrecorded goodwill is correctly valued, the resulting firm value is also correct.

This ability of the FO model to generate the same firm value regardless of the accounting policies used by the firm has an upside and a downside. On the upside, an investor who may wish to use the model to predict firm value does not in theory have to be concerned about the firm's choice of accounting policies. If the firm manager biases reported net income upwards to improve apparent performance, or biases net income downwards by means of conservative accounting, the firm value as calculated by the model is the same.[18] The reason is that changes in unrecorded goodwill induced by accounting policy choice are offset by equal but opposite changes in book values. The downside, however, is that the model can provide no guidance as to what accounting policies *should* be used.

We now see the sense in which the Ohlson clean surplus theory supports the measurement approach. Current value accounting for P.V.'s assets reduces the extent of biased accounting. In doing so, it moves more of the value of the firm onto the balance sheet, thereby reducing the amount of unrecorded goodwill that the investor has to estimate. While in theory the sum of book value and unrecorded goodwill is the same whether or not the firm uses current value accounting, in practice the firm can presumably prepare more accurate estimates of the current values of its assets and liabilities than can the investor. If so, and if the estimates are reasonably reliable, decision usefulness of the financial statements is increased, since a greater proportion of firm value can simply be read from the balance sheet. This is particularly so for investors who may not be fully rational, and who may need more help in determining firm value than they receive under the information approach.

*6.5.2 Earnings Persistence

FO then introduce the important concept of *earnings persistence* into the theory. Specifically, they assume that abnormal earnings are generated according to the following formula:

$$ \text{ox}_t^a = \omega \text{ox}_{t-1}^a + \upsilon_{t-1} + \tilde{\epsilon}_t \tag{6.2} $$

FO call this formula an **earnings dynamic**. The $\tilde{\epsilon}_t$ are the effects of state realization in period t on abnormal earnings, where the "~" indicates that these effects are random, as at the beginning of the period. As in Example 2.2, the expected value of state realization is zero and realizations are independent from one period to the next.

The ω is a persistence parameter, where $0 \leq \omega < 1$. For $\omega = 0$, we have the case of Example 2.2, that is, abnormal earnings do not persist. However, $\omega > 0$ is not unreasonable. Often, the effects of state realization in one year will persist into future years. For example, the bad-state realization in year 1 of Example 2.2 may be due to a rise in interest rates, the economic effects of which will likely persist beyond the current year. Then, ω captures the proportion of the $50 abnormal earnings in year 1 that would continue into the following year.

However, note that $\omega < 1$ in the FO model. That is, abnormal earnings of any particular year will die out over time. For example, the effects of a rise in interest rates will eventually dissipate. More generally, forces of competition will eventually eliminate positive, or negative, abnormal earnings, at a rate that ultimately depends on the firm's business strategy.

Note also that persistence is related to its empirical counterpart in the ERC research. Recall from Section 5.4.1 that ERCs are higher the greater the persistence in earnings. As we will see in Example 6.1, this is exactly what clean surplus theory predicts—the higher ω is, the greater the impact of the income statement on firm value.

---

*Section 6.5.2 can be skipped without loss of continuity.

The term v_{t-1} represents the effect of other information becoming known in year $t - 1$ (i.e., other than the information in year $t - 1$'s abnormal earnings) that affects the abnormal earnings of year t. When accounting is unbiased, $v_{t-1} = 0$. To see this, consider the case of R&D. If R&D was accounted for on a current value basis (i.e., unbiased accounting) then year $t - 1$'s abnormal earnings include the change in value brought about by R&D activities during that year. Of this change in value, the proportion ω will continue into next year's earnings. That is, if R&D is valued at current value, there is no relevant other information about future earnings from R&D—current earnings includes it all.

When accounting is biased, v_{t-1} assumes a much more important role. Thus, if R&D costs are written off as incurred, year $t - 1$'s abnormal earnings contain no information about future abnormal earnings from R&D activities. As a result, to predict year t's abnormal earnings it is necessary to add in as other information an outside estimate of the abnormal earnings in year t that will result from the R&D activities of year $t - 1$. That is, v_{t-1} represents next period's earnings from year $t - 1$'s R&D.

In sum, the earnings dynamic models current year's abnormal earnings as a proportion ω of the previous year's abnormal earnings, plus the effects of other information (if accounting is biased), plus the effects of random state realization.

Finally, note that the theory assumes that the set of possible values of $\tilde{\epsilon}_t$ and their probabilities are known to investors, consistent with ideal conditions. It is also assumed that investors know ω. If these assumptions are relaxed, rational investors will want information about $\tilde{\epsilon}_t$ and ω and can use Bayes' theorem to update their subjective state probabilities. Thus, nothing in the theory conflicts with the role of decision theory that was explained in Chapter 3.

Example 6.1
Present Value Model Under Uncertainty and Persistence

We now extend Example 2.2 to allow for persistence. Continue all the assumptions of that example and add the further assumption ω = 0.40. Since ideal conditions imply unbiased accounting, $v_{t-1} = 0$. Recall that abnormal earnings for year 1 are −$50 or $50, depending on whether the bad state or good state happens. Now, 40% of year 1 abnormal earnings will persist to affect operating earnings in year 2.

Assume that the bad state happens in year 1. (A similar analysis applies if the good state happens.) Then, we calculate P.V.'s market value at time 1. We begin with the formula based on expected future dividends.

$$PA_1 = \frac{0.5}{1.10} [(\$110 - (0.40 \times \$50) + \$100)] + \frac{0.5}{1.10} [(\$110 - (0.40 \times \$50) + \$200)]$$

$$= \left(\frac{0.5}{1.10} \times \$190 \right) + \left(\frac{0.5}{1.10} \times \$290 \right)$$

$$= \$86.36 \times \$131.82$$

$$= \$218.18$$

Note the effect of persistence—40% of year 1 abnormal earnings will persist to reduce year 2 cash flows. Otherwise, the calculation is identical with Example 2.2. We see that the effect of persistence of the bad state is to reduce the time 1 firm value by $236.36 - 218.18 = \$18.18$, the present value of the $20 of reduced future cash flows.

Now, moving from the dividends formula to the clean surplus formula for firm value (Equation 6.1), FO use the earnings dynamic equation (Equation 6.2) to show that the firm's goodwill g_t can be expressed in terms of the current year's abnormal earnings, giving a market value of:

$$PA_1 = bv_t + (\alpha \times ox_t^a) \tag{6.3}$$

where $\alpha = \omega/(1 + R_f)$ is a capitalization factor.[19] Note, as mentioned above, that the higher is the persistence parameter ω the higher is the impact of current earnings information on share price PA_t. In our example, for $t = 1$:

Cash on hand	= $100.00
Book value of asset, as per Example 2.2	= $136.36
bv_t	= $236.36

This gives:

$$PA_1 = bv_t + (\alpha \times ox_t^a)$$

$$= \$236.36 + \left(\frac{0.40}{1.10} \times -\$50\right)$$

$$= \$236.36 - \$18.18$$

$$= \$218.18$$

which agrees with the market value based on expected future dividends.

The implications of the FO model with persistence are twofold. First, even under ideal conditions, *all the action is no longer on the balance sheet.* The income statement is important too, since it reveals the current year's abnormal earnings, 40% of which will persist into future periods. Thus, we can regard abnormal earnings as 40% persistent in this example.

Second, the formula (Equation 6.2) implies that investors will want information to help them assess persistent earnings, since these are important to the future performance of the firm. Our discussion of extraordinary items in Section 5.5 showed how accountants can help in this regard by appropriate classification of items with low persistence. Also, the formula is consistent with the empirical impact of persistence on the ERC as outlined in Section 5.4.1, where we saw that greater persistence is associated with stronger investor reaction to current earnings.[20]

6.5.3 Estimating Firm Value

The FO model can be used to estimate the value of a firm's shares. This can then be compared to the actual market value, to indicate possible over- or undervaluation by the market, and to aid in investment decisions. The following example applies the model to Canadian Tire Corporation, Limited. The methodology used in this example is based on the procedures outlined in Lee (1996).

Example 6.2
Estimating the Value of Common Shares of Canadian Tire Corporation

From Canadian Tire's 2006 annual report (not reproduced here), we take 2006 net income (NI_{2006}) as $357, before minority interest (all dollar figures are in millions), its book value as $2,511.1 at December 31, 2005, and $2,785.2 at December 30, 2006 (bv_{2006}) (both including minority interest). This gives Canadian Tire's 2006 return on opening equity (ROE_{2006}) as 0.14. Somewhat arbitrarily, we assume that this return will continue for the next seven years, after which return will equal Canadian Tire's cost of capital. We will return to this assumption shortly.

Dividends totalled $53.8 for 2006, giving a dividend payout ratio of 53.8/357 = 0.15. We assume that this ratio will also continue for seven years.

To estimate Canadian Tire's cost of equity capital, we use the CAPM (Section 4.5):

$$E(R_{jt}) = R_f(1 - \beta_j) + \beta_j E(R_{Mt})$$

where firm j is Canadian Tire and t is March 2007. That is, we assume the market became aware of Canadian Tire's 2006 annual report during March 2007. $E(R_{jt})$ thus represents the rate of return demanded by the market for Canadian Tire shares at that time or, equivalently, its cost of capital. We take the risk-free rate of interest as $R_f = 0.06$ per annum, the bank prime rate in March 2007. To this rate, we add a market risk premium[21] of 4%, to estimate the expected annual rate of return on the market portfolio as 0.10. To estimate beta, we use the formula from Section 3.7:

$$\beta = \frac{Cov(j,M)}{Var(M)} = \frac{0.000615}{0.000906} = 0.68$$

where Cov (j, M) and Var (M) are estimated from returns data[22] for Canadian Tire and the S&P/TSX 300 index for March 2007. Then, our estimate of the firm's cost of equity capital in March 2007 is:

$$E(R_{jt}) = 0.06(1 - 0.68) + 0.68 \times 0.10 = 0.06 \times 0.32 + 0.07 = 0.02 + 0.07 = 0.09$$

We assume that this 9% cost of capital will stay constant.

Next, we evaluate Canadian Tire's unrecorded goodwill. As stated earlier, goodwill is the present value of expected future abnormal earnings, which we evaluate over a seven-year horizon from December 2006. First, we use the clean surplus relation to project end-of-year book values:

$$bv_{2007} = bv_{2006} + NI_{2007} - d_{2007}$$

where d is dividends. Using the relationship $d_t = kNI_t$, where k is the dividend payout ratio, this becomes:

$$
\begin{aligned}
bv_{2007} &= bv_{2006} + (1 - k)NI_{2007} \\
&= bv_{2006}(1 + (1 - k)ROE) \\
&= 2{,}785.2\,(1 + (0.85 \times 0.14)) \\
&= 2{,}785.2 \times 1.12 \\
&= \$3{,}119
\end{aligned}
$$

Similar calculations give:

$$
\begin{aligned}
bv_{2008} &= \$3{,}494 \\
bv_{2009} &= \$3{,}913 \\
bv_{2010} &= \$4{,}382 \\
bv_{2011} &= \$4{,}908 \\
bv_{2012} &= \$5{,}497
\end{aligned}
$$

Now abnormal earnings are defined as the difference between actual earnings and accretion of discount. Accretion of discount is cost of capital times opening book value. Actual earnings for a given year are projected as ROE times opening book value. Thus expected abnormal earnings for 2007 are:

$$
\begin{aligned}
ox^a_{2007} &= [ROE - E(R)]bv_{2006} \\
&= (0.14 - 0.09) \times 2{,}785.2 \\
&= 0.05 \times 2{,}785.2 \\
&= \$139
\end{aligned}
$$

Similar calculations give:

$$
\begin{aligned}
ox^a_{2008} &= \$156 \\
ox^a_{2009} &= \$175 \\
ox^a_{2010} &= \$196 \\
ox^a_{2011} &= \$219 \\
ox^a_{2012} &= \$245 \\
ox^a_{2013} &= \$275
\end{aligned}
$$

The present value of these abnormal earnings, that is, goodwill, at December 30, 2006, discounted at Canadian Tire's cost of capital, is

$$g_{2006} = \frac{139}{1.09} + \frac{156}{1.09^2} + \frac{175}{1.09^3} + \frac{196}{1.09^4} + \frac{219}{1.09^5} + \frac{245}{1.09^6} + \frac{275}{1.09^7}$$

$$= \$972$$

Finally, we add in December 30, 2006, book value (i.e., bv_{2006}):

$$PA_{2006} = 2,785.2 + 972$$

$$= \$3,757.2$$

Canadian Tire had 81,575,556 common shares outstanding[23] during 2006, giving an estimated value per share of $46.06.

Canadian Tire's actual share price around the end of March 2007 was $74, considerably more than our estimate. While one could adjust estimates of the risk-free interest rate, dividend payout ratio, and cost of capital, reasonable changes to these estimates would not affect the calculation significantly.

Consequently, the discrepancy between estimated and actual share price in Example 6.2 seems rather large. One possible explanation is that Canadian Tire's shares may be affected by the momentum behaviour described in Section 6.2.1. However, returns for both Canadian Tire shares and the S&P/TSX 300 index showed little evidence of momentum during March 2007.

Another possibility lies with the ROE used in our earnings projections. We have assumed that Canadian Tire's ROE stays constant at 0.14. Perhaps the market expects that ROE will increase. That is, our estimate may not have fully used all available information. Dechow, Hutton, and Sloan (1999), in a large sample of U.S. firms over the period 1976–1995, report that estimates of firm value based on the FO model that ignored other information were too low. To gain some insight into this possibility, consider analysts' forecasts of Canadian Tire earnings. We have used only information from the 2006 financial statement in our estimates, whereas analysts can bring considerably more information to bear. Canadian Tire reports earnings per share for 2006 of $4.35, and from reuters.com in July 2007, the average of analysts' earnings per share forecasts was $4.93 for 2007 and $5.63 for 2008. These forecasts represent earnings increases of 14% per year. This compares with an annual earnings increase of (ROE × (1 − k)) 12% implicit in our analysis. Thus, while it may be a bit low, our ROE estimate seems reasonably consistent with analysts' estimates.

Another earnings-related concern arises from recognition lag. For example, firms that conduct R&D will have their reported net income and net worth biased downwards relative to share values, since the market will look through these biased amounts to the expected value of the R&D. To the extent that R&D will increase *future* earnings, we may wish to increase our projected ROE by adding back to reported earnings all or part of R&D expense. This would increase our estimate of share value. However, as a practical matter, estimating the future value of R&D is difficult, and, in the case of Canadian Tire, there is little R&D to add back.

Market expectations of growth opportunities for Canadian Tire could also contribute to the discrepancy. Instead of an ROE of 14%, assume an ROE of 16.5%, which could arise as Canadian Tire expands its profitable operations in future. Then, given the dividend payout ratio of 15%, expected growth rate of earnings is (0.165 × 0.85) 14%, equal to analysts' expected growth in earnings for 2007 and 2008 given above. With this assumption, estimated share value rises to $55.68.

Yet another possibility for the discrepancy is the persistence of abnormal earnings. We have assumed that Canadian Tire generates abnormal earnings of (0.14 − 0.09) 0.05 for seven years and zero thereafter. That is, current abnormal earnings are assumed to be completely persistent for seven years and then immediately fall to zero. Other persistence assumptions are possible. Since Canadian Tire is well established in a stable industry, perhaps abnormal earnings will persist longer. If we were to extend the number of years, this would increase the estimated share value in our example. For example, an assumption that ROE of 14% will continue for 14 and 20 years, with other assumptions unchanged, raises estimated share value to $60.46 and $75.17, respectively.

However, it is not clear that these adjustments should be made. Even for well-established firms, competitive pressures operate to reduce growth rates and eliminate abnormal earnings over time. Supporting this refusal, Dechow, Hutton, and Sloan (1999) present tentative evidence that investors may not fully anticipate the extent to which future abnormal earnings decline.

In sum, the most likely explanation for the excess of market value over our estimate is that the market expects earnings to grow more than 12% per annum, and that abnormal earnings will persist considerably longer than our assumption of seven years.

Despite discrepancies such as this between estimated and actual share value, the FO model can be useful for investment decision-making. To see how, suppose that you carry out a similar analysis for another firm—call it Firm X—and obtain an estimated share value of $40. Which firm would you sooner invest in if they were both trading at $74? Canadian Tire, with estimated share value of $46.06, may be the better choice, since it has a higher ratio of model value to actual share value. That is, more of its actual share value is "backed up" by book value and expected abnormal earnings. Indeed, Frankel and Lee (1998), who applied the methodology of Example 6.2 to a large sample of U.S. firms during 1977–1992, found that the ratio of estimated market value to actual market value was a good predictor of share returns for two to three years into the future. Thus, for the years following 2006, Frankel and Lee's results suggest that Canadian Tire's share return should outperform that of Firm X.

We conclude that while our procedure to estimate Canadian Tire's share price is on the right track, the market seems to have considerably higher earnings expectations than ours. This leads to an examination of empirical studies of the ability of the clean surplus approach to predict earnings and share price.

6.5.4 Empirical Studies of the Clean Surplus Model

Clean surplus theory has generated much empirical research. One aspect of this research compares the relative predictive ability of the dividend, cash flow, and residual income models. Recall from Section 6.5.1 that under ideal conditions all three models produce identical valuations. However, when conditions are not ideal, the model that produces the best predictions is an empirical matter. For example, it is argued that the clean surplus model has an advantage because it uses financial statement information, which includes accruals. Since accruals anticipate future cash flows, they, in effect, bring these cash flows forward onto the balance sheet. Thus, to the extent accruals are value relevant, much of the forecasting work is already done. Cash flow and dividend models have "more" to predict, since they must predict total future flows. It is also argued that the clean surplus model is more convenient to apply than the cash flow model. It uses readily available financial statement information and does not have to back cash flows out of accrual accounting-based reports.

Our discussion in Sections 6.5.1 and 6.5.2 assumed that earnings, cash flows, and dividends were known for the complete future of the firm (only two years for P.V. Ltd.). In reality, the life of the firm and its future earnings, cash, and dividend flows are not known. What is usually done when using clean surplus to estimate firm value is to predict earnings for a **forecast horizon** of a few years into the future, and then estimate a **terminal value**, that is, the present value of abnormal earnings for all remaining years of the firm's life. A major practical problem in applying all three models is the choice of forecast horizon, and what amount, if any, to assign to the terminal value. Our Canadian Tire estimate used a forecast horizon of seven years, with a terminal value of zero on the grounds that competitive pressures are expected to eliminate abnormal returns beyond that time. Of course, this zero terminal value assumption is rather arbitrary. Perhaps a better (but still arbitrary) assumption is that Canadian Tire's abnormal earnings would not fall to zero, but rather start to decline after seven years. Then, terminal value is greater than zero, which would increase our value estimate. Indeed, if the firm has opportunities for future growth that outweigh competitive pressures, abnormal earnings will increase, rather than decrease, beyond the forecast horizon, further increasing terminal value.

An alternative terminal value approach is based on analysts' long-range forecasts. In this regard, Courteau, Kao, and Richardson (2001), for a sample of U.S. firms over the period 1992–1996, studied the relative predictive ability of the dividend, cash flow, and clean surplus models, using a five-year forecast horizon. They found that predictions using arbitrary terminal value assumptions, as we did for Canadian Tire, substantially underestimated share market prices. When terminal values were based on analysts' forecasts of share price at the end of year 5, predictions of current share prices were much more accurate. Furthermore, the three models were then roughly equal in their forecasting ability, consistent with our theoretical expectation.

Conservative accounting further complicates the forecast horizon, since it biases downwards both book value and reported earnings. In Section 6.5.1, we showed that in theory this does not matter, since abnormal earnings over the life of the firm increase to counter-act the bias. As mentioned, however, in actual applications the forecast horizon is shorter than the life of the firm, so that all of the bias is not counteracted. If the terminal value estimate is not increased to recognize this shortfall, firm value estimates will be too low. This could at least partially explain why our estimate of share price for Canadian Tire is low.

A second type of empirical clean surplus research studies the prediction of future earnings, since future earnings over the forecast horizon are a main input into the good-will estimate. This represents a significant change in emphasis from research under the information approach, which studies the association between financial statement infor-mation and share returns.

For most large firms, analysts' forecasts provide readily available future earnings esti-mates (as opposed to our estimates for Canadian Tire based on ROE). However, analysts' forecasts are only as good as the analysts who prepare them. In this regard, Abarbanell and Bushee (1997), in an extension of the approach used by Lev and Thiagarajan (1993) (Section 5.7), showed how certain "fundamental signals" from the current financial state-ments, such as changes in sales, accounts receivable, inventories, gross margin, and capital expenditure, could improve the prediction of next year's earnings changes. They went on to show that analysts appeared to underuse the fundamental signals when predicting earn-ings. In a similar vein, Begley and Feltham (2002) added analysts' forecasts and current capital expenditures as other information in the earnings dynamic. They found that this significantly improved prediction of unrecorded goodwill for their sample firms. Overall, these results suggest that analysts' earnings forecasts would benefit from greater attention to the full information potential of financial statements.

Finally, another use of the theory is to estimate a firm's cost of capital. In Example 6.2, note that any four of the five variables—share price, book value, expected future earnings, risk-free interest rate, and cost of capital—can be used, in principle, to solve for the other one. Thus, the clean surplus model provides an alternative to the CAPM for cost of capital estimation. Indeed, clean surplus offers some advantages over the CAPM by eliminating the need to estimate beta and the expected return on the market portfolio (see Section 4.5).

6.5.5 Summary

Clean surplus theory has had a major impact on financial accounting theory and research. By demonstrating that firm value can equally well be expressed in terms of financial accounting variables as in terms of dividends or cash flows, it has led to increased research attention to earnings prediction. Much of this research explores how current financial statement information can be used to improve this prediction. Better earnings prediction enables better estimates of unrecorded goodwill, leading to better predictions of firm value and hence better investment decisions.

The theory also leads to a measurement approach, since more current values reported on the balance sheet means a lower proportion of firm value included in unrecorded goodwill, hence less the potential for investor mistakes in estimating this complex component of firm value. This can improve investor decision-making and proper securities market operation, particularly if securities markets are not fully efficient.

6.6 AUDITORS' LEGAL LIABILITY

Perhaps the main source of pressure for the measurement approach, however, comes as a reaction to spectacular failures of large firms. Many such events have taken place in the United States. During the early 1980s, numerous financial institutions, specifically savings and loan associations, failed.[24] While these failures preceded the Enron and WorldCom financial reporting disasters (see Section 1.2), they remain important because they generated many of the pressures leading to the measurement approach.

The savings and loan debacle began with an inverted yield curve in the late 1970s. That is, short-term interest rates became higher than long-term rates. As a result, the savings and loans had to pay more interest to depositors than they earned from their long-term loans. Failure to write these loans down to current value resulted in overstatement of net assets on the audited balance sheets, with resultant overstatements of earnings. Auditors are often under considerable pressure from management, or even politicians, to bend or "stretch" GAAP, so that legal capital requirements, earnings targets, and/or analysts' forecasts will be met. Indeed, such stretching was a major contributing factor to the savings and loan failures. But, yielding to such pressure can result in substantial legal liability. For example, an article in *The Wall Street Journal* (March 11, 1994, p. A2) reported lawsuits against the audit firm of Deloitte and Touche totalling $1.85 billion. The charges arose from alleged clean audit opinions issued to savings and loan associations that, in retrospect, were insolvent. The article described a proposed settlement of these lawsuits in excess of $300 million. While considerably less than the amounts at suit, this was the second-largest liability settlement surrounding the savings and loan debacle. (The largest was a $400 million settlement by Ernst and Young for similar charges.)

How can auditors protect themselves against pressures and potential liabilities such as these? One response, of course, is ethical behaviour. Auditors should recognize that the long-run interests of the accounting/auditing profession are served by not yielding to inappropriate pressures to stretch GAAP.

Ethical behaviour, however, can be bolstered by conservative accounting. As we have mentioned previously, the lower-of-cost-or-market rule for inventories is a long-standing example. Furthermore, historical cost accounting contains conservative elements, such as recording profitable capital assets at cost even though current value is higher, and retaining inventories at historical cost until reliable evidence of realization is obtained.

Nevertheless, GAAP did not at the time of the savings and loan failures require recognition of current value decreases for major classes of assets and liabilities if the firm intended to hold them to maturity. Examples include certain financial assets, capital assets, intangibles, and long-term debt. Retention of these items at cost or amortized cost was justified by the going concern assumption of historical cost accounting. But, as mentioned above, overvaluation of net assets was a major criticism of financial reporting following the savings and loan failures.

It seemed that a stronger form of conservatism, requiring an extension of lower-of-cost-or-market thinking, was needed. Standard setters have implemented several standards of this nature in the years following the savings and loan debacle, such as **ceiling tests** for capital assets and goodwill. These tests represent a partial application of the measurement approach.[25] If undiscounted net future cash flows from an asset are less than book value, the asset is written down to its current value. Then, perhaps, the fact that such writedowns are required by GAAP will help auditors resist management pressure to overstate net assets. Furthermore, auditors can reduce their liability exposure by pointing out that, with ceiling tests, the financial statements proper incorporated the negative value changes leading to bankruptcy, merger, downsizing, environmental liabilities, etc. Indeed, to the extent negative value changes are inside information, their disclosure via ceiling tests informs the market about the existence and magnitude of such changes. Of course, determination of current value requires greater use of estimates and judgement but, because of legal liability, the relevance/reliability tradeoff may have shifted towards greater relevance.

The incidence of conservative financial reporting in the United States was investigated by Basu (1997). He measured conservatism by the correlation between net income and share returns. Basu argued that an efficient securities market will bid up the share prices of firms that are performing well and bid down the prices of firms that are performing poorly. Under conservative accounting, the earnings of firms that are performing well *will not* include the unrealized increases in assets that characterize a firm that is doing well. However, the earnings of firms that are performing poorly *will* include decreases in the values of their assets. It follows that the correlation between share returns and earnings will be higher for firms that are performing poorly than for firms that are performing well. As Basu puts it, earnings are more timely in their recognition of poor performance than of good performance. The difference between these two correlations can thus be viewed as evidence of conservative accounting. In a large sample of firms over the years 1963–1990, Basu found significantly higher correlation across firms in his sample that were doing poorly than for firms that were doing well, consistent with his argument.

Using this measurement approach, Basu went on to examine the period 1983–1990. This period has been identified as a period of high growth in litigation against auditors and corresponds roughly to the aftermath of the savings and loan failures described above.

He found that conservatism increased in this period relative to earlier periods of low litigation growth. This suggests that standard setters reacted to investor losses and auditors' legal difficulties by increasing conservatism, as in the ceiling test standards referred to above. Indeed, the trend to increasing conservatism continues. Ball and Shivakumar (2006) document increasing conservatism to 2002, a period ending after the Enron and WorldCom failures. It seems that investor losses, auditor liability, and severe penalties for managers who overstate earnings following these failures have further reinforced conservative accounting. For more discussion of these litigation and regulation-based explanations for conservatism, see Watts (2003).

6.7 ASYMMETRY OF INVESTOR LOSSES

These explanations for conservatism can also be supported by the decision theory out-lined in Chapter 3. To see this, consider the following examples.

*Example 6.3
Asymmetry of Investor Losses I

Bill Cautious, a rational investor, has an investment in the shares of X Ltd., with current market value of $10,000. He plans to use this amount to live on over the next two years. After that time, he will have graduated and will have a high-paying job. Consequently, he is not concerned right now about planning beyond two years. His goal is to maximize his total utility over this period. For simplicity, we assume that X Ltd. pays no dividends over these two years. Bill is risk-averse, with utility in each year equal to the square root of the amount he spends in that year.

It is easy to see that Bill's total utility will be maximized if he spends the same amount each year. Thus, he sells $5,000 of his shares now and plans to sell the remaining $5,000 at the beginning of the second year.[26]

Suppose, however, that as at the beginning of year 1, certain X Ltd. assets have fallen in value. The loss is unrealized, and the X Ltd. auditor fails to recognize it. Consequently, the loss remains as inside information, and the market value of Bill's unsold shares remains at $5,000. The loss becomes realized during year 1, and Bill's remaining shares are worth $3,000 at year-end.

Calculate Bill's utility for the two years, evaluated as at the end of year 1:

$$EU^a \text{ (Overstatement)} = \sqrt{5,000} + \sqrt{3,000}$$
$$= 70.71 + 54.77$$
$$= 125.48$$

where EU^a denotes Bill's actual utility, being the utility of the $5,000 he spends in the first year plus the utility to come in year 2 from the sale of his shares for $3,000.[27]

If Bill knew at the beginning of the first year that his wealth was only $8,000, he would plan to spend $4,000 each year. His expected utility would have been:

$$EU \text{ (Overstatement)} = \sqrt{4,000} + \sqrt{4,000}$$
$$= 63.25 + 63.25$$
$$= 126.50$$

---

*Examples 6.3 and 6.4 can be skipped without loss of continuity.

where EU denotes Bill's utility if he knew the ultimate value of his shares. Thus Bill loses utility of $126.50 - 125.48 = 1.02$ as a result of an opening $2,000 wealth overstatement.

Now assume instead that the X Ltd. assets have risen in value by $2,000 at the beginning of year 1. Again, the unrealized gain is not recognized by the auditor at the beginning of year 1, and it remains as inside information. The gain becomes realized during the year, and Bill's shares are worth $7,000 at year-end. His actual utility over the two years is:

$$EU^a \text{ (Understatement)} = \sqrt{5{,}000} + \sqrt{7{,}000}$$
$$= 70.71 + 83.67$$
$$= 154.38$$

Whereas, if Bill had known his wealth was $12,000:

$$EU \text{ (Understatement)} = \sqrt{6{,}000} + \sqrt{6{,}000}$$
$$= 77.46 + 77.46$$
$$= 154.92$$

Thus, Bill loses utility of $154.92 - 154.38 = 0.54$ as a result of an opening wealth understatement. Note that even though Bill's total consumption will be $2,000 higher than he had originally expected, he still suffers a loss of utility, since the understatement costs him the opportunity to optimally plan his spending over time.[28]

The main point of the example is that while the amount of misstatement is the same, Bill's loss of utility for an overstatement is almost twice the loss for an understatement. The loss arises because Bill misallocates his consumption over time due to errors and bias in reporting his wealth. Bill will be upset in either case, but he is more upset about an overstatement. Consequently, the auditor is more likely to be sued for overstatement errors.[29] For a more formal model to demonstrate this asymmetry, see Scott (1975).

Anticipating the investor's loss asymmetry, the auditor reacts by being conservative. When current value has decreased, writing assets down to current value benefits the investor in our example by avoiding the utility loss of 1.02, thereby decreasing the likelihood of the investor suing the auditor. Regulators, who would also like to see fewer investor losses and lawsuits, will encourage this conservatism with punitive laws for firms and their managers who fail to release bad news in a timely manner, and with new accounting standards such as ceiling tests.

Example 6.3 illustrates conditional, or *ex post*, conservatism (see Chapter 3, Note 8). The economic loss in value has already occurred, although it has not been realized at the beginning of year 1. Example 6.3 suggests a rationale for recognizing the unrealized loss—lower investor losses and less exposure to lawsuits.

In sum, one way that accountants and auditors can bolster ethical behaviour, increase usefulness for investors, and protect themselves against legal liability is to expand conditional conservatism. Note that since conditional conservatism requires measurement of current values, we can regard it as an asymmetric (i.e., one-sided) version of the measurement approach.

Of course, Example 6.3 raises the question, why not write assets up to current value as well? Recognizing a $2,000 unrealized asset increase at the first of year 1 would have increased Bill's utility by 0.54. While not as great as the utility increase from recognizing a $2,000 unrealized loss, this would constitute a further improvement in financial statement usefulness. A possible answer is that the auditor may be concerned about the reliability of current values. The increase in usefulness and decrease in lawsuit exposure from writing assets down may be high enough to outweigh reliability concerns, whereas the benefits from writing assets up may not be. Also, in addition to the investor-oriented motivation illustrated here, conditional conservatism has contracting and corporate governance motivations (to be discussed in Section 8.5.2). Writing assets up works against these motivations.

This asymmetry of utility losses, which is driven by the concavity of a risk-averse investor's utility function, constitutes an investor demand for conservatism, which underlies the litigation and regulation explanations for conservatism outlined in Section 6.6.

Example 6.4
Asymmetry of Investor Losses II

To pursue conservatism further, continue the assumptions above, except that now there has been no change in X Ltd. asset value as at the beginning of year 1. However, asset value, hence Bill's share value, may change in future. Specifically, assume that the auditor expects that as at the end of year 1, assets will either have fallen in value by $2,000 or risen in value by $2,000, each with probability of 0.5. What asset value should the auditor report at the beginning of year 1? Specifically, should the assets be reported at their expected value (i.e., current value) of $10,000?

To answer this question, assume that the auditor wants to maximize financial statement usefulness for Bill. That is, he/she wants to assist Bill to maximize his expected utility of consumption over the two years. Bill's expected utility (EU) at the beginning of the first year is:

$$EU = \sqrt{x/2} + 0.5\sqrt{8,000 - x/2} + 0.5\sqrt{12,000 - x/2} \qquad (6.4)$$

where x is the value of wealth that Bill uses for planning purposes, and x/2 is his consumption in the first year. Second year consumption is either $8,000 minus first year consumption or $12,000 minus first year consumption, each with probability 0.5.

Now, if Bill uses x = $10,000, and X Ltd. assets are worth $8,000 at year-end, he will suffer a utility loss of 1.02, as calculated in Example 6.3. Similarly, he will lose utility of

0.54 if X Ltd. assets turn out to be worth $12,000. Given this loss asymmetry, Bill should base his first year consumption on a wealth estimate less than $10,000. In fact, to maximize EU, he should use a wealth estimate of x = $9,400, yielding EU = 140 in Equation 6.4. If Bill uses a wealth estimate of x = $10,000 (i.e., the expected value of his wealth), his EU falls to 139.93.[30]

Anticipating this loss asymmetry, the auditor may value X Ltd. assets at $9,400 at the beginning of year 1, rather than their current value of $10,000. This alerts Bill to use a conservative wealth value for his consumption planning.[31] Also, legal liability is reduced, since auditors are also likely to be sued for failing to anticipate losses (as opposed to Example 6.3, where the auditor is sued for failing to report a loss that has already occurred). Experimental evidence consistent with auditors' greater avoidance of potential overstatements relative to understatements in the presence of litigation risk is reported by Barron, Pratt, and Stice (2001). Example 6.4 provides a rational underpinning to evidence such as this.

This example illustrates *ex ante* or **unconditional conservatism**, under which risky assets are reported at less than their current value even though an economic gain or loss has not yet taken place. Note that, unlike Example 6.3, no change in current value has yet taken place. However, unconditional conservatism does convey information to investors. Given that the auditor has better information about the distribution of future asset value than the investor, the conservative valuation of $9,400 represents the auditor's estimate of the most decision useful value for risk-averse investors who need a wealth estimate for decision-making purposes.

In practice, there are several ways that unconditional conservatism is implemented. For example, profitable capital investments are valued at historical cost, inventories are retained at historical cost until an increase in value is realized through sale, and amortization expense may run ahead of economic depreciation. Also, historical cost accounting requires certain expenditures on intangibles, such as research costs, to be expensed as incurred. Some of these policies can be justified on grounds of reliability. However, they can also be viewed as a response to an investor demand for unconditional conservatism.

Of course, as an alternative to reporting a single value for an asset, the auditor could report the various possible asset values and their probabilities. In Example 6.4, the $8,000 and $12,000 possible end-of-year 1 values and their probabilities could be reported as supplementary risk information. Then, Bill could pick whatever wealth value he wants for planning purposes, rather than rely on a single number from the financial statements. As a practical matter, however, this would involve overcoming possible manager objections and, for such a report to be credible, would require auditing a large multivariate probability distribution of the current values of all assets and liabilities, complete with covariances. Thus, even though the auditor will have a better estimate of this distribution than the investor, it is more reliable, and almost as relevant, to report conservative net income and balance sheet values instead.[32]

Note that unconditional conservatism pre-empts conditional conservatism (the lower is asset valuation now, the less there is to write down later). If the X Ltd. asset was valued at the beginning of year 1 at $9,400, as per this example, and a $2,000 loss on the asset is realized in year 1 as per Example 6.3, the writedown would be only $1,400 ($2,000 − $600), since $600 of the loss is pre-empted by the initial conservative asset valuation. Thus, the utility loss Bill suffers in Example 6.3 is reduced.

The extent of unconditional conservatism can be measured by a firm's market-to-book value ratio, since an efficient market will bid up the value of a firm with unrecorded goodwill and profitable assets even though value increases have not yet been recognized in the accounts. Thus, following from the previous paragraph, there should be a negative relationship between market-to-book and conditional conservatism. Both market-to-book and conditional conservatism may contain error as a conservatism measure, though, since they are also affected by matters such as the firm's future growth prospects, past write-downs, possible market inefficiency, and earnings management tactics. However, in a large sample of U.S. firms over 1970–2001, Pae, Thornton, and Welker (2005) documented empirically that market-to-book and conditional conservatism did exhibit the predicted negative relationship.[33]

6.8 CONCLUSIONS ON THE MEASUREMENT APPROACH TO DECISION USEFULNESS

The information approach to financial reporting is content to accept the historical cost basis of accounting and rely on full disclosure to enhance earnings quality and usefulness to investors. The form of disclosure does not matter, since it is assumed that there are enough rational, informed investors to quickly and correctly incorporate any reasonable form into the efficient market price, thereby price protecting investors who may not wish to conduct their own in-depth analyses. Empirical research has confirmed that the market finds net income information at least to be useful. In effect, empirical research under the information approach accepts the efficient market price and evaluates the usefulness of accounting information in terms of its association with this market price.

However, there are a number of questions about the information approach. First, securities markets may not be as fully efficient as had previously been believed, suggesting that investors might need some help in figuring out the full implications of accounting information for future returns. Behavioural theory suggests that help may be supplied by moving current value information from financial statement notes into the financial statements proper. Second, a market share of 2 to 5% for net income seems low and, despite theoretical support, it has been difficult to find much direct market reaction at all to non-earnings accounting information. In addition, legal liability may force accountants, auditors, and managers to increase conservatism in the financial statements by adopting an asymmetric version of current value measurement.

The measurement approach is reinforced by the development of the Ohlson clean surplus theory, which emphasizes the fundamental role of financial accounting information in determining firm value. This theory implies a more basic role for financial statements in reporting on firm value than the information approach, which views accounting information as one of many information sources competing for the attention of the efficient market. Thus, the clean surplus theory leads naturally to the measurement approach.

Of course, the measurement approach runs into problems of reliability. Consequently, we do not expect this approach to extend to a complete set of financial statements on a current value basis. Rather, the question is one of degree—to what degree will current values supplant costs in financial reporting? Consequently, in the next chapter we review GAAP from a current valuation perspective. There always has been a substantial present value and market value component to the financial statements. But, as we shall see, recent years have witnessed a number of new current value standards.

Questions and Problems

1. Why does a measurement approach to decision usefulness suggest more value-relevant information in the financial statements proper, when efficient securities market theory implies that financial statement notes or other disclosure would be just as useful?

2. What will be the impact on relevance, reliability, and decision usefulness of financial statement information as accountants adopt the measurement approach?

3. Explain in your own words what "post-announcement drift" is. Why is this an anomaly for securities market efficiency? Does post-announcement drift necessarily imply that investors are not rational?

4. Explain in your own words why the market response to accruals, as documented by Sloan (1996), is an anomaly for securities market efficiency.

5. An investor considers two mutual funds. Based on past experience, the first fund has expected return of 0.08 and standard deviation of 0.05. The second fund has expected return of 0.07 and standard deviation of 0.06. There is no reason to assume that future performance of these funds will differ from past performance. However, the second fund has a guarantee attached that return in any year will not be negative.

   The investor buys the second fund. Use prospect theory to explain why.

6. Lev, in his article "On the Usefulness of Earnings" (1989), points out the low ability of reported net income to explain variations in security prices around the date of release of earnings information. Lev attributes this low value relevance of earnings to low earnings quality.

   Required

   a. Define earnings quality. Relate your answer to the concept of an information system in single-person decision theory.

   b. What other reasons than low earnings quality might there be for the low value relevance of earnings?

   c. How might an increased measurement approach to financial reporting increase earnings quality, and hence the impact of earnings on security prices?

7. In Section 6.4, the concept of value relevance of net income is introduced. It appears that the value relevance of reported earnings, as measured by R^2 or ERC, is low, and falling over time. Use single-person decision theory to explain why value relevance of reported earnings can be measured by R^2 or ERC. Is it possible for abnormal share return to increase but R^2 and ERC to fall? Explain.

8. For what reasons might transactions costs, including investors' time to figure out and operate strategies that appear to beat the market, not be a completely adequate explanation for the efficient securities market anomalies?

9. Define two barriers to arbitrage, and explain why these might explain the continued existence of efficient securities market anomalies such as post-announcement drift and the accruals anomaly.

10. Reproduced below is the Economic Value Added (EVA) disclosure from the MD&A section of the 1996 annual report of Domtar, Inc. Some of the uses of EVA are outlined in Domtar's discussion in the disclosure. Of interest here is the close relationship between the EVA measurement formula and the clean surplus-based valuation procedure outlined in Example 6.2. Note that the EVA for a given year is equivalent to abnormal earnings (ox_t^a) for that year in our example. Recall that goodwill is calculated as the present value of expected future abnormal earnings.

   It is not clear whether Domtar continues to use EVA, since there is no mention of it in its 2006 annual report. Since 1996 was the last year it gave details of its EVA calculation, we will continue with its 1996 disclosure.

Economic Value Added (EVA)

At the end of 1995, the Corporation adopted a new management system known as Economic Value Added, or EVA®, to ensure that the decision-making process at Domtar is aligned with the objective of increasing shareholder value.

In 1996, this concept was implemented throughout the Corporation and is being used for measuring performance, evaluating investment decisions, improving communication and for incentive compensation. EVA® training courses were developed and are being provided to a large number of employees in on-going efforts to develop a value creation culture at Domtar.

The EVA® measurement formula is as follows:

$$\text{EVA}® = \text{NOPAT}[1] - \text{Capital Charge}[2]$$

[1] Net operating profit after tax
[2] Capital employed × Cost of capital for the Corporation

This simple formula highlights the notion that in order to create value for Domtar shareholders, every business unit must generate returns at least equal to its cost of capital, including both debt and shareholders' equity.

Following a record year in 1995 when $316 million of EVA® was created, EVA® for Domtar in 1996 was $120 million negative, due to the decline in selling prices.

$$EVA® = NOPAT - Capital\ Charge$$

1995	316	=	539	−	223
1996	(120)	=	88	−	208

Domtar remains committed to creating long-term shareholder value and will intensify its efforts in 1997, especially in areas under its control, such as productivity, costs, customer service, and capital management. Domtar will also benefit from an overall lower cost of capital going forward as a result of its debt management program completed in 1996.

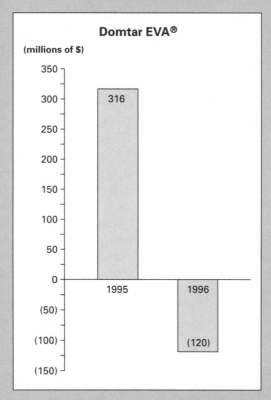

Source: Economic Value Added disclosure from Domtar, Inc.'s annual report (1996). Reproduced with permission.

Required

a. Evaluate the usefulness of this approach to communicating information to investors. Consider both relevance and reliability issues.

b. If you were the top manager of a company using EVA, would its use encourage or discourage you from initiating major, capital intensive expansion projects? Explain why or why not.

c. You are an investor in a fast-growing, high-tech company that reports EVA. The assets of the company are primarily intangible (patents, skilled workforce) and are unrecorded on the company's books, hence not included in the EVA capital charge. How would the unrecorded, intangible nature of the assets of such a company affect your interpretation of its EVA? Explain.

d. Note that reporting of EVA is voluntary. Domtar reports this information for 1996 even though its EVA is negative. Does Domtar's willingness to report this information add credibility to its claim that it "will intensify its efforts in 1997"? Explain.

11. A firm is expected to earn $100 net income for next year, at the end of which time the firm will be wound up. The $100 expected earnings includes gains and losses from disposals of assets and liabilities, and all other winding up costs. The firm's book value at the beginning of the year is $500, and its cost of capital is 14%. What is the firm's market value as at the beginning of the year?

    a. $526.32

    b. $570.00

    c. $587.72

    d. $600.00

12. Obtain the most recent annual report of a publicly traded company, and use the procedure outlined in Section 6.5.3 to estimate the value per common share of the company. Compare this value with the company's actual market value per share about three months after the company's year-end. Explain any difference. In your explanation, include consideration of possible effects of recognition lag, and justify your assumption about the persistence of abnormal earnings.

13. You are the senior accountant of a large, publicly traded company that is experiencing a decline of business that management feels is temporary. To meet earnings projections given in its previous year's MD&A, management asks you to find an additional $5 million of reported earnings for the current year. After some study, you determine that to increase earnings by this magnitude, it is necessary to recognize additional revenue on contracts in process, even though the contracts are far from completion and it is questionable whether or not any profits will actually be realized. A careful study of accounting standards relating to revenue recognition leads you to the conclusion that to recognize $5 million of profits at this stage would not be in accordance with GAAP. Consequently, the auditors will be expected to object.

    You report this to management, but are instructed to proceed anyway. Management assures you that next year's business will be much better and the premature revenue recognition will never be noticed. Furthermore, management is sure it can convince the auditor of this as well.

    Required

    What will you do in response to this ethical dilemma? Give reasons for and against your decision.

14. Recent years have seen considerable litigation against auditors in the United States. A major source of this litigation arises from the pressure firms feel to meet analysts' earnings expectations. To avoid reporting lower-than-expected earnings, firms sometimes use

earnings management, such as premature revenue recognition and other devices, to raise reported net income. To avoid a qualified audit report, the firm may pressure its auditor to "stretch" GAAP. This puts the auditor in a difficult ethical position. The auditor's primary responsibility is to the shareholders. However, it is management that influences the audit committee and pays for auditor appointments. If the auditor does not go along, he or she may lose the audit client, and also any non-audit services also provided. Furthermore, he or she will inevitably be drawn into lawsuits when the earnings management becomes known (as it eventually must, since accruals reverse).

One can sympathize with company managers for wanting to meet earnings expectations. The market will severely penalize their stock price if they do not. For example, in 1997, Eastman Kodak announced that revenue would not meet expectations due to the high value of the U.S. dollar, and analysts reduced their estimate of first quarter, 1997, earnings from $0.90 per share to $0.80. Kodak's share price fell by $9.25 to $79 in heavy trading. Subsequently, Kodak reported earnings per share for the quarter of $0.81, and share price rose $2.25 to $75.37.

This market reaction has been repeated many times since. An article in *The Wall Street Journal* in April 2000 quoted a prominent investment manager as saying that the market is "overdiscounting" changes in earnings expectations and that it is "reacting too much."

Required

a. Why might an auditor be tempted to go along with client pressure to manage reported earnings so as to meet analysts' expectations? What are some of the possible longer-run costs to the auditor if he or she goes along?

b. To what extent would increased use of a measurement approach to financial reporting reduce auditor exposure to client pressure and lawsuits?

c. Use concepts from behavioural finance to explain why the market may "overreact" to changes in earnings expectations.

d. Is the $9.25 reduction in Kodak's share price reported above inconsistent with efficient securities market theory? Use the relationship between change in analysts' earnings estimates and share price change to explain why or why not.

15. In its 2005 annual report, TD Bank Financial Group (TD) reports **economic profit** of $1,062 million. Its calculation of economic profit is summarized as follows (millions of dollars):

Average common shareholders' equity for the year	$14,600
Add goodwill/intangibles amortized to date	3,213
Average invested capital before goodwill amortization	17,813
Net income per income statement	$ 2,229
Capital charge at 10.1% per annum, estimated using CAPM	1,799
Economic profit after amortization of intangibles and items of note	430
Amortization of intangibles ($354) and items of note ($278)	632
Economic profit before amortization of intangibles and items of note	$ 1,062

Required

a. What is the relationship between TD's calculation of economic profit and the calculation of firm value using clean surplus theory, illustrated in Example 6.2?

b. Does TD have unrecorded goodwill? Explain why or why not.

c. Amortization of intangibles of $354 million is added back to 2005 GAAP net income of $2,229 for purposes of calculating economic profit, on the grounds that net income before amortization of intangibles better measures bank performance. The goodwill and other intangibles arise because of TD's acquisitions of Canada Trust in 2000 and Banknorth in 2005. Items of note of $278 are also added back. Items of note are defined in the annual report as items that management does not believe are indicative of underlying business performance. They include a charge for legal liability, costs of preferred share redemption, restructuring charge, loss on derivatives, and several related items.

As an investor in TD Bank shares, do you find economic income more or less useful than reported net income for predicting future bank performance? Explain. Focusing on economic income, do you find economic income before or after adding back amortization of intangibles and items of note to be most useful? Explain.

16. Philip Services Corp. was a large Canadian company with shares traded in Canada and the United States. Its extensive operations included recovery and recycling of scrap metals. In 1997, the company filed a prospectus in the United States, from which it raised additional common share capital. The prospectus included unqualified audited financial statements for 1995 and 1996, together with unaudited financial statement information for nine months of 1997.

In 1998, Philip revealed that it was unable to account for a large quantity of its copper inventory, costing about U.S. $80 million. In addition, it disclosed writeoffs of almost $200 million in restructuring costs and goodwill writedowns arising from acquisitions of other companies over 1993–1996. Its share price quickly fell from about $25 to pennies per share. The company subsequently went into bankruptcy protection.

A number of lawsuits and charges followed. In 2004, the Royal Canadian Mounted Police announced criminal fraud charges against the head of Philip's metals group. In 2006, the Ontario Securities Commission announced that it had banned five senior officers of Philip from serving as officers or directors of a public company for periods of up to 12 years. Furthermore, each officer was fined Can. $100,000 to meet the costs of the OSC investigation.

In March 2007, the Canadian arm of Deloitte and Touche, Philip's auditor, agreed to pay U.S. $50.5 million to settle a class action lawsuit by U.S. investors who claimed to have been misled by the 1997 prospectus. Officers and directors of Philip agreed to pay another $18 million. In December 2007, the Ontario Securities Commission announced a 20-year ban from serving as officer or director of a public company on the head of Philip's metals group. He was also banned from trading securities for 10 years and agreed to pay costs of $125,000.

Required

a. Does the share price reaction to the missing inventory and other writeoffs suggest securities market inefficiency? Explain.

b. Would current value accounting for Philip's metals inventory have helped to reduce the possibility of losing $80 million of copper inventory? Explain.

c. In retrospect, ceiling tests should have been applied to Philip's capital assets, such as its recorded goodwill, prior to the 1998 writedowns. Explain why ceiling tests may help reduce auditor liability.

Notes

1. It should be noted that Daniel and Titman's investment strategy used hindsight to pick stocks with high and low momentum. The strategy would not be implementable in real time.

2. In mathematical terms, the utility function is continuous but not differentiable at zero.

3. This supports the argument of Fama (1970) (see Section 4.3.1) that a sufficient number of sophisticated investors can drive the efficient market security price.

4. Vassalou (2003), in an empirical study, found that news related to future growth in gross domestic product (a proxy for the risk of an upturn or downturn in the economy) predicted stock returns as well as did book-to-market. This supports the argument that investors are concerned about the risk of a downturn (or upturn) in the economy, and buy low (or high) B/M firms accordingly.

5. Non-stationarity provides an alternative to noise trading, discussed in Section 4.4.1, for the non-collapse of share prices on an efficient market. When share price parameters, such as beta, are non-stationary, investors will have differing opinions as to whether current share prices reflect their current beta values, and will trade on the basis of these opinions.

6. While it does not apply directly to beta, further CAPM support is provided by Durnev, Morck, Yeung, and Zarowin (2003) (DMYZ). Recall from Section 4.5 (Equation 4.4) that the residual term ϵ_{jt} of the market model includes the firm-specific portion of share return (whereas the $\alpha_j + \beta_j R_{Mt}$ term captures the market- and industry-wide portion). DMYZ found that the variance of the market model residual is positively related to amounts of future abnormal earnings. Now the variance of ϵ_{jt} can be interpreted as an inverse measure of **synchronicity** (see Chapter 4, Note 7), since the residual variance captures the amount of firm-specific information, relative to the amount of industry- and economy-wide information, incorporated into share price—relatively more firm-specific information generates a bigger variance, or lower synchronicity. Later (since net income lags in recognizing many relevant events), this information shows up as gains and losses in net income. In effect, consistent with the results of Ball and Brown (Figure 5.3), the market anticipates much of the GN and BN in earnings and capitalizes it into share price before the earnings are reported. This result supports the CAPM and the efficient markets theory on which it is based, because, as originally suggested by Roll (1988), the low ability of the CAPM to explain share returns may be due in part to the large amount of firm-specific information constantly being developed by investors, rather than just to the CAPM leaving out important risk variables. DMYZ found no support for an alternative interpretation of the variance of ϵ_{jt} as simply the result of noise trading or investor limited attention.

7. The magnitude of PAD seems to depend on the earnings expectation construct used by the researcher. Most PAD studies measure the GN or BN in quarterly earnings based on quarterly seasonal earnings changes (a time series approach). However, Livnat and Mendenhall (2006) report that PAD is significantly greater when GN and BN are measured based on analysts' forecasts.

8. An alternative possibility is that firms' betas may shift when they announce good or bad earnings news. If the beta shifts were positive for GN firms and negative for BN, this could explain post-announcement drift as simply an artifact of the higher (for GN firms) and lower (for BN firms) returns that investors would demand to compensate for the changes in risk—as discussed in Sections 3.4, 3.5, and 3.6, investors trade off risk and return. While BT present evidence that, following earnings announcements, betas do shift in the manner described above, the magnitude of the shifts is much smaller than what would be required to explain the magnitude of the post-announcement drift.

9. Narayanamoorthy draws on accounting conservatism to argue that the positive correlation between current and next quarters' seasonal earnings changes will be lower for BN firms than for GN firms.

This is because with conservatism at least some of the BN is driven by writedowns, which forces future reported earnings up—a writedown of plant and equipment reduces future amortization expense, for example. For such firms, an increase in future earnings works *against* the positive correlation of current and future quarters' seasonal earnings changes, which is at the heart of PAD. GN firms are less likely to have suffered conservative writedowns, so that this effect does not then operate. Thus, given PAD, there are more profits to be made from investing only in GN firms, which is what Narayanamoorthy demonstrates.

10. Chordia and Shivakumar (CS) base their argument on the Modigliani and Cohn (1979) inflation illusion hypothesis, which states that common stock investors do not seem to incorporate the effects of inflation levels on the nominal growth rate of firms' earnings. CS point out that firms are affected differently by inflation—some firms' earnings benefit and some suffer. The inflation illusion hypothesis predicts that shares of firms that benefit are undervalued, and vice versa. That is, instead of *anticipating* the effects of inflation on future earnings growth, investors seem to wait until the increased or decreased earnings actually show up. Thus share prices drift upwards or downwards over time, depending on whether the firm benefits or suffers from inflation. CS' evidence in favour of this argument is drawn from a large sample of U.S. firms over 1971–2004. CS conclude that inflation provides at least a partial explanation for PAD.

11. Suppose that transactions costs were 5% of the amount invested. Then, if it was possible to gross 5% by a strategy of buying GN firms and selling short BN firms, transactions costs would consume the 5% profit, so investors would not bother. Thus, what might appear to be a profitable investment strategy may merely reflect the level of transactions costs required to earn those profits.

12. These findings resemble a "mega" version of PAD, likely due to basing the measure of earnings surprise on analysts' forecasts rather than quarterly seasonal earnings changes (see Note 7). Other reasons for the findings are the concentration on the extreme top and bottom of GN and BN firms, rather than on all GN and BN firms, and the fact that transactions costs and other barriers to arbitrage by sophisticated investors are high for the extreme firms in their sample.

13. The proportion of variability is measured by the R^2 statistic from the regression of abnormal security returns on unexpected earnings.

14. Interestingly, Kim and Kross also report that the association between share price and *book value* has *increased* over 1973–2000. This could possibly be due to greater use of current value accounting over this period.

15. The clean surplus model can be extended to allow for some information asymmetry, although under restrictive conditions. See Feltham and Ohlson (1996).

16. In the FO model, the firm's life is assumed infinite.

17. The "o" stands for "operating." If the firm has financial assets, such as cash or securities, these are assumed to earn the risk-free rate of interest. Consequently, financial assets do not contribute to goodwill, which is the ability to earn *abnormal* earnings.

18. The investor may wonder *why* the manager chose these particular accounting policies, however. That is, the manager's choice of accounting policies may itself reveal inside information to the market. Then, it is not completely correct to say that the investor need not be concerned about accounting policy choice. This is considered in Chapter 11.

19. Our expression for α differs slightly from that of FO. They assume that the firm has an infinite life, whereas our assumption is that P.V. Ltd. has a two-year life.

20. The persistence parameter ω can be related to the three types of earnings events distinguished by Ramakrishnan and Thomas (1991) (RT) (Section 5.4.1), namely permanent, transitory, and price-irrelevant, with ERCs of $(1 + R_f)/R_f$, 1, and 0, respectively. First, consider a \$1 permanent abnormal earnings event occurring in year t for a firm with an infinite life. This will increase bv_t, in FO notation, by \$1. In addition, ω of this will persist to year $t + 1$, ω^2 to year $t + 2$, etc. Thus, the total effect, discounted at the rate R_f, of the \$1 of year t abnormal earnings on PA_t, that is, the ERC, is

$$ERC = 1 + \frac{\omega}{1 + R_f} + \frac{\omega^2}{(1 + R_f)^2} + \frac{\omega^3}{(1 + R_f)^3} + \ldots$$

$$= \frac{1 + R_f}{1 + R_f - \omega}$$

In RT terms, permanent abnormal earnings have an ERC of $(1 + R_f)/R_f$. To express this ERC in terms of ω, we have

$$\frac{1 + R_f}{1 + R_f - \omega} = \frac{1 + R_f}{R_f}$$

which holds for $\omega = 1$.

Thus permanent abnormal earnings have $\omega = 1$. Note that this is outside the range of ω in the earnings dynamic (Equation 6.2). That is, for an infinite firm horizon the FO model is not defined for permanent earnings.

RT transitory abnormal earnings have an ERC of 1. Thus

$$\frac{1 + R_f}{1 + R_f - \omega} = 1$$

which holds for $\omega = 0$. Thus, transitory earnings have an ω of zero.

For price-irrelevant abnormal earnings, with ERC of 0, we have

$$\frac{1 + R_f}{1 + R_f - \omega} = 0$$

which is satisfied only in the limit as $\omega \to \pm\infty$. Since this is again outside the allowed range for ω, the FO model is not defined for price-irrelevant abnormal earnings.

21. The market risk premium is the additional return, over and above the risk-free rate, demanded by investors to compensate them for bearing the systematic risk of the market portfolio. The 4% estimate of this premium is taken from Palepu, Healy, and Bernard (2000), p. 13–9.

22. Website values for Canadian Tire's beta range from 0.60 to 0.89. Since I do not know the point in time to which these values relate, and since the values vary, I have calculated beta from its formula, as given. Specifically, Cov (j, M) and Var (M) are calculated from daily returns data for Canadian Tire and the S&P/TSX 300 index for March 2007 (21 observations).

23. Canadian Tire Corporation, Ltd. has two classes of common shares outstanding—voting and non-voting, with most of the shares non-voting. For purposes of this example, we combine the two classes.

24. For further information about the 1980s savings and loan debacle, see Zeff (2003, pp. 272–273), and the references therein.

25. Some accountants deny this statement, arguing that ceiling tests are a modified version of historical cost. That is, they regard the written-down value as the new "cost."

26. To verify this, Bill's utility from spending the same amount in each year is

$$\sqrt{5{,}000} + \sqrt{5{,}000} = 70.71 + 70.71 = 141.42$$

Any other spending allocation has lower utility. For example, if he spends $4,500 in year 1 and $5,500 in year 2, his utility is

$$\sqrt{4{,}500} + \sqrt{5{,}500} = 67.08 + 74.16 = 141.24$$

For simplicity, we assume that Bill has zero time preference for consumption. That is, a dollar of spending in year 1 has the same utility as in year 2, and vice versa. We also assume that Bill's utility function in year 2 is not affected by the level of consumption in year 1.

27. Strictly speaking, Bill's second year utilities should be discounted, since a dollar's worth of consumption next year is worth less than the same consumption today. However, this would complicate the example without changing the point to be made.

28. Basu (1997), described earlier, assumes that the market becomes aware of unrealized gains and losses as they occur from sources other than the financial statements, whereas our example assumes that the auditor misstatements remain as inside information, hence unknown to the market until their existence is later revealed. To the extent that Basu's assumption is valid, the force of our example is reduced. However, Basu's assumption relies heavily on availability of public information about gains and losses from other sources. It also relies on market efficiency with respect to this information. To the extent that inside information remains and markets are not fully efficient, our example applies. To argue that the market fully figures out inside information is to deny that financial statements have information content and to deny auditor liability.

29. If Bill holds a diversified portfolio, overstatement errors by one firm may cancel out against understatement errors by another. If they do, Bill's wealth at the end of year 1 is correctly stated on average, with no net loss of utility. However, the auditor is not off the hook, since it is unlikely that Bill, or the courts, will forgive one error because the auditor of another firm in his portfolio made an opposite error—we do observe auditor liability for valuation errors. In effect, "two wrongs do not make a right."

30. To find the x that maximizes Bill's EU, take the first derivative of Equation 6.4 with respect to x and equate to zero. With some simplification, this yields:

$$\frac{\partial EU}{\partial x} = x^{-1/2} - \frac{1}{2}\,[(16,000 - x)^{-1/2} + (24,000 - x)^{-1/2}] = 0$$

It can be verified that x = 9,400 satisfies this equation. Substitution of x = 9,400 into Equation 6.4 yields EU = 140.

If Bill uses the expected value of his wealth, substituting x = $10,000 into Equation 6.4 yields EU = 139.93.

31. Instead of reporting a conservative valuation, the auditor could report the asset at current value and disclose the conservative valuation in the financial statement notes. However, the auditor may feel that disclosure is not a substitute for recognition in the financial statements proper, due to investor behavioural biases and/or bounded rationality.

32. We say almost as relevant because to report an asset value that exactly maximizes Bill's expected utility, the auditor needs to know Bill's utility function. Alternatively, the auditor could report an asset value that minimized *his/her own* expected legal liability, on the assumption that legal liability awards accurately reflect investor utility losses. Such an assumption seems heroic, however.

33. Since the market-to-book ratio and the Basu measure are both measures of conservatism, a negative relationship between them has led to criticism of the Basu measure, on grounds that two measures of the same construct (i.e., conservatism) should be positively, not negatively, correlated. However, Basu's measure is of conditional conservatism, whereas we regard market-to-book as primarily a measure of unconditional conservatism. Since these are different conservatism concepts, it is not clear that this criticism is valid.

In this regard, Roychowdhury and Watts (2007) suggest a reconciliation. They point out, as we have, that a firm's market value includes its unrecorded goodwill and unrecognized increases in the economic value of recorded net assets. They also point out a negative association between market-to-book and reported earnings—the higher is opening market-to-book, the lower is its association with reported earnings for the period. This is because high market-to-book means that the firm has lots of unrecorded goodwill and unrecognized increases in net assets. Consequently, if some event lowers firm value, it is unlikely that net income will be lowered, for two reasons. First, since goodwill is not recognized in the first place, there is nothing to write down. Second, since past increases in net asset values are unrecognized due to conservative accounting, a "buffer" is created so that net assets do not need writedown unless their value has declined sufficiently to overcome the buffer. The higher is opening market-to-book, the stronger this effect. If some event increases firm value, book value does not increase under conservative accounting, so that the association between market-to-book and reported earnings is also negative.

Roychowdhury and Watts then assert that there is some persistence in the market-to-book ratio over short periods. For example, a firm with a high opening market-to-book ratio will tend to also have a high ratio at the end of the year. Then, the higher is *closing* market-to-book, the lower its association with reported net income. Thus, for a single short period, the association between a closing market-to-book measure of conservatism and net income is negative, whereas, as documented by Basu, his measure of conservatism for the period (correlation between share return and net income when share return is negative less correlation between share return and net income when share return is positive) is positive. Thus, the association between these two measures is negative over short periods, consistent with the results of Pae, Thornton, and Welker.

Consider what happens over several periods, however. If a firm appreciates in value over several periods, market-to-book rises and the gap between firm market value and conservative book value increases, strengthening the negative association between ending market-to-book and reported earnings. If a firm falls in value over several periods, however, market-to-book falls and reported earnings will also fall since the effects of recognition lag decrease for longer periods. This weakens the negative relationship between ending market-to-book and reported earnings. Combining these two effects, firms with high market-to-book ratios exhibit lower association with reported earnings as the time period lengthens, and firms with low ratios exhibit higher association. That is, the Basu conservatism measure increases. Thus, the association between the Basu measure and market-to-book becomes positive for longer periods. Roychowdhury and Watts present empirical evidence consistent with these predictions.

Chapter 7
Measurement Applications

Figure 7.1 Organization of Chapter 7

7.1 OVERVIEW

Despite the pressures for a measurement approach discussed in Chapter 6, the movement of accounting practice in this direction encounters some formidable obstacles. The first is reliability. The decision usefulness of current value-based financial statements will be compromised if too much reliability is sacrificed for greater relevance. Second, management's skepticism about RRA that we saw in Section 2.4.3 carries over to current value accounting in general, particularly since the measurement approach implies that current values, and the volatility that accompanies them, are incorporated into the financial statements proper. However, firms do operate in a volatile environment. To the extent that the volatility of current value accounting captures economic reality, one can argue that the financial statements should reflect the risks facing the firm. Nevertheless, in later chapters we shall see reasons why managers may dislike volatile financial statements.

Third, managers, investors, and auditors may prefer conservative accounting to current value accounting in some circumstances. Arguments that conservative accounting can contribute to investor decision-making and reduction of auditor liability were given in Section 6.7. Arguments concerning the role of conservatism in corporate governance will be discussed in Chapter 8.

Despite these obstacles, recent years have seen major new measurement-oriented standards, with more on the horizon. In this chapter, we review and evaluate some of these standards.

Before doing so, however, we will discuss the two bases of current value measurement that were introduced in Section 1.2. One is **fair value**. The most recent definition of fair value comes from SFAS 157 of the U.S. Financial Accounting Standards Board. The IASB is currently considering a similar definition.

> **Fair value** is the price that would be received to sell an asset or paid to transfer a liability in an orderly transaction between market participants at the measurement date.

This basis of valuation is also termed **exit price**. Exit price measures the **opportunity cost** to the firm of the intended use of its assets and liabilities. By using them, the firm gives up the opportunity of putting them to their next-best use, which could be to sell them or redeem them at their exit price.

Ideally, fair value is based on the market selling price of an asset or the amount the firm has to pay to dispose of a liability. When market value is not available, a variety of alternative approaches to estimating fair value are suggested in SFAS 157, including the use of mathematical models. These alternative approaches must be documented, so that outside parties, including auditors, can see how fair value has been determined.

The second basis is **value-in-use**. Value-in-use can be measured, for example, by the discounted present value of cash expected to be received or paid with respect to the use of the asset or liability, or with respect to groups of assets and liabilities if they are used jointly. Present value accounting as illustrated in Examples 2.1 and 2.2 is based on value-in-use.

Now recall our definition of relevant information, namely that it informs the investor about the firm's future economic prospects. One might then conclude that value-in-use is the ultimate in relevance, since it measures the expected cash flows to or from the firm. However, this is subject to a major qualification—management might change how it intends to use the asset or liability. For example, an impaired capital asset that has been written down to its value-in-use at the balance sheet date might instead be sold later for a higher amount. Also, amounts expected to be paid under employee retirement plans might be reduced should the firm subsequently renegotiate benefits. Consequently, the amounts of cash ultimately received or paid can differ materially from the amounts expected at the measurement date. Thus, value-in-use is a shifting sand upon which to build a measurement approach.

Fair value is less subject to this change-of-use possibility. Its relevance derives from the fact that it measures the amount that market participants are willing to pay for the asset or liability under present economic conditions. Presumably, management will retain an asset or liability, rather than dispose of it, if it believes value-in-use is greater than fair value. If so, future cash flows should be at least as great as fair value.

With respect to reliability, value-in-use is subject to the problems of estimation errors and possible manager bias that we saw with respect to RRA (Section 2.4). In addition, it is subject to the possibility that management may bias the intended use of the asset or liability, thereby biasing expected future cash flows. Fair value is quite reliable if a well-working market value is available. Otherwise, fair value is subject to similar estimation and bias problems as value-in-use. However, some reliability is retained since SFAS 157 requires documentation of how fair value is determined—recall that verifiability is a component of reliability.

We can also consider current value accounting from a revenue recognition point of view. Value-in-use recognizes revenues before they are realized, since anticipated future revenues are capitalized into asset values. More generally, current value accounting can result in gains or losses when assets are acquired or liabilities created. For example, a firm might acquire an asset for an amount less than its exit price. Then, valuation of the asset at fair value results in the recording of a gain on acquisition. Similarly, a gain can be recognized if liabilities can be disposed of for less than their book value.

It should also be noted that current value accounting changes the nature of the income statement. Under historical cost accounting, net income is the result of the matching of costs and revenue, with revenue recognized when it is considered to be realized. Under value-in-use accounting, net income is simply accretion of discount, plus or minus changes in management's estimates. Under SFAS 157's fair value version of current value accounting, net income shifts towards a report on manager stewardship. That is, the manager is charged with the opportunity cost of net assets used in the business, and, assuming reasonable reliability, his/her success is measured by the firm's ability to use these net assets to generate a return over and above their opportunity cost. Thus, despite the balance-sheet approach inherent in current value accounting (see Section 2.2), the income statement, particularly its core earnings component, retains importance under SFAS 157 since it measures the manager's stewardship performance.

Figure 7.1 outlines the organization of this chapter.

7.2 LONGSTANDING MEASUREMENT EXAMPLES

Even though financial statements are based on a mixed measurement model, they contain a substantial current value component. To preface a discussion of more recent measurement-oriented standards, we will review some common longstanding instances of current value-based measurements.

7.2.1 Accounts Receivable and Payable

For most firms, current accounts receivable (net of allowance for doubtful accounts) and accounts payable are valued at the expected amount of cash to be received or paid. Since the length of time to payment is short, the discount factor is negligible, so that this basis of valuation approximates present value.

7.2.2 Cash Flows Fixed by Contract

There are numerous instances where cash flows are fixed by contract. Then, initial valuation is based on present value if the contract provides reliable estimates of amounts and timing of future cash flows and interest rate. For example, if a firm issues long-term debt and uses the compound interest method to amortize any premium or discount, it can be shown that the resulting net book value of the debt equals the present value of the future interest and principal payments, discounted at the effective rate of interest of the debt established at the time of issue. Of course, under historical cost accounting, equality of current value and book value is lost as relevant interest rates and/or the firm's credit rating change.

As another example, IAS 17 requires finance lease contracts[1] and related leased assets to be initially valued at the lower of the fair value of the leased asset or the present value of minimum lease payments, using the interest rate implicit in the lease or the lessee's incremental borrowing rate when the implicit rate is impracticable to determine. As is the case for long-term debt, this initial equivalence between current value and book value may be lost over time. However, leased assets are subject to the ceiling test of IAS 36 (discussed below), which requires a writedown if their current value amount falls below book value. Also, IAS 16 (discussed below) allows, but does not require, a revaluation option under which capital assets are accounted for at fair value. Consequently, finance lease accounting is reasonably consistent with the measurement approach.

7.2.3 The Lower-of-Cost-or-Market Rule

The lower-of-cost-or-market rule, traditionally applied to inventories, is a long-established example of a partial measurement approach. Under IAS 2, when the net realizable value of inventory falls below cost, it is written down to the lower value. If net realizable value subsequently increases, the inventory may be written up, but not above cost. U.S. GAAP also includes a lower-of-cost-or-market rule under Accounting Research Bulletin 43. However, subsequent writeup of written-down inventory is not allowed.[2]

The lower-of-cost-or-market rule can be justified in terms of conservatism. It is more difficult to justify in terms of decision usefulness, however, since one would think that if current value information is useful, it would be useful when value is greater than cost as well as when it is less than cost. However, as argued in Sections 6.6 and 6.7, conservatism reduces the likelihood of overstatement errors, and auditors, along with managers, feel with some justification that their exposure to legal liability is greater for an asset overstatement than for an equivalent amount of understatement. Consequently, the rule remains as a partial application of the measurement approach.

7.2.4 Revaluation Option for Property, Plant, and Equipment

While historical cost accounting for property, plant, and equipment is the norm under accounting standards in Canada and the United States, IAS 16 allows a **revaluation option**. As an alternative to historical cost, tangible capital assets can be valued at fair value, providing this can be done reliably. Once assets are revalued, fair values must be kept up to date, so as not to differ materially from fair value at the balance sheet date. These revaluations may increase or decrease carrying value. This option constitutes another major example of the measurement approach.

7.2.5 Ceiling Test for Property, Plant, and Equipment

Standard setters have imposed a **ceiling test** for capital assets, such as property, plant, and equipment. Ceiling tests help protect the auditor from legal liability, and, since they force writedowns of assets that would otherwise be overvalued, contribute to the increase in conditional conservatism documented by Basu (1997), as discussed in Section 6.6. Like lower-of-cost-or-market, we shall regard ceiling tests as a partial application of the measurement approach.

Under IAS 36, an impairment loss for property, plant, and equipment is recognized if book value is greater than the **recoverable amount**, where recoverable amount is the greater of fair value less costs to sell or value-in-use.

Impairment losses for property, plant, and equipment can be reversed if the recoverable amount has increased, but not above the book value the assets would have had if no impairment loss had been recorded.

Under FASB rules, ceiling tests are somewhat different. SFAS 144 lays down a two-step procedure. First, it is determined if the asset is **impaired**. This is the case if book value exceeds the sum of *undiscounted* expected future direct net cash flows. If an asset is deemed impaired, the second step is to determine its fair value under the procedures laid down in SFAS 157, where fair value is based on the "highest and best" use of the asset by market participants. For example, many assets, such as machines used in a production process, are best used in conjunction with other machines. Then, fair value is the amount that would be received from a sale assuming the asset is to be used in this manner. In other cases, the highest and best use is stand-alone. This basis could apply to a piece of land, for example. Ideally, the fair value of the highest and best use is determined on the basis of quoted value in a well-working market. However, for property, plant, and equipment, such values may not be available. Then, as mentioned earlier, SFAS 157 lays down a variety of other approaches, including discounted expected value. In all cases, however, the fair value focus is on what market participants would pay, not on value-in-use to the firm owning the asset.[3]

Under both IASB and FASB standards, impairment losses are charged against current earnings.[4] However, unlike IAS 36, SFAS 144 does not allow for subsequent reversals of these writedowns. Thus, IAS 36 is somewhat closer to a full measurement approach than SFAS 144.

Nevertheless, despite the asymmetric nature of their application, ceiling tests represent an important extension of the measurement approach to a major class of assets.

7.2.6 Pensions and Other Post-Employment Benefits

Defined benefit pension plans[5] present a major challenge for the measurement approach, since estimating pension plan liability and expense requires numerous estimates stretching far into the future. Measuring the earnings from pension plan assets, which fund the future pension payments, presents additional challenges. Furthermore, estimates change frequently. We saw the effects of changes in estimates in RRA (Section 2.4). For pensions, changes in benefits, actuarial assumptions, discount rates, expected rate of increase in employee compensation, and expected return on plan assets produce large pension gains and losses. Their importance is compounded because pensions affect the financial statements proper, whereas RRA is supplementary information only.

Inclusion of pension gains and losses in net income, which would be required under a full application of the measurement approach, would greatly increase reported earnings volatility. For this reason, pension accounting standards have typically allowed pension gains and losses to be smoothed, by leaving them off the books and, if their amount is material, amortizing them into pension expense over periods as long as 10 to 20 years.

Pension expense for the period includes service cost (the present value of plan benefits attributed to services rendered by employees during the period), interest cost (accretion of discount on opening plan liability), and any current period's amortization of pension gains and losses, reduced by earnings attributed to pension plan assets.[6]

Since pension accounting in the United States is currently somewhat more advanced towards measurement than internationally, we begin with an overview of FASB standards. For most defined benefit plans, SFAS 87 (1987) requires the service cost component of pension expense for the period to include the effects of future expected employee compensation increases (as opposed to being based on current period compensation only).[7] The firm's total pension liability, allowing for expected compensation increases, is called the **projected benefit obligation (PBO)**.

Note, however, that the PBO includes the impact of pension gains and losses. For example, suppose a firm decides to increase its pension benefits, or the interest rate used to discount future pension payments falls, or the actuarial assumption about employee mortality increases. All of these changes increase the PBO. However, as pointed out above, the unamortized portion of pension gains and losses is off-balance-sheet. Consequently, the PBO is partially off-balance-sheet.

SFAS 87, and several subsequent standards, required that information about the PBO be reported in the financial statement notes. Omission of the PBO from the financial statements proper is not consistent with a measurement approach, however, since pension liability on the balance sheet may be understated. In a 2005 report[8] the SEC estimated the total amount of this understatement, net of pension plan assets, as $414 billion for the firms under its jurisdiction. To the extent that securities markets are not fully efficient, and assuming reasonable reliability of the PBO, this suggests that decision usefulness could be increased by bringing the full amount of the PBO into the financial statements proper. Indeed, Picconi (2006) reports on a study of analyst and investor reaction to the information disclosed under SFAS 87. He finds that investors fail to fully incorporate pension information in financial statement notes into firms' share prices in a timely manner.

In this regard, SFAS 158, effective since 2006, moves pension information into the financial statements proper. It requires the full PBO, net of the fair value of pension plan assets, to be reported on the balance sheet. Thus, if a plan is underfunded, a net liability will be shown, and vice versa.

While SFAS 158 is a movement in the measurement direction, it stops short of a full measurement approach. Pension gains and losses are still not all included in net income as they are realized or incurred. Instead, some are included in **other comprehensive income**, from which they are amortized into net income over a period of years. As mentioned, this amortization is a component of pension expense for the period. Thus, as far as net income is concerned, pension gains and losses continue to be amortized much as before.

A statement of other comprehensive income was created in the United States by SFAS 130. In addition to some pension gains and losses, other comprehensive income includes gains and losses from adjustments to fair value of available-for-sale securities (discussed below), foreign currency translation adjustments, and several other types of unrealized gains and losses. Other comprehensive income is reported separately from net income. As these gains and losses are realized or amortized, they are transferred to net income. The sum of net income and other comprehensive income is called **comprehensive income** by SFAS 130. IASB standards (IAS 1, revised) also impose a statement of other comprehensive income, beginning in 2009.[9]

In 1990, SFAS 106 extended much of pension accounting to **other post-employment benefits (OPEBs)**, such as health care and insurance provided to current and retired employees. SFAS 158 continues this extension, except that the balance sheet includes the **accumulated benefit obligation (ABO)** instead of the PBO. Unlike the PBO, the ABO does not include an estimate of future benefits increases.[10] OPEB expense for the period includes service cost and accretion of discount, less the return on any plan assets.

Prior to SFAS 106, most firms accounted for OPEBs on a pay-as-you-go basis, recognizing an expense only as cash payments were made. Thus, adoption of SFAS 106 usually resulted in the recording of a substantial liability to catch up on accumulated OPEB obligations to current and retired employees. The standard allowed the offsetting charge to go directly to retained earnings (retroactive application) or to be amortized over future years (prospective application), thus avoiding a substantial earnings hit in the year of adoption.

For firms that used the retroactive option, the amount of the OPEB writeoff was often surprisingly large. For example, *The Globe and Mail* (February 2, 1993) reported a $20.8 billion one-time charge by General Motors Corp. to record its OPEB obligation upon adoption of SFAS 106 (see Chapter 4, question 8). This reduced its shareholders' equity by about 75%!

For our purposes, the important aspect of pension and OPEB accounting is its use of discounted present value using current interest rates and estimates of future benefits to calculate benefit liabilities and expense. Indeed, SFAS 106 and 158 go further towards a measurement approach than lower-of-cost-or-market and ceiling tests, since, under U.S. standards, written-down inventories and property, plant, and equipment may not be written up again. However, subsequent changes in benefit plan assumptions and interest rates require revisions, up or down, to liability and expense calculations.

At present, IAS 19, the IASB pension standard, is broadly similar to SFAS 87. One difference is that IAS 19 allows three options for pension gains and losses. They can be included in current net income, recognized in a statement similar to other comprehensive income, or deferred off-balance-sheet and amortized along the lines of SFAS 87. However, unlike SFAS 158, IAS 19 does not allow firms that choose the other comprehensive income option to amortize the gains and losses, on the grounds that there is no rational way to do so.

IAS 19 also applies to OPEBs. Again, this standard is broadly similar to SFAS 106.

7.2.7 Summary

The above is only a partial listing of current value-based measurements in generally accepted accounting principles. For our purposes, the main point to realize is that a considerable amount of measurement approach is inherent in the mixed measurement model.

These examples, however, understate the extent of measurement in current GAAP. We now turn to a consideration of other recent current value-oriented accounting standards.

7.3 FINANCIAL INSTRUMENTS

7.3.1 Introduction

Financial instruments are defined as:

> A *financial instrument* is a contract that creates a financial asset of one firm and a financial liability or equity instrument of another firm.

Financial assets and liabilities are defined quite broadly. Thus, a financial asset is:

- cash,
- an equity instrument of another firm,
- a contractual right
  - to receive cash or another financial asset from another firm
  - to exchange financial instruments with another firm under conditions that are potentially favourable[11]

Similarly, a financial liability is any liability that is

- a contractual obligation
    - to deliver cash or another financial asset to another firm
    - to exchange financial assets or financial liabilities with another firm under conditions that are potentially unfavourable

Thus, financial assets and liabilities include items such as accounts and notes receivable and payable, debt and equity securities held by the firm, and bonds outstanding. These are referred to as primary instruments. Also included are **derivative instruments**, to be discussed in Section 7.3.4.

7.3.2 Valuation of Debt and Equity Securities

IAS 39 classifies financial assets into four categories:

- **Available-for-sale** These are non-derivative financial assets that the firm designates upon acquisition as available for sale or are not classified into one of the other three categories. They are valued at fair value with most unrealized gains and losses included in other comprehensive income. Upon disposition, unrealized gains and losses are transferred from other comprehensive income to net income.

- **Loans and receivables** These are non-derivative financial assets with fixed or determinable future payments that do not have active market values, such as bank loans. They are valued at amortized cost, subject to an impairment test. If the discounted present value of their future receipts falls below their book value they are written down to the lower amount, with the unrealized loss included in net income. The discount rate is the effective interest rate on the asset as established at time of issuance. If the value of a written-down asset subsequently increases, it is written up, but not above its current book value if there had been no writedown.

- **Held-to-maturity** These are non-derivative financial assets with fixed or determinable payments that the firm intends to hold to maturity. A portfolio of bond investments could meet this definition, for example. They are valued at amortized cost, subject to an impairment test similar to that for loans and receivables. If the value of a written-down asset subsequently increases, the writedown may be reversed under certain conditions.

- **Financial assets at fair value through profit and loss** This category includes all derivatives not held for hedging (to be discussed later) and non-derivative financial assets **held for trading**, that is, held for a short time for the purpose of selling. It also includes any other financial assets that the firm has designated at acquisition to belong to this category. This ability to designate illustrates an interesting characteristic of IAS 39, called the **fair value option**. Under the fair value option, the firm can opt to value assets and liabilities at fair value, even though fair value is not required.

As the category name suggests, unrealized gains and losses on financial assets in this category are included in net income.

With respect to financial liabilities, IAS 39 recognizes two categories:

- **Financial liabilities at fair value through profit and loss** This category includes financial liabilities held for trading, and financial liabilities that the firm has designated to belong to this category under the fair value option.

- **Other financial liabilities** These are valued at cost or amortized cost. This category includes, for example, bonds outstanding.

In the United States, SFAS 115 contains broadly similar provisions, although it does not apply to financial liabilities. Nor does it apply to loans and receivables, which are accounted for under SFAS 114, with provisions similar to those of IAS 39. Unlike IAS 39, SFAS 115 does not allow reversals of previous writedowns. SFAS 115, like IAS 1 revised, requires that unrealized gains and losses on available-for-sale securities be included in other comprehensive income.

One of the purposes of these standards is to constrain **gains trading**, also called "cherry picking." This is a practice that financial institutions, including those involved in the savings and loan debacle discussed in Section 6.6, have used as a way to manage their reported earnings. Gains trading could be employed when investment portfolios were valued at cost or amortized cost, and when at least some securities had risen in value. Then, the institution could realize a gain by selling securities that had risen in value, while continuing to hold securities that may have fallen in value. No loss was typically recognized on these latter securities. They continued to be carried at cost on grounds that they would be held to maturity.

Note that gains trading is not possible if all financial assets are valued at fair value, with unrealized gains and losses included in net income—if changes in fair value are recorded as they occur, then there is no gain or loss on disposal. Then, the firm has no discretion to cherry pick (but see problem 7). However, as described above, IAS 39 and SFAS 115 allow held-to-maturity securities to be valued on a cost basis. Thus they are, at least in theory, still available for gains trading. Furthermore, these standards theoretically have the potential to make the problem of gains trading worse rather than better. If securities are transferred from held-to-maturity to held-for-trading, this would trigger a change in valuation basis from cost to fair value, with any gain or loss included in net income. Thus, to gains trade, the firm would need only reclassify held-to-maturity securities as trading—no sale of securities would be needed.

However, IAS 39 and SFAS 115 provide strong disincentives for such behaviour, so that there is really little opportunity for gains trading in practice. Should a firm sell or reclassify a held-to-maturity security, IAS 39 prevents use of the held-to-maturity category for two years, thereby eliminating the firm's ability to value financial instruments at cost for this period. SFAS 115 contains even more stringent provisions to discourage gains trading.

If full fair value accounting prevents gains trading, one might reasonably ask why not value all financial instruments at fair value, rather than impose the complex and seemingly inconsistent juxtaposition of valuation bases described above? One reason, of course, is reliability. If reasonably reliable measurements cannot be made, fair value is unlikely to be decision useful, despite its relevance. For example, IAS 39 does not allow equity instruments to be carried at fair value if they cannot be reliably valued. Instead, they are valued on a cost basis.

Other financial items can also be very difficult to fair value reliably. For example, financial institutions are a major industry affected by fair value accounting. Demand deposits held by these institutions are currently valued at face value (i.e., a cost basis), since this is the amount that depositors can demand. Valuation of deposits at fair value, however, leads to the problem of valuing a related asset, namely **core deposit intangibles**.

Core deposit intangibles arise from customers' acceptance of a lower-than-market rate of interest on their deposits, due to goodwill, habit, location, etc. As a simple example, suppose that a bank pays 1% interest on a customer's $100 deposit but lends the customer's money at 5%. Then, as long as the customer keeps the $100 on deposit, the bank's $100 deposit liability is accompanied by a core deposit intangible asset that will generate $4 per year.

It thus seems that if deposit liabilities are fair valued, core deposit intangibles should be fair valued as well. However, valuing this intangible asset introduces problems of reliably estimating the timing of withdrawals and discounting, which are currently not generally accepted. Furthermore, the value of core deposit intangibles will change as interest rates change. In the face of these difficulties, IAS 39 and SFAS 115 do not allow fair value accounting for demand deposits.

While prohibiting fair valuing of deposit liabilities sidesteps the issue of fair valuing core deposit intangibles, the basic difficulty facing standard setters does not go away. This is the problem of **mismatch**, or earnings volatility in excess of the real volatility facing the firm. Mismatch arises when some assets or liabilities are fair valued but related liabilities or assets are not. For example, many firms hold financial assets and liabilities with similar duration and other characteristics. These create a **natural hedge** of changes in values. Thus, a firm with long-term debt issued at a fixed interest rate may hold fixed interest-bearing securities of similar amount and maturity. If interest rates, say, go down, the fundamental value of the firm goes down due to the increase in the fair value of the debt. However, this will be offset by the increase in the fair value of the interest-bearing securities. Net income will not reflect this offsetting, however, if it includes unrealized gains and losses from fair valuing the firm's interest-bearing securities while excluding losses and gains on long-term debt carried at cost. As a result, the volatility of net income is greater than the real volatility the firm has chosen through its natural hedging activities, that is, there is a mismatch. It is for this reason, presumably, that IAS 39 and SFAS 115 stipulate that certain securities (held-to-maturity) need not be carried at fair value and that gains and losses on others (available-for-sale) are excluded from net income. If unrealized gains and losses on these financial assets do not enter into net income, the mismatch that creates excess earnings volatility is again sidestepped.

However, another way to reduce mismatch is to adopt the fair value option so that "both sides" of the natural hedge are fair valued. Thus the firm could choose to fair value its long-term debt, in which case unrealized losses and gains are included in earnings under this option. These will offset the gains and losses on its interest-bearing securities. Under IAS 39, use of the fair value option is restricted. One restriction is that this option is used to reduce a mismatch such as the one just described.

In the United States, SFAS 159 creates a similar fair value option, although SFAS 159 does not restrict choice of this option to mismatch situations. Consequently, under U.S. GAAP, a firm could record a gain as its credit risk increases even though it had not hedged the interest rate risk of its debt.[12] This can produce results that may seem strange, however. For example, suppose that a firm receives a downgrade from a credit-rating agency. As a result, the fair value of its debt falls in response to the increased **credit risk** borne by lenders, where credit risk is the risk that the firm will be unable to meet its contractual liabilities as they come due. The firm could use the fair value option of SFAS 159 to fair value its debt, and, in the absence of hedging, there will be no offsetting loss on hedging instruments. The firm will thus report a gain as its credit risk increases.

While recording a gain following a credit downgrade may seem strange, it does have a rationale. By definition, a firm suffering deterioration in its credit quality is experiencing a reduction in the economic value of its net assets. One can then argue that recording a gain when credit quality decreases offsets a portion of the loss in value. That is, both lenders and shareholders must share the loss in firm value. The gain arising from fair valuing debt represents the lenders' portion of this loss—the whole loss of a credit downgrade is not borne by the shareholders.

7.3.3 Conclusion

We conclude that despite their various compromises short of fair-valuing all financial instruments, IAS 39, SFAS 114, 115, and 159 represent clear extensions of the measurement approach beyond the realm of supplemental disclosure and into the financial statements proper. Major classes of financial instruments are fair-valued, with unrealized gains and losses included in other comprehensive income.

7.3.4 Derivative Instruments

Derivative instruments are contracts, the value of which depends on some **underlying** price, interest rate, foreign exchange rate, or other variable. A common example is an option, such as a call option, that gives the holder a right to buy, say, 100 shares of a firm's common stock for $20 each during, or at the end of, some specified period. The notional amount of the contract is $2,000. The underlying is the market price of the shares. The higher the market price, the higher the value of the option, other things equal. Other examples of derivatives include futures, forward and swap contracts, interest rate caps and floors, and fixed-rate loan commitments. Generally, these instruments convey a benefit to the holder if there is a favourable movement in the underlying. If the underlying moves unfavourably, there may or may not be a loss to the holder.

A characteristic of derivative instruments is that they generally require or permit settlement in cash—delivery of the asset associated with the underlying need not take place. Thus, the option contract above need not involve the holder actually buying the shares, but only receiving the value of the option in cash at time of settlement. As another example, suppose a firm needs to borrow a large sum of money in six months' time. It is concerned that interest rates may rise over this period. It buys a bond futures contract giving it the right and obligation to sell government bonds at a specified price on a settlement date six months hence. If interest rates go up, the underlying market value of the bonds goes down, and the value of the futures contract rises to offset the higher borrowing cost. If this contract had to be settled physically, the firm would have to enter the bond market on the settlement date, buy the requisite amount of government bonds, and sell them to the party on the other side of the contract at the contract price to realize the value of the contract. With cash settlement, the firm can simply receive, or pay, cash equal to the value of the contract, thereby saving both sides the costs of physical buying and selling. The ability to settle derivative instruments in cash has contributed to the great increase in their use over the past number of years.

Derivative instruments may or may not require an initial net investment. For example, a firm may enter into an interest rate swap contract that requires no cash outlay. If an initial cash outlay is required, it is for less than the notional amount of shares times the underlying. In the option example above, if the current share price is, say, $18, the cost to the holder of the option contract will certainly be less than $1,800, the amount that would be required to buy the shares outright. This is reasonable, because while the holder of the option will participate in any price increase of the shares during the option term, other rights of ownership, such as dividends, are excluded. In effect, the option holder is buying only the rights to future appreciation in value over some time period, not the shares themselves. In our bond futures contract example, the firm could also have protected itself by borrowing now, to lock in the current interest rate. But, this would require an additional interest cost for six months on the full amount needed.

These three examples illustrate the leverage aspect of derivatives—a lot of protection can be acquired at relatively low cost. Leverage is another reason for the great increase in the use of derivatives in recent years. Of course, leverage is a two-edged sword. If derivatives are used to speculate on the underlying price rather than to manage risk, the amount that can be lost, for a low initial investment, can be very large indeed.[13] This low initial investment characteristic of derivatives is a reason why accountants have found them difficult to deal with under historical cost accounting. Since there is little or no cost to account for, all or part of the contract is off-balance-sheet. Then, it is difficult, or impossible, for investors to figure out the firm's derivative dealings and exposures from the financial statements proper. Accountants have responded to this difficulty by requiring supplemental disclosure. However, in view of behavioural characteristics such as limited attention, such disclosure may not be completely effective.

In this regard, the accounting for derivative instruments has moved substantially towards a measurement approach by IAS 39 and SFAS 133. These standards require that all derivatives be measured at fair value for balance sheet purposes. Since these two standards are quite similar at a conceptual level, our discussion will apply to both.

How does one value a derivative? If a derivative is traded on a market that works reasonably well, fair value is measured by its market value. If it is not traded, models of derivative value can be used. To illustrate, consider our example of a call option to purchase 100 shares at $20, where the current market price is $18 per share. Assume that the option can be exercised at the end of two months. Assume also that the shares change their price only at the end of each month, and that these price changes follow a random walk (see Section 4.2.1). Specifically, assume that share price will increase each month by $2 with probability 0.5 or decrease by $2 with probability 0.5. This price behaviour is depicted in Figure 7.2.

Looking ahead from time 0 (now), at the end of the first month the 100 shares will have a market value of $2,000 with probability 0.5, and a value of $1,600 with probability 0.5. At the end of the second month (the expiry date of the option) their market value will be $2,200 with probability 0.25 (i.e., 0.5 × 0.5), $1,800 with probability 0.5 (0.25 + 0.25) or $1,400 with probability 0.25.

Figure 7.2 A Simple Option Pricing Model

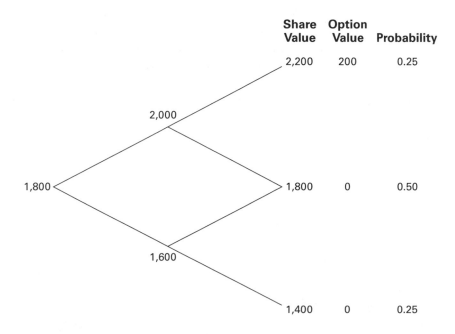

Share Value	Option Value	Probability
2,200	200	0.25
1,800	0	0.50
1,400	0	0.25

Now the option will only be exercised if the value of the shares is $2,200. Since the exercise price is $20 per share, or $2,000 in total, the value of the option is then $200. For the other two possible share values, the option will not be exercised, so that its value is then $0.

The question then is, what is the fair value of the option at time 0, its date of issuance? If we assume that the risk-free interest rate in the economy is zero, this fair value is simply $200 × 0.25 = $50, the expected value of the option at maturity.[14]

Of course, our assumption that the share price changes only at the end of each month is unrealistic. In reality, many share prices change almost continuously. This can be modelled in our example by increasing the number of times that price changes in Figure 7.2 (but holding the time to expiration constant at two months). As the number of times the price changes goes to infinity (i.e., share price varies continuously) the fair value of the option is given by the famous Black/Scholes (1973) option pricing formula,[15] which values the option as a function of the following five variables:

- Current market price of the share—$18
- Variability of return of the share
- Exercise price of option—$20
- Time to expiration
- Risk-free interest rate

The first two of these inputs to the formula are characteristics of the underlying share price. Thus, given values for the last three variables, we see how the value of the option derives from the current market price and return variability of the share. Given the exercise price, the higher the current price, the more valuable is the option. Given the current market price, the lower the exercise price the more valuable is the option. The greater the variability of the price, the more valuable is the option since there is a greater likelihood that the price will rise by the expiry date (there is also a greater likelihood that the price will fall but, in that case, the option need not be exercised). Since Black/Scholes, models to value other, more complex derivative instruments have been developed. Thus, under appropriate conditions, models provide a way to implement the calculations required by fair value accounting standards.

Changes in fair value of derivative instruments are recognized in net income under IAS 39 and SFAS 133, except for certain hedging contracts, which we will discuss in Section 7.3.5.

The Blackstone Group is a large investment company whose operations include investing in public companies and taking them private. A major component of its earnings from these investments derives from "carried interest." This is a management fee based on a preferential interest in the profits earned by unconsolidated companies in which it has invested. For example, a typical arrangement would be for Blackstone to receive an annual payment of 20% of a company's profits in excess of a hurdle rate of return on equity. These payments could continue for, say, five years, after which Blackstone would plan to sell its interest in the company.

Under historical cost accounting and the equity method of accounting for unconsolidated subsidiaries, carried interest fees would be recorded as revenue each period, if and as they are earned, with the offsetting debit to the investment account. Note, however, that Blackstone's preferential right to receive future fees conditional on a hurdle rate of return on the equity of a firm in which it has invested has option-like characteristics, expiring in five years in the above example.

In 2007, Blackstone planned an initial public offering of its stock. In its preliminary prospectus, dated March 22, it revealed that for many of its unconsolidated investments it would use the fair value option of SFAS 159 to value future carried interest fees on a fair value basis, with the offsetting credit to current earnings. Presumably, an option pricing model, such as Black/Scholes, would be used to determine fair value, as allowed by SFAS 157. If this accounting had been applied in 2006, Blackstone indicated that its 2006 earnings would have increased by $595,205, relative to earnings reported using the equity method of accounting for its unconsolidated investments.

Note that fair value has to be re-evaluated each period. Blackstone pointed out that this could introduce considerable volatility into its reported earnings. It seemed that Blackstone was willing to bear this volatility in order to secure earlier revenue recognition.

Concerns about the reliability of Blackstone's proposed accounting soon appeared in the financial media, despite the greater relevance of this approach. A major source of concern was that since bought-out companies are typically taken private, the amount of public information about them is minimal. This makes it particularly difficult for the market to assess Blackstone's valuation, and puts considerable onus on Blackstone to fully disclose its assumptions in determining fair value. Concern was also expressed that Blackstone could bias its financial results by means of these assumptions.

In its final prospectus, dated June 25, Blackstone changed its mind, announcing that it would not adopt SFAS 159. Instead, it would recognize carried interest quarterly based on its share of non-consolidated companies' quarterly earnings. Nevertheless, this episode illustrates the potential of the fair value option to implement the measurement approach.

7.3.5 Hedge Accounting

Firms issue or acquire financial instruments for a variety of reasons. For example, they may manage their capital structure by means of convertible debt. They may manage their cash flows by issuing zero-coupon debt. Interest rate swaps and bond futures contracts may enable lower financing costs. Perhaps the major reason why firms deal in derivative financial instruments, however, is to help manage risk.[16] In this regard, derivatives help to reduce market incompleteness, since they enable the firm to purchase protection against risks that would otherwise be difficult to control. It is this risk-management role of financial instruments that we concentrate on here.

The term "manage" risk is used advisedly. The goal of risk management is to produce a desired level of firm-specific risk, not necessarily to reduce it to zero. Zero risk may be too costly, or not even possible. Indeed, it may not even be desirable, since investors can reduce firm-specific risk for themselves through portfolio diversification.

A variety of derivative financial instruments has been developed to enable firms to better manage risks. Many of these risks are **price risks** (also called market risks), arising from changes in interest rates, commodity prices, and foreign exchange rates. Other risks arise from credit risk. The accounting for these financial instruments involves difficult issues of recognition and valuation.

Since natural hedges are ultimately a management decision, any evaluation of a firm's susceptibility to risk should also consider natural hedging. In effect, hedging with derivatives takes over where natural hedging leaves off. In this regard, Core and Kothari (2003) studied the hedging practices of a sample of U.S. non-financial firms. They found that on average the proportions of the sample firms' interest rate, foreign exchange, and commodity price risks hedged with derivatives is quite small relative to risk exposures. One explanation for this result derives from cost and portfolio diversification issues mentioned above. Another explanation, not inconsistent with cost and diversification, is that natural hedging also provides risk protection.

There are different types of hedges. Derivative instruments designated as hedges of recognized assets and liabilities are called **fair value hedges**. The essence of a fair value hedge is that if a firm owns, say, a risky asset, it can hedge this risk by acquiring a **hedging instrument**—some other asset or liability whose value moves in the direction opposite to that of the **hedged item**. Accounting for hedges of transactions that take place entirely within the current period is relatively straightforward. The gain or loss on the hedged item and the loss or gain on the hedging instrument can both be recorded in current net income, which then includes a realized loss or gain only to the extent the hedge is not completely effective. Hedges may not be completely effective because there may not exist a hedging instrument that will completely offset the hedged item's gain or loss. For example, a bank may have trouble finding a perfect hedge for the risk of changing interest rates on its deposit liabilities. The risk resulting from the absence of a perfectly effective hedge is called **basis risk**.

Frequently, however, hedging transactions do not take place entirely within the current period. For example, suppose that during the year a firm, concerned that selling prices might decline, hedges the price risk on its inventory by entering into a forward contract to sell the inventory at its current market price. Thus, the inventory is the hedged item and the forward contract is the hedging instrument. Suppose that, at year-end, the inventory is still on hand and its market price has fallen. As a result, the fair value of the forward contract has risen.

Under IAS 39 and SFAS 133, gains and losses on fair value hedges are included in current net income. The related loss or gain on the hedged item is also included in current net income. Thus, our firm writes its inventory down to market value and writes the forward contract up, so that net income is affected only to the extent that the hedge is not completely effective. On the balance sheet, the value of the forward contract is added to the inventory. In effect, the firm can avoid the effect on net income of lower-of-cost-or-market and, more generally, ceiling tests and other fair value changes, by appropriate hedging strategy.

Firms also may hedge *anticipated* transactions, for example to reduce risk arising from future price changes of the firm's products. Such contracts are called **cash flow hedges**. Firms engage in cash flow hedging for a variety of reasons. Perhaps the most important of these is to help ensure cash availability for future investment projects, where these are to be financed internally. Firms may wish to finance internally when, for example, their ability to raise outside capital is reduced by investor concerns about information asymmetry.

Under IAS 39 and SFAS 133, cash flow hedges are fair-valued, with unrealized gains and losses included in other comprehensive income until the transactions affect net income. Then, any accumulated gain or loss is transferred into net income for that period. For example, an oil and gas producer may wish to hedge next period's sales. These cash receipts are risky because of fluctuations in oil and gas prices and, if the oil and gas is sold in foreign markets, fluctuations in foreign exchange rates. Including unrealized gains and losses on cash flow hedges in other comprehensive income reduces net income volatility by delaying their effect on net income until the next period, when the anticipated cash flows are realized.[17]

An instrument must meet certain criteria if it is to be eligible for hedge accounting. Non-derivative instruments are generally prohibited from being eligible. Also, options issued as stock-based compensation are excluded. For instruments that are eligible, management must **designate** the instrument as a hedge at the inception of the hedge, identify the hedged item, and document the nature of the risk being hedged. The rationale is that reported net income would lose reliability if management had the discretion to designate a hedging instrument at any time it wanted. For example, faced with a major loss on derivatives held as a speculation, management could decide to retroactively designate them as cash flow hedges of forecasted transactions. Then, the loss could be excluded from net income, thereby at least delaying its impact.

Another criterion for designation as a hedge is that the derivative instrument must be "highly effective" in offsetting changes in the fair value of the hedged item. IAS 39 and SFAS 133 do not lay down specific rules for determining high effectiveness except that management's documentation of hedge effectiveness should be consistent with the firm's established risk management objective and strategy. However, highly effective essentially means that there is high negative correlation between the fair values of the hedging instrument and the hedged item.

One way of estimating this correlation is the *cumulative dollar offset* method. For example, suppose that a firm borrows at a variable interest rate. It hedges its cash flow risk by purchasing a treasury bill futures contract, whereby it can sell a given number of treasury bills at some future date at a fixed price. Suppose that, due to rising interest rates, its interest payments increase by $1,500, and the fair value of its treasury bill futures contract rises by $1,300. Then the ratio of loss to gain is $-1,500/+1,300 = -1.15$. Since this is reasonably close to a perfect ratio of -1, this supports continuing the designation of the futures contract as a hedge.

Theory in Practice 7.2

To illustrate how an attempt to avoid the effects of ceiling test writedowns on reported net income by means of hedging can go wrong, consider the case of El Paso Corporation, a large Texas-based producer and distributor of natural gas. During 1999–2002, El Paso Production Co., a subsidiary, entered into forward contracts to lock in the price it received for its future gas production. These forward contracts were with El Paso Merchant Energy, another El Paso subsidiary. Merchant Energy then entered into a set of similar contracts with outside third parties. Since outside parties were now involved, the corporation as a whole was, at this point, protected against future natural gas price changes. El Paso accounted for these forward contracts as cash flow hedges under SFAS 133. As a result, unrealized gains and losses on these derivatives were included in other comprehensive income.

However, Merchant Energy then entered into a second set of similar, but opposite, forward contracts with third parties, thereby effectively unwinding the company's price protection. Nevertheless, it continued to designate the original set of contracts between Production and Merchant Energy as hedges under SFAS 133.

During 2001, the price of natural gas had fallen to the point where the ceiling test applied, and El Paso's gas reserves would normally have

had to be written down to fair value. However, since the original contracts were designated as hedges, a writedown was not made on grounds that the hedges protected the firm against natural gas price declines.

In 2004, El Paso announced that following a review by the company and its auditors, and investigation by regulatory authorities, it had decided that its cash flow hedges did not qualify for hedge accounting under SFAS 133, presumably because of the unwinding referred to above. As a result, the ceiling test for 2001 kicked in retroactively, and El Paso was forced to write its reserves down in 2004 by $1.6 billion—the amount that should have been written off in 2001. (While the price of natural gas has risen considerably since 2001, recall that the FASB ceiling test does not allow for subsequent writeup if fair value increases.)

The stock market reacted calmly to these events, perhaps due to the company's emphasis that cash flows were not affected and that future depletion expense would be reduced. On August 10, 2004, the date the company announced it was discontinuing hedge accounting, El Paso's share price fell by only 6 cents, to $7.65. On August 23, the date it announced that the writedown was $1.6 billion, share price rose by 24 cents to $8.05.

As the El Paso vignette illustrates, if a derivative cannot be designated, it does not enjoy the benefits of hedge accounting, such as deferring loss recognition to other comprehensive income (cash flow hedge) or offsetting gains or losses on the derivative by fairvaluing the hedged item (fair value hedge).[18] Denial of these benefits may increase the volatility of reported net income over and above the volatility due to the real risks faced by the firm.

High net income volatility has adverse effects on firms with high debt loads by increasing the probability of financial distress. Also, growth firms may want to hedge their risks, but tend to have relatively few hedgeable items. Then, their use of derivatives to control risk is constrained. Such firms would need to rely on natural hedges. In effect, IAS 39 and SFAS 133 may reduce mismatch volatility, but accounting standards per se do not reduce the real volatility faced by the firm.[19] For further discussion of these issues, see Guay (1999).

Another designation problem is that many firms, particularly financial institutions, actively manage large portfolios of financial assets and liabilities in a coordinated manner as part of their interest rate risk management strategy. It is difficult to designate each derivative instrument in a large portfolio, particularly since active management results in frequent purchases and sales. In response, IAS 39 allows a limited form of **macro hedging** of interest rate risk. Under macro hedging, the firm identifies a *portfolio* of financial assets and liabilities it wishes to hedge. It then designates a portfolio of derivatives whose fair value moves opposite to changes in the fair value of the hedged portfolio. Both unrealized gains and losses from changes in fair value of the hedged portfolio and unrealized losses and gains from changes in the fair value of the hedging portfolio are included in net income. This reduces any mismatch that would result if the firm found it too difficult and costly to separately identify and designate each item in its portfolios. In effect, macro hedging is hedging applied at the portfolio level. To reduce the possibility that the firm may abuse macro hedging to manipulate its earnings, IAS 39 requires that to qualify for macro hedging a portfolio must be managed internally on a fair value basis in accordance with a documented risk management or investment strategy and that portfolio information is supplied to management on this basis.

Finally, it should be noted that the possibility of speculation threatens, in theory, the informativeness of fair value accounting for financial instruments under some conditions.

This possibility was modelled by Gigler, Kanodia, and Venugopalan (2007) (GKV). They assume a firm that acquires cash flow hedges to protect itself against future price decreases for its product, and also acquires additional derivatives to speculate. On average, investors expect the firm to make speculation profits, since they believe that management has the best information about future product prices. Consequently, they do not object to speculation *a priori*. Of course, in any particular period, the firm may lose on speculation, since management's information, analysis, and judgement is not perfect. Consequently, it is possible that the firm is entering financial distress because of speculation losses.

However, investors do not know from the financial statements proper the extent of any speculative losses. This is because, under historical cost accounting, no unrealized gains or losses on derivatives are reported and, under fair value accounting, unrealized gains and losses are reported in total, but investors do not know how much is due to speculation.

The question then is, is fair value accounting superior to historical cost in warning investors if the firm is heading for financial distress? GKV show that the answer is "not always." For example, suppose that the firm incurs a speculation loss.[20] Under historical cost accounting, failure to report unrealized losses, combined with investors' belief that on average the firm gains from speculation, leads to overvaluation of the firm. Under fair value accounting, a loss on derivatives is reported. However, investors' belief that on average the firm gains from speculation now leads them to regard the reported loss on derivatives as coming primarily from fair-valuing of hedging instruments. But, unlike for speculation losses, hedging losses will reverse next period, so investors disregard this loss, again overvaluing the firm. GKV show that if the speculation loss is large enough, over-valuation under fair value accounting exceeds that under historical cost. Consequently, under these conditions, if the firm's speculation loss is large enough to put it into financial distress, investors are less likely to realize this under fair value accounting than under historical cost.

Like any model, the GKV analysis is a simplified representation of hedging and speculation reality. For example, corporate governance may constrain the manager's ability to engage in speculation. However, some possibility of speculative losses remains (see Note 13). The point of GVK is not that fair value accounting for derivatives should be abandoned, Rather, their analysis points to the need for supplementary disclosure of the firm's risk management strategy and details of the derivatives it holds. Then, rational investors are better able to estimate the breakdown of reported derivative losses into hedging and speculation components, thereby reducing any firm overvaluation that would otherwise occur. In this regard, IAS 39 and SFAS 133 contain numerous full disclosure requirements. In addition, IFRS 7 requires extensive supplementary disclosure, as do SFAS 107 and SFAS 119.

7.3.6 Conclusion

We conclude that IAS 39 and SFAS 133 represent substantial steps towards the measurement approach for derivative instruments. However, full disclosure is necessary to protect investors, since firms may also use derivatives to speculate.

7.4 ACCOUNTING FOR INTANGIBLES

7.4.1 Introduction

Intangible assets are capital assets that do not have physical substance, such as patents, trademarks, franchises, a good workforce, location, restructurings, information technology, Internet site names, and, more generally, goodwill.

Some intangibles are accounted for much like property, plant, and equipment. If they are purchased, or self-developed with reasonable certainty of future benefits and costs can be reliably determined, they are valued at cost and amortized over their useful lives. If they are acquired in a business combination and fair value can be determined reliably, cost is equal to their fair value at acquisition. Such intangibles are subject to the ceiling test described in Section 7.2.5.

Intangible assets are important assets for many firms and, for some firms, comprise most of firm value. However, unless they satisfy the criteria of the previous paragraph, their fair values, and even their costs, are difficult to establish reliably, particularly if they are self-developed. This is because the costs of intangibles may be spread over many years and, as these costs are incurred, it may not be known whether they will ever produce future benefits. An example is the costs of research and development, which can lead to many of the intangibles mentioned above. Since it is so difficult to predict future payoffs from these costs, it is not reliably known whether they will be recovered, let alone what their fair value is. As a result, IAS 38 requires that research costs not appear on the balance sheet at all—they are charged to expense as incurred. Costs of developing a product or process resulting from research may be capitalized if the results of the research are technically and commercially feasible and the costs can be measured reliably. In the United States, SFAS 2 requires that all R&D costs be written off in the year they are incurred. Consequently, self-developed intangibles resulting from the firm's research will not appear on the balance sheet at all under U.S. GAAP.

However, it is important to realize that intangibles are "there" even if they are not on the balance sheet. Instead, due to recognition lag, they appear through the income statement. That is, since historical cost accounting waits until value is realized as sales and earnings, the income statement contains the current "instalment" of the value of intangibles. If these instalments are positive, the firm has goodwill.[21] That is, goodwill exists if the firm earns more than its cost of capital on its net assets, including any separately identified intangibles. This mirrors exactly our procedure in Section 6.5.3, where Canadian Tire's unrecorded goodwill was calculated as the present value of expected future abnormal earnings.

The question then is, should goodwill remain off the balance sheet, with the implication that the income statement reports on it as realized, or should its fair value be measured and reported on the balance sheet? Reporting the fair value of goodwill has potential for increased decision usefulness, since this may reveal management's inside information about future expected earning power (which is what creates the goodwill), and it is management that has the best information about what this earning power is. But, reporting the fair value of goodwill creates serious problems of reliability.

At this point, it is helpful to distinguish between self-developed goodwill and purchased goodwill. We first consider purchased goodwill.

7.4.2 Accounting for Purchased Goodwill

When one firm acquires another in a business combination, the **purchase method** of accounting for the transaction requires that the tangible and identifiable intangible assets and the liabilities of the acquired company be valued at their fair values for purposes of the consolidated financial statements. Goodwill is then the difference between the net amount of these fair values and the total purchase price paid by the acquiring company. We illustrate the traditional accounting for purchased goodwill with an example.

Example 7.1
Accounting for Purchased Goodwill

JDN Ltd. is a rapidly expanding "high-tech" firm. As at January 1, 2008, it had 100 shares outstanding, trading at $10. Its balance sheet was as follows:

JDN Ltd.			
Balance Sheet			
As at January 1, 2008			
Capital Assets	$500	Liabilities	$100
		Shareholders' Equity	400
	$500		$500

S Ltd. is also growing rapidly, and is in a business similar to that of JDN. Its balance sheet as at January 1, 2008, was as follows:

S Ltd.			
Balance Sheet			
As at January 1, 2008			
Capital Assets	$300	Liabilities	$140
		Shareholders' Equity	160
	$300		$300

On January 1, 2008, JDN purchases all the 160 outstanding shares of S Ltd. in exchange for 40 shares of JDN's stock valued at $10 each, for a total purchase price of $400. The balance sheet of JDN immediately after the acquisition was:

JDN Ltd.			
Balance Sheet (Post-Acquisition)			
As at January 1, 2008			
Capital Assets, Excluding		Liabilities	$100
Investment in S	$500		
Investment in S	400	Shareholders' Equity	800
	$900		$900

As mentioned, the identifiable assets and liabilities of the purchased company must be valued at their fair values for purposes of preparing a consolidated balance sheet, with any excess of the purchase price over net fair value reflected as goodwill. Assume that as at the date of acquisition the fair value of S Ltd.'s capital assets was estimated as $340, and its liabilities as $140. The consolidated balance sheet of JDN and its wholly owned subsidiary S Ltd. as at date of acquisition was thus:

JDN Ltd. and Subsidiary			
Consolidated Balance Sheet			
As at January 1, 2008			
Capital Assets,		Liabilities	$ 240
Excluding Goodwill	$ 840		
Goodwill	200	Shareholders' Equity	800
	$1,040		$1,040

Goodwill is determined as the amount paid for S Ltd. ($400) less the fair value of net assets acquired ($200).

Until 2001 in Canada and the United States, and 2004 internationally, this goodwill was amortized over its useful life, consistent with the matching concept of historical cost accounting. Management strongly complained about goodwill amortization, however, since it forced down consolidated net income following the acquisition, making it more difficult to demonstrate that the acquisition was a successful business strategy. Obviously, management has an incentive to demonstrate, through increased earnings, its good business judgement in entering into a business combination.

In response, many managers attempted to circumvent the effects of goodwill amortization by emphasizing **pro-forma income** (also called cash income[22] and a variety of other terms) rather than GAAP net income, where pro-forma income is defined as net income before goodwill amortization, restructuring charges, and a variety of other unusual, non-recurring, and extraordinary items selected by management. Under this tactic, the GAAP income statement itself is not affected. However, pro-forma income is emphasized in earnings announcements, messages to shareholders, MD&A, etc. In this way, management seeks to convince investors that goodwill amortization and related items do not matter, in the sense that they are not relevant to the evaluation of the performance of the consolidated entity.

A criticism of pro-forma income was that to the extent management succeeded in convincing investors that this is a better profit measure than GAAP net income, there was less discipline for managers to avoid overpaying in business acquisitions. The excessive goodwill amortization that results from overpaying was simply ignored. Another criticism is that it may mislead investors, since there are no standards to determine just what items are excluded from GAAP income. This is of particular concern if securities markets are not fully efficient.

In response to tactics such as these, standard setters have eliminated the amortization of goodwill. This was accomplished in the United States by SFAS 142, effective in July 2001. In Canada, the CICA *Handbook* contains similar requirements, as does IFRS 3 (2004). These standards constitute a substantial movement towards the measurement approach. Specifically, goodwill is retained on the consolidated balance sheet at its value established at time of purchase, unless there is evidence of impairment, in which case a ceiling test is to be applied to write goodwill down to its new fair value. A goodwill write-down may not be reversed if fair value subsequently increases. Since goodwill amortization was a major management complaint, this elimination has reduced the incentive for management to emphasize pro-forma income.

7.4.3 Self-Developed Goodwill

Unlike purchased goodwill, no readily identifiable transactions exist to determine the cost of self-developed goodwill. Consequently, costs that may create goodwill, such as R&D, are mostly written off as incurred. As mentioned, any goodwill that develops from these costs shows up as abnormal earnings in subsequent income statements. This recognition lag is a major reason why share price responds to earnings announcements, as documented in Chapter 5. The market watches net income carefully for clues as to future earning power.

Nevertheless, the proportion of abnormal share return explained by net income is low, and may be declining over time, as discussed in Section 6.4. Reasons for this low market share were examined by Lev and Zarowin (1999) (LZ). Recall that their study was introduced in Section 6.4, where we noted their findings of declining earnings value relevance over time. Here, we consider LZ's investigation into reasons for this falling market share. They argue that this is due primarily to a failure to account properly for self-developed intangibles.

LZ's argument is easy to see. Consider a firm's current R&D expenditures. Since they are expensed, these costs force reported net income down. However, an efficient market will not penalize the firm for the resulting lower reported earnings to the extent it expects positive results from the R&D, and may even reward it with a higher stock price. Obviously, if the firm's share price responds positively to costs that force current net income down, this will show up as a low association between abnormal share return and net income, and a low, possibly negative, ERC. Furthermore, LZ suggest most firms' expenditures on self-developed intangibles increase over time, driven by deregulation, innovation, and competition. If so, the low association intensifies. In effect, current accounting for R&D results in a mismatch of the costs of intangibles with the revenues generated by those intangibles. These effects, LZ argue, are a prime contributor to low and declining R^2s and ERCs.

To investigate this argument, LZ examined a sample of U.S. firms with high research intensity, that is, firms whose research costs have grown at an increasing rate. While research is only one intangible, they focused on it on grounds that research is a major contributor to self-developed goodwill. LZ found a significantly lower association between share returns and reported earnings for this sample than for a second sample of firms with low research intensity, consistent with their argument.

The question then is, what might be done to improve the accounting for intangibles? One suggestion made by LZ is for a type of successful efforts accounting for R&D. They propose that the accumulated costs of an R&D project be capitalized if the project passes a feasibility test, such as a working model or a successful clinical trial. LZ argue that while capitalization at this point reduces reliability, it provides a reasonable tradeoff with relevance, and reveals inside information to the market about the firm's R&D efforts. The capitalized costs would then be amortized over their estimated useful life. This proposal can be regarded as an extension of IFRS 3, which, as mentioned above, allows development costs to be capitalized once a research project attains technical and financial feasibility.

Clearly, standard setters' reluctance to capitalize research costs is due to concerns about reliability. However, an interesting argument is made by Kanodia, Singh, and Spero (2005) (KSS) that maximizing the value to investors and society of reporting capitalized research and development costs may require some degree of unreliability.

To see KSS' argument, suppose that, contrary to present standards but consistent with LZ's suggestion, the firm capitalizes the costs of research projects as they are expected to be successful, and writes the costs of unsuccessful projects off currently. Assume initially that this separation of successful and unsuccessful R&D is completely reliable. Thus, the market knows exactly the cost of successful R&D.

There are two components of the efficient market's reaction to these successful R&D costs. First, it will react positively to the increased expected profits these costs create. However, the amount invested in R&D also has a signalling effect. That is, the greater the firm's research *potential* (driven by competent research personnel, superior ability to identify promising research areas, and the expected profitability of future patents resulting from the research), the more it will invest in R&D. While the market will not know the details of this research potential (this is inside information of management), it interprets the amount spent on R&D as a signal of what this research potential is. This creates a second component of the market reaction to R&D cost—the more the firm spends, the higher its potential must be. For both of these reasons, the higher is the capitalized R&D cost the more the market will bid up the price of the firm's shares.

Now, consider this scenario from management's standpoint. Perceiving the "extra" market reaction to its R&D, management will *overinvest* in R&D. More precisely, it will push its R&D investment beyond the point where marginal costs equal marginal benefits, thereby reducing future profitability.

Investors, having purchased shares at inflated prices, will soon realize that the firm is not as profitable as they thought, due to the overinvestment in R&D. Thus, they will lower their expectations of R&D profitability. Share price will fall until it reflects actual profitability. However, the firm's R&D overinvestment remains, since these costs have already been incurred. This outcome is called a **fully revealing signalling equilibrium** (Spence, 1974). Firms signal their profitability by their choice of investment level. It is called fully revealing because in equilibrium firms' share prices are consistent with their actual levels of profitability.

Such an outcome is unfortunate, however. Overinvestment is hardly desirable from shareholders' or society's perspective. Notice that it occurs here as a result of complete reliability of reporting of R&D costs.

Now consider a more realistic scenario, where reporting is not completely reliable. Specifically, some of the firm's capitalized R&D costs will not be profitable, and some written-off costs may be profitable after all.

From an investor's standpoint, lack of knowledge of R&D profitability creates estimation risk. As a result, investors do not bid up the firm's share price in response to reported R&D as much as under complete reliability. Consequently, the firm's incentive to overinvest is reduced. KSS show that as the information asymmetry between shareholders and the manager about R&D profitability increases (the manager's inside information advantage about R&D is likely to be quite high) the lower should be reliability. We may conclude that, in theory, considerable unreliability in the reporting of R&D costs can be tolerated, supporting LZ's suggestion.

7.4.4 The Clean Surplus Model Revisited

Another approach to valuing goodwill is to use the clean surplus model discussed in Section 6.5. Recall that our valuation of the share value of Canadian Tire Corporation,

Limited in Section 6.5.3 resulted in a goodwill estimate of $972 (million). Perhaps this amount could be formally incorporated into the financial statements as the fair value of Canadian Tire's goodwill. While we discussed at the time some of the reliability issues surrounding this estimate, if the estimate was to be prepared by management it would convey relevant information about Canadian Tire's expected future earning power.[24]

Alternatively, the clean surplus goodwill calculation could possibly serve as a ceiling test for purchased goodwill. If, in the case of Canadian Tire, the book value of its purchased goodwill exceeds $972, this suggests that purchased goodwill should be written down so as not to exceed this value.[25, 26] Such a procedure, however, clouds the distinction between purchased and self-developed goodwill. For example, the purchased goodwill might be worthless, in which case it should be written down to zero, and the $972 would then be entirely self-developed. For further discussion of the possible use of the clean surplus model to account for goodwill, see AAA Financial Accounting Standards Committee (2001).

7.4.5 Summary

Accounting for intangibles is the ultimate test of the measurement approach. Application of the measurement approach to accounting for goodwill creates severe reliability problems. These problems may be somewhat mitigated for purchased goodwill, since at least a cost figure is available. Yet, even for purchased goodwill, amortization was essentially arbitrary due to the difficulty of establishing useful life. Furthermore, management disliked being charged for goodwill amortization and took steps to avoid it. Standard setters have moved towards a measurement approach to purchased goodwill by introducing standards to write it down only if there is evidence of impairment. The clean surplus model may provide a framework to structure the estimation of the fair value of goodwill.

When goodwill is self-developed, further reliability problems arise, and standard setters usually react by requiring immediate expensing of the costs of intangibles that underlie self-developed goodwill. However, this creates a mismatch between costs and revenues, and, arguably, is the root cause of low value relevance of reported earnings. A suggestion to improve the accounting for self-developed goodwill is capitalization and amortization of successful research projects.

7.5 REPORTING ON RISK

7.5.1 Beta Risk

The theory underlying the CAPM suggests (Section 4.5) that a stock's beta is the sole firm-specific risk measure for a rational investor's diversified portfolio. We discussed this theory in Section 6.2.3, concluding that despite evidence that other measures may also explain share price, beta remains as an important risk concept.

The usual way to estimate beta is by means of a regression analysis based on the market model. However, beta is subject to estimation risk, particularly if it is not stationary.

Financial statement information may help here, since beta and certain financial statement–based risk measures are correlated. Furthermore, these measures can indicate the direction and magnitude of a change in beta sooner than the market model, which would require several periods of new data for re-estimation.

Beaver, Kettler, and Scholes (1970) (BKS) were the first to examine formally the relationship between beta and financial statement–based risk measures. For a sample of 307 New York Stock Exchange firms over two time periods, 1947–1956 and 1957–1965, they used a market model regression analysis to estimate betas for their sample firms for each time period. Then they calculated various financial statement–based risk measures for the same periods. The correlations between three of these risk measures and betas are shown in Table 7.1.

Table 7.1 Correlation Coefficients Between Accounting Risk Measures and Beta, for Five-Security Portfolios

Accounting Risk Measures	Period 1 1947–56	Period 2 1957–65
Dividend payout	–0.79	–0.50
Leverage	0.41	0.48
Earnings variability	0.90	0.82

Source: Beaver, Kettler, and Scholes (BKS), Table 5, 1970. Reprinted by permission.

Dividend payout is the ratio of common share cash dividends to net income. Leverage is the ratio of senior debt securities to total assets. Earnings variability is the standard deviation of the firm's price/earnings ratio over the period.

Notice that the signs of the correlations are what we would expect (for example, the higher the dividend payout, the lower the risk, since a firm facing significant risks would likely retain its earnings for protection rather than pay them out) and that most of the correlations are quite high. Furthermore, there is reasonable consistency between Period 1 and 2. Indeed, BKS report that their most highly correlated accounting variable was a better predictor of a stock's beta than its current beta, supporting our suggestion above that accounting-based risk measures may provide timely indications of shifts in beta.

These correlation results may seem surprising since, *a priori*, it is not obvious why a market-based risk measure has anything to do with accounting variables. However, Hamada (1972) showed that, under ideal conditions, there is a direct relationship between debt-to-equity and beta. Lev (1974) showed a direct relationship, also under ideal conditions, between operating leverage and beta (operating leverage is the ratio of fixed to variable operating costs). BKS' results suggest that these relationships carry over at least in part to non-ideal conditions. The rationale for these results is not hard to see. The higher a firm's financial and operating leverage, the more it will benefit if business conditions improve, and suffer if they deteriorate, since high leverage means a high proportion of fixed costs in the firm's cost structure. Then, earnings are highly affected by changes in the level of activity. The market will be aware of this and, the higher the leverage, the more it will bid up share price when business conditions improve, and vice versa. The stock market index will also rise and fall with business conditions. Since beta measures how strongly the firm's share price varies as the market varies, the greater the leverage the higher is beta.

BKS' findings have financial reporting implications. Hamada's study implies that off-balance-sheet liabilities should be brought onto the balance sheet at current value. IAS 17, which requires current value accounting for finance leases (see Section 7.2.2), is a longstanding example. By including all liabilities on the balance sheet, measurement of the debt component of the debt-to-equity ratio is improved. Under IAS 39 and SFAS 133, (Section 7.3.4), unrealized gains and losses on fair-valuing derivative instruments are included in income, and thus in equity, improving the equity component of the ratio. In both cases, correlation of beta with debt-to-equity is increased.

Lev's study implies that firms should separate fixed and variable operating costs, if investors are to infer beta from the financial statements. Surprisingly, financial reporting seems of little help here. Indeed, Ryan (1997) points out that absorption cost accounting, which includes fixed operating costs in inventory, actually increases the difficulty of evaluating operating leverage.

7.5.2 Why Do Firms Manage Firm-Specific Risk?

While the BKS results are encouraging, they do not answer the questions of why firms manage their firm-specific risk, and why accounting standards require disclosures of firm-specific risks and how they are managed. In other words, if investors diversify their portfolios, is information about firm-specific risk decision useful, since investors can manage this risk for themselves? However, several reasons for managing and reporting on firm-specific risk can be suggested:

- Estimation risk. As noted in Section 4.5, the CAPM does not include for estimation risk. Reporting on the firm's risk management strategies may reduce investor concerns about adverse selection. In this regard, refer to the risk disclosures in Canadian Tire Corp.'s MD&A reproduced in Section 4.8.2, and note that disclosure risk and insider trading risk are among those controlled.

- Firms that are planning large capital expenditures may wish to ensure cash is available when needed. This reason applies particularly to firms that are growing rapidly and to firms that find it expensive to raise external capital. Risk management, such as by hedging, can reduce cash flow risk.

- Managers may use derivatives to speculate, as discussed in Section 7.3.4. This is a form of risk management that increases risk rather than reduces it. It may be difficult for investors to diversify speculation risk, since losses can be very large and can threaten the existence of the firm itself. Then, as implied by the study of Gigler,

Kanodia, and Venugopalan (2007) outlined in Section 7.3.5, full disclosure of the firm's risk management strategies, and the fair values of its various derivatives and their unrealized gains and losses, is crucial.

- Legal liability. As argued in Sections 6.6 and 6.7, conservative accounting can help reduce legal liability. However, hedging to manage risk may prevent losses from arising in the first place.

- Yet another reason, to be discussed in Section 10.4.3, is that managers whose compensation is based on earnings may use derivatives to reduce the volatility of their compensation.

7.5.3 Stock Market Reaction to Other Risks

In the previous section, we suggested several reasons why firms may wish to manage and report on firm-specific risk despite the theory underlying the CAPM and beta. We have already seen in Section 4.8.2 that MD&A requires a discussion of risks and uncertainties, particularly with respect to downside risk. Also, as pointed out in Section 7.3.5, many of the disclosures required by IAS 39, IFRS 7, SFASs 133, 107, and 119 are risk-related. These disclosures include supplementary information about exposures to market and credit risks and about the firm's risk management policies.

These various motivations for reporting on risk raise the question, does the stock market react to firm risks other than beta? Much of the empirical research in this area relates to interest rate risk of financial institutions. For such firms, financial assets and liabilities comprise most of book value, and it is to financial assets and liabilities that many of the risk-related disclosure standards relate. Barth, Beaver, and Landsman (1996) (BBL) examined the effects of supplemental SFAS 107 fair value disclosures on the market value of equity for a sample of 136 U.S. banks for 1992 and 1993. They found a market reaction to the fair values of banks' loans portfolios, suggesting that the relevance of fair value reporting of these assets outweighs reliability difficulties in measuring loan value.

Interestingly, BBL found that the market response to fair value of loans was smaller for banks in lower-than-average financial condition (measured by their regulatory capital ratios). This implies that the market evaluates such banks as riskier—a bank in poor financial condition is less likely to be around to realize the unrealized gains and losses on its loan portfolio.

Schrand (1997) studied the effect on interest rate risk of derivatives-based hedging activities, for a sample of 208 savings and loan associations during 1984–1988. She measured the interest rate sensitivity of her sample firms by their one-year "maturity gap," the amount of their interest-sensitive assets maturing in one year less their interest-sensitive liabilities maturing in one year. The greater the gap, the greater the sensitivity of their share returns to unexpected changes in interest rates.

Note that maturity gap corresponds to the concept of natural hedging introduced in Section 7.3.2—the narrower the gap the more the institution is coordinating the maturities of its on-balance-sheet, interest-sensitive assets and liabilities so as to reduce its interest rate risk. For most of her sample firms, Schrand found that the gap was negative. That is, Schrand's firms were not completely eliminating their interest rate risk by means of natural hedging (if they were, the gap would be zero). For each sample firm, Schrand then evaluated the effect of the firm's[27] derivatives hedging activities on its one-year maturity gap. She found that the more a firm reduced its gap in this way, the less sensitive its share price was to unexpected interest rate changes, particularly for the larger institutions in her sample (which were more active users of derivatives).

Hodder, Hopkins, and Whalen (2006) (HHW) studied interest rate risk for a sample of U.S. banks over 1996–2004. They first calculated what they called full fair value income (FFV), for each bank. This earnings measure adds to net income the unrealized gains and losses on all of a bank's financial assets and liabilities, including an estimate of core deposit intangibles (see Section 7.3.2). Sources of information for their FFV calculations include comprehensive income (which reports unrealized gains and losses on available-for-sale investments and cash flow hedges), supplementary disclosures under SFAS 107 and 133, and various filings with regulatory authorities.

HHW then calculated the variance of FFV income. Think of FFV volatility as a measure of a bank's unhedged interest rate risk. HHW found that over their sample period the volatility of FFV income greatly exceeded that of comprehensive income for most of their sample banks. This finding implies that comprehensive income contains only a relatively small amount of information about a bank's interest rate risk. Other sources of interest rate risk not reported on by other comprehensive income include deposit liabilities (not fair-valued) and held-to-maturity securities (written down if current value declines, but not subsequently written up under U.S. GAAP). The finding also implies, as in earlier studies, that banks do not fully hedge their interest rate risk (if they did, volatility of FFV would be much lower, and less than that of comprehensive income).

HHW also found that the additional volatility of FFV income was negatively related to share price, and positively related to cost of capital, after controlling for other factors affecting interest rate risk such as maturity gap, again suggesting that investors are sensitive to firm-specific risk. Indeed, these findings suggest that extension of fair value accounting towards reporting FFV income would be decision useful, since it could help investors to better evaluate firm risk.

In sum, evidence of market response to interest rate risk suggests that this risk is not fully hedged by banks and that investors do not, or cannot, fully diversify the risk that remains. Furthermore, comprehensive income seems ineffective relative to FFV income in reporting on interest rate risk, implying that increased adoption of a measurement approach could convey useful information in this regard.

We would expect that if other sources of risk than beta were to be useful for investors, it would be for interest rate risk of financial institutions. However, firms in other industries also face price risks, raising the question of whether the market also responds to these. Wong (2000) examined the foreign exchange risk of a sample of 145 manufacturing firms during 1994–1996. He found that, for some firms in his sample, share price was affected by foreign currency exposure, implying that investors do not fully diversify foreign exchange risk. However, unlike Schrand, neither the fair value nor the notional amount of firms' foreign exchange derivatives positions explained the magnitude of the sensitivity. One possible explanation is that investors sufficiently diversify their holdings so that they are not sensitive to firms' foreign exchange risks. However, Wong attributed the lack of results to shortcomings of hedging disclosures in annual reports (much of Schrand's data was taken from regulatory filings, which would not be available for industrial firms). He recommended more disaggregated disclosures in annual reports of notional amounts, fair values, long and short positions, and maturities by class of instrument. Much of this disclosure is now required by IFRS 7.

7.5.4 A Measurement Approach to Risk Reporting

The disclosures discussed in the previous section are primarily oriented to the information approach—they involve the communication of information to enable investors to make their own risk evaluations. However, like valuations of assets and liabilities, reporting on risk is also moving towards increased measurement.

In this regard, consider the risk disclosure requirements laid down by the SEC (1997), as described by Linsmeier and Pearson (1997). These include quantitative price risk disclosures, which can take the following forms: (1) a **tabular presentation** of fair values and contract terms sufficient to enable investors to determine a firm's future cash flows from financial instruments by maturity date; (2) a **sensitivity analysis** showing the impact on earnings, cash flows, or fair values of financial instruments, resulting from changes in relevant commodity prices, interest rates, and foreign exchange rates; or (3) **value at risk**, being the loss in earnings, cash flows, or fair values resulting from future price changes sufficiently large that they have a specified low probability of occurring.

Much of this risk information is reported as part of MD&A—see our discussion of Canadian Tire's risk disclosures in Section 4.8.2.

While the tabular presentation is oriented to an information approach, the latter two alternatives are of interest because they are measurement-oriented. The firm, rather than investors, prepares the quantitative risk assessments. We would expect that it is the firm that has the most accurate estimates of its own risks. Hence, these latter two risk measures have the greater potential for decision usefulness. Indeed, IFRS 7 requires a sensitivity analysis of price risks of financial instruments. This requirement is of interest because it moves sensitivity analysis away from MD&A (a securities commission regulation) into supplementary financial statement information (an audited accounting regulation).

Table 7.2 shows a sensitivity disclosure from the 2006 annual report of Suncor Energy, Inc. The table shows the impact on cash flows and earnings of relevant commodity and foreign exchange rate risks.

Note that oil and gas price sensitivities are given net of hedging activities, while exchange rate sensitivities are not. Presumably, the after-hedging sensitivities are of greater relevance, which raises the question of why exchange rate risk is reported before hedging. The answer, it seems, is that Suncor does not hedge its exchange rate risk by

Table 7.2 Sensitivity Analysis[1]

	2006 Average	Change	Approximate Change in Cash Flow from Operations ($ millions)	After-tax Earnings ($ millions)
Oil Sands				
Price of crude oil ($/barrel)[2]	$68.03	US$1.00	82	55
Sweet/sour differential ($/barrel)	$8.84	US$1.00	37	25
Sales (bpd)	263 100	1 000	13	9
Natural Gas				
Price of natural gas ($/mcf)[2]	$7.15	0.10	5	4
Production/sales of natural gas (mmcf/d)	191	10	16	7
Consolidated				
Exchange rate: Cdn$/US$	0.88	0.10	43	29

[1]The sensitivity analysis shows the main factors affecting Suncor's annual cash flow from operations and earnings based on actual 2006 operations. The table illustrates the potential financial impact of these factors applied to Suncor's 2006 results. A change in any one factor could compound or offset other factors.
[2]Includes the impact of hedging activities.

Source: Reprinted by permission of Suncor Energy Inc.

means of derivatives. Suncor states in its MD&A that exchange rate gains or losses would be partially offset by losses or gains on its U.S. dollar-denominated debt, implying that the company feels natural hedging provides sufficient protection.

Sensitivity estimates are subject to relevant range problems. Thus, if the price of oil were to change by, say, $3/bbl, it is unlikely that the impact on earnings would be three times the impact of the $1/bbl change given in the table. Another problem is with co-movements in prices, as Suncor points out in Note 1 to the table. It is unlikely, for example, that changes in the prices of crude oil and natural gas are independent. Yet, each change estimate in Table 7.2 holds the other prices constant. Finally, nothing is said about the probabilities of price changes. These would have to be assessed by the investor.

The value at risk approach addresses some of these problems. Consider, for example, a firm's portfolio of financial instruments at year-end. To calculate value at risk, the firm first needs to assess a joint probability distribution of the various price risks that affect the fair value of the portfolio over some holding period, say one day. This, in turn, is converted into a distribution of the changes in the fair value of the portfolio. The value at risk is then the loss in fair value that has only a $2\frac{1}{2}$% (or some other low probability) chance of occurring over the holding period. In effect, a loss greater than the value at risk is a rare event. The approach can also be extended to cash flow and earnings value at risk.

Microsoft Corporation is a well-known user of value at risk. It faces foreign currency, interest rate, commodity, and securities price risks, which it hedges by means of options and other derivatives. Microsoft does not fully hedge these risks; this is likely to be too costly. However, it uses value at risk to estimate its unhedged exposure and reports the results in its annual report. Presumably, Microsoft adjusts the extent of its hedging activities so as to attain the level of price risk it is willing to bear.

Microsoft's 2006 annual report discloses that there is a $97^1/_2\%$ probability that the loss on its assets subject to interest rate, currency, commodity, and equity price risks would not exceed $158 million over a one-day holding period (thus, only a $2^1/_2\%$ probability of a loss greater than this amount).

As Microsoft points out, a prolonged market decline extending for more than one day could result in a larger loss. Nevertheless, given Microsoft's 2006 reported net income of $2,195 million, the investor knows that a one-day loss due to price risks of more than 7% of earnings is unlikely.

While primarily geared to downside risk, there appears to be no reason why value at risk could not be applied to upside risk as well. Thus, assuming the price distribution is symmetric, Microsoft is unlikely to gain more than $158 million in one day if prices move in its favour.

A challenging aspect of value at risk, however, is the need to assess the joint price distribution, including correlations between the price risks. Keeping track of past price changes is one way to do this. Nevertheless, if there are, say, 10 price risks faced by a portfolio, then 10 expected values, 10 variances, and 45 correlations need to be estimated. Microsoft keeps track of 1,000 price risks, and explains that it bases its calculations on the past behaviour of relevant market prices. It cautions, however, that the distribution of past prices may change, reducing the accuracy of the value at risk calculations.

Banks also use value at risk as a risk measure for their trading operations, and the variability of a bank's trading securities portfolio can be an important component of its total risk. Liu, Ryan, and Tan (2004) examined the one-day value at risk disclosures of a sample of 17 large U.S. banks over 1997–2002. They found that value at risk enabled improved predictions of next-quarter trading income for their sample. This suggests that despite concerns about accuracy, this risk measure has potential to be decision useful.

7.5.5 Summary

We conclude that information about firm risk, in addition to beta, is valued by the stock market, particularly for financial institutions. This is documented by the reaction of share returns of these institutions to risk exposures and to the impact of hedging on these exposures. Financial reporting has responded by increased reporting of fair values for financial instruments, supplemented by discussion of risks and how they are managed, and by disclosure of financial instrument information. This enables investors to better evaluate the amounts, timing, and uncertainty of returns on their investments.

Financial reporting is also moving towards providing investors with quantitative risk information, such as sensitivity analyses and value at risk. Despite methodological challenges, these represent important steps in moving risk disclosures towards a measurement approach.

7.6 CONCLUSIONS ON MEASUREMENT APPLICATIONS

There are numerous instances of the use of current values in financial reporting, and the list is growing. Many uses involve only partial application of a measurement approach, as in lower-of-cost-or-market, long-term debt, and ceiling tests. Thus, under lower-of-cost-or-market and ceiling tests, subsequent writing up of previously written-down assets is either disallowed or subject to restrictions. Nevertheless, partial applications of fair value have the potential to be decision useful to the extent they reveal a material change in the firm's financial position and prospects.

However, several standards extend the measurement approach so as to periodically measure both value increases and decreases. Thus, pensions and OPEBs are reported at present value each period, and trading and available-for-sale securities are fair-valued each period. Several accounting standards require supplemental disclosure of fair value and risk information for a variety of financial instruments. Even the accounting for business combinations and purchased goodwill is becoming measurement-oriented, as witnessed by standards that apply a ceiling test to purchased goodwill. Securities commission regulations require disclosure of quantitative risk measures, some of which are also required by recent accounting standards.

Certainly, it appears that decision usefulness is moving more and more into the arena of measurement. Reasons for this were suggested in Chapter 6. They include the low value relevance of historical cost-based net income, reactions to theory and evidence that securities markets may not be as fully efficient as originally believed, increasing acceptance of a theory that expresses firm value in terms of accounting variables, and auditor legal liability resulting from abuses of the historical cost system. The combined effect of these factors seems to have convinced accounting standard setters that striving for greater relevance is worthwhile, even at the cost of some sacrifice of reliability.

Whether the measurement-oriented standards described in this chapter will increase the market share of financial accounting information in explaining share returns and will reduce auditor liability remain to be seen. Furthermore, only time will tell whether the downturn in economic activity triggered in the early 2000s by the collapse of share prices of many technology firms will slow down or accelerate the measurement approach. On the one hand, this collapse may remind accountants of the lesson from the Great Depression of the 1930s, that values are fleeting, thereby reinforcing the historical cost basis and accounting conservatism. On the other hand, the measurement approach may be reinforced, as accountants strive to ensure current values, whether higher or lower than cost, are promptly and fully reported.

Questions and Problems

1. Accounts receivable are usually valued on the balance sheet at current value, namely the amount owing from customers less an allowance for uncollectible accounts. Does this violate the historical cost basis of accounting? Explain.

   Note: A good answer will consider the point in the operating cycle at which revenue is realized.

2. A firm receives cash this period as payment for services to be rendered next period. The firm records the amount of cash received as a deferred liability on its balance sheet, to be transferred to revenue next period in accordance with the matching principle of historical cost accounting. Explain why the reporting of a deferred liability like this is inconsistent with the measurement approach. Assuming that unrealized gains and losses are included in other comprehensive income, how would this transaction be recorded under the measurement approach?

3. Explain why a firm may not necessarily reduce its price risks to zero by means of hedging transactions. (CGA-Canada)

4. On August 31, 1999, an article in *The Globe and Mail*, "2000: New year, new accounting, new costs," anticipated the introduction of Section 3461 of the *CICA Handbook*, requiring accrual accounting for OPEBs. This standard is similar to SFAS 106 and IAS 19 described in the text. The article noted that firms have the option of recording the accumulated OPEB liability as a direct charge to retained earnings, or to defer the amount of the liability over the next several years and amortize it. The article quotes Mr. Ken Vallillee, a partner of a large accounting firm, as saying, "Most companies will opt for the one-time charge if they can." The article also points out that Section 3461 replaces the previous method of accounting for OPEBs, charging cash payments for OPEBs to expense as they are made.

   Required

   a. Explain the extent to which the new standard will increase the decision usefulness of financial statements for investors. Consider both issues of relevance and reliability in your answer.

   b. Do you agree with Mr. Vallillee that most firms will opt for the one-time charge? Explain why or why not.

   c. What effects will the reporting of the OPEB liability have on the market value of affected firms' shares? Will the effect depend on how the firm chooses to record the liability? In your answer, consider situations where share price might fall, remain unchanged, or rise. Assume in your answer that securities markets are efficient.

5. Refer to the El Paso Corporation vignette (Theory in Practice 7.2) in Section 7.3.5.

   Required

   a. As a U.S. corporation, El Paso is subject to U.S. GAAP. Why are unrealized gains and losses on derivative instruments designated as cash flow hedges included in other comprehensive income under SFAS 133?

   b. The ceiling test applies to proved reserves of oil and gas companies that use successful-efforts accounting (SFAS 144). Explain why effective cash flow hedging of future production can reduce or avoid ceiling test writedowns for oil and gas reserves.

c. Use the "highly effective" criterion for a hedge to evaluate whether El Paso's decision that its cash flow hedges of its oil and gas production were not valid was a correct one.

d. Suppose that El Paso did not revise its cash flow hedge accounting. That is, suppose that it continued to designate these hedges as effective cash flow hedges. Suppose also that media reports began to question whether El Paso's natural gas reserves were correctly stated. Outline some possible consequences for El Paso of this questioning.

e. Do you feel that the management of El Paso, and its auditor, behaved ethically during this episode? Explain why or why not.

6. Share prices of many "high-tech" firms are quite volatile relative to the stock market index. In an article in *The Wall Street Journal* (reprinted in *The Globe and Mail,* May 16, 2001), Greg Ip discusses a reason why. He points out that high-tech firms have high fixed costs, consisting mainly of R&D driven by rapid technological progress. They also have low variable costs, since the direct production costs of their products tend to be very low. In effect, high-tech firms have high operating leverage.

For example, Yahoo Inc. incurred a drop in revenue of 42% in the first quarter of 2001, but its costs barely dropped. It reported an operating loss of $33 million for the quarter, compared to a profit of $87 million in the last quarter of 2000.

Required

a. Use high operating leverage to explain high stock price variability.

b. Use the argument that beta is non-stationary (Section 6.2.3) to explain high stock price volatility.

c. Use the behavioural finance concepts of momentum and bubbles to explain high stock price volatility.

d. Are these three sources of volatility mutually exclusive? Explain.

7. Under IAS 39 and SFAS 115, most loan assets held by banks are held in the loans and receivables or held-to-maturity categories, where they are valued at amortized cost. Of course, if the fair value of a loan should fall below this amount, the impaired loans standards require a writedown. Following the 2000 economic downturn, investors watched loan writedowns with particular care. Major writedowns will likely result in a decline in the bank's share price, as investors interpret the writedown as a sign of loan quality problems to come. For example, in Canada, *The Globe and Mail*, March 7, 2001, reported "Scotiabank profit overshadowed by impaired loans." The bank reported a substantial increase in first quarter, 2001, net income. However, it also reported a 44% increase in impaired loans. Its share price on the Toronto Stock Exchange fell by $3.46, closing at $42.44.

Faced with reactions such as these, banks may wish to disguise the extent of major loan writedowns. An article in *The Economist*, March 22, 2001, "Shell game," describes how some U.S. banks have responded to similar situations.

The trick, according to *The Economist*, is to transfer problem loans to the available-for-sale category. Under SFAS 115, available-for-sale securities are valued at their fair value. Thus, the transferred loans must be written down. However, the writedown will be buried in larger totals and the market would not know how much of the total adjustment to fair value belongs to the loans transferred. Furthermore, unrealized gains and losses from fair-valuing available-for-sale securities are included in other comprehensive income under SFAS 115, so that writedowns do not affect net income. Another consequence is that the book value of held-to-maturity loans on the balance sheet is reduced, so that any existing loan loss allowance will appear more adequate.

Whether banks actually sell the transferred problem loans is an open question. *The Economist* points out that the dollar amount of secondary trading has risen dramatically in recent years. However, the length of time that banks can hold loans in the available-for-sale category without selling them is a "grey area." Presumably, the banks' auditors will be aware of these practices and will take steps to discourage them. However, *The Economist* quotes an official of the Office of the Comptroller of the Currency (a U.S. banking regulator) as saying auditors "too often side with their clients" in grey areas.

Required

a. What is the likely effect on banks' share prices and on the operation of capital markets of the above practice? Explain.

b. Why do IAS 39 and SFAS 115 allow loans and receivables and held-to-maturity loans to be valued at cost, or amortized cost, instead of at fair value like held for trading and available-for-sale securities? To what extent would amending these standards to require fair value accounting for all financial instruments be feasible? Explain.

c. If you were the auditor of a bank engaging in the above practice, would you qualify your audit report if the bank refused your request to stop? Discuss why or why not. In your answer, consider both principles of ethical behaviour and your own reputation and economic well-being.

8. On March 11, 2000, *The Globe and Mail* reported "Ballard losses double." The reference was to Ballard Power Systems Inc., a Canadian developer of fuel cell technology. On March 10, 2000, Ballard reported an operating loss of $26 million for the fourth quarter of 1999, bringing its loss for the year to $75.2 million on revenues of $33.2 million. Its loss for 1998 was $36.2 million on revenues of $25.1 million. The reason for the increased loss in 1999, according to Ballard, was a huge increase in R&D spending for its fuel cell technology.

On March 10, 2000, Ballard's share price closed at $189 on the Toronto Stock Exchange, up $14 on the day for an increase of 8%.

Required

a. Does the increase in Ballard's share price on March 10, 2000, on the same day that it reported an increased loss, imply a high or low R^2 and ERC for the relationship between the return on Ballard's shares and abnormal earnings? Explain, using the arguments of Lev and Zarowin (1999). Assume that the risk-free interest rate and the change in the TSE 300 index on March 10, 2000, were both zero, so that all of the return on Ballard's shares on that day was abnormal.

b. How do Lev and Zarowin propose to improve the accounting for R&D but yet retain reasonable reliability? Explain how this proposal could affect R^2 and the ERC. Do you see any problems resulting from reliably accounting for the results of R&D? Explain.

c. Does Ballard's share price behaviour on March 10, 2000, suggest securities market efficiency or inefficiency? Explain.

9. As mentioned in Theory and Practice 7.3, JDS Uniphase Corporation reported a preliminary loss of $50.558 billion for the year ended June 30, 2001. In a July 26, 2001, news release accompanying its financial statements, JDS also presented a "pro-forma" income statement that showed a profit for the year of $67.4 million. The difference is summarized as follows ($ million):

Net loss, as reported	$50,558.0
Add:	
Write-off of purchased goodwill	$44,774.3
Write-off of tangible and intangible assets from acquisitions	5,939.2
Losses on equity investments	1,453.3
Gain on sale of subsidiary	(1,768.1)
Non-cash stock option compensation	385.6
Income tax	(158.9)
	50,625.4
Pro-forma net income	$ 67.4

Required

a. The purchased goodwill arose primarily from business acquisitions paid for in shares of JDS Uniphase. In *The Globe and Mail*, July 27, 2001, Fabrice Taylor stated that in JDS' case, "most of the goodwill on the books comes from overvalued stock." In a separate article, Showwei Chu quotes a senior technology analyst as saying, "They paid what the companies were worth at the time." While currently trading in the $4 range, JDS' shares were trading between $100 and $200 when most of the acquisitions were made.

 i. Assume securities markets are fully efficient. Does the $44,774.3 write-off of purchased goodwill represent a real loss to JDS Uniphase and its shareholders, given that no cash is involved? If so, state precisely the nature of the loss and who ultimately bears it.

 ii. Would your answer change if securities markets are subject to momentum and bubble behaviour? Explain.

b. What additional information is added to the publicly available information about JDS Uniphase as a result of the supplementary pro-forma income disclosure?

c. Why did JDS Uniphase management present the pro-forma income disclosure?

d. To the extent that investors accept pro-forma income as a measure of management performance, how might this affect management's propensity to overpay for future acquisitions? Explain.

10. Refer to the sensitivity analysis of Suncor Energy Inc. reproduced in Table 7.2. The analysis discloses the potential effects of changes in prices and production of oil and natural gas, and of changes in the Can./U.S. dollar exchange rate, on 2006 cash flows and earnings.

Required

a. Evaluate the relevance and reliability of this method of disclosing risk information.

b. The analysis indicates that the sensitivity of earnings to its oil and natural gas activities is net of hedging. As an investor, would you find sensitivity information net of hedging, or before hedging, more useful? Explain.

c. Suncor's price risks arise from changes in the market prices of crude oil and natural gas, with associated foreign exchange risk because market prices are largely based on the U.S. dollar. Suncor reports elsewhere in its MD&A (not reproduced) that its board of directors has approved hedging of up to 30% of its 2007 and 2008 crude oil production against price risks. Why would Suncor's board impose this limitation on management's ability to manage risk? Give reasons based on corporate governance, cost, and investor diversification considerations.

11. EnCana Corp. a large Canadian oil and gas company, reported net income of $393 million U.S. (EnCana reports in U.S. dollars) for its third quarter, 2004. This compares with net income of $290 million for the same quarter of 2003. However, third quarter, 2004, earnings would have been even higher but for a $321 million after-tax unrealized loss on cash flow hedges of future oil and gas sales charged against operations. In accordance with Canadian GAAP at the time, EnCana accounted for these financial instruments at fair value, with unrealized gains and losses included in net income. The loss was due to the dramatic increase in oil prices during 2004, and illustrates that while hedging may protect the firm from losses if product prices decline, it also shuts them out of gains if prices increase.

Required

a. Explain why EnCana reported a loss on its hedging activities.

b. Assuming that its hedges qualified for hedge accounting under IAS 39 or SFAS 133, how would EnCana's unrealized hedging loss have been accounted for under these standards?

c. Give reasons why firms such as EnCana typically hedge at least part of their price risk of future anticipated sales.

12. In a press release dated April 23, 2005, Canadian Natural Resources Limited (CNRL) reported a loss of $679 million from cash flow hedges of its crude oil and natural gas production, for the quarter ended March 31, 2005.

CNRL reported that the hedges in question did not meet the requirements for hedge accounting. Consequently, they had to be fair-valued as at March 31 with the loss included in net income. The company indicated that fair value was determined by the hedges' market values at March 31.

Required

a. The purpose of hedging is to shield the firm from the impacts of changing prices. If so, explain how a loss on cash flow hedging can arise in net income.

b. Suppose that CNRL's hedges had met the requirements for hedge accounting laid down by IAS 39 or SFAS 133 and were duly designated and accounted for by CNRL according to that standard. How would the $679 million loss be accounted for?

c. CNRL stated in its press release that the $679 million loss did not affect cash flows for the quarter ended March 31, 2005. As an investor in CNRL, do you find the information about the loss to be decision useful? Explain why or why not.

13. Refer to Theory in Practice 7.1, describing how The Blackstone Group proposed to account for the carried interest to be received from future earnings of unconsolidated firms it has invested in.

Required

a. As a rational investor in the shares of Blackstone's initial public offering, would you find fair value accounting more or less decision useful than historical cost accounting for the value of Blackstone's carried interest? In your answer, consider issues of relevance, reliability, and full disclosure.

b. As a rational investor, would the increased volatility of Blackstone's earnings resulting from fair value accounting affect the amount you would be willing to pay for its shares? Explain your answer.

c. Why do you think that Blackstone changed its mind?

14. A serious problem with fair-valuing complex financial instruments was revealed by the August 2007 meltdown of markets for collateralized debt obligations (CDO) and other asset-backed securities.

The meltdown arose in the U.S. mortgage market. Many mortgage loans had been made to poor credit risks who, the market feared, would be unable to meet increased variable-rate mortgage payments due to rising interest rates or expiration of low introductory rates.

Many of these mortgages had been repackaged by the original lenders into CDOs, that is, tranches of similar credit risk, and resold to other financial institutions. A claimed advantage of these tranches was that a CDO's mortgage default risk (i.e., credit risk) was dispersed across many different mortgages, and that it was unlikely that all, or even a few, of these homeowners would default. Furthermore, credit risk was often further dispersed by means of credit default swaps (CDS). These are financial instruments whereby, for a fee, the CDO investor would be reimbursed by the CDS issuer for all or part of any credit losses sustained. In effect, CDSs bootstrapped the quality of CDOs backed by poor-credit-risk mortgages. Many of these CDOs were purchased by hedge funds and mutual funds, including funds in Europe and elsewhere.

Other major CDO purchasers included "conduits." These are financial institutions that financed their CDO purchases by issuing asset-backed commercial paper (ABCP), which is short-term commercial paper secured by CDOs. ABCP was very popular as a vehicle whereby firms could safely invest excess cash temporarily. Other major ABCP purchasers included money-market mutual funds. While the interest rate paid by ABCP was low, it was higher than that of, for example, government treasury bills, another common short-term investment. The perception of ABCP safety was further enhanced because they generally received top ratings from credit-rating agencies. Conduits earned their profits from the spread between the interest earned on their CDOs and the lower interest they paid on their ABCP.

As evidence (e.g., increasing default rates) that the U.S. mortgage market was in trouble grew in the months leading up to August 2007, concerns about the security of CDOs also grew. Matters came to a head when two hedge funds operated by Bear Stearns Co. in New York declared bankruptcy because of CDO losses. Shortly afterwards, on August 9, BNP Paribas, France's biggest bank, halted redemptions of three of its mutual funds because it was unable to determine the fair value of the CDOs they contained. Several German funds followed suit.

While CDOs and CDSs were effective in dispersing risk, models used to establish their fair value had not anticipated the effects of lack of transparency concerning the quality of the mortgages underlying them. Once concern about mortgage defaults appeared, investors lost confidence in all CDOs, leading to a herd effect whereby no one was willing to hold them. Thus, the market collapsed. Instead of eliminating risk, it seems that CDOs and CDSs had merely transferred it from credit risk to liquidity risk.

Since ABCP was secured by CDOs, concerns about the security of ABCP also grew. Eventually no one would buy ABCP either. As a result, conduits were unable to redeem maturing ABCP from the proceeds of new ABCP issues, which spread the liquidity crisis to the short-term credit market. Since the CDOs securing the ABCP were virtually unsaleable, many firms and funds had to sell other assets to obtain needed cash, putting downward pressure on stock markets.

Central banks responded to these events by lowering interest rates and making it easier for banks and others to borrow funds. However, it quickly became apparent that the world financial system suffered from serious structural problems that would take some time to fully understand and fix.

Required

a. Why was BNP Paribas unable to determine the fair value of its CDOs?

b. Why did CDS not prevent the collapse of public confidence in CDOs and ABCP?

Notes

1. A finance lease, also called a capital lease, is a lease that transfers the significant risks and rewards of ownership to the lessee. In essence, the lessee has purchased the asset, financing it by means of the lease.

2. The U.S. rule, however, is based on the lower of cost or current replacement cost, subject to the constraints that market value should not exceed net realizable value and should not be so low as to produce a greater-than-normal profit margin.

3. An effect of the two-step procedure is to avoid writedowns of assets that are only mildly impaired or for which the decline in fair value is viewed as temporary. For example, the undiscounted future direct net cash flows of an asset with book value of $100 might be estimated as $105, despite a fair value of $90. Then, the asset need not be written down. However, if undiscounted cash flows are, say, $95, the asset is written down to fair value.

4. This assumes the firm does not use the revaluation option (Section 7.2.4). If this option is used, accounting for impairment losses is more complex.

5. A defined benefit pension plan specifies the benefits to be received by an employee, such as 75% of salary at time of retirement. This type of plan is distinguished from a defined contribution plan, where the contribution to be made by the employer is specified. In a defined contribution plan, the pension benefits received by the employee depend on the amounts contributed and the earnings of the plan assets. For a defined benefit plan, the employer bears the risk of fluctuations in the value of plan assets. For a defined contribution plan, this risk is borne by the employee.

6. Pension expense also includes amortization of prior service costs, which we do not consider here.

7. Benefits under many defined benefit plans are based on the employee's compensation in the final years of service. Many employees, especially senior executives, enjoy large compensation increases in their final years. If service cost was based on current period compensation only, this would result in large increases in pension expense in these final years. SFAS 87 smooths pension expense by anticipating these large expected compensation increases over the employee's working life.

8. See SEC, "Report and Recommendations Pursuant to Section 401(c) of the Sarbanes-Oxley Act of 2002 On Arrangements with Off-Balance Sheet Implications, Special Purpose Entities, and Transparency of Filings by Issuers." This report was prepared when share prices were still recovering from the aftermath of Enron and WorldCom. It is possible that today, pension plan assets may have increased to the point where the deficit is lower.

9. Note that a full application of the measurement approach would not require other comprehensive income, since all unrealized gains and losses from adjusting assets and liabilities to current value would be included in net income. It appears that the creation by standard setters of other comprehensive income represents a political compromise with management. This is discussed further in Section 13.3.2.

10. Service cost for pensions does, however, include an estimate of future cost increases for the benefits earned during the current period. An argument for excluding future increases in benefits for OPEBs is that it is easier for a firm to reduce or cancel OPEBs than pensions. Consequently, it is questionable if any expected increases in future OPEB benefits constitute a liability.

11. These definitions omit some components of the full definitions contained in the accounting standards. See, for example, IAS 39.

12. This statement does not apply to deposit liabilities, however, since SFAS 159 does not allow deposit liabilities to be fair valued.

13. Examples of speculation using derivatives that resulted in bankruptcy or near bankruptcy include Orange County, California; Barings Bank; and Long-term Capital Management. For accounts of these disasters, see Boyle and Boyle (2001), Chapter 8.

14. If the risk-free interest rate is greater than zero, the option fair value is more complex. Also, options are usually fair-valued by an equivalent approach, called a **replicating portfolio**. This is a portfolio consisting of an investment in the underlying share plus a short position in a risk-free asset, where the amounts of each security are determined each period so that the replicating portfolio yields the same return as the option for each possible end-of-period value of the option. Since the underlying share and the risk-free asset have readily available market values, and since the return on the option is the same as that of the replicating portfolio, arbitrage forces the fair value of the option to equal the value of the replicating portfolio. For details, see Boyle and Boyle (2001), Chapter 4.

15. Boyle and Boyle (2001) (Chapter 5, p. 89), call this formula the Black/Scholes/Merton formula, due to important contributions by Robert Merton (1973).

16. It should be apparent that risk goes both ways. That is, assets (and liabilities) may decrease or increase in value. Thus, if an asset is fully hedged against price risk, the firm will not suffer from a decline in asset value but will not enjoy an increase in value either (see problems 11 and 12). This is a statistical notion of risk. Nevertheless, we will sometimes use the term *risk* in the sense of downside risk only. Credit risk, for example, is the risk of loss from the failure of the other party to a contract to fulfill its obligations.

17. Standard setters disagree in principle with deferring unrealized gains and losses on cash flow hedges in other comprehensive income, arguing that instead these should be included in net income. The reason is that the hedged transactions have not yet occurred, so that an unrealized gain or loss on a cash flow hedge is not "associated with the measurement of another existing asset or liability" (SFAS 133, paragraph 326). In effect, the future hedged transactions depend on management intent and, as we suggested in Section 7.1, management intent is a shifting sand upon which to base a measurement approach. A counterargument, however, is that denying the anticipation of future transactions denies the going concern assumption.

18. With the advent of the fair value option (Section 7.3.2), this statement may need modification. Unrealized gains and losses from fair-valuing an undesignated hedging instrument are included in net

income, rather than other comprehensive income. However, the firm could apply the fair value option to the hedged item, so that unrealized losses and gains on this item are also included in net income. Assuming the hedge is completely effective, there is thus no net effect on net income.

19. Of course, to the extent that the standards encourage firms to engage in more hedging than they would otherwise undertake, real volatility is reduced.

20. If the firm qualifies for hedge accounting, this loss is reported in other comprehensive income, otherwise it is reported in net income.

21. The abnormal earnings instalments could also be negative. This simply means that the firm is expected to earn less than its cost of capital, that is, it has "badwill."

22. Of course, this is not really "cash" income since it includes other accruals, such as sales on credit. It is not known where the term originated.

23. The company's preliminary net loss for the year was increased by further goodwill writedowns of $5.3 billion reported in its audited financial statements for the year.

24. Management may not be willing to reveal this estimate, on grounds that it may reveal important information to competitors.

25. This requires that purchased goodwill be excluded from opening book value for purposes of the clean surplus goodwill calculations.

26. Canadian Tire reports purchased goodwill and other intangibles of $52.4 million in its 2006 annual report.

27. This information was off-balance-sheet, since Schrand's study predated SFAS 133.

Chapter 8
Economic Consequences and
Positive Accounting Theory

Figure 8.1 Organization of Chapter 8

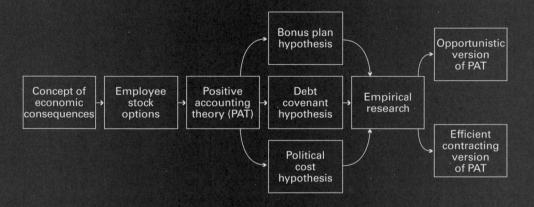

8.1 OVERVIEW

You may have noticed that there has been little discussion of management's interests in financial reporting to this point other than several references to management skepticism about current value accounting. As mentioned earlier, a thesis of this book is that motivation of responsible manager performance, that is, providing information to evaluate manager stewardship, is an equally important role of financial accounting as the provision of useful information to investors.

It should be noted, however, that standard setters do not fully agree with this dichotomy. In Section 3.8, we described the acceptance by standard setters of the decision usefulness approach, where the first objective of financial reporting is to provide useful information to present and potential investors for rational decision-making. Thus, reporting on stewardship is not a main objective. Indeed, in its 2006 *Preliminary Views on an Improved Conceptual Framework for Financial Reporting*, the IASB regards reporting on stewardship as part of its broader objective of providing useful information, but states (paragraph BC1.38) that "to make stewardship a separate objective might exaggerate what is feasible for financial reporting to accomplish." It seems that they feel it is not possible to separate the effects of manager stewardship from random state realization when reporting on firm performance. Interestingly, though, the SFAS 157 opportunity cost approach to fair value accounting can be interpreted from a stewardship perspective—see our discussion in Section 7.1.

Nevertheless, regardless of the standard setters' position, it is necessary that accountants understand and appreciate management's interests in financial reporting given the extensive interaction and conflict between managers, accountants, and auditors.

This will involve us in a new line of thought that, at first glance, differs sharply from the investor decision-based and efficient market-oriented theories discussed earlier. Our first task is to understand the concept of **economic consequences**. In the process, we will also learn about some of the accounting problems in a major area of accounting policy choice—stock-based compensation.

> **Economic consequences** *is a concept that asserts that, despite the implications of efficient securities market theory, accounting policy choice can affect firm value.*

Essentially, the notion of economic consequences is that firms' accounting policies, and changes in policies, *matter*. Primarily, they matter to management. But, if they matter to management, accounting policies matter to the investors who own the firms, because managers may well change the actual operation of their firms due to changes in accounting policies. For example, managers may cut maintenance and R&D to compensate for a new accounting policy that lowers the bottom line.

It is important to point out that the term "accounting policy" refers to *any* accounting policy, not just one that affects a firm's cash flows. Suppose that a firm changes from declining-balance to straight-line amortization. This will not in itself affect the firm's operating cash flows. Nor will there be any effect on income taxes paid, since tax authorities have their own capital cost allowance regulations. However, the new amortization policy will certainly affect reported net income. Thus, according to economic consequences doctrine, the accounting policy change will matter, despite the lack of cash flow effects. Under efficient markets theory the change will not matter (although the market may ask *why* the firm changed the policy) because future cash flows, and hence the market value of the firm, are not directly affected.

An understanding of the concept of economic consequences of accounting policy choice is important for two reasons. First, the concept is interesting in its own right. Many of the most interesting events in accounting practice derive from economic consequences. Second, a suggestion that accounting policies do not matter is at odds with accountants' experience. Much of financial accounting is devoted to discussion and argument about which accounting policies should be used in various circumstances, and many debates and conflicts over financial statement presentation involve accounting policy choice. Economic consequences are consistent with real-world experience.

The presence of economic consequences raises the question of why they exist. To answer this question, we begin with **positive accounting theory**. This theory is based on the contracts that firms enter into, in particular executive compensation contracts and debt contracts. These contracts are frequently based on financial accounting variables, such as net income and various measures of liquidity. Since accounting policies affect the values of these variables, and since management is responsible for the firm's contracts, it is natural that management be concerned about accounting policy choice. Indeed, management may choose accounting policies so as to maximize the firm's interests, or its own interests, relative to these contracts. Positive accounting theory attempts to predict what accounting policies managers will choose in order to do this.

Figure 8.1 outlines the organization of this chapter.

8.2 THE RISE OF ECONOMIC CONSEQUENCES

One of the most persuasive accounts of the existence of economic consequences appears in an early article by Stephen Zeff (1978) entitled "The Rise of 'Economic Consequences.'" The basic questions that it raises are still relevant today.

Zeff defines economic consequences as "the impact of accounting reports on the decision-making behaviour of business, government and creditors." The essence of the definition is that accounting reports can *affect* the real decisions made by managers and others, rather than simply *reflecting* the results of these decisions.

Zeff documents several instances in the United States where business, industry associations, and governments attempted to influence, or did influence, accounting standards set by the Accounting Principles Board (predecessor to the FASB) and its predecessor, the Committee on Accounting Procedure (CAP).

This "third-party intervention," as Zeff calls it, greatly complicated the setting of accounting standards. If accounting policies did not matter, choice of such policies would be strictly between the standard-setting bodies and the accountants and auditors whose task was to implement the standards. If only these parties were involved, the traditional accounting model, based on well-known concepts such as matching of costs and revenues, realization, and conservatism, could be applied and no one other than the parties involved would care what specific policies were used. In other words, accounting policy choice would be *neutral* in its effects.

As an example of an economic consequences argument, Zeff discusses the attempts by several U.S. corporations to reduce reported earnings by implementing replacement cost accounting during 1947 to 1948, a period of high inflation. Here, the third-party constituency that intervened was management, who, unlike their more recent skepticism about current value accounting, argued in favour of replacement cost amortization to bolster arguments for lower taxes and lower wage increases, and to counter a public perception of excess profitability. The efficient market argument would be that such intervention was unnecessary because the policy change would not affect cash flows, and the market would see through the high reported net incomes produced by historical cost amortization during inflation. If so, it should not be necessary to remind users by formal adoption of replacement cost amortization. It is interesting to note that the CAP held its ground in 1948 and reaffirmed historical cost accounting.

Zeff goes on to outline the response of standard-setting bodies to these various interventions. As described in Section 1.9.5, one response was to broaden constituency representation on the standard-setting bodies themselves. Also, the use of exposure drafts of proposed new standards became common as a device to allow a variety of constituencies to comment on proposed accounting policy changes.

As Zeff puts it, standard-setting bodies face a dilemma. To retain credibility with accountants, they need to set accounting policies in accordance with the financial accounting model and its traditional concepts of matching and realization (recall that Zeff is describing practices prior to the increased emphasis on the measurement approach). Yet, such historical cost-based concepts seldom lead to a unique accounting policy choice, as we saw in Section 2.5.2 with respect to amortization policy and the full-cost versus successful-efforts controversy in oil and gas accounting. That is, since net income does not exist as a well-defined economic construct under non-ideal conditions, there is no theory that clearly prescribes what accounting policies should be used, other than a vague requirement that some tradeoff between relevance and reliability is necessary. This opens the door for various other constituencies to get into the act and argue for their preferred accounting policies. In short, standard-setting bodies must operate not only in the accounting theory domain, but also in the political domain. Zeff refers to this as a "delicate balancing act." That is, without a theory to guide accounting policy choice, we must find some way of reaching a consensus on accounting policies. In a democratic setting, this implies involvement in the political domain. While a need for delicate balancing complicates the task of standard setters, it makes the study of the standard-setting process, and of accounting theory in general, much more challenging and interesting.

8.2.1 Summary

Despite the implications of efficient market theory, it appears that accounting policy choices have economic consequences for the various constituencies of financial statement users, even if these policies do not directly affect firm cash flows. Furthermore, different constituencies may prefer different accounting policies. Specifically, management's preferred policies may be at odds with those that best inform investors.

Economic consequences complicate the setting of accounting standards, which require a delicate balancing of accounting and political considerations. Standard-setting bodies have responded with due process, such as bringing different constituencies onto their boards and by issuing exposure drafts to give all interested parties an opportunity to comment on proposed standards.

8.3 EMPLOYEE STOCK OPTIONS

We now examine an area where economic consequences have been particularly apparent. This is the accounting for stock options issued to management and, in some cases, to other employees, giving them the right to buy company stock over some time period. We will refer to these options as **ESOs**.

Until relatively recently, accounting for ESOs in the United States and elsewhere was based on the 1972 Opinion 25 of the Accounting Principles Board (APB 25). This standard required firms issuing fixed[1] ESOs to record an expense equal to the difference between the market value of the shares on the date the option was granted to the employee (the **grant date**) and the exercise, or strike, price of the option. This difference is called the **intrinsic value** of the option. Most firms granting ESOs set the exercise price equal to the grant date market value, so that the intrinsic value is zero. As a result, no expense for ESO compensation was recorded. For example, if the underlying share has a market value of $10 on the grant date, setting the exercise price at $10 triggers no expense recognition, whereas setting the exercise price at $8 triggers an expense of $2 per ESO granted.

In the years following issuance of APB 25, this basis of accounting became widely recognized as inadequate. Even if there is no intrinsic value, an option has a fair value on the grant date, since the price of the underlying share may rise over the term to expiry (the **expiry date**) of the option. Failure to record an expense understates the firm's compensation cost and overstates its net income. Furthermore, a lack of earnings comparability across firms results, since different firms have different proportions of options in their total compensation packages. These problems worsened as a result of a dramatic increase in the use of ESO compensation since 1972, particularly for small, start-up, high-tech firms. These firms particularly like the non-cash-requiring aspect of ESOs and their motivational impact on the workforce, as well as the higher reported profits that result compared to other forms of compensation.

Also during this period, executive compensation came under political scrutiny, due to the high amounts of compensation that top executives received. Firms were perhaps motivated to award seemingly excessive amounts of ESO compensation since such compensation was "free." Charging the fair value of ESOs to expense would, some felt, help investors to see the real cost to the firm of this component of compensation. Indeed, in February 1992, a bill was introduced into the U.S. Congress requiring ESOs to be valued and expensed.

One of the reasons why the APB had not required fair value accounting for ESOs was the difficulty of establishing this value. This situation changed somewhat with the advent of the Black/Scholes option pricing formula (see Section 7.3.4). However, several aspects of ESOs are not captured by Black/Scholes. For example, the model assumes that options can be freely traded, whereas ESOs cannot be exercised until the **vesting date**, which is typically one or more years after they are granted. Also, if the employee leaves the firm prior to vesting the options are forfeited or, if exercised, there may be restrictions on the employee's ability to sell the acquired shares. In addition, the Black/Scholes formula assumes that the option cannot be exercised prior to expiry (a European option), whereas ESOs are an American option (can be exercised prior to expiry). Nevertheless, it was felt by many that Black/Scholes provided a reasonable basis for estimation of ESO fair value.

Consequently, in June 1993, the FASB issued an exposure draft of a proposed new standard. The exposure draft proposed that firms record compensation expense based on the fair value at the grant date (also called *ex ante* value) of ESOs issued during the period. Fair value could be determined by Black/Scholes or other option pricing formula, with adjustment for the possibility of employee retirement prior to vesting and for the possibility of early exercise. Early exercise was dealt with by using the *expected* time to exercise, based, for example, on past experience, rather than the time to expiry, in the Black/Scholes formula.

The exposure draft attracted extreme opposition from business, which soon extended into the U.S. Congress. Concerns were expressed about the economic consequences of the lower reported profits that would result. These claimed consequences included lower share prices, higher cost of capital, a shortage of managerial talent, and inadequate manager and employee motivation. This would particularly disadvantage small start-up companies that, as mentioned, were heavy options users. To preserve their bottom lines, firms would be forced to reduce ESO usage, with negative effects on cash flows, motivation, and innovation. This, it was claimed, would threaten the competitive position of American industry. Business was also concerned that the draft proposal was politically motivated. If so, opponents of the proposal would feel justified in attacking it with every means at their disposal.

Another series of questions related to the ability of Black/Scholes to accurately and reliably measure ESO fair value. To see these concerns, we first need to consider just what the costs to the firm of ESOs are, since, unlike most costs, ESOs do not require a cash outlay. Essentially, the cost is borne by the firm's existing shareholders through dilution of their proportionate interests in the firm. Thus, if an ESO is exercised at a price of, say, $10 when the market value of the share is $30, the *ex post* cost to the firm and its shareholders is $20. This $20 is called the *ex post* cost since after an ESO is exercised, its actual cost is known. We can also think of the $20 as an opportunity cost since, by admitting the new shareholder at $10, the firm forgoes the opportunity to issue the share at the market price of $30. That is, the $20 opportunity cost measures the dilution of the existing shareholders' interests.

The fair value of the ESO at the grant date, hence the *ex ante* cost to the firm, is the expected present value of the *ex post* cost.[2] Recognizing this cost as an expense increases relevance, since future dividends per share will be reduced to the extent dividends are diluted over a larger number of shares. The reduction in earnings from expensing ESOs anticipates these lower dividends, thereby helping investors to better predict future cash flows from their investments.

But, this ESO expense is very difficult to measure reliably. As mentioned, the employee may exercise the option at any time after vesting up to expiry. The *ex post* cost to the firm will then depend on the difference between the market value of the share and the exercise price at that time. In order to know the fair value of the ESO it is necessary to know the employee's optimal exercise strategy.

This strategy was modelled by Huddart (1994). As Huddart pointed out, determining the employee's strategy requires knowledge of the process generating the firm's future stock price, the employee's wealth and utility function (in particular the degree of risk aversion), whether the employee holds or sells the acquired shares (many firms require senior officers to hold large amounts of company stock) and, if sold, what investment alternatives are available. Matters are further complicated if the firm pays dividends on its shares and if the motivational impact of the ESO affects share price.

By making some simplifying assumptions (including no dividends, no motivational impact), Huddart showed that the Black/Scholes formula, assuming ESOs held to expiry date, does indeed overstate the fair value of an ESO at the grant date. To see why, we first note three option characteristics:

1. The expected return from holding an option exceeds the expected return on the underlying share. This is because the option cannot be worth less than zero, but the share price can fall below the option's exercise price. As a result, a risk-neutral employee would not normally exercise an ESO before maturity.

2. The "upside potential" of an American option (its propensity to increase in value) increases with the time to maturity. The longer the time, the greater the likelihood that during this interval the underlying share price will take off, making the option more valuable. Early exercise sacrifices some of this upside potential.

3. If an option is "deep-in-the-money," that is, if the value of the underlying share greatly exceeds the exercise price, the set of possible payoffs from holding the option and their probabilities closely resembles the set of payoffs and probabilities from holding the underlying share. This is because for a deep-in-the-money option the probability of share price falling below exercise price is low. Then, every realization of share price induces a similar realization in the option value. As a result, if the employee is required to hold the shares acquired, he or she might as well hold the option to maturity. The payoffs are the same and, due to the time value of money, paying the exercise price at expiry dominates paying it sooner.

The question then is, are there circumstances where the employee will exercise the option early? Huddart identifies two. First, if the ESO is only slightly in-the-money (substantial risk of zero payoff), the time to maturity is short (little sacrifice of upside potential), and the employee is required to hold the shares acquired, risk aversion can trigger early exercise. Since there is substantial risk of zero return, the risk-averse employee (who trades off risk and return) may feel that the reduction in risk from exercising the option now rather than continuing to hold it outweighs the lower expected return from holding the share.

The second circumstance occurs when the ESO is deep-in-the-money, the time to expiry is short, and the employee can either hold the acquired share or sell it and invest the proceeds in a riskless asset. If the employee is sufficiently risk-averse, the riskless asset is preferred to the share. Because the option is deep-in-the-money, the payoffs and their probabilities are similar for the share and ESO. Thus the employee is indifferent to holding the ESO or the share. Since holding the riskless asset is preferred to holding the share, it is also preferred to holding the option. Then, the employee will exercise the option, sell the share, and buy the riskless asset.

In a follow-up empirical study to test the early exercise predictions, Huddart and Lang (1996) examined the ESO exercise patterns of the employees of eight large U.S. corporations over a ten-year period. They found that early exercise was common, consistent with Huddart's risk aversion assumption. They also found that the variables that explained empirically the early exercises, such as time to expiration and extent to which the ESO was in-the-money, were "broadly consistent" with the predictions of the model.

The significance of early exercise is that the fair value of ESOs at grant date is less than the value determined by Black/Scholes which, as mentioned, assumes the option is held to expiry. This is particularly apparent for the first early exercise scenario outlined above. If the ESO is barely in-the-money, the *ex post* cost of the option to the employer (share price less exercise price) is low. While the cost savings from the second circumstance are less, the cost to the employer is still less than Black/Scholes, as Huddart shows.

Subsequent research has tended to confirm the tendency of Black/Scholes to overstate *ex post* ESO cost. Hall and Murphy (2002), using a different approach than Huddart, also demonstrated a substantial probability of early exercise, and showed that this significantly reduces the firm's ESO cost below Black/Scholes. Their analysis also suggested considerable variability in employees' exercise decisions.

Early exercise, presumably, is the reason the 1993 FASB exposure draft proposed using expected time to exercise, rather than expiry date, in the Black/Scholes formula.

However, as Huddart pointed out, use of expected time to exercise reduces the overstatement of ESO cost, but does not eliminate it, as also demonstrated by Hemmer, Matsunaga, and Shevlin (1994) (HMS).[3] In an empirical study, Marquardt (2002) examined the accuracy of the Black/Scholes formula based on expected time to exercise. In a sample of 966 option grants by 57 large U.S. companies over 1963–1984, she found that Black/Scholes tended to produce positively biased estimates of *ex post* ESO cost, consistent with the analyses of Huddart and HMS. She also found that the accuracy of this estimated cost varied widely for different firms.

We conclude that ESO fair value estimates may be unreliable, due both to upward bias and the need to estimate the timing of employees' early exercise decisions in the face of wide variability of these decisions. Furthermore, other Black/Scholes model inputs, such as the share variability parameter, create additional reliability problems.

As one can imagine, theory and evidence suggesting that the exposure draft, if implemented, may not produce accurate estimates of ESO expense would be seized upon by critics, particularly if the estimates tended to be too high. As a result, in December 1994 the FASB announced that it was dropping the exposure draft, on the grounds that it did not have sufficient support. Instead, the FASB turned to supplementary disclosure. In SFAS 123, issued in 1995, it urged firms to use the fair value approach suggested in the exposure draft, but allowed the APB 25 intrinsic value approach provided the firm gave supplementary disclosure of ESO expense, determined by amortizing over their vesting periods the fair value of awarded ESOs based on expected time to exercise.

More recently, financial reporting scandals such as Enron and WorldCom led to renewed pressure to expense ESOs. In retrospect, it seems that manipulations of stock price by these and other companies were often driven by senior executives' tactics to increase the values of their ESOs.

One of these tactics was **pump and dump**, whereby managers would take actions to increase share value shortly before exercising options, then sell the shares before share price fell back (sometimes in a manner to disguise the transaction) and, presumably, invest the proceeds in less risky securities.

Bartov and Mohanram (2004) tested a sample of 1,218 U.S. companies with large ESO exercises by senior executives, during 1992–2001. They found a significant decrease in average abnormal share price and earnings in the two years following such exercises, relative to a control sample of similar firms with no large ESO exercises. They also show evidence of abnormally large income-increasing accruals in the two years prior to exercise. The authors concluded that the senior managers in their test sample were aware of deteriorating profitability, and pumped up earnings and share price to delay the market's awareness of the deterioration. They then exercised their ESOs and, presumably, dumped the acquired shares immediately so as to maximize their cash proceeds. The lower earnings and share prices in the two years following exercise were driven by the reversal of the prior accruals and the market's belated awareness of the declining profitability.

Another strategy was reported by Aboody and Kasznik (2000) (AK), who studied the information release practices of CEOs around ESO grant dates. They confined their study to CEOs because it is the CEO that controls the firm's release of information. Their results are based on a sample of 4,426 ESO awards to CEOs of 1,264 different U.S. firms during 1992–1996. Of these awards, 2,039 were by firms with *scheduled* grant dates. That is, awards were made on the same dates each year.[4] Thus, CEOs of these firms knew when the ESO awards were coming. AK found that, on average, CEOs of firms with scheduled ESOs used a variety of tactics to manipulate share price downwards just prior to the grant date, and to manipulate price up shortly after. One tactic was to make an early announcement of an impending BN quarterly earnings report, but to make no such announcement for an impending GN report. Other tactics included influencing analysts' earnings forecasts and selective timing of release of their own forecasts.

It also appears that some managers manipulated the ESO award date itself. This was investigated by Yermack (1997), who reported evidence that managers pressured compensation committees to grant unscheduled ESOs shortly before good earnings news (a tactic called spring loading). This gives the CEO a low exercise price and subsequent benefit as share price rises in response to the GN.

Yet another tactic was **late timing**. Late timing is the backdating of ESO awards to a date when share price was lower than at the actual ESO grant date. This confers an immediate benefit on the recipient, since, in effect, the ESO was in-the-money on the actual grant date; that is, intrinsic value was positive. While awarding ESOs that are in-the-money is not in itself illegal, backdating of ESO awards does violate GAAP. This is because, under APB 25, in effect when much of the late timing took place, an expense had to be recognized for ESOs awarded with positive intrinsic value. Late timing disguised this expense recognition. Discovery of late timing thus leads to restatement of prior years' earnings. If ESOs were expensed, earnings would still be overstated since, holding share price constant, a decrease in exercise price increases ESO fair value. Other parameter inputs to Black/Scholes (Section 7.3.4) may also change.

Lack of disclosure of the late timing also subjects those involved to liability under securities laws. SEC and company board investigations of late timing have led to a number of CEO resignations, and their widespread nature threatens to erode public confidence in financial reporting at least as much as the Enron and WorldCom scandals.

The common theme of all these tactics is to increase the likelihood that ESOs will be deep-in-the-money. This increases the likelihood of early exercise since, according to Huddart's analysis, deep-in-the-money ESOs are more likely to be exercised early.

Obviously, managers would be unlikely to admit to the behaviours just described. Nevertheless, if ESOs had to be expensed, their usage as a compensation device would decrease, thereby reducing managers' scope to manipulate ESO values for their own benefit. This undoubtedly added fuel to their economic consequences arguments against ESO expensing.

Theory in Practice 8.1

On July 20, 2006, the SEC announced criminal and civil charges for securities fraud against the former CEO, vice-president human resources, and CFO of Brocade Communications Systems, Inc., a California-based developer of networking data storage products.

These were the first charges resulting from SEC investigations of numerous companies for late timing of ESO awards. The defendants, it was alleged, backdated employee ESO awards to a time when the company's share price was lower than the real date of the award, thereby conferring an immediate benefit on the recipients by lowering the exercise price. In effect, the ESOs were issued in-the-money. Under APB 25, in effect at the time, an expense had to be recorded for in-the-money options, but this was disguised by the backdating.

In 2005, possibly in anticipation of forthcoming SEC charges, Brocade issued revised financial statements for 1999–2004 inclusive to correct for the APB 25 earnings overstatements. It increased compensation expense and decreased reported earnings by a total of $285 million. In July 2006 the company issued a statement indicating that the executives involved were no longer with the company and reporting a provision of $7 million for settlement of its own liability resulting from the actions of its former executives. In May 2007 the financial media reported that Brocade agreed to pay a $7 million U.S. penalty to settle the SEC charges.

In August 2007 the former Brocade CEO was found guilty by a jury in San Francisco on conspiracy and fraud charges for misleading investors. He faces millions of dollars in fines and up to 20 years in prison.

The combined effect of the above-described abuses, plus improved ability of accountants to model complexities such as early exercise, enabled standard setters to overcome the opposition. SFAS 123R, effective in 2005, requires ESO expensing, as does IFRS 2 of the IASB. These standards were implemented despite the raising by many managers of economic consequences and reliability concerns similar to those expressed over the 1993 exposure draft.

As expected, an economic consequence of ESO expensing has been to greatly reduce the usage of ESOs as a compensation device. For example, *The Economist* (2006) quotes an investment banker's estimate that the fair value of options granted by the top 500 U.S. firms fell from $104 billion in 2000 to $30 billion in 2005.

While, in this case, the standard setters ultimately "won," we may conclude that the accounting for ESOs is a prime illustration of Zeff's argument that third-party intervention greatly complicates the setting of accounting standards. The intensity of management's economic consequences arguments is particularly noteworthy given that ESO expensing does not directly affect operating cash flows.

8.4 THE RELATIONSHIP BETWEEN EFFICIENT SECURITIES MARKET THEORY AND ECONOMIC CONSEQUENCES

At this point, we may have another anomaly. Efficient securities market theory predicts no price reaction to accounting policy changes that do not impact underlying profitability and cash flows. If there is no securities price reaction (implying no change in firms' costs of capital), it is unclear why management and regulators should be particularly concerned about the accounting policies that firms use. In other words, efficient market theory implies the importance of full disclosure, including disclosure of accounting policies. However, once full disclosure of accounting policies is made, the market will interpret the value of the firm's securities in the light of the policies used and will not be fooled by variations in reported net income that arise solely from differences in accounting policies.

Yet, in an important area of accounting policy choice, namely the accounting for ESOs, we have seen that the management constituency has indeed reacted to paper changes in accounting policy. The strength of management reaction seems particularly surprising, even involving appeals to government authority to intervene on its behalf. These various reactions are summarized in the concept of economic consequences. That is, accounting policy choice can matter even in the absence of cash flow effects.

Thus, accounting policies have the potential to affect real management decisions, including decisions to intervene either for or against proposed accounting standards. This "tail wagging the dog" aspect of economic consequences is all the more interesting in view of the empirical results described in Chapter 5. These results are remarkable in the sophistication they document of the market's response to financial accounting information. The question then is, does the existence of economic consequences reinforce the theory and evidence that securities markets are not fully efficient, as discussed in Section 6.2, or can efficient securities markets and economic consequences be reconciled?

Our next task is to do what any discipline does when confronted with observations, specifically, economic consequences, that are inconsistent with existing theory. We search for a more general theory that may include the existing theory but that also has the potential to explain the inconsistent observations. This brings us to positive accounting theory.

8.5 THE POSITIVE THEORY OF ACCOUNTING

8.5.1 Outline of Positive Accounting Theory

For our purposes, the term "positive" refers to a theory that attempts to make good predictions of real-world events. Thus:

> **Positive accounting theory (PAT)** *is concerned with predicting such actions as the choices of accounting policies by firm managers and how managers will respond to proposed new accounting standards.*

For example, can we predict different degrees of manager opposition to expensing ESOs, or predict which managers will react favourably to fair value accounting standards for financial instruments and which will be opposed? While PAT may not capture the actual thought processes of individuals, it does help us to understand the important factors that underlie their actions.

PAT takes the view that firms[5] organize themselves in the most efficient manner, so as to maximize their prospects for survival[6]—some firms are more decentralized than others, some firms conduct activities inside while other firms contract out the same activities, some firms finance more with debt than others, etc. The most efficient form of organization for a particular firm depends on factors such as its legal and institutional environment, its technology, and the degree of competition in its industry. Taken together, these factors determine the set of investment opportunities available to the firm, and hence its prospects.

A firm can be viewed as a **nexus of contracts**, that is, its organization can be largely described by the set of contracts it enters into. For example, contracts with employees (including managers), with suppliers, and with capital providers are central to the firm's operations. The firm will want to minimize the various **contracting costs** associated with these contracts. These include costs of negotiation, costs arising from moral hazard and monitoring of contract performance, costs of possible renegotiation or contract violation should unanticipated events arise during the term of the contract, and expected costs of bankruptcy and other types of financial distress. Contracting costs also affect the firm's cost of capital, since bonds and shares represent contracts between the firm and its capital providers. Contracts with the lowest contracting costs are called **efficient contracts**.

Many of these contracts involve accounting variables. Thus, employee promotion and remuneration may be based on accounting-based performance measures such as net income, or the meeting of pre-set individual targets, such as cost control. Contracts with suppliers may depend on liquidity and financing variables. Lenders may demand protection in the form of maintenance of certain financial ratios such as debt-to-equity or times interest earned, or minimum levels of working capital or equity.

PAT argues that firms' accounting policies will be chosen as part of the broader problem of attaining efficient corporate governance. As an illustration of efficient corporate governance, consider the study by Mian and Smith (1990), a seminal study in this area. They examined the accounting policy choice of whether to consolidate a subsidiary company. They argue that the greater the interdependence between parent and subsidiary the more efficient it is (that is, the lower the contracting costs) to prepare consolidated financial statements. The reason is that the greater the interdependence the more desirable it is to evaluate the *joint* results of parent and subsidiary operations. Consolidated financial statements provide a basis for joint evaluation. It is more efficient to monitor manager performance by use of consolidated financial statement–based performance measures than by performance measures based on separate parent and subsidiary financial statements when interdependence is high. Thus Mian and Smith predicted that the greater the integration between parent and subsidiary the more likely the parent will prepare consolidated statements. This argument can be extended to predict that if consolidated financial statements are prepared for internal monitoring of manager performance, it is less costly to also prepare consolidated statements for external reporting. Mian and Smith presented empirical evidence consistent with these predictions.

It should be noted that PAT does not go so far as to suggest that firms (and standard setters) should completely specify the accounting policies they will use. This would be too costly. It is desirable to give managers some flexibility to choose from a set of available accounting policies so that they can adapt to new or unforeseen circumstances. For example, a new accounting standard that lowers reported net income, such as the expensing of ESOs, may reduce a firm's times interest earned ratio to the point where violation of debt covenants is of concern. It would probably be less costly for management to, say, switch from the LIFO to the FIFO inventory method,[7] or liquidate LIFO inventory layers, or issue preferred stock in place of debt than to renegotiate the debt contract or suffer the expected costs of technical violation.

Usually, the set of available accounting policies can be taken as those allowed under GAAP, although there is no reason, other than cost, why the set cannot be further restricted by contract. However, giving management flexibility to choose from a set of accounting policies opens up the possibility of **opportunistic behaviour** *ex post*. That is, given the available set, managers may choose accounting policies from the set for their own purposes, thereby reducing contract efficiency.

This recognition of the possibility of opportunistic behaviour points out an important assumption. PAT assumes that **managers are rational** (like investors) and will choose accounting policies in their own best interests if able to do so. That is, managers maximize their own expected utility. Thus, PAT does *not* assume that the manager will simply act so as to maximize firm profits. Rather, the manager will only maximize profits if he/she perceives this to be in his/her own best interests. For example, managers of actively exploring oil companies whose remuneration contracts are based on reported net income may choose full-cost accounting over successful-efforts so as to smooth out income and increase the expected utility of their bonus streams, even though higher reported income under full-cost may increase firm taxes and encourage entry of additional firms into the industry. Of course, such opportunistic behaviour will be anticipated when the manager's remuneration contract is being negotiated and the firm will price-protect itself by lowering the manager's formal remuneration by the expected amount of opportunism. That is, given competition in the labour market for managers, managers will be willing to work for a lower compensation from the company if they can augment their utility by means of opportunistic behaviour. As a result, given the remuneration contract, managers have an incentive to behave opportunistically to the extent they have the ability to choose from a set of accounting policies.

The optimal set of accounting policies for the firm then represents a compromise. On the one hand, tightly prescribing accounting policies beforehand will minimize opportunistic accounting policy choice by managers, but incur costs of lack of accounting flexibility to meet changing circumstances, such as new accounting standards that affect net income. On the other hand, allowing the manager to choose from a broad array of accounting policies will reduce costs of accounting inflexibility but expose the firm to the costs of opportunistic manager behaviour.

PAT emphasizes the need for empirical investigation to determine how the tradeoff between cost of capital and contracting costs, the flexibility for managers to choose from a set of accounting policies, and, indeed, the corporate governance structure itself, varies from firm to firm depending on its environment. Ultimately the objective of the theory is to predict managerial accounting policy choice in different circumstances and across different firms.

Thus, PAT does not attempt to tell individuals or constituencies what they *should* do. Theories that do this are called **normative**. This book draws on both positive and normative theories. The single-person decision theory and the theory of investment described in Chapter 3 can be interpreted as normative theories—if individuals wish to make a decision in the face of uncertainty so as to maximize expected utility, they should proceed as the theories recommend.

Whether normative theories have good predictive abilities depends on the extent to which individuals actually make decisions as those theories prescribe. Certainly, some normative theories have predictive ability—we do observe individuals diversifying their portfolio investments, for example. However, we can still have a good normative theory even though it may not make good predictions. One reason is that it may take time for people to figure out the theory. Individuals may not follow a normative theory because they do not understand it, because they prefer some other theory, or simply because of inertia. For example, investors may not follow a diversified investment strategy because they believe in technical analysis[8] and may concentrate their investments in firms that technical analysts recommend. But, if a normative theory is a good one, we should see it being increasingly adopted over time as people learn about it. However, unlike a positive theory, predictive ability is not the main criterion by which a normative theory should be judged. Rather, it is judged by its logical consistency with underlying assumptions of how rational individuals should behave.

Some people become engaged in the question of which theoretical approach is the correct one.[9] For our purposes, however, it is sufficient to recognize that both normative and positive approaches to theory development and testing are valuable. To the extent that decision-makers proceed normatively, positive and normative theories will make similar predictions. By insisting on empirical testing of these predictions, positive theory helps to keep the normative predictions on track. In effect, the two approaches complement each other.

8.5.2 The Three Hypotheses of Positive Accounting Theory

The predictions made by PAT are largely organized around three hypotheses, formulated by Watts and Zimmerman (1986). We will give these hypotheses in their opportunistic form, since according to Watts and Zimmerman (1990), this is how they have most frequently been interpreted. By opportunistic form we mean that managers choose accounting policies in their own best interests, which may not necessarily also be in the firm's best interests.

1. **The bonus plan hypothesis** All other things being equal, managers of firms with bonus plans are more likely to choose accounting procedures that shift reported earnings from future periods to the current period.

   This hypothesis seems reasonable. Firm managers, like everyone else, would like high remuneration. If their remuneration depends, at least in part, on a bonus related to reported net income, then they may be able to increase their current bonus by reporting as high a net income as possible. One way to do this is to choose accounting policies that increase current reported earnings. Of course, due to the nature of the accrual process, this will tend to lower future reported earnings and bonuses, other things equal. However, the present value of the manager's utility from his or her future bonus stream will be increased by shifting it towards the present.

   Note also that if the manager is risk-averse, he/she will prefer accounting policies that smooth reported earnings, since a less variable bonus stream has higher expected utility than a volatile one, other things equal.

2. **The debt covenant hypothesis** All other things being equal, the closer a firm is to violation of accounting-based debt covenants, the more likely the firm manager is to select accounting procedures that shift reported earnings from future periods to the current period.

   The reasoning is that increasing reported net income will reduce the probability of technical default. Most debt agreements contain covenants that the borrower must meet during the term of the agreement. For example, a borrowing firm may covenant to maintain specified levels of interest coverage, debt-to-equity, working capital, and/

or shareholders' equity. If such covenants are violated, the debt agreement may impose penalties, such as constraints on dividends or additional borrowing.

Clearly, the prospect of covenant violation constrains management's actions in running the firm. To prevent, or at least postpone, such violation, management may adopt accounting policies to raise current earnings. According to the debt covenant hypothesis, as the firm approaches default, or if it actually is in default, it is more likely to do this.

Again, the manager may object to accounting policies that increase earnings volatility, since this increases the probability of future covenant violation.

3. **The political cost hypothesis** All other things being equal, the greater the political costs faced by a firm, the more likely the manager is to choose accounting procedures that defer reported earnings from current to future periods.

The political cost hypothesis introduces a political dimension into accounting policy choice. For example, political costs can be imposed by high profitability, which may attract media and consumer attention. Such attention can quickly translate into political "heat" on the firm, and politicians may respond with new taxes or other regulations. This has happened to oil companies during periods of restricted crude oil supply and rising gasoline prices. In the past, resulting public anger has led, in the United States, to special taxes on oil companies to take back the excess profits. As a result, oil company managers may feel that, for example, switching to LIFO would reduce the likelihood of this happening again.

Often, sheer size can lead to political costs. Very large firms may be held to higher performance standards, for example with respect to environmental responsibility, simply because they are felt to be large and powerful. If the large firms are also highly profitable, such political costs will be magnified.

Also, firms may face political costs at particular points in time. Foreign competition may lead to reduced profitability unless affected firms can influence the political process to grant import protection. One way to do this would be to adopt income-decreasing accounting policies in an attempt to convince the government that profits are suffering.

These three hypotheses form an important component of PAT. Note that they all lead to empirically testable predictions. For example, managers of firms with bonus plans are predicted to choose less conservative and less volatile accounting policies, such as full-cost accounting, than managers of firms without such plans. Also, we would expect that managers of firms with bonus plans would oppose proposed accounting standards that may lower reported net income, such as the expensing of OPEBs (Section 7.2.6). Such standards would make it more difficult to maximize current reported earnings by choice of accounting policy. Also, managers may object to volatility-increasing accounting standards, such as those based on current value accounting, particularly if unrealized gains and losses are included in net income.

Similarly, the debt covenant hypothesis predicts that managers of firms with high debt-to-equity ratios will choose less conservative accounting policies than managers of firms with low ratios, and will be more likely to oppose new standards that limit their ability to do this and/or that increase earnings volatility. The political cost hypothesis predicts that managers of very large firms will choose more conservative accounting policies than managers of smaller firms, and will be less likely to oppose new standards that may lower reported net income.

Theory in Practice 8.2

To illustrate how serious economic consequences can arise from the bonus plan hypothesis, consider Fannie Mae, established by the U.S. federal government in 1938, and converted to a public company in 1968. Its mandate is to facilitate home-owning by providing financing to mortgage lenders, including purchasing home mortgages from these institutions. Fannie Mae is the second-largest U.S. corporation in terms of assets. Its stability is essential to the U.S. housing market.

In 2004, the Office of Federal Housing Enterprise Oversight (OFHEO) issued a report highly critical of Fannie Mae. OFHEO is an office of the U.S. government created to oversee the operations of Fannie Mae and a related organization (Freddie Mac). One concern was about the amortization of discount and premium on Fannie Mae's large mortgage portfolio, going back to 1998. In that year, falling interest rates led to a large volume of mortgage repayments, as homeowners scrambled to refinance at lower rates. This created a need for Fannie Mae to accelerate amortization of discount and premium on these mortgages. For 1998, according to OFHEO, extra amortization expense of $400 million was required. However, Fannie Mae only recorded $200 million in that year, deferring the rest to 1999. This deferral did not affect operating cash flows. Nevertheless, the volatility of earnings was reduced and, of particular concern to OFHEO, management bonuses would not have been paid if the 1998 net income of Fannie Mae was reduced any further.

Another concern was with Fannie Mae's accounting for hedges. Fannie Mae claimed to account for these under SFAS 133 (see Section 7.3.5) and, by the end of 2003, had about $12.2 billion of unrealized hedging losses accumulated in other comprehensive income. However, according to OFHEO, Fannie Mae did not properly designate its hedges and did not evaluate their effectiveness. Consequently, it did not qualify for the benefits of hedge accounting under SFAS 133 (recall that one of these benefits is that unrealized gains and losses on hedging instruments are included in other comprehensive income rather than in net income). As a result, Fannie Mae's net income was overstated over several years. Furthermore, transfer of this amount back against net income threatened the adequacy of Fannie Mae's regulatory capital.

OFHEO obtained an agreement from Fannie Mae's board of directors to, among other things, bring its accounting into conformity with GAAP. In February 2006 a report commissioned by the board termed the company's accounting system at the time as grossly inadequate, and accused the then CFO of failing to provide adequate oversight of the system. The report also noted flawed accounting practices, including a drive to show smooth earnings growth and to report earnings that met analysts' forecasts. The SEC also weighed in, announcing that Fannie Mae should revise its earnings. Later, it fined the company $400 million for fraudulent accounting.

In December 2004 the board dismissed its CEO and CFO, and announced a review of their bonus and severance payments. Fannie Mae's auditor was also dismissed. In December 2006 OFHEO revealed plans to sue Fannie Mae's former CEO and CFO to recover excess compensation, and Fannie Mae launched a $2 billion lawsuit against its former auditor.

The three PAT hypotheses can also be interpreted from an efficient contracting perspective, rather than opportunistically as just illustrated. With respect to the bonus plan hypothesis, firms will benefit by excluding from their accounting policy set policies that lower reported net income or produce volatile earnings. Lower or more volatile earnings reduce the expected utility of future bonuses for risk-averse managers, forcing the firm to pay more to compensate. With respect to the debt covenant hypothesis, firms will also benefit by excluding accounting policies that lower earnings or increase their volatility, since such policies increase the probability of debt covenant violation and resulting expected costs of financial distress. With respect to the political cost hypothesis, policies that lower reported earnings help to avoid political costs, thereby maintaining profits. In all three cases, shareholders benefit from lower contracting and political costs.

Conservative accounting can also contribute to efficient contracting, as argued by Watts (2003). Consider the debt covenant hypothesis. Debtholders will suffer if the firm cannot meet its interest and principal payments. Consequently, they will benefit if the firm uses conservative accounting, due to a reduced likelihood that the firm will make excessive dividend payments—conservative accounting makes it more difficult for the manager to pay excessive dividends by introducing a persistent downward bias into retained earnings. Furthermore, conservative accounting increases the protection provided by debt covenants, other things equal. For example, suppose the debt agreement includes a covenant whereby the firm must maintain a debt-to-equity ratio of not more than two, otherwise no dividends can be paid. Since conservative accounting lowers the denominator, it increases the ratio. Thus, in real terms, the firm must retain more net assets to avoid violation, increasing the debtholders' security. This increased security increases the firm's future cash flows by enabling it to issue its debt at a lower interest rate than otherwise.

8.5.3 Empirical PAT Research

Positive accounting theory has generated a large amount of empirical research. Much of this research has been devoted to testing the implications of the three hypotheses described above. For example, the bonus plan hypothesis was investigated by Healy (1985), who found evidence that managers of firms with bonus plans based on reported net income systematically adopted accrual policies so as to maximize their expected bonuses. Healy's paper and some of the research that followed from it are discussed in Section 11.3.

Dichev and Skinner (2002) (DS) examined the debt covenant hypothesis. They studied a large sample of private[10] lending agreements. They concentrated on agreements with covenants based on maintenance of a specified current ratio or on maintenance of a specified amount of net worth.

For each sample firm, DS calculated the *covenant slack*, for each quarter during which the loan is outstanding. For example, for the current ratio, covenant slack for a loan's first quarter is the difference between the firm's actual current ratio at the end of that quarter and the current ratio the firm is required to maintain under the lending agreement. This calculation was repeated for each sample firm for all quarters, for both current ratio and net worth covenants. According to the debt covenant hypothesis, managers will want to maintain zero or positive slack.

DS found in their sample that the number of quarters with zero or slightly positive slack is significantly greater than would be expected if firms were not managing their covenant ratios. Also, the number of quarters where slack is slightly negative is significantly less than expected. These results are consistent with the debt covenant hypothesis, since they suggest that managers choose accounting policies to maintain their covenant ratios so as to meet or exceed the levels required.

This tendency to maintain zero or positive slack is particularly strong for quarters leading up to and including a *first* covenant violation. DS pointed out that the costs of an initial violation are higher than for subsequent violations, since the lender will quickly take action to protect its interests, and much of the damage to manager and firm reputation occurs when a violation first occurs. Consistent with these higher costs, the evidence suggests that managers work particularly hard to manage covenant ratios so as to avoid an initial violation. This finding supports PAT's assumption that managers are rational—we would expect managers to work harder when the costs of failure are higher.

With respect to the political cost hypothesis, much empirical investigation has been based on firm size. However, this measure of political cost is complicated by the correlation of size with other firm characteristics, such as profitability and risk. Also, the bonus plan and debt covenant hypotheses work in the opposite direction to size in their accounting policy predictions, so that it is necessary to control for their effects.

These considerations suggest that empirical investigation of the political cost hypothesis should look at situations where political costs are particularly salient. One such situation occurs when firms are under pressure from foreign imports.

Jones (1991) studied the actions of firms to lower reported net income during import relief investigations. The granting of relief to firms that are affected by foreign competition is, in part, a political decision. Trade legislation allows for the granting of assistance such as tariff protection to firms in industries that are unfairly affected by foreign competition. In the United States, the International Trade Commission (ITC) is responsible for investigating whether there is injury. This investigation will consider economic factors such as sales and profits of affected firms. However, there is also a considerable political dimension to the granting of relief, since consumers will end up paying higher prices, and there may be retaliation by foreign countries. A determination of injury by the ITC goes initially to the president, who has 60 days to decide whether to grant relief. If relief is not granted, Congress may step in and override the president.

Thus, it is by no means clear that a deterioration of profitability is sufficient for relief to be granted. As a result, affected firms have an incentive to choose accounting policies to lower their reported net income even more, so as to bolster their case. Of course, this incentive will be known to the ITC, politicians, and the public. However, as Jones points out, these constituencies may not have the motivation to adjust for any downward manipulation of earnings. For example, the effect of higher prices that would follow the granting of relief to an industry may not be sufficiently great for it to be cost effective for consumers to lobby against it. Even the ITC may not be fully motivated to adjust for manipulation of earnings if it was *a priori* sympathetic to the petitioning firms. These disincentives to unwind any earnings manipulation are strengthened if it is difficult to detect.

An effective way to reduce reported earnings in a hard-to-detect manner is to manipulate accounting policies relating to accruals. For example, a firm may increase amortization charges, it may record excessive liabilities for product guarantees, contingencies, and rebates, and it may record generous provisions for doubtful accounts and obsolescence of inventories. These are called **discretionary accruals**.

Jones examined whether firms used discretionary accruals to lower reported earnings. She collected a sample of 23 firms from five industries involved in six import relief investigations by the ITC over the period 1980–1985 inclusive.

It is easy to determine a firm's **total accruals** for the year. One approach, pointed out in Section 6.2.6, is to take the difference between operating cash flows and net income. Accruals are interpreted quite broadly here, being the net effect of all recorded operating events during the year other than cash flows. Changes in accounts receivable and payable are accruals, as are changes in inventories. Amortization expense is a negative accrual, being that portion of the cost of capital assets that is written off in the year. Jones used an alternate approach, taking the change in non-cash working capital for the year from the comparative balance sheets, plus amortization expense, as her measure of total accruals.

However, separating total accruals into discretionary and non-discretionary components presents a major challenge. This is because non-discretionary accruals are correlated with the level of business activity. For example, if a firm is suffering from foreign competition it may have lower receivables, it may have to delay payment of current liabilities, and it may have to write off large amounts of slow-moving inventory. These are negative accruals, but they can hardly be regarded as discretionary. How can the researcher, who does not have access to the firm's records and so must work from the financial statements, separate them out of total accruals so as to get at the discretionary component?

Jones' approach to this problem was to estimate the following regression equation for each firm j in her sample, over a period prior to the year of the ITC investigation:[11]

$$TA_{jt} = \alpha_j + \beta_{1j}\Delta REV_{jt} + \beta_{2j}PPE_{jt} + \epsilon_{jt}$$

where:

TA_{jt} = total accruals for firm j in year t. A positive TA_{jt} is income increasing, and vice versa

ΔREV_{jt} = revenues for firm j in year t less revenues for year t − 1

PPE_{jt} = gross property, plant, and equipment for firm j in year t

ϵ_{jt} = a residual term that captures all impacts on TA_{jt} other than those from ΔREV_{jt} and PPE_{jt}

The coefficients α_j, β_{1j}, and β_{2j} are simply constants to be estimated. In particular, β_1 and β_2 have nothing to do with a stock's beta discussed in Section 3.7.1. We expect β_{1j} to be positive, since the purpose of ΔREV_{jt} is to control for non-discretionary accruals of current assets and liabilities on the grounds that these depend on changes in business activity as measured by revenues—more business activity, more non-discretionary accruals. Also, PPE_{jt} controls for the non-discretionary component of amortization expense, on the grounds that this depends on the firm's investment in capital assets. Since amortization is income-reducing, β_{2j} is expected to be negative.

With this regression model estimated for each sample firm, Jones used it to predict non-discretionary accruals during the ITC investigation years. That is:

$$U_{jp} = TA_{jp} - (\alpha_j + \beta_{1j}\Delta REV_{jp} + \beta_{2j}PPE_{jp})$$

where p is the year of investigation, TA_{jp} is firm j's total accruals for this year, and the quantity in brackets is the predicted non-discretionary accruals for the year from the regression model. The term U_{jp} is thus an estimate of discretionary accruals for year p for firm j.[12] The political cost hypothesis predicts that the U_{jp} will be negative, that is, total accruals less than non-discretionary accruals, implying that the firm is using discretionary accruals to force down reported net income.

Jones found evidence of the predicted behaviour. For almost all firms in the sample, discretionary accruals as measured above were significantly negative in the ITC investigation years. Significant negative accruals were not found in the years immediately preceding and following the investigations. These results, while perhaps not as strong as might be expected, suggest that affected firms were systematically choosing accrual policies so as to improve their case for import protection, consistent with the political cost hypothesis.

The above are just a few of numerous studies to test the predictions of PAT. More extensive discussions are contained in Watts and Zimmerman (1986, 1990). It does appear that these three hypotheses have empirical validity in explaining differential manager reaction to accounting policy choices. Estimation of discretionary accruals is an important component of much PAT research. We will return to it in our review of earnings management in Chapter 11.

While these three PAT hypotheses may predict manager reaction, the evidence is less strong that they can predict *investor* reaction to accounting policy change, despite the possibility that economic consequences affect firm value. If accounting policies affect contract efficiency and management's operation of the firm, we would expect this to affect investor buy/sell decisions, leading to share price response to accounting policy changes such as those required by new accounting standards. However, Bernard (1989) states that evidence that the market responds to the economic consequences of new accounting standards has generally been hard to come by. Whether market value effects are present, but existing empirical methodology cannot uncover them, or whether the three hypotheses are not good predictors of securities market reaction to economic consequences appears to be an open question.

8.5.4 Distinguishing the Opportunistic and Efficient Contracting Versions of PAT

The three hypotheses of PAT have been stated above in opportunistic form, that is, they assume that managers choose accounting policies to maximize their own expected utility relative to their given remuneration and debt contracts and political costs. As mentioned, these hypotheses can also be stated in efficiency form, on the assumption that compensation contracts and internal control systems and, more generally, good corporate governance, limit opportunism, and motivate managers to choose accounting policies to control contracting costs, thereby benefiting the firm and its shareholders.

Frequently, these two forms of PAT make similar predictions. For example, from the bonus plan hypothesis a manager may choose straight-line amortization over declining-balance so as to opportunistically increase remuneration. However, this same policy could be chosen under the bonus hypothesis for efficiency reasons. Suppose that straight-line amortization best measures the opportunity cost to the firm of using its capital assets. Then, straight-line amortization results in a reported income that better measures manager performance. As a result, this policy would more efficiently motivate the manager (which is the purpose of the bonus in the first place) relative to other possible amortization policies.

Consequently, it can be difficult to tell whether firms' observed accounting policy choices are driven by opportunism or efficiency. Yet, without being able to distinguish these possibilities, it can hardly be said that we understand the process of accounting policy choice.

PAT research addresses this problem. We have already referred to the study of Mian and Smith in Section 8.5.1, who report evidence that firms make efficient decisions with respect to preparation of consolidated financial statements. Also, Christie and Zimmerman (1994) investigated the extent of income-increasing accounting choices in a sample of firms that had become takeover targets. Their reasoning was that if opportunistic accounting policy choice was taking place, it would be most rampant in firms that subsequently were taken over, as existing management struggled to fend off the takeover bid by maximizing reported net income and financial position. Christie and Zimmerman found that, even in such a sample, the effects of income-increasing accounting choices were relatively small. From this, they reasoned that the extent of opportunism in the population of firms at large was even less.

The research of Dechow (1994) also relates to the two versions of PAT. She argued that if accruals are largely the result of opportunistic manipulation of reported earnings, an efficient market will reject them in favour of cash flows, in which case cash flows should be more highly associated with share returns than net income. Alternatively, if accruals reflect efficient contracting, net income should be more highly associated with share returns than cash flows. Her empirical tests found net income to be more highly associated with returns than cash flows.

Dechow also argued that when accruals are relatively large (as, for example, in rapidly growing firms), net income should be even more highly associated with share returns, relative to cash flows, than when the firm is in steady state (in which case cash flows and net income will be equal). Her empirical tests found this to be the case, adding further support to efficient contracting.

The study of Dichev and Skinner (2002), outlined above, also provides evidence that the efficient contracting version of PAT is operative. They calculated the *variability* over time of each firm's covenant ratios. The more variable a ratio is, the greater the probability of covenant violation at some point over the term of the loan, other things equal. For example, the current ratio will be more variable under current value accounting for inventories than under historical cost accounting, with the result that the probability the ratio falls below its covenant level is increased. DS found that, on average, the greater the variability of a covenant ratio, the greater the slack at the inception of the loan. This suggests efficiency because both contracting parties suffer costs from covenant violation. Since the probability of incurring these costs increases with covenant ratio variability, it is efficient for the contracting parties to allow more slack at inception as the probability of violation goes up, perhaps setting a slightly higher interest rate to compensate.

Guay (1999) studied the derivatives activities of firms in the year that they first began to use them. He argued that efficient compensation contracts will encourage managers to reduce firm-specific price risks (e.g., an oil and gas company hedges the price risk of next year's production), since this reduction in risk encourages the (risk-averse) manager to take on other firm-specific risks that are in the shareholders' interests, such as R&D, exploration, and new investment—hedging of price risks ensures an adequate future cash balance to finance these undertakings.

Some managers, however, may use derivatives to speculate. This is often regarded as opportunistic behaviour, since speculation increases total firm risk, throwing out of balance the risk–return tradeoffs of diversified shareholders. Consequently, evidence that firms use derivatives primarily to hedge is consistent with efficient contracting.[13]

In a sample of 254 U.S. firms that first began to use derivatives during the period 1991 to 1994, inclusive, Guay found that these new users experienced a significant reduction in several measures of firm risk[14] relative to a control sample of firms that did not initiate new derivatives activity, consistent with a hedging motivation. He also documented a consistency between type of risk exposure and type of hedging instrument used. For example, a majority of test firms with high interest rate risk used hedging instruments that reduced interest rate risk, such as interest rate swaps. Furthermore, the variability of daily share returns (a measure of total firm risk) of the test sample firms fell in a manner consistent with efficient contracting following initiation of derivatives use. For example, firms with high leverage experienced high risk reductions, and vice versa. This suggests that those firms with the greatest economic incentive to hedge their risk did in fact make greater use of derivatives.

Ahmed, Billings, Harris, and Morton (2000) (ABHM) studied the role of conservatism in efficient debt contracting. They pointed out that the concern of debtholders about excessive dividends increases with the riskiness of the firm's operations, with the proportion of debt in its capital structure, and with its dividend payout ratio.

Consequently, ABHM predict that if debt contracts are efficient, the firm's accounting will be more conservative the higher are these three measures of concern.

ABHM's measure of conservatism is based on the firm's book-to-market ratio, that is, the ratio of a firm's shareholders' equity to the market value of its shares. The lower this ratio the more conservative the accounting, other things equal, since an efficient market will see through the lower shareholders' equity thus generated. They predicted that the higher is a firm's operating risk (measured by the standard deviation of past return on equity), debt-to-equity ratio, and dividend payout ratio, the more conservative that firm's accounting will be. For a sample of firms over 1993–1998, they found that this was indeed the case. They also found that the more conservative its accounting, the higher a firm's debt ratings, leading to lower interest costs, other things equal. These results are consistent with efficient debt contracting since they suggest that firms become more conservative when the need is greatest. If managers behaved opportunistically, they would be less concerned about interest costs and would work out from under the threat of debt covenant violation by shifting current reported earnings from future periods. These contracting-based rationales for conservatism augment the investor-oriented rationale given in Section 6.7.

8.6 CONCLUSIONS ON ECONOMIC CONSEQUENCES AND POSITIVE ACCOUNTING THEORY

Despite the downgrading of stewardship by standard setters, it is important for accountants to appreciate the interests of management in financial reporting, due both to the extensive interaction of accountants and managers and to our thesis that reporting on manager performance is equally important to society as reporting to investors. These two reporting objectives do not coincide, due to the fundamental problem of financial accounting theory.

To understand management's interests in financial reporting, it is necessary to appreciate the concept of economic consequences, namely that accounting policies matter, and the role of positive accounting theory (PAT) in explaining why they matter.

PAT attempts to understand and predict firms' accounting policy choices. At its most general level it asserts that accounting policy choice is part of the firm's overall need to minimize its cost of capital and other contracting costs. The accounting policies that do this are largely determined by the firm's organizational structure, which in turn is determined by its environment. Thus, accounting policy choice is part of the overall process of corporate governance.

PAT has led to a rich body of empirical literature. Three aspects of the firm's organizational structure and environment have been particularly singled out for study—its management compensation contracts, its capital structure, and its exposure to political costs.

PAT does not imply that a firm's accounting policy choice should be uniquely specified. Rather, it is usually more efficient to have a set of accounting policies from which management may choose. This set can be taken as the set of policies allowed by GAAP or it can be further restricted by contract. Allowing management some flexibility in accounting policy choice enables a flexible response to changes in the firm's environment, such as new accounting standards, and to unforeseen contract outcomes. However, it also opens the door to opportunistic management behaviour in accounting policy choice.

From the perspective of PAT, it is not hard to see why accounting policies can have economic consequences. From an efficiency perspective, the set of available policies affects the firm's flexibility. From an opportunistic perspective, the ability of management to select accounting policies for its own advantage is affected. Either way, changes in the set of available policies will matter to management. Accounting standards may restrict the allowable accounting policies, as for example, in standards that propose mandatory successful-efforts accounting for the costs of oil and gas exploration—standards to require mandatory successful-efforts will likely be imposed in Canada as the AcSB adopts IASB standards by 2011, for example. Other standards may lower reported net income, as in the accounting for OPEBs, or in standards to record an expense for employee stock options. Still other standards may increase earnings volatility, as in standards that require current value accounting.

Thus, we would expect management to react, and the more a new standard interferes with existing contracts and/or reduces accounting policy choice, the stronger this reaction is likely to be. Nothing in this argument conflicts with securities market efficiency—security prices can still fully reflect all publicly available information in the presence of economic consequences.

While, as mentioned, managers' concerns about accounting policies and standards may be driven by opportunism or by efficient contracting, there is significant evidence in favour of the efficient contracting version of PAT. This suggests that firms are able to align managers' interests with those of shareholders. We now turn to consideration of how this important aspect of corporate governance may be accomplished.

Questions and Problems

1. Explain the difference between a normative and a positive theory. Give an example of each.

2. Can a positive theory make good predictions on average, even though it may not capture exactly the underlying decision processes by which individuals make decisions? Explain.

3. How is a firm's susceptibility to political costs often measured in positive accounting theory? Do you think this is a good measure? Explain.

4. In his article "The Impact of Accounting Regulation on the Stock Market: The Case of Oil and Gas Companies," Lev (1979) examined the daily returns on a portfolio of oil and gas companies' common shares affected by the exposure draft of SFAS 19. This standard required firms to use the successful-efforts method of accounting for the costs of oil and gas exploration. Firms that were using the full-cost method would be required to switch to successful-efforts. The standard became effective in December 1977.

SFAS 19 was objected to particularly strongly by small oil and gas firms, especially if they were actively exploring, who argued that successful-efforts accounting would reduce their ability to raise capital, with consequent effects on oil and gas exploration and on the level of competition in the industry.

Lev found that there was an average decline of 4.5% in the share prices of firms that would have to switch to successful-efforts, during a three-day period following the release of the exposure draft (July 18, 1977). This study is one of the few that have detected a securities market reaction to an accounting policy change that would have no direct impact on cash flows.

Required

a. Why did Lev examine share returns around the date of the exposure draft (July 18, 1977) rather than the date SFAS 19 was issued (December 5, 1977)?

b. Use efficient securities market theory and positive accounting theory to explain why the stock market reacted as it did to the exposure draft of SFAS 19.

c. Suppose that, pursuant to the theory and evidence described in Section 6.2, securities markets are not fully efficient. What reaction to SFAS 19 would you then expect? Explain.

d. Explain, for a specific affected firm, how you would distinguish whether the bonus plan hypothesis or the debt covenant hypothesis was most likely to be driving the negative market reaction to that firm's shares.

5. Use the efficient contracting form of positive accounting theory to explain why managers would prefer to have GAAP allow a *set* of generally accepted accounting policies from which to choose, rather than have GAAP set so restrictively as to completely prescribe accounting policy choice.

Use the opportunistic form of positive accounting theory to explain the same thing.

6. A new accounting standard requires a firm to accrue major new liabilities for employee pensions and benefits. As a result, its debt-to-equity ratio rises to the point where technical violation of covenants in its borrowing agreements is threatened. Management knows that renegotiation of these covenants would be difficult and costly.

Suggest some accounting policy choices that could reduce the likelihood of technical violation. Ideally, any changes in policies should not violate GAAP, not affect the firm's real operations, and not reduce cash flows. Justify your suggestions.

7. Use positive accounting theory to explain how conservative accounting can contribute to efficient contracting.

8. Standard setters have introduced standards requiring current value accounting for OPEBs (IAS 19, SFAS 106, 158). According to SFAS 106 (paragraph 124), "accrual accounting will more appropriately reflect the financial effects of an employer's existing promise to provide those benefits and the events that affect that promise in financial statements, as those events occur." Furthermore, SFAS 106 (paragraph 20) states that "the expected postretirement benefit obligation for an employee is the actuarial present value as of a particular date of the post-employment benefits expected to be paid by the employer's plan to or for the employee . . . ."

Prior to these standards, most OPEB benefits were accounted for on a cash basis, allowing companies to expense these benefits as they were paid to employees.

These new standards created economic consequences, whereby firms moved to reduce their postretirement benefits. For example, as reported in *The Wall Street Journal* (November 4, 1992), McDonnell Douglas Corp. cut benefits to retired employees upon realizing that it faced a $1.2-billion charge against earnings from SFAS 106.

Required

a. What is the after-tax impact on a firm's cash flows following adoption of current value accounting for OPEBs, assuming benefits are not cut?

b. Why would some firms move to reduce retiree benefits following adoption of current value accounting for OPEBs?

c. Give an argument for how a firm's share price might rise following the reporting of a major charge from adopting current value accounting for OPEBs.

9. *The Globe and Mail* (November 6, 2002, p. B1), reported "New accounting rules sow confusion about oil earnings." This refers to changes, effective January 2002, to Section 1650 of the *CICA Handbook*. These changes required firms with monetary items denominated in a foreign currency to include, and disclose, gains and losses from translating these items into Canadian dollars in the current period's income statement. Previously, such gains and losses could be deferred and amortized over the life of the monetary item.

Many Canadian oil companies have long-term debt denominated in U.S. dollars. Under the new standard, fluctuations in the value of the Canadian dollar relative to the U.S. dollar increase the volatility of the reported earnings of Canadian oil companies. For example, according to the *Globe* article, EnCana Corp. reported an after-tax loss of $145 million on its foreign currency–denominated debt for its third quarter, 2002, reducing its reported earnings by about 40%. This loss followed a foreign currency conversion gain of approximately the same amount in its second quarter. The article went on to quote the managing director of research of a Calgary investment firm as saying that earnings are "going up and down like a toilet seat."

Required

a. In a follow-up article in the *Globe* on November 8, 2002 ("Accounting rule change burns big oil," p. B2), Deborah Yedlin reports the president and CEO of EnCana Corp. as commenting that the new accounting rules could deter companies from being able to lock in financing at the current low interest rates.

   Evaluate this comment from the standpoint of efficient securities market theory.

b. Evaluate the comment in part **a** from the standpoint of positive accounting theory.

10. Following the 1990 Iraqi invasion of Kuwait, the price of crude oil soared, as did retail gasoline prices. This led the major U.S. oil companies to try to hold down their reported earnings.

The oil companies were anxious to avoid a repeat of an earlier episode when crude oil and gasoline prices peaked during the 1970s, and earnings soared. The public outrage was so great that the U.S. Congress imposed an excess profits tax, taxing back several billion dollars of excess profits. Warnings of similar taxes were repeated in 1990.

To limit their 1990 profits, the major oil companies did exercise some price restraint to keep prices at the pump from rising as much as they otherwise would. They also engaged in a number of accounting practices, such as increased provisions for future environmental costs, increased maintenance, and large provisions for legal liabilities.

Required

a. What pricing and accounting policy choices are predicted by the bonus plan and debt covenant hypotheses of positive accounting theory, in response to increasing crude oil prices? Explain.

b. Use the political cost hypothesis of positive accounting theory to explain why the *major* oil companies would be the ones most concerned.

c. What inventory accounting policy would the oil companies find most effective in holding down profits? Explain.

d. Do you think the strategy of holding down reported profits by means of accounting policy choice will be effective in avoiding a backlash? Explain why or why not.

11. Many companies issue large numbers of stock options to executives and other employees. These companies frequently buy back some of their shares on the open market. For example, Microsoft Corp., which until relatively recently was a major issuer of ESOs, bought back over $20 billion of its shares over a five-year period up to 2003. In February 2005 ConocoPhillips, a large oil company based in Houston, Texas, announced a $1 billion buyback program over the next two years. ConocoPhillips was also a major ESO issuer.

Required

a. Why would firms with large ESO plans buy back their stock? Explain.

b. Normally, companies that buy back their shares do so over time, to avoid the increased demand bidding up share price, thus raising the cost of buying them back. As the shares are bought back, the company then records the reduction in outstanding shares and the cash payment. However, according to an article in *The Globe and Mail* (January 31, 2006, p. B13), "Watch out for the loophole: buybacks have hidden costs," (reproduced from *The Wall Street Journal*), many companies have engaged in "accelerated share repurchase." Under this tactic, firms record their total planned buyback all at once at their shares' current market price, even though they have not yet bought back the shares. This maximizes the increase in current earnings per share. Would you, as a potential investor in firms using this tactic, be concerned? Why or why not?

12. For large public corporations, SFAS 123R was effective for periods beginning after June 15, 2005. However, the exposure draft of this standard met considerable opposition, mostly from large technology companies. These companies formed an anti-expense lobby group, the International Employee Stock Options Coalition, to fight the proposal. As a result, several bills were introduced in the U.S. Congress to override or modify the FASB proposal. Suggested modifications included expensing only ESOs for the firm's top five executives, and setting share price variability to zero in the Black/Scholes formula.

The FASB's stand was strengthened, however, because numerous companies, including General Motors Corp., Microsoft Corp., and Exxon Mobil Corp., voluntarily decided to expense their ESOs. Also many firms reduced their ESO awards. For example, the Bank of

Montreal reduced options issued as compensation by two-thirds, replacing them with increased cash bonuses and stock awards.

In October 2004 the FASB announced it was delaying implementation of its proposal for six months, to June 15, 2005. However, except for the implementation delay, it did not back down on this standard.

Required

a. Evaluate the relevance and reliability of Black/Scholes as a measure of the fair value of ESOs.

b. Some critics of the proposed standard claim that the cost of ESOs is zero. Why? Explain to these critics why their claim is incorrect.

c. Why are some firms strongly opposed to expensing of ESOs?

d. Why would a firm voluntarily adopt expensing of ESOs?

13. On October 25, 2002, *The Globe and Mail* (p. B2) reported "Former Big Bear head denies manipulation." The article describes accusations against the former CEO of Big Bear Exploration Ltd. in a hearing before the Alberta Securities Commission. The accusations are that the former CEO fed the market gloomy news about Blue Range Resources Corp., a newly acquired subsidiary of Big Bear, in order to drive down Big Bear's stock price and benefit personally from a subsequent rebound in stock price when Blue Range sprang back from some financial difficulties that were revealed shortly after it was acquired by Big Bear.

Big Bear's former CEO strenuously denied these charges, which had not been proven at the time of the article.

Required

a. Are these accusations consistent with the findings of Aboody and Kasznik (2000)? Explain why or why not.

b. If the accusations are proven, with which version of PAT (efficient contracting or opportunistic) is this episode most consistent? Explain.

c. If, as a result of a rebound at Blue Range, Big Bear's CEO's options became deep-in-the-money, would the Black/Scholes option value formula have reliably measured their fair value at grant date? Explain why or why not.

14. Recent years saw a significant increase in "covenant-lite" debt, under which debt contracts had few if any debt covenants. For example, a private equity firm may issue such debt to finance a planned takeover. One estimate is that, in 2007, covenant-lite debt accounted for 35% of all debt issued in the United States.

This debt is typically bought by financial institutions, such as banks. A bank may then combine this loan with other similar loans and slice the total up into tranches, that is, into packages of debt of similar credit quality, called asset-backed securities or collateralized debt obligations (CDO). It will then sell these tranches to investors on a secondary loan market. The purchaser will receive his/her share of the interest and principal payments paid by the firms whose debt is in that tranche. Thus, the investor can buy interest-bearing debt with the level of default risk he/she desires, and pay accordingly. The effect is to disperse credit risk through the economy. It is expected that even for a tranche of low quality there will be no more than a few defaulting firms, so that any credit losses are spread over all the investors in that tranche.

Furthermore, it is possible to increase the credit quality of a CDO by buying credit default swaps (CDS). These are derivative instruments under which the issuer of the CDS, for a fee, agrees to compensate tranche investors for credit losses incurred by that tranche. If CDSs are bought to protect, say, 25% of the underlying debt in the tranche, the effect is to increase the credit quality of the tranche significantly. This further disperses credit risk, since now at least part of the risk is borne by the CDS issuers.

Required

a. If you were an investor in interest-bearing securities, would you be willing to invest a substantial amount of your capital in tranches secured by covenant-lite debt? Explain why or why not.

b. Concerns are sometimes expressed that issuing covenant-lite debt creates a moral hazard problem. What is the problem?

c. What would be the effect of covenant-lite debt on the validity of the debt covenant hypothesis of PAT?

d. The ability to increase the credit quality of high-risk debt by means of CDSs seems almost "magical." From the standpoint of a CDO investor, do you see a downside to investing in CDOs, particularly if protected by CDSs? Explain.

Notes

1. APB 25 distinguishes between variable and fixed ESO plans. A variable plan is one under which the number of shares the employee may acquire and/or the price to be paid are not determinable until some time after the grant date. Under a fixed plan, the number of shares and the exercise price are known at the grant date.

2. This assumes that the number of shares to be issued by means of options is not large enough to affect the market price of the firm's shares.

3. Concavity is the source of the overstatement. To see this, note first that the Black/Scholes value of an option is increasing in time to expiry, since the longer time to expiry the greater the likelihood that share price will take off. Also, recall that under APB 25, most ESOs are issued with exercise price equal to underlying share price at the grant date. When exercise price and grant date share price are equal, the Black/Scholes value may be an increasing, *concave* function of time to expiry, as argued by HMS. If so, the option value increases at a decreasing rate. The significance of concavity is that if an employee exercises his/her ESOs *before* expected time to exercise (note that expected time to exercise is an average across employees), the reduction in *ex post* cost to the firm is greater than the increase in cost if an employee exercises a similar time *after* expected time to exercise. That is, use of expected time to exercise in Black/Scholes upwardly biases ESO cost relative to *ex post* cost. When this upward bias is put together with the considerable variability of employees' exercise decisions, the bias can be significant. Using a procedure suggested by HMS to approximate the effects of this concavity, Marquardt (2002) finds the tendency of Black/Scholes to bias ESO cost is reduced.

4. AK's argument assumes that investors do not know the scheduled date. If they did, they could discount the CEO's information release to adjust for manager biases. AK argue that there is considerable uncertainty that a firm will maintain its scheduled ESO grant dates, and whether or not it does is not known by the market until after the fact. Also, it would take several years before the market could identify that the firm was, in fact, adhering to a fixed schedule. AK present evidence in support of their argument.

5. In the following discussion it will be helpful to distinguish between the firm and its manager. We can think of the firm as represented by the board of directors.

6. This is the "economic Darwinism" argument of Alchian (1950).

7. LIFO inventory is currently permitted under Canadian and U.S. accounting standards, but not under IASB standards.

8. Technical analysis is an approach to investing that studies past market performance for systematic patterns and attempts to predict future market performance by projecting these patterns. It is inconsistent with securities market efficiency, which predicts that share return fluctuations will be random.

9. See, for example, Boland and Gordon (1992) and Demski (1988).

10. Private lending agreements are loans that are not publicly traded, in contrast to public lending agreements where investors can buy or sell bonds and other credit instruments on the market. The private lending agreements studied by Dichev and Skinner consist of loans made by U.S. banks to large corporations. They report that such loans are the main form of private lending.

11. To standardize for firm size, Jones divides both sides of this equation by total assets.

12. This procedure, called the "Jones model," will be recognized as conceptually related to the use of the CAPM to separate security returns into expected and abnormal components, as illustrated in Figure 5.2. The contexts in which the two models are applied is quite different, however.

13. This argument does not completely agree with the argument of Gigler, Kanodia, and Venugopalan (2007), whose research was outlined in Section 7.3.5, and who stated that shareholders would support some speculation to the extent that they felt speculation would on balance be profitable. However, assuming usage of derivatives for speculation is small relative to use for hedging, the two arguments are reasonably consistent.

14. Risk measures used by Guay include interest rate exposure, exchange rate exposure, "total" risk (based on the standard deviation of the firm's daily stock returns), firm-specific risk (based on the standard deviation of the firm's daily stock returns after using the market model to remove economy-wide effects), and beta. By and large, Guay's result that new derivatives users do so to reduce risk holds for all of these risk concepts.

Chapter 9
An Analysis of Conflict

Figure 9.1 Organization of Chapter 9

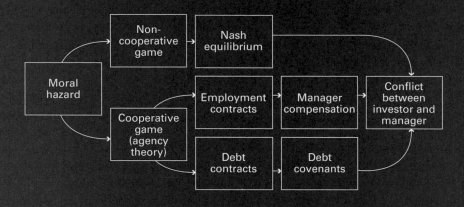

9.1 OVERVIEW

In this chapter, we consider the questions of manager/shareholder alignment that underlie economic consequences and positive accounting theory. To properly understand management's interests in financial reporting, it is necessary to consider some models from **game theory**. Game theory attempts to model and predict the outcome of **conflict** between rational individuals. Certainly, as we saw in the disputes leading up to expensing of ESOs in Chapter 8, economic consequences are characterized by conflict. We will also consider **agency theory**. This is a version of game theory that models the process of **contracting** between two or more persons. Since each party to a contract attempts to get the best deal for him/herself, agency theory also involves conflict.

As pointed out in Chapter 8, business firms enter into many contracts. Two particularly important contracts are **employment contracts** between the firm and its managers and **lending contracts** between the firm and its lenders. Both of these types of contracts often depend on the firm's reported earnings. Employment contracts frequently base managerial bonuses on net income, and lending contracts usually incorporate protection for the lenders in the form of covenants that, for example, bind the firm not to go below a stated times-interest-earned ratio, or not to pay dividends if working capital falls below a specified level.

Game theory can help us understand how managers, investors, and other affected parties can rationally deal with the economic consequences of financial reporting. Consequently, game theory and agency theory are relevant to accounting. Accounting policies can have economic consequences when important contracts are affected by those policies. Game theory helps us to see why contracts frequently depend on financial statements.

Reported net income has a different role in a contracting context than in reporting to investors. Its role is to predict the payoff from current manager activities. In so doing, it monitors and motivates manager performance. For this, net income needs to be sensitive to manager effort and precise in its measurements of the payoff from that effort. The characteristics needed to best fulfill this role are not necessarily the same as those that provide the most useful information to investors, leading to the fundamental problem of financial accounting theory outlined in Section 1.7.

Finally, the contract-based role for financial statements that emerges from game theory helps us to see how the theory of efficient securities markets is not necessarily inconsistent with economic consequences. Securities markets can be efficient and accounting policies can have economic consequences once the conflict implications for financial reporting are understood.

Figure 9.1 outlines the organization of this chapter.

9.2 UNDERSTANDING GAME THEORY

In this chapter, we will study the **economic theory of games**, or **game theory** for short. This is a large topic—we can only scratch the surface here. Nevertheless, we will see that game theory underlies many of the current issues in financial accounting theory.

Essentially, game theory models the interaction of two or more *players*. Frequently, this interaction occurs in the presence of uncertainty and information asymmetry. Each player is assumed to maximize his or her expected utility, just as the investors did in our decision theory and investment decision examples in Chapter 3. The difference is that game theory, in addition to taking into account any uncertainty arising from random realization of states of nature, requires that the players formally take the actions of the other players into account. Actions of other players can be extremely difficult to predict, since the action chosen by one player will depend on what action that player thinks the other players will take, and vice versa. Consequently, game theory tends to be more complex than decision theory and the theory of investment. However, the formal recognition of conflict between rational parties greatly expands the range of situations addressed by the theory.

Another way to view game theory is that the actual number of players lies "in between" the number in single-person decision theory and in markets. At one extreme, in decision theory, there is a *single* player, playing a game against nature—nature's play may be thought of as the realization of one of the states of nature. At the other extreme, we can think of a market as a game with a *large* number of players. If the market is perfect in the economic sense, or, in our terminology, if the market works well, the number of players is so large that the actions of any one player cannot influence what happens on the market—this is the notion of a *price-taker* in economics, as in our investment decisions in Examples 3.1 and 3.2, where the decision-makers took the market prices of securities as given.

However, in game theory the number of players, while greater than one, is sufficiently small that the actions of one player *do* influence the other players—hence the conflict aspect of a game where the players take the actions of the other players into account. The decision problems facing firms in cartels or in oligopolistic industries (where each of a few producers affect, but do not control, the market) can be modelled as games, for example.

There are many different types of games. One basis for classifying games is as **cooperative** or **non-cooperative**. In a cooperative game, the parties can enter into a **binding agreement**. A cartel is an example of a cooperative game. Cartels work best where it is possible to enforce binding agreements on members not to bolt the cartel in favour of high short-term profits. If such agreements are not possible, the cartel would be more like a non-cooperative game. An oligopolistic industry is an example of a non-cooperative game, at least in jurisdictions where agreements in restraint of trade are illegal. We will illustrate both types of games in our development.

9.3 A NON-COOPERATIVE GAME MODEL OF MANAGER–INVESTOR CONFLICT

In Section 3.2, we introduced the concept of **constituencies** of financial statement users. Conflict between constituencies can be modelled as a game, since the decision needs of different constituencies may not coincide. As we explored in Chapter 3, investors will desire relevant and reliable financial statement information to assist in assessing the expected values and risks of their investments. Managers, however, may not wish to reveal all the information that investors desire. They may prefer to omit certain liabilities from the balance sheet, on the grounds that this will make it easier to raise capital by facilitating contracts with lenders. Also, they may prefer not to reveal which accounting policies are being used so as to have room to manage reported profits by discretionary accruals or changes of accounting policy. In addition, management may fear that releasing too much information will benefit their competition. These are just some of the actions that managers may take to present the firm in the best light by biasing, or otherwise managing, the financial statements for either efficient contracting or opportunistic purposes. The investor, of course, will be aware of this possibility and will take it into account when making an investment decision. Firm management, in turn, will be aware of possible investor reaction when preparing the financial statements. Game theory provides a formal framework for studying this conflict situation and for predicting the decisions the parties will make.

We will model this situation as a **non-cooperative game**, since it is difficult to envisage a binding agreement between manager and investor about what specific information is to be supplied. For one thing, such an agreement could be very costly, since similar agreements would have to be negotiated with all users. But different users may have varied decision problems and hence different information needs, so that many different sets of financial statements would be needed. Even if such binding agreements were made, they would be difficult and costly to enforce, because each user would need to conduct, or hire, an audit investigation of the firm to monitor management compliance with the agreement. In other contexts, binding agreements may be illegal, as when an oligopolistic industry enters into an agreement in restraint of trade.

To illustrate this game between the manager and the investor, consider Example 9.1.

Example 9.1
Manager–Investor Relations as a Non-Cooperative Game

We assume the manager has two strategies, one of which must be chosen (see Table 9.1.) We will call one of these "distort" (D), which we can think of as underinvesting in corporate governance and choosing accounting policies to maximize or otherwise bias reported net income. The other strategy is to choose "honest" (H), which we can think of as maintaining strong corporate governance and preparing useful financial statements for investors. The investor also has two strategies—to buy shares in the manager's firm or to refuse to buy, denoted by B and R, respectively.

Table 9.1 Utility Payoffs in a Non-Cooperative Game

		Manager	
		HONEST (H)	**DISTORT (D)**
Investor	**BUY (B)**	60, 40	20, 80
	REFUSE TO BUY (R)	35, 20	35, 30

The numbers in Table 9.1 represent the utility payoffs to the investor and manager respectively for each possible strategy combination. Thus, if the manager chooses H and the investor B, the investor receives a utility of 60 and the manager receives 40, and so on for the other three pairs of numbers in the table. You should analyze the relationship between the payoffs to make sure they appear reasonable. For example, if the investor chooses B, a higher utility is attained by the investor when the manager is honest (60) than when the manager distorts the information (20). Similarly, if the investor refuses to buy, the manager would prefer to choose D (if the manager distorts the information, less money and effort is put into corporate governance and decision-useful reporting).

It is important to emphasize the assumption here that each party has *complete information* about the other. Thus, the investor knows the strategies available to the manager and the manager's payoffs and vice versa. Game theory can be extended to relax these assumptions, but this is beyond our scope. This completeness of information does not extend to choice of strategy, however. Each player in this example chooses his or her strategy without knowing the strategy choice of the other in this game.

What **strategy pair** will be chosen? The term means simply a statement of the strategy chosen by each player. Thus, BH is a strategy pair whereby the investor buys (B) and the manager is honest (H). Review Table 9.1 and make your own prediction before reading on.

We can rule out the RH and BD strategy pairs easily. If the manager were to choose H, the investor would reason that it would be better to choose B, because it yields a utility of 60 as opposed to one of 35 from R. Thus, RH would be unlikely to happen. Similarly, if the manager were to choose D, the investor would reason that it would be better to choose R, so BD would be unlikely.

Now consider the BH pair. If the investor were to choose B, the manager would then prefer D. Thus, it seems BH must be ruled out also. The only strategy pair not subject to this problem is RD. If the manager was to choose D, the investor would prefer R. Similarly, if the investor was to choose R, the manager would prefer D. RD is the only strategy pair such that *given* the strategy choice of the other player, each player is content with his or her strategy. Such a strategy pair is called a **Nash equilibrium**. Thus, RD is the predicted outcome of the game.

However, RD is not a completely satisfactory outcome of the game in Example 9.1. Notice that *both parties would be better off* if BH were chosen rather than RD. The strategy pair BH is called the **cooperative solution**. But, as we have argued, if the investor were to choose B rather than R, he or she knows that the rational manager would then prefer D and the investor would end up with 20 rather than the 35 from choosing R. Consequently, the investor would not choose B. The Nash equilibrium outcome RD in this game is unfortunate, because it means, at least for payoff values assumed, that the market for the firm's shares would not work very well—no one would buy them.

It is interesting to speculate what might happen next. Perhaps the parties would get together and enter into a binding agreement to choose BH, after all. However, the investor would have to be convinced the agreement was in fact binding on the manager and could be enforced.

Another approach would be to think of the game in a *long-run* perspective. If this game was repeated indefinitely, and the manager always acted ethically by choosing H, a reputation for honesty would be established and investors would start choosing B. This would give the manager a long-run average of 40, rather than the 30 that would be obtained on a one-shot basis.

A related argument derives from the folk theorem (see Chapter 1, Note 10). Each player threatens that if the other player deviates from the cooperative solution, he/she will switch strategy the next time the game is played. Thus the deviating player will be punished by receiving only the Nash equilibrium payoff for the remainder of the game. The threat is credible because the Nash equilibrium *is* an equilibrium. For this to work, however, the players must not have too high a discount rate. For example, if the investor buys, the value to the manager of an immediate payoff of $80 may exceed the present value of the $10 reduction in each future period (i.e., $40 − $30) when the investor punishes the manager by switching to R.

While this game model is a relatively simple one, it is not hard to see how it relates to the accounting and auditing scandals and resulting declines in stock markets in Canada and the United States in the early 2000s. In Table 9.1, if we start with the players at the cooperative solution BH, certain managers, such as those at Enron and WorldCom (see Section 1.2), moved to a distort strategy D. They felt that the immediate payoff by departing from the cooperative solution outweighed the longer-run costs of investor reaction. This short-run strategy generated high payoffs for them. For example, the distortions they incorporated into their financial statements increased reported earnings and removed debt from the balance sheet. The resulting increase in share prices generated huge profits for them from ESOs. When the market became aware of the financial statement distortions, investors immediately punished management by moving to R, and share price fell precipitously. However, management had already realized their ESO profits.

Management appeared to have ignored, at its peril, another way to maintain the cooperative solution. This is for central authority, such as government, the courts, and standard setters, to change the payoffs of the game by introducing new regulations and/or threatening penalties for distortion. The threat is credible to the extent that the regulations and penalties are enforced. An increase in penalties may lower the manager's payoffs for BD and RD to, say, zero. Then it can be verified that BH would be a Nash equilibrium.

Attempts by central authorities to restore investor confidence in financial reporting can be interpreted as changes in the payoffs of the game. We have already mentioned the Sarbanes-Oxley Act and Sections 1100 and 1400 of the *CICA Handbook* in Section 1.2. The *Handbook* standards tighten up the concept of generally accepted accounting principles, increasing the cost of distortion for the manager. In addition, the Public Company Accounting Oversight Board in the United States and the Canadian Public Accountability Board were created. These boards consist of prominent persons independent of the accounting and auditing profession whose role is to enforce tougher rules on auditors. Hopefully, any Enron and WorldCom-style financial statement distortions will be deterred. To the extent these bodies succeed in their mission, the manager's payoff under strategy BD will be reduced to the point where the Nash equilibrium becomes BH. In effect, the change in payoffs increases investor confidence that the manager will not distort, with the result that the investors resume buying.

For our purposes, however, the main point to note is that there will always be situations where managers perceive the short-run benefit of opportunistic behaviour as exceeding the expected costs of punishment. Hopefully, the manager will then behave ethically and "do the right thing." However, experience shows that this does not always happen. Consequently, the relationship between investors and managers remains as one of conflict.

Note the essential difference between single-person decision theory and game theory approaches. In our earlier decision theory Example 3.1, Bill Cautious assessed probabilities of what would happen—he ended up with a 0.77 probability of the high payoff, and so on. The assumption in decision theory is that the high or low payoffs are generated by some random mechanism called nature. Thus, a decision theory problem is sometimes called a game against nature, because some impartial force (nature) is assumed to generate the high or low payoffs with the probabilities as given. While we gave considerable attention to how investors may assess these probabilities and revise them as new information is obtained, we made an implicit assumption throughout Example 3.1 that the particular decision chosen by the investor would not affect what these probabilities were. That is, nature does not "think."

This assumption is fine for many decision problems. Indeed, as we outlined in Chapters 3 and 4, much progress has been made in understanding the decision needs of users through study of the decision theory approach. However, the approach breaks down when the payoffs are generated by a thinking opponent (the manager) rather than by nature. In Example 9.1, the manager will reason that if the investor buys, his/her best act is to distort, and the investor knows this. Thus, it is not correct for the investor to assign probabilities to the manager's action choice when the manager's action is not chosen probabilistically. Similarly, it would not be correct for the manager to assign probabilities to the investor's action.[1] Such behaviour, by either or both decision-makers, would be unlikely to lead to good decisions in the conflict situation.

How can we use a game such as the one modelled in Example 9.1 in financial accounting theory? The essential point to realize here is that such models enable us to better understand the process of accounting policy choice. Recall that in Chapter 3 we developed a considerable body of theory to enable us to understand the information needs of investors. In that chapter we showed that major professional accounting standard-setting bodies appear to have adopted the decision usefulness approach that follows from the theory. What we did *not* consider in those chapters, however, was whether firm management would be *willing* to adopt the full disclosure policies that accounting standard setters have proposed. Indeed, the important message in Chapter 8 was that managers appear unwilling to sit idly by and adopt whatever accounting policies are suggested by the standard setters (representing the interests of investors). The assumption of positive accounting theory that managers are rational, leading to the possibility of opportunistic behaviour, makes it clear that management has *its own* interests at stake in accounting policy choice and cannot be assumed to necessarily adopt full disclosure or other accounting policies solely on the ethical grounds that they will be useful to shareholders and other investors. This is shown in our Example 9.1 by the utility of the manager being lower under H than under D. As concluded above, the interests of the investor and manager constituencies may *conflict*.

By modelling this conflict situation as a game, we can understand the problems surrounding policy choice more clearly. In particular, we see that, depending on the payoffs of the game, it may indeed be in a manager's own interests to distort the financial statements, at least in the short run. Thus, any accounting body concerned about implementing a new pronouncement must be concerned with the resulting payoffs to *both* investors and management. Only by ensuring that the payoffs to management are such that management will accept the new policy can a smooth implementation be assured.

Of course, any accountant with practical experience in choosing a firm's accounting policies will know about management's interest in and concern about these policies, without having to be convinced by a game theory example. Our point is that such interest and concern is exactly what is predicted by the game theory. Better understanding of this conflict situation by standard setters will result in more realistic accounting policy choices, which should avoid the economic consequences disputes that were documented in Chapter 8.

There are other conflict situations in financial accounting that can be studied in a game context. For example, Darrough and Stoughton (1990) (DS) analyze a game between a monopolistic firm (the incumbent) and a potential entrant to the industry (the entrant). The incumbent needs to raise equity capital for a new project. It has inside information about itself that can be either favourable or unfavourable about its future prospects. If the information is favourable, its disclosure will lower the incumbent's cost of capital for its new equity issue. However, the entrant will revise upwards its prior probability of good future prospects in the industry upon seeing the favourable disclosure. This will encourage the entrant to enter. If the information is unfavourable, its disclosure[2] will deter the entrant but raise cost of capital. What should the incumbent do—disclose or not disclose?

The answer depends on how profitable the incumbent is. If existing monopoly profits are high and the need for equity capital is moderate, the dominant consideration for the incumbent is to deter entry. Then, DS show that if the entrant has high prior probability that the incumbent's inside information is favourable and/or the costs of entry to the industry are low (i.e., the threat of entry is high), the incumbent firm will fully disclose its inside information, favourable or unfavourable. If its inside information is unfavourable, its loss of profits if the entrant enters outweighs the higher cost of capital, so the incumbent will disclose so as to discourage entry. If its inside information is favourable, the incumbent will disclose even if this attracts entry since profits will still be satisfactory, particularly in view of the lower cost of capital following the favourable disclosure.

Other outcomes are possible, however. DS show that if the entrant has low prior probability that the incumbent's inside information is favourable (low threat of entry), the incumbent will not disclose favourable or unfavourable information. Even the incumbent with favourable news will be better off not disclosing if the higher profits from discouraging entry outweigh the higher cost of capital that results.

These conclusions are of interest, because they suggest that the question of full disclosure extends into industry structure. In the DS model, the greater the competition in an industry (measured by the threat of entry), the better the disclosure. This reinforces our conclusion from positive accounting theory that full disclosure to investors is not the only consideration affecting managers' accounting policy choices.

Indeed, it also reinforces the claim of Merino and Neimark (Section 1.2) that, prior to the creation of the SEC in 1933, the primary role of full disclosure was to enable potential entrants to identify high-profit industries. Presumably, the higher an incumbent firm's monopoly profits the more incentive it had to keep the threat of entry low by means of distorted or incomplete financial reporting.

Thus, the implications of the DS analysis have a deeper significance. By delineating conditions under which firms may or may not disclose voluntarily, conditions under which standard setting may be less needed are identified.

Since DS, other papers have refined and extended the above considerations. See, for example, Darrough (1993), Newman and Sansing (1993), Feltham and Xie (1994), Pae (2002), and Arya and Mittendorf (2005). In the Arya and Mittendorf model, a firm's voluntary disclosure (assumed truthful) reveals valuable information to a competitor. However, when third parties (e.g., analysts, credit rating agencies) follow the firm, their information-gathering activities will also generate information available to the competitor. But, by voluntarily releasing some information, the firm may be able to "herd" the third parties to accept the firm's information, thereby pre-empting third parties' own information-gathering activities. While revealing inside information will reduce firm profits by giving competitive advantage to the competitor, the reduction may be less than what would be revealed if the third parties pursued their other information-gathering activities. If so, the firm will disclose voluntarily.

9.3.1 Summary

Non-cooperative game theory enables us to model the conflict situation that often exists between different constituencies of financial statement users. Even a very simple game-theoretic model shows that an accounting standard-setting body that fails to consider the interests of all constituencies affected by accounting policy choice is in danger of making policy recommendations that are difficult to implement. Furthermore, conflict analysis can be used to examine conditions under which standards may or may not be needed, since under some conditions firms may be motivated to release even unfavourable information voluntarily.

9.4 SOME MODELS OF COOPERATIVE GAME THEORY

9.4.1 Introduction

While the non-cooperative game in Example 9.1 illustrates some of the implications of conflict between user constituencies, many other areas of accounting reflect **cooperative behaviour**. Recall that the essence of cooperation here is that the players in a conflict situation can enter into agreements that they perceive as binding. Such agreements are often called **contracts**. There are many such contractual agreements that have accounting implications.

In this section we will be concerned with two important types of contracts that have implications for financial accounting theory. These are **employment contracts** between the firm and its top manager and **lending contracts** between the firm manager and the bondholder. In these contracts, we can think of one of the parties as the principal, and the other the agent. For example, in an employment contract, the firm owner is the principal and the top manager is the agent hired to run the firm on the owner's behalf. This type of game theory is called **agency theory**.

> **Agency theory** *is a branch of game theory that studies the design of contracts to motivate a rational agent to act on behalf of a principal when the agent's interests would otherwise conflict with those of the principal.*

Actually, agency theory contracts have characteristics of both cooperative and non-cooperative games. They are non-cooperative in that both parties choose their actions non-cooperatively. The two parties do not specifically agree to take certain actions; rather, the actions are motivated by the contract itself. Nevertheless, each party must be able to commit to the contract, that is, to bind him/herself to "play by the rules." For example, it is assumed that the manager in an employment contract will not grab the total firm profits and head for a foreign jurisdiction. Such commitment may be enforced by the legal system, by use of bonding or escrow arrangements, and by ethical behaviour and reputations of the contracting parties. Consequently, for our discussion, we will include them under cooperative games.

9.4.2 Agency Theory: An Employment Contract Between Firm Owner and Manager

We begin with a single-period owner–manager contract example that introduces many of the concepts of agency theory and illustrates the basic moral hazard conflict between owner and manager. This section also illustrates how the owner can design an employment contract to control moral hazard.

It should be noted in our example that the use of two persons is a modelling device to keep things as simple as possible. The owner and the manager are proxies for a large number of similar investors and managers with conflicting interests. In effect, the firm exhibits a separation of ownership and control, captured by modelling the firm as two rational individuals with conflicting interests.

Example 9.2
A Firm Owner–Manager Agency Problem

Consider a simple firm consisting of a single owner (the principal) and a single manager (the agent). The contract is single-period. Specifically, the owner hires the manager for one year. The firm faces risk, which, as usual, we express in the form of random states of nature. Assume that there are two such states, denoted by θ_1 and θ_2. State θ_1 represents "good times" and θ_2 "bad times." If good times occur, the firm's payoff will be $x_1 = \$100$. Given bad times, the payoff will be $x_2 = \$55$.

We will think of the payoff here as the cash flows resulting from the manager's activities during the year. Many of these cash flows will be realized within the year. Activities aimed at cost control, for example, will generate cash savings with little delay. Advertising activities, if successful, will generate extra sales currently.

Other activities, such as R&D, however, may not pay off until next year, since it can take considerable time, if ever, for the results of current research to generate cash flow. In addition, current activities may generate future liabilities. Extraction of natural resources may generate environmental liabilities that may not be known for some time, for example. In effect, *the full payoff is not observable until after the current compensation contract has expired*.

It is this payoff that is the owner's ultimate interest. That is, the rational owner wishes to maximize the expected payoff, net of manager compensation.

Before proceeding with our example, we further simplify by getting rid of the need to refer specifically to the states of nature. As mentioned, each state realization leads to a specific payoff. If θ_1 occurs, net income $= x_1 = \$100$, and if θ_2 occurs, $x_2 = \$55$. Thus, we can model firm risk just as well with the probabilities of the payoffs as with the probabilities of the states of nature themselves. That is, the probability that θ_1 happens is the same as the probability that the payoff is x_1, and so on. If the probability of θ_1 is 0.6, we can say that the probability of x_1 is 0.6, rather than the more awkward "the probability of θ_1 is 0.6 and, if θ_1 occurs, $x_1 = \$100$." Consequently, we will suppress direct reference to states of nature for the remainder of this section.

Now, assume that the owner does not operate the firm. This is the responsibility of the manager. Consistent with what we observe in real employment situations, the manager will be paid at year-end, despite the payoff not being observable at that time.

Assume also that, after being hired, the manager has two action choices—**work hard**, denoted by a_1, or **shirk**, denoted by a_2. These represent all of the manager's activities during the year.

The action choice of the manager will affect the probabilities of the payoffs. Let these probabilities be as follows:

■ If the manager works hard:

$$P(x_1/a_1) = 0.6$$
$$P(x_2/a_1) = \underline{0.4}$$
$$= \underline{\underline{1.0}}$$

- If the manager shirks:

$$P(x_1/a_2) = 0.4$$
$$P(x_2/a_2) = \underline{0.6}$$
$$= \underline{\underline{1.0}}$$

Recall that x_1 represents the high payoff. If the manager works hard the probability of x_1 is greater (0.6) than it would be under shirking (0.4). In statistical terms, the payoff distribution conditional on a_1 stochastically dominates (in the first degree) the distribution conditional on a_2. This is a critical point to realize—the action of the agent affects the probabilities of the payoffs. In particular, the greater the effort put into the operation of the firm by the manager, the higher the probability of the high payoff and the lower the probability of the low payoff.

Of course, this is just what we would expect. Hard work by the manager increases the probability that the firm will do well, but it is still possible for the low payoff to occur. In our example, there is a 40% probability that the payoff will be low even though the manager works hard, since hard work cannot always overcome the risks faced by the firm. Similarly, if the manager shirks, it is still possible for the high payoff to occur, since the shirking manager may be "bailed out" by good economic times. In our example, there is a 40% probability of the high payoff even though the manager shirks. In general, the harder the manager works, the lower the probability of the low payoff.

Finally, note that effort is interpreted quite broadly. Effort goes beyond a literal interpretation as the number of hours worked, and includes such factors as the care the manager takes in running the firm, the diligence with which subordinates are motivated and supervised, the absence of perquisite-taking, and so on. In effect, effort is a modelling device that encompasses the whole range of activities undertaken by a manager during the year.

We summarize the example up to this point in Table 9.2. The dollar amounts in the table represent the payoffs under each of the four payoff/act combinations. The probabilities are conditional on the chosen act, that is, if a_1 is chosen by the manager the probability of x_1 is 0.6, whereas it is 0.4 if a_2 is chosen, and so on.[3]

Table 9.2 Payoffs for Agency Example

| | Manager's Effort | | | |
| | a_1 (work hard) | | a_2 (shirk) | |
	Payoff	Probability	Payoff	Probability
x_1 (high payoff)	$100	0.6	$100	0.4
x_2 (low payoff)	55	0.4	55	0.6

As mentioned, the payoff is not observable until after the expiration of the current period. Figure 9.2 shows a timeline of the agency model.

Figure 9.2 Timeline for Agency Model

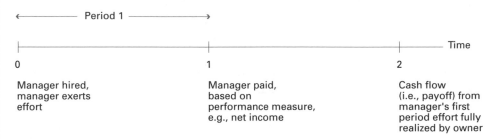

Now, consider this problem from the standpoint of the owner of the firm. The owner wishes to hire the manager to operate the firm for the year, that is, the owner will have no direct control over the act taken. Indeed, it is unlikely that the owner can even observe which act the manager takes. Nevertheless, to maximize the expected payoff, the owner would like the manager to work hard, that is, to choose a_1, because the probability of the high payoff is higher conditional on a_1 than on a_2.

To illustrate this more formally, assume that the owner is risk-neutral and that the owner's utility from a given payoff is equal to the dollar amount of that payoff. Assume also that the manager receives a fixed salary of $25 for the period. Then, the owner's expected utility conditional on each act is:

$$EU_O(a_1) = 0.6(100 - 25) + 0.4(55 - 25)$$
$$= 0.6 \times 75 + 0.4 \times 30$$
$$= 45 + 12$$
$$= 57$$

$$EU_O(a_2) = 0.4(100 - 25) + 0.6(55 - 25)$$
$$= 0.4 \times 75 + 0.6 \times 30$$
$$= 30 + 18$$
$$= 48$$

where $EU_O(a_1)$ denotes the owner's expected utility given that the manager chooses a_1, and similarly for a_2. Just as in decision theory, we assume the players wish to maximize their expected utilities. Consequently, the owner wants the manager to choose a_1, because its expected utility to the owner is greater. It should be clear that this result will hold for any probabilities such that the probability of x_1 given a_1 is greater than it is given a_2.

Now consider matters from the manager's standpoint. Let the manager be risk-averse. Specifically, assume that his or her utility from remuneration equals the square root of the remuneration.

Will the manager *want* to work for the owner? Assume that there is a reasonably efficient **managerial labour market**. This market puts a value on the manager's services, where the value depends on the manager's ability, including training, experience, and reputation. If the manager is to be willing to work for the owner for the current period, the compensation offered must be sufficiently large that his/her expected utility is at least equal to its opportunity cost, that is, the utility that could be attained by the manager in the next best employment opportunity. This is the concept of **reservation utility**. We assume that the manager's reservation utility is 3. If the contract does not offer at least this amount, the manager will go elsewhere. Of course, the manager would prefer to receive a utility greater than 3. However, other managers would also like to work for this firm. If the manager asks for more than 3, the owner may well hire someone else. Consequently, given reasonable competition in the labour market for managers, we expect the manager to be willing to work for a utility of 3.

Now, given that the manager is hired, will a_1 in fact be chosen, as desired by the owner? First, it is important to remind ourselves again that in game theory, and in agency theory in particular, one player will not choose an act desired by another player just because that player says so. Rather, each player chooses the act that maximizes his or her own expected utility. This observation is consistent with positive accounting theory, as discussed in Chapter 8.

Consequently, if the manager chooses a_1, it must be because the manager's expected utility is at least as great for a_1 as for a_2. Note that this assumption differs from much economic analysis, where it is simply *assumed* that firms act in a manner to maximize their profits. This expected utility-maximizing behaviour by all parties is one of the important and distinguishing characteristics of positive accounting theory and the economic theory of games.

Next, assume that the manager is **effort-averse**. This means that the manager dislikes effort and that the greater the level of effort the greater the dislike. In effect, the disutility of effort is subtracted from the utility of remuneration.

Consequently, we will assume:

$$\text{Disutility of effort level } a_1 = 2.00$$
$$\text{Disutility of effort level } a_2 = 1.71$$

We can now calculate the manager's expected utility, net of the disutility of effort, for each act. Recall that the manager is offered a salary of $25.

$$EU_m(a_1) = \sqrt{25} - 2.00 = 3$$
$$EU_m(a_2) = \sqrt{25} - 1.71 = 3.29$$

where $EU_m(a_1)$ denotes the expected utility of the manager, given that the manager chooses a_1, and similarly for a_2. The manager will choose a_2.[4]

This result is not very surprising. Most people, even managers, would prefer to take it easy, all other things being equal. Here, other things *are* equal, because the manager receives a salary of $25 regardless. This tendency of an agent to shirk is an example of moral hazard.

Designing a Contract to Control Moral Hazard The question now is, what should the owner do in a situation such as that described in Example 9.2? One possibility is for the owner to refuse to hire the manager. But any other rational salaried manager would also choose a_2. Consequently, the owner could either go out of business or run the firm him/herself. These possibilities are unlikely, however. The running of an organization is a complex and specialized task for which the owner may not have the required skills, and, after all, we do witness a separation of ownership and management in all but the smallest organizations. In fact, our owner has a number of other options, which we will now consider.

Hire the manager and put up with a_2 The owner could proceed anyway, letting the manager get away with a_2 and putting up with a utility of 48 rather than 57. This also seems unlikely, however, since we will see that the owner can do better than this.

Direct monitoring If the owner could costlessly observe the manager's chosen act, this would solve the problem. Then, the contract could be amended to pay the manager a salary of $25 if a_1 was taken and, say, $12 otherwise. It is easy to verify that the manager would then choose a_1, because choosing a_2 would result in only $12 remuneration and expected utility of 1.75.

A contract where direct monitoring is possible is called **first-best**. It gives the owner the maximum attainable utility (57) and gives the agent his/her reservation utility (3). Under the assumptions of Example 9.2, no other contract can improve on this.

The first-best contract also has desirable **risk-sharing** properties. Note that under this contract the manager bears none of the firm's risk, because a fixed salary is received regardless of the payoff. Since the manager is risk-averse, this is desirable. The owner bears all the risk of the random payoff. Since the owner is risk-neutral, he or she does not mind bearing risk. Indeed, we could argue that a function of business ownership is to bear risk. If the owner was risk-averse, rather than risk-neutral, the first-best contract would involve the owner and manager sharing the risk. However, demonstration of this is beyond our scope.

Unfortunately, the first-best contract is frequently unattainable. This would seem to be the case in an owner–manager contract, because it is unlikely that the owner could monitor the agent's effort in a managerial setting. The nature of managerial effort is so complex that it would be effectively impossible for a remote owner to establish whether the manager was in fact "working hard." We thus have a case of **information asymmetry**—the manager knows the effort level, but the owner does not. As mentioned previously, this particular form of information asymmetry is called moral hazard.

Indirect monitoring Given that managerial effort is not directly observable, it may be possible under some conditions to impute the effort. To illustrate, let us change our example slightly. See Table 9.3. The only difference between this table and Table 9.2 is that the payoff for (x_2, a_2) is now $40 rather than $55. In agency theory terms, this is a case of **moving support**, that is, the set of possible payoffs is different (it moves) depending on which act is taken. Table 9.2 is a case of **fixed support**—the set of possible payoffs is fixed at (100, 55), regardless of the action choice.

Table 9.3 Payoffs for Agency Example

	Manager's Effort			
	a₁ (work hard)		a₂ (shirk)	
	Payoff	Probability	Payoff	Probability
x_1 (high payoff)	$100	0.6	$100	0.4
x_2 (low payoff)	55	0.4	40	0.6

It is apparent from Table 9.3 that if the owner observes a payoff of $40 it will be known that the manager chose a_2 even though effort is not directly observable. Then the owner could amend the contract to offer the manager a salary of $25 unless the payoff turns out to be $40, in which case the manager would be obligated to later return $13 to the owner as a penalty, for a net salary of $12. It is easy to check that the manager would then choose a_1:

$$EU_m(a_1) = \sqrt{25} - 2 \qquad\qquad = 3$$

$$EU_m(a_2) = 0.4\sqrt{25} + 0.6\sqrt{12} - 1.71 = 2.37$$

The penalty of $13 if the $40 payoff happens is sufficient cause for the agent to choose a_1. This contract is also first-best, since the agent works hard, bears no risk, and receives reservation utility, thereby maximizing the owner's expected payoff.

Indirect monitoring will *not* work for the fixed-support case of Table 9.2, however. The reason is that if a payoff of $55 is observed, this is consistent with either a_1 or a_2, and similarly for the $100 payoff. Thus, the owner cannot impute the act from the payoff.

It seems, then, that we cannot rely on indirect monitoring to ensure that the first-best contract will be attained. First, many contracting situations may be characterized by fixed support. For example, in many cases the payoff may be any positive or negative number. If the payoff is, say, a loss of $1 million the owner cannot be certain whether this loss resulted from low manager effort or an unfortunate realization of the firm's risk.

Second, even if moving support holds, legal and institutional factors may prevent the owner from penalizing the manager sufficiently to force a_1. For example, it may be difficult for the owner to collect $13 from the manager after the current one-year contract has expired.

Owner rents firm to the manager At this point, the owner may well be tempted to say to the manager, "O.K., I give up—*you* take the firm and run it, taking 100% of the profits after paying me a fixed rental of $51." Then, the owner no longer cares what action the manager takes, since a rental of $51 is received regardless. This is referred to as **internalizing** the manager's decision problem.

Such arrangements do exist, or they have existed in the past, in the form of tenant farming. Tenant farming is usually regarded as inefficient, however, and it is easy to see why. The manager's expected utility would be:

$$EU_m(a_1) = 0.6 \sqrt{100 - 51} + 0.4 \sqrt{55 - 51} - 2$$
$$= 0.6 \times 7 + 0.4 \times 2 - 2$$
$$= 4.2 + 0.8 - 2$$
$$= 3.00$$

$$EU_m(a_2) = 0.4 \sqrt{100 - 51} + 0.6 \sqrt{55 - 51} - 1.71$$
$$= 0.4 \times 7 + 0.6 \times 2 - 1.71$$
$$= 2.80 + 1.20 - 1.71$$
$$= 2.29$$

Thus, the manager will choose a_1 and receive reservation utility of 3.

Note, however, that the owner receives a utility of 51 in this contract, compared to 57 in the first-best contract. Consequently, the owner is worse off. The reason is that this contracting arrangement has inefficient risk-sharing characteristics. The owner is risk-neutral, and hence is willing to bear risk, but there is no risk for the owner because a fixed rental is received. The risk-averse manager, who dislikes risk, is forced to bear it all. The owner must lower the rental from $57 to $51 to enable the manager to receive reservation utility of 3, costing the owner 6 in lost utility. The 6 is called an **agency cost** (Jensen and Meckling, 1976), and is another component of contracting costs, which the owner will want to minimize.

Give the manager a share of the profits Finally, we come to what is often the most efficient alternative if the first-best contract is not attainable. This is for the owner to give the manager a share of firm performance. However, the owner immediately runs into a problem. The payoff is not fully observable until next period. Yet the manager must be compensated at the end of the current period.

A solution to the problem is to base compensation on a **performance measure,** that is, on some jointly observable variable that reflects the manager's performance[5] and is available at the end of the first period. Net income is such a performance measure. Net income tells us *something* about manager performance, since much of manager effort shows up in current earnings. Effort devoted to cost control, maintenance, employee morale, and advertising will typically affect net income with little lag, for example. We then say that net income is **informative** about manager effort.

Unfortunately, net income is not *fully* informative about effort. One reason is the failure of corporate governance, such as weak internal controls, which allow random error or bias into net income. Recognition lag is another reason, since, as mentioned above, several components of manager effort may not fully pay off during the current period. R&D is a common example. While most R&D costs are written off currently, the realization of revenues from current R&D expenditures may be delayed until after the current period. As a result, a random understatement of the ultimate payoff is introduced into net income. Alternatively, or in addition, current manager effort may have a side-effect of creating environmental or legal liabilities that may not be known until next period, with the result that net income contains a random overstatement of the payoff.

Of course, through accruals, net income anticipates at least some of the ultimate cash flows from current manager performance. Thus, under IASB and Canadian accounting standards, development costs may be capitalized, and estimated environmental liabilities may be accrued. This is consistent with the FASB's argument in SFAC 1 (Section 3.8) that earnings based on accrual accounting generally provide a better indicator of future cash flows than do current cash flows.

Nevertheless, since accruals are subject to error and bias, and since reliability concerns prevent them from completely removing recognition lag, net income does not tell the full story about current manager performance. Thus, the research component of R&D is expensed, and legal and environmental liabilities may be too unreliable to accrue. However, we assume in this section that despite net income not telling the full story, it is unbiased or noisy. While net income may be understated or overstated relative to the payoff, the expected value of the various understatements and overstatements is zero.

In sum, in this section, we regard net income as a noisy, unbiased **message** about the payoff.

Example 9.3
Net Income as a Performance Measure

To illustrate the use of net income in compensation contracts, we extend Example 9.2. Recall from Table 9.2 that if the manager works hard (a_1) the probability of the high payoff ($100) is 0.6, with 0.4 probability of the low payoff ($55). If the manager shirks (a_2), the probabilities of the high and low payoffs are 0.4 and 0.6, respectively. As explained at the time, the reason why the payoff can be low even if the manager works hard, and vice versa, is because of the various risks faced by the firm. Despite hard work, bad economic times may result in the low payoff. Alternatively, good times may rescue the manager who shirks. These risks can be reduced by manager effort, but cannot be eliminated, as reflected in the 0.4 probability of low payoff given a_1 and the 0.4 probability of high payoff given a_2. In sum, while the manager can increase the probability of the high payoff by working hard, a high payoff cannot be guaranteed. Nor can it be guaranteed that shirking will result in a low payoff.

Furthermore, noisy net income introduces a second source of compensation risk for the manager—given the ultimate payoff, compensation will still vary depending on which net income is realized. To reflect the noise in net income, assume the following:

- If the payoff is going to be $100, net income for the current period will be $115 with probability 0.8 and $40 with probability 0.2.

- If the payoff is going to be $55, net income for the current period will be $115 with probability 0.2 and $40 with probability 0.8.

The noise in net income could result from the random effects of internal control failure and recognition lag, as discussed earlier.

There are thus two possible net income numbers. The manager who works hard requires a 0.3237 share of net income to attain reservation utility of 3. This is verified as follows:

$$
\begin{aligned}
EU_m(a_1) &= 0.6\left[0.8\sqrt{0.3237 \times 115} + 0.2\sqrt{0.3237 \times 40}\right] \\
&\quad + 0.4\left[0.2\sqrt{0.3237 \times 115} + 0.8\sqrt{0.3237 \times 40}\right] - 2 \\
&= 0.6\left[0.8\sqrt{37.2255} + 0.2\sqrt{12.9480}\right] \\
&\quad + 0.4\left[0.2\sqrt{37.2255} + 0.8\sqrt{12.9480}\right] - 2 \\
&= 0.6 \times 5.6007 + 0.4 \times 4.0989 - 2 \\
&= 3.3604 + 1.6396 - 2 \\
&= 3.00
\end{aligned}
$$

Recall that the manager's utility for money is given by the square root of the amount received and that the effort disutility of working hard is 2. The expression in the first set of square brackets is the expected utility of compensation given the high payoff. That is, if the payoff is going to be $100, net income will be $115 with probability 0.8 or $40 with probability 0.2. The result is then multiplied by the probability of the high payoff (0.6). A similar interpretation applies to the second expression, given the low payoff.

If the manager shirks, expected utility is 2.9896, net of effort disutility of 1.71, as follows:

$$
\begin{aligned}
EU_m(a_2) &= 0.4 \times 5.6007 + 0.6 \times 4.0989 - 1.71 \\
&= 2.2403 + 2.4593 - 1.71 \\
&= 2.9896
\end{aligned}
$$

Consequently, the manager will work hard.[6]

As in Example 9.2, the owner is risk-neutral, with utility equal to the dollar amount of the payoff, net of manager compensation. The owner's expected utility is now:

$$
\begin{aligned}
EU_0(a_1) &= 0.6\left[0.8(100 - (0.3237 \times 115)) + 0.2(100 - (0.3237 \times 40))\right] \\
&\quad + 0.4\left[0.2(55 - (0.3237 \times 115)) + 0.8(55 - (0.3237 \times 40))\right] \\
&= 0.6\left[0.8(100 - 37.2255) + 0.2(100 - 12.9480)\right] \\
&\quad + 0.4\left[0.2(55 - 37.2255) + 0.8(55 - 12.9480)\right] \\
&= 0.6 \times 67.6300 + 0.4 \times 37.1965 \\
&= 40.5780 + 14.8786 \\
&= 55.4566
\end{aligned}
$$

> The first expression in square brackets is the expected payoff net of manager compensation, given the high payoff. This is multiplied by the probability of the high payoff. A similar interpretation applies to the second expression given the low payoff.

Note that the owner's utility is greater than the utility of 51 under the rental contract. Thus the profit-sharing contract is more efficient. However, it is less efficient than the first-best contract of Example 9.2, where the owner's utility is 57. The agency cost is now $57 - 55.4566 = 1.5434$.

These differences in the owner's utility can also be explained in terms of the agent's compensation risk. In the first-best contract, the manager bears no risk, since a salary of $25 is expected regardless of the amount of net income (i.e., zero profit share). In the rental contract (i.e., a 100% profit share), the manager bears all of the risk. In Example 9.3, the manager bears only part of the risk (i.e., a 0.3237 profit share). Given the effort level, the more risk borne by the manager, the higher the profit share needed to overcome the manager's risk aversion and enable reservation utility to be attained.[7] The higher the profit share to the manager, the less there remains for the owner or, equivalently, the higher the agency cost. Thus, the agency costs are zero, 1.5434, and 6 for the first-best, profit sharing, and rental contracts, respectively. The most efficient contract short of first-best is called **second-best**.[8]

Note that it is the *contract* that motivates the manager to work hard in this example. Given the terms of the contract, the manager *wants* to take a_1. This aspect of the contract is called **incentive-compatibility**, since the agent's incentive to take a_1 is compatible with the owner's best interests. (The first-best contract, if it is attainable, is also incentive-compatible, because the prospect of reduced remuneration following a_2 motivates the manager to take a_1.) We then say that the owner's and manager's interests are **aligned**, since they both want the firm to do well.

Agency costs are one of the costs of contracting that are part of positive accounting theory. As discussed in Section 8.5.1, the firm will want to arrange its corporate governance as efficiently as possible, and we pointed out there that efficient contracts will depend on the firm's form of organization and its environment. Since the firm in Example 9.3 is organized with a separation of ownership and control, we would expect it to design and adopt profit-sharing contracts with the lowest agency costs. Such contracts impose the minimum compensation risk needed to motivate the manager to work hard.

This raises the question, can accountants improve the ability of net income to reflect manager effort and improve payoff prediction? This question is an important one for accountants. A less noisy net income will reduce compensation risk, enabling a lower profit-sharing proportion for the manager and increased contracting efficiency. This enhances the role of net income as a performance measure in managerial compensation plans.

Example 9.4
Less Noisy Net Income

A possible way to improve payoff prediction is to reduce recognition lag. To illustrate, suppose that improvements in estimating environmental liabilities, and new accounting standards to reliably determine fair value of R&D, enable reduced noise in net income compared with Example 9.3, while retaining unbiasedness.

Assume that the lower noise in net income is as follows:

- If the payoff is going to be $100, net income for the current period will be $110 with probability 0.8462 and $45 with probability 0.1538.

- If the payoff is going to be $55, net income for the current period will be $110 with probability 0.1538 and $45 with probability 0.8462.

The differences from Example 9.3 are that net income, while still noisy and unbiased, falls within a narrower range of the ultimate payoffs and has a greater probability of reporting high when the payoff is going to be high, and a greater probability of reporting low when the payoff is going to be low. It can be verified that the manager now requires 0.3185 of profits to attain reservation utility, down from 0.3237 above (see problem 19). Also, the manager continues to work hard.

The owner's expected utility is now:

$$
\begin{aligned}
EU_o(a_1) &= 0.6\big[0.8462(100 - (0.3185 \times 110)) + 0.1538(100 - (0.3185 \times 45))\big] \\
&\quad + 0.4\big[0.1538(55 - (0.3185 \times 110)) + 0.8462(55 - (0.3185 \times 45))\big] \\
&= 0.6[0.8462(100 - 35.0350) + 0.1538(100 - 14.3325)] \\
&\quad + 0.4[0.1538(55 - 35.0350) + 0.8462(55 - 14.3325)] \\
&= 0.6 \times 68.1491 + 0.4 \times 37.4834 \\
&= 40.8895 + 14.9934 \\
&= 55.8829
\end{aligned}
$$

The owner's expected utility is greater than that of the noisier contract of Example 9.3 (55.4566), reflecting reduced agency cost of $57 - 55.8829 = 1.1171$ in place of 1.5434 in Example 9.3. The improvement in accounting precision enables a more efficient compensation contract.

9.5 MANAGER'S INFORMATION ADVANTAGE

9.5.1 Earnings Management

In Section 9.4, we assumed that the payoff was not observable by the owner or the manager until the next period. Net income, which *is* observable currently by both parties, was viewed as a noisy, unbiased message about what the payoff will be.

Consequently, the manager had no reporting discretion in Section 9.4. Net income was viewed simply as a noisy number produced by an accounting system. The manager could not control or manage this number since the noise resulted from the characteristics of the system rather than from anything the manager does. Of course, as we showed in Example 9.4, even in the absence of earnings management, accountants can increase contracting efficiency by reducing the noise through improved measurement.

Nevertheless, as any accountant knows, managers frequently do engage in earnings management. Indeed, this is a prediction of positive accounting theory. To better understand the role of net income as a performance measure, we must allow for the possibility that the manager may bias or otherwise manage reported earnings.

There is a variety of forms that manager information advantage can take. One possibility is that the manager may have information about the payoff prior to signing the contract (called **pre-contract information**). For example, the manager may have information that the high payoff will occur, and, unless the owner can extract this information, may enter into the contract with the intention of shirking, taking advantage of the high payoff to generate high earnings and compensation. Alternatively, the manager may obtain payoff information after signing the contract but prior to choosing an act (**pre-decision information**). If the payoff information is sufficiently bad, the manager may resign unless this situation is allowed for in the contract. Yet another possibility is that the manager receives information after the act is chosen (**post-decision information**). For example, the manager may learn what net income is before reporting to the owner. If the owner cannot observe unmanaged net income, the manager may manage earnings so as to maximize compensation.

Here, we will examine a case of post-decision information. Specifically, we extend Example 9.3 by adding an assumption that the owner cannot observe which of the two possible net income numbers is actually realized. Only the manager can observe this. What the owner does observe is an earnings number *reported by* the manager. This assumption seems reasonable since the manager has the ability to influence the accounting system, creating the possibility that reported net income may be biased for his/her own purposes.[9]

Example 9.5
Biased Reporting

Recall from Example 9.3 that there were two possible net income numbers. If the payoff is going to be $100, unmanaged net income will be $115 with probability 0.8 or $40 with probability 0.2. If the payoff is going to be $55, unmanaged net income will be $115 with probability 0.2 or $40 with probability 0.8. When the owner cannot observe which of these is actually realized, reporting may be delegated to the manager. Then, it is not hard to see how the manager will opportunistically exploit this information advantage in a single-period contract. Given that the manager bears no costs to manage earnings, and that the owner is committed by contract to pay the manager a portion of reported net income, the manager will shirk and report net income of $115 regardless of what unmanaged net income is. More formally:

$$EU_m(a_1) = 0.6[0.8 \sqrt{115k} + 0.2 \sqrt{115k}] + 0.4[0.2 \sqrt{115k} + 0.8 \sqrt{115k}] - 2$$
$$= \sqrt{115k} - 2$$

$$EU_m(a_2) = 0.4[0.2 \sqrt{115k} + 0.8 \sqrt{115k}] + 0.6[0.2 \sqrt{115k} + 0.8 \sqrt{115k}] - 1.71$$
$$= \sqrt{115k} - 1.71$$

where k is the profit-sharing proportion. Obviously, the manager will choose a_2 for any k. To receive reservation utility, the manager now requires $k = 0.1929$:

$$EU_m(a_2) = \sqrt{0.1929 \times 115} - 1.71$$
$$= \sqrt{22.1835} - 1.71$$
$$= 4.7099 - 1.71$$
$$= 3$$

The owner's expected utility is now:

$$EU_O(a_2) = 0.4(100 - (0.1929 \times 115)) + 0.6(55 - (0.1929 \times 115))$$
$$= 0.4(100 - 22.1835) + 0.6(55 - 22.1835)$$
$$= 0.4 \times 77.8165 + 0.6 \times 32.8165$$
$$= 31.1266 + 19.6899$$
$$= 50.8165$$

This is less than the owner's utility in the contract of Example 9.3 (55.4566). The reduction arises because the manager can report the maximum net income regardless of effort. Consequently, the manager will shirk, and the owner's expected utility reflects the resulting lower expected payoff. Note also that the manager bears no risk, since the same compensation is received regardless of the payoff. We know from Example 9.3 that the manager bears risk if the work-hard effort alternative is to be chosen.

While the owner's utility is lower in Example 9.5 than in Example 9.3, Example 9.5 more closely approximates the actual situation of a firm owner, since we would normally *expect* the manager to have an information advantage, possibly using it to manage earnings. Given separation of ownership and control, it is unlikely that the owner would be able to observe the detailed workings of the firm's accounting and reporting systems. Then, the question arises, can the owner do anything to control this obviously unsatisfactory situation?

Example 9.6
The Revelation Principle[*]

In Example 9.5, the manager does not report truthfully. Can truthful reporting be motivated? If so, this would at least eliminate earnings management, regardless of its effect on effort. The answer is a qualified yes. To illustrate, suppose that the owner offers the following amended contract in Example 9.5:

If net income is reported as \$115, $k = 0.1929$

If net income is reported as \$40, $k = 0.5546$

It is easy to verify that the manager still receives compensation of \$22.18 as in Example 9.5, regardless of what net income is reported (e.g., if net income of \$40 is reported, compensation is $40 \times 0.5546 = 22.18$). Consequently, since no risk is borne, he/she will continue to shirk, receiving reservation utility of 3 as before. The owner continues to receive expected utility of 50.8165. *What is different is that there is now* no incentive for the manager to distort reported net income, since the same compensation is received regardless of what amount is reported.[10] This example illustrates what is called the **revelation principle** (Myerson, 1979; see also Christensen, 1981, and Arya, Glover, and Sunder, 1998). For any contract under which the manager has an incentive to lie about his/her private information, an equivalent contract can be designed that motivates truth-telling.

The revelation principle raises an intriguing question. Why not design real compensation contracts to motivate truth-telling? Then, opportunistic earnings management would be a thing of the past. While managers would tend to shirk, the shirking would be no greater than what would take place without truth-telling, and the owner's expected utility would be the same. The benefit would be a reduced adverse selection problem due to increased investor confidence that reported net income is free of manager distortion and bias.

---

[*]The remainder of this section, and Section 9.5.2, can be skipped with little loss of continuity.

However, the revelation principle is not a panacea. There are several conditions that must be met if it is to hold. One such condition is that the owner must be able to commit that the truth will not be used against the manager. For example, if the manager anticipates that truthfully reporting net income of $40 in Example 9.6 may result in being fired by an angry owner, he/she is unlikely to report the truth.

A second condition is that there must be no restrictions on the form of contract. For example, many compensation contracts do not provide for a bonus unless performance exceeds some specified level, such as earnings greater than 10% of shareholders' equity. In addition, the amount of bonus may be capped so that no bonus is payable on earnings greater than, say, 25% of equity. When such restrictions exist, we cannot be sure that the contract that motivates truth-telling will meet these restrictions. For example, if no bonus is paid on earnings greater than 25% of equity, it is hard to say that the owner is not using the truth against the manager.

A third condition is that there are no restrictions on the manager's ability to communicate his/her information. Suppose, for example, that a manager has a forecast of next year's earnings, but that honest reporting of the forecast is potentially very costly to the manager personally, due to loss of reputation and possible legal liability if the forecast is not met. A contract to motivate truthful reporting of the forecast would impose so much risk on the manager that the level of compensation needed to attain reservation utility may be more than the owner is willing to pay. Honest communication is effectively blocked. Consequently, the owner may allow the manager to report a biased forecast, or no forecast at all.

The impact of these restrictions is that we cannot rely on the revelation principle to assure us that the most efficient possible compensation contract involves truth telling. Under the assumptions of Example 9.5, a profit-sharing contract of 0.1929 of reported net income to the manager, with owner's utility of 50.8165, *is* the most efficient one available. If the revelation principle applies, we know from Example 9.6 that an equivalent contract involving reporting the truth yields the same utility to the owner. However, if the revelation principle does not apply, motivation of truthful reporting may require an increase in manager compensation, lowering the owner's expected utility below that of a contract that allows earnings management.

To illustrate, suppose that net income is reported as $40 and the manager receives high compensation (i.e., $22.18) despite low reported earnings. Angry shareholders and media reports would likely adversely affect the manager's reputation. Suppose that the manager anticipates that these costs have a personal monetary equivalent of $3. Then, if he/she is to report this amount truthfully, a profit share of 0.6295 is needed, giving compensation of $0.6295 \times 40 = 25.18. Allowing for the reputation costs of $3, the manager's net compensation is $22.18, the same as before. However, paying the extra $3 of compensation lowers the owner's expected utility. The owner is better off to revert to the contract of Example 9.5, which allows earnings management, thereby saving $3 in compensation and restoring expected utility of 50.8165.

In effect, it is unlikely that the revelation principle can eliminate earnings management. Yet, Example 9.5 illustrates how earnings management can lead to manager shirking. Can accountants help? An answer lies in GAAP.

While GAAP allows discretion in choosing among different accounting policies, it does limit the amount by which earnings can be managed. In Example 9.5, if unmanaged net income of, say, $40 is realized, could the manager really increase reported earnings to $115? Hopefully, accounting standards do not allow distortion of this magnitude, particularly when the financial statements are audited. By delegating some reporting discretion to the manager, but controlling through GAAP the magnitude of the resulting earnings management, the manager's incentive to work hard can be restored and the owner made better off.

*9.5.2 Controlling Earnings Management

A way to control earnings management is to limit it by means of GAAP, to the point where the manager's incentive to work hard is restored. Consider the following example.

Example 9.7
Limiting the Bias in Net Income

Extend Example 9.5 to replace each possible net income number (i.e., $115, $40) with a $5 range. Thus, net income of $115 is replaced by the range [$111–$116]. Similarly, net income of $40 is replaced with the range [$36–$41].

This range assumption recognizes the flexibility allowed by GAAP as discussed in Section 8.5.1. Straight-line and declining-balance amortization of capital assets are both acceptable methods, for example. Consequently, net income will differ depending on which method is chosen. The assumption of a range for unmanaged net income is also consistent with our argument in Section 2.6 that true net income does not exist.

The payoff probabilities are assumed unchanged. For example, if the manager works hard, the probability of the high payoff is still 0.6. We assume that the owner knows the two possible earnings ranges, and knows which range has occurred. For example, if the manager reports $116, the owner knows that while the manager may have biased this number, at least GAAP net income is in the range [$111–$116]. This captures the fact that GAAP does impose some discipline on reported earnings. However, the owner does not know the actual unmanaged net income within that range.

To maximize compensation in a single-period contract, the rational manager will report the upper end of the appropriate range. For example, suppose that unmanaged net income is $112, that is, it is in the [$111–$116] range. Think of the $112 as the

---

*This section can be omitted with little loss of continuity.

earnings number that results from the accounting policies and methods used by the firm *before* discretionary accruals or other earnings management devices are applied. We can also think of $112 as the net income number most useful to investors.

Given information advantage, however, the manager will engage in earnings management to bias reported earnings up to $116. This could be accomplished, within GAAP, in a number of ways. For example, the manager may accelerate revenue recognition, or switch from declining-balance to straight-line amortization. Note, however, unlike Example 9.5, that the manager cannot switch between ranges without violating GAAP. Thus, if unmanaged net income falls in the [$36–$41] range, reporting a net income of $116 would incur auditor qualification.

Knowing that the manager will report the upper end of the range, a compensation contract of 0.3193 of reported net income enables the manager to attain reservation utility. To verify, suppose a_1 is taken. Then, the manager's expected utility is:

$$
\begin{aligned}
EU_m(a_1) &= 0.6\big[0.8\ \sqrt{0.3193 \times 116} + 0.2\ \sqrt{0.3193 \times 41}\,\big] \\
&\quad + 0.4\big[0.2\ \sqrt{0.3193 \times 116} + 0.8\ \sqrt{0.3193 \times 41}\,\big] - 2 \\
&= 0.6\big[0.8 \times 6.0860 + 0.2 \times 3.6182\big] + 0.4\big[0.2 \times 6.0860 + 0.8\ \times 3.6182\big] - 2 \\
&= 0.6 \times 5.5924 + 0.4 \times 4.1118 - 2 \\
&= 3.3554 + 1.6447 - 2 \\
&= 3.00
\end{aligned}
$$

The first quantity in square brackets is the manager's expected compensation if the high payoff occurs. Under the high payoff, net income is in the range [$111–$116] with probability 0.8 and [$36–$41] with probability 0.2. As mentioned, the manager will report the upper end of the range. This expected compensation is multiplied by the probability of the high payoff (0.6). A similar interpretation applies to the second quantity.

If act a_2 is taken:

$$
\begin{aligned}
EU_m(a_2) &= 0.4\big[0.8\ \sqrt{0.3193 \times 116} + 0.2\ \sqrt{0.3193 \times 41}\,\big] \\
&\quad + 0.6\big[0.2\ \sqrt{0.3193 \times 116} + 0.8\ \sqrt{0.3193 \times 41}\,\big] - 1.71 \\
&= 0.4 \times 5.5924 + 0.6 \times 4.1118 - 1.71 \\
&= 2.99
\end{aligned}
$$

Thus the manager will now take a_1. The restrictions imposed by GAAP and auditing on the ability to misreport does not eliminate the manager's ability to exploit his/her information advantage, but reduces it to the point where hard work must be undertaken to attain reservation utility.

As might be expected, this limitation on the manager's ability to misreport benefits the owner. In fact, the owner's expected utility is now:

$$EU_o(a_1) = 0.6[0.8(100 - (0.3193 \times 116)) + 0.2(100 - (0.3193 \times 41))]$$
$$+ 0.4[0.2(55 - (0.3193 \times 116)) + 0.8(55 - (0.3193 \times 41))]$$

$$= 0.6[0.8(100 - 37.0388) + 0.2(100 - 13.0913)]$$
$$+ 0.4[0.2(55 - 37.0388) + 0.8(55 - 13.0913)]$$

$$= 0.6(0.8 \times 62.9612 + 0.2 \times 86.9087) + 0.4(0.2 \times 17.9612 + 0.8 \times 41.9087)$$

$$= 0.6 \times 67.7507 + 0.4 \times 37.1192$$

$$= 40.6504 + 14.8477$$

$$= 55.4981$$

The owner is thus better off than under the contract of Example 9.5, where expected utility was 50.8165. This is because the limitation imposed by GAAP on the manager's ability to manage net income has enabled a contract that restores an incentive to work hard. Note, however, that the contract does allow for some earnings management since, unless unmanaged net income is at the upper end of its range, the manager will bias it upwards.[11] In this sense, some degree of within-GAAP earnings management can be "good," even in a one-period contract.[12] We will return to this point in Chapter 11.

9.6 DISCUSSION AND SUMMARY

In this section, we have studied a single-period agency model. This model illustrates several important aspects of agency theory:

1. Observability of an agent's effort seems unlikely in an owner–manager context, because of the separation of ownership and control that characterizes firms in a developed industrial society. This is an example of information asymmetry leading to moral hazard. The rational manager will, if possible, take advantage of the lack of effort observability to shirk. Agency theory, a branch of game theory, studies the problem of designing a contract to control moral hazard. The most efficient contract does so with the lowest possible agency cost.

2. The nature of the most efficient contract depends crucially on what can be jointly observed. Contracts can only be written in terms of performance measures that are jointly observable by both principal and agent:

   ■ If the agent's effort can be jointly observed, directly or indirectly, a fixed salary (subject to a penalty if the contracted-for effort level is not taken) is most efficient when the principal is risk-neutral. Such a contract is called first-best. There is no agency cost. Here, *effort* is the performance measure.

   ■ Unless the firm is of very short duration, it is unlikely that the payoff from the current period's manager effort can be observed until after the end of the current period. This is because the cash flows from certain types of manager effort, such as R&D, will not be realized until a subsequent period, that is, until after the current compensation contract has expired. Given that the manager must be paid periodically, compensation cannot be based on the payoff.

- If the agent's effort cannot be jointly observed, but net income can, the most efficient contract may give the agent a share of net income. However, net income is a risky performance measure for the manager, both because the payoff is risky and because current period net income is a noisy measure of this payoff. Since the manager shares in net income, he/she bears compensation risk from both sources. Here, *net income* is the performance measure.

- If effort, payoff, and net income are all unobservable, the optimal contract is a rental contract, whereby the principal rents the firm to the manager for a fixed rental fee, thus internalizing the agent's effort decision. Such contracts are inefficient because they impose all of the firm's risk on the agent, resulting in maximum agency cost. Here, there is *no* performance measure.

3. Since the agent is assumed risk-averse, imposing compensation risk reduces his/her expected utility of compensation. This requires the principal to increase the share of net income so as to maintain the agent's reservation utility. The second-best contract is the contract that imposes the lowest amount of risk on the manager while maintaining reservation utility and the manager's incentive to work hard. Accountants can improve the efficiency of compensation contracts by improving the precision of net income as a payoff predictor.

4. When net income is the performance measure, the manager has a further information advantage over the owner. This is because the manager controls the firm's accounting system, while the owner can observe only the net income number reported by the manager. This leads to the possibility of earnings management. In theory, it may be possible to design a compensation contract to motivate the manager to report unmanaged earnings (i.e., to completely eliminate earnings management), but this is unlikely in practice since it is too costly. However, by using GAAP to limit the range over which earnings can be managed, accountants may be able to maintain the manager's incentive to work hard. This leads to a conclusion that some degree of earnings management can be "good."

9.7 AGENCY THEORY: A BONDHOLDER–MANAGER LENDING CONTRACT

We now consider another moral hazard problem, namely a contract between a lender and a firm, such as a bondholder and the firm manager. We will regard the bondholder as the principal and the manager as the agent.

Example 9.8
A Lender–Manager Agency Problem

A risk-neutral lender faces a choice of lending $100 to a firm or investing the $100 in government bonds yielding 10%. The firm offers 12% interest, contracting to repay the loan one year later, that is, to repay $112. However, unlike for government bonds, there is credit risk, that is, a possibility that the firm will go bankrupt, in which case the lender would lose both the principal and the interest.

The firm manager can choose one of two acts. The first act, denoted by a_1, is to pay no dividends while the loan is outstanding. The second act, a_2, is to pay high dividends. If the manager chooses a_1, assume that the lender assesses the probability of bankruptcy as 0.01, so that there is a 0.99 probability of receiving repayment, including $12 interest. However, if a_2 is chosen, the lender assesses the probability of bankruptcy as 0.1, because the high dividends will reduce the firm's solvency. Thus, under a_2, the probability of repayment will be only 0.9.

Assume that the manager is paid by means of an incentive contract consisting of a salary plus a bonus based on the firm's net income. Then, since dividends are not charged against income, the manager's remuneration is unaffected by the act chosen, that is, the manager is indifferent between the two acts. Thus, there is no compelling reason to assume that the manager will or will not take a_1, the lender's preferred act. After thinking about this, the lender assesses equal probabilities for each act of the manager, that is, the probability of a_1 is 0.5 and similarly for a_2. Table 9.4 summarizes this scenario.

Table 9.4 Payoffs for Lender–Manager Contract

	Manager's Act			
	a_1 (no dividends)		a_2 (high dividends)	
	Payoff	Probability	Payoff	Probability
x_1 (interest paid)	$ 12	0.99	$ 12	0.9
x_2 (bankrupt)	−100	0.01	−100	0.1

The payoff amounts in the table exclude the $100 loaned. Thus, the lender either earns an interest income of $12 or loses the $100 investment. We could add $100 to each payoff, to express returns gross of the $100 loaned, without affecting the results.

The probabilities in the table are conditional on the manager's chosen act. Thus, if a_1 is taken, the probability of the lender receiving the interest is 0.99; hence, the probability of the lender receiving nothing is $1.00 - 0.99 = 0.01$, and so on. Recall that we have also assumed that the chances are 50/50 that a_1 will be chosen.

Will the lender be willing to lend $100 to the firm? The alternative is to buy government bonds, with a return of 10%, or $10 in total. The expected profit from investing in the firm is:

$$ETR = 0.5[(12 \times 0.99) - (100 \times 0.01)] + 0.5[(12 \times 0.9) - (100 \times 0.1)]$$

$$= (0.5 \times 10.88) + (0.5 \times 0.80)$$

$$= 5.44 + 0.40$$

$$= 5.84$$

where ETR denotes expected total return.

The first term in brackets represents the lender's expected return conditional on a_1. There is a 0.5 probability that a_1 will be chosen. Similarly, the second term in brackets is the expected return conditional on a_2, also multiplied by the 0.5 probability that a_2 will be chosen.

Thus, the ETR is only $5.84 or 5.84% on the amount loaned. The reason, of course, is the probability of bankruptcy, particularly if a_2 is taken, which forces the expected return down to well below the nominal rate of 12%. Our lender, who can earn 10% elsewhere, will not make the loan.

What nominal rate would the firm have to offer in order to attract the lender? This can be calculated as follows:

$$10.00 = 0.5[0.99R - (100 \times 0.01)] + 0.5[0.9R - (100 \times 0.1)]$$

where R is the required nominal rate. The left side is the lender's required total return. Upon solving for R, we obtain:

$$R = \frac{15.50}{0.945} = 16.40$$

Thus, the firm would have to offer a nominal rate of return of over 16% in order to attract the lender.

The 16% interest rate in Example 9.8 would probably seem too high to the manager, particularly if he or she shares in net income. Consequently, the manager may try to find some more efficient contractual arrangement that would lower the interest rate. One possibility would be to *commit* to take a_1. This could be done by writing covenants into the lending agreement. An example of a covenant would be to pay no dividends if the interest coverage ratio is below a specified level. Another example would be to not undertake any additional borrowing (which would dilute the security of existing lenders) if shareholders' equity is below a specified level. Since covenants are legally binding, the lender will change the assessed probabilities of the acts. Assume the probability that the manager will take a_1 is now assessed by the lender as 1, and 0 for a_2. Thus, if the firm offers a nominal rate of 12%, the lender's ETR is:

$$ETR = 1[(12 \times 0.99) - (100 \times 0.01)] + 0[(12 \times 0.9) - (100 \times 0.1)] = 10.88$$

Since this exceeds the required $10, the lender would now make the loan.

9.7.1 Summary

The main point to realize in Example 9.8 is the existence of a moral hazard problem between lenders and firm managers—managers may act contrary to the best interests of the lenders. Rational lenders will anticipate this behaviour, however, and raise the interest rates they demand for their loans. As a result, the manager has an incentive to commit not to act in a manner that is against the lenders' interests. This can be done by inserting covenants into the lending agreement whereby the manager agrees to limit dividends or additional borrowing while the loan is outstanding. Consequently, the firm is able to borrow at lower rates.

9.8 IMPLICATIONS OF AGENCY THEORY FOR ACCOUNTING

9.8.1 Is Two Better Than One?

In a widely referenced paper, Holmström (1979) gives a rigorous extension of the agency model to allow more than one performance measure. We now review aspects of his model from an accounting perspective.

Holmström assumes that the agent's effort is unobservable by the principal but that the payoff is jointly observable at the end of the current period. This is contrary to our Examples 9.2 to 9.7. However, Feltham and Xie (1994) show that Holmström's model carries over to the case of payoff unobservable, holding the set of possible manager acts constant. Consequently, we shall continue to assume the payoff is unobservable for purposes of this discussion.

Holmström shows formally that a contract based on a performance measure such as net income is less efficient than first-best, consistent with Example 9.3. As in that example, the source of the efficiency loss is the necessity for the risk-averse agent to bear risk in order to overcome the tendency to shirk.

This raises the question of whether the second-best contract could be made more efficient by basing it on a second performance measure in addition to net income. For example, share price is also informative about manager performance. Rather than basing manager compensation solely on net income, would basing the contract on *both* net income and share price reduce the agency costs of the second-best contract?

Holmström shows that the answer to this question is yes, provided that the second measure is also jointly observable and conveys some information about manager effort beyond that contained in the first measure.[13] This should be the case for share price, since it is jointly observable and based on more information than just accounting information. Granted, share price reflects the information content of net income (Sections 5.3 and 5.4). However, share price on an efficient securities market also reflects other information. For example, it reflects expected future benefits of R&D, and expected future environmental and legal liabilities, sooner than the accounting system. Furthermore, share price may be less subject to manager bias than net income. Consequently, we would expect share price to reveal information about manager effort different from that in reported earnings. Net income, however, may be less subject than share price to volatility created by economy-wide events. Nevertheless, Holmström's analysis shows that no matter how noisy the second variable is, it can increase the efficiency of the second-best contract if it contains at least some additional effort information.[14] In effect, net income and share price can together better reflect current manager effort than either variable alone.

Example 9.9
A Two-Variable Agency Contract*

To illustrate this argument, we now add a second performance measure, namely share price, to Example 9.3.

Recall from Example 9.3 that the payoffs are $100 or $55. Continue the assumptions of that example. That is, net income is unbiased. Also, if the manager works hard, the probability of the high payoff is 0.6 and the probability of the low payoff is 0.4. If the manager shirks, the high and low payoff probabilities are 0.4 and 0.6, respectively. The payoff is not observable until after the manager's contract ends, and net income is used as a performance measure.

Now, however, share price is added to the contract as a second performance measure. Assume that share price at the end of period 1 can be high ($80) or low ($50). Let the joint probabilities of the performance measures be as follows:

Table 9.5 Joint Performance Measure Probabilities

		Payoff High Net Income		Payoff Low Net Income	
		High ($115)	Low ($40)	High ($115)	Low ($40)
Share Price	High ($80)	0.6	0.1	0.1	0.2
	Low ($50)	0.2	0.1	0.1	0.6

---

*Note: This example can be ignored with little loss of continuity.

There are four possible net income/share price combinations. Like net income, share price anticipates the ultimate payoff. If the payoff is going to be high, the probability of a high share price (0.6 + 0.1 = 0.7) is greater than the probability of low share price (0.3). If the payoff is going to be low, these probabilities are reversed. However, the anticipation is not perfect since, for example, there is a (1 − 0.7) 0.3 probability of low share price if the payoff is going to be high. This is because of random economy-wide events (e.g., changes in interest rates) that affect share price.

A 0.308 share of net income and a 0.018 share of share price will motivate the manager to work hard (a_1). This is verified as follows:

$$EU_m(a_1) = 0.6\big[0.6 \sqrt{115 \times 0.308 + 80 \times 0.018} + 0.1 \sqrt{40 \times 0.308 + 80 \times 0.018}$$

$$+ 0.2 \sqrt{115 \times 0.308 + 50 \times 0.018} + 0.1 \sqrt{40 \times 0.308 + 50 \times 0.018}\,\big]$$

$$+ 0.4\big[0.1 \sqrt{115 \times 0.308 + 80 \times 0.018} + 0.2 \sqrt{40 \times 0.308 + 80 \times 0.018}$$

$$+ 0.1 \sqrt{115 \times 0.308 + 50 \times 0.018} + 0.6 \sqrt{40 \times 0.308 + 50 \times 0.018}\,\big] - 2$$

$$= 0.6\big[0.6 \sqrt{36.860} + 0.1 \sqrt{13.760} + 0.2 \sqrt{36.320} + 0.1 \sqrt{13.220}\,\big]$$

$$+ 0.4\big[0.1 \sqrt{36.860} + 0.2 \sqrt{13.760} + 0.1 \sqrt{36.320} + 0.6 \sqrt{13.220}\,\big] - 2$$

$$= 0.6\big[3.643 + 0.371 + 1.205 + 0.364\big] + 0.4\big[0.607 + 0.742 + 0.603 + 2.182\big] - 2$$

$$= 0.6 \times 5.583 + 0.4 \times 4.134 - 2$$

$$= 3.350 + 1.654 - 2$$

$$= 3.004$$

$$= 3.00 \; approx.$$

If the manager shirks (a_2):

$$EU_m(a_2) = 0.4 \times 5.583 + 0.6 \times 4.134 - 1.71$$

$$= 2.233 + 2.480 - 1.71$$

$$= 3.003$$

$$= 3.00 \; approx.$$

Thus the manager will choose a_1 and receive reservation utility of 3.

The owner's expected utility is:

$$EU_o(a_1) = 0.6\big[0.6(100 - 36.86) + 0.1(100 - 13.76) + 0.2(100 - 36.32)$$
$$+ 0.1(100 - 13.22)\big] + 0.4\big[0.1(55 - 36.86) + 0.2(55 - 13.76)$$
$$+ 0.1(55 - 36.32) + 0.6(55 - 13.22)\big]$$

$$= 0.6 \times 67.922 + 0.4 \times 36.998$$

$$= 40.753 + 14.799$$

$$= 55.552$$

The owner's utility is higher than in Example 9.3 (55.4566) Thus, the two-performance-measure contract is more efficient, consistent with the analyses of Holmström and Feltham and Xie. The greater efficiency arises because introduction of a second performance measure provides the manager with some diversification of compensation risk, enabling reservation utility to be attained with lower expected total compensation.[15] Lower compensation shows up as higher expected utility for the owner.[16]

Given the potential for increased contracting efficiency from basing compensation on more than one performance measure, the question then becomes one of the relative *proportion* of compensation based on net income, versus based on share price, in compensation contracts. Hopefully, from an accountant's standpoint, this proportion will be high. Thus, an interesting implication of the Holmström model is that, just as net income competes with other information sources for investors under efficient securities market theory, it competes with other information sources for motivating managers under agency theory.

This raises the question of what characteristics a performance measure should have if it is to contribute to efficient compensation contracts. One important characteristic is its **sensitivity**. Sensitivity is the rate at which the expected value of a performance measure increases as the manager works harder, or decreases as the manager shirks. Sensitivity contributes to efficient compensation contracts by strengthening the connection between manager effort and the performance measure, thereby making it easier to motivate that effort.

Ideally, if the manager changes effort, the expected value of the performance measure should change accordingly. This may not happen, however, to the extent that the performance measure does not capture all aspects of current effort. For example, if an increase in effort is devoted to R&D, current net income would include little, if any, of the payoff from this effort. A move towards current value accounting for R&D can be regarded as a way to increase earnings sensitivity. By recognizing changes in current value sooner, more of the results of manager effort are captured in current income.

Another important characteristic of a performance measure is its **precision** in predicting the payoff from current manager effort. Precision is measured as the reciprocal of the variance of the noise in the performance measure. When a performance measure is precise, there is a relatively low probability that it will differ substantially from the payoff. Thus, net income in Example 9.4 is a more precise performance measure than in Example 9.3, since it has less variance. Precision contributes to efficient compensation contracts, other things equal, by reducing the manager's compensation risk.

When net income is biased, there is a tradeoff between sensitivity and precision. Attempts to increase sensitivity of net income by adopting current value accounting may reduce precision, since current value estimates tend to be imprecise. For example, precision may be a serious problem if accountants were to adopt fair value accounting for R&D, due to problems of estimating its fair value.

If we think of RRA net income as a performance measure, RRA can also be viewed as an attempt to increase sensitivity, since RRA reflects manager effort devoted to proving oil and gas reserves sooner than historical cost accounting. However, RRA suffers from low precision. We see this with a vengeance in Suncor's RRA income statement (Table 2.3), where changes in estimates dominated the income calculation. While Suncor's RRA earnings may be relatively sensitive to current manager exploration and development efforts, they are an imprecise measure of these efforts since the ultimate payoff may differ considerably.

The characteristics needed by net income if it is to be a sensitive and precise performance measure are not necessarily the same as those needed if it is to be a useful input into investment decisions. RRA, for example, may provide useful information to investors (if its relevance outweighs its low reliability) while it may not contribute to efficient compensation contracts (if its lack of precision outweighs its sensitivity).

We conclude that the challenge for accountants to maintain and increase the role of net income as a manager performance measure is to produce a net income number that represents the best possible tradeoff between sensitivity and precision. This tradeoff is not necessarily the same as the best tradeoff between relevance and reliability in informing investors.

9.8.2 Rigidity of Contracts

Agency theory assumes that the courts have authority to costlessly enforce contract provisions and adjudicate disputes. While the parties to a contract could agree among themselves to amend contract provisions following an unforeseen realization of the state of nature, this can be surprisingly difficult. Contracts tend to be *rigid* once signed. The reasons for this rigidity need some discussion. Otherwise, we might ask, if economic consequences have their roots in the contracts that managers enter into, why not just *renegotiate* the contracts following a change in GAAP, or other unforeseen state realization?

Note first that it is generally impossible to anticipate all contingencies when entering into a contract. For example, unless the contract is of very short duration, it would be difficult to predict changes in GAAP that could affect the contract. In Example 9.8, the firm's ability to avoid debt covenant violation would be reduced if, say, a new accounting standard restricts the firm's ability to switch between amortization methods. Such a standard would preclude the manager from managing covenant ratios by changing amortization method. Consequently, the probability of covenant violation increases. It is unlikely that the contract could anticipate the change in GAAP that caused this increase.

Contracts that do not anticipate all possible state realizations are termed **incomplete**. The contracts in Examples 9.3 to 9.9 are **complete**. Thus, in Example 9.3, the only possible state realizations are θ_1 and θ_2, leading to payoffs x_1 and x_2, respectively. While the set of possible state realizations could be expanded in the examples, in an actual contract the parties could not anticipate all possibilities.

For example, suppose that a new GAAP accounting policy lowers reported net income and increases its volatility. The manager goes to the bondholder and explains that, through no one's fault, the accounting rules have changed and requests that the coverage ratio covenant be reduced from 3:1 to 2:1. This, the manager argues, would maintain the bondholder's protection at what it was before the rule change. Why should the bondholder agree to such a request? In doing so, he or she is giving something away— namely the increased protection against excessive dividends that resulted from the new accounting policy. To be willing to do this, the bondholder may well require something in return, such as a higher interest rate. The problem for the manager is further complicated if, as is usually the case, there are many bondholders. Agreement would then be required from all of them, or, at least, a majority. The manager's compensation contract with the firm owner would be similarly difficult to amend. If the manager requests, say, a higher bonus rate, to correct for an accounting policy change that lowers reported net income and/or increases its volatility, the compensation committee of the board of directors may want something in return, or even reopen the entire contract for renegotiation.

Building a formal commitment for renegotiation into the contract *beforehand* is possible, but if the renegotiation is generous towards the manager (e.g., it may let the manager "off the hook" following an unfortunate state realization), the prospect of such renegotiation reduces the manager's effort incentive, which would not be in the owner's best interests.[17]

In effect, a consequence of entering into contracts is just that—they are contracts, and hence tend towards rigidity. Thus, unforeseen state realizations impose costs on the firm and/or the manager. The manager who is unfavourably affected by a change of the accounting rules in midstream may be forced to take out his or her displeasure on the accountants who introduced the rule change rather than on the other parties to the contract. It is contract incompleteness that drives the economic consequences discussed in Chapter 8.

Theory in Practice 9.1

The severe consequences of contract incompleteness and rigidity are illustrated by Mosaic Group Inc., a large designer of marketing programs for major companies.

In its third quarter, 2002, report, Mosaic Group reported an operating loss of over $395 million, after a writedown of goodwill of $347.6 million. The company had been hit by bad economic times and the loss of several major customers, state realizations that were unanticipated when its debt contracts were signed. The large loss put the firm into violation of its debt covenants. Its lenders were unwilling to waive the covenant requirements or amend the credit agreements.

Mosaic filed for bankruptcy protection in 2003. Its shares were delisted by the Toronto Stock Exchange in April 2004.

9.9 RECONCILIATION OF EFFICIENT SECURITIES MARKET THEORY WITH ECONOMIC CONSEQUENCES

We now see how firms are able to align manager and shareholder interests, consistent with the efficient contracting version of positive accounting theory. Agency theory demonstrates that the best attainable compensation contract usually bases manager compensation on one or more measures of performance. Then, managers have an incentive to maximize performance. Since higher performance leads to higher expected payoff, this is a goal also desired by shareholders.

This alignment explains why accounting policies have economic consequences, despite the implications of efficient securities market theory. Under efficient securities market theory, only accounting policy choices that affect expected cash flows create economic consequences. The contracting-based argument we have given for economic consequences does not depend on accounting policy choices having direct cash flow effects. This argument is the same whether direct cash flow effects are present or not.

Rather, it is the rigidities produced by the signing of binding, incomplete contracts that create managers' concerns, and that lead to their intervention in the standard-setting process. These rigidities have nothing to do with whether accounting policy changes affect cash flows.

Thus, economic consequences and efficient securities markets are not necessarily inconsistent. Rather, they can be reconciled by positive accounting theory, with normative support from agency theory that suggests *why* firms enter into employment and debt contracts that depend on accounting information. Nothing in the above arguments leading to managerial concern about accounting policies conflicts with securities market efficiency.

Similarly, nothing in the theory of efficient securities markets conflicts with managerial concern about accounting policies. Joint consideration of both theories, though, helps us to see that managers may well intervene in accounting policies, even though those policies would improve the decision usefulness of financial statements to investors. Thus, in the final analysis, the interaction between managers and investors is a game.

9.10 CONCLUSIONS ON THE ANALYSIS OF CONFLICT

The various conflict-based theories described in this chapter have important implications for financial accounting theory. These can be summarized as follows:

1. Conflict theories enable a reconciliation of efficient securities markets and economic consequences. Early applications of efficient market theory to financial accounting (as, for example, in Beaver's early article, discussed in Section 4.3) suggested that accountants concentrate on full disclosure of information useful for investors' decision needs. The form of disclosure and the particular accounting policies used did not matter, as the market would see through these to their ultimate cash flow implications.

Certainly, accountants have adopted the decision usefulness approach and its full-disclosure implications, and there is extensive empirical evidence that markets do respond to accounting information much as the theory predicts. Frequently, however, as noted in Chapter 8, management intervened in the standard-setting process. This was not predicted by efficient securities market theory, since under that theory the market value of a firm's securities should be independent of its accounting policies, unless cash flows were affected. Why would management care about accounting policies if these do not affect its cost of capital? An answer is that changes in accounting policies can affect provisions in contracts that firm managers have entered into, thereby affecting their expected utility and the welfare of the firm.

The reason why accounting policies can affect manager and firm welfare should be carefully considered. The basic problem is one of information asymmetry. In an owner–manager context, the manager knows his or her own effort in running the firm on the owner's behalf, but typically the owner cannot observe this effort. Knowing this, the manager faces a temptation to shirk. Thus, there is a moral hazard problem between owner and manager. To control moral hazard, the owner can offer the manager a share of reported net income. This profit sharing motivates the manager to work harder. However, it also means that the manager has a personal interest in how net income is measured. The firm will want to induce the desired effort as efficiently as possible.

When managers enter into borrowing contracts with lenders, similar implications for manager and firm welfare occur. Borrowing contracts typically contain covenants that restrict the payment of dividends depending on the values of certain financial statement-based ratios, such as interest coverage. Since covenant violations can be costly to the firm, both the manager and the firm will have a personal interest in accounting policy changes that affect the probability of covenant violation, particularly if they share in firm profits.

Thus, economic consequences can be seen as a rational result of the rigidities introduced by entering into binding, incomplete contracts. The conflict situation between managers, who may object to accounting policies that have adverse economic consequences for them and their firms, and investors, who desire full disclosure, can be modelled as non-cooperative or cooperative games.

2. An implication of agency theory is that net income has a role to play in motivating and monitoring manager performance. Arguably, this role is equally as important in society as facilitating the proper operation of capital markets by providing useful information to investors. The characteristics needed for net income to fulfill an important role in efficient contracting differ from those needed to provide useful information to investors. The ability of net income to fulfill a manager performance-enhancing role depends on its sensitivity and precision as a measure of the payoff from current manager effort while usefulness for investors depends on its ability to reliably provide relevant information about future firm performance.

3. Net income competes with other performance measures, such as share price. If accountants can improve the precision and sensitivity needed for a good performance

measure, they may expect to see an increase in the role of net income in manager compensation plans.

4. If carried to the extreme, earnings management allows manager shirking, with resulting low payoffs to owners. Complete elimination of earnings management is not cost effective. However, by controlling earnings management through GAAP, accountants can restore the manager's incentive to work hard, thereby increasing payoffs to owners.

For these various reasons, game theory is an important component of financial accounting theory. In addition to enabling a better understanding of the conflicting interests of various constituencies affected by financial reporting, it has encouraged research into executive compensation and earnings management. Chapters 10 and 11 will review some of this research.

Questions and Problems

1. Why is manager effort usually unobservable to the firm's owners? What problem of information asymmetry results? If the manager receives a straight salary, what is the effect of this information asymmetry on the manager's effort in a single-period contract? Would the effect of information asymmetry on effort change if the contract is multi-period?

2. Give some reasons why the payoff from the manager's current-period effort is typically not fully observable until a subsequent period.

3. If net income is an unbiased (i.e., noisy) measure of manager performance, less noise enables a more efficient compensation contract. Explain why. Suggest ways that accountants can reduce noise in net income.

   Does the argument that less noise enables more efficient compensation contracting change if the assumption that net income is biased is dropped? Why?

4. Why do debt contracts typically impose covenants based on accounting information such as working capital, interest coverage, and debt-to-equity?

5. Why is net income not fully informative about manager effort?

6. Define the concepts of sensitivity and precision of a performance measure. How can accountants increase sensitivity? Precision? Why do these two desirable qualities have to be traded off?

7. Suppose in Example 9.3 that net income turns out to be $25, despite the assumption that net income can only be one of $115 and $40. How could this happen, and what does it say about the completeness of the compensation contract in the example? How might the manager react to this lower net income number?

8. U-Haul, a "do-it-yourself" moving company, is doing a booming business these days. The reason is that some companies relocating employees are changing the way they reimburse moving expenses. Before the change, moves were very expensive, because the companies paid for everything. Now, the companies pay a fixed amount to the employee, who can keep the savings, if there are any. Explain this change using agency theory concepts. Also,

U-Haul offers to reimburse customers for the cost of oil used during the move, while customers have to pay for their own gasoline. Why? (CGA-Canada)

9. The controversy over expensing of ESOs can be analyzed as a non-cooperative game. Let the two players be the large, powerful corporations who wish to prevent expensing, and the standard setter. Each player faces two strategies. The "cooperate" strategy happens when a player accedes to the demands of the other, or, at least, expresses a willingness to compromise. One compromise, for example, could be to expense only ESOs granted to senior officers, with those granted to all other employees reported only as supplementary information. Another could be to delay an expensing decision to give time to work out a compromise. The "strong" strategy involves a player sticking to its own preferred policy and attempting to win support from business and government.

Hypothetical, but reasonable, payoffs for each player are summarized in the following table.

		Standard setter	
		Cooperate	**Strong**
	Cooperate	30, 30	8, 40
Corporations			
	Strong	20, 10	12, 15

In each box, the first number represents the corporations' payoff and the second number the standard setter's payoff. Consider the lower left payoffs. Here, the corporations play strong, that is, they vigorously oppose expensing and proceed to gather support for their position from business and government. The standard setter backs down, as the FASB did in 1994, and allows all ESO expense to continue to be reported in the financial statement notes. The corporations' payoff is 20 in this case, because it is seen as the dominant player. However, because this strategy erodes their relationship with the standard setter, generates political controversy, and alienates other constituencies who feel that standard setting should be done in the private sector, its payoff is less than the 30 it would receive if both players had cooperated to reach a compromise solution. The standard setter receives a very low payoff of 10, because it is perceived as capitulating to the corporations' demands. If the corporations cooperate, however, and formulate a compromise, with payoffs of 30 each, the standard setter may seize on this as an expression of weakness and force through its preferred expensing option. Then, the standard setter's payoff is 40, since it is seen as the dominant player, and the corporations suffer an embarrassing defeat with payoff of only 8. If both parties play strong, no agreement is possible and the question of ESO expensing has to be settled by another authority, such as government. Here, both parties lose, with low payoffs as shown in the lower right of the table.

Required

a. Given the payoffs as shown, which strategy pair do you predict the players will choose?

b. Is this strategy pair a Nash equilibrium? Explain.

c. Both parties would be better off if they cooperated. Explain why this strategy pair is unlikely to be chosen.

10. The shareholders of X Ltd. will vote at the forthcoming annual meeting on a proposal to establish a bonus plan, based on firm performance, for X Ltd. management. Proponents of the plan argue that management will work harder under a bonus plan and that expected cash flows will thereby increase. However, a dissident shareholder group argues that there is little point in granting a bonus plan, because management will bias or otherwise manage earnings to increase their bonus, rather than working harder.

Upon investigation, you estimate that if the bonus plan is granted, expected operating cash flows will be $150 if management does not manage earnings, and $140 if it does, *before* management remuneration in each case (cash flows are lower in the latter case because management uses earnings management to disguise shirking). Management remuneration, including the bonus, would be $50 if it does not manage earnings and $60 if it does. Assume that cash flows not paid as management remuneration will go to the shareholders. If the bonus plan is not granted, expected cash flows will be $140 before management remuneration if management does not manage earnings and $100 if it does. Management remuneration would be $30 in either case, with the balance of cash flows going to the shareholders.

Required

a. Prepare a payoff table for the above game between shareholders and management.

b. Which strategy pair will be chosen? That is, identify a Nash equilibrium for the game. Assume both players are risk-neutral.

c. What is the main advantage of a game theory approach to modelling the management's decision whether to manage earnings, rather than modelling it as a single-person decision theory problem of the manager?

11. The following table depicts a non-cooperative game between an investor in a firm's shares and the firm's auditor.

		Auditor	
		Work for investor	**Work for manager**
	Invest	5, 4	2, 6
Investor			
	Do not invest	3, 1	3, 3

The investor has two strategies—invest or not invest. The auditor can choose to work for the investor by ensuring that the firm's financial statements are free of opportunistic earnings management, or to work for the manager by allowing opportunistic earnings management, which may mislead the investor but benefit the manager.

The number pairs in the table represent the utility payoff to the investor and auditor respectively, for each strategy combination. The rationale for these payoffs is as follows:

Invest, Work for investor: The investor receives high-quality information, but the auditor incurs high audit costs due to time spent arguing with the manager and possible loss of audit engagement.

Invest, Work for manager:	The investor receives low-quality information, but the auditor's costs are lower.
Do not invest, Work for investor:	The investor buys lower-yielding securities. The firm's cost of capital rises due to lower demand for its shares. As a result, its earnings fall. Auditor incurs high audit costs, and manager demands lower audit fee due to lower firm earnings.
Do not invest, Work for manager:	The investor buys lower-yielding securities. The auditor's audit costs are lower due to less arguing with manager but audit fee is still low due to lower firm earnings.

Required

a. Identify the Nash equilibrium of this game and explain why this is the predicted outcome of the game.

b. Identify the cooperative solution. Explain why it is unlikely to be attained in a single-play of this game.

c. Outline three possible ways that the cooperative solution may be attained.

12. Pierre's small business has grown to the point where he plans to hire a full-time manager. Pierre, an architect, has little inclination and ability to manage a medium-sized, fast-growing business himself. He plans to semi-retire, devoting his working hours to consulting on issues of design and project management. Pierre's accounting system is quite simple. There is no R&D or other recognition lags. Consequently, the firm's payoff and its net income for the year are equal.

Pierre is negotiating with Yvonne as a possible manager. He wants the manager to work hard, since his past experience is that hard work generates a net income (before any manager compensation) of $2,000 90% of the time, and $900 10% of the time. Pierre's recent experience, when he has not worked hard, is that the $2,000 net income is generated only 10% of the time, otherwise net income is $900.

During the negotiations, Pierre ascertains that Yvonne is both risk- and effort-averse. Her utility for money is equal to the square root of the amount of money received. Her disutility for effort is 4 if she works hard and 1.1 if she shirks. Her reservation utility is 11.

Pierre decides that Yvonne is ideal for the job. He quickly offers her annual cash compensation of a $100 salary plus 10% of net income before manager compensation. Yvonne immediately accepts.

Required

a. Show calculations to demonstrate why Yvonne accepts the position.

b. After two years, Pierre is worried because net income has been $900 each year. He decides to change Yvonne's compensation contract. After consulting a compensation specialist, he offers her a salary of $52.30 plus a profit share of 9.21% of net income before manager compensation. Yvonne hesitates, but decides to accept. Show calculations to demonstrate why she hesitates but accepts.

Note: Take calculations to two decimal places.

c. Pierre is risk-neutral, with utility equal to the amount of profit received after manager compensation. Is Pierre's expected utility higher or lower under the new contract in part **b**, compared to the original contract in part **a**? Show calculations and explain why there is a difference.

13. Growth Ltd. is a high-tech firm whose owner does not have the required management expertise to run the firm. The owner wants to hire a manager with the required expertise. The continued success of Growth Ltd. depends crucially on how hard the new manager works.

   If the manager works hard (a_1), firm net income will be $500 with probability 0.7 and $200 with probability 0.3. If the manager shirks (a_2), net income will be $500 with probability 0.2 and $200 with probability 0.8. In both cases, profits are before manager compensation.

   The owner is interviewing a prospective manager, and finds out that she is risk-averse, with utility for compensation equal to the square root of the dollar compensation received. Like most people, however, she is also effort-averse. If she works hard, she suffers a disutility of effort of 2 units of utility. If she shirks, her effort disutility is zero.

   Required

   a. Growth Ltd. offers the manager a one-period contract with a salary of $41 per period plus 20% of net income before manager compensation. If she accepts the job, will the manager take a_1 or a_2? Show your calculations.

   b. Instead, Growth offers the manager zero salary plus 30% of net income before manager compensation. Assuming the manager accepts, will she take a_1 or a_2? Show your calculations.

   c. Does the manager's effort decision change between parts **a** and **b** above? Explain why or why not.

   d. Many executive compensation contracts base the manager's compensation on *both* net income and share price performance. Explain an advantage of using two performance measures rather than one in compensation contracts.

14. Tom operates a small, fast-growing electronics business. His workload has expanded to the point where he decides to hire a full-time manager, so that he can concentrate on the technical aspects of the business.

   Tom is negotiating with Lily for the manager job. He ascertains that Lily is risk-averse, with utility for money equal to the square root of the dollar compensation received.

   Lily advises Tom that she already has a job offer, which yields her an expected utility of 6. She is not willing to work for less than this, but would accept an expected utility of 6 from Tom. Lily also advises that she is effort-averse, with disutility of effort of 2 if she works hard, and 1 if she does not work hard.

   Tom's business has, in previous years, earned net income (before manager compensation) of $725 75% of the time, and income of $0 25% of the time. Tom has always worked hard (a_1), and reckons that if he did not work hard net income would have been $725 only 20% of the time and zero for 80% of the time. He expects this earnings pattern to continue into the future with a new manager. Tom realizes that he must motivate Lily to work hard, and offers her compensation based on a proportion of reported net income before manager compensation.

Required

a. What proportion of net income must Tom offer Lily so that she will accept the position and work hard? Show calculations.

b. Assuming that Lily accepts Tom's offer, verify that she will in fact work hard.

c. Having accepted the position, Lily soon realizes that she can opportunistically manage earnings so as to *ensure* that net income of $725 is reported, even if she does not work hard. Calculate whether or not, in a one-year contract, Lily is better off to work hard and not manage earnings or to not work hard and manage earnings.

d. State and explain two reasons why a manager who may be tempted to *not* work hard and cover up by opportunistic earnings management would not do so.

15. Henri owns and operates a small successful sporting goods store. He has not had a holiday for three years. He decides to take an extensive one-year trip around the world and is negotiating with Marie to operate the store while he is away. The store's earnings are highly dependent on how hard the manager works, as per the following table:

| | a_1: Work Hard | | a_2: Shirk | |
	Net Income	Prob.	Net Income	Prob.
x_1: High Earnings	$300	0.7	$300	0.2
x_2: Low Earnings	$80	0.3	$80	0.8

Marie, like most people, is risk-averse and effort-averse. Her utility for money is equal to the square root of the amount of money received. If she works hard, her effort disutility is 2. If she shirks, her effort disutility is 1.6.

Marie informs Henri that she is willing to accept the manager position but that she must receive at least an expected utility of 3.41, or she would be better off to work somewhere else. Henri, who is not an agency theory expert, offers Marie a salary of $20 plus 5% of the store earnings (after deducting $20 salary from the earnings in the table). Marie immediately accepts.

Required

a. If Henri hires her, which act will Marie take? Why did she immediately accept? Show calculations.

b. Henri's bank manager, to whom he has turned for advice, suggests that if he hires an agent, the store's annual earnings should be audited by a professional accountant. Explain why.

c. Assume that Henri hires Marie under the contract proposed, that is, $20 salary plus 5% of profits after salary. Shortly after he leaves, a new accounting standard requires that estimated customer liability be accrued. This lowers the high earnings to $286 and the low earnings to $40 in the table above. The payoff probabilities are unaffected. Which act will Marie now take? Show calculations. Will Marie be concerned about the new standard? Explain why or why not.

16. Mr. K, a risk-neutral investor, is contemplating a one-year 8% loan of $500 to firm J. Mr. K demands at least a 6% expected return per annum on loans like this. K is concerned

that the firm may not be able to pay the interest and/or principal at the end of the year. A further concern is that if he makes the loan, firm J may engage in additional borrowing. If so, K's security would be diluted and the firm would become more risky. Since firm J is growing rapidly, K is sure that the firm would engage in additional borrowing if he makes the loan.

K examines firm J's most recent annual report and calculates an interest coverage ratio (ratio of net income before interest and taxes to interest expense) of 4, including the contemplated $500 loan.

Upon considering all of these matters, K assesses the following probabilities:

PAYOFF	PROBABILITY
θ_1: Interest and principal repaid	0.80
θ_2: Reorganization, principal repaid but not interest	0.18
θ_3: Bankruptcy, nothing repaid	0.02
	1.00

Required

a. Should Mr. K make the loan? Show calculations.

b. Firm J offers to add a covenant to its lending agreement with Mr. K, undertaking not to engage in any additional borrowing if its interest coverage ratio falls below 4 before the next year-end. Mr. K estimates that there is a 60% probability that the interest coverage ratio will fall below 4. If it does, there would be no dilution of his equity by additional borrowing under the firm J offer, and he feels the lower coverage ratio would still be adequate. He assesses that his payoff probabilities would then be:

PAYOFF	PROBABILITY
θ_1	0.95
θ_2	0.04
θ_3	0.01

If the coverage ratio does not fall below 4, the resulting additional borrowing and dilution of security would cause him to assess payoff probabilities as:

PAYOFF	PROBABILITY
θ_1	0.85
θ_2	0.14
θ_3	0.01

Should Mr. K now make the loan? Show calculations. (CGA-Canada)

17. Toni Difelice is contemplating lending $10,000 to Tech Enterprises Ltd. Tech offers her 8% interest with the principal to be repaid at the end of the year. Toni carefully examines the financial statements of Tech Enterprises and is concerned about its interest coverage ratio,

which is currently at 1.8:1. She feels that there is a 5% chance that Tech will go bankrupt, in which case she would only recover $2,000 of her principal and no interest. She suggests a debt covenant in the lending contract, whereby Tech promises not to issue any more debt beyond what Toni invests if its interest coverage ratio falls below 1.6:1. With such covenant protection, Toni assesses only a 1% probability of bankruptcy and subsequent recovery of only $2,000.

The manager of Tech Enterprises agrees to this request, providing that Toni reduces her interest rate to 5%.

Toni is risk-averse, with a mean-variance utility function:

$$U(a) = 2x_a - \sigma_a^2$$

where a is her investment act, x_a is the expected return on a, and σ_a^2 is the variance of the return of a.

Required

a. Which act should Toni take?

a_1 : 8% interest, no debt covenant

a_2 : 5% interest, debt covenant

b. Explain why the manager of Tech Enterprises would be concerned about new accounting standards that may come into effect after the lending contract with Toni is concluded. Consider both standards that will tend to lower reported net income and standards that will increase its volatility.

18. Arnold is the successful owner and operator of a small business. He plans to take a one-year vacation and is interviewing Minnie for the position of manager while he is away.

On the basis of extensive past experience, Arnold knows that if the manager works hard (a_1), the cash flow (payoff) from the year's operations will be $505 with probability 0.8 and $345 with probability 0.2. If the manager shirks (a_2), cash flow will be $505 with probability 0.2 and $345 with probability 0.8. Payoffs are *before* any manager compensation.

However, cash flow will not be known until some time after Arnold returns, since all sales are on long-term credit, and advertising costs incurred in the year continue to generate sales well after year-end. However, Minnie demands to be paid at year-end.

Arnold decides to base compensation on net income, a performance measure available at year-end. He knows that due to random effects of states of nature, if the payoff is going to be $505, net income will be $625 with probability 0.7 and $225 with probability 0.3. If the payoff is going to be $345, net income will be $625 with probability 0.3 and $225 with probability 0.7. Net income is *before* any manager compensation.

Upon interviewing Minnie, Arnold finds that her reservation utility is 2.6, that her utility for money equals the square root of the amount of money received, and that her disutility of effort if she works hard is 8. If she shirks, her effort disutility is 7. Arnold decides to offer Minnie a one-year contract with compensation based on a percentage of audited net income before compensation. Minnie accepts.

Required

a. What percentage of net income before compensation did Arnold offer Minnie? Verify that Minnie will work hard.

b. Why did Arnold specify that net income be audited?

c. Suppose that instead of what is given above, if Minnie shirks, net income will be $505 with probability 0.2 and $400 with probability 0.8. What contract would Arnold now offer Minnie? Explain.

19. Refer to Example 9.4. Show calculations to verify the statement in the example that with a profit share of 0.3185 the manager will work hard and receive reservation utility.

Explain why the contract of Example 9.4 is more efficient than the contract of Example 9.3. How can accountants contribute to this greater efficiency when net income is unbiased?

20. A problem with many games is that they can have multiple Nash equilibria. This makes it difficult to predict the outcome of the game.

As an illustration of a non-cooperative game with multiple equilibria, consider the following payoff table:

		Country 1	
		Keep	**Violate**
	Keep	100, 100	50, 200
Country 2	**Violate**	200, 50	50, 50

Required

a. Identify three Nash equilibria of this game.

b. Suppose that this game will be repeated a known, finite number of times. Suppose that the current equilibrium is in the lower left portion of the table. Describe an action by country 1 that would cause a shift to a new equilibrium.

c. Suppose that the game will be repeated an indefinite (i.e., infinite) number of times. What equilibrium would you then predict? Explain.

21. The owner of a medium-size electronics company is concerned about cash flow. The company operates in a growing industry and produces a product that is in high demand. The owner feels that cash flow should be higher than it has been lately and fears that the company manager may be shirking, despite receiving a generous salary.

Company shares are all held by the owner and are not traded. However, audited financial statements are prepared annually, in accordance with GAAP.

The owner has decided to replace the current manager and to hire a new manager under a one-year contract, with compensation paid at the end of the year. You are hired to recommend a contract that will align the manager's interests with those of the owner.

Upon reviewing the company's history of past performance, you determine that if the manager works hard (a_1), cash flows of $600 are generated with probability 0.7 and $200 with probability 0.3. If the manager shirks (a_2), the probability of $600 cash flow falls to 0.3, with the probability of $200 rising to 0.7.

You also note that while these cash flows result from the manager's effort during the year, they are not fully received until the end of the following year. This is because the company conducts R&D, and also incurs risks of legal liability, which do not fully pay off for some time.

Your study of past financial statements reveals that net income is a noisy predictor of cash flows. Specifically, if cash flows are going to be $600, net income for the year is $725 with probability 0.8 and $100 with probability 0.2. If cash flows are going to be $200, net income for the year is $725 with probability 0.16 and $100 with probability 0.84. This is because of recognition lag—given the complex nature of R&D and legal liability, it is not possible to report a net income that perfectly predicts future cash flows.

You interview a prospective manager, and find that her reservation utility is 5. Also, she is risk-averse, with utility of compensation equal to the square root of the dollar amount of compensation received. She is also effort-averse, with disutility of effort of 2 units of utility if she works hard and 1 unit of utility if she shirks.

Required

a. You decide to recommend a compensation contract based on a percentage of audited annual net income before manager compensation. What percentage of net income should you recommend? Show calculations.

b. Why did you decide that net income should be audited to serve as a basis for payment of compensation?

c. Based on the percentage of net income that you recommend, verify that the manager will work hard. Show calculations.

d. Suppose that improvements to GAAP reduce the noise in net income, as follows. If cash flows are going to be $600, net income for the year is $650 with probability 0.9 and $150 with probability 0.1. If cash flows are going to be $200, net income for the year is $650 with probability 0.1 and $150 with probability 0.9. Will your recommended percentage of net income be higher or lower than the percentage you recommended in part **a**? Explain why. Calculations not required.

22. Sensitivity of a performance measure is the rate at which the expected value of the performance measure increases as the manager works harder. Precision, or noise, is the reciprocal of the variance of the performance measure.

Required

Refer to Example 9.7. Calculate the percentage increase in the expected value of reported net income (i.e., its sensitivity) as the manager's effort increases from shirk (a_2) to work hard (a_1). Also calculate the precision of net income in this example, given that the manager works hard.

23. You are engaged by the owner of a small firm to recommend a one-year compensation contract for the firm's top manager. The owner is concerned about cash flow and feels that, in previous years, the manager may have been shirking.

You ascertain that, if the manager works hard (a_1), the firm's ultimate cash flow from current year operations will be one of $225 or $100 (before manager compensation) with probability 0.6, 0.4, respectively. If the manager shirks (a_2), cash flow will be $225 or $100 with probability 0.2, 0.8, respectively. Cash flow, however, will not be known until after the manager's one-year contract has expired.

As an expert in GAAP, you know that if cash flow is going to be $225, net income for the year will be $300 with probability 0.7 and $50 with probability 0.3. If cash flow is going to be $100, net income will be $300 with probability 0.2 and $50 with probability 0.8. You recommend that the manager's contract be based on reported net income.

You interview the manager and find that he is rational, risk-averse with utility for money equal to the square root of the amount of money received, and effort-averse with disutility of effort of 2.5 if he works hard and 1.8 if he shirks. The manager's reservation utility, net of disutility of effort, is 4.

Required

a. What percentage of net income must the manager be offered so that he will accept the contract and work hard?

b. Suppose that all information given in the question is unchanged except that if the manager shirks, and cash flow is going to be $100, net income will be $300 with probability 0.3 and $30 with probability 0.7. What contract would you then recommend? Show calculations and explain your contract choice.

c. The owner is risk-neutral, with utility equal to the dollar amount of the payoff, net of the manager's compensation. What is the agency cost of the contract in part **a**? Show calculations.

Notes

1. The discussion here assumes only pure strategies, that is, strategies where one act is chosen with probability 1. It is possible to have mixed-strategy solutions, where players randomize between acts over which they are indifferent. Then, this statement would need modification.

2. Darrough and Stoughton assume that if disclosure is made, it is honest. This assumption can be motivated by an audit and/or by severe penalties for fraudulent disclosure.

3. There is an implicit assumption throughout Section 9.4 that principal and agent have the same state and payoff probabilities when the contract is being negotiated. This assumption is made in most agency models. See also Note 6.

4. For simplicity, we ignore here what might happen next. Given a reasonably efficient managerial labour market, other similar managers would also like to work for this firm. Once they see that the job promises more than reservation utility, they will offer to work for less. The resulting bidding process will drive the salary down to $22.18, so that the shirking manager earns only reservation utility, as follows:

$$EU_m(a_1) = \sqrt{22.18} - 2 = 2.71$$

$$EU_m(a_2) = \sqrt{22.18} - 1.71 = 3.00$$

Whether or not the owner opens the job up for bids, the important point is that the manager will prefer to choose a_2, contrary to the best interests of the owner.

5. If the payoff was observable at period end, it would also be a performance measure.

6. The agency models of this chapter assume rational expectations. Thus, in equilibrium, the owner and manager know the possible payoffs and have the same net income and payoff probabilities (called **homogeneous probabilities**) for each manager effort level. This is equivalent to the manager knowing the firm's production function, which is determined by the manager's ability. The owner also knows the manager's utility function and effort disutility. Without this knowledge, the owner would not be able to design the compensation contract and motivate the manager to work hard.

Since investors (recall that the owner is a proxy for a typical investor) know which act the manager will take and know the firm's production function, reported net income and payoff reveal no new information about the manager's effort and ability. This justifies taking the agent's reservation utility R as a fixed constant in the single-period model—since net income and payoff resulting from current effort reveal no new information about the manager's performance, there is no effect on reputation.

This lack of market reaction to manager performance is obviously unrealistic, since if a manager does a good job (i.e., works hard), we would expect the market to increase its probability of high future firm performance. To generate a market reaction to new information in net income about manager effort and ability would require a more complex, multi-period, agency model, which is beyond our scope here.

7. It is easy to verify what the manager's expected compensation is now:

$$
\begin{aligned}
\text{Expected comp.} &= 0.6\big[0.8(0.3237 \times 115) + 0.2(0.3237 \times 40)\big] \\
&\quad + 0.4\big[0.2(0.3237 \times 115) + 0.8(0.3237 \times 40)\big] \\
&= 0.6(0.8 \times 37.2255 + 0.2 \times 12.9480) + 0.4(0.2 \times 37.2255 + 0.8 \times 12.9480) \\
&= 0.6 \times 32.37 + 0.4 \times 17.80 \\
&= 19.44 + 7.12 \\
&= 26.56
\end{aligned}
$$

The manager's expected compensation has to be raised from $25 under the first-best contract to $26.56 under profit sharing to offset the compensation risk that the manager now bears and enable reservation utility to be attained. This increase in expected compensation accounts for the agency cost of 1.5434 now borne by the owner.

8. Agency theory seeks to find the contract with the lowest possible agency cost (i.e., the most efficient form of contract). We do not claim that the contract of Example 9.3, based on 0.3237 of net income, is necessarily the most efficient. In fact, it can be verified that a contract paying the manager a salary of $0.78 plus 0.3129 of net income (or, equivalently, 0.3197 of net income if net income is $115, and 0.3324 of net income if net income is $40) is slightly more efficient. This contract makes the manager indifferent between a_1 and a_2 (in which case it is assumed the agent will take a_1), and yields the owner expected utility of 55.6210, up from 55.4566 in our contract. The reason for the greater efficiency is that this contract places less risk on the manager, due both to the salary and the smaller profit share. This enables a lower risk premium for the agent to attain reservation utility. We use a straight profit share in the body of the text primarily for simplicity.

Note that both of the contracts here are linear in the performance measure. When there are more than two states of nature, it is possible that a non-linear contract would be more efficient. This is beyond our scope here.

9. This assumption may seem to violate our statement in Section 9.4.2 that contracts are based on variables that are jointly observable. However, this is really not the case. Reported net income (as opposed to unmanaged net income) *is* jointly observable. The question then is, does reported net income have sufficient credibility that parties are willing to contract on it? If not, other performance measures, such as share price, may take over. However, GAAP and auditing help to give the owner confidence in reported net income as a performance measure. Furthermore, as we will see in Chapter 10, actual compensation contracts are based, at least in part, on reported net income.

10. There is no incentive to report truthfully, either, since the manager receives the same utility regardless. The theory assumes that, if indifferent, the manager will report truthfully.

11. The revelation principle could in turn be applied to this contract. The owner could simply agree to pay 0.3193 times the upper limit of the range that occurs, regardless of the amount of unmanaged net income reported within that range. The manager then has no incentive to manage earnings upward. However, paying the manager on the basis of a higher net income than reported may impose costs on the manager, since such compensation may be regarded as excessive in the media and by regulators. In view of the restrictions on the revelation principle discussed in Section 9.5.1, we do not pursue this here.

12. Another way to eliminate the manager's incentive to manage earnings is to pay a constant wage. However, with a constant wage, the manager will shirk, and the owner would be back in the situation of Example 9.6.

13. More precisely, for the second performance measure to reduce agency costs it must be false that the first measure is a sufficient statistic for the pair of variables (first performance measure, second performance measure) with respect to effort.

14. Holmström points out that if the contract with the manager is confined to a limited class, such as the linear contract with a straight profit share assumed in Example 9.3, this result may not hold.

15. The manager's expected compensation is:

$$0.6[0.6 \times 36.86 + 0.1 \times 13.76 + 0.2 \times 36.32 + 0.1 \times 13.22] + 0.4[0.1 \times 36.86 + 0.2 \times 13.76 + 0.1 \times 36.32 + 0.6 \times 13.22]$$

$$= 0.4 \times 36.86 + 0.14 \times 13.76 + 0.16 \times 36.32 + 0.3 \times 13.22$$

$$= \$26.45$$

The manager's expected compensation in Example 9.3 was calculated in Note 7 as \$26.56.

16. Strictly speaking, our assumption that the firm has a share price is not consistent with the firm having a single owner. We make this assumption due to the prevalence of share price in real compensation contracts, as we shall see in the next chapter. Here, we could just as easily use a credit rating from an independent rating agency as a second performance measure. Even the weather could be a second performance measure. Obviously, the manager does not control the weather, but suppose that weather affects the probability that net income will be high or low (e.g., a sporting goods manufacturer). Then, the weather tells us something about net income, which, in turn, tells us something about effort. This is known as the principle of **conditional controllability**. Even though a manager cannot control a variable, that variable can be informative about performance. This is an important point to notice, since managers often complain that their performance should *not* be evaluated on variables they cannot control.

17. Christensen, Demski, and Frimor (2002) present a two-period agency model that allows contract renegotiation at the end of the first period, but also allows the manager to underreport first period output (i.e., conservative accounting). Since accruals reverse, any underreporting of first period output must be added to second period reported output, however. This restores some of the agent's incentive to work hard since working hard in the first period leads to extra expected compensation in the second. This provides another argument that some degree of earnings management can be good. Further pursuit of contract renegotiation is beyond our scope.

Chapter 10
Executive Compensation

Figure 10.1 Organization of Chapter 10

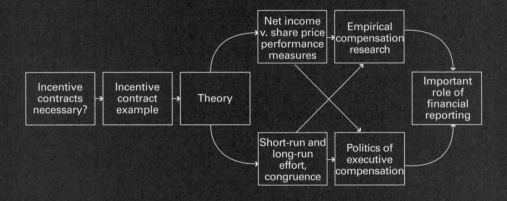

10.1 OVERVIEW

In this chapter we consider **executive compensation plans**. We will see that real incentive plans follow from the agency theory developed in Chapter 9, but are more complex and detailed, and span multiple periods. They involve a delicate mix of incentive, risk, and decision horizon considerations.

> An **executive compensation plan** is an agency contract between the firm and its manager that attempts to align the interests of owners and manager by basing the manager's compensation on one or more measures of the manager's performance in operating the firm.

Many compensation plans are based on two performance measures—net income and share price. That is, the amounts of cash bonus, shares, options, and other components of executive pay that are awarded in a particular year depend on both net income and share price performance. The analyses of Holmström (1979) and Feltham and Xie (1994) outlined in Section 9.8.1 suggest that multiple performance measures increase contracting efficiency.

The role of net income in motivating manager performance is equally as important as its role in informing investors. This is because the motivation of responsible manager performance and improving the operation of managerial labour markets are desirable social goals. They are equally as important as the enabling of good investment decisions and securities market operation. Consequently, an understanding of the properties that net income needs in order to measure manager performance is important for accountants. Unless net income has desirable qualities of sensitivity and precision, it will not be informative about manager effort. That is, it will not measure performance efficiently and will not enable the market to properly value the manager's worth. It will also be "squeezed out" of efficient compensation plans.

Figure 10.1 outlines the organization of this chapter.

10.2 ARE INCENTIVE CONTRACTS NECESSARY?

Fama (1980) makes the case that incentive contracts of the type studied in Section 9.4.2 are not necessary because the managerial labour market controls moral hazard. If a manager can establish a **reputation** for creating high payoffs for owners, that manager's market value (i.e., the compensation he or she can command) will increase. Conversely, a manager who shirks, thus reporting lower payoffs on average, will suffer a decline in market value. As a manager who is tempted to shirk looks ahead to future periods, the present value of reduced future compensation, Fama argues, will be equal to or greater than the immediate benefits of shirking. Thus, the manager will not shirk. This argument, of course, assumes an efficient managerial labour market that properly values the manager's reputation. Analogous to the case of a capital market, the operation of a managerial labour market is enhanced by full disclosure of the manager's performance.

Fama also argues that for lower-level managers, any shirking will be detected and reported by managers below them, who want to get ahead. That is, a process of "internal monitoring" operates to discipline managers who may be less subject to the discipline of the managerial labour market itself.

Since the owner knows which action the manager will take in the single-period models of Chapter 9, these models do not reveal any information about manager effort and ability.[1] Thus they cannot deal directly with the multi-period horizon that is needed for reputation formation and internal monitoring. Recall that in the single-period model, the manager's market value enters only through the reservation utility constraint—the utility of the compensation of the next-best available position. In a one-period model, this utility is taken as a constant. Fama's argument is that if the manager contemplates the downwards effect of current shirking on the reservation utility of future employment contracts, shirking will be deterred.

The agency model can be extended to deal with some of these considerations. With respect to internal monitoring, we outline the study of Arya, Fellingham, and Glover (1997) (AFG). They design a two-period model with one owner and two risk-averse managers. The managers' efforts produce a joint, observable payoff in each period. The owner cannot observe either manager's effort but each manager knows the effort of the other. One way for the owner to motivate the managers to work hard is to offer each of them an incentive contract similar to the ones in Section 9.4.2, in each period. However, AFG show that the owner can offer a more efficient contract by exploiting the ability of each manager to observe the other's effort. Since the payoff is a joint effort, shirking by either manager will reduce the payoff for *both*. Then, in the AFG contract, each manager threatens the other that he/she will shirk in the second period if the other shirks in the first. If the contract is designed properly, the threat is credible and each manager works hard in both periods. The resulting two-period contract is more efficient because it imposes less risk than a sequence of two single-period contracts. As a result, managers can attain their reservation utility with lower expected compensation.

The important point for our purposes is that the contract continues to base manager compensation on some measure of the payoff. In effect, while exploitation of the ability of managers to monitor each other can *reduce* agency costs of moral hazard, it does not eliminate them. Thus, AFG's model suggests that an incentive contract for lower-level managers is still necessary.

With respect to the ability of manager reputation to control moral hazard, Fama's argument does not consider that the manager may be able to disguise the effects of shirking, at least in the short run, by managing the release of information. That is, the manager may try to "fool" the market by opportunistically managing earnings to cover up shirking. Since persons with a tendency to do this will be attracted to the opportunity, the managerial labour market is subject to adverse selection as well as moral hazard.

Of course, GAAP limits, to some extent, the manager's ability to cover up shirking. Also, since accruals reverse, such behaviour will eventually be discovered, in which case the manager's reputation will be destroyed. The question then is, are the expected costs of lost reputation strong enough to supply the missing effort motivation? If they are, then an incentive contract would not be necessary, as Fama argues. The manager could be paid a straight salary, and the manager's reputation on the managerial labour market would prevent shirking.

In this regard, some empirical evidence on the market's ability to control the manager's incentive to shirk was presented by Wolfson (1985). He examined contracts of oil and gas limited partnerships in the United States. These are tax-advantaged contracts between a general partner (agent) and limited partners (principal) to drill for oil and gas. The general partner provides the expertise and pays some of the costs. The bulk of the capital is provided by the limited partners.

Such contracts are particularly subject to moral hazard and adverse selection problems, due to the highly technical nature of oil and gas exploration. For example, the general partner privately learns the results of the drilling. This leads to the "noncompletion incentive problem." Once drilled, a well should be completed (i.e., brought into production) if its expected revenues—call them R—exceed the costs of completion. However, for tax reasons, completion costs are paid by the general partner. If the general partner receives, say, 40% of the revenues, then, from his/her perspective, it is worthwhile to complete only if 0.40R is greater than the completion costs. Given that only the general partner knows R, a well may not be completed (i.e., the manager covers up shirking by withholding information about R) unless R is very high.

Wolfson studied two types of well-drilling: exploratory wells and development wells. The noncompletion problem is not as great for exploratory wells since, if an exploratory well does come in, the chances are that R will be high indeed.

Investors will be aware of this noncompletion problem, of course, and will bid down the price they are willing to pay to buy in, possibly to the point where the general partner cannot attract limited partners at all. The question then is, can a general partner ease investor concerns by establishing a reputation, thereby increasing his/her market value and the amounts that investors are willing to pay?

To measure reputation, Wolfson collected information on the past performance of a sample of general partners over 1977–1980. The higher a general partner's past success in generating a return for limited partners, the higher that partner's reputation was taken to be. Wolfson found that the higher the reputation of a general partner, the more he/she received from limited partners to buy in, suggesting that investors were responding to the manager's reputation.

However, Wolfson also found that investors paid significantly less to buy into development wells than into exploratory wells. As mentioned, the undercompletion problem is greater for development wells.

Combination of these two findings suggests that while market forces can *reduce* the managers' moral hazard problem, *they do not eliminate it*. If reputation-building completely eliminated the undercompletion problem, we would not see investors paying less when the problem is greater.

While Wolfson's results apply only to a small sample of oil and gas contracts, they are of more general interest because of their implication that the managerial labour market is not completely effective in controlling moral hazard, contrary to Fama's argument. An agent's past success in generating payoffs for investors does not perfectly predict that he/she always "works hard."

A more recent study, in a broader context, is consistent with Wolfson's results. Bushman, Engel, and Smith (2006) analyzed a large sample of firms over 1970–2000. They reported a correlation of .34 between security market response to a firm's earnings and the change in its managers' cash compensation. This suggests that net income is partially informative about manager effort—higher cash compensation awarded by compensation committees is accompanied by increased investor probability of high future firm performance, and vice versa. However, net income is not completely informative about effort—if it was, the correlation would be 1. Consequently, the market is not able to perfectly value a manager's reputation on the basis of accounting information. But, if the market cannot value a manager's reputation with complete accuracy, an incentive contract to motivate effort is needed.

We conclude that while internal and market forces may help control managers' tendencies to shirk, they do not eliminate them. Thus, effort incentives based on some measure of the payoff are still necessary. We now turn to an examination of an actual managerial compensation contract of a large corporation. As we will see, incentives loom large.

10.3 A MANAGERIAL COMPENSATION PLAN

In this section, we present an example of a managerial compensation plan. The following exhibit describes the plan of BCE Inc., a large Canadian corporation with shares, at the time, traded on the Toronto, New York, and Zurich Stock Exchanges. Exhibit 10.1 presents excerpts from BCE's 2004 Management Proxy Circular.

Several aspects of this compensation plan should be noted. First, officers are required to hold a significant amount of BCE shares, ranging from two to five times base salary. Second, there are three main compensation components: salary; annual short-term incentive awards, consisting of cash bonuses or, for senior officers, deferred share units (DSUs); and stock options. DSUs are BCE shares that cannot be sold while the holder remains with the company.

Observe that the short-term incentive awards depend on both corporate performance and individual creativity and initiative. Corporate performance includes the attainment of financial targets such as earnings per common share (a net income-based measure of performance) and achievement of strategic corporate business objectives such as market share and customer satisfaction. The more senior the manager, the more his/her compensation depends on corporate performance, and the less on individual performance. For example, the target award of the president and CEO is set at 125% of base salary, whereas awards for other senior executives are as low as 30%. The target award is the bonus to be paid if performance objectives for the year are met. If objectives are exceeded, higher bonuses may be paid, and vice versa.

Stock options are awarded under the long-term component of the plan. Since the value of the stock options depends on BCE's share price, these provide an incentive to increase share price.

Third, many compensation plans require that a certain level of earnings, or other performance measure, be reached before incentive compensation becomes payable. The threshold level of performance is called the **bogey**. Also, many plans contain an upper limit to compensation, called the **cap**.

In BCE's case, no formal bogey or cap is stated. However, these seem implicit. We are told that total compensation is positioned between the 50th and 75th percentiles of that of a group of comparable companies, thereby placing an upper limit on compensation. Also, the amounts of short-term incentive awards are geared to targets set at the beginning of the year. If these bogeys are not met, the awards are, presumably, zero, or at least

Exhibit 10.1
Executive Officers' Compensation, BCE Inc.

EXECUTIVE OFFICERS' COMPENSATION

The executive compensation policy is designed to attract, motivate and retain the executive officers needed to achieve and surpass BCE'S corporate objectives and to build an industry-leading company in terms of operational performance and creation of value for the shareholders.

BCE's compensation philosophy is to offer total compensation which is competitive in the marketplace. To complement this market positioning, BCE also ensures (for internal equity) that the compensation of each position fairly reflects the responsibilities of that position relative to other positions at BCE.

A substantial portion of each executive officer's cash compensation each year depends on meeting annual corporate performance objectives. In addition, BCE has in place long-term incentive programs. These are mainly stock options that are designed to:

- compensate and retain executive officers
- link the executive officers' interests to those of the shareholders
- encourage executive officers to pursue value-creating opportunities for BCE by allowing them to participate in the appreciation in share value.

The MRCC (Management Resources and Compensation Committee) periodically reviews BCE'S executive compensation policy to make sure that it continues to meet its objectives. This review also includes a specific review of the compensation of the President and Chief Executive Officer and of the executive officers. In this document, executive officers whose compensation is disclosed in the *Summary compensation table* are referred to as the "named executive officers".

In 2003, in light of the evolving internal and external environments, the MRCC conducted a comprehensive review of BCE's executive compensation policy. Following this review, changes to the compensation policy were recommended by the MRCC and approved by the board in November 2003. The changes to the compensation policy are discussed in more detail under *Change in compensation strategy for 2004 and in the future*.

TOTAL COMPENSATION

In 2003, total compensation consisted of:

- base salary
- annual short-term incentive awards
- long-term incentives
- benefits and perquisites including pension benefits, described under *Other compensation information*.

For 2003 and consistent with past practices, total compensation was positioned at the median of what is paid by the group of companies with which BCE compares itself (comparator group). Paying at the median of the comparator group means that 50% of the companies in the comparator group pay more than BCE and 50% pay less for similar positions.

In 2003, as part of its periodic reviews of the comparator group, the MRCC decided to expand the group from 22 to 43 publicly traded Canadian and U.S. companies. The 2003 comparator group includes 23 Canadian companies and 20 U.S. companies. The Canadian and the U.S. companies were selected based on one or more of the following criteria: telecommunications/high technology, strategic use of technology, most admired companies and revenues. This larger group of companies is more representative of BCE's current environment and will therefore provide a better basis for comparisons to the market.

Total compensation that the executive officers received was between the median and the 75th percentile of what the comparator group offered for similar positions, based on each individual's contribution to BCE's performance and how successful BCE was in achieving its strategic business objectives and financial targets. Consistent with past practices, the 75th percentile was reserved for those few individuals who contributed in an outstanding fashion. The 75th percentile means that 25% of the comparator group pay more than BCE and 75% of the comparator group pay less. The MRCC did not assign weightings to any elements of the total compensation.

Please see *Other compensation information — Executive compensation table* for total compensation paid to the named executive officers over the past three years.

BASE SALARY

The MRCC determines the base salary of each executive officer within a salary range to reflect individual performance and responsibilities related to the position. The mid-point of the salary range corresponds to the median of the comparator group for similar positions. The minimum for the salary range is 20% below the mid-point and the maximum is 20% above.

ANNUAL SHORT-TERM INCENTIVE AWARDS

The short-term incentive program is designed to support the achievement of corporate objectives and reward executive officers based on BCE's success. Financial targets account for 70% of the corporate performance factor while the remaining portion is based on the achievement of strategic business objectives. The board sets these objectives in the corporate mandate at the beginning of each year. Please see *Statement of corporate governance practices — How we are meeting the TSX guidelines — guidelines 1(a) and 1(c)* for more information. The MRCC determines the annual short-term incentive awards by considering both the corporate performance and the executive officer's contributions.

For the year 2003, BCE's financial targets were set with respect to net earnings applicable to common shares (EPS), revenue growth, EBITDA[1] growth, capital intensity (% of revenues), free cash flow[2] and ROIC[3]. Each of these components has a weight of 10% except the EPS which is at 20%. Strategic business objectives which account for the remaining 30% of the corporate performance factor might include, for example, a specific corporate objective with respect to a particular subsidiary, the development of new businesses, higher penetration of products and services, the improvement of management development or the strengthening of certain relationships. Further to the implementation of a new structure at Bell Canada in June 2003 and in recognition of the increased focus of BCE's executive officers on Bell Canada, BCE's core asset, the MRCC and the board decided to adjust BCE's corporate performance factor based on Bell Canada results. In 2003, Bell Canada's performance was evaluated based on NIAC[4] (45%), revenue (25%) and customer satisfaction (30%), which resulted in a Bell Canada corporate performance factor of 50%. Consequently, a corporate performance factor of 50% instead of 65% was used to determine the annual short-term incentive awards of BCE's executive officers.

The individual's contribution is evaluated based on criteria that affect corporate performance such as creativity and initiative in addressing business issues, succession planning and management development. The individual performance factor may vary between 0 and 200%.

Each year, the MRCC sets target values for the awards. In 2003 the target awards ranged from 30% of base salary for the lowest eligible officer's position to 125% of base salary for the President and Chief Executive Officer. The minimum target for the named executive officers was 75% of base salary.

---

[1] The term EBITDA (earnings before interest, taxes, depreciation and amortization) does not have any standardized meaning prescribed by Canadian generally accepted accounting principles (GAAP) and is therefore unlikely to be comparable to similar measures presented by other issuers. We define it as operating revenues less operating expenses, which means it represents operating income before amortization expense, net benefit plans credit (cost) and restructuring and other charges. EBITDA should not be confused with net cash flows from operating activities. The most comparable Canadian GAAP earnings measure is operating income.

[2] The term *free cash flow* does not have any standardized meaning prescribed by Canadian GAAP and is therefore unlikely to be comparable to similar measures presented by other issuers. Free cash flow is calculated as cash from operating activities after total dividends, capital expenditures and other investing activities. The most comparable Canadian GAAP financial measure is cash from operating activities.

[3] The return on invested capital (ROIC) is defined as the latest twelve months' net earnings divided by the most recent quarter invested capital (long-term debt plus common and preferred stock equity).

[4] NIAC (Net Income Applicable to Common Shares) is based on net revenues earned, minus the cost of conducting business. NIAC represents a good estimate of funds generated from operations available to holders of common shares. Such funds can either be distributed as dividends, or kept for reinvestment in the company.

On the basis of the above factors, the MRCC determines the size of the annual short-term incentive awards. More specifically, awards are computed based on the product of the target award, the corporate performance factor and the individual performance factor. The maximum payout is two times the target award.

In most cases, awards granted for a year are paid at the beginning of the following year.

Executive officers who are eligible to participate in the *BCE share unit plan for senior executives and other key employees (1997)* (deferred share unit plan) and in the *Employees' profit sharing plan* can elect to have up to 100% of their annual short-term incentive award paid in deferred share units (DSUs) or contributed to the *Employees' profit sharing plan*. They must decide how they wish to receive their award by the end of the year in which the award is earned. Please see *Deferred share unit plan* for more information. Contribution to the *Employees' profit sharing plan* permits tax on the incentive award to be paid by the time of the required filing date of the income tax return for the year of contribution.

Election to receive the award in the form of DSUs can be used as a means to achieve mandatory share ownership levels as described under *Share ownership requirements*.

LONG-TERM INCENTIVES

In light of BCE's internal and external environments and to create an even stronger link between executive compensation and BCE's mid-term and long-term operational and financial success, the board has approved, for 2004 and onward, a significant shift in BCE's long-term compensation strategy which includes the introduction of a mid-term incentive and a reduction in the use of stock options. These are discussed under *Change in compensation strategy for 2004 and in the future*.

STOCK OPTIONS

The MRCC may grant BCE's executive officers and other key employees, and those of certain of BCE's subsidiaries, options to buy BCE common shares under the stock option plans. The number of outstanding options is not taken into account when determining if and how many options will be awarded.

Multiples of the base salary are used as a basis to grant stock options. The multiples vary depending on the position and are designed to bring total compensation, depending on individual performance, to between the 50th and 75th percentile of what is paid by the comparator group for similar positions. The 75th percentile is reserved for those few individuals who have contributed in an outstanding fashion. The option multiples used in 2003 were reduced by an average of 20% from the 2002 levels in order to reflect the downward trend in the size of stock option grants.

The number of options granted is calculated by dividing the value of the grant by the subscription price, i.e., the market value of BCE common shares on the day before the grant is effective. The MRCC may approve special grants of stock options to recognize singular achievements or, exceptionally, to retain or motivate executive officers and key employees.

The price at which a common share may be purchased when the option is being exercised is called the exercise price. The exercise price is at least equal to the subscription price, except under certain circumstances. For example, the MRCC may set a higher exercise price when it grants the option. Or it may set a lower exercise price to maintain the economic position of the option holder. This may take place when an option to acquire shares of one of BCE's subsidiaries or of a company that BCE is acquiring is converted into an option to acquire BCE common shares. The lower price would be subject to any required approval of the stock exchanges on which BCE common shares are listed.

The term of an option is normally 10 years from the day it is granted, unless the option holder retires, leaves the BCE group of companies, dies, or the company he or she works for is no longer part of the BCE group of companies. In these cases, the term may be reduced in accordance with the stock option plan under which it was granted or in accordance with decisions made by the MRCC.

The right to exercise an option normally accrues or "vests" by 25% a year for four years from the day of grant, unless there is a change of control of BCE or of a designated subsidiary or the MRCC sets different terms. Please see *Change of control* for details.

Option holders will lose all of their unexercised options granted after 2001 if they engage in prohibited behavior after they leave the BCE group of companies. These include using BCE's confidential information for the benefit of another employer. In addition, the option holder must reimburse BCE the after-tax profit realized on exercising any options during the twelve-month period preceding the date on which the unfair employment practice began.

Prior to November 1999, some options were granted with related rights to special compensation payments (SCPs). SCPs are cash payments representing the excess of the market value of the shares on the day of exercise of the related options over the subscription price of the options. SCPs, if any, are attached to options and are triggered when the options are exercised.

Effective January 1, 2003, BCE adopted the fair value method of accounting for stock option compensation on a prospective basis.

Stock options for executive officers of BCE subsidiaries

The number of options granted to Bell Canada's executive officers in 2003 was based on the economic profit target of 2002. As the 2002 target was exceeded, their stock option grant was increased by 10% which means that they received 110% of their normal grant in February 2003. If 90% to 100% of the target had been achieved, 100% of the grant would have been awarded. If less than 90% of the target had been achieved, executive officers would have received only 50% of their grant.

In 2003, the economic profit target was replaced by the return on equity (ROE)[1] target and therefore 100% of the grant was taken into consideration when establishing the 2004 grants under the new executive compensation policy. Please see *Change in compensation strategy for 2004 and in the future* for details.

The share option plan of BCE Emergis is almost the same as BCE's stock option plans, except that the term of the options is six years and options vest by 25% after two years, 75% after three years and 100% after four years. As Chief Executive Officer of BCE Emergis until May 13, 2003, Mr. Blouin participated in the BCE Emergis share option plan.

You will find more information about options granted and exercised under these programs in the tables under *Other compensation information — Stock options*.

DEFERRED SHARE UNIT PLAN

The deferred share unit plan is designed to more closely link the interests of the executive officers to those of the shareholders. DSUs may be awarded to certain executive officers and other key employees and those of certain subsidiaries.

DSUs have the same value as BCE common shares. The number and terms of outstanding DSUs are not taken into account when determining if and how many DSUs will be awarded. There is no vesting period for DSUs.

DSUs receive payments that are equivalent to the dividends on BCE common shares. Additional DSUs are credited on each dividend payment date and are equivalent in value to the dividend paid.

Eligible executive officers can choose to have up to 100% of their annual short-term incentive award and capital efficiency incentive award paid in DSUs instead of cash. The award is converted into DSUs based on the market value of a BCE common share on the day before the award is approved by the board. These DSUs count towards the minimum share ownership requirements, which are described under *Share ownership requirements*.

The MRCC may also grant special awards of DSUs to recognize outstanding achievements or for attaining certain corporate objectives.

Holders of DSUs may not sell their units while they are employed by a company of the BCE group. Once they leave the BCE group, BCE will buy the same number of BCE common shares on the open market as the number of DSUs a participant holds in the plan, after deductions for applicable taxes. These shares are then delivered to the former employee.

SHARE OWNERSHIP REQUIREMENTS

BCE believes in substantial share ownership and is providing compensation programs designed to encourage executive officers to own shares of BCE through common

---

[1] ROE (return on common shareholders' equity) is calculated as net earnings applicable to common shares as a percentage of average common shareholders' equity.

shares or DSUs. A minimum share ownership level has been set for each position, based on a percentage of annual base salary:

- President and Chief Executive Officer — 500%
- Group Presidents and heads of major lines of business — 300%
- other officers — 200%.

These officers must meet their target within five years with the objective that 50% of their target will be reached within 3 years. The 5-year target must be reached by April 2006, or within 5 years from their date of hire or promotion, if such event occurred after April 1, 2001.

Share ownership requirements also apply to all Vice-Presidents with a target of 100% of annual base salary.

Shares or DSUs received through the following programs can be used to reach the minimum share ownership level:

- deferred share unit plan, which is described under *Deferred share unit plan*
- employees' savings plan, which is described in *Other compensation information — Executive compensation table*, footnote (6)
- shares acquired and held by exercising stock options granted under BCE's stock option plans which are described under *Long-term incentives*.

As part of the new compensation policy for 2004 and beyond, concrete measures will be taken to ensure that share ownership requirements are met.

COMPENSATION POLICY OF SUBSIDIARIES

Bell Canada's and BCE Emergis' compensation policies are similar to BCE's. Payments under their short-term incentive plans depend on achieving their respective corporate objectives, which are set out at the beginning of each year.

The board approved the recommendations of Bell Canada for grants of BCE options to Mr. Blouin, Mr. Wetmore, Mr. Roman and Mr. Sheridan in 2003. Grants of options to Mr. Blouin while he was employed by BCE Emergis were made under the BCE Emergis share option plan, according to BCE Emergis' compensation policy.

CHANGE IN COMPENSATION STRATEGY FOR 2004 AND IN THE FUTURE

BCE and its core asset, Bell Canada, are dealing proactively to the changing competitive landscape and customer needs. During the last year, the structure and business strategy have been realigned to deliver on these business realities. BCE and Bell Canada have worked to simplify both the customer experience and the internal operations. As well, the type of leadership considered essential for success now and into the future was redefined.

In light of these important changes, starting in 2004, the executive compensation policy has been redesigned to ensure close alignment and support with the company's new direction and strategic objectives. The committee has been closely involved in developing the overall design. The design delivers clear direction as to what is important to BCE executives and Bell Canada executives and what behaviors and types of results will be rewarded. Fundamentally, the new executive compensation policy is designed to drive a shift in culture toward greater individual accountability and higher levels of performance.

The underlying philosophy is to remain conservative with regards to fixed compensation (such as base salary) while placing more emphasis on variable (at risk) compensation, through the use of three different compensation vehicles, short-term, mid-term and long-term incentive plans. Each of these variable compensation vehicles contains specific performance targets which must be met in order to trigger any payments. These targets are not achievable by incremental change alone; in some cases they will require a complete process redesign.

The key components of this policy are:

- increase total compensation from the median (50th percentile), where it is today, to the 60th percentile of a specific comparator group of companies. This will provide BCE and Bell Canada with the ability to attract and retain the type of executives needed to deliver at required performance levels.

- elements within the total compensation policy at the 60th percentile
  - maintain base salaries at the median (50th percentile), their current level
  - increase the short-term annual incentive target awards from the median to the 75th percentile of the comparator group for similar positions. This will further reinforce the importance of meeting the annual financial drivers and the fashion in which they are delivered.
  - transfer approximately 50% of the value of the long-term incentive plan, where stock options are granted, into a new mid-term plan under which Restricted Share Units (RSU) are used as the vehicle:
    - dependent on their level, each executive is granted a specific number of RSUs for a two-year period. The RSUs will either vest or be forfeited two years from the grant date.
    - vesting is conditional on achieving specific operational targets by the end of a two-year performance period. These targets are directly aligned to achieving the company's strategic goals for each of the core business units of Bell Canada.
    - at the end of the performance period, subject to compliance with individual share ownership requirements, vested RSUs will be paid in BCE common shares or in cash.

- reduce the value of stock options granted in the long-term incentive plan by approximately 50% and changing the key design features:
  - vesting is subject to a combination of time and performance. The performance metric is based on meeting or exceeding the median total shareholder return of a group of North American telecommunications companies. 50% of the stock options will vest after two years and 100% after three years, subject to achieving the performance metric.
  - option period reduced from ten to six years
  - number of stock options granted cover a three-year period (front-loaded).

CONCLUSION

In the MRCC's view, the total compensation of the named executive officers for 2003 was appropriate and competitive in the marketplace. The MRCC believes that it was also consistent with the compensation policy of linking a large part of executive officers' compensation to the achievement of corporate performance objectives and the creation of shareholder value.

The MRCC believes that the compensation must reflect corporate performance. As such, the annual short-term incentive award of the named executive officers was based on a corporate performance factor of 50% as the corporate objectives were not fully achieved.

Overall, the MRCC is confident that this approach to compensation has allowed BCE to attract, motivate and retain executive officers, while aligning their interests with those of its shareholders. The new compensation strategy implemented in 2004 will help further support the company's goal to become the best telecommunications company in North America.

Report presented March 10, 2004, by: **P.M. Tellier, Chairman; R.A. Brenneman; A.S. Fell; B.M. Levitt; J.H. McArthur;** and **V.L. Young**.

Source: Reproduced with permission from BCE Inc.

reduced. Also, the short-term awards are capped at two times the amount based on the target.

It should be noted that the compensation committee of BCE's board of directors (MRCC) has the ultimate say in the amounts of salary, bonus, and option awards, within the above guidelines. The compensation committee is a corporate governance device, to deal with the fact that the BCE plan, like all real compensation contracts, is *incomplete* (see the discussion of complete and incomplete contracts in Section 9.8.2). While contracts tend to be rigid, the compensation committee may have some discretion to deal with the effects on compensation of an unanticipated outcome. For example, we are told that short-term incentive awards were reduced by 50% of target since corporate objectives for 2003 were not fully achieved. One might expect that if targets are not achieved, no bonus is payable. However, the MRCC must have felt that sufficient progress was made that some bonus was justified.

Fourth, the incentive effects of BCE's compensation plan should be apparent. For highest-ranking officers, annual incentive awards are based primarily on attainment of financial targets, such as earnings per share and return on capital, and are paid either in cash or DSUs. Since the short-term incentive awards depend largely on current year's performance, this creates an incentive to maximize the current year's levels of the performance measures. Note, however, that maximizing current reported performance, such as earnings per share, may be at the expense of the firm's longer-run interests, leading to dysfunctional tactics such as deferral of maintenance, underinvestment in R&D, premature disposal of facilities in order to realize a gain, and other opportunistic earnings management techniques. However, the requirement of substantial share ownership gives officers a longer-term interest in the success of the firm. Presumably, this reduces the temptation to engage in dysfunctional practices such as those mentioned.

To reinforce these longer-term considerations, all executives and other key employees participate in the stock option-based long-term incentive plan. Here, recipients will benefit to the extent that BCE's common share price when an option is exercised exceeds the price when the option is granted. Note that the exercise price of the option is generally equal to the market value of a BCE share on the day prior to the effective date of the grant (the subscription price). In terms of our discussion of ESOs in Section 8.3, the option's intrinsic value is zero. Accounting for ESOs changed, however, beginning in 2004, when Canadian accounting standards required ESO expensing—see our discussion in Section 8.3. Note that BCE has anticipated this requirement by voluntarily expensing its ESOs from January 1, 2003.

The options have a 10-year term, and, normally, the right to exercise early is not fully available until four years after the grant date.

Fifth, the *mix* of short- and long-term incentive components in a compensation plan is important. As mentioned above, a high proportion of long-term incentive components should produce a longer manager decision horizon, and vice versa. The MRCC can influence the mix, since it determines the size of the annual short-term incentive awards. That is, since options are awarded to bring an executive's total compensation up to the 50th to 75th percentile of that of comparable corporations, the greater the size of the short-term award the smaller the options award and vice versa, other things equal. We will outline in Section 10.4.2 why some flexibility in the short-term/long-term incentives mix is desirable.

Finally, consider the risk aspects of BCE's plan. Certainly, compensation is risky for BCE managers since economy and industry-wide events, which may not be informative about the manager's effort, will affect both earnings per share and share price. However, aspects of the BCE plan operate to limit compensation risk. Base salary, of course, is relatively risk-free. Also, the lower limit on both short-term incentive awards and stock option value is zero. This reduces downside risk since, if the bogey is not attained or if share value falls below the exercise price, the manager does not have to pay the firm. In addition, as mentioned, total compensation is adjusted to the 50th to 75th percentile of that of the comparison group. By setting total compensation in this way, an averaging effect is introduced, which would tend to make a BCE executive's total compensation less subject to variations in the performance of BCE itself.

In sum, the BCE compensation structure appears to be quite sophisticated in terms of its incentives, decision horizon, and risk properties. For our purposes, the most important point to note is that there are two main incentive components: short-term incentive awards based on earnings and individual achievement, and longer-term stock options whose value depends on share price performance. Thus, both accounting and market-based performance incentives are embedded in the plan. These give management a vital interest in how net income is determined, both because earnings per share is a direct input into compensation and because, as we saw in Chapter 5, net income affects share price.

Of particular interest are the changes in compensation strategy for 2004. Two aspects of the new strategy should be particularly noted:

- An increase in total compensation (to help retain executive talent) combined with a greater proportion of total compensation depending on performance.

- A shortening of the decision horizon, by increasing the weight of the short-term incentive awards, creation of a new mid-term compensation component, and reductions in the value and vesting period of stock options.

The reduced role of stock options consists of a 50% reduction in the value granted plus a reduction of term to expiry from 10 to six years. These reductions are due, presumably, to the "pump and dump" ESO abuses in recent years whereby it seems that many CEOs artificially inflated share price so as to increase the value of their vested options (see Section 8.3). In effect, ESOs seem to have motivated very short-run decision horizons— the opposite of the longer-run horizons that were intended. While no such allegations have been made against BCE, it is one of several large companies that have reduced their usage of ESOs.

The shortening of decision horizon is of particular interest. As mentioned earlier, BCE did not achieve all of its short-term corporate objectives in 2003. It seems that the company wants to increase incentives to attain these objectives in future. However, this raises the possibility of dysfunctional behaviour to increase reported performance in the short run, as described above. Consequently, the company has created a mid-term compensation plan. This plan introduces a two-year performance period, and pays compensation in the form of **restricted share units**. These are units of company stock that will only be awarded if one or more targets are met, such as attainment of a specified return on assets and/or a specified share price. In the case of BCE, the restricted stock vests only if some specific two-year operational objectives are attained. Presumably, the combination of a two-year performance period and a reduction in ESOs will control tendencies for dysfunctional short-run behaviour.

We now turn to a more general consideration of the compensation issues raised above.

10.4 THE THEORY OF EXECUTIVE COMPENSATION

10.4.1 The Relative Proportions of Net Income and Share Price in Evaluating Manager Performance

Much of the theory of executive compensation derives from the agency models developed in Chapter 9, despite their single-period orientation. In particular, the analysis of Holmström (Section 9.8.1) predicts that the efficiency of a compensation contract may be increased if it is based on two or more performance measures. The BCE Inc. contract discussed above is consistent with this prediction. The question then is, what determines the relative importance of net income and share price in evaluating manager performance? This is an important question for accountants, since motivation of manager performance is an important social goal. If financial reporting is to contribute to attainment of this goal, it must successfully complement other performance measures, such as share price. What determines the relative weights (i.e., the mix) of net income and share price in evaluating the manager's overall performance?

This question was studied by Banker and Datar (1989). Banker and Datar demonstrated conditions under which the linear mix of performance measures depends on the product of the sensitivity and precision of those measures. These concepts were introduced in Section 9.8.1, where sensitivity was defined as the rate at which the expected value of the measure responds to manager effort, and precision as the reciprocal of the variance of the noise in the measure.[2] Banker and Datar showed that the lower the noise in net income and the greater its sensitivity to manager effort, the greater should be the proportion of net income to share price in determining the manager's overall performance.

There are a number of ways that accountants can increase the sensitivity of net income. One possibility, raised in Section 9.8.1, is to reduce recognition lag by moving to current value accounting. Reduced recognition lag increases sensitivity since more of the payoffs from manager effort show up in current net income.

However, current value accounting is a double-edged sword in this regard, since it also tends to reduce precision. As mentioned above, Banker and Datar show that lower precision reduces the optimal proportion of a performance measure in the contract. It is thus unclear whether adoption of current value accounting would result in a net gain in importance for net income. Indeed, if the negative precision effect of current value accounting outweighs its positive sensitivity effect, a bit of conservatism, such as in historical cost accounting, may be preferable to current value for compensation contracting.[3]

Another approach to increasing sensitivity is through full disclosure, particularly of unusual and non-recurring items. Full disclosure increases sensitivity by enabling the compensation committee to better evaluate manager effort and ability, and also to evaluate earnings persistence. Persistent earnings are a more sensitive measure of current manager effort than transitory or price-irrelevant earnings, which may arise independently of effort. Notice also that GAAP can reduce the scope for opportunistic earnings management, as illustrated in Example 9.7. Reduced earnings management increases sensitivity by reducing the manager's ability to disguise shirking.

With respect to share price, a major reason for its relatively low precision derives from the effects of economy-wide factors. For example, if interest rates increase, the expected effects on future firm performance will quickly show up in share price. These effects may say relatively little about current manager effort, however. As a result, they mainly add volatility to share price. Nevertheless, as we pointed out in Section 9.8.1, Holmström's analysis shows that share price could never be completely replaced as a performance measure as long as it contains some additional effort information. The sensitivity of share price is sufficiently great that it will always reveal additional payoff information beyond that contained in net income. Thus, we may expect both measures to coexist.

This coexistence, however, creates an opportunity for the compensation plan to influence the length of the manager's decision horizon. To explain, assume two types of manager effort—short-run and long-run. The owner can adjust the relative proportions of net income–based and share price–based compensation to exploit the fact that current net income aggregates the payoffs from only some manager activities in the current period. For example, to encourage more R&D (i.e., long-run effort), the owner can reduce the proportion of the manager's compensation based on net income and increase the proportion based on share price. Compensation will now rise more strongly due to securities market response to an increase in R&D, and there will be less compensation penalty from writing R&D costs off currently. Consequently, it will be in the manager's interest to increase R&D. More generally, firms with substantial investment opportunities will want to increase the proportion of share price–based compensation.[4]

Alternatively, suppose that the firm has to cut costs (i.e., short-run effort) due, for example, to an increase in competition or an increase in the domestic exchange rate. Net income will aggregate the favourable cash flow effects of cost cutting quickly and accurately, perhaps even more so than share price, particularly if the cost-cutting measures are complex or constitute inside information, or if the market is concerned about the longer-run effects of cost cutting. Also share price may not perfectly aggregate the cost-cutting information in the presence of noise trading or market inefficiencies. Then, the firm may wish to increase the weight of net income relative to share price in the manager's compensation.

In effect, when share price and net income differentially reflect the short- and long-run payoffs of current manager actions, the length of the manager's decision horizon can be influenced by the mix of share price–based and net income–based compensation— more share-based compensation produces a longer decision horizon and vice versa. This was demonstrated theoretically by Bushman and Indjejikian (1993). As we pointed out in Section 10.3, the BCE compensation plan allows the compensation committee some flexibility with respect to the mix of short- and long-term compensation. Furthermore, the 2004 revisions to BCE's compensation plan seem to shorten the decision horizon.

The mix of performance measures was further studied by Datar, Kulp, and Lambert (2001). Their analysis suggests that decision horizon must be traded off with the sensitivity and precision of performance measures. For example, the owner will increase the weight on a performance measure, even if this results in a manager decision horizon that is not exactly what the owner wants, if that performance measure is sensitive and precise. The reason is that such a performance measure "tells more" about effort, hence enables a more efficient contract. This greater efficiency is traded off against the benefits of controlling the manager's decision horizon. Consequently, sensitivity and precision remain as important characteristics in the presence of more than one type of managerial effort.

*10.4.2 Short-Run and Long-Run Effort

Our discussion of agency theory in Chapter 9 assumed that manager effort is single-dimensional—a modelling device to encompass the whole range of managerial activities. Thus, we were interested in the *intensity* of effort, and envisaged two levels of intensity—"working hard" or "shirking." To enable us to better understand executive compensation, we now extend the agency model to regard effort as multi-dimensional. Specifically, we pursue the assumption in the previous section that effort consists of **short-run effort** (SR) and **long-run effort** (LR). Now, however, we view these two effort components as separate manager decisions.

SR is effort devoted to activities such as cost control, maintenance, employee morale, advertising, and other day-to-day activities that generate net income mainly in the current period. LR is effort devoted to activities such as long-range planning, R&D, and acquisitions. While LR effort may generate some net income in the current period, most of the payoffs from these activities extend into future periods. Our development here is based on Feltham and Xie (1994).

The manager can either work hard or shirk along either or both effort dimensions. Then, we can regard current period net income (NI) as being generated by the following equation:

$$NI = \mu_1 SR + \mu_2 LR \pm \text{random factors with expected value zero} \qquad (10.1)$$

where SR and LR are the quantities of short-run and long-run effort, respectively. There are now two sensitivities of net income rather than one. Thus μ_1 is the sensitivity of earnings to SR effort and μ_2 is sensitivity to LR effort. The assumption that the random factors affecting net income have expected value of zero implies that net income is not subject to manager manipulation and bias, consistent with our assumption in Section 9.4.2.

The firm's payoff x is also affected by these SR and LR activities. Thus, we can write the payoff as:

$$x = b_1 SR + b_2 LR \pm \text{random factors with expected value zero} \qquad (10.2)$$

where b_1 and b_2 are sensitivities of the payoff to SR and LR effort, respectively. We assume here that the manager exerts effort only in the first period, and that net income is reported at the end of this period. However, consistent with our assumption in Chapter 9, the payoff is not fully observable until the next period. That is, the full payoffs from the manager's

---

*This section can be omitted with little loss of continuity.

SR and LR first-period effort decisions are not realized until that time. Net income is a message that predicts what these payoffs will be. The manager is compensated based on first-period net income. The payoff in the next period goes wholly to the owner.

Recognition of effort as a set of activities introduces a new concept—the **congruency** of a performance measure. To illustrate congruency, consider the following example.

Example 10.1
A Congruent Performance Measure

Assume that the manager can work hard or shirk on both SR and LR effort, and that the net incomes and payoffs are as given in Table 10.1:

Table 10.1 Expected Net Incomes and Payoffs for Congruent Performance Measure

| | Manager's Effort | | | |
| | Short-run Effort (SR) | | Long-run Effort (LR) | |
	Work Hard	Shirk	Work Hard	Shirk
Expected Net Income E(NI)	$4	$1	$3	$2
Expected Payoff E(x)	$6	$1.5	$4.5	$3

If the manager allocates all effort to SR and works hard, expected net income is $4. However, some of this effort, such as cost control, may remain to benefit next period, assuming that at least some of the lower costs will persist. Let these future benefits amount to $2. Then the expected *payoff* from SR effort totals $6. If the manager works hard at LR effort, say, by devoting time to R&D, this generates expected net income of $3 currently but is expected to create additional payoff of $1.5 next period, for a total of $4.5. Similar comments apply if the manager shirks.

From Table 10.1, the *increases* in expected payoffs if the manager works hard, compared to shirking, are given in Table 10.2:

Table 10.2 Increases in Net Incomes and Payoffs from Working Hard

| | Manager's Effort | |
	Short-run Effort (SR)	Long-run Effort (LR)
Expected Net Income E(NI)	$\mu_1 = \$3$	$\mu_2 = \$1$
Expected Payoff E(x)	$b_1 = \$4.5$	$b_2 = \$1.5$

The μ_1 and μ_2 in Table 10.2 are the sensitivities of net income to SR and LR effort, respectively—see Equation 10.1. Similarly, b_1 and b_2 are the sensitivities of the payoff to effort—see Equation 10.2. Note that b_1 is in the *same proportion* to μ_1 (4.5:3 = 3:2) as b_2 is to μ_2 (1.5:1 = 3:2). Then, net income is said to be **congruent** to the payoff. That is, an increase of expected net income by, say, $1 will increase the expected payoff by $1.5 regardless of whether the increase in expected net income comes from LR or SR effort or any combination of the two.

This being the case, the owner can design a contract that compensates the manager on the basis of reported net income for the first period without worrying about how the manager allocates effort between short-run and long-run activities. Given the contract, the manager will choose an effort intensity and allocation to maximize his/her expected utility of compensation, net of effort disutility. This was illustrated in Examples 9.3–9.7.

In sum, if there is more than one dimension to manager effort, and if net income is congruent to the payoff, the owner need not be concerned how the manager allocates effort across the dimensions. Each type of effort is equally effective in generating payoff.

Unfortunately, congruent net income is unlikely to be the case. Again, the reason derives from recognition lag. Consider Table 10.1 once more. While SR effort, such as cost control, may be an effective way to generate current net income, this is unlikely to be as effective in generating payoff in the next period, contrary to our assumption above. While some of the lower costs may persist, the cost-cutting nature of SR effort is likely to reduce employee morale and organization effectiveness in the next period, and this effect is not recognized in current net income. A more likely payoff from SR effort is, say, $2 if the manager works hard (i.e., the net income of $4 in the current period is reduced by $2 in the next, giving a net payoff of $2) and, say, $1.5 if he/she shirks. LR effort, however, is likely to have an opposite effect. Effort devoted to R&D, for example, will likely generate a high longer-run payoff, say $9 if the manager works hard and $4 if he/she shirks. Tables 10.3 and 10.4 summarize these assumptions:

Table 10.3 Expected Net Incomes and Payoffs for Noncongruent Performance Measure

	Manager's Effort			
	Short-run Effort (SR)		**Long-run Effort (LR)**	
	Work Hard	Shirk	Work Hard	Shirk
Expected Net Income E(NI)	$4	$1	$3	$2
Expected Payoff E(x)	$2	$1.5	$9	$4

Table 10.4 Increases in Net Incomes and Payoffs from Working Hard

	Manager's Effort	
	Short-run Effort (SR)	**Long-run Effort (LR)**
Expected Net Income E(NI)	$\mu_1 = \$3$	$\mu_2 = \$1$
Expected Payoff E(x)	$b_1 = \$0.5$	$b_2 = \$5$

Now, for SR effort, the proportion of b_1 to μ_1 is 0.5:3 = 1/6. For LR effort, the proportion is 5:1 = 5. Thus net income is **noncongruent** to the payoff—it *does* matter to the owner which type of effort generates net income. An increase of $1 in net income from SR effort will increase expected payoff by $1/6 whereas an increase in net income of $1 from LR effort will increase it by $5.

In our example, the owner will want high R&D, because of its high ultimate payoff (i.e., b_2 is greater than b_1 in Table 10.4). But the manager, whose compensation is based on first period net income, will tend towards a short-run decision horizon since effort allocated to SR activities generates greater expected net income and compensation (i.e., μ_1 is greater than μ_2 in Table 10.4). The compensation contract must now consider not only the intensity of manager effort but also the *allocation* of effort across activities. Raising the manager's profit share will not serve to lengthen the manager's decision horizon—it will simply encourage more SR effort. As a result, the owner settles for less LR effort than he/she would like.

The question, then, is what might the owner do about this? One possibility is to replace net income with a more congruent performance measure, such as share price. It is not hard to see that share price is more congruent with payoff than net income, since it is less subject to recognition lag. Then, favourable share price sensitivity to R&D will motivate the manager to increase LR effort. However, share price is less precise than net income. Consequently, it is not clear that basing compensation only on share price would increase contracting efficiency.

A second possibility is to use both performance measures. As noted in Section 9.8.1, Feltham and Xie show conditions under which Holmström's (1979) result continues to apply when effort is multi-dimensional. Then, theory predicts that compensation will depend on both net income and share price, consistent with what we observe in real compensation contracts.

10.4.3 The Role of Risk in Executive Compensation

We can also consider the manager's effort from a risk perspective since, as pointed out in Chapter 9, in the presence of moral hazard the manager must bear some compensation risk if effort is to be motivated. Since managers, like other rational, risk-averse individuals, trade off risk and return, the more risk managers bear the higher must be their *expected* compensation if reservation utility is to be attained. Thus, to motivate the manager at the lowest cost, designers of efficient incentive compensation plans try to get the most motivation for a given amount of risk imposed or, equivalently, the least risk for a given level of motivation.

It is important to realize that compensation risk affects how the manager operates the firm. If not enough risk is imposed, the firm suffers from low manager effort. If too much risk is imposed, the manager may underinvest in risky projects even though such projects would benefit diversified shareholders.

There are several ways to control compensation risk. Perhaps the most important of these from a theoretical perspective is **relative performance evaluation** (RPE). Here, instead of measuring performance by net income and/or share price, performance is measured by the *difference* between the firm's net income and/or share price performance and the average performance of a group of similar firms, such as other firms in the same industry. The theory of RPE was developed by Holmström (1982). By measuring the manager's performance relative to the average performance of similar firms, the systematic or common risks that the industry faces will be filtered out of the incentive plan, especially if the number of firms in the industry is large. To see this, note that when there are noisy performance measures in the contract, there will be some risks that are common to all firms in the industry.[5] For example, at least some of the effects on share price and earnings of a downturn in the economy, such as a reduction in sales, will also affect other firms in the industry. RPE deducts the average earnings and share price performance of other firms in the industry from the manager's performance measures, leaving a net performance that more precisely reflects the manager's efforts in running the firm in question. Thus, under RPE, it is possible for a manager to do well even if the firm reports a loss and/or share price is down, providing the losses are lower than those of the average firm in the industry.

If the RPE theory is valid, we would expect to observe total manager compensation negatively related to average industry performance. For example, when industry performance is low, high earnings and/or share price performance for the firm in question is even more impressive since it overcomes negative factors affecting the whole industry. Consequently, the compensation committee will award higher bonuses. When industry performance is high, high earnings and/or share price for the firm in question is less impressive, so that lower bonuses are awarded.

However, despite RPE's theoretical appeal, strong statistical evidence that managers are compensated this way has been hard to come by. Antle and Smith (1986) found weak evidence for RPE, and, according to Pavlik, Scott, and Tiessen (1993), a survey of RPE articles shows that the ability of RPE to predict manager compensation is modest. A possible reason for the weak empirical support is given by Sloan (1993), who argues that net income is less affected in the current period by economy-wide risks than share price, that is, share price is less precise. Inclusion of net income as a performance measure in addition to share price shields manager compensation from these economy-wide effects. As a result, Sloan concludes, RPE is not needed since basing compensation on both share price and net income accomplishes a similar result.

Also, it is possible that strategic factors work against finding empirical evidence of RPE. For example, Aggarwal and Samwick (1999) (AS) present a model of firms in an oligopolistic industry, where the demand for a firm's product depends not only on its own product price but also on the prices of its competitors' products.[6] That is, the lower are competitors' prices the lower is the demand for the product of the firm in question, and vice versa. This creates an incentive for managers to engage in cooperative pricing behaviour to "soften" competition, as AS put it. This raises profits for all firms in the industry. To encourage this cooperative behaviour, compensation plans put positive, not negative, weight on other firms' performance. Furthermore, the magnitude of this positive weight should be stronger the greater the degree of competition in the industry. AS report empirical evidence consistent with this prediction. The BCE plan has a similar characteristic, since total compensation is positioned at the median of that paid by a group of comparable companies. To the extent that profits, and thus compensation, of BCE's competitors are high, BCE's compensation will also rise. The difficulty of finding empirical support for RPE could be due to countervailing effects such as these.

Another way to control risk is through the bogey of the compensation plan. Consider the manager in Example 9.3 who receives compensation of 0.3237 of earnings. Suppose the firm loses $50 million. That is, earnings are negative, and so would be the manager's compensation. Instead of receiving compensation, the manager would have to pay the firm over $16 million! Under such a risky contract, the average level of compensation needed for the manager to attain reservation utility would be prohibitive. In other words, fear of personal bankruptcy is probably not the most efficient way to motivate a manager to work hard. For this reason, compensation plans usually impose a bogey. That is, incentive compensation does not kick in until some level of financial performance—10% return on equity, for example—is reached. The effect is that if the bogey is not attained, the contract does not award any incentive compensation. However, an ancillary effect is that the manager does not have to pay the firm if there is a loss.[7]

If downside risk is limited, it seems reasonable for upside risk to be limited too; otherwise the manager would have everything to gain and little to lose, which could encourage excessive risk taking. As a result, many plans impose a cap, whereby incentive compensation ceases beyond a certain level. For example, no bonus may be awarded for return on equity exceeding, say, 25%. Note that the BCE plan imposes a cap on short-term incentive awards of two times the target award.

Conservative accounting also controls upside risk by delaying recognition of unrealized gains and discouraging premature revenue recognition. Watts (2003) argues that conservative accounting promotes contract efficiency by constraining the manager's ability to inflate current earnings, and hence compensation, by recording unrealized gains. However, basing compensation on conservative earnings gives the manager little incentive to invest in risky projects. No compensation will be received unless and until a project starts to generate realized profits. This creates a role for share-based compensation. Since share price will quickly reflect unrealized profits on long-term projects, managers can be encouraged to invest in such projects (equivalently, to incur upside risk) by basing compensation on share price performance. For example, ESOs provide this incentive since, if they succeed, they can become very valuable. Yet, if they do not succeed, the lowest the ESOs can be worth is zero.

Indeed, ESOs may be too effective in this regard. While they encourage upside risk, they impose little downside risk, and so may promote excessive risk taking. Thus, ESOs seem to have been a driving force behind horror stories such as Enron and WorldCom, as described in Section 1.2. It seems that manager effort was diverted away from value-increasing projects into opportunistic actions to increase share price, hence the value of their ESOs. The resulting risky and deceptive practices eventually led to the firms', and the managers', downfall.

Nevertheless, one should not conclude that ESOs should be eliminated from compensation plans. In this regard, it is interesting to recall BCE's changes to compensation for 2004, in Exhibit 10.1. These include a 50% reduction in ESO awards, not their elimination. Rajgopal and Shevlin (2002), in a sample of oil and gas firms over 1992–1997, found that ESOs did motivate managers to increase firm risk. This increased risk showed up both in increased exploration risk and reduced hedging activity. Rajgopal and Shevlin also found, however, that the effect of ESOs in their sample firms was to encourage risk-averse managers to undertake risky projects when these projects were economically desirable, not to encourage excessive risk taking. In effect, as in the results of Guay (1999) outlined in Section 8.5.4, their findings are consistent with efficient contracting.[8]

In sum, we arrive once again at a conclusion that a mix of performance measures is desirable. Compensation in the form of ESOs and/or company shares encourages upside risk and a longer-run decision horizon, while net income–based compensation imposes downside risk to discourage excessive risk taking that pure share-based compensation may create.

Another approach to controlling risk is through the compensation committee. As we saw in the BCE plan, this committee has the ultimate responsibility to determine the amounts of cash and stock compensation, and it has the flexibility to take special circumstances into account. For example, if the firm reports a loss, or earnings below the bogey, it may award a bonus anyway, particularly if it feels that the loss is due to some low-persistence item such as an unusual, non-recurring, or extraordinary event. However, the committee must exercise some restraint in this regard. If it is overly generous in not penalizing the manager for state realizations that are not his/her "fault," this will destroy contract rigidity and reduce effort incentive.

Given the amount of risk imposed on the manager by the compensation plan, it is important that the manager not be able to work out from under this risk. The manager can shed compensation risk by, for example, selling shares and options acquired and investing the proceeds in a risk-free asset and/or a diversified portfolio. However, compensation plans typically constrain this possibility by restricting the manager's ability to dispose of shares and options. Thus the BCE plan requires officers to hold from two to five times annual base salary in BCE shares. Also, stock options will not be fully exercisable until three years after the grant date.

The manager can also shed risk by excessive hedging. Not only is hedging costly, but effort incentive will suffer if the manager works out from under risk this way. Consequently, the firm may limit the manager's hedging behaviour.

Theory in Practice 10.1

Suncor Energy Inc., in its 2006 annual report MD&A (p. 31), describes how it controls possible excess hedging in its oil and gas cash flow hedg- ing program. Suncor's board has restricted cash flow hedging to a maximum of 30% of crude oil production up to December 31, 2008.

10.5 EMPIRICAL COMPENSATION RESEARCH

The research of Rajgopal and Shevlin outlined above provides some evidence that real compensation plans are designed efficiently. In this section, we review other empirical studies bearing on the relation between compensation theory and practice, concentrating on studies that examine the role of accounting information.

An early study in this area was conducted by Lambert and Larcker (1987) (LL). Using a sample of 370 U.S. firms over 1970–1984 inclusive, LL investigated the relative ability of return on shares and return on equity to explain managers' cash compensation (salary plus bonus). If, for example, compensation plans and compensation committees primarily use share return to motivate manager performance, then share return should be significantly related to cash compensation. Alternatively, if they primarily use net income as a motivator, return on equity (a ratio based on net income) should be significantly related to cash compensation.

Note that LL examined only cash compensation. Empirically, accounting variables do not seem to explain the options component of manager compensation. Indeed, this can be seen in the BCE plan. While short-term incentive awards are based on individual achievement and net income, stock option awards are not. Rather, they are made to bring total compensation up to the 50th to 75th percentiles of that paid by the group of comparison companies. Consequently, many studies of the role of net income in compensation concentrate on cash awards.

LL found that return on equity was more highly related to cash compensation than was return on shares. Indeed, several other studies have found the same results. This supports the decision horizon-controlling and risk-controlling roles for net income in compensation plans that were suggested in Sections 10.4.1 and 10.4.3.

LL also found that the relationship of these two payoff measures to cash compensation varied in systematic ways. For example, they found some evidence that the relationship between return on equity and cash compensation strengthened when net income was less noisy relative to return on shares. They measured the relative noisiness of net income by the ratio of the variability of return on equity over 1970–1984 to the variability of return on shares over the same period. The lower the noise in net income, the better it predicts the payoff, as illustrated in Example 9.4. This finding is also consistent with Banker and Datar's analysis.

LL also found that managerial compensation for growth firms' executives tended to have a lower relationship with return on equity than average. This too is consistent with

Banker and Datar, since, for growth firms, net income is relatively less sensitive to manager effort than it is for the average firm. Historical cost-based net income tends particularly to lag behind the real economic performance of a growth firm, because this basis of accounting does not recognize value increases until they are realized. The efficient market, however, will look through to real economic performance and value the shares accordingly. Thus, return on equity should be related less to compensation than share return for such firms, consistent with what LL found.

Perhaps the most interesting finding of LL, however, was that for firms where the correlation between share return and return on equity was low, there tended to be a higher weight on return on equity in the compensation plan, and vice versa. In other words, when net income is relatively uninformative to investors (low correlation between share return and return on equity) that same net income is relatively informative about manager effort (higher weight on return on equity in the compensation plan). This provides empirical evidence on the impact of the fundamental problem of financial accounting theory—the investor-informing and the manager performance-motivating dimensions of usefulness must be traded off.

Further evidence of efficient compensation contracting was provided by Indjejikian and Nanda (2002). In a sample of 2,981 senior executives over 1988–1995, they found that, on average, the lower the variability of return on equity the higher the target bonus[9] relative to base salary. This suggests that firms substitute out of salary (riskless, but little incentive effect) into bonus (risky, but greater incentive) as firm risk is less. This is consistent with efficient contracting since, when firm risk is relatively low, the incentive benefits of a bonus can be attained with relatively low compensation risk loaded onto the manager. Indjejikian and Nanda also found that target bonuses, especially for the CEOs in their sample, tended to increase, relative to base salary, with the volatility of return on shares. One interpretation is that firms in high-risk environments (hence, more volatile share prices) rely more on accounting-based performance measures relative to those based on stock price performance. Again, this is consistent with theory.

Bushman, Indjejikian, and Smith (1996) found that CEOs of growth firms, and of firms with long product development and life cycles, derived a greater proportion of their compensation from *individual* performance measures relative to net income- and stock price–based measures. This is consistent with theory since net income, and perhaps even stock price, will be low in both sensitivity and precision for such firms, hence relatively uninformative about individual effort. Sensitivity and precision of net income and stock price, being based on overall firm performance, will also be low for managers who are lower down in the organization. Recall that BCE's compensation plan bases short-term incentive awards on individual creativity and initiative in addition to earnings.

In Section 10.4.1, we suggested that full disclosure could improve the sensitivity of net income to manager effort by enabling identification of persistent earnings by the compensation committee. Evidence that suggests compensation committees do value persistent earnings more highly for compensation purposes than transitory or price-irrelevant earnings is provided by Baber, Kang, and Kumar (1999). In a sample of firms over the years 1992 and 1993, their results include a finding that the effect of earnings changes on compensation increases with the persistence of those earnings changes.

In sum, the above empirical results suggest that, like investors, compensation committees are on average quite sophisticated in their use of accounting information. Just as full disclosure of reliable, value-relevant information will increase investors' use of this information, full disclosure of precise, "effort informative" (i.e., sensitive) information will increase its usage by compensation committees, thereby maintaining and increasing the role of net income in motivating responsible manager performance.

10.6 THE POLITICS OF EXECUTIVE COMPENSATION

The question of manager compensation has been a longstanding one in the United States and Canada. Many have argued that top managers are overpaid, especially in comparison to those in other countries, such as Japan.

In 1990, Jensen and Murphy (JM) published a controversial article about top manager compensation. They argued that CEOs were not overpaid, but that their compensation was far too unrelated to performance, where performance was measured as the change in the firm's market value (that is, the change in shareholder wealth). They examined the salary plus bonus of the CEOs of the 250 largest U.S. corporations over the 15 years from 1974 to 1988. For each year, they added the current year's and next year's salary and bonus and found that on average the CEOs received an extra 6.7 cents compensation over the two years for every $1,000 increase in shareholder wealth. When they added in other compensation components, including stock options and direct share holdings, the CEOs still received only $2.59 per $1,000 increase in shareholder wealth.

Other aspects of JM's investigation were consistent with these findings. For example, the variability (as measured by the standard deviation) over time of CEOs' and regular workers' compensations were almost the same. JM concluded that CEOs did not bear enough risk to motivate good performance, and consequently recommended larger stock holdings by managers. With respect to the BCE plan, note again that there are guidelines that require substantial stock holdings by officers.

However, some counterarguments can be made to JM.[10] First, we would *expect* the relationship between pay and performance to be low for large firms, simply because of a size effect. Suppose that a large corporation increased in value by billions of dollars last year (for example, BCE Inc.'s 2006 net income was $2.007 billion). An increase of even a small proportion of this amount in the CEO's remuneration would likely attract media attention.

Second, for large corporations at least, it is difficult to put much downside risk on an executive, as we argued in Section 10.4.3. An executive whose pay is highly related to performance would have so much to lose from even a small decline in firm value that this would probably lead to excessive avoidance of risky projects. As a result, the compensation committee may, for example, exclude extraordinary losses when deciding on bonus awards, particularly if the extraordinary loss is low in persistence and thus relatively uninformative about manager effort. Extraordinary losses do, however, lower company value and net income. Consequently, such exclusions lower the pay–performance relationship. If, in addition, upside risk is limited, the relationship is further lowered. While excluding extraordinary items from compensation does lower the CEOs' risk, it may be that this risk reduction is consistent with efficient contracting since, as mentioned, extraordinary items may be low in persistence and informativeness.

Theory in Practice 10.2

To illustrate the treatment of extraordinary items in compensation, it is worthwhile to consider BCE Inc.'s accounting for the results of telecommunications deregulation in Canada during the 1990s. In 1997, BCE Inc. reported a net loss of $1.536 billion, compared to net earnings of $1.152 billion for 1996. Nevertheless, 60,881 share units were awarded to six senior officers for 1997 under the short-term compensation plan in effect at that time, compared to 55,299 share units in 1996. Salaries were also up for 1997, as were stock options awarded under the long-term incentive plan.

BCE's 1997 net loss resulted from an extraordinary item of $2.950 billion for "stranded costs." That is, increasing competition as a result of telecommunications deregulation resulted in BCE's inability to recover the full costs of certain assets from revenues. The extraordinary charge represented a writedown of these assets to estimated future cash flows, consistent with the ceiling test of the *CICA Handbook*. BCE's 1997 earnings before this extraordinary item were $1.414 billion.

One could argue that deregulation of the telecommunications industry has little to do with manager effort, consistent with BCE's treatment of the writedown as an extraordinary item under Section 3480 of the *CICA Handbook* (see Section 5.5). In effect, the item is transitory, hence of low persistence. Low persistence supports a low weighting in determining compensation. Nevertheless, exclusion of the writedown for bonus purposes also supports an argument that a low pay–performance relationship is to be expected.

BCE's exclusion of an extraordinary loss, as just described, is consistent with the results of Gaver and Gaver (1998). For a sample of large U.S. firms over the years 1970–1996, these authors found that while extraordinary gains tended to be reflected in CEO cash compensation, extraordinary losses were not. A possible explanation is that compensation committees feel that reducing manager compensation for extraordinary losses imposes excessive downside risk on the manager, since the extraordinary loss may be the result of a market downturn rather than manager shirking. Of course, to the extent that extraordinary losses *are* informative about manager effort, their exclusion from bonus calculations is questionable, since their anticipation reduces the manager's effort incentive.

While extraordinary losses may not lead to reduced compensation, there is evidence that extraordinary gains do lead to increased compensation. The results of Gaver and Gaver just described provide such evidence with respect to cash compensation. Bertrand

and Mullainathan (2001) find a similar result for ESO compensation, particularly for firms with weak corporate governance.

Despite these counterarguments to JM, compensation concerns continue to appear. For example, political attention grew in the 1990s and early 2000s with respect to ESOs. For CEOs of large U.S. corporations, the market value of these awards often ran into the hundreds of millions of dollars. This attention intensified as the proportion of compensation based on ESOs steadily increased during the 1990s. For example, according to Hall and Murphy (2002), option grants to CEOs of the S&P 500 industrial firms increased from 22% of median total compensation in 1992 to 56% in 1999. Furthermore, option grants continued to rise in the early 2000s, despite a severe decline in the stock market.

Another focus of political attention involves "golden parachutes." These components of compensation contracts often oblige a company to pay multi-million dollar settlements to executives who leave, for whatever reason.

Theory in Practice 10.3

The Economist (October 9, 2003) reports the objections of the shareholders of GlaxoSmithKline, a large pharmaceutical company, to severance pay included in the compensation contract with its CEO, of $37.5 million U.S. This would be paid even if he was dismissed for poor performance. Angry shareholders voted down the contract at the firm's 2003 annual meeting. However, the vote was advisory only, and the company went ahead despite the vote. GlaxoSmithKline's chairman announced that the company was reviewing its remuneration policy.

Since ESOs bear little downside risk, and golden parachutes reward even poor performance, some support is provided for JM's claim that executives do not bear enough risk. BCE's move to award restricted stock units (payable in BCE shares) from 2004 instead of ESOs is consistent with an intent to increase manager risk. In effect, the BCE manager who receives restricted share units is forced to hold company shares for two years, assuming they vest, whereas BCE's ESOs vested at the rate of 25% per year. Thus, with restricted stock, the BCE manager is less able to work out from under compensation risk by immediately disposing of vested shares.

To fully understand the politics of executive compensation, however, it is important to realize that the value of a given amount of risky compensation to a manager is lower than it might appear at first glance. For example, the cost of ESOs to the firm is usually based on an option pricing model such as Black/Scholes. This provides a reasonable measure of the *firm's* ESO cost, since this is the opportunity cost of issuing ESOs to managers (see Section 8.3). However, Black/Scholes assumes that options can be freely traded, whereas compensation plan ESOs usually vest over a period of several years. If a manager is forced to hold ESOs, he/she cannot diversify compensation risk by, for example, selling the acquired shares and buying a diversified portfolio. These restrictions reduce ESO value to the manager. The more risk-averse the manager, and the less diversified the manager's other wealth, the greater the reduction.

This effect was studied by Hall and Murphy (2002) (HM), building on an earlier analysis by Lambert, Larcker, and Verrecchia (1991). HM report, for example, that the median 1999 total compensation of CEOs of S&P 500 industrial firms was $5.695 million U.S., of which 74% was in the form of ESOs and company stock (ESOs valued on a Black/Scholes basis). For a moderately risk-averse and diversified CEO, however, the cash-equivalent value of this compensation, after allowing for restrictions on disposal, was $3.420 million, a reduction of almost 40%. For a more risk-averse CEO, the reduction was almost 55%. By ignoring risk and diversification factors, media and politicians substantially overstate CEO compensation.

From an optimal contracting perspective, whether restricted stock is a more efficient compensation device than ESOs depends on a number of factors, such as employee risk aversion and the volatility of the firm's operations. HM's analysis, for example, supports the increasing use of restricted stock in place of ESOs. If an increase in stock-based compensation is accompanied by a reduction in CEO cash compensation, as opposed to simply being added on to existing compensation (this is consistent with the manager not receiving more than reservation utility),[11] the firm is better off to use restricted stock rather than ESOs with a positive strike price.[12] The reason, according to HM, derives from the fact that, other things equal, a share of restricted stock is preferred by the CEO to an ESO (since the ESO requires payment of the strike price while no payment is required for a share). Consequently the CEO is willing to give up more cash compensation for restricted stock than for ESOs. Then, for a given reduction in cash compensation, the firm can issue more shares via restricted stock than via ESOs, increasing the CEO's incentive to work hard.[13]

If restricted stock can be a more efficient motivator than ESOs, why have ESOs been a more popular compensation vehicle? The answer seems to be that issuing restricted stock has always required expensing, whereas ESOs have required expensing only since 2004. Some firms were apparently willing to use a less efficient compensation device (ESOs) in order to report higher net income. Once ESO expensing was required, this advantage disappeared. We would thus expect to see many firms moving towards more restricted stock compensation over time.

To summarize, requirements to expense ESOs will likely result in many firms reducing ESO usage in favour of restricted stock. Furthermore, the risky component of CEO compensation is less than it may appear at first glance, and seems justified in relation to shareholder value created. Nevertheless, sensitivity of shareholders, media, and politicians to perceived excessive compensation remains.

10.7 THE POWER THEORY OF EXECUTIVE COMPENSATION

Our discussion to this point has generally supported the efficient contracting view of executive compensation. Thus, we concluded in Section 10.5 that compensation committees are quite sophisticated in their use of accounting information and, in Section 10.6, that CEO compensation may be less than it seems at first glance. However, our discussion contained hints of another theory, the **power theory** of executive compensation. This theory suggests that executive compensation in practice is driven by manager opportunism, not efficient contracting.

The power theory is set forth by Bebchuk, Fried, and Walker (2002) (BFW). They argue that managers have sufficient power to influence their own compensation, and that they use this power to generate excessive pay, at the expense of shareholder value. If so, managers receive more than their reservation utility, contrary to our assumption in Chapter 9 that market forces prevent this. In effect, the power theory questions the efficient operation of the managerial labour market, much like behavioural finance questions efficient securities market theory (Section 6.2).

The source of manager power, BFW argue, is the ability of the CEO to influence the board of directors, including the compensation committee. Even though a majority of the board may be nominally independent, the CEO can influence their appointment. Furthermore, once appointed, even an independent director may feel that if he/she blocks excessive CEO compensation awards, an anti-management reputation will quickly be acquired. Such a reputation will hamper his/her interaction with other directors and reduce the likelihood of appointment to other boards.

The theory acknowledges that there are limits to the manager's power over compensation, namely "outrage." If compensation awards become too high, they attract negative publicity and at some point the board will have to step in to exercise its responsibility. However, as BFW point out, there are ways to "camouflage" excessive compensation. One way is to hire a compensation consultant to add legitimacy to compensation awards. However, since the CEO also has influence over their appointments, compensation consultants may well feel that if they recommend a compensation plan that is unfavourable to the CEO, this will quickly get around and they will have difficulty obtaining other consulting engagements.

Another camouflage device is to tie total compensation to a peer group of similar companies. Recall that BCE Inc. adjusts total compensation to the 50th to 75th percentiles of its comparison group. BFW point out that most companies do this. Obviously, if companies pay more than the average compensation of their peer groups, total compensation will ratchet up over time.

The power theory raises several questions about the efficient contracting view of executive compensation. For example, BFW ask, why are ESO awards not adjusted downwards for gains that are not under manager control? The results of Bertrand and Mullainathan referred to earlier provide empirical support for this question.[14] Another question is why managers have so much freedom to control the exercise of ESOs. Recall from Section 8.3 that ESOs can be exercised any time between vesting date and expiry. Indeed, it is this exercise date flexibility that has complicated accountants' efforts to estimate the cost of ESO awards, since exercise date has to be estimated. Furthermore, after exercise, managers have considerable freedom to sell the acquired shares. Under efficient contracting, a manager's ability to manage compensation risk would be more constrained.

Additional support for the power theory is provided by Core, Holthausen, and Larcker (1999), whose study of a sample of 205 U.S. firms revealed that a significant portion of CEO compensation is explained by corporate governance variables—poorer governance is associated with greater excess compensation. If the efficient contracting version of compensation held, there would be no excess compensation, since compensation would depend only on CEO quality.[15]

Revelations of **late timing** of ESO awards, discussed in Section 8.3, are a recent example of the power theory in action. Many firms, especially in the United States, backdated their ESO grant dates to create instant gains for the manager since the ESOs were, in effect, in-the-money when they were actually awarded.

Scandals such as late timing suggest that the power theory does hold, at least to some degree. The question then is, how can manager compensation practice be moved towards more efficient contracting? One response is to improve corporate governance, particularly since studies such as Bertrand and Mallainathan, and Core, Holthausen, and Larcker, referenced above, suggest that pay is more excessive when governance is weak. The Sarbanes-Oxley Act and related regulations in Canada (Section 1.2) provide an impetus towards better governance.

Accountants can also assist the governance process. Full disclosure enables better identification of earnings components with low persistence and informativeness. This helps compensation committees to tie pay to performance, and, if they do not, improves the ability of investors and media to diagnose excessive pay. Expensing of ESOs also plays a role, since an effect of expensing is to encourage firms to move to possibly more efficient compensation vehicles, such as restricted stock.

Of course, if the efficiency of compensation plans is to be controlled, politicians, media, and investors must know how much compensation the manager is receiving. In this regard, the SEC imposed regulations in 1992 to require firms to give more disclosure of their executive compensation, including a detailed explanation of the compensation of the five highest-paid executives and a report from the compensation committee justifying the pay levels. Similar requirements were adopted in Canada in 1993. These requirements were extended by the SEC in 2006 to include a Compensation Discussion and Analysis, a clear statement of total compensation received by five senior officers, and extensive disclosure of share-based compensation. Also required are disclosures of any late timing of ESO awards and of any golden parachutes. Similar requirements are currently proposed in Canada. Presumably, the securities commissions feel that if investors have enough information to intelligently evaluate manager compensation levels and components, they will take appropriate action if these appear excessive.

Some evidence that full disclosure of compensation does have the desired effect was reported by Lo (2003). Lo studied the subsequent operating performance (measured by ROE and ROA) and share price performance of firms that had lobbied against the 1992 SEC regulations, relative to a control sample of similar firms that did not lobby. Note that if a firm's compensation contract is biased in the manager's favour, so that the manager receives excess compensation, that firm's manager has an incentive to lobby against fuller disclosure of compensation plan details. Lo found that on average both the operating and share returns of the lobbying firms improved relative to the control firms subsequent to the new regulations. This improved performance is consistent with more efficient compensation contracts, imposed on the lobbying managers as more compensation information became available.

A further attempt to control excessive pay is to limit the amount of manager compensation deductible for tax purposes. In the United States, compensation in excess of $1 million is not tax deductible, except for compensation based on achievement of performance targets set by the compensation committee. However, since ESOs are regarded as performance based (their value derives from share price performance), this exception may have been another contributor to the tremendous increase in ESO awards during the 1990s, rather than contributing to reduced total compensation.

We conclude that regulators and accountants are responding to the political pressures that result when compensation reflects manager power. To the extent these responses are successful, the operation of managerial labour markets is improved.

10.8 THE SOCIAL SIGNIFICANCE OF MANAGERIAL LABOUR MARKETS THAT WORK WELL

In a capitalist economy, manager performance contributes to social welfare. Welfare is increased to the extent managers "work hard," that is, make good capital investment decisions and bring about high firm productivity.

Attainment of these desirable social goals is hampered to the extent that measures of manager performance are not fully informative. More informative performance measures enable more efficient compensation contracts and better operation of the managerial labour market, resulting in higher firm productivity and social welfare. Accountants can contribute to informativeness both by an appropriate tradeoff between sensitivity and precision of net income and by full disclosure.

10.9 CONCLUSIONS ON EXECUTIVE COMPENSATION

Managerial labour markets undoubtedly reduce the severity of moral hazard. However, past manager performance is not an iron-clad indicator of future performance. Also, labour markets are subject to moral hazard and adverse selection problems, such as earnings management to disguise shirking. Consequently, incentive contracts are still necessary even if managers' reputations on managerial labour markets fully reflect publicly available information.

Executive compensation contracts involve a delicate balancing of incentives, risk, and decision horizon. To properly align the interests of managers and shareholders, an efficient contract needs to achieve a high level of motivation while controlling compensation risk.

Too little risk discourages manager effort. Too much risk may shorten a manager's decision horizon, encourage earnings-increasing tactics that are against the firm's longer-run interests, lead to avoidance of risky projects, and encourage excessive hedging. Managers are particularly sensitive to risk, because the compensation contract may restrict their ability to diversify it away, unlike shareholders.

To attain proper alignment, incentive plans usually feature a combination of salary, bonus, and equity-based compensation such as restricted stock and options. These components of compensation are usually based on two performance measures—net income and share price. We can think of these as two noisy measures of the future payoff from current-period manager effort. Theory predicts that the relative proportion of each in the compensation plan depends on both their relative precision and sensitivity, and the length of manager decision horizon that the firm wants to motivate. Empirically, it appears that executive compensation is related to performance but that the strength of the relationship is low. However, for large firms at least, this low relationship is to be expected. Also, the relative proportion of net income–based and share price–based compensation components seems to vary as the theory predicts.

Executive compensation is surrounded by political controversy. Much of this controversy results from CEOs who exploit their power, using it to generate excessive compensation. Regulators have responded by expanding the information available to shareholders and others, on the assumption that they will take action to eliminate inefficient plans, or the managers and firms that have them. There is some evidence that expanded information is having the desired effect. However, politicians, media, and shareholders should realize that the value of risky compensation to risk-averse managers is usually less than it may seem at first glance.

We conclude that financial reporting has an important role in motivating executive performance and controlling manager power. This role includes full disclosure, so that compensation committees and investors can better relate pay to performance. It also includes expensing of stock option awards to help control their abuse and encourage more efficient compensation vehicles. As a result, responsible manager performance is motivated and the extent to which manager reputation is based on incomplete or biased information is reduced. This improves the operation of the managerial labour market, a goal equally important to society as promoting good investor decisions and improving the operation of securities markets.

Questions and Problems

1. Below is a portion of a 2008 proxy form sent to shareholders of Miracle-J Corporation. It reveals that Miracle-J has a bonus plan for its three senior executives that allocates them 10% of before-tax profits. Also, under the Employee Stock Option Plan, share options up to 12% of capitalization may be granted to directors or employees.

Miracle-J Corp.

Executive and Management Compensation

The Corporation's five executive officers were remunerated, in total, $440,000 by way of fees, salaries, and bonuses for the fiscal year ended May 31, 2008.

Included in the aforesaid sum was $280,000 paid to the three senior executive officers as full-time employees of the Corporation, pursuant to individual four-year Management Agreements made between the Corporation and those senior executive officers, effective June 1, 2006. Under the terms of the Agreements, the three senior executives are entitled to receive an aggregate bonus of 10% of before-tax profits earned by the company and their base salaries are to be increased 10% per year. For the 2008 fiscal year, the three senior executive officers waived their bonus entitlements to the extent that each received dividends on shares of the Corporation held by them which dividend was declared and paid for the fiscal year ended May 31, 2008.

It is to be noted that the Directors have adopted a form of Employee Stock Option Plan under which share options of up to 12% of the capitalization of the Corporation may be granted to Directors or employees. There are presently reserved, to that end, 930,000 common shares of the Corporation; but the Corporation has not granted any option to any Director or employees as of the date of this Information Circular.

Required

a. Explain the reason for the 10% bonus plan for senior executives. Are there any possible dysfunctional consequences of the bonus plan resulting from the apparent lack of a cap? Why is the bonus based on before-tax profits, rather than after-tax?

b. Explain reasons for the Employee Stock Option Plan in addition to the bonus plan for senior executives. Why does the Plan apparently apply to all employees?

c. To what extent would the bonus plan cause management to be concerned about accounting policies and changes in GAAP?

2. Agency theory suggests that a way to motivate managers to act in the best interests of the owners/shareholders is to link managerial compensation to performance measures, such as net income or share price. However, such a linkage imposes risk on the manager.

Required

a. Why is it important to control or reduce some of the risk thus imposed on managers? Explain.

b. Explain *two* methods by which risk imposed on the managers could be reduced. What happens if too much compensation risk is eliminated?

c. Many managerial compensation packages impose restrictions on *when* managers can sell stock granted to them as a part of their compensation. For example, some compensation packages indicate that restricted stock awards may be forfeited unless the manager continues to work for the firm for a certain number of years after the granting of the award. Discuss the justification behind such restrictions.

d. Inclusion of shares and options in managerial compensation packages has been attributed to the desire of the owners/shareholders to provide managers an incentive to undertake policies that benefit the firm's long-term rather than short-term interests. If this is true, why not compensate the manager only on the basis of share return (for example, only by stock options or restricted stock)? In other words, under these circumstances, what is the justification for having a cash or bonus element in the compensation package?

3. A proponent of ESOs argues that no expense should be recorded for ESOs issued to managers and other employees, since they do not cost the employer anything. On the contrary, the employer *receives* cash equal to the ESOs' exercise price.

Do you agree that no expense should be recorded? Explain why or why not.

4. Explain why the value of ESOs and restricted stock to a manager is generally less than their fair values, such as Black/Scholes value for ESOs, or stock market value for restricted stock.

5. Explain why, for large corporations, a low pay–performance relationship is to be expected.

6. Firms A and B are roughly the same size, but operate in different industries. Firm A bases a high proportion of its executive compensation on net income and a relatively low proportion on share price performance. For firm B, these proportions are reversed. Yet, both firms appear to be well managed, consistently profitable, and growing. Use the concepts of sensitivity and precision of a performance measure to explain why both firms' compensation plans are efficient, despite the differing proportions.

7. In the BCE compensation plan, outlined in Section 10.3, short-term incentive awards are based less heavily on corporate performance and more on individual creativity and initiative as the employee is less senior. Why?

8. In 2002, the Toronto-Dominion Bank (TD) announced that it would voluntarily expense ESOs, starting with its 2003 fiscal year beginning November 1, 2002. Accounting standards in Canada did not require ESO expensing until fiscal years beginning on or after January 1, 2004. In the MD&A section of its 2003 annual report, TD stated that it had charged to expense for 2003 an amount of $9 million for ESOs, using the fair value method.

TD's reported net income for 2003 was $1.076 billion, compared to a net loss of $67 million for 2002.

Suggest reasons why TD would voluntarily expense its ESOs.

9. Microsoft Corp. announced in 2002 that it was discontinuing its employees' stock option plan in favour of restricted stock, vesting over a five-year period. At that time, many of its already-granted ESOs were under water (i.e., exercise price greater than share market value).

In 2003, no expense needed to be recorded for ESOs if they were granted with an intrinsic value of zero, since an FASB standard requiring expensing ESO fair value was not effective until fiscal years beginning after June 15, 2005. However, generally speaking, the fair value of restricted stock issued to employees *is* charged to expense.

For 2003, Microsoft reported earnings per share of 14 cents, after stock-based compensation expense of $2.17 billion U.S. Its 2003 earnings were 17 cents per share. Microsoft reported that before stock-related expenses its 2002 earnings would have been 34 cents per share, compared with analysts' consensus estimate of 30 cents.

Required

a. Give a reason why Microsoft's share price would be unaffected by the news of its reduction in reported earnings due to the 2003 stock-based compensation expense. Give reasons why stock price may fall.

b. Give reasons why Microsoft's share price might rise as a result of this news.

c. Why might Microsoft, and numerous other large corporations, such as BCE Inc. (Section 10.3), have eliminated or reduced the usage of ESOs in their compensation plans?

10. In its 2004 proxy statement to shareholders, the compensation committee of General Electric Company (GE) reported that in 2003 it had discontinued ESOs for its CEO, Jeffrey Immelt. In their place, GE awarded 250,000 restricted share units. One-half of these units entitle Mr. Immelt to one share each in 2008 if operating cash flow growth, adjusted for the effect of unusual events, increased at an average rate of 10% or more during 2003–2007. Otherwise, the share units would be cancelled. The other 125,000 units entitled him to one share each in 2008 if the total return on GE shares over 2003–2007 meets or exceeds the return on the S&P 500 Index for the same period. Otherwise, the share units would be cancelled. GE's shares were trading for about $30 U.S. at the time of this announcement.

For 2003, Mr. Immelt's compensation also included a base salary of $3 million plus a cash bonus of $4.325 million. The amounts of cash bonuses are determined by GE's compensation committee upon evaluation of an individual's performance for the year, including contribution to financial performance. According to the compensation committee, after taking into account cash bonus and restricted share units, more than 75% of Mr. Immelt's potential compensation for 2003 was at risk. GE also required that its CEO own six times salary in company shares.

Required

a. What balance between short-run and long-run CEO effort is the GE compensation plan likely to induce? Explain.

b. What are some of the dysfunctional effects for the firm of too much risk imposed on a risk-averse manager?

c. One-half of the restricted share units awarded to Mr. Immelt are based on meeting an operating cash flow target. Evaluate the relative precision and sensitivity of operating cash flow and net income as performance measures. Also, evaluate the effects on manager motivation of eliminating "unusual events" from the performance measure.

d. To what extent are the restricted share units awarded to Mr. Immelt based on shareholder return subject to the "pump and dump" behaviour that some managers seem to adopt when their compensation is based on ESOs?

11. In 1993, the Ontario Securities Commission implemented new executive compensation disclosure rules (OSC, Form 40, Securities Act, Regulation 638/93). Similar requirements were already in place in the United States. These disclosure rules specified that shareholder proxy statements contain tables spelling out compensation for the five highest-paid executives, plus a report from the board's compensation committee explaining the firm's compensation practices. (The BCE Compensation Committee report in Exhibit 10.1 is an example of reporting under these rules.)

Required

a. To what extent do you think that such disclosure requirements will assist an efficient managerial labour market to work well? Explain. Include a definition of an efficient managerial labour market in your answer.

b. If the managerial labour market is fully efficient (that is, analogous to an efficient securities market), would manager incentive plans based on risky performance measures such as share price and reported net income be needed? Explain why or why not.

12. On November 18, 2002, *The Globe and Mail* (p. B4) reported "CEO assails pay disclosure rules." This referred to a speech by Claude Lamoureux, CEO of Ontario Teachers Pension Plan Board. The board is a major owner of and shareholder in numerous companies, hence vitally interested in questions of executive motivation and compensation. Mr. Lamoureux's concern is with the OSC rules requiring firms to disclose and explain the compensation of their five most highly paid employees. He argues that the effect of these rules is simply to put upward pressure on pay levels, as executives demand raises to meet or exceed that of their peers in other companies.

In this regard, the BCE Compensation Committee states (Exhibit 10.1) that an executive's total compensation is positioned at the median of what is paid by a group of similar companies. In the changes to the BCE plan for 2004, the committee advises that total compensation will be increased to the 60th percentile of that paid by the comparable companies.

Required

a. Explain the argument in favour of companies disclosing compensation information of their senior executives. Why do you think that Mr. Lamoureux, CEO of a very large and powerful institutional investor, rejects this argument?

b. How do you think the policy of BCE Inc. of fixing its total executive compensation at the 60th percentile of that paid by the comparable companies will affect the level of executive compensation in the telecommunications industry?

13. Refer to Theory in Practice 10.2 in Section 10.6 concerning BCE Inc. Reproduced on p. 395 are the 1997 consolidated statement of operations and Note 2 to the financial statements of BCE. The statement of operations shows an extraordinary charge of $2.950 billion for stranded costs. After this extraordinary charge, operations showed a net loss for the year of $1.536 billion.

Required

a. Does the charge for stranded costs meet the definition of an extraordinary item under Section 3480 of the *CICA Handbook* (see Section 5.5)? Discuss.

b. Regardless of whether or not the $2.950 billion is an extraordinary item, as a member of BCE's compensation committee would you support exclusion of the charge from earnings for the purpose of managers' short-term incentive awards? Discuss.

c. What is the persistence of the $2.950 billion component of 1997 earnings? Your answer should be in the range [0–1]. Explain your answer.

d. On April 23, 1998, *The Globe and Mail* reported "Earnings results fuel BCE shares to 52-week high." This headline refers to BCE's record reported earnings for its first quarter, 1998, of 48 cents per share excluding "onetime items." This is a 46% increase over 33 cents per share for the same quarter of 1997. The article quoted the CEO of BCE as saying, "We continue to see solid growth in all areas of our operations." According to the article, these first-quarter results suggest a good performance by BCE in 1998, after a $1.5 billion loss in 1997 due to a record $2.9 billion charge at its telephone company subsidiary.

Give another reason, in addition to "solid growth," that may explain the record first-quarter results. As a member of the BCE compensation committee contemplating the 1998 annual short-term incentive awards, would you support basing these awards on the record first-quarter earnings? Explain your position.

Consolidated Financial Statements—BCE Inc.
Consolidated Statement of Operations

	($ million, except per share amounts)		
For the years ended December 31	1997	1996	1995
Revenues	33,191	28,167	24,624
Operating expenses	25,795	22,011	19,434
Research and development expense	2,911	2,471	2,134
Operating profit	4,485	3,685	3,056
Other income	365	393	238
Operating earnings	4,850	4,078	3,294
Interest expense – long-term debt	1,111	1,160	1,154
– other debt	121	141	172
Total interest expense	1,232	1,301	1,326
Earnings before taxes, non-controlling interest and extraordinary item	3,618	2,777	1,968
Income taxes	(1,522)	(1,118)	(819)
Non-controlling interest	(682)	(507)	(367)
Net earnings before extraordinary item	1,414	1,152	782
Extraordinary item	(2,950)	—	—
Net earnings (loss)	(1,536)	1,152	782
Dividends on preferred shares	(74)	(76)	(87)
Net earnings (loss) applicable to common shares	(1,610)	1,076	695
Earnings (loss) per common share[1]			
Net earnings before extraordinary item	2.11	1.70	1.12
Extraordinary item	(4.64)	—	—
Net earnings (loss)	(2.53)	1.70	1.12
Dividends per common share[1]	1.36	1.36	1.36
Average number of common shares outstanding (millions)[1]	636.0	632.7	622.9

[1]Reflects the subdivision of common shares on a two-for-one basis on May 14, 1997.

Extraordinary Item

As at December 31, 1997, BCE determined that most of its telecommunications subsidiary and associated companies no longer met the criteria necessary for the continued application of regulatory accounting provisions. As a result, BCE recorded an extraordinary non-cash charge of $2,950 million, net of an income tax benefit of $1,892 million and a non-controlling interest of $38 million. Also included in the extraordinary item is an after-tax charge of $97 million representing BCE's share of the related extraordinary item of its associated companies.

The operations of most of BCE's telecommunications subsidiary and associated companies no longer met the criteria for application of regulatory accounting provisions due to significant changes in regulation including the implementation of price cap regulation which replaced rate-of-return regulation effective January 1, 1998, and the concurrent introduction of competition in the local exchange market. Accordingly, BCE adjusted the net carrying values of assets and liabilities as at December 31, 1997, to reflect values appropriate under GAAP for enterprises no longer subject to rate-of-return regulation.

The determination by BCE that most of its telecommunications subsidiary and associated companies no longer met the criteria for the continuing application of regulatory accounting provisions is the result of a review, which began in 1997, to assess the impact of the introduction of price cap regulation coupled with the introduction of competition in the local exchange market. Before the advent of these two factors, accounting practices were based on a regulatory regime which provided reasonable assurance of the recovery of costs through rates set by the regulator and charged to customers. These regulatory accounting provisions resulted in the recognition of certain assets and liabilities along with capital asset lives which were substantially different from enterprises not subject to rate-of-return regulation.

The extraordinary charge consists of a pre-tax charge of $3,602 million related to capital assets and a pre-tax charge of $1,181 million to adjust the carrying values of other assets and liabilities to arrive at carrying values appropriate for enterprises not subject to rate-of-return regulation. The amount of the charge related to capital assets was determined based upon an estimate of the underlying cash flows using management's best estimate assumptions concerning the most likely course of action and other factors relating to competition, technological changes and the evolution of products and services. The net carrying values of capital assets were adjusted primarily through an increase in accumulated depreciation. The primary component of the $1,181 million charge relates to the write-off of deferred business transformation and workforce reduction costs.

Source: BCE Inc., 1997 annual report. Reprinted by permission.

---

14. Many firms "reprice" ESOs following major declines in their share price by lowering the exercise price. This is because ESOs issued before the decline are deep out of the money, hence unlikely to be of any value. Such moves usually outrage shareholders, who have seen the value of their shares also fall but who receive no comparable benefits, and are prominently reported in the media.

Saly (1994) was an original analytical study of the repricing of ESOs. Her analysis applies to repricing after a market downturn, such as the downturn experienced in the early 2000s, and not to a firm-specific fall in share price that may be due to manager shirking.

As Saly points out, compensation contracts are incomplete. That is, it is unlikely that provisions for adjustments to compensation following a market downturn are anticipated and written into the compensation plan. The question then is, should the contract be "renegotiated" following a market downturn by repricing ESOs? If so, this would violate the general rule that, once signed, contracts tend to be rigid.

In Saly's model, the answer is yes. Renegotiation of the ESOs' strike price increases the correlation between manager effort and the performance measure (share price), since a market downturn is not a result of low manager effort. Without the possibility of renegotiation, the risk-averse manager would have to be compensated for the risk inherent in the possibility of a market downturn to attain reservation utility. If a downturn occurs and there is no repricing, the manager's expected utility will fall, since the expected proceeds from ESOs are effectively zero. This will cause him/her to either shirk or leave the company.

In June 2001, Nortel Networks Corp. announced that it was cancelling its existing ESOs and replacing them with new ESOs with a lower strike price. Nortel's share price, which had been in excess of $100 when many of the ESOs were issued, suffered following the market collapse of share prices of high-tech firms, and was trading in the $20 range at the time of the announcement. Nortel's move was widely reported in the financial media and drew significant negative comment. For example, *The Globe and Mail* (June 5, 2001) quoted Carol Bowie of the Investor Responsibility Research Center as saying " . . . you can't make the 50-yard kick. So we'll cut it down to 35." It also quoted J. Richard Finlay, head of the Center for Corporate and Public Governance, as saying "We'd all like to be told our high school physics test where we got 35 out of 100 is now 35 out of 50, but shareholders don't have that luxury."

Nortel defended its move by claiming it was necessary to retain key employees, pointing out that top manager ESOs were not being repriced (this would require shareholder approval) but only those of lower level employees. In the same issue of the *Globe*, Brian Milner pointed out that the cost to Nortel of repricing the ESOs is zero, and that no further dilution of shareholders' equity will result since the old ESOs are being cancelled. Nevertheless, Milner comments that in the public eye the repricing is still "a reward for crummy performance."

Required

a. In the light of Saly's model, do you agree with Nortel's ESO repricing? Explain why or why not.

b. Nortel planned to cancel existing ESOs and replace them with new ones, rather than simply repricing the existing options to a lower exercise price. Recall that in 2001, GAAP did not require expensing of ESOs. Rather, most firms, including Nortel, followed APB 25 (see Section 8.3) in the financial statements proper, reporting the fair value of ESO expense in a note to the financial statements. Why do you think Nortel replaced the old ESOs with new ones, rather than simply repricing the existing ones?

c. In its 2003 proxy statement, the Compensation Committee of General Electric Company reported that the company has a policy of not repricing ESOs. Why would a company have such a policy?

15. In January 2007, Zions Bancorporation announced that it had received SEC permission to use a market-based approach to valuation of its ESOs. Zions is a large U.S. financial services company that operates numerous banks in several states.

Zions' approach is to create special securities, called "Employee Stock Option Appreciation Rights Securities" (ESOARS), to be sold to outside investors. These give the holder the right to receive a portion of the gain realized by Zions' employees when they exercise their ESOs. Thus, the ESOARS are subject to all of the conditions attached to the ESOs. The fair value of the ESOs, Zions argued, can then be inferred from the market value of the ESOARS. For example, if ESOARS give the holder 25% of the employees' ESO gains, the ESO fair value is four times the ESOARS' market value.

In May 2007, Zions announced a successful auction of ESOARS. There were 43 bidders, with an average price paid of $12.06. Thus, if the ESOARS entitle the holder to 25% of ESO gains, ESOs would be worth about $48.24. This implied ESO fair value was about one half of the value estimated from an ESO valuation model, such as Black/Scholes. Zions indicated that it would use this implied fair value to measure its stock option expense under SFAS 123R.

Required

a. Why would Zions Bancorporation use a market-based approach to estimating its stock option expense, instead of a model-based approach?

b. Why is the ESOARS-based ESO value so much lower than the model-based value? Assume that ESOARS purchasers are risk-averse.

c. Do you agree with Zions' approach? Explain why or why not.

16. Grein, Hand, and Klassen (2005) studied the stock price reaction to repricing of ESOs. They examined a sample of 72 Canadian companies that repriced ESOs during 1994–2001. They found a 4.9% average positive abnormal share price reaction for their sample firms over a narrow window of three days surrounding the repricing announcement. Furthermore, the lower the stock market return on the firm's shares for the six-month period leading up to the repricing (and thus the greater the fall in value of employee ESOs), the more positive the stock market's reaction to the repricing.

They also found that the probability a firm would reprice its ESOs was greater when the firm had poor corporate governance (their proxy for poor governance was that the CEO and the board chair were the same person).

Required

a. Explain reasons why firms may reprice their ESOs. Use positive accounting theory and agency theory concepts in your answer, where appropriate.

b. Which of the reasons you identified is most likely to predict the researchers' finding that share prices for their sample firms increased on average following ESO repricing? Does this finding support efficient securities market theory? Explain.

17. Ittner, Larcker, and Rajan (1997) studied the relative weights placed on financial and non-financial performance measures in CEO bonus contracts for a sample of 317 U.S. firms across 48 industries for 1993–1994. Recall that BCE Inc. (Section 10.3) has both types of performance measures in its short-term incentive awards. Non-financial performance measures in the BCE plan are based on individual creativity and initiative, succession planning, and management development. Financial performance measures include earnings per share, revenue growth, earnings growth, capital intensity, free cash flow, and return on invested capital.

Ittner, Larcker, and Rajan find empirical support for the following hypotheses about the relative weights on financial and non-financial performance measures in compensation plans:

i. *Noise.* The lower the correlation between manager effort and net income (measured by the correlation between stock market and accounting-based returns), the less the relative weight on financial performance measures.

ii. *Firm strategy.* "Prospector firms" (growth and innovation oriented, identify and adapt quickly to new product/service opportunities) will have greater relative weight on non-financial performance measures than "defender" firms (stable set of products/services, emphasis on increasing efficiency to reduce operating costs).

iii. *Product quality.* The greater the firm commitment to quality, the greater the relative weight on non-financial performance measures.

iv. *Regulation.* Regulated firms will have greater relative weight on non-financial performance measures than non-regulated firms.

Required

a. Give intuitive arguments to explain these four hypotheses.

b. Which of these four hypotheses might explain the inclusion by BCE Inc. of non-financial performance measures in its short-term incentive awards?

18. Note: This question integrates several topics from earlier sections of the text.

UnitedHealth Group, Inc. is a large U.S. health insurance company. In a May 11, 2006, SEC filing, the company revealed a significant deficiency in its stock option granting practices, leading to a potential reduction of 2003, 2004, and 2005 reported earnings totalling about $286 million from correction of late timing of ESO grants. Of this amount, $150 million related to 2005, a reduction in reported earnings of 4.5%. The company also disclosed that it would stop issuing ESOs to CEO William McGuire and other senior managers.

UnitedHealth shares fell $1.80 on May 11, closing at $44.37.

On October 15, 2006, Mr. McGuire resigned, following a report from a law firm engaged by the board that he had benefited from late timing of ESO grants and had not disclosed a conflict of interest with the chair of UnitedHealth's compensation committee.

On November 8, 2006, the company announced that it had agreed with Mr. McGuire to reprice ESOs awarded to him since 1994 to the highest share price for the year the ESOs were awarded, resulting in a material reduction in the value of the awards. Similar repricing applied to other senior officers. The company also announced that its financial statements from 1994 to 2005 could no longer be relied on, and that it would delay filing its financial results for third quarter, 2006, until the amounts of earnings restatements were fully determined. In December 2007, Mr. McGuire agreed to return about $468 million of ESOs and other benefits to the company.

Required

a. Use efficient contracting theory to explain why a company awards ESOs as compensation.

b. Use the power theory of compensation to explain why a company may engage in late timing of ESO awards.

c. UnitedHealth shares are listed on the New York Stock Exchange. On May 11, 2006, the Dow Jones Index fell by 141.92 points, a decline of 1.22%. UnitedHealth's stock beta at this time was 0.4, according to Reuters/business. The risk-free interest rate was 5%, or about 0.0001 per day. Calculate the abnormal return on UnitedHealth shares for May 11.

d. The company stated that there would be no effect on cash flows as a result of its reductions in reported earnings (presumably, it felt any effect on income tax would be negligible). If so, give reasons why its share price fell on May 11.

e. During the years of UnitedHealth's late timing, the rules of APB 25 applied. Explain why correcting the late timing results in an increase in compensation expense under APB 25. Suppose instead that the late timing took place entirely after the effective date of SFAS 123R. Would any correction of previous earnings be needed? Explain.

f. What effect, if any, would late timing of ESOs have on their expected time to exercise? Explain.

g. In what other ways can CEOs manipulate the value of their ESO awards?

19. Refer to Theory in Practice 4.2.

Required

The Kmart CEO charged by the SEC was hired in May 2000 and fired in March 2002. Despite Kmart losses of $3.9 billion for the five quarters ended April 2002, the CEO received total compensation of almost $23 million during his tenure. Presumably, much of this compensation was in the form of Kmart shares and ESOs. To what extent does awarding manager compensation in the form of company shares and ESOs discourage the type of opportunistic behaviour charged against the Kmart executives?

Notes

1. See Chapter 9, Note 6.

2. When there is more than one performance measure in the contract, the sensitivity concept becomes more complex. An increase, say, in effort increases the expected value of *all* of the performance measures. In our context, an effort increase has a direct effect of increasing the expected value of net income. However, the expected value of share price also increases. To the extent that there is positive covariance between net income and share price, the increase in expected share price dilutes the ability of net income to convey information about effort, reducing its sensitivity and hence its weight in the mix of performance measures. A similar phenomenon reduces the sensitivity of share price.

This argument can also be interpreted from a risk standpoint. Covariance between net income and share price measures the extent to which random factors affecting net income also affect share price, that is, the *common noise*. To avoid impacting the manager's compensation twice for the same noise, the weights on the performance measures are reduced by an amount that depends on the covariance between them.

3. A compromise is to record unrealized gains and losses from current valuation of assets and liabilities in other comprehensive income. Then, net income omits the sensitivity and precision effects of current value accounting.

4. For a methodology to estimate a firm's investment opportunities, and evidence that the proportion of share price-based compensation in firms' compensation contracts increases with investment opportunities, see Baber, Janakiraman, and Kang (1996).

5. In statistical terms, the performance measures covary.

6. In economics, a situation where an oligopolist chooses product price is known as Bertrand competition. This is contrasted with Cournot competition, where the firm chooses the amount of production.

7. In technical terms, compensation from plans that limit downside risk but not upside risk is a convex function of performance. Thus plans with a bogey but no cap are convex, as are ESO plans.

8. However, if the ESOs are deep-in-the-money, the manager may avoid adopting risky projects to reduce the likelihood that share price, hence ESO value, will fall. That is, the expected payoff from holding a deep-in-the-money ESO is similar to that of holding the share, as pointed out in Section 8.3. This effect also applies to the manager's holdings of company stock. These possibilities illustrate the difficulties of evaluating the effects of compensation risk on managerial actions. These effects will vary depending on the manager's risk aversion, the extent to which the manager must hold an equity position in the company, on the manager's outside wealth, and on the extent to which the manager may be able to compensate for compensation risk by diversification and hedging.

9. A target bonus is the bonus a firm pays if the executive's performance reaches a predetermined level. If performance is greater than target, a larger bonus is paid, and vice versa. The BCE plan contains a target bonus, and this bonus increases with corporate performance (the corporate performance factor).

10. These arguments are based on R.A. Lambert and D.F. Larcker, "Firm Performance and the Compensation of Chief Executive Officers," working paper, January 1993.

11. Note that in the revised BCE compensation plan, issuance of restricted stock is accompanied by a reduction in ESO compensation, not cash compensation. The reason, presumably, is that BCE is moving to shorten managers' decision horizons at the same time.

12. Restricted stock is equivalent to an ESO with a zero strike price.

13. This assumes that the CEO cannot work out from under the increased incentive by selling existing holdings of company stock and/or increasing the diversification of other wealth.

14. However, gains can still be informative about effort, even if not under manager control—see Chapter 9, Note 16. Consequently, Bertrand and Mullainathan's findings are not completely inconsistent with efficient contracting. What is inconsistent, however, is that uncontrollable losses are adjusted for, but uncontrollable gains are not, as reported by Gaver and Gaver (1998).

15. However, due to contract rigidity, a firm's compensation contract may depart from full efficiency, at least for a time. If so, what might appear to be excess compensation due to manager power could instead be due to costs of amending contracts.

Chapter 11
Earnings Management

Figure 11.1 Organization of Chapter 11

11.1 OVERVIEW

Earnings management can be viewed from both a financial reporting and a contracting perspective. From a financial reporting perspective, managers may use earnings management to meet analysts' earnings forecasts, thereby avoiding the reputation damage and strong negative share price reaction that quickly follows a failure to meet investor expectations. Also, they may record excessive write-offs, or emphasize earnings constructs other than net income, such as "pro-forma" earnings. Some of these tactics suggest that managers do not fully accept securities market efficiency.

There is another view of earnings management, however. Management may use it to report a stream of smooth and growing earnings over time. Given securities market efficiency, this requires management to draw on its inside information. Thus, earnings management can be a vehicle for the communication of management's inside information to investors. Interpreted this way, income smoothing leads to the interesting, and perhaps surprising, conclusion that some earnings management can be useful from a financial reporting perspective.

From a contracting perspective, earnings management can be used as a way to protect the firm from the consequences of unforeseen events when contracts are rigid and incomplete. Also, as we saw in Chapter 9, managerial compensation contracts that allow some earnings management can be more efficient than ones that do not, due to the high costs of eliminating earnings management completely.

Too much earnings management, however, may reduce usefulness for investors. This is particularly so if the earnings management is buried in core earnings or otherwise not fully disclosed. Also, earnings management affects the manager's motivation to exert effort, because managers can use earnings management opportunistically to smooth their compensation over time, thereby reducing compensation risk. But, we have seen that managers need to bear some risk if they are to work hard.

For whatever reason, it should be apparent that managers have a strong interest in the bottom line. Given that managers can choose accounting policies from a set of policies (for example, GAAP), it is natural to expect that they will choose policies so as to help achieve their objectives. They may also take real actions affecting earnings, such as cutting R&D. As mentioned, these choices can be motivated either by efficient markets and contracts, or by opportunism and rejection of market efficiency. Whatever the reason, this is called **earnings management**.

An understanding of earnings management is important to accountants, because it enables an improved understanding of the usefulness of net income, both for reporting to investors and for contracting. It may also assist accountants to avoid some of the serious legal and reputation consequences that arise when firms become financially distressed. Such distress is often preceded by serious abuse of earnings management.

> **Earnings management** is the choice by a manager of accounting policies, or actions affecting earnings, so as to achieve some specific reported earnings objective.

Thus, earnings management includes both accounting policy choice and real actions. We consider accounting policy choice first. It should be mentioned that choice of accounting policies is interpreted quite broadly. While the dividing line is not clear-cut, it is convenient to divide accounting policy choice into two categories. One is the choice of accounting policies per se, such as straight-line versus declining-balance amortization, or policies for revenue recognition. The other category is discretionary accruals, such as provisions for credit losses, warranty costs, inventory values, and timing and amounts of non-recurring and extraordinary items such as write-offs and provisions for reorganization.

Regardless of its rationale, it is important to realize that there is an "iron law" surrounding accruals-based earnings management, which will be familiar from introductory accounting. This is that *accruals reverse*. Thus, a manager who manages earnings upwards to an amount greater than can be sustained will find that the reversal of these accruals in subsequent periods will force future earnings downwards just as surely as current earnings were raised.[1] Then, even more earnings management is needed if reporting of losses is to be further postponed. In effect, if a firm is performing poorly, earnings management cannot indefinitely postpone the day of reckoning. Thus, the possibility that earnings management can be good should not be used to rationalize misleading or fraudulent reporting. The accountant treads a fine line between earnings management and earnings mismanagement. Ultimately, the location of this line must be determined by effective corporate governance, reinforced by securities and managerial labour markets, standard setters, securities commissions, and the courts.

The iron law of accruals reversal leads to an important aspect of earnings management. All of the models of earnings management in Chapter 9 were single-period. Even then, we showed that earnings management could, in theory, be beneficial. However, to better understand earnings management, we need to think in terms of multiple periods. Then, further earnings management potential, such as income smoothing and "big bath," is revealed. Indeed, the three hypotheses of positive accounting theory (Section 8.5.2) implicitly assume a multi-period horizon.

Yet, multi-period horizons also operate to inhibit earnings management. For example, to what extent is a manager's propensity to over- or understate reported net income reduced by the knowledge that such misstatements will inevitably reverse? To what extent do markets, such as the securities market and the manager's reputation on the managerial labour market, help to control opportunistic earnings management? We saw some evidence in Wolfson's (1985) study of oil and gas limited partnerships in Section 10.2 that reputation effects reduce but do not eliminate the moral hazard problem. While a multi-period horizon increases the potential for earnings management, it also operates to constrain the practice.

Another way to manage earnings is by means of *real* variables, such as advertising, R&D, maintenance, timing of purchases and disposals of capital assets, stuffing the channels, etc. These devices may be costly, since they directly affect the firm's longer-run interests. Nevertheless, managers may use them since the costs of managing earnings using accounting variables has increased of late, due to reporting failures such as Enron and WorldCom and resulting legislation, notably Sarbanes-Oxley (see Section 1.2). Indeed, Graham, Harvey, and Rajgopal (2005), in a survey of chief financial officers of 312 U.S. public companies, report that most respondents indicated a willingness to manage real variables in order to meet earnings targets and/or smooth earnings, even though such actions may compromise longer-term objectives. Use of accounting policy variables for these purposes received relatively little support from the respondents. Note that earnings management by real variables manages cash flows as well as earnings. Nevertheless, we concentrate primarily on management of accounting variables rather than real variables due to their historical importance, their relevance to accounting, and the likelihood that the lessons of Enron and WorldCom will grow dim over time.

Figure 11.1 outlines the organization of this chapter.

11.2 PATTERNS OF EARNINGS MANAGEMENT

Managers may engage in a variety of earnings management patterns. Here, we collect and briefly summarize these patterns.

1. **Taking a bath** This can take place during periods of organizational stress or reorganization. If a firm must report a loss, management may feel it might as well report a large one—it has little to lose at this point. Consequently, it will write-off assets, provide for expected future costs, and generally "clear the decks." Because of accrual reversal, this enhances the probability of future reported profits. In effect, the recording of large write-offs puts future earnings "in the bank."

2. **Income minimization** This is similar to taking a bath, but less extreme. Such a pattern may be chosen by a politically visible firm during periods of high profitability. Policies that suggest income minimization include rapid write-offs of capital assets and intangibles, expensing of advertising and R&D expenditures, successful-efforts accounting for oil and gas exploration costs, and so on. Income tax considerations, such as for LIFO inventory in the United States, provide another set of motivations for this pattern, as does enhancement of arguments for relief from foreign competition.

3. **Income maximization** From positive accounting theory, managers may engage in a pattern of maximization of reported net income for bonus purposes, providing this does not put them above the cap. Firms that are close to debt covenant violations may also maximize income.

4. **Income smoothing** This is perhaps the most interesting earnings management pattern. From a contracting perspective, risk-averse managers prefer a less variable bonus stream, other things equal. Consequently, managers may smooth reported earnings over time so as to receive relatively constant compensation. Efficient compensation contracting may exploit this effect, and condone some income smoothing as a low-cost way to attain the manager's reservation utility.

   We considered covenants in long-term lending agreements in Section 9.7. The more volatile the stream of reported net income, the higher the probability that covenant violation will occur. This provides another smoothing incentive—to reduce volatility of reported net income so as to smooth covenant ratios over time.

   Managers may feel, with some justification, that they may be fired when reported earnings are low. Income smoothing reduces the likelihood of reporting low earnings.

   Finally, firms may smooth reported net income for external reporting purposes. As we have suggested, smoothing can convey inside information to the market by enabling the firm to communicate its expected persistent earning power.

It should be apparent that these various earnings management patterns can be in conflict. Over time, the pattern chosen by a firm may vary due to changes in contracts, changes in levels of profitability, and changes in political visibility. Even at a given point in time, the firm may face conflicting needs to, say, reduce reported net income for political reasons, increase it to meet analysts' forecasts, or smooth it for borrowing purposes.

11.3 EVIDENCE OF EARNINGS MANAGEMENT FOR BONUS PURPOSES

A paper by Healy (1985), entitled "The Effect of Bonus Schemes on Accounting Decisions," is a seminal investigation of a contractual motivation for earnings management. Healy observed that managers have inside information on the firm's net income before earnings management.[2] Since outside parties, including the board itself, may be unable to learn what this number is, he predicted that managers would manage net income so as to maximize their bonuses under their firms' compensation plans. Here, we will review Healy's methods and findings.

Healy's paper is based on positive accounting theory (Section 8.5). It attempts to explain and predict managers' choices of accounting policies. More specifically, it is an extension of the bonus plan hypothesis, which states that managers of firms with bonus plans will maximize current earnings. By looking more closely at the structure of bonus plans, Healy comes up with specific predictions of how and under what circumstances managers will engage in this type of earnings management.

Healy's study was confined to firms whose compensation plans are based on current reported net income only. These will be called **bonus schemes** for the rest of this section. As we saw for BCE Inc. in Section 10.3, net income-based financial targets are a major input into short-term incentive awards. We also pointed out, in Section 10.4.3, reasons why bonus schemes may have bogeys and caps. Figure 11.2 illustrates a typical bonus scheme.

In the figure, the bonus increases linearly (for example, 10% of net income) between the bogey and the cap. Below the bogey, bonus is zero. If there is no cap, the bonus would increase along the dotted line. Otherwise, the bonus becomes a constant for net income

Figure 11.2 Typical Bonus Scheme

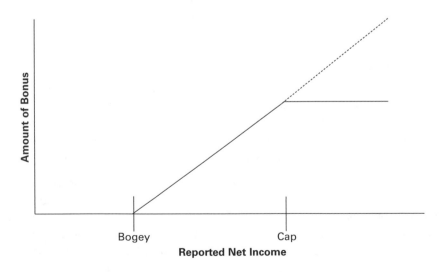

greater than the cap. Such bonus plans are called **piecewise linear**. A piecewise linear bonus scheme is simpler than that of BCE's short-term incentive plan, where the bogey and cap are implicit. Nevertheless, the basic idea of compensation increasing in earnings performance carries over. The question then is, do managers manage earnings as predicted by the bonus hypothesis?

To explore this question, consider the incentives to manage reported net income faced by a manager subject to such a scheme. If net income is low (that is, below the bogey), the manager has an incentive to lower it even further, that is, to take a bath. If no bonus is to be received anyway, the manager might as well adopt accounting policies to further reduce reported net income.[3] In so doing, the probability of receiving a bonus the following year is increased since current write-offs will reduce future amortization charges. Similarly, if net income is high (above the cap), there is motivation to adopt income minimization policies, because bonus is permanently lost on reported net income greater than the cap.

Only if net income is between the bogey and cap (except for the case in Note 3) is the manager motivated to adopt accounting policies to increase reported net income. Thus, Healy refines the bonus plan hypothesis—it really only applies when net income is between the bogey and the cap.

How does a manager manage net income? Healy assumed that managers use accruals. To illustrate how accruals may be used to manage earnings, we begin by repeating again the formula given in Sections 5.4.1 and 6.2.6:

Net income = cash flow from operations ± net accruals

This can be broken down into:

Net income = cash flow from operations ± net non-discretionary accruals
± net discretionary accruals

The concept of discretionary accruals was introduced in Section 8.5.3. These are accruals over which the manager can exercise some control. As pointed out there, the estimation of discretionary accruals by researchers poses a major challenge.

To illustrate the interplay between discretionary and non-discretionary accruals, consider the hypothetical example in Table 11.1.

Table 11.1 Discretionary and Non-Discretionary Accruals

Cash flow, as per cash flow statement		$1,000
Less: Amortization expense	− 50	
Add: Increase in (net) accounts receivable during the year	+ 40	
Add: Increase in inventory during the year	+100	
Add: Decrease in accounts payable and accrued liabilities during the year	+ 30	120
Net income, as per income statement		$1,120

In the table, a positive sign for an accrual means that, for given cash flow, it increases net income, and vice versa. The information in the table could be taken from the statement of cash flows.[4] For simplicity, we have assumed that there are no extraordinary income statement items and no income tax expense. Assume that explanations for the four accrual items are as follows:

■ **Amortization expense** Annual amortization expense is laid down by the firm's amortization policy and its estimates of assets' useful lives. Given this policy, amortization expense is a non-discretionary accrual. Of course, the firm might change its policy, for example by changing estimates of useful life, in which case amortization expense would contain a discretionary component.

■ **Increase in net accounts receivable** Assume that this derives from a decrease in the allowance for doubtful accounts, resulting from a less conservative estimate than in previous years. This accrual is discretionary, since management has some flexibility to control the amount. Other reasons for the increase could include earlier revenue recognition, a more generous credit policy, keeping the books open beyond the year-end, or simply an increase in volume of business. The first three of these accruals are discretionary, the fourth is non-discretionary.

Thus, we see that there can be several reasons for an increase in receivables. A researcher with access only to the comparative financial statements would be unlikely to know what particular reason or reasons accounted for the increase or whether the increase was discretionary or non-discretionary or both. Nevertheless, it is clear that the manager who wishes to increase reported net income through accounts receivable accruals has several means available.

■ **Increase in inventory** Assume that this derives from the firm manufacturing for stock during a period of excess manufacturing capacity. The result is to include fixed overhead costs in inventory rather than charging them off to expense as unfavourable volume variances. This accrual is discretionary, and illustrates the use of a real variable to manage earnings. However, non-discretionary reasons for the increase could be an inventory buildup in anticipation of a strike, or simply increased demand.

While other reasons for the increase are possible, just as in the case of accounts receivable, discretionary, income-increasing accruals are available for inventory as well.

■ **Decrease in accounts payable and accrual liabilities** Assume that this derives from the firm being more optimistic about warranty claims on its products than it has been in previous years. Alternatively, or in addition, the decrease could be due to regarding certain borderline items as contingencies rather than accruals. Again, we see that there can be ample room for discretionary accruals in accounts payable.

The main point to note is that the manager has considerable discretion to manage reported net income. While it is easy to determine the change in account balances, the reasons for the change are typically unknown to the investor and researcher. Also, for many of these discretionary accruals, it would be difficult for the firm's auditors to discover the earnings management or, if they did discover it, to object, since all of the techniques mentioned, with the exception of holding the books open past the year-end, are within GAAP. A similar set of discretionary accruals to decrease reported net income is available to the manager, simply by reversing those described above.

Healy did not have access to the books and records of his sample firms, and was unable to determine the specific discretionary accruals made by those firms' managers. As a result, he used another approach, namely to take total accruals as a proxy for discretionary accruals. Thus, in our example, he would estimate discretionary accruals as +$120, instead of the +$170 that would be used if he had full information. The +$170 of discretionary accruals will raise total accruals by $170, regardless of what other non-discretionary accruals may be present; that is, higher total accruals contain higher discretionary accruals, and vice versa.

Healy obtained a sample of 94 of the largest U.S. industrial companies. He followed each company over the period 1930–1980 and obtained a total of 1,527 usable observations, that is, 1,527 firm years where the bogey and (if applicable) cap for a firm's bonus scheme could be calculated. Of these, 447 observations included both a bogey and a cap.

Each observation was then classified into one of three categories, or "portfolios" as Healy calls them. Portfolio UPP consisted of observations where earnings were above the cap, portfolio LOW of observations where earnings were below the bogey, and portfolio MID where they were between the bogey and cap. If the bonus plan hypothesis is valid, total accruals should be greater for the MID portfolio than for UPP and LOW.

For the 447 observations that had both a bogey and a cap, the results are summarized in Table 11.2. We see that 46% of the 281 observations in the MID portfolio had total accruals that were positive, that is, income-increasing. The average accrual of these 281 observations was +0.0021 of total assets (accruals were deflated by total assets so that they could be compared across firms of different sizes). For the observations in the LOW and UPP portfolios, the proportions with positive total accruals were much lower—only 9% and 10%, respectively. In fact, the average accruals for these observations were negative (income-decreasing). These results are consistent with Healy's arguments that firm managers whose net incomes are below the bogey and above the cap will tend to adopt income-decreasing accruals and only managers with net income between the two will tend to adopt income-increasing accruals. Thus, Healy's predictions of earnings management by managers subject to bonus schemes were supported by the empirical results.

It should be emphasized that empirical earnings management studies face severe methodological problems. As mentioned earlier, a major difficulty is that discretionary accruals cannot be directly observed. Consequently, some proxy must be used. Using total accruals, as Healy did, introduces measurement error into the discretionary accruals variable, making it more difficult to detect earnings management should it exist. For example, the amount of non-discretionary accruals is likely correlated with net income. As Kaplan (1985) pointed out, a firm with reported net income above the cap of its bonus plan may have low non-discretionary accruals if its high income is due to an unexpected increase in demand that runs down inventory. Then, the low total accruals that are used to infer

Table 11.2 Observations With Both a Bogey and a Cap

	PROPORTION OF ACCRUALS WITH GIVEN SIGN		NUMBER OF OBSERVATIONS	AVERAGE ACCRUALS
	Positive	**Negative**		
LOW	0.09	0.91	22	−0.0671
MID	0.46	0.54	281	+0.0021
UPP	0.10	0.90	144	−0.0536
			447	

Source: P. M. Healy, "The Effect of Bonus Schemes on Accounting Decisions," *Journal of Accounting and Economics* (April 1985), p. 96, Table 2. Reprinted by permission.

earnings management are really due to the level of the firm's real economic activity and not to low discretionary accruals. Healy was aware of these problems and conducted additional tests to control for them, which he interpreted as confirming his findings.[5]

McNichols and Wilson (1988) also studied the behaviour of accruals in a bonus context. They confined their investigation to the provision for bad debts, on the grounds that a precise estimate of what the bad debts allowance should be (that is, the non-discretionary portion of the bad debts accrual) can be made. Then, discretionary accruals can be taken as the difference between this estimate and the actual bad debts provision. A precise estimate of non-discretionary accruals will reduce the problem of measurement error in the discretionary accruals variable. This approach also reduces the problem of correlation between net income and non-discretionary accruals, since the impact on the bad debts provision of the firm's level of economic activity is captured by their estimate of what the bad debts allowance should be. They found that, over the period 1969–1985, discretionary bad debt accruals were significantly income-reducing both for firm years that were very unprofitable and those that were very profitable (and thus likely to be below and above the bogeys and caps, respectively, of the bonus agreements). For firm years that were between these profitability extremes, discretionary accruals were much lower, and usually income-increasing. These results are consistent with those of Healy.

The methodology used by Jones (1991), described in Section 8.5.3, provides a more refined way to estimate non-discretionary accruals (Healy's study preceded development of this approach). In this regard, Holthausen, Larcker, and Sloan (1995) (HLS) also studied managers' accruals behaviour for bonus purposes. They were able to obtain data on whether managers' annual earnings-based bonuses were in fact zero, greater than zero but less than the maximum bonus, or at the maximum. These are substantially better data than Healy, who had to estimate whether earnings before discretionary accruals were below bogey, between bogey and cap, or above cap on the basis of available descriptions of bonus contracts, and *assume* that if earnings were below the bogey the manager would not receive a bonus, etc.

Using a version of the Jones (1991) model to estimate non-discretionary accruals for a sample of 443 firm-year observations over 1982–1990, HLS found that managers who received zero bonus did not use accruals to manage earnings downward, which differed from Healy's findings (row 1, Table 11.2). They concluded that methodological problems arising from Healy's procedures for estimating discretionary accruals explained why he appeared to find negative accruals for his low portfolio.[6] However, HLS did find that managers who were at their bonus maxima managed accruals so as to lower reported earnings. This is consistent with Healy's results—see row 3 of Table 11.2.

We may conclude that, despite methodological challenges to Healy's seminal study, there is significant evidence that, on average, managers use accruals to manage earnings so as to influence their bonuses, particularly when earnings are high. This evidence is consistent with the bonus plan hypothesis of positive accounting theory.

However, we can think about consistency with the bonus plan hypothesis in two ways. Perhaps the most natural way is to view it as opportunistic behaviour by managers to exploit their power in the organization, by maximizing their utility at the expense of the firm's shareholders and other investors who may find it prohibitively costly to unravel discretionary accruals. More visible earnings management techniques, such as accounting policy changes, timing of capital gains and losses, and provisions for restructuring can also be difficult to interpret. For example, is a firm's sale of one of its divisions driven by necessity or by timing considerations, or is a provision for restructuring excessive? Answers to questions such as these are typically private, inside information of the manager.

A second way to think about earnings management, however, is from an efficient contracting perspective. When setting compensation contracts, firms will rationally anticipate managers' incentives to manage earnings and will allow for this in the amount of compensation they offer. This was illustrated in Example 9.7, where a contract that allowed for some earnings management was less costly than eliminating it completely. Consequently, even boards of directors may not be motivated to unravel earnings management.

Nevertheless, whether we view them from an opportunistic or efficient contracting perspective, compensation contracts do create earnings management incentives.

11.4 OTHER MOTIVATIONS FOR EARNINGS MANAGEMENT

Healy's study applies to bonus contracts. However, managers may engage in earnings management for a variety of other reasons. Now, we will consider some of these.

11.4.1 Other Contracting Motivations

Debt contracts typically depend on accounting variables, arising from the moral hazard problem between manager and lender analyzed in Section 9.7. To control this problem, long-term lending contracts typically contain covenants to protect against actions by managers that are against the lenders' best interests, such as excessive dividends, additional borrowing, or letting working capital or shareholders' equity fall below specified levels, all of which dilute the security of existing lenders.

Earnings management for covenant purposes is predicted by the debt covenant hypothesis of positive accounting theory. Given that covenant violation can impose heavy costs, firm managers will be expected to avoid them. Indeed, they will even try to avoid being close to violation, because this will constrain their freedom of action in operating the firm. Thus, earnings management can arise as a device to reduce the probability of covenant violation in debt contracts.

Earnings management in a debt covenant context was investigated by Sweeney (1994). For a sample of firms that had defaulted on debt contracts, Sweeney found significantly greater use of income-increasing accounting changes relative to a control sample, and also found that defaulting firms tended to undertake early adoption of new accounting standards when these increased reported net income, and vice versa.

DeFond and Jiambalvo (1994) also examined earnings management by firms disclosing a debt covenant violation during 1985–1988. They found evidence of the use of discretionary accruals to increase reported income in the year prior to and, to a lesser extent, in the year of the covenant violation.

Somewhat different results are reported by DeAngelo, DeAngelo, and Skinner (1994), however. They studied a sample of 76 large, troubled firms. These were firms that had three or more consecutive loss years during 1980–1985 and that had reduced dividends during the loss period. For 29 of these firms, the cut in dividends was forced by binding debt covenant constraints.

After controlling for the influence of declining sales and cash flows on accruals, DeAngelo et al. failed to find evidence that these 29 firms used accruals to manage earnings upward in years prior to the cut in dividends, relative to the remaining sample firms that did not face debt covenant constraints. Rather, all the 29 firms exhibited large negative (that is, earnings-reducing) accruals extending for at least three years beyond the year of the dividend cut. DeAngelo et al. attribute this conservative behaviour as due in part to large, discretionary non-cash write-offs. Apparently, these were to signal to lenders, shareholders, unions, and others that the firm was facing up to its troubles, and to prepare the ground for subsequent contract renegotiations that frequently took place.

It thus seems that when its troubles are profound, the firm's behaviour transcends that which is predicted by the debt covenant hypothesis and, instead, earnings management becomes part of the firm's (and its manager's) overall strategy for survival.

Earnings management incentives also derive from **implicit contracts**, also called relational contracts. These are not formal contracts, such as the compensation and debt contracts just considered. Rather, they arise from continuing relationships between the firm and its stakeholders (e.g., employees, suppliers, lenders, customers) and represent expected behaviour based on past business dealings. For example, if the firm and its manager develop a reputation for always meeting formal contract commitments they will receive better terms from suppliers, lower interest rates from lenders, etc. In effect, the parties act *as if* such favourable contracts exist. In terms of our game theory Example 9.1, the manager and the firm's stakeholders trust each other sufficiently that they play the cooperative solution rather than the Nash equilibrium.

Earnings management for implicit contracting purposes was investigated by Bowen, DuCharme, and Shores (1995) (BDS). They argued that the manager's implicit contracting reputation can be bolstered by high reported profits, which increase stakeholders' confidence that the manager will continue to meet contractual obligations.[7] For example, they predicted that firms with relatively high cost of goods sold and notes payable (used as proxies for high continuing involvement with suppliers and short-term creditors, respectively) would be more likely to choose FIFO inventory and straight-line amortization accounting policies than LIFO and accelerated amortization policies. FIFO and straight-line amortization are regarded as income-increasing since they tend to produce higher reported earnings over time than their LIFO and accelerated amortization counterparts.

Based on a large sample of U.S. firms over 1981–1993, BDS found that firms with a high level of continuing involvement with stakeholders were more likely to choose FIFO and straight-line amortization policies than firms with lower levels of continuing involvement, consistent with their prediction. Furthermore, this tendency was still evident after they controlled for other earnings management motivations, such as those arising from the compensation and debt contracts discussed above. The survey results of Graham, Campbell, and Harvey (2005) support BDS' findings. They report that managers ranked relations with other stakeholders as an important reason to meet earnings targets.

11.4.2 To Meet Investors' Earnings Expectations and Maintain Reputation

Investors' earnings expectations can be formed in a variety of ways. For example, they may be based on earnings for the same period last year, or on recent analyst or company forecasts.

Firms that report earnings greater than expected typically enjoy a significant share price increase, as investors revise upwards their probabilities of good future performance. Conversely, firms that fail to meet expectations suffer a significant share price decrease. Bartov, Givoly, and Hayn (2002), in a study over the years 1983–1997, documented significantly greater abnormal share returns for firms that exceeded their most recent analysts' earnings forecasts, relative to firms that failed to meet their forecasts. Skinner and Sloan (2002), in a study over 1984–1996, documented negative share returns for firms that failed to meet earnings expectations. These were significantly greater in magnitude than the positive returns for firms that exceeded expectations. This suggests that the market penalizes firms that fall short of expectations by more than it rewards firms that exceed them.[8]

As a result, managers have a strong incentive to ensure that earnings expectations are met, particularly if they hold ESOs or other share-related compensation. One way to do this is to manage earnings upwards.[9] Rational investors will be aware of this incentive, of course. This makes meeting expectations all the more important for managers. If these are not met, the market will reason that if the manager could not find enough earnings management to avoid the shortfall, the firm's earnings outlook must be bleak indeed, and/or the firm is not well managed since it cannot predict its own future. This could explain the more severe market penalty for failure to meet expectations, particularly if the shortfall is small.

Of course, managers who miss earnings expectations may offer explanations. Some explanations candidly face up to the firm's problems. Others, however, are simply excuses. For example, the weather may be blamed for disappointing results when the real reason is that the firm does not have adequate strategies to cope with the risks it faces. Barton and Mercer (2005) provide experimental evidence on analyst reaction to manager explanations for poor performance. They find that if an explanation is plausible, analysts will increase both their earnings forecasts and their opinion of management. However, if the explanation is not plausible, earnings forecasts and opinion of management decrease. This latter finding is of particular interest since one might think that implausible information would simply be ignored.

Failure to meet investors' earnings expectations thus has serious consequences. There is a direct effect on the firm's share price and cost of capital as investors revise downwards their probabilities of good future performance. There can also be an indirect effect through manager reputation, particularly if the shortfall is small and if manager explanations are perceived as excuses. Consequently, meeting earnings expectations and maintaining reputation are powerful earnings management incentives.

11.4.3 Initial Public Offerings

By definition, firms making initial public offerings (IPOs) do not have an established market price. This raises the question of how to value the shares of such firms. Presumably, financial accounting information included in the prospectus is a useful information source. For example, Hughes (1986) showed analytically that information such as net income can be useful in helping to signal firm value to investors, and Clarkson, Dontoh, Richardson, and Sefcik (1992) found empirical evidence that the market responds positively to earnings forecasts as a signal of firm value. This raises the possibility that managers of firms going public may manage the earnings reported in their prospectuses in the hope of receiving a higher price for their shares.

Teoh, Welch, and Wong (1998) investigated the stock market performance of a sample of firms issuing IPOs during 1980–1992, following their share returns for several years after the IPO. They estimated the discretionary accruals of these firms around the IPO date, using a version of the Jones model (Section 8.5.3). They concentrated on working capital accruals, on grounds that these were relatively easy for managers to manage (e.g., revenue recognition) and relatively difficult for investors to decipher (e.g., lack of prior financial data, strong firm growth). After extensive tests to control for other factors affecting accruals and share returns, they found that the subsequent abnormal stock market returns of IPO firms with high discretionary accruals were significantly negative relative to IPO firms with low accruals. This suggests that many IPO firms do manage earnings upwards and that lower reported earnings in subsequent years, driven by accrual reversals, contribute to poor share return performance.

11.5 THE GOOD SIDE OF EARNINGS MANAGEMENT

In Section 11.1, we suggested that earnings management can be good. Here, we review these arguments, and outline theoretical and empirical evidence in their favour.

11.5.1 Blocked Communication

An argument in favour of good earnings management is based on the **blocked communication** concept of Demski and Sappington (1987) (DSa). Frequently, agents obtain specialized information as part of their expertise, and this information can be prohibitively costly to communicate to the principal, that is, its communication is blocked. For example, it may be difficult for a physician to communicate to the patient exact details of an examination and diagnosis. Then, the physician's act (e.g., operating on the patient) must stand in not only for the physician's surgical skills but also for the information acquired during the diagnosis. DSa show that the presence of blocked communication can reduce the efficiency of agency contracts, since the agent may shirk on information acquisition and compensate by taking an act that, from the principal's standpoint, is sub-optimal—the physician may simply sew up a badly cut hand on the basis of a cursory examination that fails to check for possible tendon or nerve damage, for example. If so, the principal has an incentive to try to eliminate or reduce the blocked communication.

There is a variety of ways to reduce blockage. Gu and Li (2007) report an increased positive market reaction to disclosures of business strategy by high-tech firms when the disclosures are preceded by a credible gesture of confidence in the firm by management, namely insider stock purchases. Hirst, Koonce, and Venkataraman (2007) report, based on an experimental study, that disaggregation of a good news forecast (i.e., forecasting sales and expenses as well as net income) increases its credibility. They argue that disclosure of line items reduces the ability of managers to use earnings management to attain the forecast, thereby offsetting investor suspicions that the forecast may be biased upwards.

In our context, earnings management can also be a device to reduce blockage. To illustrate, suppose that the manager desires to communicate the firm's expected long-run, persistent earnings potential. Assume that this amount is $1 million per annum. This earnings potential is complex inside information of the manager. If the manager simply announced it, the announcement would not be credible, since the market would find it prohibitively costly to verify. Suppose, however, that the firm has just realized a profit of $200,000 from the sale of a division. Suppose also that this item increases current reported net income to $1,180,000, well above its sustainable level of $1 million. Rather than report a net income substantially higher than what is expected to persist in the long run, the manager decides to record a provision for restructuring of $180,000, thereby reducing current earnings to the $1 million the manager feels will persist.

This "unblocking" of the manager's inside information by means of large discretionary accruals to produce a desired result has credibility. The market knows that a manager (except one with a very short decision horizon) would be foolish to report higher earnings than can be sustained, since the inevitable reduction in future earnings would severely punish him/her through capital and labour market reaction. Notice that the market cannot unravel this earnings management, since it is based on inside information about sustainable earning power. However, the market can use the earnings management to infer what this inside information is.

Arguments for good earnings management are strengthened by a further paper by Demski and Sappington (1990) (DSb), who show conditions under which management's inside information can always be conveyed by means of earnings management, should management wish to do so. DSb point out that operating cash flows, or some other relatively unmanaged performance measure such as core earnings (see Section 5.5), convey *some* information about future firm performance. However, management typically has additional information about future performance, such as new firm strategies, changes in firm characteristics, or changes in market conditions. While quite relevant, this information is likely to be sufficiently complex that its direct communication is blocked. Then, DSb show that judicious choice and disclosure of discretionary accruals can reveal this information to investors.[10]

*11.5.2 Theory and Empirical Evidence of Good Earnings Management

We first outline some other theoretical models that suggest earnings management can be good, and then consider empirical evidence in this regard.

Stocken and Verrecchia (2004) argue that while earnings management can be used to reveal inside information to investors as just described, it also imposes a cost since, if it is buried in operations, the ability of investors to make good investment decisions is reduced. That is, the ability of current net income to predict future performance is "jammed." For example, the inside information may be unreliable since, by definition, it has not yet been recognized by the firm's accounting system (if it was, it would no longer be inside). We saw in Chapter 5 that investors find current net income useful. We also know, however, that low reliability reduces (jams) this usefulness. To the extent investors' decisions are jammed, the firm faces higher cost of capital and reduced profits. This cost affects both shareholders and, through lower compensation, the manager.

---

*This section can be skipped with little loss of continuity.

The manager also faces another cost of earnings management. He/she may be held liable for excessive earnings management, as illustrated, for example, by the Qwest Communications vignette in Section 1.2. Here, early revenue recognition, which Qwest's managers may, at the time, have felt revealed relevant inside information about future earnings, was proven unreliable by later events.

Stocken and Verrecchia go on to show conditions under which earnings management can be good, that is, under which the benefits of revealing inside information outweigh the two costs just mentioned. Essentially, these are that the firm's environment is volatile (so that there is lots of potential for inside information to be useful) and the amount of inside information is high. Then, earnings management benefits both investors and the manager.

The good side of earnings management is also supported by efficient contracting theory. Some support was provided in Chapter 9 in a single-period context. However, as argued above, a multi-period horizon increases both the potential for and the constraints on earnings management. In this regard, Evans and Sridhar (1996) (ES) present a two-period contract where the manager has an information advantage. Specifically, the manager knows the firm's unmanaged earnings, but the owner can only observe the net income reported by the manager.

The potential for earnings management in the ES analysis is determined by GAAP, which they view as changing over time. The probability that GAAP completely specifies the firm's accounting and accrual policies next period is termed the *flexibility* of its accounting system. If this probability is high, leaving little likelihood of earnings management, the system has low flexibility, and vice versa. Nevertheless, for given GAAP, there will typically be *some* flexibility. The extent to which the firm exploits this earnings management discretion will be determined by the firm's detailed accounting and accrual policies. These policies are assumed to be inside information of the manager. Furthermore, they are sufficiently complex and technical that their communication to the owner is blocked. This creates the potential for low manager effort to be concealed by earnings management.

Since the ES model spans two periods, any earnings overstatement in the first period will reverse in the second, and vice versa. The question then is, will the manager still manage earnings? ES show that the answer is yes, under two conditions. First, the probability of earnings management being caught and/or the penalty if caught must be sufficiently low that the manager can attain reservation utility. Second, the accounting system must have low flexibility (i.e., strong GAAP).

To explain this strong GAAP result, note first that in a two-period contract, a manager's utility is maximized, other things equal, if the same compensation is received in each period. However, it is possible that first-period unmanaged earnings might be low due to random state realization. Then, if the manager reports a low earnings amount, compensation will be low. This creates an incentive for earnings management. The manager faces less compensation risk if some earnings can be "borrowed" from the expected earnings of the second period, thereby smoothing compensation across periods. If unmanaged first-period earnings are high, the manager can accomplish the same thing by deferring earnings from the current period to the next.

This risk reduction through earnings management enables the manager to attain reservation utility with a lower profit share than if earnings management was not possible. In effect, in the ES model, a contract that allows for earnings management can be more efficient than one that does not.

The reason why this result only works when there is strong GAAP is that if GAAP is weak the manager can shed too much risk through earnings management. Then, the incentive to exert effort falls. In effect, the manager "overdoses" on earnings management, resulting in an inefficient contract. We saw a similar effect in Chapter 9. There, the limitation on earnings management created by GAAP enabled a contract whereby the manager worked hard (Example 9.7). When GAAP is weak or non-existent (Example 9.5), the manager shirked. As a result, the owner was better off under strong GAAP.

Dye (1988) also investigated the possibility of earnings management. In a multi-period analysis that allows for accruals reversal, he showed conditions under which current shareholders will prefer a compensation contract that motivates the manager to smooth reported income. This contract benefits current shareholders not only by efficiently implementing a desired level of manager effort, as in the Evans and Sridhar analysis, but also by maximizing the proceeds received by current shareholders when they sell their shares to new investors.

It may seem that maximizing the proceeds received by current shareholders benefits one class of investors relative to another. However, this is not the case if markets have rational expectations, as Dye assumes. The reason is that since investors cannot control or directly observe the extent of any earnings management, the manager cannot credibly commit *not* to manage earnings, and investors realize that the manager has an incentive to manage earnings. If the efficient market has rational expectations, it will correctly anticipate the earnings management incentives and will adjust for any overstatement or understatement of earnings in setting the firm's share price, even though investors do not know specific details of what the earnings management is. Thus, when current shareholders sell their shares, they receive what the shares are really worth, not some lower amount.

When markets have rational expectations, the manager may as well go ahead and manage earnings since the market anticipates it. For example, if the manager in Dye's model does not smooth earnings as expected, investors will nevertheless think that earnings have been smoothed. They will then conclude that the firm's real earnings are lumpier than they actually are, and bid down share price accordingly. Then, the proceeds received by current shareholders will not be maximized, adversely affecting the manager's compensation as well as the current shareholders' welfare. Thus, when markets have rational expectations, earnings management is good in the sense that it avoids this market penalty.

More recently, Chen, Hemmer, and Zhang (2007) (CHZ) analyzed a related model in which the owner of a firm plans a future sale of the firm to outside investors.

The firm is operated by a manager whose compensation is based on net income. To maximize the proceeds of the sale, the owner's incentive is to manage current earnings upwards. As in the Dye model, investors are assumed to have rational expectations. Consequently, the firm owner does not benefit from the upward earnings management, since the market correctly anticipates this and adjusts its valuation of the firm accordingly. Nevertheless, the firm has to engage in this earnings management since investors expect it.

However, as we know from the analysis in Chapter 9, managing earnings upwards decreases the informativeness of net income about manager effort. That is, knowing that the owner supports managing earnings upwards, the manager has an incentive to shirk, but still receive high compensation. Consequently, the firm is in a bind—it has to manage earnings upwards since the market anticipates this, but doing so decreases contract efficiency, thereby lowering firm value.

CHZ then introduce conservative accounting (regarded here as a form of earnings management). Conservative accounting further decreases contract efficiency since it is now more likely that high manager effort will result in low reported net income and compensation. At the same time, conservative accounting increases contract efficiency by reducing the need for upward earnings management (to rational investors, a low reported net income generated by conservatism is not really as bad as it looks). A reduction in earnings management benefits the firm by reducing the manager's incentive to shirk. CHZ then show conditions (essentially, that the manager is reasonably risk-averse) under which the net of these two effects is positive.

In sum, the CHZ model predicts that managing earnings through conservative accounting can be good through its effect in reducing compensation contract inefficiency.

We conclude on the basis of the models described above that the possibility of good earnings management for both contracting and financial reporting purposes is predicted by theory.

However, given the variety of motivations for earnings management, and the difficulty of discovering and interpreting discretionary accruals including extraordinary items, it is a complex task to establish empirically whether the stock market reacts to earnings management as the theory predicts. In particular, does the market react to earnings management as if it is good? The answer to this question is important to accountants since they are prominently involved in the techniques and implementation of earnings management, and will get drawn into the negative publicity and lawsuits that inevitably follow the revelation of bad earnings management practices. Also, to the extent that earnings management is good, excessive standard setting to overly limit accounting choice may not be cost effective.

Subramanyam (1996) provided some evidence on this issue. He separated accruals into discretionary and non-discretionary components, using the Jones model (Section 8.5.3), for a large sample of firms over the years 1973–1993. Subramanyam found, after controlling for the effects of operating cash flows and non-discretionary accruals on share returns, that the stock market responded positively to the current period's discretionary accruals, consistent with managers, on average, using earnings management responsibly to reveal inside information about future earning power.

As Subramanyam pointed out, however, this finding is subject to different interpretations. For example, the market may be responding naïvely to the higher/lower reported earnings that result from high/low discretionary accruals. If so, managers may be exploiting a securities market anomaly similar to that of Sloan (1996) (Section 6.2.6).

Subramanyam conducted extensive tests, though, that tend to support that the market responds efficiently to the discretionary accruals.

However, a study by Xie (2001) questions this interpretation. For a large sample of firms over the years 1971–1992, Xie used the Jones model to estimate discretionary and non-discretionary accruals for each firm-year observation. He then estimated the persistence of these two accruals components. As we would expect, he found the persistence of discretionary accruals to be less than that of non-discretionary accruals. As a result, the efficient market should assign a lower ERC to a dollar of discretionary accruals than to a dollar of non-discretionary. However, Xie found, consistent with Sloan (1996), that the ERCs for discretionary accruals in his sample were significantly higher than their low persistence would suggest. In other words, rather than reacting to discretionary accruals as if they were good, the market appears to overvalue them.

Thus, evidence on whether the market reacts to discretionary accruals as if they are good appears mixed. However, a more direct test of this argument was conducted by Tucker and Zarowin (2006). They argued that to the extent income smoothing increases investors' ability to predict future earnings (i.e., good earnings management), the response of share return to reported earnings (which we documented in Chapter 5) will increase, assuming securities market efficiency. Conversely, if smoothing makes it more difficult for investors to predict future earnings, this response will decrease.

The authors measured income smoothing by the correlation of changes in discretionary accruals with changes in pre-smoothed earnings (measured by reported earnings minus discretionary accruals). For example, if a smoothing firm's pre-smoothed earnings are up this year, we would expect it to adopt more income-decreasing discretionary accruals to reduce reported earnings, and vice versa. Thus, the correlation should be negative, and a more negative correlation implies greater smoothing.

Based on a large sample of U.S. firms over 1993–2000, Tucker and Zarowin report that greater smoothing behaviour is accompanied by increased market response, consistent with the good earnings management argument.

All of these findings depend on the ability of the Jones model to separate accruals into discretionary and non-discretionary components in a manner consistent with how the market interprets them. Like any model, the validity of the Jones model has been extensively debated. This suggests that alternate approaches to studying the market's reaction to earnings management are desirable. For example, Liu, Ryan, and Wahlen (1997) examined the quarterly loan loss accruals (a vehicle for earnings management) of a sample of 104 U.S. banks over 1984–1991. After separating these accruals into expected and unexpected components, they found a significantly positive share price reaction to unexpected increases in loan loss provisions for "at-risk" banks (banks with regulatory capital close to legal minimums), but only in the fourth quarter. For banks not at risk, share price reaction to unexpected loan loss provisions was negative. These results suggest that at-risk banks, by managing their earnings downwards, credibly convey to the market that they are taking steps to resolve their problems, which should improve their future performance. This good news was strong enough to outweigh the bad news of the fact of the loan write-downs per se, particularly since the market may have already reacted to the banks being at risk. For banks not at risk, there is less need to take steps to resolve problems, with the result that the bad news component dominated the market's reaction. The reason why the at-risk banks' share prices rose only in the fourth quarter appears to be due to auditor involvement in that quarter. Presumably, management, and investors, take loan loss provisions more seriously when auditors are involved.

In addition to providing further evidence of how earnings management can convey inside information, Liu, Ryan, and Whalen's results suggest considerable sophistication in the securities market's response, supporting the efficient market interpretation of the findings of Subramanyam, and Tucker and Zarowin.

Additional evidence consistent with responsible earnings management is provided by Barth, Elliott, and Finn (1999). From a large sample of U.S. corporations over the years 1982–1992, they report evidence that firms with patterns of steadily increasing earnings for five years and longer enjoy higher price/earnings multiples than firms with equivalent levels and variability of earnings growth but absent the steadily increasing pattern. To the extent the steadily increasing earnings patterns are created by earnings management, the market appears to reward earnings management that does not overstate future earning power.

It should be noted that in deriving their result, Barth, Elliott, and Finn control for earnings persistence. Thus, the increased market valuation of their subject firms derives from factors beyond the use of earnings management to reveal persistent earning power. The most likely explanation, they suggest, is that the increasing earnings patterns reveal inside information about growth opportunities. For a specific example of a firm that reports steadily increasing earnings, see problem 9.

Callen and Segal (2004) also studied the market response to accruals. They point out that increases in expected future share returns (implying from the CAPM, an increase in firm risk) drive down current share returns, much like increases in expected future interest rates drive down current bond prices. After allowing for this effect in a large sample of firms over 1962–2000, they report that both accrual information and operating cash flow information have a positive effect on annual abnormal share returns, with some evidence that the accrual effect is the stronger of the two.

While Callen and Segal do not break accruals into discretionary and non-discretionary components, their findings of a positive relationship between accruals and annual share returns suggest that, on balance, accruals have information content for investors. If opportunistic earnings management overwhelmed the information content of accruals, an efficient market would not react positively to them.

Another approach to whether discretionary accruals are perceived as good or bad is to use the Dechow and Dichev procedure described in Section 5.4.1 to determine accrual quality. Francis, LaFond, Olsson, and Schipper (2005) (FLOS) studied a large sample of U.S. firms over 1970–2001, yielding 91,280 observations. For each firm, for each year, they measured accrual quality residuals ϵ_t. They then estimated the portion of these residuals arising from "innate" firm characteristics such as the volatility of its operations. More volatile firms need to record larger accruals to meet earnings expectations and to smooth earnings for compensation and covenant reasons. FLOS then regarded the remaining portion of the Dechow and Dichev residuals as discretionary, representing earnings management activities.

The question, then, is how does the market react to these accrual quality components? FLOS reported a positive market reaction to the innate components. This is to be expected if accruals are doing their job. That is, it seems that larger innate accruals convey useful information to the market, despite the potential for greater estimation error in a more volatile environment.

FLOS also reported a positive market reaction to the discretionary accrual components, although less positive than to the innate components. From this, they argued that managers use discretionary accruals responsibly to convey useful information to investors, also supporting the efficient contracting results of Subramanyam outlined above. This finding, on balance, supports the good side of earnings management. However, to the extent the market reaction is less than to the innate accruals component, it seems that some bad earnings management is mixed in with the good.

We conclude that there is substantial theory and evidence that earnings management can both inform investors and enable more efficient contracting. However, the possibility that opportunistic earnings management is mixed in with the good cannot be ruled out.

11.6 THE BAD SIDE OF EARNINGS MANAGEMENT

11.6.1 Opportunistic Earnings Management

Despite theory and evidence of responsible use of earnings management, there is also evidence of bad earnings management. From a contracting perspective, this can result from opportunistic manager behaviour. The tendency of managers to use earnings management to maximize their bonuses, as documented by Healy, can be interpreted this way, for example.

Further evidence is supplied by Dechow, Sloan, and Sweeney (1996), who examined the earnings management practices of a test sample of 92 firms charged in the United States by the SEC with alleged violation of GAAP (i.e., bad earnings management), compared to a control sample of firms of similar size and industry. Their investigation revealed a number of motivations for such earnings management. A common one was closeness to debt covenant constraints. The firms in their test sample had, on average, significantly greater leverage and significantly more debt covenant violations than the control sample.

It seems that at least some firms follow the opportunistic version of the debt covenant hypothesis.

As mentioned earlier, another motive for bad earnings management arises when a manager intends to raise new share capital and wants to maximize the proceeds from the new issue. A variety of discretionary accruals can be used to increase reported net income in the short run, such as speeding up revenue recognition, lengthening the useful life of capital assets, underprovision for environmental and restoration costs, etc. The iron law of accruals reversal is of less concern due to the short decision horizon. To the extent that earnings management to raise the issue price is unanticipated, the current shareholders benefit at the expense of new ones. Dechow, Sloan, and Sweeney (1996), mentioned above, also studied the financing decisions of their sample firms. They found that their charged firms (which, by definition, were heavy users of earnings management) issued, on average, significantly more securities during the period of earnings manipulation than the control sample.

Hanna (1999) discussed another type of earnings management. This is the frequent recording of excessive charges for non-recurring items such as writedowns under ceiling test standards, and provisions for reorganization. Hanna asserted that manager bonuses are typically based on core earnings. Furthermore, analysts' forecasts are typically of core earnings. Thus non-recurring charges do not affect manager bonuses and do not take away from the ability to meet earnings forecasts. But, excessive non-recurring charges increase *future core earnings*, by putting them in the bank through reduced future amortization charges and absorption of future costs that would otherwise be charged to operating expense when incurred. Then, the manager benefits both ways. Major costs that may have been accumulating for several years (i.e., the non-recurring charges) do not affect bonuses or ability to meet earnings forecasts, and the future expense reductions increase future core earnings, on which the manager *is* evaluated.

Furthermore, the upwards effect on future core earnings is very difficult to detect, since reduced future amortization charges and other expense reductions are buried in larger totals. In effect, poor disclosure of the effects of past non-recurring charges enables managers to engage in this type of earnings management. Nevertheless, the market does appear to react to earnings management of this nature. As mentioned in Section 5.5, Elliott and Hanna (1996) found that the ERC for a dollar of quarterly core earnings is lower for firms that have frequently recorded large unusual and non-recurring charges than for firms that have not recorded such charges. This is consistent with the market using the frequency of non-recurring charges as a proxy for the extent to which core earnings may be overstated. Of course, if accountants would disclose the effect on core earnings of past non-recurring write-offs, a proxy such as this would not be needed.

The earnings management practices discussed by Hanna are illustrated by the following vignette.

Earnings management in an international context was studied by Leuz, Nanda, and Wysocki (2003). They evaluated the extent of earnings management in each of 31 countries during 1990–1999. Their measures of earnings management differed from the discretionary

In April 2004, Nortel Networks Corp. announced that it had fired its CEO, Chief Financial Officer, and Controller. Its share price, over $11 prior to the announcement, fell to $5.26. The company later announced that several more senior managers were also fired. It appears that Nortel's 2003 reported net income of $734 million U.S. was substantially overstated.

The overstatement arose out of the collapse of the technology boom in the early 2000s. This left many of Nortel's customers and subsidiary companies in financial distress. Accruals were recorded by Nortel in 2001 and 2002 to provide for costs of contract cancellations, bad debts, layoffs, and plant closures. By mid-2002, about $5 billion of such accruals were on Nortel's balance sheet.

It appears, however, that many of these accruals were excessive, and in 2003 the company reversed them. The reversals, which were not disclosed to investors, were credited to operating expense. In retrospect, Nortel's 2001 and 2002 losses were overstated and its 2003 profit was overstated.

The significance of the 2003 profit overstatement was that Nortel's compensation plan provided for bonuses if the company returned to profitability, where profits were defined as quarterly pro-forma income (see Section 7.4.2). The company reported pro-forma income of $40 million U.S. in the first quarter of 2003 and $34 million U.S. in the second. Consequently, most employees received cash bonuses, including the CEO, who received $3.6 million U.S. However, after the effects of excessive accrual reversals are taken into account, it appears that the first two quarters of 2003 may have been loss quarters.

The company issued restated 2001–2003 results in January 2005, reporting first and second quarter 2003 net losses of U.S. $146 and $128 million, respectively, compared with an originally stated first quarter loss of $16 million and a second quarter profit of $40 million. In February 2005, the company announced that it was suing three former executives to recover $13 million in bonuses and, in March 2007, the SEC began civil proceedings against four former executives.

In February 2006, Nortel agreed to a $2.5 billion U.S. settlement of class-action lawsuits resulting from this incident. In May 2007, it agreed to pay $1 million to the Ontario Securities Commission to meet the costs of the Commission's investigation. No penalty was paid, although the company formally agreed that its 2002 and 2003 financial statements were misleading. On March 1, 2007, Nortel announced a revenue timing restatement, reducing earnings for 2005 and prior by $134 million. It also indicated that the restatement would put it into violation of certain debt covenants.

accruals approach of Jones. One measure was based on the variability of operating income—lower variability implies less income smoothing. Another measure was based on the correlation between accruals and cash flow—low correlation implies, for example, that firms in a country may be recognizing revenue well before it is received in cash. A third measure was the magnitude of total accruals—high total accruals contain high discretionary accruals, similar to the reasoning of Healy. Finally, drawing on the implication of prospect theory that small losses are more serious than small gains (Section 6.2.2), they calculated each country's ratio of small earnings losses to small gains. A low ratio suggests earnings management to avoid small losses.

Leuz, Nanda, and Wysocki combined these measures into a score for each country. For example, the United States scored 2, Canada 5, Hong Kong 15.5, and Germany 21.5, where lower scores imply less earnings management. Then, they related these scores to various country institutional characteristics, such as the level of investor protection. They found that lower investor protection was associated with more earnings management. This suggests that in countries with poor investor protection, opportunistic earnings management is more prevalent.

We conclude from these various results that accountants must scrutinize manager motivations with great care if they are to detect opportunistic earnings management.

11.6.2 Do Managers Accept Securities Market Efficiency?

The earnings management techniques just outlined, including those of Nortel, are not necessarily inconsistent with securities market efficiency. They rely on poor disclosure and limited investor attention to keep the extent of earnings management as inside information. Yet, other results question management's acceptance of efficiency itself.

We reported in Section 11.5.2 on the finding of Barth, Elliott, and Finn (1999) that the market favours firms with steadily increasing earnings patterns. Their interpretation is that the efficient market responds to the persistence and growth information implicit in the increasing earnings. However, Barth, Elliott, and Finn do not rule out an alternative, inefficient market interpretation, which is that momentum trading (see Section 6.2.1) in response to the increasing earnings pattern drives the favourable market reaction.

Schrand and Walther (2000) report yet another form of earnings management. They analyzed a sample of firms that reported a material, non-recurring gain or loss on disposal of property, plant, and equipment in the *prior year's* quarter but no such gain or loss in the same quarter of the *current year*. In news releases that typically accompany earnings announcements, managers compare the current quarter's performance with the prior year's quarter. This is consistent with the survey results of Graham et al. (Section 11.1), who report that same-quarter earnings of the previous year are a very important earnings benchmark for managers. The question then is, in these news releases, do managers remind investors of the non-recurring gain or loss in the prior quarter? Schrand and Walther found that the likelihood of such a reminder was significantly greater if the prior quarter's non-recurring item was a gain rather than a loss. In this way, the lowest possible prior period benchmark was emphasized (i.e., managed), thereby showing the change in earnings from the prior quarter in the most favourable light.

Pro-forma earnings (see Section 7.4.2) represent another form of earnings management that questions managers' acceptance of market efficiency. Managers who emphasize pro-forma earnings claim that this measure better portrays the firm's (and their own) performance than GAAP net income. However, since there are no standards to determine pro-forma earnings, managers may be tempted to leave out expense items that do contain relevant, persistent information, in order to meet earnings targets, maximize compensation, and/or improve reputation. Since the GAAP-based income statement is also available, an efficient market would quickly adjust for the omitted items. Consequently, managers' emphasis on pro-forma earnings suggests they do not accept efficiency.

Investor reaction to pro-forma earnings was studied by Doyle, Lundholm, and Soliman (2003) (DLS). They obtained a large sample of firms that reported pro-forma quarterly earnings over 1988–1999 and, for each firm and quarter, calculated the difference from GAAP net income. They found, contrary to management's claim, that many expenses excluded from GAAP net income (for example, provisions for reorganization) did have significant future effects on operating cash flows, persisting for up to three years from the dates of the quarterly announcements. Consequently, investors who look only at pro-forma earnings ignore useful information.

DLS also examined abnormal share returns of their sample firms over a three-day window surrounding the date of their quarterly earnings announcements. After controlling for other factors that affect share returns, they found that the greater the difference between pro-forma and GAAP earnings (recall that since there are no rules surrounding pro-forma earnings, some managers may leave out more expenses than others) the lower the abnormal share return over the three days. This suggests that the market does not ignore the excluded items—if it did, the abnormal returns would not be affected by the amounts of omitted expenses.

However, the market's reaction was not complete. DLS report that the lower share returns for firms with greater pro-forma–GAAP discrepancies continued for up to three years. If the market was fully efficient, all of the negative reaction would have taken place within the three-day window.

The important point from the Schrand and Walters and DLS studies is that these earnings management policies make little sense if securities markets are efficient. Consequently, managers who engage in them must not fully accept efficiency. Furthermore, despite our suggestion in Section 9.9, rejection of efficiency implies that contracting variables do not completely reconcile economic consequences and market efficiency. That is, accounting policies without cash flow effects can matter to managers simply because they believe that the market will not see through them.

11.6.3 Implications for Accountants

The implication for accountants who wish to reduce bad earnings management, however, is not to reject market efficiency, but to *improve disclosure*. As argued in Section 6.2.7, full disclosure helps investors to evaluate the financial statements, thereby reducing their susceptibility to behavioural biases and reducing managers' ability to exploit poor corporate governance and market inefficiencies. For example, clear reporting of revenue recognition policies, and detailed descriptions of major discretionary accruals such as writedowns and provisions for reorganization, will bring bad earnings management into the open, reducing managers' ability to manipulate and bias the financial statements for their own advantage. Other ways to improve disclosure include reporting the effects on core earnings of previous write-offs and, in general, assisting investors and compensation committees to diagnose low-persistence items. Managers would then bear the full consequences of their actions and bad earnings management would decrease.

11.7 CONCLUSIONS ON EARNINGS MANAGEMENT

Earnings management is made possible by the fact that true net income does not exist (Section 2.6). Furthermore, GAAP do not completely constrain managers' choices of accounting policies and procedures. Such choices are much more complex and challenging than simply selecting those policies and procedures that best inform investors. Rather, managers' accounting policy choices are often motivated by strategic considerations, such as meeting earnings expectations, contracts that depend on financial accounting variables, new share issues, discouraging potential competition, and unblocking of inside information. In effect, accounting policy choice has characteristics of a game. Economic consequences are created when changes in GAAP adversely affect managers' abilities to play the game. That is, managers will react against rule changes that reduce their flexibility of accounting choice. As a result, accountants need to be aware of the legitimate needs of management, as well as of investors. Actual financial reporting represents a compromise between the needs of these two major constituencies.

Despite the reduction of reliability and sensitivity that often accompanies earnings management, strong arguments can be made that it is useful if kept within bounds. First, it gives managers flexibility to react to unanticipated state realizations when contracts are rigid and incomplete.

Second, earnings management can serve as a vehicle for the credible communication of inside information to investors.

Both of these arguments are consistent with efficient securities markets and the efficiency version of positive accounting theory.

Nevertheless, some managers may abuse the communications potential of GAAP by pushing earnings management too far, with the result that persistent earning power is overstated, at least temporarily. This behaviour can result from a failure to accept securities market efficiency or from an ability to hide bad earnings management behind poor disclosure, or both. To the extent managers do not accept securities market efficiency, believing instead that they can fool the market by their disclosure decisions, positive accounting theory does not fully reconcile market efficiency and economic consequences.

Thus, whether earnings management is good or bad depends on how it is used. Accountants can reduce the extent of bad earnings management by bringing it out into the open. This can be accomplished by improved disclosure of low-persistence items and reporting the effect of previous write-offs on core earnings. In addition to assisting share prices to more closely reflect fundamental firm value, improved disclosure assists corporate governance, since compensation committees and the managerial labour market can better reward good manager performance and discipline managers who shirk. The resulting improvements in allocation of scarce investment capital and firm productivity increase social welfare.

Questions and Problems

1. Explain why a firm's manager might both believe in securities market efficiency and engage in earnings management.

2. For an income management strategy of taking a bath, the probability of the manager receiving a bonus in a future year rises. Explain why. (CGA-Canada)

3. A manager increases reported earnings by $1,300 this year. This was done by reducing the allowance for credit losses by $500 below the expected amount, and reducing the accrual for warranty costs expense to $800 below the expected amount. Explain why, other things equal, this will lower next year's earnings by $1,300.

4. You are a CEO operating under a bonus plan similar to the one assumed by Healy (Section 11.3). Explain whether you would react favourably or negatively to an exposure draft of a proposed change in GAAP that has the following effects on your financial statements. Treat each effect as independent of the others.

    a. The effect will be to increase liabilities. Examples of such GAAP changes include capitalization of long-term leases (Section 7.2.2), and recording of pension plan obligations and other postretirement benefits (Section 7.2.6).

    b. The effect will be to increase the volatility of reported net income. An example would be a standard that required unrealized gains and losses on capital assets and securities to be included in net income.

    c. The effect will be to exert downward pressure on reported net income. An example is the expensing of employee stock options (Section 8.3) and the ceiling tests for property, plant, and equipment (Section 7.2.5), and purchased goodwill (Section 7.4.2).

    d. The effect will be to eliminate alternative ways of accounting for the same thing. For example, a new standard might remove LIFO inventory method from GAAP.

5. The firms in Healy's study of earnings management (Section 11.3) would have been using the historical cost basis of accounting. Given that accounting standards have moved to fair value accounting for financial instruments, as described in Section 7.3.2, would this increase or decrease the potential for opportunistic earnings management for bonus purposes? Explain.

6. The comparative balance sheet of JSA Ltd. as at June 30, 2008 is as follows:

	June 30, 2008	June 30, 2007
	Assets	
Current assets:		
Accounts receivable (net)	$ 76	$ 60
Inventories	35	53
Prepaid expenses	2	1
	113	114
Capital assets (net)	37	39
Long-term investments	2	2
Prepaid development costs	40	39
	$192	$194
	Liabilities and Shareholders' Equity	
Current liabilities:		
Bank indebtedness	$ 18	$ 4
Accounts payable	64	71
Customer advances	13	8
Current portion of long-term debt	1	2
Current portion of future income taxes	2	1
	98	86
Long-term debt	5	3
Liability for future income taxes	0	6
Share capital	73	71
Retained earnings	16	28
	$192	$194

JSA Ltd.'s 2008 income statement is as follows:

Sales		$233
Expenses:		
Cost of sales	184	
Administrative and selling	35	
Research and development	4	
Depreciation and amortization	14	
Interest	3	240
Loss before undernoted items		(7)
Income tax recovery		7
Provision for reorganization		(12)
Net loss for the year		$ (12)
Cash flow from operations for 2008 was $7.		

Required

a. Calculate the various accruals on an item-by-item basis. For each accrual indicate the extent to which that accrual may contain a discretionary component and briefly explain why.

b. Briefly describe two other ways that researchers have used to estimate the discretionary component of total accruals.

c. A manager, whose bonus is related to reported net income, finds that net income for the year (before bonus) is below the bogey of the incentive plan. What type of earnings management might the manager then engage in? Which of the accruals in part **a** would be most suitable for this purpose? Explain.

7. A common tactic to manage earnings is to "stuff the channels," that is, to ship product prematurely to dealers and customers, thereby inflating sales for the period. A case in point is Bristol-Myers Squibb Co. (BMS), a multinational pharmaceutical and baby food company headquartered in New York. In August 2004, the SEC announced a $150 million penalty levied against BMS. This was part of an agreement to settle charges by the SEC that the company had engaged in a fraudulent scheme to inflate sales and earnings in order to meet analysts' earnings forecasts.

The scheme involved recognition of revenue on pharmaceutical products shipped to its wholesalers in excess of the amounts demanded by them. These shipments amounted to $1.5 billion U.S. during 2001–2002. To persuade its wholesalers to accept this excess inventory, BMS agreed to cover their carrying costs, amounting to millions of dollars per quarter. In addition, BMS understated its accruals for rebates and discounts allowed to its large customers.

According to the SEC, the company also engaged in "cookie jar" accounting. That is, it created phony reserves for disposals of unneeded plants and divisions during high-profit quarters. These would be transferred to reduce operating expenses in low-profit quarters when BMS' earnings still fell short of amounts needed to meet forecasts.

Required

a. Give reasons why managers would resort to extreme earnings management tactics such as these.

b. Evaluate the effectiveness of stuffing the channels as an earnings management device. Consider both from the standpoint of a single year and over a series of years.

c. Evaluate the effectiveness of cookie jar accounting as an earnings management device. What earnings management pattern did BMS appear to be following by means of this tactic?

8. The potentially serious consequences of bad earnings management are illustrated by the case of Atlas Cold Storage Income Trust, which operates a system of refrigerated warehouses across Canada and the United States. During June 2004, the Ontario Securities Commission filed quasi-criminal charges under the Ontario Securities Act against four senior officials of the company, including its CEO. The company itself was not charged because it cooperated with the investigation and took steps to remedy the problems.

The OSC charged that during 2001–2003, Atlas had engaged in several types of financial statement manipulations. One tactic was to capitalize certain costs that, according to

GAAP, should have been charged to expense. Another involved deferring recognition of a large customer claim for damaged goods from 2001, where it belonged, to 2002. A third tactic was to disguise breaches of debt covenants by a subsidiary company by advancing money to the subsidiary at financial statement dates. These advances were repaid shortly thereafter. According to revised financial statements filed by the company, net income was originally reported too high by $5.2 million for 2001 and $32.4 million for 2002. The company also faced a class-action lawsuit by investors.

Required

a. Evaluate the short-run (i.e., one year) and long-run effectiveness of capitalizing expenses as an earnings management device.

b. The motivation for some of the claimed manipulations was apparently to meet earnings targets. Why is it important to managers to meet earnings targets? Use concepts of market efficiency and investor rationality in your answer.

c. With respect to earnings targets, Coca-Cola Co. announced in December 2002 that it was discontinuing the provision of quarterly and annual earnings forecasts to analysts. Some other large public companies, including BCE Inc., have taken similar action. Why would they do this?

9. General Electric Company (GE) is a large United States-based conglomerate, with operations extending from a large variety of industrial equipment and services, to healthcare, to TV and entertainment, to commercial finance. The sheer complexity and industry diversity of GE makes it particularly difficult for even financial analysts to fully understand the company, since it is unlikely, if not impossible, for anyone to be an expert in all the industries in which the company operates. As a result, it is very difficult for investors to predict GE's future performance. This puts a strong onus on GE management to assist investors in this regard.

Table 11.3 shows reported earnings for GE for the years indicated. What is striking is the steady increase in reported earnings. Only in 2005, when net income was pulled down by a large loss on discontinued operations, is there a small break in this impressive pattern of earnings growth.

Table 11.3 General Electric Company Reported Net Income, 1993–2006, Incl.

Year	Reported Net Income	Year	Reported Net Income
2006	$20,829	1999	$10,717
2005	16,711	1998	9,296
2004	17,160	1997	8,203
2003	15,002	1996	7,280
2002	14,118	1995	6,573
2001	13,684	1994	4,726
2000	12,735	1993	4,315

Source: Annual Reports, General Electric Company.

GE has long been regarded as using earnings management to smooth its reported earnings to a pattern of steady growth. Some of the techniques with earnings management potential that it has used are:

- Changes to the expected rate of return on pension plan assets.

- Sales of divisions. Such sales generally lead to large non-recurring gains.

- Restructuring charges. These are charges to current earnings to provide for expected costs of restructuring the operations of one or more of its many divisions. It is claimed that GE manages the amounts and timing of these charges so as to offset large non-recurring gains, such as from sales of divisions. The objective is to avoid reporting higher earnings than can be sustained in future years.

- Buying profitable businesses. GE is constantly acquiring new subsidiary companies. If needed to prevent reporting an earnings decrease, management of the timing and identity of such acquisitions can achieve an immediate contribution to consolidated reported earnings in the year of acquisition.

- Conservative accounting. Rapid amortization of, for example, leased aircraft by GE's commercial finance division enables large profits to be recorded when the aircraft are eventually sold. The timing of such sales can be managed by GE.

- Allocation of purchased goodwill upon acquisition of subsidiary companies. When GE acquires a subsidiary, it may decide, or be required, to dispose of segments of the acquired business. The flexibility under GAAP of allocation of the excess of amount paid for a subsidiary company over the fair value of assets acquired enables GE to record a gain on such dispositions, by allocating a relatively small amount of amount paid to any subsidiary segments that it intends to dispose of.

The important point about the array of earnings management techniques available to GE is that they can be used in concert to report a smooth earnings sequence. Table 11.3 suggests that GE has been quite successful in this regard.

Required

a. Evaluate restructuring charges as an earnings management device. Relate your answer to the claims of Hanna (1999) about misuse of restructuring charges.

b. Under securities markets efficiency, share prices always fully reflect all public information about a firm's securities. Given its complexity, would GE's share price always reflect all public information about GE? Explain why or why not.

c. Is earnings management by GE good or bad? Explain.

10. The article "Dangerous Games," by Jonathan Laing is here reproduced from *Barron's* (June 8, 1998). The article describes apparent earnings management devices used by Sunbeam Corp., with "Chainsaw Al" Dunlap as CEO, to "largely manufacture" its 1997 reported earnings of $109.4 million.

Dangerous Games

Did "Chainsaw Al" Dunlap manufacture Sunbeam's earnings last year?

Albert Dunlap likes to tell how confidants warned him in 1996 that taking the top job at the small-appliance maker Sunbeam Corp. would likely be his Vietnam. For a time, the 60-year-old West Point graduate seemingly proved the Cassandras wrong. As the poster boy of 'Nineties-style corporate cost-cutting, he delivered exactly the huge body counts and punishing airstrikes that Wall Street loved. He dumped half of Sunbeam's 12,000 employees by either laying them off or selling the operations where they worked. In all, he shuttered or sold about 80 of Sunbeam's 114 plants, offices and warehouses.

Sunbeam's sales and earnings responded, and so did its stock price, rising from $12.50 a share the day Dunlap took over in July 1996 to a high of $53 in early March of this year.

But last month Sunbeam suffered a reversal of fortune that was as sudden and traumatic for Dunlap as the Viet Cong's Tet offensive was to U.S. forces in 1968. After several mild warnings of a possible revenue disappointment, Sunbeam shocked Wall Street by reporting a loss of $44.6 million for the first quarter on a sales decline of 3.6%. In a trice, the Sunbeam cost-cutting story was dead, along with "Chainsaw Al" Dunlap's image as the supreme maximizer of shareholder value. Now Sunbeam stock has fallen more than 50% from its peak, to a recent $22.

And just as suddenly, what was supposed to be an easy sprint, Dunlap's last hurrah as a corporate turnaround artist, has turned into a grinding marathon. Lying in tatters is his growth scenario for Sunbeam, based on supposedly sexy new offerings such as soft-ice cream makers, fancy grills, home water purifiers and air-filter appliances. Many of the new products have bombed in the marketplace or run into serious quality problems. Moreover, Sunbeam has run into all manner of production, quality and delivery problems. It recently announced the closing of two Mexican manufacturing facilities with some 2,800 workers, citing the facilities' lamentable performance. Dozens of key executives, members of what Dunlap just months ago called his Dream Team, are bailing out. And now he faces another year or more of the wrenching restructuring that's needed to meld Sunbeam with its recently announced acquisitions, including the camping-equipment maker Coleman Co., the smoke detector producer First Alert and Signature Brands USA, best known for its Mr. Coffee line of appliances. These acquisitions will double the size of a company whose wheels are coming off. This may not be Vietnam, but it sure ain't Kansas, Toto.

Sunbeam declined to discuss the company's problems with *Barron's*. In some ways, Dunlap seems to have morphed into a latter-day Colonel Kurtz of the movie *Apocalypse Now*, increasingly out of touch with the grim realities of Sunbeam's situation and suspicious of friend and foe alike. For example, Wall Street is still buzzing over a confrontation that Dunlap had with PaineWebber analyst Andrew Shore at a Sunbeam meeting with the financial community in New York three weeks ago. Shore had the temerity to ask several questions that Dunlap deemed impertinent, and Dunlap snarled, "You son of a bitch. If you want to come after me, I'll come after you twice as hard."

Shore, the first major analyst to downgrade Sunbeam's stock in April when word began to circulate of a possible first-quarter earnings debacle, is still upset over the incident.

"As far as I'm concerned, Al is the most overrated CEO in America," he grouses. "He's nothing but a bully who speaks in sound bites and completely lacks substance."

Despite Sunbeam's latest reversal of fortune, don't expect Al Dunlap to be headed for the poorhouse any time soon. Though the swoon in Sunbeam shares has vaporized the value of the options held by most of the company's executives and managers, Dunlap's large option and stock grants are still worth about $70 million, down from a peak value of over $300 million when the stock was at its high. Moreover, in February Dunlap negotiated a new contract, doubling his annual base salary of $2 million. Under a rich benefits package, Sunbeam even foots the bill for Dunlap and his wife's first-class air fare from Florida, where Sunbeam is headquartered, to Philadelphia so that Dunlap can visit his personal dentist to keep his latest bridge comfy and pearly white. Limo charges and overnights at the Four Seasons hotel are included as well. All this from the self-styled champion of shareholder value.

We can't say we are surprised by Sunbeam's current woes. In a cover story last year entitled "Careful, Al" (June 16), we cast a skeptical eye on Dunlap's growth objectives in the low-margin, cutthroat small-appliance industry. We also pointed out the yawning gap between Sunbeam's performance claims and reality. We took special note of Sunbeam's accounting gimmickry, which appeared to have transmogrified through accounting wizardry the company's monster 1996 restructuring charge ($337 million before taxes) into 1997's eye-popping sales and earnings rebound. But to no avail. Wall Street remained impressed by Sunbeam's earnings, and the stock continued to rise from a price of $37 at the time of the story.

Sunbeam's financials under Dunlap look like an exercise in high-energy physics, in which time and space seem to fuse and bend. They are a veritable cloud chamber. Income and costs move almost imperceptibly back and forth between the income statement and balance sheet like charged ions, whose vapor trail has long since dissipated by the end of any quarter, when results are reported. There are also some signs of other accounting shenanigans and puffery, including sales and related profits booked in periods before the goods were actually shipped or payment received. Booking sales and earnings in advance can comply with accounting regulations under certain strict circumstances.

"We had an amazing year," Dunlap crowed in Sunbeam's recently released 1997 annual report, taking an impromptu victory lap for the profit of $109.4 million, or $1.41 a share, on sales of $1.2 billion. Sunbeam had every incentive to try to shoot the lights out in 1997. Dunlap and crew were convinced they would be able to attract a buyer for the company just as they had done in the second year of their restructuring of Scott Paper in 1995, when Dunlap managed to fob Scott off on Kimberly Clark for $9 billion. They openly shopped Sunbeam around in the second half of last year, but the offer never came. The rising stock price made the company too expensive, and would-be buyers were also deterred by the nightmares Kimberly Clark experienced after buying Scott.

Yet, sad to say, the earnings from Sunbeam's supposed breakthrough year appear to be largely manufactured. That, at least, is our conclusion after close perusal of the company's recently released 10-K, with a little help from some people close to the company.

Start with the fact that in the 1996 restructuring, Sunbeam chose to write down to zero some $90 million of its inventory for product lines being discontinued and other perfectly good items. Even if Sunbeam realized just 50 cents on the dollar by selling these goods in 1997 (in some cases, they reportedly did even better), that would account for about a third of last year's net income of $109.4 million.

One has to go to the 1997 year-end balance sheet to detect more of mother's little helpers. One notes a striking $23.2 million drop, from $40.4 million in 1996 to $17.2 million in 1997, in pre-paid expenses and other current assets. There's no mystery here, according to a former Sunbeam financial type. The huge restructuring charge in 1996 made it a lost year anyway, so Sunbeam prepaid everything it could, ranging from advertising and packaging costs to insurance premiums and various inventory expenses. The result: Costs expensed for 1997 were reduced markedly, if unnaturally. This artifice alone probably yielded an additional $15 million or so in 1997 after-tax income.

Why did Sunbeam's "Other Current Liabilities" mysteriously drop by $18.1 million and "Other Long-Term Liabilities" fall by $19 million in 1997? The answer is simple, according to folks close to the company. Various reserves for product warranties and other items that were set aside during Sunbeam's giant 1996 restructuring were drained down in 1997, creating perhaps an additional $25 million or so in additional net income for the year.

On top of all that, as part of the 1996 restructuring charge, Sunbeam reduced the value of its property, plant, equipment and trademarks by $92 million. Though some of these charges applied to assets Sunbeam was selling off, the bulk of the charge related to ongoing operations. This allowed Sunbeam to lower its depreciation and amortization expense on the 1997 income statement by nearly $9 million. That would create about $6 million of additional after-tax income.

Oddly enough, the figure for net property, plant and equipment on Sunbeam's balance sheet still rose during 1997, to $241 million from $220 million the year before. This is likely an indication that such costs as product development, new packaging and some advertising and marketing initiatives were capitalized or put straight on the balance sheet instead of being expensed in the year they were incurred, as was the previous practice. In this manner, expense could have been shifted from 1997 into future years, when they can be burned off at a slower, more decorous pace afforded by multi-year depreciation schedules. Why else would Sunbeam's advertising and promotion expense drop by some $15 million, from $71.5 million in 1996 to $56.4 million last year? Particularly when Sunbeam trotted out a splashy national television ad campaign in 1997 to boost consumer demand for its new products. This advertising shortfall alone contributed another $10 million to Sunbeam's 1997 profits.

The company also got a nice boost from a 61% drop in its allowance for doubtful accounts and cash discounts, from $23.4 million in 1996 to $8.4 million in 1997. And this decline occurred despite a 19% rise in Sunbeam's sales last year. The milking of this bad debt reserve in 1997 likely puffed net income by an additional $10 million or so.

Then there's the mystery of why Sunbeam's inventories exploded by some 40%, or $93 million, during 1997. Quite possibly, Sunbeam was playing games with its inventories to help the income statement. By running plants flat out and building inventories, a company can shift fixed overhead costs from the income statement to the balance sheet where they remain ensconced as part of the value of the inventory until such time as the inventory is sold. To be conservative, let's assume this inventory buildup might have helped Sunbeam's profits to the tune of, say, $10 million.

Lastly, there are more than superficial indications that Sunbeam jammed as many sales as it could in 1997 to pump both the top and bottom lines. The revenue games began innocently enough early last year. Sales were apparently delayed in late 1996, a lost year anyway, and rammed into 1997. Likewise, *The Wall Street Journal* reported several instances of "inventory stuffing" during 1997, in which Sunbeam either sent more goods than had been ordered by customers or shipped goods even after an order had been cancelled. But these are comparatively venial sins that companies engage in all the time to make a quarter's results look better. Besides, Sunbeam gave the plausible excuse at the time that glitches in a computer system consolidation in the first quarter had them flying blind for a time.

But as 1997 dragged on and the pressure to perform for Wall Street intensified, Sunbeam began to take greater and greater liberties with sales terms to puff current results. The latest 10-K, for example, discloses that in the fourth quarter of last year Sunbeam recorded some $50 million in sales of cooking grills under an "early buy" program that allowed retailers to delay payment for the items as long as six months. Moreover, some $35 million of these "early buys" were categorized "bill and hold" sales and never even left Sunbeam's warehouses.

Sunbeam engaged in bill-and-hold transactions in other product lines, too, according to a number of people in the appliance industry. In the second quarter, for example, Sunbeam booked a sale and "shipped" some $10 million of blankets to a warehouse it had rented in Mississippi near its Hattiesburg distribution center. They were held there for some weeks for Wal-Mart. The company also pumped millions of dollars of goods into several national small-appliance distributors on such easy payment terms as to call into question whether a sale ever took place. Some with knowledge of Sunbeam's business practices say the appliance maker in some instances transferred title for the goods to distributors but then agreed to not only delay payment but actually pay the distributors what amounted to a storage charge for taking the goods. These sources also said that in some cases distributors also had the right to return the items to Sunbeam without suffering any loss.

How much did various types of questionable sales add to 1997's net income? No outsider can know for sure. But we can make an educated guess based on the fact that Sunbeam's receivables, or unpaid customer accounts, jumped by 38%, or $82 million, in 1997. Taking into account Sunbeam's profit margins, it seems that questionable sales could have boosted 1997 net income by as much as $8 million.

We by no means are privy to all Sunbeam's techniques for harvesting current earnings from past restructuring charges and future sales. Deconstructing Al Dunlap is a daunting task. But to save our gentle readers the effort, our total estimate of artificial profit boosters in 1997 came to around $120 million compared with the $109.4 million profit the company actually reported. Thus, one is left to wonder whether Sunbeam made anything at all from its actual operations, despite Dunlap's claim to have realized some $225 million in cost savings as a result of his restructuring prowess.

Our dour view of Sunbeam's current financial health is only confirmed by the company's consolidated statement of cash flow in the latest 10-K. These numbers, of course, are harder to finesse because they track the actual cash that flowed in and out of the company during 1997. And the statement doesn't paint a pretty picture. Despite 1997's eye-catching $109.4 million net profit, Sunbeam still suffered negative cash flow from operations of $8.2 million, after taking into account the explosion in Sunbeam's inventory and accounts receivable during the year. And that operating cash flow deficit would have been an even larger $67.2 million if not for the sale of $59 million in receivables in the last week of 1997. After capital expenditures of $58.3 million is thrown into the equation, Sunbeam's free cash flow deficit amounts to more than $125 million.

Sunbeam's first-quarter earnings debacle is yet another sign of a company that's in anything but the pink of health. Despite management assertions into April that Sunbeam's first-quarter sales would finish comfortably ahead of those for the first quarter of 1997, they ended up declining 4%. Even more shocking to Dunlap's fans was the $44.6 million loss in the March quarter compared with a profit in the year earlier period of $6.9 million. Sure, $36.8 million of that first-quarter loss was the result of nonrecurring charges, mostly a handsome new pay package Dunlap managed to negotiate in February. But the operating loss Sunbeam suffered of $7.8 million was a clear sign of its true earnings power once the tank from the 1996 restructuring charge had run dry.

Dunlap trotted out a whole raft of excuses for the company's lamentable first-quarter performance. He cited dumb deals his former No. 3 executive had made with major retailers before Chainsaw fired him in April, the effect of bad weather on grill sales caused by El Nino, and so forth.

Whatever the case, the first-quarter disaster wasn't the result of any lack of effort on Sunbeam's part to pump up the results. The company recorded $29 million of additional "buy now, pay later" grill sales. In fact, the company is now holding so many grills, in various warehouses around its Neosho, Missouri, grill plant that it has had to lease warehouse space in nearby Oklahoma. Who knows how many of these grills will ever make it to the selling floor?

Sunbeam also extended its quarter by three days, from March 28 to March 31. This allowed the company to book an extra $20 million in sales both from ongoing Sunbeam operations and two days of sales from Coleman (its acquisition closed on March 30). But to no avail. Sunbeam still fell $9 million short of last year's sales of $253.5 million.

Reports are rife that Sunbeam tried to strong-arm suppliers into "recutting" their invoices for various goods and services so that Sunbeam would officially owe less money. The proviso was that the suppliers would be allowed to add back the amount forgone, plus interest, in invoices submitted after the first quarter had ended. A Sunbeam financial official denies the "recutting" charge and characterizes the activity by the company's procurement department as the normal give-and-take that goes on between suppliers and companies seeking rebates.

But that's not the understanding held by an official at one China-based supplier. When contacted by *Barron's*, this official readily acknowledged that he had sent Sunbeam a check for $500,000, or 5% of the business he does annually with the company, in late March. "The only reason I sent them a check rather than a new invoice is that we had no invoices outstanding at the time we received the call," he explained. "We figure our contribution dropped right down to the bottom line if Sunbeam actually booked it. I don't know what happened, though."

For the next few quarters, expect the recent acquisition of Coleman, First Alert and Mr. Coffee to restore a measure of calm to Sunbeam's financial performance. The giant restructuring charges that Sunbeam is taking to integrate the new units, at $390 million before taxes, will give the company plenty of fodder with which to play earnings games.

The company is even forecasting earnings of $1 a share this year and $2 next year—before extraordinary items, naturally.

But Dunlap's days at Sunbeam may be numbered. The already-ailing company now has to struggle under $2 billion of additional debt and a negative tangible net worth of $800 million. And his enemies, including disenchanted shareholders, angry securities analysts, and bitter former employees, are growing in number and circling ever closer to the company's headquarters in Delray Beach. Of course, Dunlap could always escape by using the building's flat roof to chopper out, should it come to that. One can only hope he'll remember to take the American flag with him.

Required

a. Jonathan Laing notes that Sunbeam's prepaid expenses declined from $40.4 million at December 31, 1996, to $17.2 million at December 31, 1997, a reduction of $23.2 million. He points out that 1996 was a "lost year anyway" (because of a 1996 restructuring charge of $337 million), so Sunbeam "prepaid everything it could." Laing then states that this "artifice alone probably yielded" $15 million in 1997 after-tax income.

   Do you agree with Laing's analysis of the effect of the decline in prepaid expenses during 1997 on 1997 net income? Explain why or why not.

b. Laing reports that 1997 operating cash flow was –$8.2 million. Since net income was reported as $109.4 million, net income-increasing accruals must have totalled $117.6 million. Use the information in the article to itemize the impacts on net income of the various earnings management devices described. How close does your itemized list come to $117.6 million? In arriving at your itemized total, take your answer to part **a** into account. Do you agree with Laing's statement that 1997 earnings "appear to be largely manufactured"? Explain why or why not.

c. On the last page, the article refers to Sunbeam's acquisition of Coleman, First Alert, and Mr. Coffee, indicating that Sunbeam is taking restructuring charges of $390 million to integrate these firms into its operations. Explain how this will "give the company plenty of fodder with which to play earnings games."

d. Use the "iron law" of accruals reversal to help explain why there was a substantial first quarter 1998 loss.

11. Barton (2001) studied managers' use of derivatives and discretionary accruals to smooth reported earnings. As Barton points out, both of these devices have smoothing potential—since earnings can be expressed as the sum of operating cash flows and total accruals, smoothing can be accomplished through operating cash flows (which can be hedged by derivatives—a real earnings management device) and/or through accruals (by means of the discretionary portion).

   From a sample of large U.S. firms during 1994–1996, inclusive, Barton found that managers trade off the use of derivatives and discretionary accruals in order to maintain (i.e., smooth) earnings volatility at a desired level. Specifically, firms that were heavy derivatives users tended to be low users of discretionary accruals, and vice versa. Other things equal, this suggests that managers are sensitive to the costs of smoothing earnings. That is, firms appear to use the combination of smoothing devices that are, for them, the least costly.

Required

a. Give reasons why managers may want to smooth earnings.

b. What are some of the costs of opportunistic smoothing of earnings? Why would managers trade off these two earnings smoothing devices, rather than using only one or the other?

c. Are Barton's results more consistent with the opportunistic or efficient contracting version of positive accounting theory? Why?

12. Refer to Theory in Practice 11.1 in Section 11.6.

Required

a. Which earnings management policy did Nortel appear to be using in 2001 and 2002? Why? Which policy did it appear to be using in 2003? Why?

b. Discuss the possible impacts on manager effort of the Nortel compensation plan's tying of bonuses to a return to profitability.

c. Assuming that the accruals recorded by Nortel in 2001 and 2002 were justified by pessimistic economic conditions at the time, where did Nortel management go wrong? Explain.

13. You are an expert on generally accepted accounting principles and the quality of financial reporting, with extensive experience in rational investing. You determine the current quality of financial reporting as summarized in the following information system:

		GN	BN
	High	0.9	0.1
State of Nature			
	Low	0.2	0.8

The states of nature refer to future firm performance. GN (good news) and BN (bad news) summarize the information content of current financial statements.

You are a shareholder of CG Ltd., which has just released its quarterly financial report, and are evaluating this report to decide whether to sell your shares now or hold them for another quarter.

Your prior probability of the high state is 0.7. The current market value (i.e., your payoff if you sell now) of your CG Ltd. shares is $81. If CG is in the high state, your payoff will be $100 if you sell at the end of the next quarter. If CG is in the low state, your payoff will be $36. You are risk-averse, with utility equal to the square root of your payoff.

Required

a. CG Ltd. has reported steadily increasing earnings for several years. This quarter is no exception, with earnings up 10% from the same quarter last year, and exactly equal to analysts' consensus forecast. However, you notice a large, non-recurring loss in net income. Does the current financial report show GN or BN? Explain.

b. Based on your evaluation in **a**, should you sell or hold your CG shares? Show calculations.

c. Assume the same scenario as in **a**, but that CG's earnings per share are 1 cent below analysts' consensus forecast. Would your evaluation of the GN or BN in earnings change? Explain why or why not.

14. On March 10, 2006, Nortel Networks Corp. announced that it would delay filing its 2005 financial reports with the SEC. The delay arose because Nortel and its auditors decided that certain revenue recognized in prior periods should have been deferred. The estimated deferral of revenue previously recognized in the first nine months of 2005 totalled $162 million U.S., reducing 2005 earnings from continuing operations by $95 million. For 2004 and prior years, the corresponding amounts were deferral of $704 million of previously recognized revenue and a reduction of prior years' earnings of $279 million.

Nortel explained that these changes follow from Statements of Position issued by the AICPA (Nortel follows U.S. GAAP), which require that revenue from longer-term contracts involving "multiple deliverables," such as hardware, software, and services, should be deferred until delivery.

On the same day, Nortel announced an estimated, unaudited, net loss from 2005 continuing operations of $2.421 billion. This loss included an expense of $2.474 billion to settle shareholder litigation resulting from previous accounting restatements (see Theory in Practice 11.1).

On March 10, 2006, Nortel's share price on the TSX composite index fell 11 cents in heavy trading to $3.50 Can., for a return of −3.05% for the day. On the same day, the TSX composite index rose 68.28 points to 11,833.61, for a return of 0.58%. According to Reuters' web site, Nortel's beta on the TSX at this time was 1.96. The risk-free interest rate R_f was 4.5%, or 0.0001 per day.

Required

a. Evaluate the effect of Nortel's revenue deferral on the relevance and reliability of its 2005 financial statements.

b. What earnings management pattern did Nortel appear to be following for 2005? Why?

c. Calculate the abnormal return on Nortel's shares, relative to the return on the TSX, for March 10, 2006. Do you feel that the abnormal return arose primarily from the news of the revenue deferral or from the $2.474 billion shareholder litigation expense? Explain.

Hint: According to the market model and CAPM, $\alpha_j = R_f (1 - \beta_j)$.

d. Nortel included the $2.474 billion shareholder litigation expense as part of continuing operations, rather than as an extraordinary item. Do you agree? Explain.

15. In April 2005, the SEC announced settlement with Coca-Cola Company of charges of fraud and false and misleading financial reporting. The charges arose from "gallon pushing" at Coca-Cola's Japanese subsidiary during 1997 to 1999, whereby the subsidiary shipped more concentrate to its bottlers than needed to meet sales volumes.

According to the SEC, in the first quarter of 1997 over 3.3 million extra gallons were pushed, generating additional revenue for Coca-Cola of $46.2 million for the quarter. Amount pushed increased over the two years, reaching 10.1 million gallons in the fourth quarter of 1999, generating almost $209 million in extra revenue for that quarter. Coca-Cola granted extended credit terms to its bottlers to assist them in carrying the excess inventory.

The result of these activities was to increase Coca-Cola's quarterly earnings by 1 or 2 cents per share. This increase enabled Coca-Cola to meet analysts' earnings per share projections in eight of the 12 quarters under investigation. However, by the end of 1999, Japanese bottlers' inventories had risen to the point where additional gallonage could not be pushed. In January 2000, Coca-Cola announced a worldwide inventory reduction program to "optimum" levels. The company estimated that this would create a one-time reduction of earnings per share of 11 to 13 cents in the first two quarters of 2000, with about 5 cents of this reduction coming from Japan alone.

According to the SEC, Coca-Cola did not disclose the existence of the gallon-pushing program, its impact on earnings per share, or its likely impact on future reported earnings. The company was charged with violations of the U.S. Securities Act. Under the April 2005 settlement, Coca-Cola agreed, without admitting or denying liability, to remedial actions, including establishment of an Ethics and Compliance Office and a Disclosure Committee, close monitoring of any extended payment terms to customers, and adding an independent legal advisor experienced in securities law disclosure issues to its Audit Committee.

Required

a. Evaluate revenue recognition as an earnings management device. Give possible reasons why Coca-Cola managed its reported earnings upwards.

b. Explain why Coca-Cola had to increase the gallonage pushed over the 12 quarters in order to maintain a 1 to 2 cents per share increase of earnings per share each quarter.

c. Why did Coca-Cola undertake the inventory reduction program in 2000? Consider the effect of the program on core earnings and earnings from continuing operations as well as on net income.

Note: Problem 14 of Chapter 7 should be read prior to answering the following problem.

16. On October 3, 2007, Deutsche Bank AG announced that it would record a writedown of EUR 2.2 billion. Most of the writedown applied to its investments in asset-backed securities and related financial instruments, following from the August meltdown of the market for these investments. This writedown materially reduced third quarter, 2007, earnings. At the same time, the Deutsche Bank CEO reaffirmed the company's previous earnings guidance for 2008, which was for a profit of EUR 8.4 billion. However, he qualified this forecast with the comment that this assumed "normally functioning markets."

Comments appeared in the financial press, following these announcements, about the difficulties faced by Deutsche Bank in determining the new fair value of these written-down investments, since market values were not readily available. Some comments suggested the possibility that the company was taking a bath, thereby creating a "cookie jar" that could be used to augment future earnings. Other commentators were concerned that the writedowns may have been understated, rather than overstated, so as to disguise losses, and that further writedowns would likely follow. The company assured investors, however, that it had used "a rigorous process applying appropriate accounting principles."

In the face of these events, the share price of Deutsche Bank rose 2.1% on October 3, compared with a rise of about 0.6% on that day for the Dow Jones Stoxx European banking index. On October 4, Deutsche Bank shares closed unchanged, compared with a 0.96 increase in the banking index.

Required

a. Give reasons why Deutsche Bank's share price rose on October 3.

b. Give reasons why Deutsche Bank may want to take a bath.

c. Give reasons why Deutsche Bank may want to understate its writedown.

d. You are an auditor of Deutsche Bank. Prior to the writedown, the bank suggests that the investments in question be reclassified from held-for-trading (their present classification under IAS 39) to held-to-maturity. What is your reaction to this suggestion? Explain.

Notes

1. This assumes that the manager stays with the firm throughout the period required for the accruals to reverse. Should this not be the case, the manager may escape some of the accrual reversal consequences.

2. This is a case of post-decision information. See Section 9.5.1.

3. Healy points out that if net income is just below the bogey, the manager might instead adopt policies to increase net income, so that at least some bonus would be received.

4. An alternative is to take changes in working capital items from the comparative balance sheets. However, Hribar and Collins (2002) caution that this may bias the accruals estimates. The reason is that many firms engage in acquisitions and divestitures. Then, working capital items are increased or decreased on the consolidated balance sheet but these changes do not affect net income, and thus are not subject to earnings management. Changes in working capital items on the statement of cash flows do not include these non-earnings-related changes.

5. For further discussion of methodological issues in this area see McNichols and Wilson (1988), Schipper (1989), Dechow, Sloan, and Sweeney (1995), and Bernard and Skinner (1996).

6. Evidence for an alternative explanation is provided by Abarbanell and Lehavy (2003). They argue that if managers are also compensated based on share price performance (recall that Healy studied only bonus plans, which are typically based on earnings), they will want to avoid the negative share price reaction that follows bad earnings news.

7. This assumes that stakeholders do not unwind the earnings management. Consistent with our argument in Section 11.3, BDS argue that it is not cost effective for them to do so since it is difficult to isolate effects on reported income of continuing use of, for example, FIFO inventory or accelerated amortization, particularly since many stakeholders have limited ability to process information and may not have enough at stake to warrant careful evaluation of reported earnings.

8. Skinner and Sloan studied growth firms (firms with a high ratio of market value to book value). They argue that investors overestimate the future performance of growth firms, due to behavioural factors such as self-attribution bias discussed in Section 6.2. Failure to meet earnings expectations brings investors "back to earth," resulting in a major share price decline.

9. Another way is to lower investors' expectations by "talking down" analysts, to the point where reported earnings meet or exceed the analysts' revised, lower forecasts. This was studied by Matsumoto (2002), who found that firms in her sample used both approaches. As Matsumoto points out, however, her study preceded regulation FD (an SEC regulation introduced in 2000 to prohibit firms from releasing material information only to analysts). Subsequent to 2000, the incidence of talking down analysts should decrease.

10. As DSb point out, the information conveyed by the financial statements in their model does not purport to fully convey the value of the firm. All that is claimed is that *some* value-relevant information is conveyed by net income. That is, their model does not get around our general observation that net income is only well defined under ideal conditions.

Chapter 12
Standard Setting: Economic Issues

Figure 12.1 Organization of Chapter 12

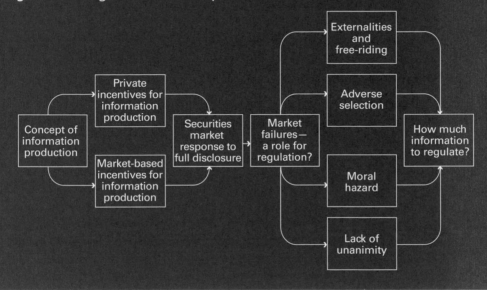

12.1 OVERVIEW

We now return to the role of standard setting that was introduced in Chapter 1. Recall that we view the standard setter as a mediator between the conflicting interests of investors and managers. The fundamental problem of financial accounting theory is how to conduct this mediation, that is, how to reconcile the financial reporting and efficient contracting roles of accounting information or, equivalently, how to determine the socially "right" amount of information. We define the right amount as that amount that equates the marginal social benefits of information to the marginal social costs.[1]

Of course, we should not take for granted that regulation is necessary for this reconciliation. Much of the required mediation can be accomplished by market forces. Nevertheless, substantial arguments can be made that market forces alone are unable to drive the right amount of information production. Our purpose in this chapter is to review and evaluate these arguments.

The extent of standard setting is a challenging one for accountants. Many aspects of firms' information production are regulated, and many of these regulations are laid down by accounting standard-setting bodies themselves, in the form of GAAP. Furthermore, the extent of regulation is increasing all the time, as more and more accounting standards are promulgated.

As you are aware, many industries in recent years have been deregulated. Airlines, trucking, financial services, telecommunications, and electric power generation are examples of industries that have seen substantial deregulation. What would happen if the information industry was deregulated? Would this produce a flood of competition and innovation, or would information production collapse into chaos? At present, the answers to these questions are not known. However, discussion of the pros and cons of standard setting helps us to see the tradeoffs that are involved and to appreciate the crucial role of information in society.

Figure 12.1 outlines the organization of this chapter.

12.2 REGULATION OF ECONOMIC ACTIVITY

There are numerous instances of regulation of economic activity in our economy. Firms that have a monopoly, such as electricity distribution, local telephone companies, and transportation companies, are common examples. Here, regulation typically takes the form of regulation of rates, regulation of the rate of return on invested capital, or both. Public safety is an area subject to frequent regulation as, for example, in elevator inspection laws, standards for automobile tire construction, and fire protection regulations. Communications is another area that, in many countries, is deemed sufficiently sensitive to attract regulation.

Other sets of regulations affect financial institutions and securities markets. The primary reason for such regulation is to protect individuals who are at an information disadvantage. This points up the fact that information asymmetry underlies the regulation of information production. If there was no information asymmetry, so that managerial actions and inside information were freely observable by all, there would be no need to protect individuals from the consequences of information disadvantage.

Information asymmetry is thus frequently used to justify regulations to protect the information-disadvantaged. Insider trading rules, executive compensation disclosures in management proxy circulars, public access to corporate conference calls with analysts, and regulations of full disclosure in prospectuses are examples. In addition to protecting ordinary investors, such regulations are also intended to improve the operation of capital markets by enhancing public confidence in their fairness.

Accounting practice is also strongly affected by regulations designed to protect against information asymmetry. An important role of accounting and auditing is to report useful financial information, thereby reducing information asymmetry between firm insiders, the investing public, and other users. However, this role requires that accountants and auditors be credible and competent. Thus, there are laws to regulate the accounting professions that control entry and maintain high standards. Many other regulations also affect accountants. Minimum disclosure requirements for annual reports are required by corporations acts. Government statistical agencies and taxation authorities require financial information. Quasi-governmental bodies such as securities commissions require a variety of information disclosures for firms whose shares are publicly traded. Private bodies such as stock exchanges require periodic disclosures from firms whose securities are traded on the exchange. Finally, other private bodies, such as the IASB, AcSB, and FASB, set accounting and auditing standards.

Thus, we see that accounting is a highly regulated area of economic activity. Governments are directly involved in this regulation through laws to control the creation of professional accounting bodies and their rights to public practice, and also through minimum disclosure requirements for annual reports and prospectuses. Indirect government involvement comes, for example, through securities commissions' standards, such as MD&A and management proxy circulars. Furthermore, the professions themselves do much of their own regulating by formulating and monitoring accounting and auditing standards. Henceforth, we will use the term **central authority** to refer to any of these regulatory bodies.

In this chapter our primary concerns are the regulation of minimum disclosure requirements, generally accepted accounting and auditing standards, and the requirement that public companies have audits. We will use the term **standard setting** to denote the establishment of these various rules and regulations. Note that standard setting involves the regulation of firms' external information production decisions. For our purposes, it does not matter whether these standards are set by direct or indirect regulation. In the case of indirect regulation, such as IASB, AcSB, and FASB standards, authority to set standards is allowed by government. The main point is that firms are not completely free to control the amount and timing of the information they produce about themselves. Rather, they must do so under a host of regulations that we will call standards, laid down by some central authority.

Standard setting is the regulation of firms' external information production decisions by some central authority.

In considering issues of information production, it is helpful to distinguish between two types of information that a manager may possess. The first type is called **proprietary information**. This is information that, if released, would directly affect future cash flows of the firm.[2] Examples are technical information about valuable patents and plans for strategic initiatives such as takeover bids or mergers. The costs to the manager and firm of releasing proprietary information can be quite high.

The second type is called **non-proprietary information**. This is information that does not directly affect firm cash flows. It includes financial statement information, earnings forecasts, details of new financing, and so on. The audit is also included in non-proprietary information.

12.3 WAYS TO CHARACTERIZE INFORMATION PRODUCTION

While the term "production" of information may take some getting used to, we use it for two reasons. First, we want to think of information as a commodity that can be produced and sold. Then, it is natural to consider separately the costs and benefits of information production.

Second, we want a unified way of thinking about the various ways information production can be accomplished. Information is a complex commodity. Just what do we mean when we speak of the quantity of information produced? There are several ways to answer this question.

First, we can think of **finer information**. For example, a thermometer that tells you the temperature in degrees is a finer information system than one that only tells you if the temperature is above or below freezing—the first thermometer tells you everything that the second one does, and more. It enables a finer reading of the temperature. In an accounting context, a finer reporting system adds more detail to the existing financial statements. Examples of finer reporting include expanded note disclosure, additional line items on the financial statements, segment reporting, and so on. In terms of our decision theory discussion of Chapter 3, finer information production means a better ability to discriminate between realizations of the states of nature. For example, in a decision problem where the relevant set of states of nature is the temperature, a thermometer that tells you degrees enables better discrimination between different temperature states than one that only tells you if the temperature is above or below freezing. We can also think of the information approach to decision usefulness, discussed in Chapter 5, as implying finer information production, since the information approach encourages elaboration of the financial statements proper by means of MD&A and notes.

Second, we can think of **additional information**. For example, we might add a barometer to our thermometer. In an accounting context, additional information means the introduction of new information systems to report on matters not currently included. Examples would include extensions of current value accounting to additional assets and liabilities, and future-oriented financial information included in MD&A, which expands reporting to include expected future operations. In decision theory terms, additional information means an expansion of the set of relevant states of nature upon which the firm's performance depends. Thus a thermometer–barometer reports on atmospheric pressure as well as temperature. In effect, additional information can produce greater relevance in reporting. We can think of the measurement approach to decision usefulness discussed in Chapter 6 as a move towards producing additional value-relevant information.

A third way to think about information production is in terms of its **credibility**. The essence of credibility is that the receiver knows that the supplier of information has an incentive to disclose truthfully. In our thermometer example, the purchaser knows that the manufacturer must produce an accurate product in order to stay in business. Thus, the purchaser accepts the thermometer as a credible representation of the temperature. In an accounting context, it is often suggested that a "Big Four" audit is more credible than a "non-Big Four" audit because a large audit firm has more to lose,[3] both in terms of reputation and "deep pockets"; hence, it will maintain high audit standards. Also, the greater the penalties for managers who divulge false information, the more credibility investors attach to managers' disclosures.

In this chapter we will not need to distinguish these different ways to produce information and will refer to them all, rather loosely, as **information production**. Note that however we think of its production, more information will require higher costs, some of which may be proprietary.

12.4 PRIVATE INCENTIVES FOR INFORMATION PRODUCTION

12.4.1 Contractual Incentives for Information Production

Incentives for private information production arise from the contracts that firms enter into. As we saw in Chapter 9, information is necessary to monitor compliance with contracts. For example, if managerial effort is unobservable, this leads to an incentive contract based on the results of the firm's operations. Then, information about profitability is needed to provide a measure of performance. Also, an audit adds credibility to reported net income, so that both the owner and the manager of the firm are willing to accept reported net income as a precise measure of current managerial performance.

Similarly, when a firm issues debt, it typically includes covenants in the contract. Information is needed about the various ratios on which the covenants are based, so that the firm's adherence to its covenants can be monitored over the life of the debt issue. Again, an audit adds credibility to the covenant information.

Another contractual reason for private information production arises when a privately owned firm goes public. This was modelled by Jensen and Meckling (1976). The owner–manager of a firm going public, after selling all or part interest, has a motivation to increase shirking. Prior to the IPO the shirking problem was internalized—the owner–manager bore all the costs. The costs of shirking are the reduced profits that result. Subsequent to the new issue, the owner–manager does not bear all the costs—the new owners will bear their proportionate share. Thus, shirking costs the owner–manager less after going public, so he or she will engage in more of it. This is an agency cost to the new owners of the firm.

Investors will be aware of this motivation, however, and will bid down the amount they are willing to pay for the new issue by the expected amount of agency costs. In effect, the firm's cost of capital rises. Consequently, the owner–manager has an incentive to contract to limit his or her shirking and thereby raise the issue price. For example, the contract between the owner–manager and the new investors in the firm may include a forecast, which the owner–manager will be motivated to meet (this will be recognized as the production of additional information). Alternatively, the contract may provide for a lot of detail in the financial statements (finer information), to make it more difficult for the owner–manager to hide or bury costs of perquisites. Also, the contract may provide for an audit to increase the credibility of the information production. In all of these cases, the owner–manager commits by contract to produce information that will convince investors that he or she will in fact continue to manage diligently. Investors, realizing this, will be willing to pay more for an interest in the firm than they would otherwise.

The key point here is that the firm has a private incentive to produce information in all of these contracting scenarios—no central authority is needed to force information production. Furthermore, since the types and amounts of information to be produced under the contract are negotiated and agreed to by all contracting parties, the right amount of information is produced, by definition. That is, the information production decision is internalized between the contracting parties. Then, the question of whether too much or too little information is produced does not arise. Failure to provide for information production in the contract will make it more incomplete, hence more difficult or impossible to enforce.

In principle, the contractual motivation for information production can be extended to any group of contracting parties. Consider, for example, the relationship between the firm manager and investors. The investor's decision problem was reviewed in Chapter 3, where we concluded that rational investors want information about the expected return and risk of their investments. The firm manager and each investor could contract for the desired amount of information about the firm's future cash flows, financial position, and so on. The contract could provide that the investor pay for this information or, perhaps, the manager would offer it free to raise the demand for the firm's shares. Note that different investors would, in general, want different amounts of information about the firm. One investor, adept at financial analysis, might demand a very fine projection of future operations, from which to prepare an estimate of future cash flows and returns on investment. Another investor may simply want information about the firm's dividend policy. A very risk-averse investor might demand a very credible audit, at a correspondingly high cost, while another investor would prefer the least costly audit available. Other investors may not demand any information at all, particularly if their investment portfolios are well diversified. Instead, they might rely on market efficiency to price-protect them.

Unfortunately, while direct contracting for information production may be fine in principle, it will not always work in practice. The reason should be apparent from the previous paragraph. In many cases there are simply too many parties for contracts to be feasible. If the firm manager was to attempt to negotiate a contract for information production with every potential investor, the negotiation costs alone would be prohibitive. In addition, to the extent that different investors want different information, the firm's costs of information production would also be prohibitive. If, as an alternative, the manager attempted to negotiate a single contract with all investors, these investors would have to agree on what information they wanted. Again, given the disparate information needs of different investors, this process would be extremely time-consuming and costly if, indeed, it was possible at all. Hence, the contracting approach only seems feasible when there are a few parties involved. The owner–manager incentive contracts studied in Section 9.4.2 involved only two persons. Our long-term lending contract example in Section 9.7 involved a manager and a lender.

Even if contracting parties do reach an information production agreement, another problem arises. Unless the agreement can be enforced (as in a cooperative game), parties to the agreement may be tempted to violate it for their own short-run benefit. For example, suppose that a managerial compensation contract provides for a year-end audit. Knowing this, the manager works hard during the year. Then, since the manager's effort has already been exerted, the principal would benefit from cancelling the audit, thereby saving the audit costs. But, cancelling the audit this year will reduce the incentive for the manager to work hard next year.

It seems that while contracts are an important source of private information production, we cannot rely on them completely for the information needs of society. Accordingly, we now turn to a second set of private incentives for firms' information production. We will call these **market-based incentives**.

12.4.2 Market-Based Incentives for Information Production

Private incentives for managers to produce information about their firms also derive from market forces. Several markets are involved.

The *managerial labour market* constantly evaluates manager performance. As a result, managers who release false, incomplete, or biased information will suffer damage to their reputations. While reputation considerations do not completely remove the need for incentive contracts, as discussed in Section 10.2, they do reduce the amount of incentives needed. In terms of Example 9.3, where the manager received a 32.37% profit share, a profit share of, say, 20% may be sufficient when reputation considerations are taken into account.[4] With a lower proportion of compensation at risk the (risk-averse) manager is less concerned about releasing information that affects firm value. Thus, the managerial labour market provides important incentives for information production.

Similar incentives are provided by *capital markets*. Managers are motivated by reputation and contracting considerations to increase firm value. This creates an incentive to release information to the market. The reason is that more information, by reducing concerns about adverse selection and estimation risk (see Section 4.6.1), increases investor confidence in the firm, with the result that the market prices of its securities will rise or, equivalently, its cost of capital will fall, other things being equal. This will show up in enhanced firm profitability and value, hence enhanced reservation utility and compensation for the manager.

Another market that disciplines managers is the *takeover market*, also called the market for corporate control. If the manager does not increase firm value, the firm may be subject to a takeover bid, which, if successful, frequently results in replacement of the manager. The more disgruntled the shareholders are, the more likely that such a takeover bid will be successful. Consequently, the takeover market also motivates managers to increase firm value, with implications for information production similar to those of the managerial labour and capital markets.

Formal models that relate information release to the firm's market value are presented by, for example, Merton (1987) and Diamond and Verrecchia (1991). In the Merton model, information asymmetry is modelled as only a subset of investors knowing about each firm. As a result, investors cannot fully diversify. Then, the firm's cost of capital is greater than that given by the CAPM (Section 4.5), since its risk is spread over relatively few investors. If the firm can increase the size of its subset of investors, say by the voluntary release of information, its cost of capital will fall and its market value rise, other things equal. In the Diamond and Verrecchia model, voluntary disclosure reduces information asymmetry between the firm and the market, which facilitates trading in its shares. The resulting increase in **market liquidity**[5] attracts large institutional investors who, if they have to do so in future, can then sell large blocks of shares without lowering the price they receive. The firm's share price increases as a result of this greater demand.[6]

Other models include the CAPM-based model of Lambert, Leuz, and Verrecchia (2007), described in Section 4.5, which suggests that more informative disclosure can reduce estimation risk and cost of capital.

Easley and O'Hara (2004) present a model with inside and outside information. Easley and O'Hara show that investors demand a higher expected return (i.e., higher than the CAPM) the greater the ratio of inside information to outside. The reason is that insiders can make better investment decisions than outsiders due to their information advantage. Outside investors know this but, due to noise trading, are unable to fully infer from share price what this inside information is—it could be good or bad. Thus, outsiders face estimation risk, which cannot be fully diversified away if the number of investors and securities is finite (which Easley and O'Hara assume). Consequently, investors demand a higher expected return to compensate. The more inside information there is relative to outside, the stronger this effect is. It follows that firms can reduce their costs of capital and increase market value by policies such as full disclosure, high accrual quality, and credible release of inside information.

Thus, labour markets and the market for corporate control, along with efficient securities markets, are important noncontractual sources of private information production. In all cases, it is market prices that provide the motivation—security prices and managers' market values on the labour market are affected by the quality of firms' information production decisions.

12.4.3 Securities Market Response to Full Disclosure

The theoretical arguments in Section 12.4.2 predict that the securities market will respond positively to increased disclosure. In this section, we review some empirical studies of this prediction. The Merton model was tested by Lang and Lundholm (1996).

They used financial analysts' ratings of disclosure quality, based on evaluations of firms' quarterly and annual reports and investor relations, for a large sample of firms over the years 1985–1989. The authors found that, other things equal, the higher the disclosure quality as judged by the analysts, the greater the number of analysts following the firm. A complementary relationship between disclosure quality and analyst following is not obvious, *a priori*, because one could argue that better information production by a firm reduces the need for analysts to interpret it for investors. The finding that analyst following increased suggests that analysts can do a better job when they have more information to work with; that is, increased analyst following leads to increased investor interest. Merton's model then predicts increased demand for the firm's shares, or, equivalently, lower cost of capital.

Healy, Hutton, and Palepu (1999) tested implications of the Diamond and Verrecchia model. Using the same analysts' disclosure quality ratings as Lang and Lundholm, they found that firms with improved disclosure ratings were associated with a significantly improved share price performance in the year following the rating increase, compared to other firms in their same industry. They also found a significant increase in institutional ownership. Both of these results are predicted by Diamond and Verrecchia.

Welker (1995) investigated the effect of disclosure quality on the bid–ask spread component of market liquidity (see Note 5). He predicted that shares of firms with better disclosure policies would have lower spreads, the reason being that better disclosure policy implied less investor concern about insider trading and other adverse selection problems. After controlling for other factors that also affect spread, such as trading volume,[7] Welker found a significant negative relationship between disclosure quality (as measured by analysts' disclosure quality ratings) and bid–ask spread. Again, this result is consistent with the Diamond and Verrecchia model.

Botosan and Plumlee (2002) reported the results of a direct test of disclosure quality and cost of capital. For a large sample of U.S. firms across many different industries over 1985–1996, these researchers found that superior annual report disclosure reduced cost of capital of their sample firms by an average of 0.7%, other things equal.[8] Botosan and Plumlee's estimates of disclosure quality were based on firms' disclosure ratings published by the Association for Investment Management and Research, a large international non-profit organization of investment professionals and educators.

Sengupta (1998) investigated the impact of disclosure quality on the cost of debt. He found that, on average, his sample firms enjoyed a 0.02% reduction in interest cost for every 1% increase in their disclosure quality as rated by financial analysts over 1987–1991. He also found that this result strengthened for riskier firms, where a firm's riskiness was measured by the standard deviation of the return on its shares. The reason for this favourable impact, according to Sengupta, was that lenders assigned lower credit risk to firms with superior disclosure policies.

The market response to *lack of* full disclosure is also worth noting. When investors lose faith in a firm's financial reporting, the consequences can be severe indeed. In their study of firms under investigation by the SEC for violations of GAAP, Dechow, Sloan, and Sweeney (1996) report an average drop of 9% in share price on the day the investigation is announced. The collapse of Enron Corp. and WorldCom Inc., outlined in Section 1.2, provides a dramatic example of the consequence of poor disclosure. The loss of investor confidence was so severe that these firms' costs of capital effectively became infinite.

Of course, these various results do not imply that firms should then choose the highest possible level of disclosure quality, since there are costs of disclosure. For example, the model of Darrough and Stoughton outlined in Section 9.3 implies that release of valuable information to competitors is a disclosure cost. Nevertheless, they do show that good disclosure has benefits, namely increased share liquidity, greater analyst following, and lower costs of debt and equity capital. They support theoretical arguments that market forces encourage information production.

12.5 A CLOSER LOOK AT MARKET-BASED INCENTIVES

12.5.1 The Disclosure Principle

A simple argument can be made that suggests that a manager will release all information, good or bad. This is known as the **disclosure principle**.[9] If investors know that the manager has the information, but do not know what it is, they will assume that if it was favourable the manager would release it. Thus, if investors do not observe the manager releasing it, they will assume the worst and bid down the market value of the firm's shares accordingly. For example, suppose that all investors know that a manager possesses a forecast of next year's earnings, but they do not know what the forecast is. The manager may as well release it, as failure to do so would be interpreted by the market as the lowest possible forecast.

This argument is reinforced by the manager's incentive to keep the firm's share price from falling. As mentioned earlier, a fall in share price will harm the manager through lower remuneration, and/or through lower value on the labour market for managers. Since the market will assume the worst if the information is not released, any release of credible information will prevent share price and market value from falling as low as it would otherwise.

Undoubtedly, the disclosure principle operates in many situations. However, it does not always work. This was examined by Verrecchia (1983), who sought to reconcile the disclosure principle with the empirical observation that managers do not always fully disclose. Verrecchia assumed that, if disclosure is made, it is truthful. He also assumed that there is a cost of disclosure. The cost is constant, independent of the nature of the information. For example, there may be a proprietary cost of releasing valuable patent information. He assumed that investors know that the manager has the news, and know its cost of disclosure, but do not know what the news is.

If we rank the nature of the news on a continuum from bad to good, Verrecchia showed that for a given disclosure cost there is a threshold level of disclosure. The manager, who is assumed to maximize firm value, will only disclose the information if it exceeds the threshold. Investors cannot penalize the firm for non-disclosure since they do not know whether the information is withheld because it is bad news or because it is good news but not good enough to exceed the threshold. Thus the disclosure principle fails. The lower the disclosure cost, the lower the threshold, and if disclosure cost is zero, the disclosure principle is reinstated.

However, consistent with the disclosure principle, Verrecchia assumed that the market knows that the manager has the information. What if the market is unsure about this? Is there still an incentive to voluntarily release information? Also, what if the firm has more than one item of information? Under what conditions will the manager reveal all items, some of them, or none? What if the information is non-proprietary?

Pae (2005) considered these questions. Consider, for example, a forecast of earnings and a cash flow forecast. It is costly for a firm to develop these two items of non-proprietary information. Consequently, investors do not know whether the firm has internally generated the information or not. Pae assumes that investors assess probabilities that the firm has no forecasts, only one forecast, or both. While forecasts are costly to develop, Pae assumes that there is no cost to release them (i.e., non-proprietary information). If a disclosure is made, it is assumed truthful.[10]

Pae shows that if the firm has developed both forecasts, the manager, who wants to maximize firm value, will disclose them if they are both sufficiently favourable to exceed disclosure thresholds, especially if the items tend to confirm each other (high forecast earnings and high cash flows tend to go together, for example). However, if one forecast is below a threshold and the other above, only the one above will be disclosed. If both are below thresholds, neither will be disclosed.

If the firm has developed one forecast, it will disclose it if it exceeds a threshold. Otherwise, it discloses nothing.

If the firm has not developed either forecast, it will obviously disclose nothing. Note that if a firm discloses nothing, investors do not know whether the firm has developed both forecasts but they are both below their thresholds, developed one but it is below its threshold, or has developed neither. This is what prevents the disclosure principle from operating to force full disclosure—recall that this principle requires that investors know the firm has the information.[11]

Pae's threshold results seem similar to those of Verrecchia. The difference, however, is that the information is non-proprietary, and the manager's motivation to release it derives from its effect on firm value. In Verrecchia's model, disclosure must also overcome the proprietary cost of releasing the information. Nevertheless, the general impression from both models is that the better the news the more likely it is to be disclosed voluntarily. For an example of this effect, see Theory in Practice 12.1.

Einhorn (2007) examines a scenario where the market is unsure about the manager's reporting objective. Some managers may want to maximize firm value to enhance their

This effect can be seen in the case of Mark's Work Wearhouse, Ltd., a large Canadian clothing retailer. For many years, Mark's included a high-quality forecast of next year's earnings in its MD&A. Such a forecast can be regarded as non-proprietary information since it is unlikely to directly affect future cash flows. However, Mark's did not release a forecast for 1992, a year in which it was expecting a loss. The reason, presumably, was that if Mark's released the bad news forecast, its high quality would greatly affect investors' perceptions of the firm's future prospects. In effect, the likelihood of disclosure decreases with information quality—why should a firm release a high-quality forecast of trouble ahead? Consequently, high-quality disclosures will tend to be for good news.

reputation, to increase the value of shares and ESOs they own, and/or to protect against a possible takeover bid. Other managers, however, may want to minimize firm value. For example, we saw in Section 8.3 that some managers manipulate share price downwards prior to ESO awards. The political cost hypothesis outlined in Section 8.5.2 provides another motivation to lower share price.

Suppose that a manager has inside information about firm value. Suppose also that the market feels that most managers want to maximize firm value. Consistent with the disclosure principle, the manager who wants to maximize firm value will disclose this information unless the news is very bad.

However, managers who want to minimize firm value can exploit the disclosure policy of value-maximizing managers. Since the market knows that value-minimizing managers are rare, their failure to disclose is almost as effective in lowering firm value as it is for value-maximizing managers. Unless the value-minimizing manager's information is very bad, non-disclosure will result in a value lower than what would result from disclosure. Then, the value-minimizing manager will not disclose, and the disclosure principle fails.

Einhorn (2005) analyzes voluntary disclosure in conjunction with regulation. This is a more realistic scenario than the ones just described, since much disclosure is laid down by, for example, GAAP and MD&A. Voluntary disclosure then involves going beyond minimum required disclosures, as in our discussion of Canadian Tire's MD&A in Section 4.8.2. Einhorn shows that voluntary disclosure depends crucially on the quality of mandated disclosure.

To illustrate, suppose that an oil and gas company, whose manager wants to maximize firm value, has two segments. One segment explores for and sells crude oil and natural gas. Due to high energy prices, this segment is currently very profitable. The other segment refines and markets refined oil products. Traditionally, this segment has low profit margins. The firm is concerned about reporting high profits because this creates the possibility of an excess profits tax.

Assume initially that GAAP is of low quality. Specifically, separate reporting of segments is not required. Consequently, to reduce the probability of a tax, the firm disguises, at least partially, the high profits of the exploration division by combining them with the refining division.

Now suppose that the firm has inside information about the level of crude oil and gas prices next period. Should it voluntarily release this future-oriented information? The higher are expected prices, the higher will be share price, other things equal, since investors will respond positively to higher expected future product prices. However, high expected product prices, if this inside information is reported, will increase the probability of the excess profits tax.

Einhorn shows that there is a threshold level of next-period prices above which the forecast information will be disclosed. That is, if the expected prices are high enough, the positive effect on firm value of high future prices outweighs the negative effect resulting from the increased probability of excess profits tax. Furthermore, the higher is current reported net income, the higher the disclosure threshold for the forecast. This is because high reported earnings operate to increase the prospect of the excess profits tax. Consequently, the firm can less "afford" to make matters worse by reporting the favourable forecast.

Now suppose that GAAP quality improves. Specifically, the earnings of each firm segment must now be disclosed. Then, everyone, including the tax authority, knows the high profitability of the exploration division. Reporting the high forecast would further add to the probability of an excess profits tax. Einhorn shows that the firm would prefer to disclose bad news, not good news. That is, the disclosure threshold switches so that only expected prices *below* a threshold will be voluntarily reported.[12]

In sum, regardless of whether good news or bad news is reported, it is clear that when the requirements of the disclosure principle are not fully met, all of the above models predict only **partial disclosure**. That is, while the capital market encourages voluntary release, it by no means ensures that all information will be released. As a result, a role for regulation of information production is not shut out.

Information released under the disclosure principle must be credible. That is, the market must know that the manager has an incentive to reveal it truthfully. Obviously, if a manager lies about next year's forecast of net income it can hardly be said that information is being disclosed. Information that is subject to verification after the event, such as a forecast, will be credible to the extent that misstatement can be proved and penalties applied. Another way to secure credibility is to have released information attested to by a third party, such as an auditor. However, since much inside information is not verifiable even after the fact, or subject to audit, truthful disclosure cannot always be attained.

The need for truthful disclosure has been relaxed somewhat by Newman and Sansing (1993) (NS). They analyzed a two-period model consisting of an incumbent firm, a representative shareholder, and a potential entrant to the industry. The firm manager, who is assumed to act in the shareholder's best interests, knows firm value exactly. If it were not for the potential entrant, the shareholder's best interests would be served if the firm committed to publicly disclosing this value, since the shareholder could then optimally plan consumption and investment over the two periods. However, full disclosure of firm value may trigger entry, in which case the incumbent firm will suffer a loss of profits and value. How should the firm report?

The answer depends on the costs to the entrant should it decide to enter the industry, and the resulting loss of profits to the incumbent. For example, if entry costs are high and there is substantial loss of profits upon entry, the incumbent firm may disclose imprecise information about its value. That is, instead of an exact disclosure, it will disclose an interval within which its value lies. If it reported its value exactly, its disclosures would not be credible, since everyone knows it has an incentive to deter entry.[13]

Disclosure in the NS model is truthful in the sense that the firm credibly reveals an interval within which its value lies, that is, a range estimate. Nevertheless, the firm does not fully report the truth since it does not report its value exactly. Interestingly, Cotter, Tuna, and Wysocki (2006), in their study of management's quarterly public earnings forecasts, report that range estimates are the most common form of forecast in their sample. (However, rather than preventing entry of competitors, the authors attribute the issuance of a forecast to management's attempt to "talk down" overly optimistic analyst forecasts to levels the firm can meet.)

Finally, as shown by Dye (1985), the disclosure principle can break down due to a conflict between information desired by investors and information needed for contracting purposes. Recall from our discussion in Chapter 10 that manager compensation is based, at least in part, on share price performance. Suppose, however, that the manager has a forecast of net income. The market knows the forecast exists but does not know the amount. If reported, the forecast will affect share price. This reduces the ability of share price to reflect manager effort, since this ability is swamped by the impact of the forecast on price. In effect, release of the forecast incurs an agency cost that reduces the efficiency of the manager's compensation contract. Thus, it may be desirable to discourage the reporting of forecasts even though a forecast provides useful information to investors. The best information for contracting may not be the best information for investor decision-making, and the investor information may not be reported for contracting reasons. This suggests that, like a securities market, a managerial labour market does not guarantee that information release is complete.

Dye's model provides a supplement to legal liability as a reason why reporting of forecasts is rare. A similar tradeoff between cost of capital and the costs of motivating the manager is demonstrated by Baiman and Verrecchia (1996).

We conclude that while the disclosure principle is a simple and compelling argument for release of inside information, it breaks down in numerous instances, and hence cannot be relied upon to ensure that firms always release full information.

12.5.2 Signalling

It frequently happens that firms differ in quality. For example, a firm may have better investment opportunities than other firms. Alternatively, a firm may conduct superior R&D, leading to potentially valuable patents. Such information would be of considerable usefulness to investors. Yet, disclosure of the details of high-quality projects and technology may reveal valuable proprietary information. Furthermore, even if the manager did disclose the details, he or she may not be believed by a skeptical marketplace. How can the manager credibly reveal the firm's **type**, as these underlying quality differences are called, without incurring the excessive costs?

This problem of separating firms of different types has been extensively considered by means of signalling models.

> A **signal** is an action taken by a high-type manager that would not be rational if that manager was low-type.

A crucial requirement for a signal is that it be less costly for a high-type manager than for a low-type. This is what gives a signal its credibility, since it is then irrational for a low-type to mimic a high-type, and the market knows this.

Spence (1973) was the first to formally model signalling equilibria. He did so in the context of a job market. Given that it is less costly to a high-type job applicant to obtain a specified level of education than to a low-type, Spence showed that equilibria exist where employers can rely on the applicant's chosen level of education as a credible signal of that person's underlying competence.

A number of signals have been suggested that are relevant to accounting. One such signal is **direct disclosure**. Hughes (1986) showed how such disclosure can be a credible signal. In her model, a manager makes a direct disclosure of his or her expectation of future cash flows, which determine firm value. Investors observe the firm's actual cash flows at the end of the period and revise their firm value estimate. If the manager's disclosure was sufficiently greater than this revised estimate, investors conclude that the disclosure was untrue, and penalties are applied. To avoid this cost, the manager is motivated to report truthfully, so that in equilibrium investors can correctly infer his or her expectation of firm value.

While Hughes' model does not apply to the moral hazard problem (the manager's expectation of firm value is independent of his or her effort), it does demonstrate how direct disclosure can operate to reduce adverse selection. Firms of different types can separate themselves, so that the market value of their securities is closer to fundamental firm value.

A variety of **indirect signals** have been studied to further understand disclosure issues. As Leland and Pyle (1977) show for an entrepreneur going public, the proportion of equity retained is a signal, because it would not be rational for a bad-news manager to retain a high equity position—he/she would find this too costly. Also, audit quality can be a signal of the value of a new securities issue. A rational manager would be unlikely to retain a high-quality (and high-cost) auditor when the firm is a low-type—why pay more to credibly reveal poor prospects? Similar arguments relate to the choice of underwriter for a new stock issue. Titman and Trueman (1986) and Datar, Feltham, and Hughes (1991) developed models where audit quality is a signal.

A forecast can be a signal. For example, it is less costly for a high-type firm to release a high-quality, good news forecast—a low-type firm would be unlikely to meet a good news forecast and its high quality would only increase investor backlash. In MD&A, information about future firm prospects (i.e., a forecast) is required. However, there is sufficient latitude in the MD&A requirements that firms can signal by means of their forecast quality. For example, we concluded in Section 4.8.2 that forward-looking information in Canadian Tire's MD&A went beyond minimal requirements. As a result, its disclosure has a signalling component, since in addition to the information in the disclosure itself, the firm's willingness to choose high-quality disclosure credibly reveals inside information that management has a confident and well-planned view of its future, thereby adding credibility to the forecast.

A firm's capital structure has signalling properties. There is evidence, for example, that the market value of existing common shares falls when the firm issues new shares. While dilution of existing shareholders' equity is one possibility, another explanation is the market's concern that the new shares may be issued by a low-type firm—a high-type firm would be more likely to issue bonds or finance internally. One reason is that the high-value increments would then accrue to existing shareholders. Another reason is that a high-type firm would assess its probability of bankruptcy as low (thus, the probability that the bondholders would take over the firm is low).

Dividend policy can also be a signal. A high payout ratio may signal a firm as having a confident future. However, a high payout ratio could also mean that the firm sees little prospect for profitable internal financing from retained earnings. Thus, dividend policy may not be as effective a signal as others.

Accounting policy choice also has signalling properties. For example, a firm may adopt a number of conservative accounting policies. A high-type firm can do this and still report profits, while a low-type firm would report losses. Thus, conservative accounting policies can also signal a manager's confident view of the firm's future.

Note that for signals to be applicable, the manager must have a *choice*. Indeed, Spence (1973) shows that for a viable signalling equilibrium to exist there must be a sufficient number of signals available to the manager. For example, if some central authority imposed a uniform standard of audit quality on all firms, audit quality would not be available as a signal. Furthermore, reducing the latitude to choose forecasting quality in MD&A would reduce its signalling content.

This argument, that standards to enforce uniform accounting destroy managers' abilities to signal, is important for standard setting. In Section 2.5.1 we suggested that a major problem with historical cost accounting is that there is no unique way to match costs with revenues, implying that diversity in reporting practices was "bad." This implication is correct as far as it goes. Diversity in reporting practices imposes costs on investors who want to compare the performance of different entities, because it is necessary to restate their financial statements to a common basis before valid comparisons can be made.

However, if we reconsider this implication in the light of signalling theory, we see that diversity may not be as bad as first suggested. To the extent that firms' choices of accounting policies signal credible information about those firms, diversity of reporting practices is desirable. This argument is reinforced by our discussion of earnings management in Chapter 11. We argued there that some earnings management can be good since it can serve as a vehicle for the release of inside information. Earnings management to reveal persistent earning power can be interpreted as a signal since it can be very costly for a low-type manager to report higher earnings than can be maintained (since accruals reverse). Obviously, earnings management by means of accounting policy choice is only possible if there is a sufficiently rich set of accounting policies, such as GAAP, from which to choose. Signalling theory serves as a counterargument to the continual refinement of GAAP so as to eliminate accounting policy choice.

12.5.3 Financial Policy as a Signal

In this section we review a paper by Healy and Palepu (1993) (HP). HP address the question of what managers might do to signal their inside information to the efficient market. We have already discussed how market forces motivate managers to communicate information so as to increase their firm's market value. But since, as we shall see, these forces are subject to various degrees of market failure, and also since noise trading can distort a firm's share price, managers of some firms may find their firms undervalued by the capital market relative to their inside information. The question then is, how can they best signal the real value of the firm?

HP provide an illustration of the above problem. Patten Corp.[14] acquires large undeveloped tracts of land, subdivides them into lots, and sells them, with up to 90% of the financing supplied by Patten. Revenue is recognized upon sale, that is, when at least 10% of the purchase price has been received and collection of the balance is reasonably assured. This creates a potential problem of bad debt losses. However, in its 1986 financial statements Patten provided a bad debt allowance of only $10,000 on accounts receivable of $29.4 million. The firm claimed that this low amount was justified by past experience and a low current delinquency rate.

In 1987, concern appeared in the financial media that Patten's bad debt allowance was too low. Specifically, the fear was expressed that past delinquency rates may not be representative of future delinquency. Patten's share price plunged following the publication of these concerns, as investors quickly revised their beliefs about Patten's future performance.

HP suggest several possible manager responses to convince the market of their inside information that the value of the accounts receivable is substantially as shown in the financial statements. One response is direct disclosure of credit granting and collection procedures, so as to inform the market of their integrity. Direct disclosure should be a credible signal here, since management would be foolish to overly expose itself to penalties such as loss of reputation and legal liability by disclosing incorrect information at such a critical time.

However, details of the firm's credit and collection policies are likely to be proprietary information, which could harm its competitive position—recall our discussion of the

Darrough and Stoughton model in Section 9.3 and of Newman and Sansing in Section 12.5.1. Consequently, HP suggest several financial policies that could serve as indirect signals of management's information.

One such policy would be to raise private financing and/or to sell accounts receivable without recourse to a financial institution. Our discussion of contractual incentives for information production in Section 12.4.1 suggests that when there are only a few parties involved in a contract they can agree among themselves what information to provide. Here, it may be less costly for Patten to provide a private lender with information about the real value of its receivables than to provide it to the market, since, as mentioned, providing it to the market would require public release of proprietary information. The market, upon becoming aware of the private financing, would realize that this is an indirect signal and would raise its evaluation of Patten.

Another possibility would be for Patten to engage in a hedging strategy. Then, credit losses on accounts receivable would be offset by gains on the hedging instrument. Such a policy would be prohibitively expensive if large credit losses were anticipated. Consequently, it should be a credible signal.

Yet another signalling strategy would be for management to increase its holdings of Patten shares. This would load additional risk on to management, thereby increasing their incentive to work hard as well as giving them a longer-run perspective in operating the firm.

Note the common theme in all of these signalling strategies. Management would be foolish to undertake any of them unless it really believed its inside information about asset values. This is what gives signals their credibility. The market will realize this, with the result that the fall of Patten's share price should be reversed. HP's article insightfully demonstrates the rich variety of signals available for credible communication of inside information to an efficient market.

12.5.4 Private Information Search

To this point, our investigation of private incentives for release of inside information has centred on the manager. The argument has been that a high level of information release will improve the manager's reputation, lower investors' estimation risk, and reduce the firm's cost of capital, to the firm's and manager's benefit. Thus, the onus is on the manager to release information.

Implicit in this line of reasoning is that investors are passive. They merely react to whatever information the manager releases in deciding on their demand for the firm's securities. In effect, they are price-protected by the market. It may be, however, that many investors will be active in seeking out information, particularly in the presence of noise traders or securities market inefficiencies. For example, they may conduct their own investigations and analyses of fundamental firm value, or hire financial analysts, mutual fund managers, and other experts to assist them. They may watch closely persons that they suspect have inside information and mimic their actions.

Thus, there is a variety of ways that investors or their representatives can conduct a **private information search**. Bill Cautious, in Example 3.1, did so by analysis of the annual report, using Bayes' theorem to process the resulting information. To the extent that such activities are successful, inside information is very quickly transferred to the public domain. By limiting the time available to insiders to capitalize on inside information, the severity of the adverse selection problem is reduced.

Unfortunately, private information search can be quite costly, from society's perspective, since more than one investor incurs costs to discover the same information. It would be cheaper, in terms of total resources used to generate information, if the firm produced and publicized the information only once, so that each investor would not have to rediscover it.

Hirschleifer's (1971) analysis is a classic in the area of private information search. Hirschleifer considered an exchange economy, that is, an economy without production, so that there is no scope for information search to affect the manager's effort. Then, Hirschleifer showed that the social value of information search is negative, even though individual investors may perceive it as valuable. The reason is that, without production, the amount of goods and services in the economy is fixed, so that private information search just redistributes wealth, it does not create wealth. Then, since information search has a cost, the net social effect is negative.

If we consider a production economy, private information search may improve the operation of markets, with resulting impacts on firms' costs of capital and manager effort. However, to the extent that a redistributive component to private information search remains, this will still incur a cost for society.

12.5.5 Summary

Private information search undoubtedly generates much information. However, to the extent that different persons expend time and effort to discover the same information, this imposes a cost on society. Thus, much of the onus for cost-effective private information production rests with managers. There are many private vehicles and incentives for firm managers to produce credible information, thereby reducing investors' estimation risk and increasing market liquidity. Empirical research into these private incentives suggests that firms and managers benefit from superior disclosure, and are punished when misleading information release is discovered.

However, it should be emphasized again that market forces will not motivate the release of all inside information, since there are costs to the firm of information release. In addition to proprietary costs, agency costs arise because information production for investors, which lowers cost of capital, may render compensation contracts less efficient, and vice versa.[15]

Assuming that firms choose the lowest cost point of this tradeoff between benefits and costs, it might seem that market forces can drive the right amount of information production from society's perspective. However, we now review some counterarguments, called **market failures**, which suggest that regulation is still needed.

12.6 SOURCES OF MARKET FAILURE

12.6.1 Externalities and Free-Riding

Frequently, information released by one firm will convey information about other firms. For example, if a firm reveals a sharp increase in sales and profits, this may affect the market's expectations for other firms in the industry. Also, if a firm releases proprietary information (for example, details about a valuable patent) this could affect the market's expectations of future earnings of competing firms. Interactive effects such as these are called **externalities**.

The effect of externalities is to cause the private and social values of information to diverge. The Darrough and Stoughton (1990) model, reviewed in Section 9.3, of a game between a monopolist incumbent and a potential entrant to the industry illustrates this effect. Under some conditions, the monopoly firm does not release information, so as to deter entry. While this may benefit the monopolist, it does reduce the flow of information to the market, thereby imposing a cost on society.

In Section 5.6, we noted that accounting information has characteristics of a public good. We pointed out that this makes it difficult for the firm to charge for producing this information. In effect, when the use of information by one individual does not destroy it for use by another, other investors can "free-ride" on this information. Since all investors will realize this, no one has an incentive to pay. Then, if the firm cannot recover the costs of information production it will produce less than it would otherwise.

> An **externality** is an action taken by a firm or individual that imposes costs or benefits on other firms or individuals for which the entity creating the externality is not charged or does not receive revenue. **Free-riding** is the receipt by a firm or individual of a benefit from an externality.

The crucial aspect of both externalities and free-riding is that the costs and benefits of information production as perceived by the firm differ from the costs and benefits to society. For example, if accounting information produced by one firm informs investors about other firms, this is a benefit to society for which the producing firm receives no benefit. Hence, the firm will underproduce relative to the first-best amount for society. A similar phenomenon operates for the free-rider problem.

In this regard, Anilosky, Feng, and Skinner (2007) studied the relationship between management's quarterly guidance about future earnings and aggregate stock market performance. If, for example, a large number of managers report that earnings are expected to fall, this could convey information about future performance of the economy, which would be quite useful to investors. If so, we should observe a fall in the stock market index following a lot of bad news expected earnings guidance. However, the authors find little evidence of this effect,[16] except for "bellwether" firms, being the largest 20 firms in their sample. They conclude it is likely, for most firms, that issuance of earnings guidance *follows* the performance of the economy, rather than providing information about its future performance. If more firms would issue earnings guidance sooner, this would constitute a positive externality that benefits society.

Of course, firm managers have their own, *firm-specific*, reasons for issuing earnings guidance, such as higher reputation and share price. However, market forces provide no additional benefit to the firm for the externality that timely forecasting conveys about the future state of the economy. Consequently, as found by Anilosky, Feng, and Skinner, the number and timeliness of forecasts falls short of what is socially desirable.

Thus, externalities and free-riding are well-known reasons used to justify regulation. The regulator steps in to try to restore the socially right amount of production because market forces alone fall short.

12.6.2 The Adverse Selection Problem

Given our conclusion in Section 12.5.5 that market forces do not motivate release of all inside information, estimation risk arising from the adverse selection problem remains. Persons with access to this inside information may well exploit their advantage at the expense of outside investors.

In our context, there are two versions of the adverse selection problem. First, we have the problem of insider trading, which was introduced in Chapter 4. If opportunities exist for insiders, including managers, to generate excessive profits by trading on the basis of their inside information, persons willing to do this will be attracted to the opportunity. Then, outside investors will not perceive the securities market as a level playing field and may withdraw. This will reduce market liquidity. For the market to operate well, it is necessary that there be enough traders that the buy or sell decisions of any one of them do not affect the market price of a security. This will not happen unless the market is sufficiently liquid. Thus, the ability of insiders to earn excessive trading profits constitutes a securities market failure.

A second version of adverse selection arises when managers who are privy to bad news about the firm's future do not release that information, thereby avoiding, or at least postponing, the negative firm consequences. This has two adverse effects. First, investors are less able to distinguish between securities of different qualities. Then, managers with low-quality, bad-news securities will be encouraged to bring them to market and managers with good-news securities may not bring them to market. If the market cannot distinguish between securities of different qualities, it will pool them into a single category, in which case the market price will reflect average quality. Second, since owners do not know that the bad news firm is doing badly, the ability of the takeover market to purge poor managers is reduced, so that the average quality of managers is lowered.

A related problem with adverse selection is unequal distribution of information across investors, as discussed by Beaver (1989). For example, the "big guys" may have more resources to find and analyze information, leaving the small investor at a disadvantage. This leads to suggestions, such as by Lev (1988), for regulation to require firms to release information to everyone, thereby enhancing public confidence in a fair marketplace and contributing to market liquidity.

Interestingly, the SEC has done just this. Regulation FD, adopted in 2000, prohibits companies from selectively disclosing information. In Canada, the Ontario Securities Act prohibits companies from releasing information to selected individuals before releasing it to the general public.

The introduction of Regulation FD was surrounded by considerable controversy, however. One prediction was that abnormal share returns between earnings announcement dates would become more volatile, since new information would be released by firms directly to the market, rather than being filtered through analysts (i.e., prior to FD, analysts might downplay or smooth out the significance of new information in return for the favour of receiving it in advance). Note that volatility of share returns is a measure of new information coming to the market. Thus, more volatility between earnings announcements implies that the market receives more information sooner—investors do not have to wait until earnings are announced. From a small investor standpoint, this is desirable, since there is then less time available for insiders and big guys to take advantage of inside information. But critics of FD claimed that to reduce the share price volatility just mentioned, firms would reduce the amount of information they released between earnings announcements. This would show up as an increased number of earnings surprises, leading to increased abnormal share return volatility around earnings announcement dates.

Francis, Nanda, and Wang (2006) examined a sample of firms spanning six quarters prior to and six quarters following the implementation of Regulation FD. They found no increase in abnormal share returns, either between or surrounding earnings announcement dates, implying that Regulation FD had little effect on the amount or timing of information coming to the market. They did find, post FD, lower abnormal share returns around the dates analysts released their earnings forecasts, suggesting that analysts' forecasts became less informative, consistent with a decline in their information advantage. Eleswarapu, Thompson, and Venkataraman (2004) examined a sample of firms over a 16-month period surrounding Regulation FD implementation. They found that the average bid–ask spread of their sample firms fell post FD, implying less investor concern about estimation risk from information asymmetry and adverse selection. They also found that spread decreased on the day that firms released their quarterly earnings. Typically, spread increases, due to increased concern by the market about information asymmetry and insider trading around earnings announcements. A finding that spread decreased suggests increased investor confidence in a fair marketplace.

We conclude that Regulation FD has had some success in reducing small investor disadvantage. However, since it seems that all of its goals have not been met, the adverse selection problem remains.

12.6.3 The Moral Hazard Problem

We suggested in Section 12.4.2 that reputation formation on the managerial labour market, in conjunction with incentive-based compensation contracts, operates to encourage managers' information production. However, these forces may not be completely effective. The reason is that managers may be able to disguise shirking, and resulting low profitability, by opportunistic earnings management and/or by reducing voluntary disclosure. Thus, despite managerial labour markets and incentive contracts, investors will also be concerned about moral hazard and (bad) earnings management.

12.6.4 Unanimity

A characteristic of economies with markets that do not work well is a lack of unanimity, which derives from the effects of adverse selection and moral hazard just described. If markets work well, shareholders will be unanimously in favour of the manager maximizing the market value of the firm. When markets do not work well because of adverse selection and moral hazard, this need not be the case. Eckern and Wilson (1974) studied this problem with respect to the physical production of the firm—that is, the types and quantities of products to be produced—and showed that the manager's choice of production plan to maximize the market value of the firm would not in general be approved by all shareholders under certain market conditions.

A similar result applies to firms' production of information. Blazenko and Scott (1986) demonstrated that in an economy where the information market does not work well, due to adverse selection, the firm manager was motivated to choose that audit quality that would maximize firm market value (recall that an audit is a form of information production). All shareholders, however, would prefer a higher-quality audit. The reason is that from the shareholders' perspective, there are two valuable functions of the audit. One is to add credibility to the firm's financial statements, as we have mentioned. The other is that if the audit catches the manager in fraud or shirking, the shareholders may recover damages. Since only the first function has value to the manager, the audit is of greater value to the shareholders. Consequently, they will demand more of it than the manager wishes to supply.

To put this argument another way, an effect of investor concerns about adverse selection and moral hazard is to lower share prices relative to their fundamental values. Even if a manager does engage in information release to maximize firm value, this maximization is with respect to a share price that is "too low." Thus, shareholders and society would benefit if the manager was to release more information than the manager feels is optimal.

12.6.5 Summary

Markets for information are characterized by externalities and free-riding. These problems, if sufficiently serious, can justify central authority intervention. Furthermore, since market forces do not motivate full release of inside information, securities and managerial labour markets do not fully protect investors from the consequences of insider trading and earnings management. As a result, shareholders will not be unanimous in their support of manager policies, even policies that involve firm value maximization.

12.7 HOW MUCH INFORMATION IS ENOUGH?

Starting from the standard economic prescription that firms should produce information to the point where its marginal social benefit equals its marginal social cost, we see that private market forces are unlikely to produce this result. One reason is externalities and free-riding—market forces are unable to give firms the full social benefits of their information production decisions and are unable to fully internalize the costs of these decisions. Even if they could, the forces of moral hazard and adverse selection lead to a fundamental lack of unanimity between managers' decisions and investors' interests, motivating investors to demand regulation to protect their interests.

Nevertheless, we must not assume that ever-increasing regulation is necessarily socially desirable. This is because regulation carries with it substantial costs. These include direct costs of the bureaucracy needed to establish and administer the regulations, and compliance costs imposed on firms. For example, to the extent that Regulation FD (Section 12.6.2) does not attain all of its goals, its benefits may be less than the costs of compliance. Of possibly greater magnitude are indirect costs. One such cost arises when standards to enforce uniform accounting and reporting reduce managers' opportunity to signal. Uniform audit standards for all firms and stricter forecasting requirements are examples of standards that would reduce signalling potential.

A second indirect cost arises because the regulator may not, and in general will not, be able to calculate the socially optimal amount of information to require.[17] This is because information is such a complex commodity, because there are conflicts between decision usefulness and contracting needs for information, and because different investors have different decision needs.[18] Since information regulations affect firms' financing, investment, and production decisions, the indirect costs of any "wrong" amount of information production can be large indeed.

Given these complex cost–benefit considerations, we simply do not know how much regulation is enough. However, it is safe to say that complete deregulation would not be socially desirable. The uncontrolled impacts of externalities, adverse selection, and moral hazard would be sufficiently serious that markets would probably cease to function. Nor is complete regulation desirable, since the costs to completely eliminate accounting policy choice would be astronomic. However, this leaves a considerable range over which to debate the extent of regulation. Much more knowledge of the benefits and costs of financial reporting will be needed before the question of extent of regulation can be answered.

In this regard, the usefulness of regulation has been studied empirically. Indeed, we have already seen some evidence in our discussion of the value relevance of earnings in Section 6.4. While the results outlined there are somewhat controversial, recall that some authors have documented a low and declining ability of net income to explain share returns (measured by R^2 and ERC), suggesting a decrease in the value relevance of earnings over time. However, the number of accounting standards has been increasing over time. If this greater extent of regulation was socially useful, we would expect to see value relevance increase, not decrease, as investors and markets responded to higher earnings quality.

A more formal test of the extent of regulation was conducted by Ely and Waymire (1999). They studied the period 1927–1993. For each year in this period they estimated the share price response to net income for a sample of 100 firms, similar to the procedure used by Lev (1989) outlined in Section 6.4. Ely and Waymire found an average R^2 of 0.185 over this period, suggesting a "market share" of slightly over 18% for net income during this time.

The researchers then examined separately four sub-periods. The first was 1927–1939. This was prior to the creation of the Committee on Accounting Procedure (CAP) of the AICPA. CAP was the first professional accounting standard-setting body in the United States. Subsequent periods examined coincided with major reorganizations of U.S. standard-setting bodies. For example, the fourth period began in 1973 with the creation of the FASB. In sum, in the 1927–1939 period there were no accounting standards. In the three subsequent periods, the number of standards increased steadily, with the FASB being the latest and most active.

If these new accounting standards were socially desirable, Ely and Waymire argued, the value relevance of net income should increase in the later periods, relative to the 1927–1939 period, and there should be further increases in each successive standard-setting regime. However, using a variety of tests, no significant increases were found. A failure to find increased value relevance of earnings as the number of accounting standards increases raises questions about the benefits of increased regulation.

Theory in Practice 12.2

Jamal, Maier, and Sunder (2003) (JMS) examined the privacy policies and practices of the web site industry. In the United States, this industry is unregulated. Consequently, there is an adverse selection problem that web sites will abuse the privacy of visitors to the site, such as bombarding them with unsolicited e-mails, including from third parties to whom the site may have sold private information.

As JMS suggest, market forces constrain such acts—web sites may feel that it is in their long-run interests to protect the privacy of their customers. They can do so, for example, by establishing and following privacy policies that enable site visitors to opt out of receiving subsequent advertising messages. These policies can be reinforced by

voluntarily hiring an assurance service. Several such services exist, including WebTrust offered by the AICPA and CICA, which includes a full audit of clients' privacy policies.

With these considerations in mind, JMS evaluated 100 high-traffic web sites. Of these, 34 had some form of assurance service and all 34 posted an easily accessible privacy policy on their sites. However, of the 66 sites without an assurance service, 63 also posted a privacy policy. This suggests that most web sites were at least aware of the benefits of protecting users' privacy.

To evaluate whether the sites actually followed their posted policy, JMS registered at each site twice, under separate identities. In one identity, they opted to allow their identity information to

(continued)

be shared with others. In the other, they did not. They then kept track of subsequent e-mails received by each identity for 26 weeks. For those registrations for which they had opted to allow identity sharing, 15,143 e-mails were received. Most of these were generated by five sites, none of which used an assurance service. For those registrations for which they opted out, only 501 messages were received. It seems that even without regulation, almost all web sites respect the privacy wishes of registrants.

JMS concluded that market forces can drive substantial voluntary use of assurance services to signal integrity, and can drive substantial respect for the interests of consumers. However, they caution that the web site industry and the accounting industry differ. For example, they are at different stages of development. Nevertheless, their findings question whether constantly increasing regulation of accounting—also intended to secure integrity and protect customers (investors)—should be taken for granted.

Despite questions about the extent of regulation, we can still ask if the efficiency of regulation can be improved. That is, how might standards generate more information at less cost? In the next section, we consider a suggestion in this regard.

12.8 DECENTRALIZED REGULATION

Information about firm segments—where segmentation may be on the basis of products and services or geography—has been required disclosure in firms' annual reports for some time. Segment information should be useful to investors, since, in evaluating the expected performance and risk of large and complex firms, relevant information, such as differing risks, rates of return, and opportunities for growth, may be buried in consolidated totals. Also, with segment disclosure it is more difficult to disguise poor performance in one segment by burying it in good performance in another, or vice versa.

IFRS 8 regulates segment reporting. A similar standard, SFAS 131, is in effect in the United States. Of interest is the basis of segmentation in these standards. They require that the firm normally report segment information on the same basis as it organizes its segments internally for top management decision-making and performance evaluation. For our purposes, two aspects of this requirement are of interest. First, of the various bases of segmentation that are possible, reporting on a basis consistent with the internal organization should be of greatest usefulness to investors, since it is management that knows best how to organize the business given the products and services it produces and the risks, returns, and opportunities for growth it faces. Thus, reporting externally on the same basis will give investors the best insights into the firm's operations. Second, the direct costs to the firm of complying with the new standard should be low since the firm is already preparing the required information internally. Evidence supportive of the usefulness of these segment disclosures is provided by Berger and Hann (2003), who report that disclosures under SFAS 131 have revealed additional information to the market.[19]

Another example of this approach is the SEC's (1997) requirement for risk disclosure, discussed in Section 7.5.4. This standard also allows management a choice of how best to report on the riskiness of its operations. Presumably, the best way to report on risk is in a manner consistent with the firm's internal risk management procedures.

We call this approach "decentralized regulation." While there is regulation involved, compliance is decentralized to the internal decisions of management.[20] This decentralization improves relevance of reporting and at the same time is less costly. Note that, unlike most standards, management retains some ability to signal through its choice of reporting methods.

12.9 CONCLUSIONS ON STANDARD SETTING RELATED TO ECONOMIC ISSUES

The question of the extent to which standards for information production should be imposed is a complex and important one for a market economy. At present, we witness substantial regulation of firms' information production decisions. These regulations include insider trading laws and laws to regulate full disclosure. They also include laws to establish accounting and auditing professions. These professions, in turn, may form bodies empowered to establish GAAP, such as the IASB, AcSB, and FASB. However, it can be argued, by analogy with other industries where regulation has been eased, that deregulation of the information industry would result in a flood of innovation and competition, to society's advantage.

Indeed, theory suggests a number of reasons why firms would produce information in the absence of standards. These derive from the information needs of contracts, and from market forces. Parties to contracts will want information to motivate effort and to reward accomplishment. Managerial labour markets and takeover markets interact with securities markets to motivate managers to release information so as to increase market value. Signalling is an important vehicle for credible information release.

Such private forces undoubtedly result in much information production. Theory also suggests, however, that even if we ignore externalities and free-riding, the amount produced by private forces alone may fall short of society's demands. The reason can be seen by means of a two-stage argument. First, contracts for information production break down when a large number of persons are involved. Consequently, we cannot rely on contracts for all of society's information needs.

Second, when contracts break down, market prices (for managerial services and for securities) must take over as motivators of information production. However, market forces may not motivate full information release in the presence of information asymmetries. Also, there are costs of releasing information and firms will trade off the costs with the benefits. As a result, some inside information remains, creating a fundamental lack of unanimity between managers' information production decisions and information demanded by investors. Investors may then demand regulation to remedy the perceived deficiency.

However, it is important to realize that private forces need not completely eliminate market failures to preclude regulation. This is because regulation also has costs. These include direct costs, such as a bureaucracy to set and enforce the standards, and compliance costs imposed on firms. More importantly, however, they include indirect costs imposed on society if the central authority mandates the wrong amount of information. Since information is such a complex commodity, this is quite likely to happen. Given the impact of information on firms' production, financing, and investment decisions, the costs to society here can be significant.

The question of standard setting then boils down to a cost–benefit tradeoff. The costs of regulation include not only the enforcement costs, but also the costs of any wrong decisions made by the regulator. The benefits lie in reduced market failures that persist after private market forces have done their best. At present, the extent to which the benefits of regulation exceed the costs is not known, although giving firms some flexibility in how they meet reporting standards may be worthwhile.

Finally, it should be noted that lack of unanimity leads directly to questions about the fairness of the distribution of information. That is, standard setting may need to draw on politics as well as economics. We will explore this suggestion in Chapter 13.

Questions and Problems

1. Information has both costs and benefits to a firm. What are the costs and benefits of information production to a firm? How much information should the firm produce? (CGA-Canada)

2. Explain why a voluntary forecast can be an indirect signal but a mandated forecast cannot. (CGA-Canada)

3. "Contracting internalizes the problem of information production." Explain what this statement means. (CGA-Canada)

4. Describe the difference between a direct and an indirect signal, using the quality of forward-looking information and risk disclosure in MD&A (see Section 4.8.2) as an example.

5. To what extent do (i) security market forces and (ii) managerial labour market forces operate to motivate managers to operate their firms in the best interests of the shareholders? In your answer, identify how financial accounting information enables the market forces to operate.

6. The notion of a market for information, unlike markets for agricultural commodities, transportation services, and so on, may be unfamiliar to most people. A main reason for this is that information is a very complex commodity.

    Give three ways that we can think about the quantity of information and explain each briefly.

7. An adverse selection problem can arise from information asymmetry between issuer and buyer of securities.

    ### Required

    a. Explain what the adverse selection problem is in this context.

    b. How can financial accounting information reduce the adverse selection problem?

c. Can financial accounting information eliminate the problem completely? Explain.

d. What other ways operate to reduce the problem of inside information?

8. The failure of managers to release bad news is a version of the adverse selection problem. Such failure indicates that the securities market is not working well.

   Required

   a. Why might a manager withhold bad news?

   b. To what extent does the disclosure principle operate to reduce the incentive of a manager to withhold bad news? Explain.

9. On September 15, 2004, the Dow Jones Industrial Index suffered its largest fall in a month, dropping by 0.8% or 86.8 points. The Standard and Poor's 100, 400, and 500 indices also dropped by similar amounts.

   According to media reports, the market declines were triggered by Coca-Cola Co. and Xilinx Inc. (a large producer of computer logic chips and related products). These companies announced that sales and profits for the third quarter 2004 would be less than analysts' estimates.

   Required

   a. Why did the whole market decline?

   b. What market failure does this episode illustrate? Explain why this is a failure.

10. In February 1998, Newbridge Networks Corp., a telecommunications equipment maker based in Kanata, Ontario, announced that its revenues and profits for the quarter ending on February 1, 1998, would be substantially below analysts' estimates. Its share price immediately fell by 23% on the Toronto and New York Stock Exchanges.

    The sale, in December 1997, of over $5 million of the company's shares by an inside director of Newbridge was widely reported in the financial media during February 1998. Details of sales by other Newbridge insiders, including its CEO, during previous months were also reported. The implication of these media reports was that these persons had taken advantage of inside information about disappointing sales of a new product line.

    Required

    a. Which source of market failure is implied by these media reports?

    b. What effects on investors, and on liquidity of trading in Newbridge shares, would media reports of such insider sales be expected to create?

    c. Suppose that Newbridge's management felt that its share price was undervalued by the market after the February earnings announcement. Describe some signals that management and directors could engage in to counter the public impression of lower-than-expected profitability.

11. On March 15, 2004, Canadian Superior Energy Inc. held a conference call concerning the recent abandonment of its Mariner E-85 exploration well off the coast of Nova Scotia. The company's CEO explained that the well was a success but that its partner, El Paso Corp., had decided not to invest more money into it. The CEO indicated his optimism that a new partner could be lined up, but refused to answer any questions from the audience.

Previously, in January 2004, Canadian Superior had issued favourable press releases about the Mariner well. However, its CEO had sold $4.3 million of his holdings of company stock in the same month. Following the news of well abandonment in March, class-action lawsuits were initiated on behalf of U.S. investors (Canadian Superior shares were traded in the United States as well as in Canada), claiming that investors had been misled.

The company's shares lost half their value in the few days following the March abandonment announcement, closing at $1.72 on the Toronto Stock Exchange on March 18, 2004.

Required

a. Obviously, the news of well abandonment was a major factor contributing to Canadian Superior's share price decline in March. However, other reasons for the decline can also be suggested. Give two other reasons.

b. What well-known problem of information asymmetry is suggested by the CEO's sale of stock in January 2004? Explain.

c. Assuming that the market's concerns about the information asymmetry problem you identified in **b** are well-founded, what is the likely effect of these concerns on the share prices of all Canadian oil and gas companies? Why?

d. Suppose that given the CEO's optimism about the ultimate success of the well, the company believes that its share price is undervalued by the market. Suggest three credible signals that the company and/or its CEO could give to increase its share price. Explain why the signals you suggest are credible.

12. Imax Corp. is a large entertainment technology company, with headquarters in New York and Toronto. Currently, it has 266 theatres in 38 countries. Its share price, which was as high as $13.89 on the Toronto Stock Exchange in 2003, had fallen to a low of $5.50 following its reporting of a loss, in accordance with U.S. GAAP, of $896,000 U.S. for the first quarter of 2004. This compared with a profit of over $2.4 million for the same quarter of 2003.

On May 14, 2004 (i.e., after reporting the first quarter loss), *The Globe and Mail* reported that a group of senior Imax executives had bought about $1 million U.S. of Imax shares on the open market. The company's share price immediately rose by $1.17 to $7.20.

Imax later reported earnings for the second quarter of 2004 of $1.552 million. However, its problems were not over. In March 2007, the company announced that it was expanding a probe into its accounting for the previous six years, following SEC and OSC investigations into its revenue recognition practices. The company also indicated that it had misclassified some expenses as capital. Imax shares were threatened with delisting by NASDAQ, the exchange on which its shares traded in the United States, since the probe delayed the filing of its financial statements. The filing delay also violated the covenants on its long-term debt. Imax shares fell by over 6%, to $5.79, on the Toronto Stock Exchange on the day following its announcement.

Required

a. What apparent information was conveyed to the market by the executive share purchase? Did the share repurchase constitute a credible signal at the time? Explain why or why not.

b. What market failures are revealed by the subsequent probes into Imax's accounting policies? Explain.

c. Why would the Imax executives have bought shares when they must have known about the opportunistic management of its reported earnings?

13. On May 16, 2002, The Toronto-Dominion Bank (TD) announced that it would voluntarily begin expensing its executive stock options, effective for its fiscal year beginning November 1, 2002. This announcement coincided with the release of its earnings for the quarter ended April 30, 2002. Net income was $132 million, down substantially from earnings of $359 million for the same quarter of 2001. While profits in TD's retail banking division were down somewhat, the main component of the earnings decrease came from write-offs of problem loans and massive provisions for further loan losses.

Required

a. Given its sharply reduced earnings, why would the bank make matters worse by expensing its ESOs?

b. Canadian accounting standards required expensing of ESOs beginning in 2004, with IASB and FASB standards following in 2005. Previously, ESO fair value was reported in the financial statement notes. TD was one of numerous firms that voluntarily decided to expense their ESOs prior to these standards coming into effect. Given this voluntary expensing, the question arises as to whether a standard is needed. Explain some of the costs and benefits of a standard requiring ESOs to be expensed.

14. XYZ Ltd. is an owner-managed retail grocery store that went public on January 1, 2008. Afterwards, Tom Jones, the fun-loving owner–manager, held 40% of the common stock and remained the chief executive of the company.

Required

a. Why is it likely that Tom Jones will shirk more after going public relative to the time he was the owner–manager of the company prior to January 1, 2008? Will this affect the amount that Tom receives for his new share issue? Explain.

b. What steps can Tom Jones take to convince potential shareholders that he will not engage in excessive shirking?

15. Regulation FD of the SEC came into effect in 2000. This standard requires firms that release material information that may affect their share price to release it to all investors simultaneously. The purpose is to stop "selective disclosure," whereby managers release information, such as changes in earnings forecasts, to a select group of analysts and institutional investors, relying on these persons to convey the information to the market.

Required

a. Explain the market failure that has led to this new standard.

b. Describe the effects on market liquidity of selective disclosure. Why is liquidity important if securities markets are to work well?

c. While research suggests that Regulation FD has been at least partially effective in levelling the playing field for outside investors, it is unclear whether or not its benefits outweigh its costs. Describe and explain sources of increased cost to firms and/or society resulting from this regulation.

16. On October 7, 2000, *The Globe and Mail* reported that Air Canada had slashed its third and fourth quarter 2000 earnings forecasts. The company had revealed this information by phone calls to a select group of analysts. Air Canada's share price dropped by 12% on the day it revealed this information, and by another 3% on the next trading day.

The selective disclosure to certain analysts immediately produced strong negative reactions by angry investors and media, and led to calls for investigation by the Ontario Securities Commission and the Toronto Stock Exchange.

This episode was particularly embarrassing to Canadian securities regulators since, a few weeks previously, the SEC had passed Regulation FD in the United States. This is a fair disclosure regulation that prohibits material information from being revealed only to investment analysts. Canadian regulators said at the time that a similar regulation was not needed in Canada because Canadian laws already prohibited such selective disclosure.

Air Canada defended its disclosure policy by claiming that the information underlying the lower earnings forecasts (e.g., higher fuel prices and increased payments to pilots) was already in the public domain. It was attempting to remind analysts that they had not properly incorporated this information into their earnings forecasts.

Subsequently, Air Canada agreed to pay a fine of $1,080,000 in settlement of charges levied against it over this incident.

Required

a. Why would Air Canada want to disclose information about lower-than-expected earnings prior to the actual release of its quarterly income statements?

b. Give two reasons why share price fell in the days following the selective disclosure.

c. Explain the impact of selective disclosure practices on the operation of the securities market.

d. *The Globe and Mail* also reported that a huge block of Air Canada shares had traded on the day prior to the selective disclosure. What problem of information asymmetry is suggested by this trade? Explain.

e. Canadian securities legislation prohibits use for personal gain of such material information by the analysts to whom it is given. Assuming that the analysts did not use the information for personal gain, do you think that Air Canada should have been charged? Explain why or why not.

17. In *The Wall Street Journal*, June 30, 1997, Suzanne McGee describes how institutional investors, such as mutual fund managers, are searching for highly liquid stocks to invest in. If the market for a stock is not liquid, these large investors will have to pay a higher price to buy in, and receive a lower price if they sell out, simply because the quantities they deal in are large enough to affect share price. These concerns are heightened, according to McGee, because many large investors adopt a strategy of selling out at the first sign of trouble and buying back in at the first sign of recovery.

McGee points out that liquidity has a favourable effect on share price. For example, highly liquid stocks such as Coca-Cola are selling at 46 times earnings, whereas the Standard and Poor's 500-stock index trades at 22 times earnings. In effect, McGee argues, the market pays a premium for liquidity.

Required

a. Given its size and number of shares outstanding, how can a firm increase the liquidity of its shares? Consider both depth and bid–ask spread in your answer.

b. What are some of the costs to a firm of increased disclosure?

18. The following article by John Partridge appeared in *The Globe and Mail*, August 23, 2001. It discusses the decision by Canadian Imperial Bank of Commerce (CIBC) to discontinue separate disclosure of gains on sales of portions of its "bonanza" investment in Global Crossing Ltd.

Silence on Global Gains Seen Helping CIBC

When Canadian Imperial Bank of Commerce reported its third-quarter results on Monday, it kept its mouth firmly shut about its bonanza investment in Global Crossing Ltd. for the first time since 1999.

Analysts say that CIBC's sudden reticence about the rich gains it has been making on its original $30-million (U.S.) stake in the Bermuda-based telecommunications company could help start a recovery in the bank's lagging stock market valuation—although some of them contend that the change in disclosure is a step backwards.

"We debated whether we should continue to disclose the [gains on] Global Crossing and other large merchant banking investment, and we concluded that we wouldn't be going forward," Tom Woods, CIBC's chief financial officer, told analysts during the quarterly conference call.

Despite the new vow of silence, Global Crossing has given CIBC a lot to crow about.

Back in 1999, the value of the bank's initial investment in Global Crossing soared to more than $4.3-billion as the Bermuda company caught the updraft of the telecom and high-tech boom. Its shares skyrocketed to a high of $54.

CIBC made a pretax gain of $583-million (Canadian) by selling some of its Global Crossing stock that year, and another $697-million in 2000. This second sale translated to $397-million after tax, equal to nearly 20 percent of the bank's $2.06-billion profit last year.

And in this year's second quarter, when CIBC put a total of $426-million on the bottom line, Global Crossing gains brought it another tidy $314-million before taxes.

The Bermuda company's shares have plummeted to less than $5 (U.S.) apiece in the telecom and tech meltdown, but CIBC had already hedged much of its remaining stake in the company through forward sales contracts. According to its annual report for 2000, the hedges mature between this year and 2003, and are at prices ranging from a "floor" or low of $20 to $28 a share to a "ceiling" of $46 to $64.

Analysts figure CIBC still has about $1.5-billion (Canadian) in unrealized but locked-in gains on its big score. "It's a huge number," one said.

During Monday's conference call, Mr. Woods didn't explain why the bank has decided to stop breaking out these gains.

But analysts are pretty sure they know the reason. CIBC, they say, figures it has been penalized for disclosing them, and is betting that silence on the topic may be golden for its share price.

That price could unquestionably do with a bit of help. Despite rallying this week, CIBC's stock currently carries the worst "beta" or volatility rating among the five biggest domestic banks, and the lowest price–earnings multiple.

"Everybody would strip out the Global Crossing gains from the numbers," one analyst said, explaining how he and his colleagues have used the information until now.

"They're saying 'Well, how is it that when we do well you take it out, but when we do badly you analysts leave it in? We're not getting any credit for it, so we're going to bury it in our earnings, and you guys can do whatever you want to do.'"

CIBC's new approach will instead allow it to use the Global Crossing gains to discreetly smooth and manage—and make more predictable—its overall financial results, without observers being able to divine precisely how this was done. This is a practice already widely followed by other banks in similar situations, and as another analyst put it, CIBC was simply "trying to be too honourable."

Some observers are unhappy that the bank has decided to go quiet on Global Crossing. For instance, in a report issued Tuesday, analyst James Bantis of Credit Suisse First Boston called the move "a step back" after two years in which the bank has "made great strides towards improving the level of financial disclosure and source of earnings."

Mr. Bantis complained that no longer disclosing the Global Crossing gains—which he considers non-recurring—"reduces the quality and transparency of CIBC's earnings over the medium term."

Still, the view is that over time, CIBC's market valuation will benefit because there are few things investors like banks to have more than "earnings visibility," that is, predictable results.

"Historically, CIBC has not been prepared to smooth their earnings, but that changed in this quarter," one of the analysts said. "What it means is that there's going to be much better earnings visibility out of the Commerce, because they've got $1.5-billion in gains left and total flexibility about bringing it in whenever they want... Intuitively, they're going to book them when they most need them."

Another analyst concurred, saying that the new approach will likely be a positive influence on Bay Street's profit forecasts for the bank, and that this, in turn, "will be positive for their valuation."

Source: Reprinted with permission from *The Globe and Mail*.

Required

a. Will this reduction of disclosure affect the market's ability to evaluate the persistence of CIBC's earnings? Explain.

b. Accounting standards in Canada require separate income statement disclosure of gains and losses that do not have all of the characteristics of extraordinary items but which are not expected to occur frequently over several years or do not typify normal business activities (see Section 5.5). Do you feel that CIBC's reduction of disclosure violates this requirement? Explain why or why not.

c. How do you think the securities market will react to this reduction of disclosure? Explain.

d. In this case, it seems that private market forces to motivate information production have failed. Should new regulations be put into place to strengthen requirements for separate disclosure of gains and losses on sales of this nature? Explain why or why not.

19. In November 2006, the financial media reported a 12-year jail sentence to Sanjay Kumar, ex-CEO of Computer Associates International, a large computer software company (now called CA Inc.). In addition, Mr. Kumar was ordered to pay $8 million in fines and restitution. Six other senior executives of the company were also sentenced.

    The defendants were found guilty of a massive fraud during 1999–2000. Tactics used were to hold the books open after period-end and to backdate sales contracts to the current period, to meet Wall Street expectations. In 2004, Computer Associates restated its revenue in the amount of $2.2 billion, the amount of sales fraudulently booked.

    Mr. Kumar joined Computer Associates in 1987, and, through a combination of brilliance and hard work, rose through the ranks to become CEO in 2000. He resigned in 2004, when the magnitude of revenue misstatement had become apparent.

    Mr. Kumar apologized to the court for his conduct, for which he accepted full responsibility.

    Required

    a. Would the revenue overstatements carried out by Mr. Kumar have affected Computer Associates' total net income over a period of several years? Explain why or why not.

    b. Would an accounting standard mandating more conservative revenue recognition policies have prevented the revenue misstatements? Why or why not?

    c. Give reasons why a manager would overstate current period revenue. Which reason do you feel is the most likely one in this case? Explain.

    d. What source of market failure is most likely at work here? Outline the effects of this failure on investors and on the operation of securities markets.

20. A number of firms, such as BCE Inc., Coca-Cola, and McDonalds, have discontinued their practice of issuing quarterly earnings forecasts, thereby lowering their disclosure quality. The reason usually given is that the severe negative consequences of not meeting quarterly targets gives management a short-run focus, distracting it from the attainment of longer-term goals. Consequently, the firm is better off not to issue a forecast in the first place. For example, in a 2005 speech to Wall Street analysts, Thomas Donohue, head of the U.S. Chamber of Commerce, stated "companies sacrifice creating long-term value if it means missing quarterly earnings projections. Some managers forgo making investments and cut expenditures on R&D and marketing to ensure that they hit quarterly numbers, even if they believe that the cuts are destroying business value over the long term."

    Others disagree. In a 2003 speech, Sheryl Kennedy, deputy governor for financial markets of the Bank of Canada, encouraged firms to increase their forecasting, arguing that corporations should provide quarterly outlooks so that investors could better value companies. She did not say specifically that such forecasting should be in the form of earnings forecasts (MD&A, which does not specifically require earnings forecasts, provides an alternative vehicle for forward-looking disclosures, for example). Nevertheless, her arguments suggest that the market would not look favourably on discontinuance of earnings forecasts.

In this regard, another reason can be suggested to explain why firms may discontinue forecasts, namely, to disguise poor performance. Chen, Matsumoto, and Rajgopal (2006) analyzed a sample of 76 firms that discontinued forecasting of quarterly earnings during 2001–2004. They found that the average stock market return on the shares of these firms for the year prior to discontinuance was significantly less than the return on the shares of a control sample of similar firms that had not discontinued forecasting. The discontinuing firms also had a higher proportion of prior loss quarters, and a higher proportion of quarters for which earnings were less than the same quarter of the preceding year (recall that earnings of the prior year's quarter is a proxy for expected earnings of the current quarter). All of these findings are consistent with relatively poor performance for the discontinuing firms.

The stock market seems to agree with this latter reason. Chen, Matsumoto, and Rajgopal reported a negative stock market return for the sample firms over a three-day window surrounding the date of announcement of forecast discontinuance, suggesting that investors revised downwards their probabilities of good future performance. The researchers also report some evidence that the betas of the sample firms increased following their announcements, suggesting an increase in cost of capital. If the main reason for discontinuance of quarterly earnings forecasts was that this created management distraction from longer-term goals, we would expect the market to react positively to the announcements, rather than negatively.

Required

a. Outline some of the costs to firms of issuing quarterly earnings forecasts.

b. Outline some of the benefits to firms of issuing quarterly earnings forecasts.

c. Why does the market penalize the share price of firms that do not meet their earnings targets? Include in your answer an explanation of why the disclosure principle has not motivated these firms to continue their forecasts.

d. Why would managers forgo capital investments, and cut R&D and marketing costs, in order to meet earnings targets, rather than meeting earnings targets by means of income-increasing discretionary accruals? Explain.

21. General Electric Corp. (GE) is a large and complex United States–based conglomerate, with operations extending from industrial and medical equipment to aircraft leasing and mortgage lending. Its share price fell considerably during 2000–2002, following the Enron scandal and resulting stock market collapse and economic recession. This fall occurred despite there being no evidence that GE had engaged in any irregular accounting practices.

GE adopted a number of strategies to halt and reverse its share price decline. Several of these strategies involved increased disclosure. GE's CEO was quoted as saying "If the annual report . . . has to be the size of the New York City phone book, that's life." For example, GE's 2001 annual report, issued in March 2002, disclosed separate revenue and operating profits for 26 of its business segments, up from 12 segments previously. The company also provided extensive discussion of its SPEs, in view of the abuses of these off-balance entities by Enron. It disclosed that none of its SPEs were allowed to hold GE stock, and that none of them engaged in speculative activities, or were used to hedge any of GE's operations. Furthermore, GE employees were not allowed to invest in any of its SPEs.

Also, the CEO reaffirmed the firm's 2002 earnings forecast, and GE began providing quarterly conference calls and webcasts, available to analysts and investors, to answer questions and provide additional information about its earnings announcements.

GE also announced in 2002 that it would voluntarily begin to record options to employees (ESOs) as an expense. (An FASB standard requiring expensing of ESOs did not come into effect until 2005.)

Required

a. Give reasons why GE's share price fell during 2001–2002. Give reasons why increased disclosure exerts upwards influence on a firm's share price.

b. Evaluate the likely effects of GE's SPE disclosures, increased earnings announcement disclosures, and its early adoption of ESO expensing on its share price.

c. Despite GE's increased segment disclosure, numerous analysts and investors were concerned that the company's increased disclosure did not extend to reporting how much of its consolidated earnings came from the earnings of new subsidiaries and how much from previously acquired ones. The source of these concerns appeared to be GE's practice of "buying earnings" by acquiring profitable companies whose earnings exceeded the cost of financing the acquisitions (see Chapter 11, question 9). To what extent will GE's increased segment disclosures reduce investor concerns about low transparency of GE's financial reporting?

22. In December 2006, after a lengthy hearing, the Alberta Securities Commission found that former officers and directors of Blue Range Resources Corp. had "failed to make fair, accurate, public disclosure of material information during 1997 and 1998." Blue Range was an Alberta corporation engaged in exploring for and selling natural gas.

The defendants were found to have overstated physical quantities of reserves and production volumes. This was accomplished by adding a "heat adjustment" to actual volumes, on the grounds that the company's natural gas had greater-than-average energy content. These practices were not disclosed and appeared to depart from industry practice.

The company had also announced a 30% increase in new natural gas production, without disclosing that its 1999 total production volume was expected to decline by 20%. A related charge was that the company over-contracted to deliver natural gas, but did not disclose the risks resulting from having to buy natural gas on the open market to meet its commitments.

Note: For an earlier episode involving Blue Range, see Chapter 8, question 13.

Required

a. This episode contributed to the adoption of increased regulation of disclosures of oil and gas reserves in Canada (National Instrument 51-101 of the Canadian Securities Administrators, 2003). The new regulations go considerably beyond the requirements of SFAS 69 in the United States (see Chapter 2, question 24 for details). What are the costs and benefits of increased regulation of oil and gas disclosures?

b. The new disclosure regulations allow firms to seek an exemption from the new regulations and instead report in accordance with SFAS 69. Many large companies have applied for and received such exemption. Why would these companies do this?

c. Suppose that a Canadian firm is eligible to obtain exemption from the Canadian regulations but decides instead to adopt them for reporting purposes. Use the disclosure principle and signalling theory to explain why.

Notes

1. This is a purely economic definition. Note that it is in terms of *total* information production. The benefits and costs of information production are aggregated across all members of society. The reason why economists define the socially right amount of information this way derives from a desire to attain the largest possible information "pie" in the economy (equating marginal total benefits with marginal total costs does this). Also of concern, however, is the *distribution* of total information across investors. Economists may not feel that they have a comparative advantage in advising how the pie should be carved up. To illustrate, hold total information production constant at a level that satisfies the definition and consider two scenarios. In the first, 80% of the benefits of information production go to the wealthiest 10% of investors. In the second, the benefits are distributed equally across all investors. Most people would not feel that the two scenarios were equivalent. Thus, issues of distribution quickly get caught up in ethical and political debate—they are no longer strictly economic.

   In this chapter, we are primarily concerned about aggregate information production. In Chapter 13, we examine the role of accounting standard-setting bodies in promoting distribution of information in a manner that is fair to managers and investors.

2. The dividing line between proprietary and non-proprietary information is somewhat ambiguous. For example, as we saw in our review of Darrough and Stoughton (Section 9.3), the release of information that may seem non-proprietary (such as a financial forecast) could affect future cash flows if it attracts entry to the industry. Nevertheless, the distinction is a useful one. For further discussion of the interrelationships between proprietary and non-proprietary information, see Dye (1986).

3. See, for example, L. DeAngelo (1981).

4. It would be necessary to top up the manager's contract with, say, a fixed salary to meet the manager's reservation utility.

5. By market liquidity we mean the ability of investors to quickly buy and sell large quantities of securities at the market price with reasonable transactions costs. Liquidity is a composite of market **depth**—the number of shares that investors are willing to buy or sell at any given price—and the **bid–ask spread**—the contemporaneous difference between buying price and selling price of a share. Information asymmetry is one of the factors affecting the spread. The more investors are wary of buying a lemon, the greater the asymmetry—the market protects itself from asymmetry by increasing the spread. Information asymmetry also reduces depth, by causing investors to leave the market.

6. For these effects on cost of capital to operate, the market must perceive the information released to be credible. Devices to attain credibility include lawsuits, audits, and stock exchange or country of listing. Hiring a higher-quality auditor implies a commitment to greater information release. Alternatively, or in addition, a manager could commit to a higher level of information production by moving the firm to an exchange, possibly in a different country, with higher information standards. For example, Lang, Lins, and Miller (2003) report lower cost of capital for a sample of non-U.S. firms that cross-list their shares in the United States. Such cross-listing commits the firm to increased disclosure.

7. Lee, Mucklow, and Ready (1993) found that a share's spread increases when its trading volume is unusually high. They suggest that the market interprets the high volume as due to insiders or other traders with superior information trading on the basis of this information. Without knowing what this information is, the market becomes more uncertain about the share's future return prospects, and increases the spread to protect itself.

8. Botosan and Plumlee also found a *positive* relationship between cost of capital and the quality of more timely disclosures (i.e., more timely than the annual report) such as quarterly reports. It seems

that superior disclosure of more timely information increases cost of capital in their sample, contrary to expectation. Their suggested explanation is that superior timely information attracts short-term, transient investors whose actions increase share price volatility. Increased volatility can increase a stock's beta, thereby increasing cost of capital according to the CAPM. More generally, there is evidence that investors demand a higher return (i.e., higher cost of capital) in periods leading up to scheduled announcements, such as quarterly earnings, due to non-diversifiable uncertainty about what the announcement will reveal. To the extent that quarterly earnings announcements pre-empt the information content of annual earnings announcements, this volatility effect on cost of capital will be less for annual announcements. See Cohen, Dey, Lys, and Sunder (2007).

9. The disclosure principle is attributed to Grossman (1981) and Milgrom (1981).

10. A similar model, with one information item, was developed by Penno (1997).

11. These thresholds have to be consistent with each other. In Pae's model, investors have rational expectations, consequently, they know the various thresholds (which depend, among other things, on investors' probabilities that the firm has developed the information). If thresholds differ depending on whether the firm has developed one or both forecasts, investors would know how many forecasts the firm has developed, and the disclosure principle would operate to force their release regardless of whether they are above or below their thresholds.

12. Refer to Chapter 8, question 10, pertaining to the 1990 Iraqi invasion of Kuwait, for an illustration of how oil companies found themselves in a situation somewhat similar to that envisaged by Einhorn.

13. This type of game is called a **cheap talk game**, since, unlike the signalling models to be discussed next, there is no *direct* cost of disclosure to the manager. However, there is an indirect disclosure cost. This is because the reporting of imprecise interval information to deter entry reduces the ability of the shareholder to optimally plan consumption. It is this tension between deterring entry and reporting accurately to the shareholder that drives the reporting of imprecise information. Such games were first modelled by Crawford and Sobel (1982).

14. For further discussion see Healy and Palepu (1993). Data on Patten Corp. are from Harvard Business School case #9-188-027.

15. Another cost arises if we recognize more than one type of investor. Large institutional investors will have greater ability and resources to analyze information than ordinary investors. Ordinary investors may feel that this disadvantage will increase as more firm information is released, and they may reduce their demand for the firm's shares at the same time that demand from institutional investors is increasing. (As an example, consider the practice of many firms of giving "guidance" to analysts, or releasing information in conference calls with a select group of analysts and large institutions. The SEC has prohibited this practice with Regulation FD, on the grounds that it puts ordinary investors at a disadvantage—see Section 12.6.2.) If ordinary investors leave the market, this puts a brake on the increase in market liquidity, which will cause the firm to stop short of full information release.

16. Note that management's earnings guidance is subject to blockage, as discussed in Section 11.5.1. To the extent that a large number of managers report similar earnings guidance, this is another way to overcome blockage.

17. The impossibility of accounting standards that are "right" from society's perspective follows from the Possibility Theorem of Arrow (Section 1.2). Demski (1973) demonstrates that, even for a single individual, such standards do not in general exist independently of the decision problem and utility function of that individual. Scott (1977) shows, however, that socially right standards are possible for a special case of decision problem (the "single-peakedness" condition), and argues that this condition is quite common.

18. Indeed, this complexity is recognized by standard setters. Thus SFAC 1.23 of the FASB (see Section 3.8) states " . . . the benefits from financial information are usually difficult or impossible to measure objectively, and the costs often are; different persons will honestly disagree about whether the benefits of information justify its costs."

19. While direct costs may be low, SFAS 131 disclosures may incur proprietary costs. For example, the disclosures may reveal segments that are very profitable, possibly encouraging competitors to enter, or incurring political costs. Also, the disclosures may reveal poorly performing divisions, identification of which may lead to increased monitoring of management by the firm's corporate governance system. More generally, the disclosures may reveal that the firm is having trouble coordinating and controlling its various divisions. In this regard, Berger and Hann also report that firms that were forced to reveal previously hidden information suffered a decline in market value, and that they may have tightened up their monitoring of divisions as a result. Increased monitoring suggests that SFAS 131 has economic consequences, as some firms change their internal organization to reduce proprietary costs.

20. Section 1701 of the *CICA Handbook* calls this the "management approach."

Chapter 13
Standard Setting: Political Issues

Figure 13.1 Organization of Chapter 13

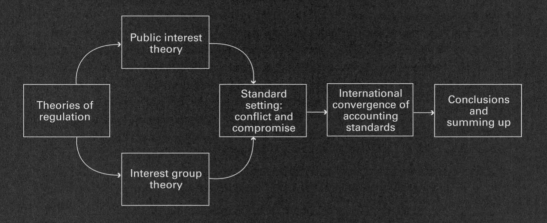

13.1 OVERVIEW

In Chapter 12 we saw that, from an economics perspective, the question of extent of regulation of accounting and reporting standards is unsettled. While we can suggest a number of contractual and market-based incentives for private information production in the absence of regulation, we simply do not know whether increased market failures that would follow from deregulation of firms' information production would be more or less costly to society than the various costs of the standard-setting process. It does appear, however, that the problem of market failure is quite fundamental. Information asymmetry (and the resulting problems of moral hazard and adverse selection), which creates the demand for information production by firms, also creates a demand for regulation of that information production. This is because of the problem of unanimity—the amount of information that firms would privately produce need not, and in general will not, equal the amount that investors want. As a result, investors may push for regulation to remedy the perceived deficiency.

This suggests that standard setting is fundamentally as much a political process as an economic one. Such a viewpoint is consistent with the concept of constituencies of accounting, with the political cost hypothesis of positive accounting theory, and with the game theoretic and agency theoretic views of constituency conflict in Chapter 9. It seems natural to expect that the various accounting constituencies would appeal to the political process when their conflicting interests cannot be resolved by contractual or market forces.

Our first objective in this chapter is to review two theories of regulation. The first, the **public interest theory**, takes the view that regulation should maximize social welfare. This was the viewpoint of Chapter 12. The second, the **interest group theory** of regulation, suggests that individuals form coalitions, or constituencies, to protect and promote their interests by lobbying the government. These coalitions are viewed as being in conflict with each other to obtain their share of benefits from regulation. We shall conclude that the process of standard setting is most consistent with the interest group theory.

Our second objective is to consider the criteria that standard setters need to consider if their standards are to be acceptable. While decision usefulness and reduction of information asymmetry are necessary for any standard, we shall see that much more is needed. Specifically, the standard must be acceptable to its various constituencies. This requires a careful attention to due process by the standard setter.

Finally, we shall consider the additional challenges to financial reporting and standard setting resulting from global integration of capital markets and international convergence of accounting standards.

Figure 13.1 outlines the organization of this chapter.

13.2 TWO THEORIES OF REGULATION

13.2.1 The Public Interest Theory

The public interest theory of regulation was implicit in our examination of standard setting in Chapter 12. This theory suggests that regulation is the result of a public demand for correction of market failures. In this theory, the central authority, also called the regulatory body or the regulator, is assumed to have the best interests of society at heart. It does its best to regulate so as to maximize social welfare. Consequently, regulation is thought of as a tradeoff between the costs of regulation and its social benefits in the form of improved operation of markets. Chapter 12 addressed these various costs and benefits.

While this view represents an ideal of how regulation should be carried out, there are problems with its implementation. It can be argued, from the standpoint of how regulation works in practice, that the theory is superficial and perhaps naïve. Our discussion here is based on Stigler (1971), Posner (1974), and Peltzman (1976).

One problem with the public interest theory is the very complex task of deciding on the right amount of regulation. This is particularly true for a complex commodity like information where, as Chapter 12 makes clear, it is effectively impossible to please everyone. Then, the door is left open for other theories of how the amount of regulation is determined.

An equally serious problem, however, lies in the motivation of the regulatory body. Given the complex nature of its task, it is difficult for a legislature to monitor the operations of the regulator. In effect, the ability of the legislature to force the regulatory body to act in the public interest is weak, because of the complex nature of regulation and the fact that costly and lengthy hearings would be needed for the legislature to know whether the regulator is doing a good job. This creates a moral hazard problem—the possibility that the regulatory agency will operate on its own behalf rather than on behalf of the public. The situation here is reminiscent of the manager in our agency theory discussion of Example 9.2, who was motivated to shirk because his or her action was unobservable to the owner. Thus, the public interest theory represents a sort of first-best approach to regulation. In practice, the first-best solution may not be attainable, because of problems of implementation. This leads directly to another theory.

13.2.2 The Interest Group Theory

The interest group theory of regulation takes the view that an industry operates in the presence of a number of interest groups (or constituencies, as we have used the term in earlier chapters). Consider any manufacturing industry as an example. The firms in the industry comprise an obvious interest group, as do the firms' customers. Another interest group would be environmentalists, who would be concerned about the industry's social responsibility. These various interest groups will lobby the legislature for various amounts and types of regulation. For example, the industry itself may demand regulation to protect it against foreign price competition or against encroachments on its operations by related industries. Customers may form groups to lobby for quality standards or price controls. Environmentalists may lobby for emission control regulations and greater disclosure of environmental performance. These various constituencies can be thought of as demanders of regulation. Note that the nature and extent of the regulation demanded will differ across constituencies.

The political authority, or legislature, can also be thought of as an interest group, which has the power to supply regulation. The interests of the political authority lie in retaining power. Consequently, it will supply regulation to those constituencies that it believes will be most effective and useful in helping it retain power. The regulatory body is then in the middle. It is the vehicle whereby regulation is supplied. It attempts to maximize its own welfare while at the same time balancing the demands of the various constituencies, including the political authority.

In effect, the interest group theory regards regulation as a commodity for which there is a demand and a supply. The commodity will be allocated to those constituencies that are most politically effective in convincing the legislature to grant them regulatory favours.

While it may seem rather cynical, the interest group theory may well be a better predictor of how regulation really works than the public interest theory.

13.2.3 Which Theory of Regulation Applies to Standard Setting?

Our description of the standard-setting bodies in Section 1.9.5 emphasizes that standard setting is characterized by due process. As we saw, in Canada, the United States, and internationally, major constituencies with an interest in financial reporting are represented on the standard-setting bodies. Also, there are provisions for public hearings, exposure drafts, and, generally, for openness, as well as requirements for super-majority votes in favour before new standards are issued.

This due process characteristic is consistent with conflict-based theories of constituency interaction. The sources of market failure in the production of information discussed in Chapter 12 imply that market forces cannot always be relied upon to generate the right accounting standards and procedures. Yet, the complexities arising from the diverse information needs and interests of investors and managers make it effectively impossible for standard setters to calculate the right accounting standards either. We simply do not know how to calculate the best tradeoff between the conflicting uses of information by investors and managers that is required by the public interest theory of regulation. This is why the choice of accounting standards is better regarded as a conflict between constituencies than as a process of calculation. The AcSB, the FASB, and the IASB are players in a complex game where affected constituencies choose strategies of lobbying for or against a proposed new standard.

If the players of the game are to accept the outcome (that is, the issuance or non-issuance of a new standard and, if issued, its specific reporting requirements), they must feel that the process was fair, and that their strategy at least had a chance of working. In terms of the game theoretic Example 9.1, the players must know the strategies available to the other parties. The willingness of players to accept a new standard is enhanced if they feel that their views were heard. This explains the attention to due process as a way of moderating the inherent constituency conflict in standard setting.

These considerations suggest that the interest group theory of regulation may be a better predictor of new standards than the public interest theory, since the interest group theory formally recognizes the existence of conflicting constituencies. To pursue this question further, we next consider some of the conflict leading up to a specific IASB standard.

13.3 CONFLICT AND COMPROMISE

13.3.1 An Example of Constituency Conflict

We described IAS 39, "Financial Instruments: Recognition and Measurement," in Section 7.3.2. However, we did not consider the process that led up to IAS 39. Here, we consider aspects of this process, which provide an interesting and important example of the problems of developing a new standard.

IAS 39 was issued in December 1998, with effective date January 1, 2001. Recall that it proposed fair value accounting for major classes of financial instruments. Fair value accounting, however, has long been opposed by financial institutions, in particular, the banking industry. Since financial institutions are heavy users of financial instruments, and are crucial to the operation of the economy, the views of this important constituency cannot be ignored.

In this regard, the European Central Bank issued a comment in November 2001 entitled "Fair Value Accounting in the Banking Sector." The Bank expressed four general concerns, which we summarize as follows:

- **Short-run, long-run** Banks will reduce the earnings volatility resulting from fair valuing financial instruments by reducing their long-term lending, since the fair values of long-term loans are more subject to interest rate risk than short-term. Reduced long-term lending would hamper investment in the economy, thereby adversely affecting economic growth.

- **Reliability of fair values for bank loans** Fair values that are not derived from properly working markets or adequate mathematical models lack reliability. Furthermore, in 2001, credit derivative markets had not sufficiently developed that bank loan fair values could be inferred. These valuation problems would work against the transparency and comparability of bank financial statements.

- **Own credit risk** Fair-valuing bank liabilities, without fair-valuing corresponding assets, would result in recording a profit from deterioration in credit risk. This mismatch is counter-intuitive and misleading for shareholders.

- **Conservatism** Recognition of unrealized gains and losses in profits goes against prudent bank behaviour, which recognizes unrealized losses on financial instruments but not unrealized gains. Unrealized gains should be recognized only for marketable instruments. Abandoning conservative accounting might induce banks to behave less prudently. This could also upset banking regulators.

Nevertheless, the IASB continued with IAS 39 along the lines discussed in Section 7.3. It should be noted that IAS 39, like SFAS 115, contains provisions to reduce banks' concerns expressed above. Volatility of reported net income is reduced by inclusion of unrealized gains and losses on available-for-sale financial instruments in other comprehensive income. Also, volatility concerns are further addressed by allowing valuation of held-to-maturity instruments on a cost basis.

However, criticisms continued, particularly with respect to the fair value option originally included in IAS 39. For example, the Basel Committee on Banking Supervision is a forum of bank regulators from several European countries, Canada, Japan, and the United States. In a July 2004 comment on IASB proposals to reduce the scope of the fair value option, the Committee expressed concerns about possible use of the fair value option by companies wishing to disguise deteriorating credit risk. This could be done by reporting gains from fair-valuing own debt, particularly if applied to instruments not traded in well-working markets.

Criticisms from other constituent sources ranged from concerns that the restrictive hedging provisions of IAS 39 would result in artificial earnings volatility, to charges that in following SFAS 115 and SFAS 133 too closely the IASB was ignoring the "Europeness" of risk management. Instead, it was suggested, the IASB was using arguments for convergence of accounting standards to push its pronouncements too far in a theoretical direction.

Other European constituents were very much in favour of the fair value option of IAS 39, however. Thus, Danish regulators pointed out that mortgage loans were a very important financial liability in Denmark's financial system. Typically, mortgage loan risk was hedged by financial assets that would have to be fair-valued under IAS 39. If the full fair value option was withdrawn, Danish firms could not fair-value mortgage liabilities. But the financial assets that hedged these liabilities were to be fair-valued. The resulting reported earnings volatility, so it was claimed, would produce financial market instability that would threaten the entire Danish economy. The Accounting Standards Board of the United Kingdom also expressed concerns about artificial volatility.

In the face of these disagreements, the European Union, which was implementing IASB standards for its member states from January 1, 2005, "carved out" of IAS 39 the fair value option and the strict provisions for hedging, leaving it up to member states and individual companies whether or not to adopt them.

In response to these carve-outs, the IASB made several changes to IAS 39. One change was to introduce a form of macro hedging, described in Section 7.3, which allowed for hedging of interest rate risk on a portfolio basis as a way to reduce some of the complexities of applying hedge accounting to individual instruments. The IASB also backed off somewhat from the full fair value option. As described in Section 7.3, its use is now restricted to reducing mismatches and to situations where financial instruments are managed internally as a group. The IASB did not back down on other provisions, however. Demand deposits cannot be identified as a fair value hedged item, on grounds that demand deposits are payable immediately on demand. This reduces pressures for current value accounting for core deposit intangibles, which require an assumption that at least some deposits will be kept on deposit for an extended period. Also, the restriction of the fair value option to eliminating mismatches allows recognition of gains on deterioration of own credit risk, providing liabilities are hedged by fair-valued financial instruments.

The changes to the fair value option appear to have satisfied the European Union, despite banks' and regulators' objections to recording gains on own credit risk outlined above. Concerns about hedging remain, however. Thus, in September 2005, the Association of Corporate Treasurers (ACT), an association of UK corporate treasurers, stated that IAS 39 hedging requirements were still too strict. The UK was originally a strong supporter of IAS 39. However, the ACT feels that the hedge accounting rules continue to eliminate some valid hedging strategies, leading to excess earnings volatility.

The bottom line of this conflict between the standard setter and affected constituencies is that differences across firms in the application of the various options of IAS 39 can reduce comparability of financial statements. These differences will likely continue for some time due to objections to full fair value accounting from constituencies such as banking regulators, and management.

13.3.2 Comprehensive Income

In 1997, SFAS 130, **Comprehensive Income**, was issued by the FASB. We introduced this standard in Section 7.2.6. A similar Canadian standard was implemented in 2006. The IASB has adopted a similar standard (IAS 1, revised) effective in 2009.[1] Since SFAS 130 is the original standard in this area, we shall discuss it here.

Comprehensive income is defined as all changes in equity during the period except those resulting from investments by or distributions to owners. Thus, in addition to net income as calculated under GAAP, comprehensive income includes other items such as unrealized translation gains and losses resulting from consolidation of foreign subsidiaries under SFAS 52, unrealized gains and losses on marking-to-market available-for-sale securities under SFAS 115 (Section 7.3.2), and unrealized gains and losses on cash flow hedges of forecasted transactions under SFAS 133 (Section 7.3.5). In each of these cases, management objects to the inclusion of these items in net income, on the grounds that they are volatile, uncontrollable, and uninformative about their effort. Our study of contracting theory suggests reasons for management's concerns.

SFAS 130 requires that items such as these be included in a **Statement of Other Comprehensive Income**, which can be presented either along with the income statement or in a separate statement of changes in shareholders' equity. Once unrealized gains and losses are realized, for example by selling available-for-sale securities, the now-realized gain or loss is transferred from other comprehensive income to net income.

Comprehensive income is thus the sum of net income and other comprehensive income. To illustrate, we extend the hierarchy of earnings numbers given in Section 5.5 (again, ignoring income taxes) as follows:

Core earnings	xx
Unusual and non-recurring items	xx
Income from continuing operations	xx
Extraordinary items	xx
Net income	xx
Other comprehensive income	xx
Comprehensive income	xx

This dichotomization between realized (net income) and unrealized (other comprehensive income) earnings components brings to mind the two roles of financial reporting—providing useful information to investors and enabling the managerial labour market to evaluate manager performance. Since current market value is the best indicator of future value when markets work reasonably well, unrealized gains and losses provide relevant information to investors about future firm performance. However, to the extent that unrealized gains and losses are less informative about manager effort than realized gains and losses, net income is a more informative measure of performance for contracting. Contracting efficiency could perhaps be enhanced by moving additional items from net income to other comprehensive income, such as ceiling test writedowns where these are deemed to be uninformative about effort (recall BCE's write-off of stranded costs in Section 10.6). Of course, such an approach would need standards to control a manager's temptation to avoid responsibility for losses by shuffling informative loss items out of net income, or shuffling uninformative gains the other way. Given such controls, the dichotomization approach has some potential to relieve the fundamental problem of financial accounting theory.[2]

Despite this potential, SFAS 130 ignores any mention of the role of net income in motivating manager performance. Nevertheless, this role seems implicit. For example, the standard states (paragraph 66) that other comprehensive income is not a measure of financial performance, implying that net income is.

Theory in Practice 13.1

Under SFAS 115, unrealized gains and losses on available-for-sale securities are included in other comprehensive income (OCI). As these unrealized gains and losses are realized through sale of the securities, they are transferred to net income.

Thus, despite the intent of SFAS 115 to prevent gains trading, firms can still engage in a form of this type of earnings management—they can manage reported net income by selling available-for-sale securities. For example, to increase reported net income, it is only necessary to sell available-for-sale securities that have unrealized gains attached. Of course, this also reduces OCI, since the gain is now realized, and comprehensive income (the sum of net income and OCI) is unaffected. Nevertheless, managers may feel that investors will concentrate on net income for evaluation of firm performance.

An interesting characteristic of SFAS 130 is that it allows the firm to report OCI either below net income or as part of a statement of changes to shareholders' equity. This latter option shows OCI *apart* from net income—for example, as note information or as part of an expanded statement of retained earnings. The significance of including OCI apart from net income is that gains trading may be less noticeable—the investor has to study the OCI statement to realize that a realized gain or loss in net income is merely the result of realizing gains and losses that have already occurred and are thus of little economic significance.

This behaviour was studied by Lee, Petroni, and Shen (2004) (LPS). They obtained a sample of 82 U.S. insurance companies. Such firms hold large amounts of available-for-sale securities, typically about 40% of total assets. Consequently, the potential to manage net income by gains trading is great.

LPS classified their 82 firms into "cherry pickers" (firms that appeared to gains trade as just described so as to manage reported net income) and firms that did not exhibit this behaviour. For

(continued)

example, if a firm followed a pattern over time of reporting realized gains on securities when its net income before such gains was unusually low, it was classified as a cherry picker. The implication is that the firm was managing its reported net income upwards, perhaps to meet analysts' and investors' earnings expectations. There were 23 cherry pickers in their sample.

Then, LPS looked at the reporting option used by the 23 cherry picking firms. They found that 75% of them used the option of reporting apart from net income. Of the 59 firms not classed as cherry pickers, only 38% used this option.

LPS' evidence suggests that cherry pickers feel they have something to hide and, accordingly, choose the less transparent reporting option. Another interpretation, however, is that managers may feel that since realized gains and losses are not subject to the volatility of unrealized gains and losses, they are more informative about their efforts in running the firm.

The reporting of comprehensive income raises the question of whether it is decision useful for investors. The above vignette suggests some potential, since a careful examination of other comprehensive income may reveal earnings management. The usefulness issue was investigated by Dhaliwal, Subramanyam, and Trezevant (1999). For a large sample of U.S. firms, they calculated the association between share returns and comprehensive income, and compared the result with the association between share returns and net income. They found no clear evidence that other comprehensive income is more highly correlated with share returns than net income, implying no additional decision usefulness. Skinner (1999) pointed out that this result is what we would expect given securities market efficiency. Much of the information about the components of other comprehensive income would have been available to the market from other sources, such as supplementary information in financial statement notes.

Given a lack of decision usefulness, what is the purpose of SFAS 130, since a full application of the measurement approach would include all unrealized gains and losses in net income? It seems that the standard represents a political compromise between investors' and managers' interests. Investors benefit from the decision usefulness of current value accounting. Managers seem willing to accept current value accounting providing that resulting unrealized gains and losses are excluded from net income.

13.3.3 Conclusions Regarding Comprehensive Income

Comprehensive income is a creature of current value accounting standards. The role of current value accounting is to convey useful information to investors and to control gains trading, thereby contributing to better working capital markets.

While these are valuable improvements, it should be clear that much more is required if a standard is to succeed. An acceptable compromise between the interests of affected constituencies is also essential. With respect to SFAS 130, the compromise is to exclude from net income unrealized gains and losses over which management has relatively little control and which are relatively uninformative about manager effort. It seems that such a compromise is necessary if management is to accept current value accounting. Nevertheless, by excluding unrealized gains and losses that are relatively uninformative about manager effort from net income, other comprehensive income has the potential to improve the role of net income in reporting on manager performance.

13.4 RULES-BASED VERSUS PRINCIPLES-BASED ACCOUNTING STANDARDS

The practice versus theory vignette above leads to the distinction between **rules-based** and **principles-based accounting standards**. Rules-based standards, of which SFAS 115 is an example, attempt to lay down detailed rules for how to account. For example, an objective of SFAS 115 was to eliminate gains trading. However, as the vignette illustrates, it is difficult to lay down detailed rules to deal with every possible situation (for another illustration, see Chapter 7, problem 7). An alternative to detailed rules is for accounting standards to lay down general principles only, and rely on auditor professional judgement to ensure that application of the standards is not misleading. Thus, if the general rule is that gains trading should be eliminated, the auditor will object if the manager appears to use gains trading for opportunistic purposes.

In this regard, the SEC, in a 2003 study, "Study Pursuant to Section 108(d) of the Sarbanes-Oxley Act . . . ," recommends that the FASB adopt a principles-based approach to accounting standards. Note that such an approach puts more weight on the Conceptual Framework (see Section 3.8) to provide a framework for professional judgement. The SEC study is in broad agreement with the FASB's own 2002 "Proposal for a Principles-Based Approach to U.S. Standard-Setting." The FASB is currently working on ways to implement this approach.

Principles-based accounting standards also raise the important ethical issues discussed in Section 1.3, since there is increased emphasis on the accountant/auditor's judgement. Professional accounting bodies must strive to ensure that their members put longer-run public interests (e.g., securities and managerial labour markets should work well) ahead of shorter-run interests of clients (e.g., opportunistic earnings management). Of course, professional accounting bodies already do this, through codes of professional conduct, discipline committees, and due process in standard setting. Nevertheless, in view of major reporting failures as described in Section 1.2, even greater efforts to increase the transparency of the accounting profession are warranted, since it is also difficult to enforce good judgement.

In this regard, the organization of the standard-setting body itself has ethical implications. In Canada, the standard setting body (AcSB) and the discipline-enforcing body are both wings of the same professional organization (CICA). This creates at least the appearance of a moral hazard problem, since the body responsible for financial accounting standards is associated through the professional organization with the body responsible for enforcement. In contrast, the FASB and IASB are distinct from a professional accounting body.

13.5 CRITERIA FOR STANDARD SETTING

We have seen that there are a number of factors that affect the process of standard setting. Standards should be decision useful, but they should also be acceptable to other constituencies—in particular, management. This puts the standard setter in a conflict situation and it is difficult to predict what an acceptable resolution of this conflict will be. Nevertheless, we now suggest some criteria that should be kept in mind when trying to understand standard setting.

13.5.1 Decision Usefulness

The criterion of decision usefulness underlies the information and measurement perspectives on financial reporting, and the empirical capital market studies. Recall that the more informative about future firm performance an information system is, the stronger will be investor reaction to information produced by the system, other things equal. Thus, empirical evidence that security prices respond to accounting information suggests that investors find accounting information useful.

This suggests that a necessary condition for the success of a new standard is that it be decision useful. Of course, this can be hard to assess beforehand, since the market has not yet had a chance to respond to the standard. Nevertheless, the theory of rational investor decision-making can be used to predict decision usefulness. For example, Bandyopadhyay (1994) predicted that oil and gas companies' earnings reported under successful-efforts were more informative than under full-cost accounting, and provided evidence to this effect. Also, as argued in Chapter 6, the incorporation of current values into financial reporting will increase investor decision usefulness to the extent that this tightens up the linkage between current and future performance.

However, while decision usefulness may be a necessary criterion for a successful standard, it is not sufficient to ensure success. We saw in Section 5.6 that, because of certain public good characteristics of accounting information, we cannot be sure that the standard that has the greatest decision usefulness is best for society. Since investors do not directly pay for accounting information, they may "overuse" it. Thus, a standard could appear to be decision useful, yet society would be worse off because the costs of producing the information were not taken into account. Furthermore, changes in standards can impose contracting costs on firms and their managers. In effect, as implied by the fundamental problem of financial accounting theory, standard setters must consider criteria other than decision usefulness.

13.5.2 Reduction of Information Asymmetry

We saw in Section 12.4.2 that market forces operate to motivate management and investors to generate information. Standard setters should be aware of these forces and take advantage of them, to the extent possible, to reduce the need for standards. Unfortunately, market forces alone cannot ensure that the right amount of information is produced. As we saw in Section 12.6, one of the reasons for this is information asymmetry. Consequently, as suggested by Lev (1988), standard setters should use reduction of information asymmetry in capital and managerial labour markets as a criterion for new standards.

While the public good characteristics of accounting information complicate the ability of decision usefulness to guide standard setters, as just pointed out, these same characteristics mean that standards can be quite effective in reducing information asymmetry. That is, since the use of financial accounting information by one individual does not destroy it for use by another, expanding disclosure by means of standards works towards a fair distribution of the benefits of information to all investors. These benefits are available *directly* to those who are willing and able to use the expanded information (as in the case of Bill Cautious in Example 3.1), or *indirectly* to other investors through the price-protection mechanism of efficient securities markets (Section 4.3.1). Consequently, reduction of information asymmetry improves the operation of markets, since investors will perceive investing as more of a level playing field. This will reduce estimation risk and the "lemons" phenomenon, expand market liquidity, and generally produce social benefits from better-working markets.

Standard setters should be aware of the informativeness of market price itself as a conveyor of information. As discussed in Section 4.4, the efficient market price of a firm's shares reflects, with noise, what is publicly known about that firm. Furthermore, more is publicly known about large firms than small firms to the extent they are in the public eye and have analyst and media following. Consequently, we would expect the extent of information asymmetry between managers and investors to be greater for small firms, suggesting that standard setters should require at least as high disclosure standards for small firms as for large firms. In this regard, it is interesting that while the CICA *Handbook* applies to all profit-oriented enterprises, certain disclosure exemptions for small firms are allowed. For example, Section 3500 of the *Handbook* excludes the reporting of earnings per share by firms whose shares are not publicly traded.

However, it should be noted that reduction of information asymmetry as a criterion is again a necessary condition for a successful standard but not a sufficient one. Just as decision useful information has a cost, so does reduction of information asymmetry. Consequently, it is hard to know when standards to reduce information asymmetry cease to be cost effective.

13.5.3 Economic Consequences of New Standards

As mentioned above, one of the costs of a new standard is the cost imposed on firms and managers to meet that standard. This goes beyond the out-of-pocket costs of producing the newly mandated information. Costs are also created by contract rigidities, as in an increased probability of violating debt covenants, and effects on the level and volatility of managers' future bonus streams. These costs can affect managers' operating and financial policies. Furthermore, to the extent that new standards require the release of proprietary information, firms' future profitability can be affected by the reduction of competitive advantage.

The reduction in managers' freedom to choose from different accounting policies that frequently results when a new standard is implemented is also a source of economic consequences. We argued in Section 12.5.2 that firms can signal inside information by accounting policy choice. Also, responsible earnings management can reveal inside information, as discussed in Section 11.5. Obviously, if accounting policy choice is constrained, there is a reduction in the extent to which these private forces for information production can operate.

Finally, the Darrough and Stoughton model in Section 9.3 suggests that the greater the degree of competition in an industry the better the disclosure, other things equal. As a result, there may be less need for accounting standards in some industries than in others.

These considerations suggest that standard setters should weigh the possible economic consequences of new standards as an important source of cost that will affect both the need for the standard and the willingness of constituencies to accept it. Of course, it may be that the economic consequences of a new standard will be overstated during the debate leading to the standard. For example, would banks really stop long-term lending if their long-term investments have to be fully marked-to-market? Probably not, but the costs to banks of long-term lending would increase and, as a result, the charges to borrowers would likely rise.

13.5.4 The Political Aspects of Standard Setting

Economic consequences leads directly to our last criterion, namely the political aspects of standard setting. Standard setters, in effect, must engineer a consensus sufficiently strong that even a constituency that does not like a new standard will nevertheless go along with it. This is the "delicate balancing" act that Zeff referred to (see Section 8.2). As should be apparent from Section 1.9.5, the structure and due process of standard-setting bodies, both nationally and internationally, is designed to encourage such a consensus.

We concluded earlier that the standard-setting process seems most consistent with the interest group theory of regulation. Certainly, technical, and even theoretical, correctness is not sufficient to ensure the success of a standard. As we argued in Section 8.3, failure to record an expense for ESOs overstates net income and reduces the comparability of reported earnings across firms. Yet the FASB's 1993 exposure draft proposing fair value accounting for ESOs met with such resistance that it had to be withdrawn, and its 2005 expensing standard encountered similar resistance (see problem 4). While careful attention to due process may be time-consuming, such attention seems essential if costly and embarrassing retractions are to be minimized. Too many of these will threaten the existence of the standard-setting body itself.

13.5.5 Summary

Accounting standard setters can be guided by decision usefulness and reduction of information asymmetry. However, while these criteria are necessary, they are not sufficient to ensure successful standard setting. It is also necessary to consider the legitimate interests of management and other constituencies, and to pay careful attention to due process. Because of the fundamental problem of financial accounting theory, it seems that the actual process of standard setting is better described by the interest group theory of regulation than by the public interest theory.

13.6 INTERNATIONAL INTEGRATION OF CAPITAL MARKETS

13.6.1 Convergence of Accounting Standards

Accounting, in any country, takes place within the social, political, legal, and economic institutions of that country. In this book, we have taken North American market-oriented institutions largely for granted. However, as capital markets become more integrated worldwide, investors are increasingly investing in firms in foreign countries, whose customs, institutions, and accounting standards may differ from those of the investor's home country. It is argued that integration leads to better working capital markets, increased investment, and more efficient contracting across the integrated markets. Consequently, any evaluation of the political aspects of standard setting must now take international integration into account.

One response to capital markets integration is to pursue a common set of international accounting standards. Indeed, as noted in Section 1.9.5, this is the basic objective of the IASB. To the extent that a common set of standards becomes acceptable to securities regulators as a substitute for local GAAP, costs of multiple stock exchange listings will fall. This should lower firms' financial statement preparation costs. It may also lower their costs of capital, as they are better able to tap more liquid sources of financing. In addition, a common set of international standards will decrease **network externalities**. That is, it will reduce costs for investors who do not then have to familiarize themselves with more than one set of GAAP.

However, U.S. accounting standards have worldwide influence too, particularly for foreign firms that wish to raise capital in the United States. The convergence question then becomes, should convergence be to IASB or FASB standards? A response is to converge these two sets of standards to each other.

In this regard, the 2002 Norwalk Agreement[3] between the FASB and IASB commits the two bodies to work towards a common set of high quality standards. In Canada, the AcSB announced in March 2005 a proposal to align its standards for public companies with IASB standards by 2011, abandoning its previous policy of moving Canadian standards into alignment with those of the FASB.

Some progress has been made towards IASB/FASB standards convergence. For example, the provisions of IAS 39, dealing with the recognition and measurement of financial instruments, are substantially similar to those of FASB 115 and FASB 133, although IAS 39 applies to financial liabilities as well as financial assets (see Section 7.3). IFRS 2 requires expensing of ESOs, as does SFAS 123R. IFRS 3 requires the purchase method of accounting for purchased goodwill. Goodwill is not amortized but is subject to a ceiling test. These requirements are similar to SFAS 142 (see Section 7.4.2). IASB standards now recognize other comprehensive income (see Section 13.3.2).

Yet, differences remain. For example, IAS 16 allows upward revaluation of property, plant, and equipment, whereas historical cost is generally used in the United States and Canada. Development costs may be capitalized under IAS 38, similar to Section 3450 of the *CICA Handbook*. In the United States, almost all R&D is expensed. Given the differences that remain, full standards convergence may take some time and will likely require agreement on a common conceptual framework.

13.6.2 Effects of Customs and Institutions on Financial Reporting

As mentioned, financial reporting is affected by local customs and institutions. The legal environment in a country is an important example. Ball, Kothari, and Robin (2000) (BKR), in a study spanning 1985–1995, compared the quality of financial reporting in several common-law countries (Australia, Canada, United Kingdom, United States) to reporting quality in code-law countries (France, Germany, Japan). In common-law countries, accounting standards are set, in varying degrees, in the private sector, and are oriented primarily to investors. In contrast, standards in code-law countries were set primarily by governments, hence subject to more political influence than under common law. As a result, additional constituencies are represented *within* the corporate governance structure under code law, such as banks, business associations, and labour unions. In effect, BKR point out, there is less information asymmetry in code-law countries, since important constituencies are insiders rather than outsiders.

If so, insiders will quickly learn, for example, about major gains and losses. Consequently, there is less need for timeliness in conveying this information outside the company. Thus BKR predict that financial reporting has greater recognition lag in code-law countries relative to common-law countries.

BKR also predicted that financial reporting will be less conservative in code-law countries. Since influential insiders will already be aware of major losses, they can rapidly bring pressure to bear on management to forestall and correct them, without waiting for the pressure to arise from violation of debt covenants and capital market reaction to public disclosure of bad news. Consequently, there is less need for conservative standards, such as ceiling tests, relative to common-law countries. In effect, the agency costs of contracting between managers and owners are lower under code law.

To test their predictions, BKR studied a sample of 40,359 firm year-ends from the countries involved. They measured economic income by the change in a firm's share value over the year (adjusted for capital transactions). Recognition lag was then evaluated by the association between net income and economic income—lower association indicates greater recognition lag between the occurrence of an economic gain or loss and its incorporation into the financial statements. Their empirical results showed significantly lower associations for code-law countries, consistent with their prediction.

To test for conservative reporting, BKR used a technique similar to that used by Basu (1997) (see Section 6.6). They evaluated the association between economic income and reported net income separately for firms with negative and positive economic incomes. Recall that an efficient market will bid up share prices of firms with good economic news and bid down the prices of firms with bad news. Under conservative accounting, recognition lag is less for bad news (i.e., negative economic income) than for good news. Consequently, the association between bad economic news and net income will be higher than the association between good economic news and net income. BKR's empirical results were broadly consistent with their prediction of less conservative accounting under code law.

High recognition lag and less conservative accounting suggest that financial reporting in code-law countries is of lower quality than under common law. However, this does not imply that financial reporting under code law is necessarily more opportunistic than under common law. Rather, these differences reflect underlying differences in institutions, agency costs, and corporate governance structures.

By and large, the countries in the BKR study did not at the time use international accounting standards. For example, IASB standards had not yet been adopted by the European Union. We might then be tempted to conclude that if all countries adopted international standards, the higher costs to investors of interpreting and analyzing financial statements of foreign firms in the face of differences such as timeliness and conservatism would disappear. However, one must be careful about such a conclusion. Recall that even high quality accounting standards allow considerable judgement and discretion in the application of accounting policies (see Section 2.5).

In this regard, Ball, Robin, and Wu (2003) (BRW) studied a sample of 2,726 firm year-ends over 1984–1996 from Hong Kong, Singapore, Malaysia, and Thailand. All of these countries had adopted high quality standards, such as IASB, which have their origins in common-law countries. However, institutional characteristics in the four countries are typical of code law, namely greater family and bank influence and more private debt. These reduce the agency costs of managerial and debt contracts, since information needed for monitoring and corrective action can be communicated between insiders rather than through financial disclosure. This reduces the need for timely and conservative reporting, as in the BKR study. BRW found that financial reporting in these countries, as measured by recognition lag and conservatism, was similar to the lower quality of code-law countries even though they used high quality standards similar to those of common-law countries. This suggests that we cannot take for granted that high quality standards will, by themselves, improve financial reporting.

An additional complication of international accounting standards is that governments may influence financial reporting. In some countries, firms may be allowed, or even encouraged, to cover up large losses so as to avoid bankruptcy, which would embarrass the government. Indeed, poorly performing firms themselves have an incentive to smooth recognition of losses and accelerate recognition of gains if they fear the government may take over in the national interest. Alternatively, large gains may be smoothed so as to forestall racial tensions within the country. Smoothing of large losses and gains increases recognition lag since, instead of reporting them currently, their recognition is deferred over future periods. Also, smoothing of large losses reduces conservatism.

These issues were examined by Bushman and Piotroski (2006), who studied a sample of 38 countries during 1992–2001. They found that in countries with substantial state involvement in the economy, recognition lag for good news firms was relatively low, while the lag for bad news was relatively high. This tendency to maximize reported earnings through faster recognition of good news and smoothing of losses suggests that a desire to reduce the possibility of further state involvement dominates any concerns firms may have about lower quality financial reporting and possible racial tensions.

13.6.3 Enforcement of Accounting Standards

Accounting standards must be enforced if they are to contribute to higher quality financial reporting. Enforcement of IASB standards is of particular concern since, as pointed out in Section 1.9.5, IOSCO does not have formal enforcement powers. Enforcement is up to the countries that adopt IASB standards. Should this enforcement be less than adequate, we cannot be sure that high quality standards are applied in practice. Investors may face serious exposure to estimation risk arising from adverse selection and moral hazard if legal systems, stock exchanges, and securities regulators do not reinforce the application of accounting standards to provide a stable environment for high quality financial reporting. Furthermore, markets that do not work well reduce incentives for voluntary disclosure, since firms' share prices will be less rewarded.

A related enforcement issue is the protection of small investors. In many countries, firms are controlled by families, large institutions, or governments. Minority shareholders in firms with highly concentrated ownership may suffer at the hands of the controlling interest. This creates a different type of agency problem than the manager/owner conflict studied in this book. While concentrated ownership may reduce the moral hazard problem between managers and owners, the problem now shifts to one between controlling shareholders and minority shareholders. Minority investors will be wary of this moral hazard, and will not invest, or will demand a high return. If so, capital markets will not work well, constraining productivity and growth in the economy.

Auditing is an important enforcement mechanism. A well-functioning audit contributes to investor confidence and efficient contracting. In particular, full disclosure protects small minority investors by making it more difficult for controlling interests to expropriate firm value through, for example, excessive compensation, perquisites, and related party transactions. Yet, even large international audit firms may be under pressure from controlling interests to accept such opportunistic practices. In effect, who audits the auditor?

Guedhami and Pittman (2006) studied this issue. With a sample of firms drawn from countries worldwide (excluding Canada, the United States, and the United Kingdom), they used ownership concentration as a proxy for the extent of the agency problem between controlling interests and small investors. They found that ownership concentration was lower in countries with strong laws enforcing auditor liability. It appears that auditors do a better job on behalf of outside investors when they are more under the threat of legal liability. Small investors are then less wary of investing, reducing ownership concentration.

From a professional standpoint, this result seems unfortunate, since we would hope that ethical behaviour would drive audit performance, regardless of audit liability. However, it does reinforce our argument in Section 1.3 that reputation considerations, such as avoiding legal liability, can drive behaviour that is, in effect, ethical.

13.6.4 Benefits of Adopting High Quality Accounting Standards

Despite the problems just discussed, adoption of high quality accounting standards is potentially worthwhile, since economies with relatively weak regulatory environments may benefit from higher quality reporting and consequent strengthening of their capital markets. Hail and Leuz (2006), in a study of 40 countries over 1992–2001, report lower average costs of equity capital for countries with strong disclosure regulation and enforcement. This result is after controlling for cross-country differences in risk and growth opportunities, which also affect cost of capital. Frost and Hayes (2006), in a study of 50 stock exchanges worldwide over 1997–1998, find a positive relationship between stock exchange disclosure and enforcement regulations and the level of securities market development in the countries involved. This positive relationship was found after controlling for the effects of the legal environment and other factors affecting market development such as disclosure laws, analyst following, and media coverage. These two studies suggest that greater market development encourages more liquidity, more foreign investment, more small domestic investors and, generally, attainment of the benefits of better-working markets.

High quality accounting standards can also contribute to better-working markets, as we discussed in Section 4.7. There is some evidence that adoption of IASB standards does improve earnings quality. Barth, Landsman, and Lang (2005) examined a sample of firms from 24 countries (excluding the United States) over 1990–2004. Their sample firms had adopted IASB standards in place of their own domestic GAAP. The authors report higher earnings quality on average following the switch to international GAAP.

Empirical evidence also confirms that higher earnings quality can lead to more foreign investment. Covrig, DeFond, and Hung (2007) studied stock holdings of mutual funds for a large sample of firms from 29 countries, excluding the United States and Canada. They found that foreign mutual funds (i.e., funds not located in the same country as a sample firm) included in their portfolios a significantly higher number of shares of firms that had voluntarily adopted IASB standards, relative to firms using their domestic GAAP.

While the evidence just cited suggests that a shift from domestic GAAP to IASB GAAP benefits the economies involved, a related question is the relative quality of IASB and United States GAAP. This question is important since the SEC now allows foreign firms under its jurisdiction to report using IASB standards without reconciliation to FASB standards. Indeed, the SEC is also considering the possibility of allowing U.S. firms under its jurisdiction to report under either set of standards. In this regard, Leuz (2003) examined the market liquidity of firms traded on the German New Market. This market allows its listed firms to report under either IASB or FASB standards. Recall from Section 12.4.2 that market liquidity is a measure of information asymmetry, which, as we argued in Section 13.5.2, is an important consideration for standard setters. Information asymmetry and resulting estimation risk crucially determine the extent to which securities markets work well. Leuz measured a firm's liquidity by its bid–ask spread and share turnover, where share turnover is a proxy for market depth—see Chapter 12, Note 5. He found no significant differences between IASB and FASB standards for these measures, and concluded that there is little difference in information asymmetries between firms reporting under the two sets of standards.

However, Barth, Landsman, Lang, and Williams (2006) examined a sample of firms from 24 countries over 1990–2004, in comparison to a matched sample of U.S. firms using U.S. GAAP. Using several earnings quality measures, such as accruals quality and association with share price, they concluded that firms using IASB GAAP exhibit lower average earnings quality than their U.S. counterparts. It thus seems that the question of whether one set of standards is superior is unsettled at the present time.

13.6.5 Should Standard Setters Compete?

An alternative to standards convergence is for each country to allow firms in its jurisdiction to use either domestic accounting standards or IASB standards (or any other set of standards, for that matter). In particular, as mentioned above, suppose that the SEC was to allow all firms in its jurisdiction to use, without reconciliation, either U.S. GAAP or IASB GAAP.

This proposal, which would introduce a measure of competition to the standard-setting process, was discussed by Dye and Sunder (2001). One possible effect, they suggest, is a "race to the bottom," whereby each standard setter lowers its standards so as to attract firms and their managers away from the other. As a result, estimation risk and the potential for bad earnings management are increased. This outcome is analogous to the Nash equilibrium outcome of the game discussed in Example 9.1.

However, as Dye and Sunder discuss, there are forces to control such a tendency. There would be investor reaction to a firm that chooses low quality accounting standards.

We pointed out in Section 12.4.2 that market forces reward managers who release full and timely information. Furthermore, a race to the bottom is inconsistent with the objectives of the IASB and FASB, which include high quality accounting standards.

Granted, network externalities would increase since investors would bear costs of having to learn more than one set of accounting standards. However, Dye and Sunder suggest that these costs would be relatively low. For example, analysts and other experts could specialize in interpreting a particular set of standards. Given securities market efficiency, the results of their analyses would quickly be incorporated into share market values, thereby price-protecting ordinary investors.

A benefit of competition in standard setting derives from the impossibility of calculating the socially correct extent of regulation as concluded in Chapter 12. A standard setter with no competition may attempt to maximize its influence by imposing more and more standards, as predicted by the interest group theory of regulation. As a result, the extent of regulation may go beyond its socially optimal level. Competition among standard setters would help to control this tendency since firms that did not like one set of standards could simply adopt the other, thereby causing the overzealous standard setter to "lose customers." However, this process need not degenerate into a race to the bottom since firms could signal their commitment to quality reporting by means of the set of standards they adopt. Of course, for such a signal to be credible, some means of *enforcing* proper application of the firm's chosen set of standards is needed. Such enforcement could be provided by a securities commission with sufficient powers and, hopefully, by an ethical auditing profession.

While the question of competition between standard setters is complex, these arguments suggest that there is a tradeoff between the benefits and costs of convergence to a single set of high quality standards. The best point on this tradeoff is not necessarily at full standards convergence, but depends on a country's social, legal, and institutional environment, and the difficulties this environment creates in applying the converged standards.

13.6.6 Summary of Accounting for International Capital Markets Integration

It should be emphasized that financial reporting that seems to be of lower quality than that of North America is not necessarily opportunistic, but may instead efficiently reflect differences in customs, institutional structures, government involvement, and enforcement.

Nevertheless, capital markets worldwide are becoming increasingly integrated. Better-working capital markets contribute to social welfare through lower cost of capital and increased domestic investment. Empirical evidence suggests that strong disclosure regulations and adequate enforcement contribute to better-working markets.

High quality financial reporting standards, such as those of the IASB, have a role to play in bringing about better-working markets. Indeed, empirical studies show that adoption of IASB standards is accompanied by higher earnings quality and increased foreign investment. However, adoption of IASB standards does not by itself guarantee higher quality reporting. Application of standards needs to be enforced by a strong regulatory environment and auditor liability. Even then, investors and standard setters need to be aware that different customs and institutional structures continue to affect actual reporting. If investors who invest in another country on the strength of IASB standards suffer losses arising from reporting failures, they may react by blaming the standards rather than their failure to realize the impact of country-specific factors on reporting quality. Since it is even more difficult to change customs and institutions than accounting standards, differences in foreign environments will likely persist for many years. As a result, complete integration of accounting standards will take some time if, indeed, it is desirable at all. In the meantime, some ability of firms to choose between competing sets of accounting standards should not be ruled out.

13.7 CONCLUSIONS AND SUMMING UP

In a sense, this whole book comes to a focus on standard setting. We saw, in Chapter 2, that under ideal conditions accounting and reporting standards are not needed, since there is only one way to account, on the basis of the present values of firms' future cash flows. Indeed, under ideal conditions one can question whether financial accounting is needed at all.

Fortunately, in view of our conclusion in Section 2.6 that accountants would not be needed under ideal conditions, such conditions do not exist. As a result, financial accounting becomes much more challenging. Information asymmetry is a major source of this challenge.

We have seen two major types of information asymmetry. The first is adverse selection. That is, managers and other insiders typically know more than outside investors about the state and prospects of the firm. Here, the accounting challenge is to convey information from inside to outside the firm, thereby improving investor decision-making, limiting the ability of insiders to exploit their information advantage, and enhancing the operation of capital markets.

The second type of information asymmetry is moral hazard. That is, the effort exerted by a manager is unobservable to shareholders and lenders in all but the smallest firms. Here, the accounting challenge is to provide an informative measure of managerial performance. This enables incentive contracts to motivate manager effort, protect lenders, and inform the managerial labour market.

It is important to realize that the accounting system that best meets the first challenge is unlikely to best meet the second, so that actual financial reporting represents a compromise between the two. Specifically, investors need decision-relevant information to help them predict future firm performance. This implies current value-based information since current values are generally the best predictors of future values. However, problems of volatility and possible low reliability of fair values reduce the informativeness of net income about manager performance. To the extent that historical cost accounting or, more generally, conservative accounting is less subject to problems of measuring manager performance, it can be argued that it better meets the challenge of enabling efficient contracts. Consequently, despite standard setters' concentration on current value accounting and their downgrading of reporting on stewardship, current value- and historical cost-based accounting must be traded off.

It is this need for financial reporting to fulfill a dual role of meeting investors' information needs and the needs of efficient contracting that creates the fundamental problem of financial accounting theory. Investors, including securities commissions acting on their behalf, push for additional information, including current value information. Management pushes the other way when they perceive that proposed standards will affect their flexibility under the contracts they have entered into, inhibit their ability to credibly communicate with the market through accounting policy choice, reduce their ability to hide poor performance through opportunistic earnings management, or choose a tradeoff between full disclosure to investors and the agency costs that are thus created. As mentioned, the standard setter must then seek a compromise between these conflicting interests. The structure of standard-setting bodies is designed to facilitate such a compromise.

With the increasing globalization of commerce, including securities markets, the need for international accounting standards will continue to expand. However, the difficulties of standard setting will also increase. In addition to investor–manager conflict, new constituencies arise representing different levels of economic development, different business practices, and different cultures. Standard-setting bodies, and investors, will have to adapt to take these additional challenges into account.

Questions and Problems

1. Contrast the public interest and interest group theories of regulation with respect to:

   a. The role of the regulatory body.

   b. Their implications for the amount of the regulated commodity or service (here, information) to be supplied. (CGA-Canada)

2. The interest group theory of regulation predicts constituency conflict surrounding the design and implementation of new accounting standards.

   Required

   a. Describe how the structure of standard setting is designed to facilitate the resolution of constituency conflicts surrounding new accounting standards.

   b. Explain why a super-majority vote by IASB and AcSB members is required to pass a new standard.

3. Numerous countries have adopted, in whole or in part, IASB accounting standards. Canada plans to adopt IASB standards from 2011. What are some of the benefits and costs to a country of adopting IASB standards?

4. In March 2004, the FASB issued an exposure draft of a standard proposing the expensing of ESOs. However, the proposal faced powerful opponents. These included large corpo-

rations such as Texas Instruments, Cisco Systems Inc., Intel Corporation, and Sun Microsystems, Inc., all of which were heavy ESO users. Also, bills were introduced in the U.S. Congress to override or water down the expensing requirement. For example, one such bill would have limited ESO expensing to the firm's top five officers. These bills were of concern, since Congress has the power to override the FASB.

Objections to the proposed standard were similar to those raised when the FASB attempted to implement a similar standard in 1994. These include the confusing of investors, damage to job creation and innovation, damage to the competitive position of U.S. industry, and unreliability of fair value ESO measures.

The proposed standard also has powerful proponents, including some congressional leaders and then-Chairman Greenspan of the Federal Reserve. Also, despite the opposing arguments, by early 2004 almost 500 U.S. corporations had voluntarily decided to expense their ESOs.

Required

a. In theory, what are the advantages of ESOs as a compensation device?

b. In practice, during the boom of the late twentieth century, what were the negative effects of ESOs on some managers' incentives and actions?

c. Are ESOs an expense? Explain why or why not.

d. With what theory of regulation are the claims of opponents of the proposed standard most consistent? With what theory are the FASB's actions in implementing the new standard most consistent? Explain your answers.

e. Suppose that you are a member of the FASB. Evaluate a proposal to expense ESOs in relation to the four criteria suggested in Section 13.5.

5. The article here reproduced from *The New York Times* (October 12, 1997) describes pressures to "kill" the FASB, and hand its duties over to the SEC. The reason for the pressure seems to be due to SFAS 133 (see Sections 7.3.4 and 7.3.5), which requires firms to fair value derivative instruments.

Politicians Threaten Accounting Integrity

Sixty years ago, an intense battle was waged inside the young Securities and Exchange Commission. There was no consensus about how to fix what all agreed was the deplorable accounting that was showing up in corporate financial reports.

On one side was the commission's new chairman, William O. Douglas, who thought the commission should promulgate its own standards. On the other was the S.E.C.'s chief accountant, Carman C. Blough, who thought the Government could not do a good job and wanted it left to the private sector, with S.E.C. oversight. On a 3–2 vote of the commission in 1938, Douglas lost.

Blough then persuaded the American Institute of Certified Public Accountants that it needed to get moving. After hearing Blough give a harsh speech noting more than 30 questionable accounting practices that had been approved by accountants, the institute set up a Committee on Accounting Procedure to make rules. That body was replaced by the Accounting Principles Board in 1959 and by the Financial Accounting Standards Board in 1973, as the rule makers gained more power and independence.

The arrangements have sometimes been cumbersome and slow. It has been more than a decade since the board took up the question of accounting for derivatives, and only now is it poised to issue a rule. But the process has produced the best accounting anywhere and helped to make New York the financial capital of the world. It would be hard for the S.E.C. to match the detailed expertise of the F.A.S.B. and its staff.

Nonetheless, a campaign is on to kill the F.A.S.B. The banks are furious over the new derivatives rule, which would force users of derivatives to record the market value of those instruments in their financial reports. The banks say the rule will confuse investors and scare off some companies that would benefit from using derivatives. They have lobbied hard in Congress, and both the House and Senate have held hearings to bash the F.A.S.B. on the issue. Last week, John Reed, the chairman of Citicorp, called for abolishing the F.A.S.B. and transferring its duties to the S.E.C.

Mr. Reed's suggestion, as it happened, was published in a letter to the editor of the *Wall Street Journal* on the same day that the Senate killed campaign finance reform. The sad reality today is that injecting politics into accounting carries with it a real risk regarding accounting integrity. It is not hard to imagine a future S.E.C. budget being held up by a Congressman, or confirmation of a future S.E.C. chairman delayed by a senator, amid quiet negotiations regarding the need to change an accounting rule that threatens— quite unfairly, of course—to penalize the profits, and perhaps hurt investors and employees, of a company that has been a substantial supporter of the legislator.

The F.A.S.B.'s new derivatives rule is not perfect, but it is an improvement over current practice. If need be, it can be changed later. But the wisdom of that rule is much less important than the preservation of a process that has worked well without a hint of impropriety. If the politicians succeed in killing this rule, as they did with an earlier proposal to change accounting for employee stock options, it is hard to see how the F.A.S.B. will survive. And that would pose a real threat to continued investor confidence.

It is time for businesses, even those that don't like the derivatives proposal, to tell the politicians to leave accounting alone.

Already The Oldest

Rule makers for American accounting:

Committee on Accounting Procedure
1938–1959   *21 years*

Accounting Principles Board
1959–1973   *14 years*

Financial Accounting Standard Board
1973–present   *24 years*

Source: Copyright © 1997 by the New York Times Co. Reprinted by permission.

Required

a. Use the interest group theory of regulation to explain the reasons for the campaign to kill the FASB. Why would certain bank executives prefer accounting standards to be set by the SEC?

b. Use the public interest theory of regulation to evaluate the costs and benefits of moving financial accounting standard setting to the SEC. Include in your answer an evaluation of the structure of the FASB. Also consider the effects of such a move on investor confidence in capital markets.

6. IAS 39, *Financial Instruments: Recognition and Measurement*, requires companies using IASB standards to fair-value many financial instruments including derivatives, effective January 1, 2005. This standard moved the accounting for financial instruments into substantial agreement with SFAS 115 and 133 and similar standards in Canada. It is an example of the ongoing movement towards international harmonization of accounting standards.

However, IAS 39 met substantial opposition from the European Union (EU), which has required its members to adopt IASB standards effective in 2005. The opposition arose from concerns of European banks and insurance companies, who claimed that fair value accounting would introduce volatility into their financial statements. As a result, the EU carved out the fair value option and hedging provisions of IAS 39.

Required

a. Why would banks and insurance companies be concerned about financial statement volatility introduced by IAS 39? Consider both the balance sheet and income statement in your answer.

b. As international harmonization of accounting standards progresses, there will be increasing pressure on the SEC to accept either FASB or IASB standards for firms under its jurisdiction. What would the costs and benefits to firms and investors be if the SEC was to accept either FASB or IASB standards? In your answer, consider the possibility of a "race to the bottom."

c. How will the EU carve-outs of IAS 39 affect the likelihood that the SEC will accept either FASB or IASB standards?

7. In a June 2007 article in *The New York Times*, Floyd Norris discusses recent moves by the SEC to speed up its proposed halting of reconciliation to U.S. GAAP by foreign companies whose shares are traded in the United States and whose financial statements are prepared according to IASB accounting standards. Mr. Norris indicates that the SEC will propose halting reconciliation beginning with 2008 financial statements. At the same time, the SEC may allow U.S. companies to prepare financial statements in accordance with IASB GAAP. If so, companies would be able to choose between two sets of GAAP, resulting in a degree of competition between IASB and FASB standard-setting bodies.

Mr. Norris mentions the possibility of a race to the bottom, also raised by Dye and Sunder (2001) outlined in Section 13.6.5. However, he raises an alternate possibility, of a "race to the top."

Note: In 2007, the SEC did decide to halt reconciliation.

Required

a. What is meant by "a race to the top" in this context?

b. Assuming that standard-setting bodies wish to maximize the number of firms using their standards, why might a race to the top, rather than a race to the bottom, result?

c. Assuming the SEC does drop its reconciliation requirement, what difficulties are created for investors who wish to use financial statements for investment decisions?

8. In its report to shareholders for its quarter ended April 30, 2007, TD Bank Financial Group reported the following items ($ million) in other comprehensive income:

– Change in unrealized gains and losses on
    available-for-sale securities, net of cash flow hedges $87

– Reclassification to earnings in respect of
    available-for-sale securities   (26)

– Change in gains and losses on derivative instruments
    designated as cash flow hedges   13

Note: For purposes of this question, treat the relevant provisions of the *CICA Handbook* as identical to SFAS 115, SFAS 130, and SFAS 133.

Required

a. Explain the nature of each of these three items.

b. What is the purpose of other comprehensive income?

c. TD includes its statement of other comprehensive income in a statement of changes in equity. What alternative treatment of other comprehensive income is also acceptable under U.S. (SFAS 130) and Canadian (*CICA Handbook*, Section 1530) GAAP? Why would TD choose the changes in equity alternative to report its other comprehensive income?

d. As an investor, which earnings measure, net income or comprehensive income, is most useful to you in deciding whether to buy, hold, or sell TD shares? Explain.

e. As a member of the Compensation Committee of TD's Board of Directors, which performance measure, net income or comprehensive income, is most useful to you in deciding on the amount of cash bonuses for senior officers for 2007? Explain.

9. In its 1999 annual report, Scotiabank's auditors qualified their audit report. The problem was with the bank's provision for credit losses. During 1999, Scotiabank decided to increase its general provision for credit losses on loans receivable by $700 million. This was in addition to a specific provision for loan losses on identified problem loans. The general provision applies to loans that have not as yet been specifically identified as in arrears.

Under GAAP, the $700 million increase in the general provision should be charged as an expense of the year. However, Scotiabank obtained permission from the Superintendent of Financial Institutions of Canada (OSFI) to charge $550 million of this amount ($314 million after tax) directly to retained earnings.

As a result, Scotiabank reported net income for 1999 of $1,551 million. Net incomes for 1998 and 1997 were $1,394 million and $1,514 million, respectively.

This direct charge to retained earnings was criticized in the financial media. For example, Eric Reguly, in *The Globe and Mail*, December 7, 1999, called it "an accounting sleight-of-hand that has never been used by the Big Five Canadian banks." Reguly describes the objections of the OSC which, however, could do nothing because the federal Bank Act (administered by OSFI) overrides the Ontario Securities Act. OSFI permitted the direct charge, according to Reguly, because it wanted banks to have a "thicker safety cushion."

Required

a. Use the public interest theory of regulation to justify OSFI's permission for the direct charge to retained earnings.

b. Use the interest group theory of regulation to explain OSFI's permission for the direct charge.

c. Given that the treatment was fully disclosed in the notes to Scotiabank's annual report, in the auditors' report, and in the media, how do you think the securities market would respond to this treatment?

10. Refer to Theory in Practice 13.1, concerning SFASs 130 and 115, in Section 13.3.2.

Required

a. Why does SFAS 115 require unrealized gains and losses on available-for-sale securities to be included in OCI rather than in net income?

b. If securities markets are fully efficient, would a strategy of trying to disguise gains trading by reporting OCI in a statement of changes in shareholders' equity rather than below net income work? Explain why or why not.

c. If securities markets are not fully efficient, would such a strategy work? Explain.

d. You are the auditor of a firm using this strategy. You object to it, and management responds that the strategy is clearly in accordance with GAAP since SFAS 130 allows OCI to be included in a separate statement apart from net income. Furthermore, if you do not accept it you will be forced to resign as auditor. This will also result in your loss of systems and tax consulting work for the client. Would you resign? Explain your decision.

11. The Sarbanes-Oxley Act was passed by the U.S. Congress in 2002, following financial reporting disasters of Enron Corp. and WorldCom Inc. (see Section 1.2). Section 404 of the act requires that senior management and an independent auditor certify the proper operation of a public company's controls over financial reporting.

Undoubtedly, Sarbanes-Oxley has benefited investors and contributed to restoration of investor confidence in capital markets, since it reduces investors' estimation risk that investment values will not suddenly disappear due, for example, to opportunistic manager behaviour covered up for a time by misleading financial reporting.

However, Section 404 has drawn increasing criticism from companies, due to the costs of implementing the section. These costs have been estimated to average as high as $4.36 million U.S. per firm for 2004, and up to $10 million for very large firms. Section 404 is particularly onerous for small companies since the costs of establishing, evaluating, and auditing internal controls over financial reporting contain a significant fixed cost component—they do not decrease in proportion to lower firm size. Also, United States Treasury Secretary Henry Paulson, in a November 2006 speech, stated that excessive regulation stifles innovation, and that a significant portion of management time, energy, and expense devoted to Section 404 might have been better spent on more direct business matters.

Furthermore, it appears that U. S. capital markets are losing market share to foreign capital markets such as those in London and Hong Kong. Foreign firms that had been previously attracted to listing their shares on U.S. capital markets, because of the availability of large amounts of capital and a share price premium due to lower investor estimation risk on well-regulated markets, are going elsewhere in increasing numbers.

These concerns led to the creation in the United States of the Committee on Capital Markets Regulation, an independent panel of business and academic leaders. The Committee's first report, issued in December 2006, identified reasons for lower market share. These included foreign companies' fear of lawsuits, perceived overzealous regulation by agencies such as the SEC, and costs imposed by Section 404 of Sarbanes-Oxley. Among the Committee's recommendations were easing of Section 404 and measures to reduce the number of prosecutions and lawsuits. Also, foreign companies should be exempt from some Sarbanes-Oxley requirements if they meet similar regulations in their home countries.

In 2007, the SEC announced some relaxation of Section 404. Managers were given some flexibility to identify and test only the most critical financial reporting risks, and the audit requirements were reduced.

In Canada, NI 52-109 of the CSA proposes similar requirements to Section 404, but does not require auditor certification.

Required

a. Certifying the adequacy of companies' controls over their financial reporting is a form of information production. It is difficult for a regulator to determine the socially correct amount of information to require. What is the socially correct amount of information? Did Section 404 of the Sarbanes-Oxley Act require too much information production or too little? In your answer, consider both the costs and the benefits of Section 404.

b. The Committee report criticized the SEC, recommending that it should adopt a principles-based approach, focused on establishing general rules of behaviour for capital market participants and monitoring the operation of these rules to ensure they were accomplishing their desired effect of protecting investors (this is somewhat ironic since the SEC has urged accounting standard setters to become more principles-based—see Section 13.4). The Committee felt that the SEC was too rules-oriented—issuing too many detailed rules and regulations, the enforcement of which sidetracked it into securing settlements and convictions for violations with relatively little attention to whether the rules and regulations were cost effective in improving the operation of capital markets.

Is a principles-based approach to regulation of financial accounting and reporting feasible in the complex environment in which securities commissions, auditors, and accountants operate? Justify your answer.

12. Insurance companies have developed a product called **finite insurance**. A client firm enters into an insurance contract under which it pays annual premiums that sum to an amount equal to or close to the policy coverage. For example, a firm may take out a three-year policy to protect itself against natural disasters, with coverage of $1,500. It pays an annual premium of $500, or $1,500 over the policy term. If a loss occurs, the insurer pays

up to the $1,500 maximum. If no loss occurs, the $1,500 of premiums are returned to the firm. The insurance company will charge a fee for this service.

Note that the firm taking out the insurance bears the risk, not the insurer, since the firm does not recover its premiums paid to the extent there are policy claims. Why would a firm pay a fee for a policy such as this? A reason is that the policy acts as an income smoothing device. The firm may not be concerned about its ability to withstand the loss financially, but may be concerned about the "hit" to reported earnings in the event a major loss takes place. By taking out the finite insurance policy, the loss is recorded as an insurance expense over the term of the policy (if there is no loss, the return of premiums paid will result in a large credit to earnings, however the firm may be more concerned about avoiding a large loss than reporting a large gain).

From the insurer's standpoint, the question arises whether the premiums received from the client represent premium income, or simply a loan from the client. In this regard, the insurance industry has a 10/10 rule: the insurer should face at a minimum a 10% chance of losing 10% of the policy coverage if the premiums are to be regarded as income. Under this rule, if the total premiums to be paid are equal to or less than 90% of the policy coverage, and if there is at least a 10% chance of loss, the insurer is deemed to be bearing enough risk that premiums are regarded as income.

American International Group (AIG) is a large multinational insurance company based in the United States, with shares traded on the New York Stock Exchange. During 2000–2001, AIG assumed $500 million of finite insurance contracts from General Re Corp., another insurance company. General Re paid over the $500 million of premiums it had collected for these policies to AIG. Thus, in the relationship between the firms taking out the $500 million of finite insurance and AIG, AIG is now in the role of insurer. AIG paid General Re a $5 million fee for taking over these contracts.

At first glance, this deal seems illogical for AIG. When the finite insurance contracts expire, AIG would have to repay the $500 million received from General Re to the various firms that had taken out the finite insurance, less any claims it may have paid. Consequently, its net cash flows would be zero. Why would AIG pay a $5 million fee (instead of receiving a fee) for taking over the contracts when it had nothing to gain?

On closer scrutiny, however, it turned out that investors had been concerned that AIG did not have sufficient reserves (insurance companies are required to create reserves to help ensure they can meet policy claims). AIG credited the $500 million received from General Re to revenue, then transferred the same amount from earnings to reserves. It was thus able to increase its reserves without penalizing its earnings.

In February 2005, AIG received subpoenas from the Office of the Attorney General of the State of New York and the SEC relating to its accounting for this transaction. Its stock price plummeted. In March 2005, AIG's directors dismissed CEO Maurice "Hank" Greenberg, and CFO Howard I. Smith. The company also issued a statement that due to the lack of risk transfer, the payment from General Re should have been accounted for as a loan rather than revenue. Financial statements for five years ending with 2004 were subsequently restated. Earnings over this period were reduced by 10%, about $3.9 billion, as a result of this and other accounting manipulations.

In early 2006, media reports indicated that AIG would pay over $1.5 billion to settle lawsuits arising from the charges against it, and would make changes to its corporate governance process. The settlement did not apply to Greenberg and Smith, who also faced lawsuits of their own.

Required

a. From the standpoint of a firm that takes out a finite insurance policy, evaluate finite insurance as an income smoothing device.

b. A firm has just suffered a large non-recurring uninsured loss. The firm is concerned about securities market reaction to lower reported net income this quarter if the loss is charged to current operations. The firm approaches an insurance company with a request to *retroactively* sell it a finite insurance policy with face value equal to the amount of the loss. Under such a policy, the firm would immediately receive a payment from the insurer equal to its loss, which would be credited to current net income. The firm would then pay the policy premium quarterly, over a five-year period, with each payment charged to insurance expense for that quarter. The insurance company agrees to this arrangement.

You are the firm's auditor and are debating whether or not to qualify your report. Should you? If you did qualify, what would be your basis for qualification?

c. Do you agree that the $500 million received by AIG from General Re should have been accounted for as a loan rather than as income? Explain.

d. Should a new accounting standard to prevent the use of finite insurance contracts be implemented? In your answer, draw on the question of rules-based versus principles-based accounting standards.

Notes

1. Prior to the 2009 effective date of the revisions to IAS 1, unrealized gains and losses are included as separate items in shareholders' equity.

2. In this regard, we mentioned in Section 1.7 that standard setters are considering dichotomization of the income statement into several components, including operations and other comprehensive income. As noted there, the extent to which any such breakdown will better report on manager stewardship remains to be seen.

3. This agreement was reaffirmed in 2006.

Bibliography

ABARBANELL, J.S. and B.J. BUSHEE, "Fundamental Analysis, Future Earnings, and Stock Prices," *Journal of Accounting Research* (Spring, 1997), pp. 1–24.

ABARBANELL, J.S., W.N. LANEN, and R.E. VERRECHIA, "Analysts' Forecasts as Proxies for Investor Beliefs in Empirical Research," *Journal of Accounting and Economics* (July, 1995), pp. 31–60.

ABARBANELL, J. and R. LEHAVY, "Can Stock Recommendations Predict Earnings Management and Analysts' Earnings Forecast Errors?" *Journal of Accounting Research* (March, 2003), pp. 1–31.

ABOODY, D., M. BARTH, and R. KASZNIK, "SFAS 123 Stock-Based Compensation Expense and Equity Market Values," *The Accounting Review* (April, 2004), pp. 251–275.

ABOODY, D. and R. KASZNIK, "CEO Stock Option Awards and the Timing of Corporate Voluntary Disclosures," *Journal of Accounting and Economics* (February, 2000), pp. 73–100.

ACKERT, L.F., and B.F. SMITH, "Stock Price Volatility, Ordinary Dividends, and Other Cash Flows to Shareholders," *The Journal of Finance* (September, 1993), pp. 1147–1160.

AGGARWAL, R.K. and A.A. SAMWICK, "Executive Compensation, Strategic Competition, and Relative Performance Evaluation: Theory and Evidence," *The Journal of Finance* (December, 1999), pp. 1999–2043.

AHMED, A.S., B. BILLINGS, M.S. HARRIS, and R. M. MORTON, "Accounting Conservatism and Cost of Debt," Working paper, School of Management, Syracuse University (March, 2000).

AHMED, A.S., E. KILIC, and G.J. LOBO, "Does Recognition versus Disclosure Matter? Evidence from Value-relevance of Banks' Recognized and Disclosed Derivative Financial Instruments," *The Accounting Review* (May, 2006), pp. 567–588.

AKERLOF, G.A., "The Market for 'Lemons': Quality Uncertainty and the Market Mechanism," *Quarterly Journal of Economics* (August, 1970), pp. 488–500.

ALCHIAN, A., "Uncertainty, Evolution and Economic Theory," *Journal of Political Economy* (June, 1950), pp. 211–221.

AMERICAN ACCOUNTING ASSOCIATION COMMITTEE TO PREPARE A STATEMENT OF BASIC ACCOUNTING THEORY, "*A Statement of Basic Accounting Theory*" (American Accounting Association, 1966).

AMERICAN ACCOUNTING ASSOCIATION FINANCIAL ACCOUNTING STANDARDS COMMITTEE, "Equity Valuation Models and Measuring Goodwill Impairment" *Accounting Horizons* (June, 2001), pp. 161–170.

AMERICAN INSTITUTE OF CERTIFIED PUBLIC ACCOUNTANTS STUDY GROUP ON THE OBJECTIVES OF FINANCIAL STATEMENTS, "*Objectives of Financial Statements*" (New York, NY: AICPA, 1973).

ANILOSKI, C., MEI FENG, and D.J. SKINNER, "Does Earnings Guidance Affect Market Returns? The Nature and Information Content of Aggregate Earnings Guidance," *Journal of Accounting and Economics* (September, 2007), pp. 36–63.

ANTLE, R. and A. SMITH, "An Empirical Examination of the Relative Performance Evaluation of Corporate Executives," *Journal of Accounting Research* (Spring, 1986), pp. 1–39.

ARROW, K. J., *Social Choice and Individual Values*, Cowles Foundation Monograph (New York, NY: John Wiley, 1963).

ARYA, A., J. FELLINGHAM, and J. GLOVER, "Teams, Repeated Tasks and Implicit Incentives," *Journal of Accounting and Economics* (May, 1997), pp. 7–30.

ARYA, A., J. GLOVER, and S. SUNDER, "Earnings Management and the Revelation Principle," *Review of Accounting Studies* (1998), pp. 7–34.

ARYA, A. and B. MITTENDORF, "Using Disclosure to Influence Herd Behavior and Alter Competition," *Journal of Accounting and Economics* (December, 2005), pp. 231–246.

AUMANN, R.J., "War and Peace," Nobel Prize Lecture (December 8, 2005), available at http://nobelprize.org/nobel_prizes/economics/laureates/2005/aumann-lecture.html

BABER, W.R., S. JANAKIRAMAN, and S-H. KANG, "Investment Opportunities and the Structure of Executive Compensation," *Journal of Accounting and Economics* (June, 1996), pp. 297–318.

BABER, W.R., S-H. KANG, and K.R. KUMAR, "The Explanatory Power of Earnings Levels vs. Earnings Changes in the Context of Executive Compensation," *The Accounting Review* (October, 1999), pp. 459–472.

BAIMAN, S. and R. E. VERRECCHIA, "The Relation Among Capital Markets, Financial Disclosure, Production Efficiency, and Insider Trading," *Journal of Accounting Research* (Spring, 1996), pp. 1–22.

BALL, R. and E. BARTOV, "How Naive Is the Stock Market's Use of Earnings Information?" *Journal of Accounting and Economics* (June, 1996), pp. 319–337.

BALL, R. and P. BROWN, "An Empirical Evaluation of Accounting Income Numbers," *Journal of Accounting Research* (Autumn, 1968), pp. 159–178.

BALL, R. and S.P. KOTHARI, "Nonstationary Expected Returns: Implications for Tests of Market Efficiency and Serial Correlation in Returns," *Journal of Financial Economics* (1989), pp. 51–74.

BALL, R., S.P. KOTHARI, and A. ROBIN, "The Effect of International Institutional Factors on Properties of Accounting Earnings," *Journal of Accounting and Economics* (February, 2000), pp. 1–51.

BALL, R., A. ROBIN, and J.S. WU, "Incentives versus Standards: Properties of Accounting Income in Four East Asian Companies," *Journal of Accounting and Economics* (December, 2003), pp. 235–270.

BALL, R., and L. SHIVAKUMAR, "The Role of Accruals in Asymmetrically Timely Gain and Loss Recognition," *Journal of Accounting Research* (May, 2006), pp. 207–242.

BANDYOPADHYAY, S., "Market Reaction to Earnings Announcements of SE and FC Firms in the Oil and Gas Industry," *The Accounting Review* (October, 1994), pp. 657–674.

BANKER, R.D. and S. DATAR, "Sensitivity, Precision, and Linear Aggregation of Signals for Performance Evaluation," *Journal of Accounting Research* (Spring, 1989), pp. 21–39.

BARBERIS, N., A. SHLEIFER and R. VISHNEY, "A Model of Investor Sentiment," *Journal of Financial Economics* (1998), pp. 307–343.

BARNEA, A., J. RONEN, and S. SADAN, "Classificatory Smoothing of Income with Extraordinary Items," *The Accounting Review* (January, 1976), pp. 110–122.

BARRON, O., J. PRATT, and J.D. STICE, "Misstatement Direction, Litigation Risk, and Planned Audit Investment," *Journal of Accounting Research* (December, 2001), pp. 449–462.

BARTH, M.E., W.H. BEAVER, and W.R. LANDSMAN, "Value-Relevance of Banks' Fair Value Disclosures under SFAS 107," *The Accounting Review* (October, 1996), pp. 513–537.

BARTH, M.E., G. CLINCH, and T. SHIBANO, "Market Effects of Recognition and Disclosure," *Journal of Accounting Research* (September, 2003), pp. 581–609.

BARTH, M.E., J.A. ELLIOTT, and M.W. FINN, "Market Rewards Associated with Patterns of Increasing Earnings," *Journal of Accounting Research* (Autumn, 1999), pp. 387–413.

BARTH, M.E., W. LANDSMAN, and M. LANG, "International Accounting Standards and Accounting Quality," Working paper, Stanford University (March, 2005).

BARTH, M.E., R. LANDSMAN, M. LANG, and C. WILLIAMS, "Accounting Quality: International Accounting Standards and U.S. GAAP," Working paper, Stanford University (March, 2006).

BARTON, J. and M. MERCER, "To Blame or Not to Blame: Analysts' Reactions to External Explanations for Poor Financial Performance," *Journal of Accounting and Economics* (September, 2005), pp. 509–533.

BARTOV, E., D. GIVOLY, and C. HAYN, "The Rewards to Meeting or Beating Earnings Expectations," *Journal of Accounting and Economics* (June, 2002), pp.173–204.

BARTOV, E. and P. MOHANRAM, "Private Information, Earnings Manipulation, and Executive Stock Option Exercise," *The Accounting Review* (October, 2004), pp. 889–920.

BARTOV, E., S. RADHAKRISHNAN, and S. KRINSKY, "Investor Sophistication and Patterns in Stock Returns after Earnings Announcements," *The Accounting Review* (January, 2000), pp. 43–63.

BASU, S., "The Conservation Principle and the Asymmetric Timeliness of Earnings," *Journal of Accounting and Economics* (December, 1997), pp. 3–37.

BCE INC., *1997 Annual Report* (Montreal, QC: BCE Inc., 1997).

BEAVER, W.H., "The Information Content of Annual Earnings Announcements," *Journal of Accounting Research* (Supplement, 1968), pp. 67–92.

BEAVER, W.H., "What Should be the FASB's Objectives?" *The Journal of Accountancy* (August, 1973), pp. 49–56.

BEAVER, W.H., *Financial Reporting: An Accounting Revolution*, Second Edition (Englewood Cliffs, NJ: Prentice Hall, 1989).

BEAVER, W.H., R. CLARKE, and W.F. WRIGHT, "The Association Between Unsystematic Security Returns and the Magnitude of Earnings Forecast Errors," *Journal of Accounting Research* (Autumn, 1979), pp. 316–340.

BEAVER, W.H. and J. DEMSKI, "The Nature of Income Measurement," *The Accounting Review* (January, 1979), pp. 38–46.

BEAVER, W.H., P. KETTLER, and M. SCHOLES, "The Association Between Market-Determined and Accounting-Determined Risk Measures," *The Accounting Review* (October, 1970), pp. 654–682.

BEAVER, W.H. and W.R. LANDSMAN, *The Incremental Information Content of FAS 33 Disclosures* (Stamford, CT: FASB, 1983).

BEAVER, W.H. and S.G. RYAN, "Conditional and Unconditional Conservatism: Concepts and Modeling," *Review of Accounting Studies* (September, 2005), pp. 269–309.

BEBCHUK, L.A., J.M. FRIED, and D.I. WALKER, "Managerial Power and Rent Extraction in the Design of Executive Compensation," *The University of Chicago Law Review* (2002), pp. 751–846.

BEGLEY, J. and G.A. FELTHAM, "The Relation between Market Values, Earnings Forecasts, and Reported Earnings," *Contemporary Accounting Research* (Spring, 2002), pp. 1–48.

BENSTON, G.J., "Required Disclosure and the Stock Market: An Evaluation of the Securities Exchange Act of 1934," *American Economic Review* (March, 1973), pp. 132–155.

BERGER, P.G. and R. HANN, "The Impact of SFAS 131 on Information and Monitoring," *Journal of Accounting Research* (May, 2003), pp. 163–223.

BERNARD, V.L., "Cross-Sectional Dependance and Problems in Inference in Market-Based Accounting Research," *Journal of Accounting Research* (Spring, 1987), pp. 1–48.

BERNARD, V.L., "Capital Markets Research in Accounting During the 1980s: A Critical Review," working paper, University of Michigan (1989).

BERNARD, V.L. and R.G. RULAND, "The Incremental Information Content of Historical Cost and Current Cost Income Numbers: Time Series Analysis for 1962–1980," *The Accounting Review* (October, 1987), pp. 707–722.

BERNARD, V.L. and D.J. SKINNER, "What Motivates Managers' Choice of Discretionary Accruals?" *Journal of Accounting and Economics* (August-December, 1996), pp. 313–325.

BERNARD, V.L. and J. THOMAS, "Post-Earnings Announcement Drift: Delayed Price Reaction or Risk Premium?" *Journal of Accounting Research* (Supplement, 1989), pp. 1–36.

BERTRAND, M. and S. MALLAINATHAN, "Are CEOs Rewarded for Luck?: The Ones Without Principles Are," *Quarterly Journal of Economics* (2001), pp. 901–929.

BLACK, F. and M. SCHOLES, "The Pricing of Options and Corporate Liabilities," *Journal of Political Economy* (May/June, 1973), pp. 637–654.

BLAZENKO, G. and W.R. SCOTT, "A Model of Standard Setting in Auditing," *Contemporary Accounting Research* (Fall, 1986), pp. 68–92.

BOLAND, L.A. and I.M. GORDON, "Criticizing Positive Accounting Theory," *Contemporary Accounting Research* (Fall, 1992), pp. 147–170.

BOONE, J.P., "Revisiting the Reportedly Weak Value Relevance of Oil and Gas Asset Present Values: The Role of Measurement Error, Model Misspecification, and Time Period Idiosyncrasy," *The Accounting Review* (January, 2002), pp. 73–106.

BOTOSAN, C.A. and M.A. PLUMLEE, "A Re-examination of Disclosure Level and the Expected Cost of Equity Capital," *Journal of Accounting Research* (March, 2002), pp. 21–40.

BOWEN, R.M., L. DuCHARME, and D. SHORES, "Stakeholders' Implicit Claims and Accounting Method Choice," *Journal of Accounting and Economics* (December, 1995), pp. 255–295.

BOYLE, P. and P. BOYLE, *Derivatives: The Tools That Changed Finance* (London: Risk Books, 2001).

BRAV, A. and J.B. HEATON, "Competing Theories of Financial Anomalies," *The Review of Financial Studies* (2002), pp. 575–606.

BROWN, L.D., R.L. HAGERMAN, P.A. GRIFFIN, and M. ZMIJEWSKI, "Security Analyst Superiority Relative to Univariate Time-Series Models in Forecasting Quarterly Earnings," *Journal of Accounting and Economics* (April, 1987), pp. 61–87.

BROWN, L.D. and J.C.Y. HAN, "Do Stock Prices Fully Reflect the Implications of Current Earnings for Future Earnings for *ARI* Firms?" *Journal of Accounting Research* (Spring, 2000), pp. 149–164.

BROWN, R.G. and K.S. JOHNSTON, *Paciolo on Accounting* (New York, NY: McGraw-Hill, 1963).

BROWN, S., K. LO, and T. LYS, "Use of R^2 in Accounting Research: Measuring Changes in Value Relevance Over the Last Four Decades," *Journal of Accounting and Economics* (December, 1999), pp. 83–115.

BROWN, S.J. and J.B. WARNER, "Measuring Security Price Performance," *Journal of Financial Economics* (September, 1980), pp. 205–258.

BURGSTAHLER, D. and I. DICHEV, "Earnings Management to Avoid Earnings Decreases and Losses," *Journal of Accounting and Economics* (December, 1997), pp. 99–126.

BUSHMAN, R.M., E. ENGEL, and A. SMITH, "An Analysis of the Relation between the Stewardship and Valuation Roles of Earnings," *Journal of Accounting Research* (March, 2006), pp. 53–83.

BUSHMAN, R.M. and R.J. INDJEJIKIAN, "Accounting Income, Stock Price and Managerial Compensation," *Journal of Accounting and Economics* (January/April/July, 1993), pp. 3–23.

BUSHMAN, R.M., R.J. INDJEJIKIAN, and A. SMITH, "CEO Compensation: The Role of Individual Performance Evaluation," *Journal of Accounting and Economics* (April, 1996), pp. 161–193.

BUSHMAN, R.M. and J.D. PIOTROSKI, "Financial Reporting Incentives for Conservative Accounting: The Influence of Legal and Political Institutions," *Journal of Accounting and Economics* (October, 2006), pp. 107–148.

CALLEN, J.J. and D. SEGAL, "Do Accruals Drive Firm-Level Stock Returns? A Variance Decomposition Analysis," *Journal of Accounting Research* (June, 2004), pp. 527–560.

CANADIAN INSTITUTE OF CHARTERED ACCOUNTANTS, *CICA Handbook,* (Toronto, ON: CICA, 2006).

CHEN, Q., T. HEMMER, and Y. ZHANG, "On the Relation between Conservatism in Accounting Standards and Incentives for Earnings Management," *Journal of Accounting Research* (June, 2007), pp.541–565.

CHEN, S., M.L. DEFOND, and C.W. PARK, "Voluntary Disclosure of Balance Sheet Information in Quarterly Earnings Announcements," *Journal of Accounting and Economics* (June, 2002), pp. 229–251.

CHEN, S., D. MATSUMOTO, and S. RAJGOPAL, "Is Silence Golden? An Empirical Analysis of Firms that Stop Giving Quarterly Earnings Guidance," Working paper, University of Washington (January 3, 2006).

CHORDIA, T. and l. SHIVAKUMAR, "Inflation Illusion and Post-Earnings-Announcement Drift," *Journal of Accounting Research* (September, 2005), pp. 521–556.

CHRISTENSEN, J., "Communication in Agencies," *The Bell Journal of Economics* (Autumn, 1981), pp. 661–674.

CHRISTENSEN, P.O., J.S. DEMSKI, and H. FRIMOR, "Accounting Policies in Agencies with Moral Hazard," *Journal of Accounting Research* (September, 2002), pp. 1071–1090.

CHRISTIE, A.A. and J. ZIMMERMAN, "Efficient and Opportunistic Choices of Accounting Procedures: Corporate Control Contests," *The Accounting Review* (October, 1994), pp. 539–566.

CLARKSON, P., A. DONTOH, G.D. RICHARD-SON, and S. SEFCIK, "The Voluntary Inclusion of Earnings Forecasts in IPO Prospectuses," *Contemporary Accounting Research* (Spring, 1992), pp. 601–626.

COHEN, D.A., A. DEY, T.Z. LYS, and S.V. SUNDER, "Earnings Announcement Premia and the Limits to Arbitrage, *Journal of Accounting and Economics* (July, 2007), pp. 153–180.

COLLINS, D.W. and S.P. KOTHARI, "An Analysis of the Intertemporal and Cross-Sectional Determinants of Earnings Response Coefficients," *Journal of Accounting and Economics* (July, 1989), pp. 143–181.

CORE, J.E., R.W. HOLTHAUSEN, and D.F. LARCKER, "Corporate Governance, Chief Executive Officer Compensation, and Firm per-formance," *Journal of Financial Economics* (1999), pp. 371–406.

COTTER, J., I. TUNA, and P.D. WYSOCKI, "Expectations Management and Beatable Targets: How Do Analysts React to Explicit Earnings Guidance?" *Contemporary Accounting Research* (Fall, 2006), pp. 593–624.

COURTEAU, L., J. KAO, and G.D. RICHARDSON, "Equity Valuation Employing the Ideal versus Ad Hoc Terminal Value Expression," *Contemporary Accounting Research* (Winter, 2001), pp. 625–661.

COVRIG, V.M., M.L. DEFOND, and M. HUNG, "Home Bias, Foreign Mutual Fund Holdings, and the Voluntary Adoption of International Accounting Standards," *Journal of Accounting Research* (March, 2007), pp. 41–70.

CRAWFORD, V.P. and J. SOBEL, "Strategic Information Transmission," *Econometrica* (November, 1982), pp. 1431–1451.

DANIEL, K.D., D. HIRSHLEIFER, and A. SUBRAHMANYAM, "Investor Psychology and Security Market Investor Under- and Over-Reactions," *Journal of Finance* (December, 1998), pp. 1839–1885.

DANIEL, K.D., D. HIRSHLEIFER, and A. SUBRAHMANYAM, "Overconfidence, Arbitrage, and Equilibrium Asset Pricing," *The Journal of Finance* (2001), pp. 921–965.

DANIEL, K.D. and S. TITMAN, "Market Efficiency in an Irrational World," *Financial Analysts' Journal* (1999), pp. 28–40.

DARROUGH, M.N., "Disclosure Policy and Competition: Cournot vs. Bertrand," *The Accounting Review* (July, 1993), pp. 534–561.

DARROUGH, M.N. and N.M. STOUGHTON, "Financial Disclosure Policy in an Entry Game," *Journal of Accounting and Economics* (January, 1990), pp. 219–243.

DATAR, S.M., G.A. FELTHAM, and J.S. HUGHES, "The Role of Audits and Audit Quality in Valuing New Issues," *Journal of Accounting and Economics* (March, 1991), pp. 3–49.

DATAR, S.M., S.C. KULP, and R.A. LAMBERT, "Balancing Performance Measures, *Journal of Accounting Research* (June, 2001), pp. 75–92.

DE ANGELO, H., L.E. DE ANGELO, and D.J. SKINNER, "Accounting Choice in Troubled

Companies," *Journal of Accounting and Economics* (January, 1994), pp. 113–143.

DE ANGELO, L.E., "Auditor Size and Auditor Quality," *Journal of Accounting and Economics* (December, 1981), pp. 183–199.

DE BONDT, W.F.M. and R. THALER, "Does the Stock Market Overreact?" *The Journal of Finance* (July, 1985), pp. 793–805.

DECHOW, P.M., "Accounting Earnings and Cash Flows as Measures of Firm Performance: The Role of Accounting Accruals," *Journal of Accounting and Economics* (July, 1994), pp. 3–42.

DECHOW, P.M. and I. DICHEV, "The Quality of Accruals and Earnings: The Role of Accrual Estimation Errors," *The Accounting Review* (Supplement, 2002), pp. 35–59.

DECHOW, P.M., A.P. HUTTON, and R.G. SLOAN, "An Empirical Assessment of the Residual Income Valuation Model," *Journal of Accounting and Economics* (January, 1999), pp. 1–34.

DECHOW, P.M., R.G. SLOAN, and A.P. SWEENEY, "Detecting Earnings Management," *The Accounting Review* (April, 1995), pp. 193–225.

DECHOW, P.M., R.G. SLOAN, AND A.P. SWEENEY, "Causes and Consequences of Earnings Manipulation: An Analysis of Firms Subject to Enforcement Actions by the SEC," *Contemporary Accounting Research* (Spring, 1996), pp. 1–36.

DEFOND, M.L. and J. JIAMBALVO, "Debt Covenant Violation and Manipulation of Accruals," *Journal of Accounting and Economics* (January, 1994), pp. 145–176.

DELONG, J.B., A. SHLEIFER, L. SUMMERS, and R.J. WALDMANN, "Positive Feedback Investment Strategies and Destabilizing Rational Speculation," *Journal of Finance* (June, 1990), pp. 375–395.

DEMSKI, J., *Information Analysis* (Reading, MA: Addison-Wesley, 1972).

DEMSKI, J., "The General Impossibility of Normative Accounting Standards," *The Accounting Review* (1973), pp. 718–723.

DEMSKI, J., "Positive Accounting Theory: A Review," *Accounting, Organizations and Society* (October, 1988), pp. 623–629.

DEMSKI, J. and D.E.M. SAPPINGTON, "Delegated Expertise," *Journal of Accounting Research* (Spring, 1987), pp. 68–89.

DEMSKI, J. and D.E.M. SAPPINGTON, "Fully Revealing Income Measurement," *The Accounting Review* (April, 1990), pp. 363–383.

DHALIWAL, D.S., K.J. LEE, and N.L. FARGHER, "The Association Between Unexpected Earnings and Abnormal Security Returns in the Presence of Financial Leverage," *Contemporary Accounting Research* (Fall, 1991), pp. 20–41.

DHALIWAL, D.S., K.R. SUBRAMANYAM, and R. TREZEVANT, "Is Comprehensive Income Superior to Net Income as a Measure of Firm Performance?" *Journal of Accounting and Economics* (January, 1999), pp. 43–67.

DIAMOND, D.W. and R.E. VERRECCHIA, "Disclosure, Liquidity, and the Cost of Capital," *The Journal of Finance* (September, 1991), pp. 1325–1359.

DICHEV, I.D. and D.J. SKINNER, "Large-Sample Evidence on the Debt Covenant Hypothesis," *Journal of Accounting Research* (September, 2002), pp. 1091–1123.

DOMTAR, *Annual Report 1996* (Montreal, QC: Domtar Inc., 1997).

DORAN, B.M., D.W. COLLINS, and D.S. DHALIWAL, "The Information Content of Historical Cost Earnings Relative to Supplemental Reserve-Based Accounting Data in the Extractive Petroleum Industry," *The Accounting Review* (July, 1988), pp. 389–413.

DOYLE, J.T., R.J. LUNDHOLM, and M.T. SOLIMAN, "The Predictive Value of Expenses Excluded from Pro Forma Earnings," *Review of Accounting Studies* (2003), pp. 145–174.

DOYLE, J.T., R.J. LUNDHOLM, and M.T. SOLIMAN, "The Extreme Future Stock Returns Following I/B/E/S Earnings Surprises," *Journal of Accounting Research* (December, 2006), pp. 849–887.

DURNEV, A., R. MORCK, B. YEUNG and P. ZAROWIN, "Does Greater Firm-Specific Return Variation Mean More or Less Informed Stock Pricing?" *Journal of Accounting Research* (December, 2003), pp. 797–836.

DURTSCHI, C. and P. EASTON, "Earnings Management? The Shapes of the Frequency Distributions of Earnings Metrics Are Not Evidence Ipso Facto," *Journal of Accounting Research* (September, 2005), pp. 557–592.

DYCKMAN, T.R. and A.J. SMITH, "Financial Accounting and Reporting by Oil and Gas Producing Companies: A Study of Information Effects," *Journal of Accounting and Economics* (March, 1979), pp. 45–76.

DYE, R.A., "Disclosure of Nonproprietary Information," *Journal of Accounting Research* (Spring, 1985), pp. 123–145.

DYE, R.A., "Proprietary and Nonproprietary Disclosures," *Journal of Business* (April, 1986), pp. 331–366.

DYE, R.A., "Earnings Management in an Overlapping Generations Model," *Journal of Accounting Research* (Autumn, 1988), pp. 195–235.

DYE, R.A. and S. SUNDER, "Why Not Allow FASB and IASB Standards to Compete in the U.S.?" *Accounting Horizons* (September, 2001), pp. 257–271.

EASLEY, D. and M. O'HARA, "Information and the Cost of Capital," *The Journal of Finance* (August, 2004), pp. 1553–1583.

EASTON, P.D. and T.S. HARRIS, "Earnings as an Explanatory Variable for Returns," *Journal of Accounting Research* (Spring, 1991), pp. 19–36.

EASTON, P.D., T.S. HARRIS, and J.A. OHLSON, "Aggregate Accounting Earnings Can Explain Most of Security Returns," *Journal of Accounting and Economics* (June/September, 1992), pp. 119–142.

EASTON, P.D. and M.E. ZMIJEWSKI, "Cross-Sectional Variation in the Stock-Market Response to Accounting Earnings Announcements," *Journal of Accounting and Economics* (July, 1989), pp. 117–141.

ECKER, F., J. FRANCIS, I. KIM, P.M. OLSSON, and K. SCHIPPER, "A Returns-Based Representation of Earnings Quality," *The Accounting Review* (July, 2006), pp. 749–780.

ECKERN, S. and R. WILSON, "On the Theory of the Firm in an Economy with Incomplete Markets," *The Bell Journal of Economics and Management Science* (Spring, 1974), pp. 171–180.

EINHORN, E., "The Nature of the Interaction between Mandatory and Voluntary Disclosures," *Journal of Accounting Research* (September, 2005), pp. 593–621.

EINHORN, E., "Voluntary Disclosure under Uncertainty about the Reporting Objective," *Journal of Accounting and Economics* (July, 2007), pp. 245–274.

ELESWARAPU, V.R., R. THOMPSON, and K. VENKATARAMAN, "Measuring the Fairness of Regulation Fair Disclosure through its Impact on Trading Costs and Information Asymmetry," *Journal of Financial and Quantitative Analysis* (2004), pp. 209–25

ELLIOTT, J.A. and J.D. HANNA, "Repeated Accounting Write-Offs and the Information Content of Earnings," *Journal of Accounting Research* (Supplement, 1996), pp. 135–169.

ELLIOTT, J.A., J.D. HANNA, and W.H. SHAW, "The Evaluation by the Financial Markets of Changes in Bank Loan Loss Reserve Levels," *The Accounting Review* (October, 1991), pp. 847–861.

ELY K. and G. WAYMIRE, "Accounting Standard-Setting Organizations and Earnings Relevance: Longitudinal Evidence from NYSE Common Stocks, 1927–93,"*Journal of Accounting Research* (Autumn, 1999), pp. 293–317.

EUROPEAN CENTRAL BANK, "Fair Value Accounting in the Banking Sector," *Comment* (November, 2001).

EVANS, J.H. and S.S. SRIDHAR, "Multiple Control Systems, Accrual Accounting, and Earnings Management," *Journal of Accounting Research* (Spring, 1996), pp. 45–65.

FAMA, E.F., "Efficient Capital Markets: A Review of Theory and Empirical Work," *Journal of Finance* (May, 1970), pp. 383–417.

FAMA, E.F., "Agency Problems and the Theory of the Firm," *Journal of Political Economy* (April, 1980), pp. 288–307.

FAMA, E.F., "Market Efficiency, Long-Term Returns and Behavioral Finance," *Journal* of Financial Economics (September, 1998), pp. 283–306.

FAMA, E.F. and K.R. FRENCH, "The Cross-Section of Expected Stock Returns," *The Journal of Finance* (1992), pp. 427–465.

FELTHAM, G.A. and J.A. OHLSON, "Valuation and Clean Surplus Accounting for Operating and Financial Activities," *Contemporary Accounting Research* (Spring, 1995), pp. 689–731.

FELTHAM, G.A. and J.A. OHLSON, "Uncertainty Resolution and the Theory of Depreciation Measurement," *Journal of Accounting Research* (Autumn, 1996), pp. 209–234.

FELTHAM, G.A. and J. XIE, "Performance Measure Congruity and Diversity in Multi-Task Principal/Agent Relations," *The Accounting Review* (July, 1994), pp. 429–453.

FINANCIAL ACCOUNTING STANDARDS BOARD, *Proposal for a Principles-based Approach to U.S. Standard-setting* (Norwalk, CT: FASB, 2002).

FINANCIAL ACCOUNTING STANDARDS BOARD, *Statement of Financial Accounting Concepts No. 1, Objectives of Financial Reporting by Business Enterprises* (Norwalk, CT: FASB, 1978).

FINANCIAL ACCOUNTING STANDARDS BOARD, *Statement of Financial Accounting Concepts No. 2, Qualitative Characteristics of Accounting Information* (Norwalk, CT: FASB, 1980).

FINANCIAL ACCOUNTING STANDARDS BOARD, *Statement of Financial Accounting Standards No. 2, Accounting for Research and Development Costs* (Norwalk, CT: FASB, 1974).

FINANCIAL ACCOUNTING STANDARDS BOARD, *Statement of Financial Accounting Standards No. 19, Financial Accounting and Reporting by Oil and Gas Producing Companies* (Norwalk, CT: FASB, 1977).

FINANCIAL ACCOUNTING STANDARDS BOARD, *Statement of Financial Accounting Standards No. 25, Suspension of Certain Accounting Requirements for Oil and Gas Producing Companies* (Norwalk, CT: FASB, 1979).

FINANCIAL ACCOUNTING STANDARDS BOARD, *Statement of Financial Accounting Standards No. 33, Financial Reporting and Changing Prices* (Norwalk, CT: FASB, 1979).

FINANCIAL ACCOUNTING STANDARDS BOARD, *Statement of Financial Accounting Standards No. 52, Foreign Currency Translation* (Norwalk, CT: FASB, 1981).

FINANCIAL ACCOUNTING STANDARDS BOARD, *Statement of Financial Accounting Standards No. 69, Disclosures about Oil and Gas Producing Activities* (Norwalk, CT: FASB, 1982).

FINANCIAL ACCOUNTING STANDARDS BOARD, *Statement of Financial Accounting Standards No. 87, Employers' Accounting for Pensions* (Norwalk, CT: FASB, 1985).

FINANCIAL ACCOUNTING STANDARDS BOARD, *Statement of Financial Accounting Standards No. 106, Employers' Accounting for Postretirement Benefits Other Than Pensions* (Norwalk, CT: FASB, 1990).

FINANCIAL ACCOUNTING STANDARDS BOARD, *Statement of Financial Accounting Standards No. 107, Disclosures about Fair Value of Financial Instruments* (Norwalk, CT: FASB, 1991).

FINANCIAL ACCOUNTING STANDARDS BOARD, *Statement of Financial Accounting Standards No. 114, Accounting by Creditors for Impairment of a Loan: An Amendment of FASB Statements No. 5 and 15* (Norwalk, CT: FASB, 1993).

FINANCIAL ACCOUNTING STANDARDS BOARD, *Statement of Financial Accounting Standards No. 115, Accounting for Certain Investments in Debt and Equity Securities* (Norwalk, CT: FASB, 1993).

FINANCIAL ACCOUNTING STANDARDS BOARD, *Statement of Financial Accounting Standards No. 119, Disclosure about Derivative Financial Instruments and Fair Value of Financial Instruments* (Norwalk, CT: FASB, 1994).

FINANCIAL ACCOUNTING STANDARDS BOARD, *Statement of Financial Accounting*

Standards No.123, Accounting for Stock-based Compensation (Norwalk, CT: FASB, 1995).

FINANCIAL ACCOUNTING STANDARDS BOARD, Statement of Financial Accounting Standards No. 123R, Share-Based Payment (Norwalk, CT: FASB, 2004).

FINANCIAL ACCOUNTING STANDARDS BOARD, Statement of Financial Accounting Standards No. 130, Reporting Comprehensive Income (Norwalk, CT: FASB, 1997).

FINANCIAL ACCOUNTING STANDARDS BOARD, Statement of Financial Accounting Standards No. 131, Financial Reporting for Segments of a Business Enterprise (Norwalk, CT: FASB, 1997).

FINANCIAL ACCOUNTING STANDARDS BOARD, Statement of Financial Accounting Standards No. 133, Accounting for Derivative Instruments and Hedging Activities (Norwalk, CT: FASB, 1998).

FINANCIAL ACCOUNTING STANDARDS BOARD, Statement of Financial Accounting Standards No. 142, Goodwill and Other Intangible Assets (Norwalk, CT: FASB, 2001).

FINANCIAL ACCOUNTING STANDARDS BOARD, Statement of Financial Accounting Standards No. 144, Accounting for the Impairment or Disposal of Long-Lived Assets (Norwalk, CT: FASB, 2001).

FINANCIAL ACCOUNTING STANDARDS BOARD, Statement of Financial Accounting Standards No. 157, Fair Value Measurements (Norwalk, CT: FASB, 2006).

FINANCIAL ACCOUNTING STANDARDS BOARD, Statement of Financial Accounting Standards No. 158, Employers' Accounting for Defined Benefit Pension and Other Postretirement Plans: An Amendment of FASB Statements No. 87, 88,106, and 132R (Norwalk, CT: FASB, 2006).

FINANCIAL ACCOUNTING STANDARDS BOARD, Statement of Financial Accounting Standards No. 159, The Fair Value Option for Financial Assets and Financial Liabilities:—Including an Amendment of FASB Statement No. 115 (Norwalk, CT: FASB, 2007).

FRANCIS, J., R. LAFOND, P. OLSSON and K. SCHIPPER, "Costs of Equity and Earnings Attributes," The Accounting Review (October, 2004), pp. 967–1010.

FRANCIS, J., R. LAFOND, P. OLSSON and K. SCHIPPER, "The Market Pricing of Accruals Quality," Journal of Accounting and Economics (June, 2005), pp. 295–327.

FRANCIS, J., D. NANDA, and X. WANG, "Re-examining the Effects of Regulation Fair Disclosure using Foreign Listed Firms to Control for Concurrent Shocks," Journal of Accounting and Economics (September, 2006), pp. 271–292.

FRANCIS, J., K. SCHIPPER and L. VINCENT, "Expanded Disclosures and the Increased Usefulness of Earnings Announcements," The Accounting Review (July, 2002), pp. 515–546.

FRANKEL, R. and C.M.C. LEE, "Accounting Valuation, Market Expectation, and Cross-Sectional Stock Returns," Journal of Accounting and Economics (June, 1998), pp. 283–319.

FRIEDMAN, J.W., Game Theory with Applications to Economics (New York, NY: Oxford University Press, 1986).

FROST, C.A., E.A. GORDON, and A.F. HAYES, "Stock Exchange Disclosure and Market Development: An Analysis of 50 International Exchanges," Journal of Accounting Research (June, 2006), pp. 437–483.

GAVER, J.J. and K.M. GAVER, "The Relation Between Nonrecurring Accounting Transactions and CEO Cash Compensation," The Accounting Review (April, 1998), pp. 235–253.

GIGLER, F., C. KANODIA and R. VENUGOPALAN, "Assessing the Information Content of Mark-to-Market Accounting with Mixed Attributes: The Case of Cash Flow Hedges," Journal of Accounting Research (May, 2007), pp. 257–276.

GJESDAL, F., "Accounting for Stewardship," Journal of Accounting Research (Spring, 1981), pp. 208–231.

GONEDES, N. and N. DOPUCH, "Capital Market Equilibrium, Information Production, and Selected Accounting Techniques: Theoretical

Framework and Review of Empirical Work," *Journal of Accounting Research* (Supplement, 1974), pp. 48–129.

GRAHAM, J.R., C.R. HARVEY and S. RAJGOPAL, "The Economic Implications of Corporate Financial Reporting," *Journal of Accounting and Economics* (December, 2005), pp. 3–73.

GREIM, B.M., J.R.M. HAND, and K.J. KLASSEN, "Stock Price Reactions to the Repricing of Employee Stock Options." *Contemporary Accounting Research* (Winter, 2005), pp. 701–828.

GROSSMAN, S., "On the Efficiency of Competitive Stock Markets Where Traders Have Diverse Information," *The Journal of Finance* (May, 1976), pp. 573–585.

GROSSMAN, S., "The Informational Role of Warranties and Private Disclosure about Product Quality," *Journal of Law and Economics* (December, 1981), pp. 461–484.

GU, F. and J.Q. LI, "The Credibility of Voluntary Disclosure and Insider Stock Transactions," *Journal of Accounting Research* (September, 2007), pp. 171–810.

GUAY, W. and S.P. KOTHARI, "How Much do Firms Hedge with Derivatives?" *Journal of Financial Economics* (December, 2003), pp. 423–461.

GUAY, W.R., "The Impact of Derivatives on Firm Risk: An Empirical Examination of New Derivatives Users," *Journal of Accounting and Economics* (January, 1999), pp. 319–351.

GUEDHAMI, O. and J. PITTMAN, "Ownership Concentration in Privatized Firms: The Role of Disclosure Standards, Auditor Choice, and Auditing Infrastructure," *Journal of Accounting Research* (December, 2006), pp. 889–929.

HAIL, H. and C. LEUZ, "International Differences in the Cost of Equity Capital: Do Legal Institutions and Securities Regulation Matter?" *Journal of Accounting Research* (June, 2006), pp. 485–531.

HALL, B.J. and K.J. MURPHY, "Stock Options for Undiversified Executives," *Journal of Accounting and Economics* (February, 2002), pp. 3–42.

HAMADA, R., "The Effect of the Firm's Capital Structure on the Systematic Risk of Common Stocks," *Journal of Finance* (May, 1972), pp. 435–452.

HANNA, J.D., "Never Say Never," *CA Magazine* (August, 1999), pp. 35–39.

HANNA, J.R., D.B. KENNEDY, and G.D. RICHARDSON, *Reporting the Effects of Changing Prices: A Review of the Experience with Section 4510* (Toronto, ON: CICA, 1990).

HATFIELD, H.R., *Accounting* (New York, NY: Appleton-Century-Crofts, Inc., 1927).

HEALY, P.M., "The Effect of Bonus Schemes on Accounting Decisions," *Journal of Accounting and Economics* (April, 1985), pp. 85–107.

HEALY, P.M., A.P. HUTTON, and K.G. PALEPU, "Stock Performance and Intermediation Changes Surrounding Sustained Increases in Disclosure," *Contemporary Accounting Research* (Fall, 1999), pp. 485–520.

HEALY, P.M. and K.G. PALEPU, "The Effect of Firms' Financial Disclosure Strategies on Stock Prices," *Accounting Horizons* (March, 1993), pp. 1–11.

HEALY, P.M. and K.G. PALEPU, "The Fall of Enron," *Journal of Economic Perspectives* (Spring, 2003), pp. 3–26.

HEMMER, T.S., S. MATSUNAGA, and T. SHEVLIN, "Estimating the 'Fair Value' of Employee Stock Options with Expected Early Exercise," *Accounting Horizons* (December, 1994), pp. 23–42.

HIRSHLEIFER, D., "Investor Psychology and Asset Pricing," *Journal of Finance* (August, 2001), pp. 1533–1597.

HIRSHLEIFER, D. and S.H. TEOH, "Limited Attention, Information Disclosure, and Financial Reporting," *Journal of Accounting and Economics* (December, 2003), pp. 337–386.

HIRSHLEIFER, J., "The Private and Social Value of Information and the Reward to Inventive Activity," *American Economic Review* (September, 1971), pp. 561–573.

HIRST, D.E., L. KOONCE, and S. VENKATARAMAN, "How Disaggregation Enhances the Credibility of Management Forecasts," *Journal of Accounting Research* (September, 2007), pp. 811–837.

HODDER, L.D., P.E. HOPKINS, and J.W. WHALEN, "Risk-Relevance of Fair-Value Income Measures for Commercial Banks," *The Accounting Review* (March, 2006), pp. 335–337.

HOLMSTRÖM, B., "Moral Hazard and Observability," *The Bell Journal of Economics* (Spring, 1979), pp. 74–91.

HOLMSTRÖM, B., "Moral Hazard in Teams," *The Bell Journal of Economics* (Autumn, 1982), pp. 324–340.

HOLTHAUSEN, R.W. and D.F. LARCKER, "The Prediction of Stock Returns using Financial Statement Information," *Journal of Accounting and Economics* (June/September, 1992), pp. 373–411.

HOLTHAUSEN, R.W., D.F. LARCKER, and R.G. SLOAN, "Annual Bonus Schemes and the Manipulation of Earnings," *Journal of Accounting and Economics* (February, 1995), pp. 29–74.

HRIBAR, P. and D. W. COLLINS, "Errors in Estimating Accruals," *Journal of Accounting Research* (March, 2002), pp. 105–134.

HUDDART, S., "Employee Stock Options," *Journal of Accounting and Economics* (September, 1994), pp. 207–231.

HUDDART, S. and M. LANG, "Employee Stock Option Exercises: An Empirical Analysis," *Journal of Accounting and Economics* (February, 1996), pp. 5–43.

HUGHES, P.J., "Signalling by Direct Disclosure Under Asymmetric Information," *Journal of Accounting and Economics* (June, 1986), pp. 119–142.

INDJEJIKIAN, R. J. and D. NANDA, "Executive Bonuses and What They Imply about Performance Standards," *The Accounting Review* (October, 2002), pp. 793–819.

INTERNATIONAL ACCOUNTING STANDARDS BOARD, *Framework for the Preparation and Presentation of Financial Statements* (London: IASB, 2001).

INTERNATIONAL ACCOUNTING STANDARDS BOARD, *International Financial Reporting Standard IFRS 3, Business Combinations* (London: IASB, 2004).

INTERNATIONAL ACCOUNTING STANDARDS BOARD, *International Financial Reporting Standard IFRS 2, Share-based Payment* (London: IASB, 2005).

INTERNATIONAL ACCOUNTING STANDARDS BOARD, *International Financial Reporting Standard IFRS 6, Exploration for and Extraction of Mineral Resources* (London, IASB, 2006).

INTERNATIONAL ACCOUNTING STANDARDS BOARD, *International Financial Reporting Standard IFRS 8, Operating Segments* (London, IASB, 2006).

INTERNATIONAL ACCOUNTING STANDARDS BOARD, *International Financial Reporting Standard IFRS 7, Financial Instruments: Disclosures* (London: IASB, 2007).

INTERNATIONAL ACCOUNTING STANDARDS BOARD, *International Accounting Standard IAS 18, Revenue* (London: IASB, 1995).

INTERNATIONAL ACCOUNTING STANDARDS BOARD, *International Accounting Standard IAS 39, Financial Instruments: Recognition and Measurement* (London: IASB, 1999).

INTERNATIONAL ACCOUNTING STANDARDS BOARD, *International Accounting Standard IAS 19, Employee Benefits* (London: IASB, 2004).

INTERNATIONAL ACCOUNTING STANDARDS BOARD, *International Accounting Standard IAS 36, Impairment of Assets* (London: IASB, 2004).

INTERNATIONAL ACCOUNTING STANDARDS BOARD, *International Accounting Standard IAS 38, Intangible Assets* (London: IASB, 2004).

INTERNATIONAL ACCOUNTING STANDARDS BOARD, *International Accounting*

Standard IAS 38, Intangible Assets (London: IASB, 2004).

INTERNATIONAL ACCOUNTING STANDARDS BOARD, International Accounting Standard IAS 2, Inventories (London: IASB, 2005).

INTERNATIONAL ACCOUNTING STANDARDS BOARD, International Accounting Standard IAS 16, Property, Plant & Equipment (London: IASB, 2005).

INTERNATIONAL ACCOUNTING STANDARDS BOARD, International Accounting Standard IAS 17, Leases (London: IASB, 2005).

INTERNATIONAL ACCOUNTING STANDARDS BOARD, Preliminary Views on an Improved Conceptual Framework for Financial Reporting (London: IASB, July, 2006).

INTERNATIONAL ACCOUNTING STANDARDS BOARD, Presentation of Financial Statements IAS 1, revised September 6, 2007 (London, IASB, 2007).

ITTNER, C.D., D.F. LARCKER, and M.V. RAJAN, "The Choice of Performance Measures in Annual Bonus Contracts," The Accounting Review (April, 1997), pp. 231–255.

JACOB, J, and B.N. JORGENSEN, "Earnings Management and Accounting Income Aggregation," Journal of Accounting and Economics (July, 2007), pp.369–390.

JAMAL, K., M. MAIER, and S. SUNDER, "Privacy in E-Commerce: Development of Reporting Standards, Disclosure, and Assurance Services in an Unregulated Market," Journal of Accounting Research (May, 2003), pp. 285–309.

JENSEN, M.C. and W.H. MECKLING, "Theory of the Firm: Managerial Behavior, Agency Costs and Ownership Structure," Journal of Financial Economics (October, 1976), pp. 305–360.

JENSEN, M.C. and K.J. MURPHY, "CEO Incentives—It's Not How Much You Pay, But How," Harvard Business Review (May/June, 1990), pp. 138–149.

JONES, J., "Earnings Management During Import Relief Investigations," Journal of Accounting Research (Autumn, 1991), pp. 193–228.

KAHNEMAN, D. and A. TVERSKY, "Prospect Theory: An Analysis of Decision Under Risk," Econometrica (March, 1979), pp. 263–291.

KANODIA, C., R. SINGH, and A. SPERO, "Imprecision in Accounting Measurement" Journal of Accounting Research (June, 2005), pp. 487–519.

KAPLAN, R.S., "Comments on Paul Healy," Journal of Accounting and Economics (April, 1985), pp. 109–113.

KE, B. and S. RAMALINGEGOWDA, "Do Institutional Investors Exploit the Post-Earnings Announcement Drift?" Journal of Accounting and Economics (February, 2005), pp. 25–53.

KIM, M. and W. KROSS, "The Ability of Earnings to Predict Future Operating Cash Flows Has Been Increasing—Not Decreasing," Journal of Accounting Research (December, 2005), pp. 753–780.

KIM, O. and Y. SUH, "Incentive Efficiency of Compensation Based on Accounting and Market Performance," Journal of Accounting and Economics (January/April/July, 1993), pp. 25–53.

KIM, O. and R.E. VERRECCHIA, "Pre-announcement and Event-period Private Information," Journal of Accounting and Economics (1997), pp. 395–419.

KNETSCH, J.L., "The Endowment Effect and Evidence of Nonreversible Indifference Curves," The American Economic Review (December, 1989), pp. 1277–1284.

KORMENDI, R.C. and R. LIPE, "Earnings Innovations, Earnings Persistence, and Stock Returns," Journal of Business (July, 1987), pp. 323–346.

KOTHARI, S.P., "Capital Markets Research in Accounting," Journal of Accounting and Economics (September, 2001), pp. 105–231.

KOTHARI, S.P., A.J. LEONE, and C.E. WASLEY, "Performance Matched Discretionary Accrual Measures," Journal of Accounting and Economics (February, 2005), pp. 163–197.

KOTHARI, S.P., J. SHANKEN, and R. SLOAN, "Another Look at the Cross-Section of Expected Returns," Journal of Finance (March, 1995), pp. 185–224.

KROSS, W., "Stock Returns and Oil and Gas Pronouncements: Replications and Extensions," *Journal of Accounting Research* (Autumn, 1982), pp. 459–471.

KURZ, M., ed., *Endogenous Economic Fluctuations* (New York, NY: Springer-Verlag, 1997).

KURZ, M., "Endogenous Uncertainty: A Unified View of Market Volatility," working paper, Stanford University (September, 1997).

LAFFONT, J.J., *The Economics of Uncertainty and Information* (Cambridge, MA: MIT Press, 1989).

LAMBERT, R.A. and D.F. LARCKER, "An Analysis of the Use of Accounting and Market Measures of Performance in Executive Compensation Contracts," *Journal of Accounting Research* (Supplement, 1987), pp. 85–125.

LAMBERT, R.A. and D.F. LARCKER, "Firm Performance and the Compensation of Chief Executive Officers," working paper (January, 1993).

LAMBERT, R.A., D.F. LARCKER, and R.E. VERRECCHIA, "Portfolio Considerations in Valuing Executive Compensation," *Journal of Accounting Research* (Spring, 1991), pp. 129–149.

LAMBERT, R.A., C. LEUZ, and R.E. VERRECCHIA, "Accounting Information, Disclosure, and the Cost of Capital," *Journal of Accounting Research* (May, 2007), pp. 385–420.

LANDSMAN, W.R. and E.L. MAYDEW, "Has the Information Content of Quarterly Earnings Announcements Declined in the Past Three Decades?" *Journal of Accounting Research* (June, 2002), pp. 797–808.

LANG, M.H. and R.J. LUNDHOLM, "Corporate Disclosure Policy and Analyst Behavior," *The Accounting Review* (October, 1996), pp. 467–492.

LANG, M.H., K.V. LINS and D.P. MILLER, "ADRs, Analysts, and Accuracy: Does Cross Listing in the United States Improve a Firm's Information Environment and Increase Market Value?" *Journal of Accounting Research* (May, 2003), pp. 317–345.

LEE, C.M.C., "Measuring Wealth," *C.A. Magazine* (April, 1996), pp. 32–37.

LEE, C.M.C., "Market Efficiency and Accounting Research: A Discussion of 'Capital Market Research in Accounting' by S.P. Kothari," *Journal of Accounting and Economics* (September, 2001), pp. 233–253.

LEE, C.M.C., B. MUCKLOW, and M.J. READY, "Spreads, Depths, and the Impact of Earnings Information: An Intraday Analysis," *The Review of Financial Studies* (1993), pp. 345–374.

LEE, Y-J, K. PETRONI, and M. SHEN, "Cherry Picking, Disclosure Quality, and Comprehensive Income Reporting Choices: The Case of Property-Liability Insurers," *Contemporary Accounting Research* (Fall, 2006).

LELAND, H.E. and D.H. PYLE, "Information Asymmetries, Financial Structure, and Financial Intermediation," *The Journal of Finance* (May, 1977), pp. 371–387.

LEUZ, C., "IAS Versus U.S.GAAP: Information Asymmetry – Based Evidence from Germany's New Market," *Journal of Accounting Research* (June, 2003), pp. 445–472.

LEV, B., "On the Association Between Operating Leverage and Risk," *Journal of Financial and Quantitative Analysis* (September, 1974), pp. 627–640.

LEV, B., "The Impact of Accounting Regulation on the Stock Market: The Case of Oil and Gas Companies," *The Accounting Review* (July, 1979), pp. 485–503.

LEV, B., "Toward a Theory of Equitable and Efficient Accounting Policy," *The Accounting Review* (January, 1988), pp. 1–22.

LEV, B., "On the Usefulness of Earnings: Lessons and Directions from Two Decades of Empirical Research," *Journal of Accounting Research* (Supplement, 1989), pp. 153–192.

LEV, B., and D. NISSIM, "The Persistence of the Accruals Anomaly," *Contemporary Accounting Research* (Spring, 2006), pp. 193–226.

LEV, B. and S.R. THIAGARAJAN, "Fundamental Information Analysis," *Journal of Accounting Research* (Autumn, 1993), pp. 190–215.

LEV, B., and P. ZAROWIN, "The Boundaries of Financial Reporting and How to Extend Them," *Journal of Accounting Research* (Autumn, 1999), pp. 353–385.

LINSMEIER, T.J. and N.D. PEARSON, "Quantitative Disclosures of Market Risk in the SEC Release," *Accounting Horizons* (1997), pp. 107–135.

LINTNER, J., "The Valuation of Risky Assets and the Selection of Risky Investments in Stock Portfolios and Capital Budgets," *Review of Economics and Statistics* (February, 1965), pp. 13–37.

LIST, J.A., "Does Market Experience Eliminate Market Anomalies?" *The Quarterly Journal of Economics* (February, 2003), pp. 41–71.

LIU, C.-C., S.G. RYAN, and H. TAN, "How Banks' Value-at-Risk Disclosures Predict their Total and Priced Risk: Effects of Banks' Technical Sophistication and Learning over Time," *Review of Accounting Studies* (2004), pp. 265–294.

LIU, C.-C., S.G. RYAN, and J.M. WAHLEN, "Differential Valuation Implications of Loan Loss Provisions Across Banks and Fiscal Quarters," *The Accounting Review* (January, 1997), pp. 133–146.

LIVNAT, J. and R.R. MENDENHALL, "Comparing the Post-Earnings Announcement Drift for Surprises Calculated from Analyst and Time Series Forecasts," *Journal of Accounting Research* (March, 2006), pp. 177–205.

LO, K., "Economic Consequences of Regulated Changes in Disclosure: the Case of Executive Compensation," *Journal of Accounting and Economics* (August, 2003), pp. 285–314.

LOBO, G.J. and J. ZHOU, "Did Conservatism in Financial Accounting Increase after the Sarbanes-Oxley Act? Initial Evidence," *Accounting Horizons* (March, 2006), pp. 57–73.

LYS, T., "Mandated Accounting Changes and Debt Covenants: The Case of Oil and Gas Companies," *Journal of Accounting and Economics* (April, 1984), pp. 39–65.

MAGLIOLO, J., "Capital Market Analysis of Reserve Recognition Accounting," *Journal of Accounting Research* (Supplement, 1986), pp. 69–108.

MARQUARDT, C.A., 'The Cost of Employee Stock Option Grants: An Empirical Analysis," *Journal of Accounting Research* (September, 2002), pp. 1191–1217.

MASHRUWALA, C., S. RAJGOPAL, and T. SHEVLIN, "Why is the Accrual Anomaly not Arbitraged Away? The Role of Idiosyncratic Risk and Transactions Costs," *Journal of Accounting and Economics* (October, 2006), pp. 3–33.

MATSUMOTO, D.A., "Management's Incentives to Avoid Negative Earnings Surprises," *The Accounting Review* (July, 2002), pp. 483–514.

MCNICHOLS, M. and G.P. WILSON, "Evidence of Earnings Management from the Provision for Bad Debts," *Journal of Accounting Research* (Supplement, 1988), pp. 1–31.

MENDENHALL, R.R., "Arbitrage Risk and Post-Earnings Announcement Drift," *Journal of Business* (2004), pp. 875–894.

MERINO, D.B. and M.D. NEIMARK, "Disclosure Regulation and Public Policy: A Sociohistorical Reappraisal," *Journal of Accounting and Public Policy* (Fall, 1982), pp. 33–57.

MERTON, R.C., "Theory of Rational Option Pricing," *Bell Journal of Economics and Management Science* (Spring, 1973), pp. 141–183.

MERTON, R.C., "A Simple Model of Capital Market Equilibrium with Incomplete Markets," *The Journal of Finance* (July, 1987), pp. 483–510.

MIAN, S.L. and C.W. SMITH, JR., "Incentives for Unconsolidated Financial Reporting," *Journal of Accounting and Economics* (January, 1990), pp. 141–171.

MILGROM, P., "Good News and Bad News: Representation Theorems and Applications," *Bell Journal of Economics* (Autumn, 1981), pp. 380–391.

MODIGLIANI, F. and R.A. COHN, "Inflation, Rational Valuation and the Market," *Financial Analysts' Journal* (1979), pp. 24–44.

MYERS, J.N., "Implementing Residual Income Valuation With Linear Information Dynamics," *The Accounting Review* (January, 1999), pp. 1–28.

MYERSON, R.B., "Incentive Compatibility and the Bargaining Problem," *Econometrica* (1979), pp. 61–74.

NARAYANAMOORTHY, N., "Conservatism and Cross-Sectional Variation in the Post-Earnings Announcement Drift," *Journal of Accounting Research* (September, 2006), pp. 763–789.

NEWMAN, P. and R. SANSING, "Disclosure Policies with Multiple Users," *Journal of Accounting Research* (Spring, 1993), pp. 92–112.

NORRIS, FLOYD, "A Tower of Babel in Accounting?" *The New York Times* (June 15, 2007, late edition).

O'BRIEN, P.C., "Analysts' Forecasts as Earnings Expectations," *Journal of Accounting and Economics* (January, 1988), pp. 53–83.

ODEAN, T., "Volume, Volatility, Price and Profit When All Traders are Above Average," *Journal of Finance* (December, 1998), pp. 1887–1934.

OHLSON, J.A., "On the Nature of Income Measurement: The Basic Results," *Contemporary Accounting Research* (Fall, 1987), pp. 1–15.

ONTARIO SECURITIES COMMISSION, National Instrument 51–102, "Continuous Disclosure Obligations" (Ontario Securities Commission: March, 2004).

ONTARIO SECURITIES COMMISSION, "Statement of Executive Compensation," Form 40, Securities Act, Regulation 638/93, *The Ontario Gazette*, Vol. 126–39 (September 25, 1993), pp. 1203–1216.

PAE, J., D.B. THORNTON, and M. WELKER, "The Link between Earnings Conservatism and the Price-to-Book Ratio," *Contemporary Accounting Research* (Fall, 2005), pp. 693–717.

PAE, S., "Optimal Disclosure Policy in Oligopoly Markets," *Journal of Accounting Research* (June, 2002), pp. 901–932.

PAE, S., "Selective Disclosure in the Presence of Uncertainty about Information Endowment," *Journal of Accounting and Economics* (September, 2005), pp. 383–409.

PALEPU, K.G., P.M. HEALY, and V.L. BERNARD, *Business Analysis and Valuation* (South-Western College Publishing: Cincinnati, Ohio, 2000).

PALMROSE, Z-V. and S. SCHOLZ, "The Circumstances and Legal Consequences of Non-GAAP Reporting: Evidence from Restatements," *Contemporary Accounting Research* (Spring, 2004), pp. 139–180.

PATON, W.A. and A.C. LITTLETON, *An Introduction to Corporate Accounting Standards* (Ubana, IL: American Accounting Association, 1940).

PAVLIK, E.L., T.W. SCOTT, and P. TIESSEN, "Executive Compensation: Issues and Research," *Journal of Accounting Literature* (1993), pp. 131–189.

PELTZMAN, S., "Toward a More General Theory of Regulation," *The Journal of Law and Economics* (August, 1976), pp. 21–240.

PENNO, M.C., "Information Quality and Voluntary Disclosure," *The Accounting Review* (April, 1997), pp. 275–284.

PICCONI, M., "The Perils of Pensions: Does Pension Accounting Lead Investors and Analysts Astray?" *The Accounting Review* (July, 2006), pp. 925–955.

POSNER, R.A., "Theories of Economic Regulation," *Bell Journal of Economics and Management Science* (Autumn, 1974), pp. 335–358.

PRATT, J.W., "Risk Aversion In the Small and In the Large," *Econometrica* (January-April, 1964), pp. 122–136.

RAIFFA, H., *Decision Analysis: Introductory Lectures on Choices Under Uncertainty* (Reading, MA: Addison-Wesley, 1968).

RAJGOPAL, S. and T. SHEVLIN, "Empirical Evidence on the Relation between Stock Option Compensation and Risk Taking," *Journal of Accounting and Economics* (June, 2002), pp. 145–171.

RAMAKRISHNAN, R.T.S. and J.K. THOMAS, "Valuation of Permanent, Transitory and Price-Irrelevant Components of Reported Earnings," working paper, Columbia University Business School (July, 1991).

ROLL, R.,"R^2," *Journal of Finance* (July, 1988), pp. 541–566.

ROYCHOWDHURY, S. and R.L. WATTS, "Asymmetric Timeliness of Earnings, Market-to-Book and Conservatism in Financial Reporting," *Journal of Accounting and Economics* (September, 2007), pp. 2–31.

RYAN, S.G., "A Survey of Research Relating Accounting Numbers to Systematic Equity Risk, with Implications for Risk Disclosure Policy and Future Research," *Accounting Horizons* (June, 1997), pp. 82–95.

SALY, P.J., "Repricing Executive Stock Options in a Down Market," *Journal of Accounting and Economics* (November, 1994), pp. 325–356.

SAVAGE, L.J., *The Foundations of Statistics* (NY: Wiley, 1954).

SCHRAND, C.M., "The Association Between Stock-Price Interest Rate Sensitivity and Disclosures about Derivative Instruments," *The Accounting Review* (January, 1997), pp. 87–109.

SCHRAND, C.M. and B.R. WALTHER, "Strategic Benchmarks in Earnings Announcements: The Selective Disclosure of Prior-Period Earnings Components," *The Accounting Review* (April, 2000), pp. 151–177.

SCOTT, W.R., "Auditor's Loss Functions Implicit in Consumption-Investment Models," *Journal of Accounting Research* (Supplement, 1975), pp. 98–117.

SCOTT, W.R., "Group Preference Orderings for Audit and Valuation Alternatives, *"Journal of Accounting Research"* (Spring, 1977), pp. 120–138.

SECURITIES ACT, *Revised Statutes of Ontario*, 1990, Vol. 11, Chapter 5.5 (Toronto, ON: Queen's Printer for Ontario, 1991).

SECURITIES AND EXCHANGE COMMISSION, *Accounting Series Release No. 150* (Washington, DC: SEC, 1973).

SECURITIES and EXCHANGE COMMISSION, *Accounting Series Release No. 253* (Washington, DC: SEC, 1978).

SECURITIES AND EXCHANGE COMMISSION, *Disclosure of Accounting Policies for Derivative Financial Instruments and Derivative Commodity Instruments and Disclosure of Quantitative and Qualitative Information about Market Risk Inherent in Derivative Financial Instruments, Other Financial Instruments, and Derivative Commodity Instruments* (Washington, DC: SEC, 1997).

SECURITIES AND EXCHANGE COMMISSION, *Report and Recommendations Pursuant to Section 401(c) of the Sarbanes-Oxley Act of 2002 On Arrangements with Off-Balance Sheet Implications, Special Purpose Entities, and Transparency of Filings by Issuers* (Washington, DC: SEC, June, 2005)

SECURITIES AND EXCHANGE COMMISSION, *Study Pursuant to Section 108(d) of the Sarbanes-Oxley Act of 2002 on the Adoption by the United States Financial Reporting System of a Principles-Based Accounting System* (Washington, DC: SEC, 2003).

SENGUPTA, P., "Corporate Disclosure Quality and the Cost of Debt," *The Accounting Review* (October, 1998), pp. 459–474.

SHARPE, W.F., "Capital Asset Prices: A Theory of Market Equilibrium Under Conditions of Risk," *The Journal of Finance* (September, 1964), pp. 425–442.

SHEFRIN, H. and M. STATMAN, "The Disposition to Sell Winners Too Early and Ride Losers Too Long," *Journal of Finance* (July, 1985), pp. 777–790.

SHILLER, R.J., "Do Stock Prices Move Too Much to be Justified by Subsequent Changes in Dividends?" *The American Economic Review* (June, 1981), pp. 421–436.

SHILLER, R.J., *Irrational Exuberance* (New York, NY: Broadway Books, 2000).

SKINNER, D.J., "How Well Does Net Income Measure Firm Performance? A Discussion of Two Studies," *Journal of Accounting and Economics* (January, 1999), pp. 105–111.

SKINNER, D.J. and R.G. SLOAN, "Earnings Surprises, Growth Expectations, and Stock Returns or Don't Let an Earnings Torpedo Sink Your Portfolio," *Review of Accounting Studies* (2002), pp. 289–312.

SLOAN, R.G., "Accounting Earnings and Top Executive Compensation," *Journal of Accounting and Economics* (January/April/July, 1993), pp. 55–100.

SLOAN, R.G., "Do Stock Prices Fully Reflect Information in Accruals and Cash Flows About Future Earnings?" *The Accounting Review* (July, 1996), pp. 289–315.

SMITH, A., "Earnings and Management Incentives: Comments," *Journal of Accounting and Economics* (January/April/July, 1993), pp. 337–347.

SPENCE, M., "Job Market Signalling," *Quarterly Journal of Economics* (August, 1973), pp. 355–374.

SPENCE, M., "Competitive and Optimal Responses to Signals: An Analysis of Efficiency and Distribution," *Journal of Economic Theory* (March, 1974), pp. 296–332.

STIGLER, G.J., "The Theory of Economic Regulation," *The Bell Journal of Economics and Management Science* (Spring, 1971), pp. 3–21.

STOCKEN, P.C. and R.E. VERRECCHIA, "Financial Reporting System Choice and Disclosure Management," *The Accounting Review* (October, 2004), pp. 1181–1203.

STOREY, R.K. and S. STOREY, *The Framework of Financial Accounting Concepts and Standards* (Norwalk, CT: Financial Accounting Standards Board, 1998).

STUDY GROUP ON THE OBJECTIVES OF FINANCIAL STATEMENTS, *Objectives of Financial Statements* (New York, NY: American Institute of Certified Public Accountants, 1973). (Also called the Trueblood committee report).

SUBRAMANYAM, K.R., "The Pricing of Discretionary Accruals," *Journal of Accounting and Economics* (August-December, 1996), pp. 249–281.

SUROWIECKI, JAMES, *The Wisdom of Crowds* (New York, NY: Doubleday Division of Random House Inc., 2004).

SWEENEY, A.P., "Debt-covenant Violations and Managers' Accounting Responses," *Journal of Accounting and Economics* (May, 1994), pp. 281–308.

TEOH, S.H., I. WELCH, and T.J. WONG, "Earnings Management and the Long-Run Performance of Initial Public Offerings," *The Journal of Finance* (December, 1998), pp. 1935–1974.

The Economist (October 21–27, 2003), "Fat cats feeding," pp. 64–66.

The Economist (July 20, 2006), "Executive share options: Dates from hell," pp. 59–60.

The Globe and Mail (July 9, 2003), "Microsoft to award stock, not options to employees," p. B9 (Reprinted from an article in *The Wall Street Journal* by Don Clark).

TITMAN, S. and B. TRUEMAN, "Information Quality and the Valuation of New Issues," *Journal of Accounting and Economics* (June, 1986), pp. 159–172.

TUCKER, J.W., and P.A. ZAROWIN, "Does Income Smoothing Improve Earnings Informativeness?" *The Accounting Review* (January, 2006), pp. 251–270.

VASSALOU, M., "News Related to Future GDP Growth as a Risk Factor in Equity Returns," *Journal of Financial Economics* (2003), pp. 47–73.

VERRECCHIA, R.E., "Discretionary Disclosure," *Journal of Accounting and Economics* (December 1983), pp. 179–194.

WARFIELD, T.D. and J.J. WILD, "Accounting Recognition and the Relevance of Earnings as an Explanatory Variable for Returns," *The Accounting Review* (October, 1992), pp. 821–842.

WATTS, R.L., "Conservatism in Accounting Part I: Explanations and Implications" *Accounting Horizons* (September, 2003), pp. 207–221.

WATTS, R.L., "Conservatism in Accounting Part II: Evidence and Research Opportunities," *Accounting Horizons* (December, 2003), pp. 287–301.

WATTS, R.L. and J.L. ZIMMERMAN, *Positive Accounting Theory* (Englewood Cliffs, NJ: Prentice-Hall, 1986).

WATTS, R.L. and J.L. ZIMMERMAN, "Positive Accounting Theory: A Ten Year Perspective," *The Accounting Review* (January, 1990), pp. 131–156.

WELKER, M., "Disclosure Policy, Information Asymmetry, and Liquidity in Equity Markets," *Contemporary Accounting Research* (Spring, 1995), pp. 801–827.

WOLFSON, M.A., "Empirical Evidence of Incentive Problems and their Mitigation in Oil and Gas Tax Shelter Programs," in J.W. Pratt and R.J. Zeckhauser, eds., *Principals and Agents: The Structure of Business* (Boston, MA: The President and Fellows of Harvard College, 1985), pp. 101–125.

WONG, M.H.F., "The Association between SFAS 119 Derivative Disclosures and the Foreign Exchange Risk Exposure of Manufacturing Firms," *Journal of Accounting Research* (Autumn, 2000), pp. 387–417.

WURGLER, J., "Financial Markets and the Allocation of Capital," *Journal of Financial Economics*, Vol. 58 (2000), pp. 187–214.

XIE, H., "The Mispricing of Abnormal Accruals," *The Accounting Review* (July, 2001), pp. 357–373.

YERMACK, D., "Good Timing: CEO Stock Option Awards and Company News Announcements," *Journal of Finance* (1997), pp. 449–476.

ZEFF, S.A., "The Rise of Economic Consequences," *The Journal of Accountancy* (December, 1978), pp. 56–63.

ZEFF, S.A., "How the U.S. Accounting Profession Got Where it is Today: Part II," *Accounting Horizons* (December, 2003), pp. 267–286.

ZHANG, Y., "Revenue Recognition Timing and Attributes of Reported Revenue: The Case of Software Industry's Adoption of SOP 91–1," *Journal of Accounting and Economics* (September, 2005), pp. 535–561.

Index

camouflage devices, 387
Canada
    adoption of IASB standards, 19, 20
    historical perspective, 6–7
Canada Business Corporations Act, 6
Canadian Accounting Standards Board (AcSB). *See* Accounting Standards Board (AcSB)
Canadian Imperial Bank of Commerce (CIBC), 475–476
Canadian Institute of Chartered Accountants (CICA), 20
Canadian Natural Resources Limited (CNRL), 268
Canadian Public Accountability Board, 309
Canadian Securities Administrators (CSA), 20
Canadian Superior Energy Inc., 471–472
Canadian Tire Corporation, Limited, 121–134, 122*f*, 172, 204–207, 225*n*, 272*n*
cap, 407, 409, 409*t*
capital asset pricing model, 110–114, 149, 183–185, 223*n*
capital assets
    amortization of, 43–44
    appraisal of, 3
    and current cost accounting, 166
    international standards, 4
capital costs, 209, 480*n*
capital lease, 270*n*
capital markets, 449
capital structure, 154–157
cartels, 306
cash, 56*n*
cash flow accounting
    matching of costs and revenues, 43
    relevance, 42
    reliability, 42
    revenue recognition, 42
cash flow hedges, 245, 271*n*, 381
cash flows fixed by contract, 231
cash income, 251–252
causation, 151–152
ceiling test writedowns, 246
ceiling tests, 211, 232–233

Center for Corporate and Public Governance, 397
central authority, 445
certainty
    present value model, 25–28
    vs. uncertainty, 31
cheap talk game, 481*n*
cherry picking, 237
Chicago Daily News, 102
chief executive officers (CEOs)
    compensation. *See* executive compensation
    information release practices, 281
China, 19
Chrysler Corp., 139
CICA Handbook
    accounting policies, disclosure of, 105
    amortization of goodwill, elimination of, 252
    current cost disclosures for capital assets, 166
    decision usefulness approach, 12, 83
    and departure from GAAP, 9
    disclosure of notes to financial statements, 5
    distortion, costs of, 309
    extraordinary items, 162, 163–164
    financial statements, 122
    foreign currency translation gains and losses, 299
    management approach, 482*n*
    meaning of Canadian GAAP, 9
    origins of, 6
    other post-employment benefits (OPEBs), 264
    recognition as authoritative statement of GAAP, 6
Cisco Systems Inc., 161
classificatory smoothing, 163
clean surplus theory
    biased accounting, 200
    cost of capital estimates, 209
    described, 198
    earnings dynamic, 201
    earnings persistence, 201–203
    empirical studies, 208–209
    estimate of firm value, 204–207

    forecast horizon, 208–209
    future earnings prediction, 209
    goodwill, valuation of, 254–255
    and information asymmetry, 224*n*
    and investment decision-making, 207
    summary, 209
    terminal value approach, 208–209
    three formulae for firm value, 198–201
    unbiased accounting, 199–200
    zero goodwill, 199
Coca-Cola Company, 440–441, 471, 474, 477
collateralized debt obligations (CDO), 269–270, 301
Committee on Accounting and Auditing Research, 6
    see also Canadian Institute of Chartered Accountants (CICA)
Committee on Accounting Procedure (CAP), 275
Companies Act (1844), 2
compensation. *See* executive compensation
compensation committee, 380
compensation expense, 278
compensation risk, 323
complete contracts, 339
complexity of information, 11–12
comprehensive income, 234
Computer Associates International, 477
concavity, 302*n*
Conceptual Frameworks of the Financial Accounting Standards Board, 6, 12, 21, 83, 84, 162
conditional conservatism, 96*n*
conditional controllability, 355*n*
conduits, 269
conflict
    conclusions, 341–343
    game theory. *See* game theory
    manager-investor conflict, 306–312
    overview, 304–305

Public Company Accounting
  Oversight Board (U.S.), 9–309
public confidence, 8–9, 10, 116
public good, 165
pump and dump, 281
purchase method, 249
purchased goodwill, 249–252
pure strategies, 353n

Q

quantitative price risk disclosures,
  260
quarterly seasonal earnings
  changes, 187
Qwest Communications
  International Inc., 8

R

random walk, 101, 103–104
A Random Walk Down Wall Street
  (Malkiel), 103–104
rational, risk-averse investor,
  68–71
rational behaviour, 96n
rational decision-making, 68–69
rational decision-making theory, 5
rational expectations, 66, 83,
  108, 353n
rational investment decision
  theory, 17
rational managers, 285–286
realized net income, 26, 31
receivables, 236
  see also accounts receivable;
  notes receivable
recognition lag, 42, 152
recoverable amount, 232
regression analysis, 148, 160,
  255–256
regulation
  decentralized regulation,
    468–469
  deregulation, 16
  of economic activity, 444–445
  and incentives, 119
  indirect regulation, 445
  information asymmetry, as
    justification, 444
  market failures, 462–465
  as reaction to fundamental
    problem, 15–16
  standard setting as form of, 15
  and voluntary disclosure, 454

Regulation FD, 464, 466, 473,
  481n
relational contracts, 412–413
relative performance evaluation
  (RPE), 378
relevance, 42, 86
relevant information, 24, 26, 33
reliability, 42, 86, 166
reliable information, 24, 27–33
replicating portfolio, 271n
representational faithfulness, 27
representativeness, 179, 182
repricing of ESOs, 396–397
reputation maintenance, 413–414
research
  Ball and Brown study,
    149–153
  clean surplus theory, 208–209
  comparison of returns and
    income, 148–149
  described, 12–13
  earnings response coeffi-
    cients (ERC), 153–162
  empirical research, 143, 154
  event study, 149
  executive compensation,
    381–383
  good earnings management,
    416–422
  market response, 145–146
  market-wide factors *vs.* firm-
    specific factors, 146–148,
    147f
  narrow window studies, 152
  positive accounting theory
    (PAT), 290–293
  on prospect theory, 182–183
  research problem, and infor-
    mation approach, 145–149
  wide window studies, 152
research and development costs,
  253–254
reservation utility, 317
reserve quantity estimates, 41
reserve recognition accounting
  (RRA)
  and asset valuation, 40
  vs. cost-based approach, 44
  critique of, 31–40, 41
  example of, 31–35
  market reaction, 166
  net income, as performance
    measure, 339

prior period estimates,
  adjustments to, 176n
reliability, 40–41
summary, 41
supplementary current value
  information, 66
residual income model, 198
  see also clean surplus theory
restraint of trade, 306
restricted stock, 401n
returns
  abnormal return, 113, 142n,
    150, 176n
  comparison of, 148–149
  economy-wide factors, 74
  ex ante returns, 111
  ex post returns, 111
  expected rate of return, 73t,
    75t
  firm-specific factors, 75
  market-wide factors, 74
  meaning of, 110
  unexpected returns, 112–113
revaluation option, 232
revelation principle, 327–328,
  354n
revenue recognition, 42, 52, 230
rigidity of contracts, 339–340
risk
  basis risk, 244
  beta risk, 255–257
  compensation risk, 323
  credit risk, 239
  disclosure, 468–469
  estimation risk, 113, 193, 257
  ex ante risk, 96n
  executive compensation,
    role in, 377–380
  firm-specific risks, 76,
    257–258
  foreign exchange risk,
    259–260
  idiosyncratic risk, 193
  interest rate risk, 258–259
  market risk premium, 225n
  market risks, 244
  measurement approach to
    risk reporting, 260–262
  non-diversifiable risk, 76
  portfolio risk, 79–83
  price risks, 244
  quantitative price risk disclo-
    sures, 260